# The Illustrated Encyclopedia of Archaeology

# The Illustrated Encyclopedia of
# ARCHAEOLOGY

*Consultant Editor* Glyn Daniel

Thomas Y. Crowell Company

ESTABLISHED 1834

10E. 53rd Street, New York 10022

Opposite: a reconstruction of a waterwheel pit at Birkenhead
Gunpowder Mills, Delaware, U.S.A.

| | |
|---|---|
| *Consultant Editor* | **Professor Glyn E. Daniel**, Cambridge University |
| *Editor* | **Elaine Paintin**, British Museum |
| *Principal Contributors* | **J. W. Allan**, Ashmolean Museum, Oxford |
| | **Dr. R. Allchin**, Cambridge University |
| | **Carol Andrews**, British Museum |
| | **Peter Bellwood**, Australian National University, Canberra |
| | **Dr. P. L. Carter**, Cambridge University |
| | **Dr. Desmond Collins**, London University |
| | **Dr. Dominique Collon**, London University |
| | **Adrian Digby**, British Museum |
| | **Paul F. Healy**, Trent University, Canada |
| | **Kenneth Hudson** |
| | **Dr. Stephen Johnson**, Department of the Environment, London. |
| | **Dr. Ann Kendall**, London University |
| | **Dr. Jonathan King**, British Museum |
| | **Dr. Lloyd Laing**, University of Liverpool |
| | **Dr. Richard S. MacNeish**, R. S. Peabody Foundation for Archaeology, Mass. |
| | **Elaine Paintin**, British Museum |
| | **Jessica Rawson**, British Museum |
| | **Professor Jeremy Sabloff**, University of Utah |
| | **Dr. Andrew Sherratt**, Ashmolean Museum, Oxford |
| | **Dr. Mansel Spratling**, British Museum |
| | **Dr. Gordon R. Willey**, Harvard University |

© 1977 Reference International Publishers Ltd

Published in the USA 1977 by
Thomas Y. Crowell Company Inc., New York, N.Y.

Library of Congress Cataloging in Publication Data
Main entry under title:

The Illustrated encyclopedia of archaeology.

Includes index.
1. Archaeology—Dictionaries.   I.   Daniel, Glyn Edmund.
CC70.I44      930′.1′03      77–4817
ISBN 0–690–01473–2

A quarter of a century ago archaeologists were still thought of by many as strange remote characters not really concerned with present-day affairs: Sir Flinders Petrie, with his long white beard and patriarchal appearance, was the popular figure of an archaeologist. And to the world at large archaeology was the search for treasure—the gold in the ground from past ages. All that has now changed: archaeology is one of the most popular disciplines in American and British universities and the sale of archaeological books is large. This is for two reasons: first, that the widening interest in the past—and man is an historical animal—has now taken in all aspects of man's past cultural activities, and second, that professional archaeologists are now very properly devoting some of their time to setting out the results of their excavations, discoveries, and researches in an intelligible form. No reasonably educated person can or should now be unaware of the new perspective of his past which archaeology provides.

The word archaeology comes from two Greek words: *archaia*, meaning ancient things, and *logos*, meaning science, knowledge, or theory. The Greeks used the word to mean the study of ancient things: they did not themselves excavate or do any of the other things that modern archaeologists do—but of course they did speculate about the past. Since the time of the Classical world of Greece and Rome, the word archaeology has been used in a wide variety of ways, and mainly to mean ancient history, but from the end of the 18th century onwards it has come to mean that branch of learning which studies the material remains of man's past. Its scope is, therefore, enormous, ranging from the first stone tools made and fashioned by man perhaps over 3 million years ago in East Africa, to the rubbish thrown into our trashcans and taken to municipal incinerators and dumps yesterday. Every artifact, that is to say every tool, weapon, or construction made by human beings, is the vital concern of the archaeologist.

The importance and relevance of archaeology to the total picture of man's origins and cultural development varies with time, and with the existence or non-existence of written sources. The earliest writing occurred in Egypt and Mesopotamia 5,000 years ago: before then is prehistory or strictly speaking prewritten history, and here the archaeologist is paramount, for the only sources for prehistory are the material remains. In historic times archaeology is an adjunct to the written sources, and sometimes the archaeologist is referred to as the handmaiden of the historian. But even so, the archaeologist often supplies information of great importance unobtainable in other ways, as for example has been revealed in the study of deserted medieval villages, and of towns such as Colonial Williamsburg in Virginia; York, Winchester, and London in Britain; Dublin in Ireland; and Paris and La Couvertoirade in France. Historical archaeology is now a well recognized branch of the subject, and in the last two decades industrial archaeology has attracted a great deal of attention.

Between prehistoric archaeology and historical archaeology there is a wide zone in time where the written and material sources are of approximately equal importance and this is usually referred to as protohistory. The study of the origins of civilization in the ancient Near East and of the Anglo Saxons and Vikings in Northern Europe is protohistory.

The archaeologist is a craftsman, a scientist, and an historian. His craft is the reconnaisance and discovery of ancient sites by ground and aerial survey, their careful excavation—and the surgical examination of man's past cultural landscape is one of the main and key activities of the archaeologist—and the interpretation of the materials found by survey, digging, and, very often, by chance. In this work he uses all kinds of scientific techniques, from the analysis of rocks and materials to dating techniques like potassium-argon dating, radioactive carbon dating, and thermoluminescence. But the ultimate aim of his craft and his use of the physical and biological sciences is to write human history: to give as full and as accurate an account as possible of the development of human societies, to describe man's cultural evolution from the Old Stone Age, through the New Stone Age and Bronze Age to the early civilizations of Southwest Asia, India, China, and America and from them to the historic civilizations of the world. The archaeologist not only records the progress of man as revealed in his surviving material remains—and it is one of the sad limitations, particularly of the worker in the fields of prehistory and protohistory, that the archaeologist is restricted only to what has survived the shipwrecks of time—but also the achievements of past societies. At one time, there was argued to be a distinction between the art historian and the archaeologist, who was seen as a doubtful character with mud on his boots and who was mainly concerned with coarse pottery and flint flakes. Gone is that unhappy and unreal dichotomy between connoisseur and digger: the archaeologist studies all aspects of the societies he describes and rejoices in the Upper Palaeolithic cave paintings of Lascaux and Altamira, the treasures from Tutankhamun's tomb and the Royal Graves at Ur, the art of the Vikings, the Scythians, and the Olmecs and Maya of Central America, appreciating them all as being among the highest products of human endeavor.

Archaeology began, 150 years ago, as the study of pre-Roman and Roman remains in France and Britain, of pre-Viking remains in Scandinavia, and of the standing monuments of the Mediterranean and Egypt, such as the temples of Greece and the pyramids along the banks of the Nile. Now it is worldwide in its scope and there is archaeology from China to Peru, from Greenland to Ceylon. In the last 30 years most notable and important archaeological discovery and research has taken place in Southeast Asia, Australasia, and America.

The greatest change in archaeology in the last quarter of a century is that is has become scientific. A very wide variety of scientific techniques are now used and have to be used by the archaeologist both in the field and in the laboratory when he is analyzing his material. Analysis of stone and of metal can indicate early trade routes. It has been obvious to antiquaries and archaeologists for centuries that the great megalithic temple of Stonehenge on Salisbury Plain in Wiltshire was built of two different materials—the sarsens that came from not far away in North Wiltshire, and the so-called bluestones or foreign stones. It was careful and detailed geological and petrological analysis that proved that these foreign stones came from the Preseli hills of Southwest Wales. Here was science providing an archaeological and historical fact that could not be obtained in any other way.

But it is in the dating of the past that science has given archaeology and history its most remarkable contribution.

To a very large extent the dates given by archaeologists to their finds before 3000 BC was a matter of intelligent guesswork and reasonable speculation until the advent of radiocarbon dating. Tree-ring dating and the counting of clay varves certainly had given some exact chronology, but it was not until Professor W. F. Libby, then of the University of Chicago, expounded the theory and practice of radiocarbon dating and in 1949 announced the first dates that prehistoric and protohistoric archaeology could work to an exact chronology. Since 1949 over 20,000 archaeological radiocarbon dates have been determined and, as a result, our whole picture of early man in various parts of the world revolutionized. To take one example, we now know through radiocarbon dating that the megalithic temples of Malta and some of the megalithic tombs of Brittany were built before the pyramids of Egypt and the ziggurats of Mesopotamia and are the earliest pieces of architecture in the whole world.

No one archaeologist can now encompass the new and wide range of his subject in time and space and a large library of books is required to give even the outlines of our present-day world archaeology. There is more than ever need for archaeological works of general reference summarizing what is known from archaeology about human history in all parts of the globe. The *Illustrated Encyclopedia of Archaeology* aims to be such a work and here the general reader, the earnest student, and the professional will find an alphabetical survey, carefully illustrated and cross-referenced, which will give him ready access to all the farflung aspects of this complex and varied field. Such a book is difficult to compile because there are so many archaeologies and so many differing archaeologists. Disputes about theory must color the accounts given by various writers, but in an encyclopedia such as this our aim is to reflect the great diversity of the field rather than to set forth a single and controversial view.

Glyn Daniel

**Abbevillian.** The name often given to primitive handax assemblages in Europe, based on the type locality of Abbeville, near the mouth of the Somme valley in France. Such a stage would precede the ACHEULIAN, over 300,000 years ago. Many prehistorians are sceptical about the validity of such a stage.

**Aceramic Neolithic.** When the term Neolithic was first coined by Lord Avebury in the late 19th century, only the European material was at all well known; and it appeared that pottery was first introduced at the same time as polished axes came into use. Pottery thus came to be seen as an essential element in the Neolithic "package"—cultivation and stock rearing, settled villages, a new technology for forest clearance, and new containers for cooking.

It was a surprise, therefore, when, as recently as the 1950s, excavations on Near Eastern TELL sites revealed extensive deposits, representing long periods of a settled agricultural existence, in which no traces of pottery were to be found. JERICHO in Jordan was one such site, and some 33 ft. (10 m) of accumulation, including mud-brick buildings and a substantial stone tower, belonged to a Pre-Pottery Neolithic (PPN) period. This could be divided into PPN A and PPN B phases on the basis of changes in architecture and stone tools. Together they lasted from 8000 to 6000 BC.

Such a potteryless or aceramic Neolithic phase began to be found extensively in the Near East: at the bottom of the tell of HACILAR in Turkey, for example; at Khirokitia in Cyprus; at Ali Kosh in Iranian Khuzistan; and just into Europe itself at the bottom of some of the Neolithic tell sites in Thessaly. In Greece, however, it was a much less substantial period of time than the 2,000-years duration of the Palestinian PPN, and had more the character of a short pioneer phase before the appearance of a full ceramic assemblage.

The earliest traces of proto-pottery come from Anatolia, and areas adjacent to the southeast, around 7000 BC. These baked clay containers were thick walled and not fully portable; but by 6000 BC recognizable pottery was being made over a wide area of the Near East, and by 5000 BC there were already a multitude of different traditions of often complex painted wares.

**Achaea.** The ancient name for Greece, but in Classical times applied to an area of Greece lying to the north of the Peloponnese on the Corinthian Gulf. The Achaean Confederacy of 12 states came to prominence in the middle of the 3rd century BC. Later, Achaea was the name of the Roman province of the Greek mainland, formed in 27 BC.

**Achaemenids.** A Persian royal Dynasty named after Achaemenes (c. 700 BC). Cyrus II, the Great, defeated

An Achaemenid fire temple at Naqsh-i-Rustam, near Persepolis in Iran, dating from the 6th–5th century BC.

the MEDES and founded the Persian Empire. He gained control of LYDIA and BABYLON which brought almost the whole of the Near East under his rule, and extended his frontiers eastwards. His son Cambyses II conquered Egypt and the empire was consolidated under Darius I. The number of satrapies, or vassal states, was increased from 23 to 31 to include regions beyond the Oxus and as far as the Indus, but the empire was a threat to Greek commercial interests in the West and this led to the Persian Wars. Alexander the Great brought about the fall of the Achaemenid Empire with his capture of PERSEPOLIS and his defeat of Darius III (330 BC).

*Rulers of the Achaemenid Empire*
Cyrus II, the Great (559–529 BC)
Cambyses II (529–521 BC)
Darius I (521–485 BC)
Xerxes I (485–465 BC)
Artaxerxes I (465–424 BC)
Xerxes II (424 BC)
Darius II (424–404 BC)
Artaxerxes II 404–358 BC)
Artaxerxes III (358–338 BC)
Arses (338–335 BC)
Darius III (335–330 BC)

Royal palaces at Persepolis, Pasargadae, and SUSA, the tomb of Cyrus the Great near Pasargadae, and rockcut tombs of later rulers and a fire temple at Naqsh-i-Rustam are the principal surviving monuments. Relief sculpture, seal engraving, and metalwork all reveal a highly eclectic and technically sophisticated form of art, which nevertheless lacks a certain spontaneity.

**Acheulian.** The name, proposed in 1872 by Gabriel de Mortillet, which was originally used for an epoch or subdivision within the Palaeolithic, falling before the Mousterian epoch. The name derives from St. Acheul, a suburb of Amiens in the Somme valley of Northern France. Here, on the middle terrace of the Somme, large numbers of handaxes have been found. Today, the idea of archaeological epochs is out of fashion, and the term Acheulian is mainly used for assemblages of stone tools which contain substantial numbers of handaxes.

Handaxes are found all over Africa, except in the rain forest area, over Southern Asia, and in Western Europe from Italy to Britain. The earliest are believed to date from over a million years ago. The latest handax assemblages in Africa have associated radiocarbon dates of about 60,000 years, but this may be an underestimate.

The Acheulian type of assemblage is often regarded as a culture tradition, but its entire distribution over three continents can hardly be regarded as a single tradition, for there are clear local differences. In Africa, for example, distinctive cleavers are found in the assemblages. The main floruit in Europe, the "true" Acheulian, dates from *c.* 150,000 to 250,000 years ago.

**Acropolis.** Literally meaning "high city," the acropolis was usually a small plateau on a low-lying hill within the area of a Greek city. In very early times, the acropolis formed the defended area of the city, and often the

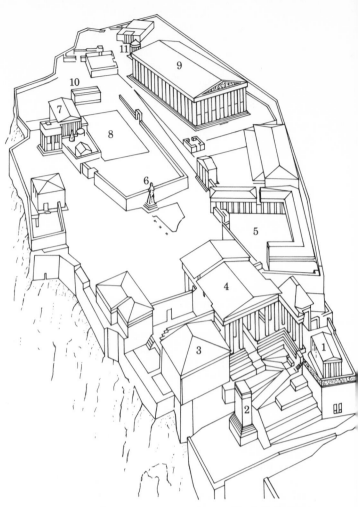

A reconstruction of the Acropolis at Athens. Key: (1) Temple of Athena Nike; (2) Agrippa's Monument; (3) Pinakotheke; (4) Propylaea; (5) Precinct of Artemis Brauronia; (6) Statue of Athene Promachos; (7) Erechtheum; (8) Site of original Temple of Athene; (9) Parthenon; (10) Great Altar; (11) Temple of Augustus and Rome.

existence of a suitable hill was a strong guiding factor in the choice of a settlement site. The Acropolis of ATHENS is typical: originally surrounded by walls of Bronze Age date, making it a strong citadel, it later became the area dedicated to Athene, patron goddess of the city, and held her temple, the PARTHENON.

**Acroterion.** Decoration, in the form of a ceramic or marble statue, for the pinnacle and the gable ends of a Greek temple.

**Adena.** A culture of the United States named after the Adena Mound group of Ross County, Ohio, dating from around 1000 BC. Adena sites, found in parts of Ohio, Indiana, Kentucky, Pennsylvania, and West Virginia, are characterized by the three main traits of the WOODLAND TRADITION: woodland pottery, burial mounds, and the beginnings of agriculture. The burial mounds are usually conical: the largest, 66 ft. (20 m) high, is the Creek Grave Mound in West Virginia. The mound enclosures or embankments, also typical of this culture, were often perfectly circular. Although burial mounds have been found within the enclosures, their use was probably ceremonial.

The tombs inside the mounds were usually rectangular timber constructions, the bodies being placed in the graves in extended positions. Grave goods included various polished stone tools such as boatstones, thin stone tablets carved with zoomorphic and curvilinear designs, and tobacco pipes such as the one carved in the form of a man from the Adena Mound. Copper was hammered into ornaments, and was occasionally used for making axes. Pottery was never used in burials; it was grit tempered and was sometimes decorated with an incised diamond pattern. In general the people of the Adena culture were probably more settled than their ARCHAIC TRADITION predecessors, growing sunflowers, squash, and gourds, as well as hunting, and centering their ritual life on the ancestor worship exemplified by the burial mounds.

A carved stone pipe, *c*, 9 in. (20 cm) high, in the form of a man, from the Adena Mound, Ohio.

**Adobe.** A term for the sun-dried mud bricks used in aboriginal America.

**Aeolis.** An area of Northwestern Asia Minor and the islands of Lesbos and Tenedos, colonized by the Greeks, and the scene of fighting between Greece and Persia in the 6th century BC.

**Afanasievo culture.** A Neolithic culture in the Yenisei valley in South Siberia. The people, who moved into the area in the 3rd millennium BC, were stock breeders, but they also depended on hunting. Most excavated sites are burials under low mounds, or kurgans, surrounded by circular stone walls. Stamped pottery, implements in stone or bronze, and a few copper ornaments are found in them.

**Africa in Prehistory.** There is a growing body of evidence to suggest that "man the toolmaker" first evolved on the African continent. It is Africa therefore that provides the greatest time depth for the study of our prehistoric ancestors. The earliest evidence for intentional toolmaking, and the remains of the toolmakers, comes from a number of localities in the Great Rift valley of East Africa in what are today the modern states of Kenya, Tanzania, and Ethiopia.

POTASSIUM–ARGON DATING has shown that the Ethiopian site of Hadar in the Northeast and the Omo valley in the far South are between 2 and 3 million years old. The Hadar site has produced a nearly complete skeleton of an Australopithecine, as well as other hominid remains and stone tools. In the Omo valley, hominid remains are not common although both robust and gracile forms of Australopithecines have been recovered. The Omo sites are best known for very rich mammalian fauna and the earliest stone tools so far recognized by prehistorians. These early stone tools are flaked pieces of quartzite from the deposits of the Shunguru formation, dating from about 2.4 million years ago.

In Northern Kenya, the country to the east of Lake Turkana (formerly Lake Rudolf) has produced an outstanding profusion of evidence relating to the origins of man and his toolkits. This evidence is still being studied and interpretations change frequently as new evidence accumulates, but we can say, as in Ethiopia, that both forms of Australopithecine occur although the record is complicated by the presence of other hominids, such as the 1470 skull that is attributed to the genus *Homo*. Somewhat later than the 1470 skull in the KBS tuff (volcanic) formation are the earliest tool occurrences at East Turkana. More than 15 separate sites are known, a number of which have been excavated. At several sites stone tools occur in association with animal bones. Particularly interesting is the "Hippo butchery site," dating from about 2.5 million years ago, where a hippopotamus skeleton was associated with stone tools that had been used to dismember the carcass.

The well known site at OLDUVAI GORGE in Northern Tanzania documents the change from the earliest, Oldowan, stage of tool development to the ACHEULIAN stage, when tool types become more standardized, sites occur outside Africa, and we have the first good evidence for the appearance of HOMO ERECTUS in the prehistoric record. Although Acheulian sites occur in Europe, Southwest Asia, and parts of India, the African evidence is still of paramount importance. During the Acheulian period

Much of the evidence for the African Stone Age comes from stratified sequences such as this site at Ha Soloja in Lesotho, where a series of layers containing Middle Stone Age tools, animal bones, and hearths have been dated to 43,000 years BP (before the present).

more than 50% of the inhabited world was in present-day Africa. The Acheulian dates from about 1.4 million to approximately 110,000 years ago, and throughout this time the diagnostic tool type was the handax and associated flake tools. The evidence from Isimilia and Olduvai in Tanzania, Olorgesaille in Kenya, Melka Kontoure in Ethiopia, and other sites outside Africa shows that Acheulian man was an effective and success-ful hunter of many different kinds of large game animals, such as elephant, buffalo, zebra, antelope, and bush pig. That the hunters were of *Homo erectus* type is clear from fossil human remains recovered in Bed (Level) II at Olduvai and at three sites in Northwest Africa (Casa-blanca and Rabat on the Moroccan coast, and Ternifine on the Algerian plateau).

About 110,000 years ago there was a major change in world climate, probably caused by variations in the eccen-tricity of the earth's orbit, which gave rise to an Ice Age in Northern latitudes and to marked precipitation changes, both of distribution and amount, on the African con-tinent. The disappearance of *Homo erectus* and the asso-ciated Acheulian toolkit appears broadly to coincide with this climatic change both in Europe and in Africa, where we have the first evidence for HOMO SAPIENS and an associated Middle Stone Age tool technology. The men of the Middle Stone Age in Africa were very similar, if not identical, to NEANDERTHAL MAN of Europe and Southeast Asia.

A virtually complete skeleton of Middle Stone Age man comes from Kabwe (formerly Broken Hill) in Zambia. The skull is unusually massive but in other respects the pelvis and limb bones associated with the skull are similar to those of modern man. Other sites that have provided comparable skeletal material are Dire Dawa in Ethiopia, Jebel Irhoud in Morocco, and the Haua Fteah in Cyrenaica (North Africa). These early representatives of modern man are associated with toolkits that are undoubtedly task specific and more efficient than the tools of *Homo erectus*. Points, both unifacial and bifacial, some of which are tanged, various scraper forms, engraving tools, and small crescent-shaped pieces that must have been hafted occur, as well as bone and wooden tools. There is a rich regional diversity of toolkit and there is little doubt that this diversity reflects a selective adaptation to different environments. Regional diversity is particularly marked in the difference between the technology practiced in sub-Saharan Africa and the technology of the North African littoral and the Magreb, but as yet we do not know why this difference occurs or what it may represent.

A similar diversity of economic practice is also apparent from the archaeological record and the controlled use of fire is well attested. Towards the end of the Middle Stone Age a series of major cultural advances, such as the development of painting and engraving and the rapidity with which all earlier forms are replaced by *Homo sapiens sapiens*, are more easily accounted for if the ability to use language was a characteristic confined to modern man.

Exactly where and when modern man first evolved is still not known. Only future discoveries may confirm or refute the claim of a German scientist, Dr. Rainer Protsch, that this evolution took place in Southern Africa. Regardless of where they originated, by 35,000 years ago men indistinguishable from modern groups occur throughout the continent. These Late Stone Age peoples no doubt had the same rational minds as ourselves and a diversity of behavior and belief made possible by the medium of speech. The increasing amount of cultural and fossil data gives us some indication of the prehistoric antecedents underlying the genetic and cultural diversity exhibited by the present-day populations.

Although the Late Stone Age peoples did not have the use of metals, their material culture and way of life was very similar to those of modern hunter-gatherer groups, such as the Bushmen of Southern Africa, the Adza of Tanzania, and the Mbuti of Eastern Zaire. Arrows were tipped with very fine and carefully made points of stone or bone, and flaked stone knives and scrapers for leatherworking were used. Hunting nets and snares were made from vegetable fibers and sinew. Leather clothing was carefully sewn with fine bone needles. A very wide range of plant and animal foods was exploited on a seasonal basis. Extensive use was made of naturally occurring rock shelters, as well as shelters constructed of timber and thatch.

By about 5000 BC, in several parts of the Sahara Desert there is evidence for economies based on formalized animal husbandry and the use of pottery. The Late Stone Age hunting economies were, however, so well adapted to the African environment that it took a considerable time for farming practices to spread throughout the continent. Although there is evidence for domestic cattle and goats in West Africa (*see* KINTAMPO NEOLITHIC) by 1500 BC, and for cattle and sheep in East Africa by 700 BC, it was not until the early years of the Christian era that formalized animal husbandry reached the Southern tip of the continent.

From 5000 BC until the present day, both hunter-gatherers and farmers have coexisted side by side and it was not until the spread of iron-using, Bantu-speaking, negroid farmers from AD 300 onwards that farming became the predominant mode of subsistence in rural Africa.

**Agade.** *See* AKKAD.

**Agora.** An open space in the center of a Greek city, in the older settlements sometimes linked with a temple, but used as a market or meeting place. Later developments included the "peristyle agora" of more formal type, usually rectangular and surrounded by columns, with two or more courtyards forming part of a larger complex, as at Miletus or Magnesia.

**Agragas** (Agrigentum). A rich and flourishing Greek and Roman city in Sicily, originally a colony of Gela, founded in 580 BC. The city walls enclosed an area of 1600 ac. (647 ha), and the site is particularly famous for its series of Doric temples (*see* ARCHITECTURE, GREEK; COLUMN).

**Agrelo culture.** The type-site of the Agrelo culture is located about 12 mi. (20 km) south of Mendoza in Northwest Argentina. It features distinctive pottery with parallel stepped incised lines, punctations, and fingernail impressions, which is typical of the Southern Andean cultural tradition. The Agrelo culture dates from AD 1 to 1000.

**Agriculture, Europe.**
*Prehistoric.* The population of Europe, as of the rest of the world, has shown much higher rates of growth in the last 10,000 years than ever before. This is due to the introduction of a number of key species, and to the artificial encouragement of others, involving radical changes in natural ecology, such as the clearance of forest to provide fields and pastures: in a word, agriculture.

In Europe, the system of cultivation based on cereal and leguminous crops, with sheep as a major stock animal along with cattle and pigs, came as a sudden introduction from the Near East, where it had slowly developed from the onset of the postglacial period some 10,000 years ago. Neither the main cereal species, nor the ancestors of sheep and goats were native to Europe. Their introduction is documented by the appearance of larger, village communities whose need to clear forest to sow their crops is reflected in changes in the frequencies of tree pollen preserved in lakes and bogs. In Southern Europe, the characteristic "Mediterranean" vegetation, with its many dwarf and browse-resistant species, dates from this time; while in Northern Europe the first clearings are shown as temporary openings in the existing dense mixed oak forest. Polished and, later, bronze axes used for tree felling are conspicuous among the new tools, and careful excavation and analysis can reveal actual remains of the animal and plant species among the rubbish of early village settlements.

*Greek and Roman.* Archaeological evidence for farming in Greek and Roman times has always been and probably will continue to be only of secondary importance beside the writings of Xenophon, Varro, Cato, Columella, and other ancient authors who described the processes of ancient agriculture in some detail. Most of the techniques would have been known from Bronze Age or Neolithic times. The history of Greek and Roman agriculture is more that of who actually used and worked the land, rather than how it was done.

With the breakdown of slave-run farms, and the passing of smaller areas of land both in Italy and the provinces to smallholders, the villa, traditionally the farmstead, came into prominence in the countryside. In the imperial period, small producers, provincials, captured enemies or peasants all learned the arts and traditions of Roman agriculture, and remains of their villas, with their living and working quarters and field systems are still discernible in many parts of the Roman world. Study of their animals, mainly from the bones of beasts jointed for the table, is as yet in its infancy, as is a systematic study of pollens, seeds, and other plant remains which provide information about the ancient environment. Some details do come from archaeological sources, notably mosaics, which show the various tasks performed by farmers and representations of their villas and beasts. Finds and drawings of equipment are common, one of the most notable being a Gallic reaping machine pushed by animals through a cornfield. Its front, rather like a bulldozer's bucket, was equipped with sharp teeth, which cut off and collected the ears of corn. (*See also* DOMESTICATION OF PLANTS AND ANIMALS, ARCHAEOLOGY OF; NEOLITHIC. *For the New World, see* CAMELID DOMESTICATION; DOMESTICATION, SOUTH AMERICA.)

An aerial view of a deserted medieval village, at Argan, East Yorkshire.

**Aguada culture.** Located on the Western slopes of the Andes in Northwestern Argentina, this culture is dated between AD 600 and 1000. Its black and yellow pottery is decorated with distinctive feline motifs.

**Air photography.** One of the archaeologist's main research tools. Its value is due to the ease with which complex largescale patterns on the ground can be understood and recorded from the air, and this is enhanced by the fact that changes in the annual cycles of land use and vegetational growth reveal traces of buried structures that are visible only briefly and could not be recorded on the ground, nor even observed, in the time available before they disappear from view.

Such underground structures lead to the formation of "crop marks," particularly in cereal crops, which are due to the amount of moisture available to the roots. Greater moisture is available to roots over filled-in pits and ditches, and less to those over foundations of walls or stone floors; these differences lead respectively to faster and slower growth, or slower and faster ripening of the crop, and are detectable by differences in the overall

A copper head of an Akkadian king, perhaps Sargon, found at Nineveh and dated to *c.* 2370 BC.

color of the crop, or by shadows cast when the sun is at a low angle in the early morning or evening. Such shadows also lead to the easy recognition of low earthworks that at other times of the day would be barely, if at all, visible.

Aerial photogrammetry, particularly using stereo cameras, is used to make archaeological maps and plans, with contours giving the relative heights of the ground's surface and archaeological features upon it. Infra-red film is also increasingly being used to detect buried structures, for it records the relative humidity of the soil (by detecting heat) and of features constructed upon or dug into the subsoil.

**Ajanta.** A Buddhist cave temple site in Maharashtra, India, unique in having paintings on the walls and porch ceilings representing scenes from the life of Buddha. Early caves and paintings date from around the 1st century BC, and the main period of excavation was under the Vakataka Dynasty (5th–6th century AD). (*See also* INDIA.)

**Akhenaten.** An Egyptian king during the 18th Dynasty, who reigned *c.* 1379–1362 BC. Originally called Amenophis IV, he changed his name when he promoted the sun's disk, the Aten, to be supreme god. In the 6th year of his reign he moved from THEBES, the capital city and cult center of AMUN, the Aten's chief rival for religious supremacy, and founded Akhenaten, a new capital city, on a virgin site now called Tell el-Amarna. The Amarna heresy did not survive Akhenaten's death: his half-brother, Tutankhamun, returned to Thebes and restored Amun as chief god (*see* TUTANKHAMUN'S TOMB).

**Akkad, Akkadians.** The name of the first Semitic Dynasty to rule over MESOPOTAMIA, founded by Sargon. He also founded its capital Agade, the present site of which has still to be located, although it must have been near BABYLON.

*Dynasty of Akkad*
Sargon (2334–2279 BC)
Rimush (2278–2270 BC)
Manishtushu (2269–2255 BC)
Naram-Sin (2254–2218 BC)
Shar-kali-sharri (2217–2193 BC)
4 kings (2192–2190 BC)
Dudu (2189–2169 BC)
Shuturul (2168–2154 BC)

Sargon himself was of humble origin and had usurped the throne of KISH. He united the various city states under his rule and proceeded to expand the frontiers of his kingdom to include the whole of Mesopotamia. He reached Lebanon and the Taurus Mountains in the West and ELAM in the East, thus controlling important trade routes. His successor, Rimush, had to deal with rebellion at the beginning of his short reign and he was killed in a palace revolt. Manishtushu seems to have lost control of Syria but led an expedition across the Persian Gulf to secure other sources of raw materials. The deified king Naram-Sin regained control of Syria and the West, built a palace at TELL BRAK and defeated the ruler of MAGAN. Under his successor, however, the empire collapsed and tribes from the Zagros Mountains to the east overran the kingdom. The GUTI gained predominance and the final rulers of the Akkadian Dynasty, in what is frequently known as the Post-Akkadian period, were mere puppet kings.

Rock reliefs in Eastern Turkey and Western Iran and seals of the Indus Valley type found in Mesopotamia bear witness to the extent of the empire and its connections. Though the site of Agade has not been found, many of the treasures it contained have been discovered during the course of excavations at SUSA, where they had been taken as booty by the Elamites. These and numerous cylinder SEALS testify to the high degree of artistic and technical achievement. A copper head of Sargon, found at NINEVEH, is a masterpiece of casting and is made of almost pure copper. Lifesize stone statues of Manishtushu have been found, and the stele of Naram-Sin shows a new feeling for composition. The few buildings ascribed to this period are compact and well designed.

**Akkadian.** The earliest written Semitic language. It is divided into Old Akkadian, succeeded by Babylonian, and Assyrian, and there are many West Semitic dialects. In the middle of the 2nd millennium BC, it became the *lingua franca* for the whole of the Near East and political archives were written in it: the "Amarna Letters" are a series of letters from Syrian, Hittite, and Kassite rulers to the Egyptian pharaohs. The language was written in cuneiform (*see* WRITING) from the middle of the 3rd millennium BC onwards and gradually became replaced in Assyrian times by ARAMAIC, which could be written alphabetically on parchment.

**Alaca Hüyük.** A site in Central ANATOLIA approached through a monumental gateway ornamented with two great stone sphinxes. This, and the buildings within the

The 13th-century BC Hittite Sphinx Gate at Alaca Hüyük in Anatolia, carved from monoliths.

gate, excavated by Turkish archaeologists, date to the period of the Hittite Empire, and the reliefs from the site are now preserved in Ankara Museum. Below these buildings, 13 rich Early Bronze Age (Period II) tombs were discovered. They were obviously built over several generations and are large, shallow, rectangular pits lined with rough stone walls and originally covered with a flat timber roof. Some contained a single burial and some the bodies of a man and a woman with weapons and ornaments, including a dagger (one of the earliest occurrences of iron), gold vessels, diadems, pins, and bronze "standards," consisting of a grill and ornamented with stags. The burials seem to have followed an elaborate ritual.

**Alaka culture.** A preceramic shell mound culture with grinding stones and choppers. It is found in Guyana, and may date from as early as 1000 BC.

**Alalakh.** *See* TELL ATCHANA.

**Alba Fucens.** A Roman colony, founded in Italy in 302 BC. It preserves remains of the forum with a temple. Various additional buildings of the time of Sulla, including a MACELLUM, a BASILICA, and a CURIA, have been revealed by excavations. The city also had a THEATER and an AMPHITHEATER.

**Albright, William Foxwell** (1891–1971). An American archaeologist who excavated many sites in the Holy Land.

**Aleppo.** An important city in Northern Syria on the route between the Euphrates and Orontes valleys, mentioned in texts from the 2nd millennium BC onwards. It was the capital of the kingdom of Yamhad (*see* TELL ATCHANA) and was known to the HITTITES as Halpa. It is still inhabited and only part of the Crusader period citadel has been excavated to reveal Neo-Hittite levels. (*See also* SYRIA-PALESTINE.)

**Alexandria.** Founded by Alexander the Great in 332 BC, Alexandria was built up by the Ptolemaic kings as the chief city of Egypt, which it remained in Roman times. It was famed for its library and especially for its lighthouse, the Pharos, built by Sostratos of Knidos between 299 and 279 BC and destroyed in AD 1326. The city was composed of quarters—Egyptian, Greek, Jewish, and the so-called "Kings quarter," which contained most of the important buildings, among them the Caesareion, which originally contained the obelisks sent to New York and London. Little of the ancient city remains visible today.

**Alphabet.** *See* WRITING.

**Altamira.** The site of a cave near Castillana, in the Canatabrian province of Santander, Spain. It contains some of the finest prehistoric paintings known, including the famous sleeping bison. The paintings were first recognized by Don Marcelino de Sautuola in 1879, but their authenticity was not proved until after 1900.

**Altar de Sacrificios.** The site of Altar de Sacrificios is situated on the south bank of the Rio Pasion, in the Southwest of the Department of Peten, Guatemala. The Pasion and Salinas Rivers are a part of the larger Usumacinta River system, the archaeological sites of whose drainage comprise the Western zone of the Southern Maya Lowlands.

The site was occupied from the Middle Preclassic Period, *c.* 800 BC, until the beginning of the Postclassic Period, *c.* AD 1000. Its phases of greatest architectural building and politico-religious activity were during the Classic Period. A series of Early Classic stelae date from between AD 455 and 524. Following a hiatus, which corresponds to a general constructional and dedicatory hiatus for the Southern Maya Lowlands as a whole, a series of Late Classic stelae at Altar de Sacrificios were erected between AD 618 and 771, and other monuments at the site may date from as late as AD 849.

The principal architecture of the site consists of three groups of platforms and pyramids (Groups A, B, and C) which are arranged compactly around plazas, the whole covering no more than 478 sq. yd. (400 m²). The construction of Group B is of particular interest, as the earlier interior structures there date back to the Middle Preclassic Period. These were covered with subsequent buildings, the latest construction phase dating from the Early Classic Period. The building stone used in Group B is unique for the Maya Lowlands as it is a soft red sandstone. Groups A and C date largely from the Late Classic Period and are of limestone. The overall settlement of the region has not been well surveyed, but a clustering of some 40 small mounds, or domestic structures, extends to the west of the main center for 0.33 mi. (0.50 km). This settlement, however, is believed to represent only a fraction of the former populations responsible for the construction and support of the center.

**Altoparaná** (or Altoparanense). A complex of crude chipped stone tools, mainly unifacial plano-convex scrapers, but including a few bifacial ax-like or pick-like arti-

facts, estimated to date from 25,000 to 9000 BC. The sites are found in the Pampas area in Argentina, the Paraná drainage of Paraguay, Uruguay, and Southern Brazil as far north as the state of São Paulo.

**Altun Ha.** A relatively small but well known MAYA site in Belize, about 35 mi. (56 km) north of Belize City. Excavated by the Royal Ontario Museum, the site ranges from the Middle Preclassic to the Late Classic Period, at which time (*c.* AD 900) it was largely abandoned, like most other ceremonial centers of the Maya subarea. The site is best known for its evidence of Preclassic long-distance contact with TEOTIHUACAN, and for Tomb B-4/7, which apparently belonged to a Classic Period Maya priest and contained the offering of a jade sculpture of the head of the Maya sun god. Weighing nearly 10 lb. (4 kg), this is the largest carved jade artifact ever recorded from the Maya subarea.

**Al 'Ubaid.** *See* UBAID.

**Amber.** This was known to and used by the prehistoric peoples of Europe from Mesolithic times. It was sometimes carved and small pieces often formed the beads of necklaces. Amber is known from Bronze Age MYCENAE and from Egypt, and it is probable that the so-called amber route—the road from Macedonia through Serbia and Hungary, leading to the Baltic regions and Prussia (the probable source of amber)—was in use from very early times. The Phoenicians were specialist traders in amber, and in the Roman imperial period the prehistoric route was also the main channel for the trade in amber. Aquileia, at the Italian end of the route, became a production center for carved amber jewelry.

**Amenophis III.** An Egyptian king of the 18th Dynasty, who reigned from *c.* 1417 to 1379 BC, when Egypt was at her most powerful and wealthy. He was the father of the heretic King AKHENATEN and husband of Queen Tiye, whose parents' burial in the Valley of the Kings at THEBES was found intact by Theodore Davis and J. E. Quibell. Amenophis III's palace at Malkata is in the process of further excavation (1977).

**Amlash.** A site in IRAN, in the mountains southwest of the Caspian Sea. Tombs in the area have produced many objects: gold and silver cups, figurines and, above all, some very fine animal-shaped pottery rhytons (ritual vessels). Unfortunately most of the burials have been looted and the objects, together with many forgeries, all indiscriminately labeled "Amlash," have appeared on the market.

**Amorites.** Semitic nomads who lived in the Syrian desert and were referred to as MAR.TU or Amurrû in Sumerian and Akkadian texts from Early Dynastic times onwards. They moved into Mesopotamia at the end of the 3rd millennium BC, and founded a series of kingdoms throughout Mesopotamia and across Northern Syria, the most important of which emerged as BABYLON and ASSUR. In Palestine their arrival has been equated with the

The most famous Roman Amphitheater: the Colosseum at Rome, built by Vespasian and Titus AD 70–80.

changes which appear in Early Bronze to Middle Bronze Age times. (*See* SYRIA–PALESTINE.)

**Ampajango.** A river terrace site with a complex of crude bifacial tools, reputedly dating from *c*. 10,000 BC, from Catamarca Province in Northwest Argentina.

**Amphitheater.** A type of theater, developed by the Romans, enclosing a sandy arena in which spectacles, usually of a gladiatorial nature, took place. The earliest amphitheaters were oval in form, and built of wood; later they were more normally stone built. The greatest of them was the Colosseum, in Rome. Seating for spectators was usually on tiered galleries, two or three stories in height, and there was provision for covering the whole area with shades against the rain or sun. Under the arena there are occasionally tunnels and passages in which wild beasts and scenery could be housed.

**Amphora.** A large, two-handled vessel, chiefly associated with the Classical world, used as a container for foodstuffs—wine, oil, or fish. It often had a pointed bottom, so that it could be sunk into the ground to keep produce cool.

**Ampurias** (Emporion). Originally a colony of Marseilles (Massalia), Ampurias was a Greek trading settlement in Spain. It became a Roman colony under Augustus (27 BC–AD 14). The excavated remains show clearly the phases of expansion from original Greek colony to Roman city.

An Athenian black-figured amphora, showing Ajax and Achilles playing draughts, painted by Exekias, *c*. 550–540 BC.

**Amun.** An Egyptian god of obscure origins who, by the 11th Dynasty, had become established at THEBES and rose to become supreme god of the Egyptian pantheon. His supremacy was challenged only once, during the reign of AKHENATEN.

**'Amuq.** A plain on the Syrian-Turkish frontier east of Antioch (Antakya). Round the lake of Antioch are several hundred tells (*see* TELL), and the Oriental Institute of Chicago University made a series of excavations in the 1930s in order to establish a chronological sequence for the area. The principal mound excavated was Tell Judeideh, but the sequence was confirmed and gaps in it were supplied by excavations at neighboring tells, among them Çatal Hüyük (not to be confused with the Anatolian site of that name). The different phases in the sequence were identified by letters. Other important tells excavated in the area are TELL ATCHANA and Tell Tayanat. (*See* SYRIA–PALESTINE; the chronological table, p. 198.)

**Anasazi.** A cultural subarea of the Southwest of the United States: it centers on the area where the four states of Arizona, New Mexico, Utah, and Colorado meet. The period of its development is from 100 BC to the present day, and concerns the development of the prehistoric Basketmaker culture into the historical Pueblo peoples. The word "Anasazi" was taken over from the Navajo, who used it to mean enemy, probably in reference to the Pueblos.

The sequence is divided into two Basketmaker periods and four Pueblo periods. The first period is Basketmaker II (100 BC–AD 400), since Basketmaker I is still hypothetical and no sites have definitely been assigned to it. The first dated Basketmaker II sites are in the Durango region of Colorado and are either cave or open village sites. The Talus Village site was one of the latter type with a series of shallow saucer-shaped pithouses, with log and mud constructions above ground. The economy of these peoples was mixed and included the growing of maize along rivers, the hunting of game and the gathering of wild plants. Basketmaker III period (AD 400–600) is characterized by the appearance of pottery, probably from the MOGOLLON area to the south. The further development of agriculture included the cultivation of the bean (*Phaseolus vulgaris*); and the greater size of the pithouse settlements. In the Quemado region of New Mexico, Basketmaker III villages had up to 50 pithouses, which were more deeply excavated in this period.

The transition from the Basketmaker to the Pueblo sequence is characterized by the change from dwellings below ground to those above ground, and by increasing

Cliff Palace, Mesa Verde, Colorado, c, AD 1100–1300. This was an Anasazi cliff dwelling with 200 rooms.

dependence on agriculture. This is best illustrated by the site of Kiatuthlanna in Eastern Arizona, which dates from the Pueblo I period (AD 700–900). This site consists of four groups of pithouses. Associated with each cluster were pole and mud plaster (*jacal*) structures, above ground, which were probably storehouses. At a slightly later period both the houses and storehouses, at other sites, are made of *jacal*. It is therefore probable that the Pueblo culture developed directly from the preceding Basketmaker. During the Pueblo II period (AD 900–1100), the settlements become more dispersed, with a greater number of small dwellings suitable for single, rather than extended, family groups. *Jacal* as a construction technique gives way to construction with stone masonry. Kivas, the circular ceremonial rooms characteristic of the Anasazi, change in their construction by the addition of wall benches, among other things (*see* KIVA). Pueblo IV period (AD 1100–1300) is the period of the construction of large Pueblo-type structures of communicating apartment houses. The huge defensive buildings, such as PUEBLO BONITO in the Chaco Canyon in New Mexico, and Cliff Palace in the Mesa Verde in Colorado, were probably built to withstand attack: this would have been either from intruding Athabascan groups (the historical Navajos and Apaches), or else due to inter-Pueblo warfare, which may have arisen because of the increasing scarcity of water at this time. In the Pueblo IV period (AD 1300–1700), the Northern Pueblo sites were abandoned; populations gathered in larger towns, particularly the historical Pecos, Zuñi, and Hopi Pueblos. This was where the earliest Spanish explorers found the descendants of the Anasazi subtradition.

The pottery of this area shows a continuous development in the increasing use of black-on-white geometric decoration, which reached its climax in Pueblo III period. In Pueblo II and III much domestic pottery is of the type called corrugated: pots were made by spiral coiling and the semiobliteration of the coils, thus producing a corrugated effect. Much historical Pueblo pottery was decorated with geometric and curvilinear polychrome designs.

From ethnographical studies of the historical Pueblos it is possible to speculate about the prehistoric social and political life of the Anasazi peoples. Each Pueblo was run by a series of elders, who were heads of the religious groups; they exercised their power in the kivas in, for example, healing and rainmaking ceremonies, and in the settlement of disputes.

**Anatolia.** This name is derived from *Anadolu*, the Turkish name for the peninsula of Asia Minor. A central plateau slopes down to the Aegean on the west, rises in the east to form a high mountainous area, and is separated from coastal plains to the north and south by further ranges of mountains. Very different cultures have flourished in these varied geographic and climatic regions, but from earliest times Anatolia has been a land bridge between East and West, North and South.

Upper Palaeolithic cultures flourished in caves in the Antalya area (Belbaşi and Beldibi *c.* 13,000–7000 BC) and have Levantine affinities. Pottery appears in the latest levels at Beldibi. OBSIDIAN was traded with Proto-Neolithic JERICHO, but no Central Anatolian sites of this period have yet been excavated. The earliest known agricultural settlements are all aceramic (without pottery): HACILAR (first half of the 7th millennium BC), Suberde in the Taurus Mountains (second half of the 7th millennium BC), and CAN HASAN (Period III: *c.* 6500 BC). The earliest excavated levels at ÇATAL HÜYÜK already have pottery and the site shows a well developed economy based on trade and an organized domestic and religious life. Hacilar, Çatal Hüyük West, and Can Hasan illustrate the transition from Late Neolithic to Chalcolithic and take us to the middle of the 5th millennium BC. To the south of the "Cilician Gates," the important pass through the Taurus Mountains, there is a sequence at MERSIN going back to Early Neolithic times, *c.* 6000 BC, which shows affinities with both the plateau and Syria and which must have been on the trade route for Central Anatolian obsidian.

The succeeding Early Bronze Age (also known as the Copper Age in Anatolia) is divided into three phases. At TROY, a small fortress was founded on virgin rock, and there were settlements on the islands of Lemnos (Poliochni) and Lesbos (Thermi), with houses built to a MEGARON plan and extramural cemeteries such as that at Yortan. To the second phase belong the settlement of Troy II with large megara and hoards of jewelry ("Priam's Treasure"), the rich tombs of ALACA HÜYÜK, Horoztepe, and Mahmatlar, and the shrines of BEYCESULTAN. The Cilician sequence is scanty at Mersin but well represented at TARSUS. With the advent of the third phase, the Anatolian preference for plain, burnished pottery is broken by the appearance of the so-called "Red Cross" bowls throughout Anatolia and of "Cappadocian" painted wares, especially at Alishar, BOĞAZKÖY, and KÜLTEPE, where the megaron also appears.

Little is known of the history of the Early Bronze Age, save for some references in Akkadian texts from MESOPOTAMIA and for what the HITTITES tell us of their predecessors, the Hattians, who spoke a language with no known affinities and lived in the sites which were later taken over by the Hittites. From the 19th century BC, however, the "Cappadocian" tablets from Kültepe and other sites give us information regarding colonies of Assyrian traders settled in Anatolia. These were destroyed at the beginning of the 18th century BC. Texts from Boğazköy have illuminated the history of the Hittite Old Kingdom and Empire during the 2nd millennium BC, but less is known about the kingdoms of Arzawa in the Southwest or Kizzuwatna (Cilicia). Around 1200 BC, however, there was a general movement eastwards into Anatolia of tribes known as the SEA PEOPLE, and they brought about the downfall of the Hittites.

Little is known about the succeeding Dark Age, but when the situation becomes clearer we find the Indo-European Lycians and Lydians and the Carians established in the West, the Phrygians in Central Anatolia, the Neo-Hittites in the Southeast, and the Urartians in the East. From *c.* 1000 BC there were Greek settlements on the Aegean coast at Miletus, and the founding of the Ionian League led to the expansion of a Greco-Anatolian

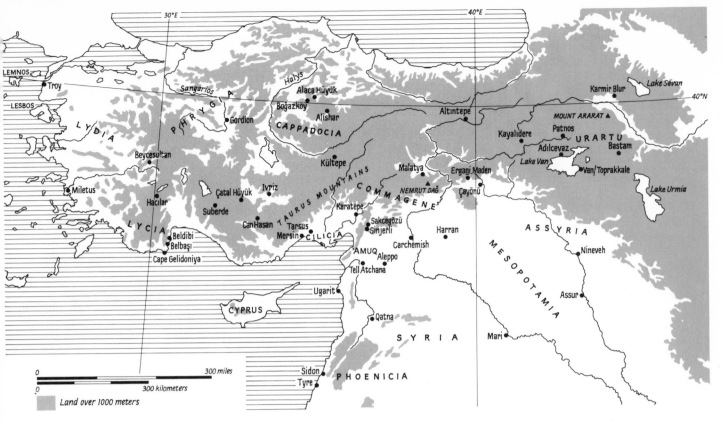

Map of Anatolia.

civilization which eventually spread throughout Anatolia.

**Ancón Yacht.** A site located in the Ancón valley on the Peruvian coast, just north of Lima. It consists of a high shell mound, with deep stratified layers containing a few chipped leaf points, abundant string, twined cloth and baskets, wooden tools, shell fishhooks, and cultivated plants, including gourds, cotton, chile peppers, and guavas. These remains date from between 2500 and 2000 BC.

**Andean chronology.** A variety of different systems of chronology of the Central Andean area have been put forward during this century and various approaches adopted. However, two main stages are generally accepted: Preceramic and Ceramic, the former being the older. The "periods of time" of the Ceramic stage are: Initial Period, 1900–1200 BC; Early Horizon, 1200–300 BC; Early Intermediate Period, 300 BC–AD 700; Middle Horizon, AD 700–1100; Late Intermediate Period, AD 1100–1438/1478; Late Horizon AD 1438–1532. Horizon periods are periods of time with widespread unity of cultural traits. Intermediate periods are periods of time of cultural diversification and nationalism.

**Andean Hunting-Collecting tradition.** Dating from *c.* 6000 to 4000 BC, this tradition is characterized by seasonal transhumance—shifting residence and a trend toward specialization into regional environmental niches.

**Andrae, Walter** (1875–1956). A German architect and archaeologist who excavated ASSUR (capital of Assyria) from 1903 to 1914.

**Androvonovo culture.** A metal-using culture established from the mid-2nd millennium BC in Siberia within the area from the Don to the Yenisei Rivers. Although the people lived in small settlements of up to 10 semisubterranean houses, grew wheat and millet and bred livestock, they were the ancestors of the nomads who later inhabited the Central Asiatic and Siberian steppes.

**Angkor Thom.** A square city, covering $5\frac{1}{2}$ sq. mi. (13.5 km²), built by the KHMER emperor Jayavarman VII (AD 1181–1219) in Cambodia. The central temple, Bayon, has no less than 54 towers rising 150 ft. (45 m), each decorated on all four sides by gigantic human faces. The temples, surrounding walls, and much of the remaining architecture is very elaborately decorated.

**Angkor Wat.** A vast stone, stepped pyramid surrounded by a moat and surmounted by five vast towers, in Angkor, Cambodia, the capital of the KHMER Empire from the time of Yasovarman I. In the tradition of the Khmer emperors, who were regarded in their lifetimes as incarnations of Hindu gods, Angkor Wat was built by Suryavarman II (AD 1113–1150) as his own mausoleum. A fine decorative frieze runs round the building.

**Anglo-Saxons.** The process of barbarian Germanic influence in England began during the Roman occupation, but it was most important in the 5th and 6th centuries AD. Several Germanic groups were represented in the English settlements—Angles from Jutland, Saxons from the North Sea coast to the north of the Elbe, along with some Franks and Frisians. To some extent, their fusion had taken place before they arrived in England.

Most of the archaeological evidence from the Pagan

Anneal

Saxon period (early 5th to mid-7th century) comes from cemeteries. Cremation, with the remains placed in distinctive urns, characterized the Anglian areas (roughly those north of the Thames), while burial in flat cemeteries or under barrows (mounds) characterized those of the Saxons. From the start Kent was one of the most important regions, from which have come rich finds from such cemeteries as Kingston Down, Crundale, Chartham Lines, Faversham, and Fairford. In Sussex, the 7th-century barrow burial at Taplow represents an extension of Kentish culture.

The mission of St. Augustine in AD 597 was followed in the 7th century AD by the widespread adoption of Christianity. Less is known of the Middle Saxon period because of the absence of grave furniture in the Christian graves. During this period the numerous kingdoms that had grown up following the settlements unified into seven, the Heptarchy, and England was led by the most powerful: in succession, Kent, East Anglia, Northumbria, Mercia, and Wessex. A number of churches or fragments of churches survive from this period. An important group in Kent centered on St. Augustine's own foundation at Canterbury, with other early churches at Brixworth (Northants.), Deerhurst (Glos.), and Bradford-upon-Avon (Somerset). The richly furnished royal ship burial at SUTTON HOO belongs to the transitional period between Pagan and Middle Saxon England.

The Late Saxon period is characterized by the growth of towns and the expansion of trade. Some late Saxon town defenses are known, notably in Mercia, from the excavations at Hereford, Tamworth, Cricklade, and South Cadbury. During the 9th century, towns were established for the first time since the Anglo-Saxon invasions, Mercia probably taking the lead and Wessex following, with *burhs* partly established to counter the Danish threat. Many were laid out with gridiron street plans. After a lull during the Danish raids, there was a revival in church building, and many fine examples, such as that at Earl's Barton (Northants.) survive. WINCHESTER became the capital of the now unified England, and its cathedral the center of the flourishing Winchester school of art, which produced light and naturalistic stone sculpture and ivories. During this period Anglo-Saxon coinage (which had been introduced in the 7th century) developed into one of the most sophisticated monetary systems in Europe. Glazed, wheelmade pottery spread to many parts of England, while ornamental metalwork flourished. The Trewhiddle style of metalwork, named after a hoard found in Cornwall, used niello infilling contrasted against a silver ground, with naturalistic animal and foliage patterns in small units of design.

Throughout the Anglo-Saxon period houses were built of timber. In the Pagan Saxon period villages of sunken-floor huts (GRUBENHAÜSER) and rectangular post-built timber buildings are both known, for example from West Stow (Suffolk), Mucking (Essex), and Chalton (Hants.). Similar villages continued to be occupied in the Middle Saxon period, and a few have been excavated—at North Elmham (Norfolk) and Maxey (Northants.). In the Late Saxon period posthole and sleeper-beam rectangular buildings predominated, as for example at Thetford (Norfolk), though a few sunken-floor huts persisted.

**Anneal.** *See* METAL TECHNOLOGY, PREHISTORIC EUROPE.

**Anshan.** *See* ELAM, ELAMITES.

**Anthropology and Prehistory.** In its widest sense, anthropology comprises the sciences of man. The branches most often studied under that name are: first, physical anthropology, the study of man's bodily characteristics, hair type, skin color, blood types, skeletal characteristics, etc.; and second, social anthropology, which takes in such problems as types of kinship recognized in primitive societies and their mode of social organization. Present-day non-literate societies tend to be the primary concern, and the term ethnography is often used to cover all such studies. In one sense, prehistory is a division of anthropology, dealing with events before history and before the ethnographic present observed by recent scholars: in America it is often taught as part of anthropology. Physical anthropology has a major bearing on prehistory in that it embraces the study of fossil man, and of the nature and stages of human emergence.

Ethnography does not include prehistory, but traditionally plays a large part in attempts to understand the prehistoric past: it has done so ever since pioneers like Sir Edward Tylor, in the 19th century, suggested that man had passed first through a hunting stage and then through a farming stage. A common approach used in making hypothetical reconstructions of the past is to see what common features are possessed by present-day peoples believed to be at the same state of development, and then to use this information to interpret material remains. Another approach is to see whether objects still in use today resemble those found by prehistorians, and thus to infer a function for them. These are called ethnographic parallels.

**Antioch** (Antiochia). A city in Asia Minor, founded in 300 BC by Seleucus I, and extended by Antiochus IV. It became a Roman city in 64 BC through the activities of Pompey, and, as capital of the province of Syria, it was one of the three most important cities of the Roman world. It reached its peak under Hadrian, suffered from Persian invasions of the 3rd century AD, but was rebuilt in large measure by Diocletian and successive emperors from the 4th century AD. Visible remains are the Byzantine wall circuit, and the rock carvings (so-called Charonion) of the time of Antiochus IV.

**An-yang.** The site, in China, of the last capital of the SHANG DYNASTY, occupied in the 12th and 11th centuries BC. It is one of the best and most extensively excavated sites in China. The excavations have revealed palaces and ceremonial complexes founded on podiums of HANG-T'U, or pisé (mud brick), workshops, and immense shaft tombs, presumably those of the kings. Large deposits of ORACLE BONES and groups of RITUAL VESSELS and JADE objects have been recovered.

**Aosta** (Augusta Praetoria). An Augustan Roman colony

at the foot of the Italian Alps. It preserves remains of the rectangular circuit of walls, gates, FORUM, THEATER, AMPHITHEATER, and an Augustan triumphal arch.

**Apadana.** A distinctive type of columned audience hall used in Achaemenid architecture.

**Apamea.** A Syrian city on the Orontes, originally a Macedonian colony, later becoming a Seleucid city and, under the Romans, capital of the province of Syria Secunda. Devastated by an earthquake in 1152, the city still preserves ruins of its defenses, a colonnaded street, and a temple dedicated to Baal.

**Apis.** *See* SERAPEUM.

**Aqueduct.** The provision of water in Greek and Roman times was usually achieved by constructing a channel with a gradient sufficient to bring water to the city from the nearest source: only occasionally was the principle of water pressure employed. The water, in a cement channel or in lead or wooden pipes, was brought to a distribution outlet within the city (*castellum divisorium*), and ensured a constant supply of water for baths, cleaning the streets, and the public mains. Rome had several well known aqueducts, which usually entered the city at or near gateways, and in the provinces some of the more spectacular engineering feats were achieved to bring water across deep ravines—for example the PONT DU GARD near Nîmes and the aqueduct at Segovia. The longest known aqueduct, at 82 mi. (132 km), is that of CARTHAGE, built in Hadrianic times.

**Aquileia.** Founded in 181 BC, Aquileia soon became a flourishing center for trade along the route north and eastwards into the Black Sea areas. The remains of the harbor, domestic quarter, and the city walls are substantial, and there is also an AMPHITHEATER. The remains of an early Christian double church, perhaps dating from Constantine (*c.* AD 320) lie in the center: several of its rooms contain exceptionally fine mosaic pavements.

**Arad.** A Biblical city west of the Dead Sea, excavated 1962–67. A walled city at the beginning of the 3rd millennium BC, it contained imported Egyptian pottery and was destroyed *c.* 2700 BC. It was resettled in the 11th century BC, and a succession of walled citadels and a temple have been found. An important find of ostraca (inscribed pieces of pottery) dates from *c.* 600 BC.

**Aramaeans.** Semitic tribes, which established themselves in Northern Syria at the end of the 2nd millennium BC and founded a series of small states, of which the foremost were Aram of DAMASCUS, Aram Naharaim, and Sam'al (SINJERLI). They lacked the necessary unity to withstand the yearly onslaughts of Tukulti-Ninurta II of Assyria, and one by one they collapsed.

**Aramaic.** The language of the Aramaeans, which became the *lingua franca* of the Near East by the 8th century BC, after the transportation and resettlement of large sections of the population by the Assyrians (*see* WRITING). Under the Achaemenids, it became the diplomatic language of the empire; it was the vernacular of the Jews and was spoken by Jesus. It was replaced by Arabic after the Arab Conquest, but is still spoken today in some remote villages of Syria.

**Araquinoid subtradition.** A pottery tradition located in the Middle Orinoco River region of Eastern Venezuela, *c.* AD 600–1200. It is characterized by geometric incised designs on the interior beveled rims of bowls.

**Archaic tradition.** A group of cultures in the Eastern United States and Canada which developed from the original migration of man from Asia during the Pleistocene, between 40,000 and 20,000 BC. They occurred east of a line from Louisiana in the South to Minnesota in the North, and south of a line from Minnesota to the estuary of the St. Lawrence River. They may have originated in the BIG GAME HUNTING TRADITION, and the economy was based on hunting and fishing, and shell and plant gathering. It is the first major tradition which delineates the Eastern Woodlands as a separate cultural area. Between 8000 and 1000 BC a series of technical achievements characterizes this tradition, which can be broken into the following periods: the Early Archaic period, 8000–5000 BC, features the mixture of the Big Game Hunting tradition with the early Archaic cultures; the Archaic tradition cultures survive by themselves in the Middle Archaic period, 5000–2000 BC, and the Late Archaic period, 2000–1000 BC. The first technical innovation is the production of polished stone artifacts, the most typical of which are the weights for throwing sticks or atlatls (*see* ATLATL). Birdstones and bannerstones begin to appear between the Early and Middle Archaic periods (*see* BIRDSTONE). The other important innovation is pottery: the earliest comes from Georgia and Northern Florida and is fiber tempered, though the first pottery from the Northeastern United States is grit tempered and somewhat later. Typical artifacts of the area and people include stone projectile points with broad blades and stems, and grooved bone axes, adzes, and gouges.

Throughout the period there was increasingly sedentary occupation of sites. A few foods, such as the sunflower and Jerusalem artichoke, may have been cultivated towards the end of the period, when milling and grinding tools became more common. The area and period can be divided into several subtraditions. In the Northeast the Archaic tradition divides into the Coastal and Boreal Archaic of New York, New England, and the Maritime Provinces of Canada. Bannerstones and grooved axes suggest that the Boreal Archaic was influenced from the South. The distinctive culture of the Great Lakes and upper Mississippi valley is the Old Copper culture dating from between 4500 and 1500 BC. Native copper was worked cold or hot, but never melted or cast. Copper artifacts include *ulu*-shaped (crescent-shaped) knives, barbed harpoon points, and copper copies of bannerstone atlatl weights. The area between New England and Virginia is characterized by vessels of steatite. In North

Carolina, the Savanna River phase of the Middle Archaic is also characterized by these vessels, as well as by numerous polished stone implements. In general, while the components of the Archaic tradition varied through time and space, the period is integrated by the continual association of the above traits.

**Architecture, Greek.** The beginnings of Greek monumental architecture after the collapse of the Mycenaean kingdoms came in the 8th century BC, with the construction of what became the prototype of the Greek temple. The Temple of Hera at SAMOS was built in wood with a narrow shrine, fronted by a row of columns. This form, completely ringed with columns forming a peristyle, was further developed in the 7th century BC with temples at Samos and Miletus. The earliest Temple of Hera at OLYMPIA was built in the "Doric style" about 600 BC: it had wooden columns and lintels, but was in many respects similar to almost contemporary temples at ARGOS, Tegea, Sparta, Eretria, and DELPHI, which now for the first time were stone built.

During the course of the 6th century BC, temples of Doric type, with strongly tapered plain columns and flattened capitals with heavy lintels, were normally built of stone. Towards the century's end, an effort was made to lighten the rather heavy effect—the height of the columns in proportion to their lower diameter was increased, and the "ideal proportions" of length to breadth were standardized. In the colonized areas of Italy and Africa, there are differences of detail within temples of 6th-century date, in the numbers and rows of columns, the placing of the cult statue, and the practice of grouping temples in clusters, as at PAESTUM or SYRACUSE.

By the 5th century BC, the Classical Doric style of temple had reached its peak of perfection. The Temple of Zeus at Olympia, built between 470 and 456 BC, is perhaps its prime example, where the design suggests lightness rather than flamboyance within the individual features. The style accrued new forms of decoration in the period 430–370 BC, and experiments were made with new forms as, for example, the THOLOS temples at Olympia, Epidauros, and Delphi.

In Classical architecture in Attica, the plainer Doric style met the Ionian and East Greek influences because of Athens' involvement with the Ionian islands. The highest peak of this style is represented by the PARTHENON on the Acropolis at ATHENS, built by Ictinus between 447 and 438 BC, and the Propylaea, built in 437–431 BC by Mnesicles, which formed the monumental entrance to the whole of the Acropolis complex. The Temple of Athena Nike and the Odeon of Pericles in the Agora are its contemporaries. Another temple on the Acropolis, the ERECHTHEUM, with its differences of level and asymmetrical plan, represents a development of this style.

In the 5th century BC, the architectural emphasis shifted again from mainland Greece to Ionia, where the Ionic style flowered. Of particular note is the Mausoleum of HALICARNASSUS (*c*. 355 BC) which was a temple in Ionic style on a high plinth. Hellenistic architecture widened its scope to embody buildings other than temples: plan-

ning of a unit was often the new scheme—temple complexes at Lindos or Cos, or a town plan at PERGAMUM. Temples themselves became less significant buildings, the main emphasis now being on their surroundings. Houses, too, started to become a feature of architectural interest, with a growth of rather more luxurious villas. It was in the Hellenistic period that two of the so-called seven wonders of the ancient world were built—the Pharos at Alexandria, built in stepped courses and standing about 426 ft. (130 m) high, and the Colossus of Rhodes, a bronze statue 98 ft. (30 m) high astride the harbor entrance.

**Architecture, Roman.** The earliest architecture of Italy is that of the Etruscans: the majority of surviving remains are of fortifications, temples, city plans, and tombs, some of which may reflect typical house patterns. Much of the domestic architecture was probably still very crude, for round Iron Age huts of Etruscan date were displayed on the Palatine Hill in ROME in late antiquity. On Rome's Capitol Hill in 509 BC, a temple to Jupiter was built, and several other temples followed in the 4th century BC within her Servian walls, which were built in 386 BC after a raid on Rome by Gallic tribesmen.

Rome's architecture was more diverse than that of Greece, following the Hellenistic tradition. Colonies of the 4th and 3rd centuries BC have a rectangular ground plan—for example COSA, ALBA FUCENS, Cremona, and Placentia, while OSTIA was established as a rectangular fort at the mouth of the Tiber. In 273 BC a FORUM and CAPITOLIUM with a basilica was established at Cosa; but Rome's first basilica was not built until 184 BC, by which time she already possessed several fora, and two public atria. A great advance was the increased use of arches and vaults, for example in the aqueduct of Aqua Maria, in 144 BC, which ran for 7 mi. (11 km) above ground, and in the Stabian Baths at POMPEII. In the realm of domestic architecture, the Italian house was improved by the addition of a Hellenistic peristyle, and wall paintings in the 1st Pompeian style.

The 1st century BC was a fruitful period in Rome; the Tabularium and the Theater of Marcellus are two of the most important monumental buildings prior to Augustus' reign: both have elaborate architectural façades, and the theater is an almost new departure in that it is freestanding, rather than terraced into a hillside. Houses were split into smaller rooms, which were given the illusion of space by *trompe-l'oeil* paintings (2nd Pompeian style).

Augustus boasted that he found Rome built of brick and left it built of marble, and the use of Carrara marble from the quarries at Luna was certainly a mark of his activity, which exceeded his predecessor's efforts not only in Rome but all over the provinces in the construction of fortifications, aqueducts, and public buildings. In Rome the major buildings were the Pantheon, the Baths of Agrippa, the Forum of Augustus and its Temple of Mars Ultor, the Basilica Julia and the Theater of Marcellus. In Northern Italy and Provence, cities such as AOSTA, Turin, Como, AUTUN, and NÎMES now received their walls and gates.

By contrast, Augustus' imperial palace on the Palatine was still an unpretentious building, but successive emperors—Tiberius and Nero in particular—conceived and carried out grand additions. Nero's Golden House, started in AD 64, was a building of great architectural importance, not only in view of its layout round a central octagon, but also because of the flexibility achieved through the use of concrete, still at that time a relatively new medium.

Later emperors added many important new buildings, among them the Colosseum (on the site of Nero's lake), and Domitian's palace by the Flavians, and architecture reached a new peak under their successors: Nerva, Trajan, and Hadrian. This was the period of many new city layouts all over the provinces: for example, Timgad and Lambaesis under Trajan, together with the complete rebuilding of Rome's harbor town of Ostia. Hadrian's Villa at TIVOLI was constructed on the site of a republican villa but it had many additional courtyards and peristyles, with copies of famous buildings from other parts of the Classical world.

Under the Severan emperors came further building— the Baths of Caracalla at Rome and Severus' Arch, as well as the Forum Urbis, a plan of the city on marble, of which portions survive. In the late empire, the emphasis was on defense, with new wall circuits constructed not only at Rome, but at most of the major cities at least in the Western half of the Roman world. Within these, there was still room for large buildings of heavy grandeur —for example, the range of new imperial palaces built at Constantinople, TRIER, MILAN, Nicomedia, and Salonica, a series begun by Diocletian with the construction of his retirement palace at SPLIT. From the period of Constantine onwards, the mainstream of architecture shifted eastwards to Constantinople and to a more Christian tradition.

**Arena.** An area, usually sand-strewn, in a Roman amphitheater or circus, where the spectacle took place.

**Arenal.** A preceramic site and culture, dating from between 6500 and 6000 BC, on the Central coast of Peru, south of Lima. The culture is characterized by large diamond-shaped chipped points with rudimentary stems, which indicate a predominantly hunting way of life.

**Areopagus.** A small hill west of the Acropolis at Athens, where the chief magistrate presided over the assembly of ex-magistrates. Little remains there to show its original function.

**Argos.** The capital of the Argolid, in the Peloponnese region of Greece. The hill of Larisa forms an acropolis to the site. It formed the Mycenaean citadel and held a Classical temple. Little of the Greek city remains, but at the foot of the hill was a Roman THEATER and small ODEUM.

**Arica.** A city in the valley of Azapa on the North coast of Chile, in the vicinity of which preceramic shell mounds were excavated at Quiani, Pichalo, and Taltal. It is dated c. AD 1200–1450.

**Arikamedu.** Situated on the Madras coast of South India near Pondicherry, this was an important trading post of the Romans after the mid-1st century BC, when a town with warehouses was built. Excavations by Sir Mortimer WHEELER in 1954 revealed ARRETINE WARE of the 1st century AD, Mediterranean amphorae, and imperial Roman coins. Other contemporary South Indian sites have both Roman imports and local imitations of ceramics and coinage. Pre-Roman remains testify to the presence of a local settlement going back several centuries. (*See also* INDIA.)

**Arles** (Arelate). A colony in Southern Gaul founded by Caesar, retaining its amphitheater and cryptoporticus dating from the 1st century BC. Constantine the Great (AD 306–337) adopted the city as one of his capitals, and the monumental baths date from his time. The city was also a mint in late Roman times and a bishop's seat.

**Armor, Europe.**
*Prehistoric.* Shields, helmets, breastplates, and greaves (shinguards) are known from the Bronze Age onwards in Europe, and they seem to be connected with the appearance of personal fighting weapons made of metal, such as daggers, swords, and spears. A wooden shield is known from Ireland, but most examples are of bronze (the metal used for armor in prehistory because of its workable properties) and they were probably originally mounted on wood or leather. Bronze Age shields were round or oblong, often decorated with embossed or cast patterns, while a notable late IRON AGE shield from Lincolnshire is long and rectangular.

Helmets are known in the Bronze Age from Eastern Europe to France: rounded and conical forms were common, often with crests and wings. In England, bronze caps and helmets are known from the late Iron Age. Like other pieces of armor, they are often found in bogs, rivers, or lakes, and this probably ritual deposition indicates their ceremonial function as well as everyday use. Armor was probably often worn as much to impress and intimidate opponents as to protect the body. Breastplates and greaves are known in the Bronze Age over a similar area to helmets, but they are much rarer in the Iron Age. This seems to be connected with the rise of the naked Celtic warrior, fearless for his own safety and scornful of protection, whom we know of through his contacts with the civilized Mediterranean world.

*Greek and Roman.* Knowledge of the earliest forms of Greek arms and armor comes from the Homeric poems (*see* HOMERIC ARCHAEOLOGY), the descriptions in which fit various forms of defensive and offensive weapons both of Mycenaean and of later (Dark Age) date. The normal soldier of Classical Greek times was the hoplite: he was a heavily armed infantryman with bronze shield, breastplate, greaves, and helmet. He carried a spear and sword of iron. Battles were fought in formation—the spear used for thrusting and the sword for close fighting. With the advent of more sophisticated fighting techniques in the 4th century BC, the troops were less heavily armed, and had longer spears and smaller shields.

The earliest Roman sophisticated infantry was

modeled on the Greek hoplite, with very similar equipment, but by the 2nd century BC, the heavily armed legionary would have a throwing spear, a two-edged sword, and a large curved shield, breastplate, and helmet. This remained standard equipment for much of the imperial period: auxiliary troops, recruited from various provincial (and sometimes extra-provincial) sources would normally carry arms and armor to which they were accustomed. By far the most spectacular archaeological finds are pieces of parade armor: fine helmets, swords, greaves, and horse armor—all of them too richly decorated for use in battle. The later Roman army, increasingly reliant on the employment of non-Roman soldiers, was lighter armed and became more and more specialized in different fields.

**Arretine ware.** A type of pottery with relief-molded decoration and orange-red slip, made in Arretium (present-day Arezzo) from 40 BC onwards. The quality of the (usually) figured reliefs is outstanding. The workshops flourished until the reign of Claudius. (*See also* TERRA SIGILLATA.)

**Arsacids.** *See* PARTHIA, PARTHIANS.

**Arsenic.** Since it gives a very hard cutting edge, arsenical copper (copper alloyed with arsenic) was widely used for a long time, until replaced by tin-bronze (tin alloyed with copper), for the manufacture of tools and weapons in prehistoric Europe and the Near East. Orpiment, the trisulphide of arsenic, was used in antiquity as a yellow pigment.

**Arslan Tash.** The site of the ancient city of Hadâtu, a provincial capital of the Assyrian kings in Northern Syria. The central TELL is surrounded by a circular wall. A French team, led by F. Thureau-Dangin, excavated here in 1927, and found a palace and a temple, together with some fine ivories—probably booty from Syria, captured at the beginning of the 8th century BC and stored there. Some Assyrian reliefs and statues were also excavated.

**Art, Prehistoric Europe.** With the advent of farming in Europe from about 6000 BC, new forms of artistic expression appear. Noteworthy are the Neolithic pottery and stone figurines from Southeast Europe, whose stylization of the human body foreshadows modern sculpture; and styles of abstract patterns, executed by burnishing, incision, and painting, are skillfully adapted to the shapes of Neolithic pots. In Western Europe some megalithic tombs were adorned with elaborate patterns of spirals, chevrons, and lozenges. Metallurgy introduced new materials (gold, silver, copper, bronze, and finally iron and steel), and smiths often produced extremely fine pieces of workmanship.

Until 1000 BC, the finest Bronze Age work in metal is seen in weaponry and jewelry, and the favorite decorative motif was the spiral. Other materials—faience, amber, ivory, and jet—were also exploited, principally for jewelry. In the centuries following 1000 BC, some of the best work went into the production of ceramic and bronze vessels in Central Europe, while in the East the SCYTHIANS developed a highly imaginative, powerful animal style. From the 5th century BC the CELTS formulated a series of original abstract syles of curvilinear decoration (based ultimately on floral patterns from Greek and Etruscan ornament), into which bodies of animals and human faces were often interwoven. In Ireland, these styles eventually developed by successive stimuli, latterly from early Byzantine and Germanic animal interlace styles, into the magnificent patterns seen on the stone crosses and illuminated Gospels of the late 1st millennium AD. (*See also* CAVE ART.)

**Aryballos.** A form of Greek vase: a small squat oil flask with a single mouth and a single band handle.

**Asine.** A pre-Classical Greek settlement near Nauplia in the Argolid Gulf. It preserves remains of the Early, Middle, and Late Helladic settlement and of Hellenistic city walls.

**Assiut.** A Lydian, Persian, Greek, and Roman city in the Troas: it retains a 6th-century BC Doric temple as well as walls and a theater.

**Assur.** The first capital of ASSYRIA, situated at the junction of a canal with the Tigris, where the present-day Qalaat-Shergat now stands. The site was excavated by a German team under W. ANDRAE from 1903 to 1914. The earliest levels date back to the beginning of the 3rd millennium BC. Towards the end of that millennium, fortifications were built on the landward side. In Old Assyrian times it became the center of trade with Cappadocia, and under Shamshi-Adad I it became a capital. The principal temples found are those of Anu-adad, Assur (each with a ZIGGURAT), Ishtar, and Sin-Shamash; there were also several palaces. In every case, earlier buildings were restored or rebuilt by later rulers. Sennacherib added a sanctuary called the *bît akitu*, which was built outside the walls and used for the New Year Festival. Rows of stelae belonging to kings and high officials were also found. Assur fell in 612 BC, at the same time as NINEVEH, and never recovered. The team of workmen trained by Andrae, and their descendants, have been used as specialized workmen on virtually all excavations in Iraq this century and are known as Shergatis. (*See* the chronological table, p. 198.)

**Assyria, Assyrians.** Originally Semitic nomads in Northern MESOPOTAMIA, who finally settled round ASSUR and accepted its tutelary god as their own. After the fall of the 3rd Dynasty of UR (2004 BC), Assyria seems to have become an independent state and its fortunes were based on its role as middleman in international trade in the Old Assyrian period (19th century BC). The exact mechanics of this trade still elude us, but copper, textiles, and perhaps tin seem to have played a part in it, and merchant colonies were established in Central Anatolia in a series of trading stations: the karum of Kanesh (KÜLTEPE) has produced several thousand tablets relating to these

A 9th-century BC relief from Nineveh, showing King Assurnasirpal II of Assyria hunting lions from his chariot.

business transactions.

The life of these colonies came to an abrupt end, but an Amorite Dynasty gained power in Assur and, under Shamshi-Adad I (1813–1781 BC), Assyria became politically active throughout Northern Syria and Mesopotamia. Shamshi-Adad installed his son Iasmah-Adad (1796–1780 BC) as governor of MARI, while his other son and successor, Ishme-Dagan, became governor of Ekallatum: their letters, found at Mari, illuminate this whole period. Hammurabi of BABYLON overthrew Ishme-Dagan in two campaigns (1756 and 1754 BC) and, though kings continued to reign in Assur, their domination of Northern Iraq was at an end, and they fell successively under Kassite and Mitannian rule (*see* HURRIANS). The Middle Assyrian King Ashur-uballit I (1365–1330 BC) obtained his country's independence, and Tukulti-Ninurta I (1244–1208 BC) overthrew the Kassite King Kashtiliash and reached the Persian Gulf; but he was killed a few years later in his new capital, Kar-Tukulti-Ninurta. Kings continued to rule in Assur during the Dark Ages which succeeded the invasion of the SEA PEOPLE.

The accession of Adad-nirari II in 911 BC heralds the Neo-Assyrian Empire. From then on, almost yearly campaigns ensured the expansion of the Assyrians southwards into BABYLONIA, eastwards into SYRIA-PALESTINE and the rich coastal cities of PHOENICIA and even into Egypt, northwards into URARTU and the Neo-Hittite and Aramaean states of Southeast ANATOLIA, and eastwards into IRAN, where the MEDES and Persians were slowly gaining power. Assyrian annals, monumental inscriptions, and reliefs have left us a record of many of these campaigns and some of the booty obtained has been found, notably ivories at ARSLAN TASH and NIMRUD. This latter city, NINEVEH, and KHORSABAD were all at one time or another the capital. Generally, the military activities of the Assyrian rulers went hand in hand with building activity, and the foremost kings can be listed as follows:

*Rulers of the Assyrian Empire*
Adad-nirari II (911–891 BC)
Tukulti-Ninurta II (890–884 BC)
Assurnasirpal II (883–859 BC)
Shalmaneser III (858–824 BC)
Tiglath-Pileser III (744–727 BC)
Sargon II (721–705 BC)
Sennacherib (704–681 BC)
Esarhaddon (680–669 BC)
Assurbanipal (668–627 BC)

Little is known of the last Assyrian kings, and Nineveh fell before the Medes in 612 BC. (*See also* BALAWAT; BAVIAN; JERWAN; MALTAI; TELL AHMAR.)

**Astronomy, Mesoamerica.** In view of the great emphasis, both religious and secular, on the calendar among all Mesoamerican peoples, astronomy was extremely important. It is clear today that Mesoamerican astronomers were able to make extremely accurate measurements of the solar year, could record the phases of the moon, and, judging from the tables of the Dresden Codex, could forecast eclipses. They also knew the length of time for a revolution of Venus and possibly also of Mars.

Their traditional method of making observations was by noting the positions of the rising and setting of the sun or moon at crucial times of the year. These sighting points were marked by the erection of monuments which gave a line of sight to the horizon. Basically these were the same methods which were used by the megalithic cultures of Europe, and are comparable to the uses of composite stone circles like STONEHENGE. For example, at COPAN there are two stelae which give a line of sight to the horizon where the sun sets on April 12th. More elaborate is a complex of buildings consisting of three temples set on a bank to the east of a pyramid, and so arranged that an observer on the steps of the pyramid would see the sun rise behind the edge of the most northerly temple at the summer solstice; behind the edge of the southerly

The Mayan astronomical observatory, called the Caracol, at Chichen Itza, Mexico.

one at the winter solstice; and over the central one at the equinoxes. This tripartite arrangement of buildings was first noticed at UAXACTUN, but similar arrangements have been noticed at other sites as well. The top of a building called the Caracol, at CHICHEN ITZA, is a chamber with apertures which gave lines of sight to the setting sun at the spring equinox and to the setting moon when it was at its maximum northern and southern declinations. Only about one-third of the circular wall of the chamber remains today, so we do not know what other lines of sight were provided by other apertures.

There are very few indications that observations were made of celestial bodies when they were high in the sky, as opposed to when they were rising or setting. One example is the shaft at Xochicalco, intended to give the time of the summer solstice. A shaft in the stairs of Building G at MONTE ALBAN may have served a comparable purpose. Recently it was suggested that the roof combs of Maya temples may have been used as gnomons, the shadow from which may have indicated the positions of the sun at various times and seasons.

Little is known of any instrumental astronomy. Pictures in the codices suggest that crossed sticks were set up in front of temples to indicate the position from which observations should be made. It has also been argued that the year glyph, used at Xochicalco and some other Central Mexican sites, consists of two trapezes which would show the position of the sun if they were set up at right angles, with one trapeze oriented north-south and the other east-west. The movement of the shadow of the north-south trapeze would reflect the time of day: that of the east-west trapeze, reflecting the changing declination of the sun, would show the seasons. The Precolumbian Mexicans, therefore, had a more sophisticated sundial than was known contemporaneously in the Old World. (*See also* CALENDAR, MESOAMERICA.)

**Asuka Period.** In Japan, the introduction of Buddhism from Korea represented an important link with the culture of mainland Korea and China. Initially, such cultural influences were confined to the court established in the Asuka region (AD 552–710), where Buddhist temples, imperial palaces, and military headquarters were constructed, a number of which have now been investigated. With the establishment of the capital at Fujiwara in AD 694, the ideas and skills hitherto confined to the court became known to a wider area and were to reach a high point in the succeeding NARA PERIOD.

**Atchana.** *See* TELL ATCHANA.

**Athens.** The city of Athens lies some 3 mi. (5 km) from the sea, and at the center of the city is the rocky outcrop known as the Acropolis. In Mycenaean times this was walled and held a palace. In the 8th and 7th centuries BC the marketplace (AGORA) lying north of the Acropolis was established, while by the 6th century BC, the Acropolis itself had become a temple area, and there were large public buildings in the agora. After the destruction of the city by the Persians in 480 BC, a new circuit of walls was built under the guidance of Themistocles. The port of

PIRAEUS was walled, too, and long walls protected the route between it and the main city. The Themistoclean circuit of walls, repaired after further destruction by Spartans, fixed the extent of the city until well into the Roman period.

Of the city's present remains, the most impressive are on the Acropolis. The PARTHENON, built in 447–432 BC, occupied the site of an unfinished temple, ruined in 480 BC. This was soon followed by the Propylaea (437–432 BC) and the Temple of Athena Nike. The ERECHTHEUM occupied the site of a 6th-century BC temple, and was built before the end of the 5th century BC.

During the course of the 5th century BC, important buildings were erected at the foot of the Acropolis. Best preserved of these are the Theater of Dionysus, the Odeon of Pericles, and, in an area known for its natural springs, the Sanctuary of Asclepius, the God of healing.

The agora lay between the main "Dipylon" gate and the Acropolis. Its earliest buildings—the Temple of Apollo Patrous and the altar of the 12 gods—date from the 6th century BC. Later were added the tholos, the Temple of Hephaestos, and the Stoa Poikile, which has not been excavated, but whose decoration is known to have included a pictorial history of Athens. Attention again turned on the agora after the completion of the Acropolis temples. A new BOULEUTERION, the Stoa of Zeus, and the South Stoa were added in the 4th century BC. Later still (in the 2nd century BC), the Stoa of Attalus II and the Metroon were built.

Plan of the agora at Athens.

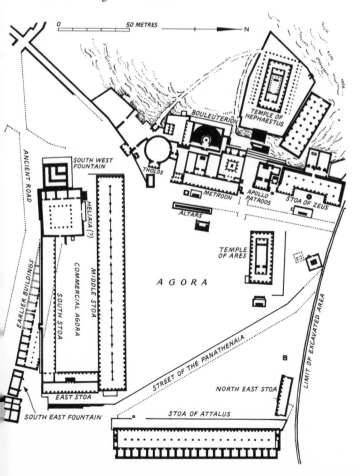

In the Roman imperial period, Athens was a university city and the seat of philosophical schools. Roman buildings in the agora and on the Acropolis were few, but they included the Odeon of Agrippa and the Temple of Augustus and Rome, next to the Parthenon. A new market, west of the agora, was built round the octagonal Temple of the Winds, built by Andronikos in the 1st century BC. Hadrian enlarged the city and completed a 6th-century BC Temple of Zeus.

Large areas were destroyed in the Herulian invasions of AD 267, and a late Roman circuit of city walls enclosed a restricted area north of the Acropolis. The temples on the Acropolis itself remained as a stronghold of paganism until the 5th century AD, and they were probably not converted into churches until the 6th century AD.

**Atlantis.** An island mentioned by Plato. It was supposed to have belonged in the far-off past to Egypt, but had sunk under the Ocean. Its location is not known, but it has been suggested that reference to Atlantis was a legendary memory of the vanished Minoan civilization.

**Atlatl.** The Aztec word for spearthrower. This is an ancient weapon aid, probably dating to Paleo-Indian times in the New World. It is usually a short, and often grooved, stick with a hook at one end. The butt end of the spear or dart fits into the hook of the atlatl, which effectively lengthens the arm of the thrower, and helps to propel the spear a greater distance. It can be considered as a kind of rigid sling. More elaborate Mexican examples have two loops for thumb and index finger grips. Ceremonial atlatls of Aztec date have beautifully carved and gilded handles. The atlatl was the missile weapon *par excellence* of Mexico until the Late Postclassic, when the bow and arrow appeared. There are many drawings of atlatls in the MIXTEC codices and on representations of Toltec warriors at Tula and CHICHEN ITZA. The spearthrower was also utilized by a number of Precolumbian New World cultures.

**Atrium.** The central courtyard of the Roman house, usually surrounded by a peristyle round which living rooms and bedrooms were ranged.

**Augst** (Augusta Raurica). Founded in 44 BC in Celtic territory, now in Switzerland, the city flourished under Hadrian. It preserves one of the most complete Roman city layouts north of the Alps, with a THEATER, FORUM, AMPHITHEATER, BATHS, and city walls.

**Aurignacian.** Recognized in 1906 as the first part of the Upper PALAEOLITHIC sequence in France, the Aurignacian has subsequently been redefined, so that only the "Middle Aurignacian" of the original classification now carries this name. It is characterized by split-based bone points and "carinate"-shaped stone tools, and is radiocarbon dated to between 33,000 and 36,000 BC.

**Aurochs.** *Bos primigenius*, the ancestor of the present-day domestic cattle, which became extinct only in the 17th century AD. Its habitat was forest, and it was widely distributed from Europe to China. It was probably independently domesticated in several places, one of the most important of which was Eastern Hungary in the 4th millennium BC.

**Australia.** In the last decade or so, the prehistory of Australia has changed more rapidly and significantly than that of any other region, and we must thus be prepared for the picture to continue to change drastically. Australia was certainly occupied more than 25,000 years ago, and probably more than 40,000 years ago. In fact the whole continent, including Tasmania and New Guinea which would have been joined by land bridges, was probably widely settled 20,000 years ago. This early occupation coincided with the later part of the last glaciation—a time of lower sea level, cooler climate, and less evaporation—and presumably the terrain was less arid. This is also the time of the Upper Palaeolithic of Europe and adjacent regions, but whether the Australian occupation should be called Upper Palaeolithic is not clear.

There are a number of fossil men from Australia. The Keilor skull from near Melbourne was the first known to belong to the time of the Ice Ages, and is now thought to be 15,000 years old or more. There are two well dated skeletons from Mungo Lake, some 186 mi. (300 km) north of Melbourne, in New South Wales; they are about 25,000 and 30,000 years old respectively. All these skulls are claimed to be as modern as those of living aborigines in type. Other skulls, notably those from Kow Swamp, 93 mi. (150 km) north of Melbourne in Victoria, appear to be more archaic, with big brow ridges and a long low skull vault. Some workers have compared them to the primitive Solo skulls and Java man from Java. Some of these more primitive skulls from Australia are only 9,000 years old or less, and thus postglacial in date. This could imply two groups of people living in Australia. Other anthropologists doubt if the archaic skulls are really different from those of other early aborigines. The question of the origin of the Tasmanians is also much disputed.

Little is known at the moment about the earliest occupied sites in Australia, but the early hunters were contemporary with the last giant marsupials, and may have contributed to their extinction. The prehistoric peoples of Australia, possibly eventually numbering about 300,000, were hunters and gatherers: many living near the coast are known to have eaten widely from the sea's resources, and on land they also no doubt exploited aquatic resources. A wide variety of stone-tool types were made, but at first blades and small blade tools were rare. Later, in the so-called Australian small tool tradition, such tools came into use, and have some analogies with the European Mesolithic.

The Mungo Lake burial is important as the earliest evidence of cremation, for it was quite heavily burned. The even earlier burial from this site had been covered with red ocher. The use of ocher crayons is known from this time and rock surfaces were decorated with painted lines and carved grooves.

Sites in Northern Territory have produced ground stone adzes or axes with hafting grooves. The hafting of spear points and other tools was undoubtedly common. Simple bone points were made by grinding. The spear-thrower was being widely used at the time of European colonization, but the bow and arrow had not arrived.

*Australopithecus.* Following the discovery of a child's skull at Taung in South Africa in 1924, a very large series of hominid (manlike) fossils were found in the Sterkfontein valley near Krugersdorp and at Makapan Limeworks. One series, *Australopithecus africanus*, according to the normal modern classification, is believed to be an adult form of the Taung skull, and a possible ancestor of man 2.5 to 3 million years ago.

The skull of *Australopithecus africanus*, from Sterkfontein.

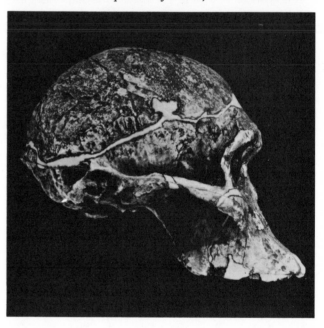

**Automobile industry.** The archaeology of automobile production covers the manufacturing, maintenance, repair, and retailing aspects of the industry. Garages, fuel pumps, multistory or underground parks and show-rooms are as relevant and as important as factories, but they are considerably more neglected and vulnerable. In England, factory buildings dating back to the 1920s survive as part of the British Leyland plants at Cowley, Oxford, and Longbridge, Birmingham, but veteran premises of this vintage are rare in the industry. Saddest and least defensible is the sweeping away in 1976 of the 1910 Ford plant at Highland Park, Mich., United States, the birthplace of the mass-production of cars on moving assembly lines. It was the cornerstone of Model T production and it was here that the famous five dollar minimum daily wage plan was put into operation.

Automobile museums exist in every industrialized country and the history of the automobile itself is adequately documented. Much work remains to be done, however, to locate and record the sites of the numerous small manufacturing firms which existed up to the 1930s.

**Autun** (Augustodunum). An Augustan Roman city foundation in Gaul: it preserves remains of city walls with two Augustan gates, a THEATER, and a native-style Temple of Janus.

**Avebury.** This site in Wiltshire, England, is one of the largest and most impressive of the class of late Neolithic (c. 2000 BC) ceremonial enclosures in England, Scotland, and Wales known as henges (see HENGE). It consists of a large bank set outside a deep ditch, with four entrances, and a ring of large stones inside the ditch and further stone circles within. The bank has a mean diameter of about 1400 ft. (427 m) and reaches up to 18 ft. (5 m) above ground, and 50 ft. (15 m) from the bottom of the ditch. It was built principally of chalk from the ditch, with turf and wood revetments in places. The ditch was about 70 ft. (21 m) wide and about 30 ft. (9 m) deep, and encloses some 28 ac. (11 ha). A little within it was a continuous ring of about 98 stones, of a tall and squat variety, set about 35 ft. (11 m) apart. Within, the southern inner circle of 340 ft. (104 m) diameter was formed of further large stones, with an internal more linear arrangement of other stones, and in the center of the northern inner circle, 320 ft. (97 m) in diameter, were 3 large stones known as the Cove. From the southern entrance ran an avenue composed of paired large stones leading to a small ceremonial enclosure over 1½ mi. (2.4 km) away at West Kennet, known as the Sanctuary. Traces exist of another avenue connecting with the west entrance. Surprisingly few finds have been recovered in excavations. Pottery indicates construction and use by late Neolithic communities, perhaps continuing into the Early Bronze Age. Like other large henges, its purpose may have been primarily ceremonial, and some archaeologists have deduced also a concern with astronomical observation from the stone settings.

**Aviation.** The archaeology of aviation, as distinct from museums, relics, and mementoes of aviation, is at a very primitive stage. Any comprehensive conservation policy admittedly faces great difficulties. Many of the old grass airfields have been built over and the simple passenger-handling facilities of the 1920s and early 1930s have mostly been swept away or, being often made of wood, burnt down. A reconstruction of one of these early airports would be valuable.

Rhinebeck, N.Y., has a replica of the kind of airdrome that was normal during World War I, and Brooks Air Force Base, San Antonio, Tex., has Hangar Nine, which is believed to be the oldest surviving military hangar in the United States. At Rockcliffe Airport, Ottawa, Canada, there is a hangar (1939) which was the prototype of the cheap, easy to erect hangar built by the score during World War II. Another historic hangar (1931) is preserved at the former American Airship Center, now Lakehurst Naval Air Station, N.J. Britain has two airship hangars at Cardington, Beds. (1917, extended 1927; and 1927), now scheduled historic monuments. The Brabazon Assembly Hall (1947) at Filton, Bristol, is notable for its 200-ton (181,437 kg) aluminum doors, which can be opened in two minutes. The first all-aluminum hangar in Britain (1951) is still in service at London Airport. The terminal building (1928) at Croydon, England, belonged to the foremost airport of its day. It is now used as offices, the airfield itself unrecognizable in its new role of an industrial estate. Few of the pre-1939 town terminals are still in use.

**Awl.** See STONE TECHNOLOGY.

**Ax, stone.** One of the last major categories of stone tool to be invented, occurring first at the end of the last ICE AGE in the PALAEOLITHIC. In Mesolithic times stone axes were usually chipped from a block of flint, and could be resharpened by the removal of a flake from the end. In the Neolithic, they were polished and often perforated to aid hafting. (See also STONE TECHNOLOGY.)

**Ayacucho complex.** Found in the lowest levels of PIKIMACHAY CAVE, about 6 mi. (10 km) north of the city of Ayacucho in Peru, this is a complex of unifacial chipped tools and bone artifacts, associated with the bone of horse, camel, and giant sloth and dating from between 13,000 and 11,000 BC.

**Ayampitin.** A site near Cordoba in Northwestern Argentina, where a great number of large, crude bifacial leaf points were found. This type of point, which was made between 8000 and 12,000 years ago, occurs over much of South America and is the diagnostic feature of the early leaf-shaped projectile point complexes.

**Aylesford.** A cemetery of cremation burials of the middle to late 1st century BC was discovered in the 1880s at Aylesford (Kent) in England. The burials contained wheel-thrown pottery, including "pedestal urns" of the Aylesford-Swarling culture, identified with the BELGAE in England. Other grave goods from the cemetery included brooches (see FIBULA) and wooden stave-built buckets with metal fittings. One of the buckets had a pair of cast bronze heads on its rim at the ends of the handle, and was bound with sheet bronze hoops decorated with *repoussé* relief designs of horses, faces, and whirligig and yin-yan patterns. The same burial, probably that of a chieftain, contained a bronze jug and pan for pouring and ladling out wine: these two vessels had been imported from Central Italy. The bucket was probably used for mixing water with the wine.

**Aymara.** The tribal group and language of the people who occupy the Titicaca basin area. They may have been responsible for the TIAHUANACO culture. They have maintained their language and much of their culture to the present day.

**Aztecs.** The Aztecs, *Mexica*, or *Tenochcas*, were one of the last of several nomadic Northern tribes which periodically moved southward into the valley of Mexico in search of better food resources. Their mythical homeland, the Seven Caves of Chicomoztoc, has not been identified but it was probably in Northwest Mexico.

Unable to establish themselves successfully in the mainland part of the valley, they finally took refuge on two inhospitable, marshy islands in Lake Texcoco, where they served as tributaries to the Tepanec town of Azcapotzalco. The Aztecs and other early settlers on the two islands were little better than exiled bandits. Much of Aztec history of this time is obscure: their island capital, TENOCHTITLAN, was probably founded about AD 1345, but dynasties for both islands were provided from outside.

In 1428, Tenochtitlan, smarting under the tyranny of the ruler of Azcapotzalco, formed an alliance with the cities of Texcoco and Tlacopan and rebelled. Azcapotzalco was defeated by this Triple Alliance and the Aztecs became principal heirs to all the cities previously paying tribute to the Tepanecs. From this time, the history of the Aztecs is one of continuous military expansion until the 16th-century Spanish Conquest.

During the Aztec reign of Itzcoatl (1428–1440), religious and military hierarchies were established, and conquests were made in the immediate neighborhood of Tenochtitlan. He was succeeded by Moctezuma I, who expanded his conquests to the north and east, bringing the Aztecs into contact with the high cultures of Puebla. In the reign of Axayacatl, who succeeded Moctezuma I in 1469, the rivalry between the twin island towns of Tenochtitlan and Tlatelolco was brought to an end by the capture and absorption of the latter. It was also in this reign that the Aztecs suffered their greatest military setback, being decisively defeated in Michoacan by the Tarascans. Otherwise, their military record through succeeding reigns, Tizoc (1481–1486), Ahuizotl (1486–1503), and Moctezuma II (1503–1520), misnamed Montezuma by the Spaniards, was a record of almost continuous conquest, or reconquest, of rebellious cities. They dominated both the Gulf, and much of the Pacific coast of Mexico and even penetrated into Guatemala. They do not seem to have occupied the Yucatan but apparently had a trading post at Xicalango. Certain isolated groups of Mesoamerica remained independent, most notably the Tlaxcalans. A number of Zapotec and Mixtec towns also successfully defended themselves through allied efforts.

The motives for the aggressive Aztec policy were partly economic, and partly religious. They wanted resources, such as cotton which would not grow in the highlands, as well as cacao and the rich luxury goods of gold, turquoise, feathers, and copal incense from the Isthmian region and Oaxaca. Their own facilities for food production were limited. They obtained fish from Lake Texcoco, and grew crops on the reclaimed CHINAMPA lands.

All through the history of Mesoamerica there had always been a tradition of long-distance trading. Among the Aztecs this tradition was carried on by a guild of merchants known as the *pochteca*. They organized trade caravans which traveled all over Mexico. They were armed and fully able to defend themselves if attacked. A frequent cause of war was the unwillingness of some towns to trade on terms the *pochteca* considered reasonable. In such cases the military flag followed trade.

The religious motive for expansion was also important because of the need for prisoners for human sacrifice to the Aztec gods. This rite, which had a long history in Mesoamerica, reached outrageous proportions under the Aztecs. If native sources can be believed, no less than 20,000 victims were sacrificed at the dedication of the great temple in the reign of Tizoc, with thousands of others during the ceremonial year. So pressing was the need for prisoners to sacrifice that, at times when no war existed, the Aztecs would resort to a ceremonial war with a friendly city. These wars, euphemistically termed the "Flowery Wars," were fought by arrangement for the purpose of obtaining prisoners for sacrifice. The overall terror of Aztec military supremacy was such that many foreign towns submitted to them without resistance.

By the time of the Spanish Conquest the population of Tenochtitlan had grown to about 300,000 people. The two islands had merged into one community through the use of causeways and CHINAMPA lands. The island was also joined to the mainland by causeways to Tepeyac, Tlacopan, and Coyoacan. The ceremonial heart of the great city, dominated by the twin temples of Tlaloc and Huitzilopochtli, was also the site of other principal temples, the ballcourt, the *Tzompantli*, where the thousands of skulls of sacrificial victims were strung, and Moctezuma's palace. The draining of the lake and the recent sprawling growth of modern Mexico City, directly over the Aztec capital, has increased the problems of archaeologists.

**Babel.** *See* BABYLON; BORSIPPA.

**Babylon.** Babylonian capital of Southern Mesopotamia, situated on the River Euphrates at Hilleh, south of Baghdad. It was excavated by the Germans under R. KOLDEWEY from 1899 to 1917. The site covers a huge area, which was originally divided into two by the River Euphrates, with the palace and more important temples on the east bank, surrounded by huge double fortifications pierced by eight gates. The most important of these is Nebuchadnezzar's Ishtar Gate, approached by a processional way and decorated with enameled bricks bearing dragons, bulls, and lions in relief. Immediately within the gate was the *Südburg*: a vast palace built by Nabopolassar and Nebuchadnezzar, which included the famous "hanging gardens"—one of the seven Wonders of the World—built at different levels over a series of vaulted chambers. Other palaces and temples were also excavated, but the famous Tower of Babel had been so robbed for its bricks that nothing survives, and the name came to be applied to the well preserved ZIGGURAT at BORSIPPA. Merkes, an important commercial quarter, was also excavated.

After Nabonidus' defeat by Cyrus II, the city came under Achaemenid rule and was captured in 331 BC by Alexander the Great, who died there in 323 BC. Babylon gradually fell into ruin and was replaced as capital by Seleucia on the River Tigris, and by CTESIPHON under the SELEUCIDS and PARTHIANS. The material from Babylon is predominantly Chaldaean and the earlier levels have become inaccessible, owing to the rising water table. However, the city was already mentioned in the middle

A reconstruction of Nebuchadnezzar's Ishtar Gate at Babylon, which dates from the early 6th century BC.

of the 3rd millennium BC, though it first became important under the kings of the 1st Dynasty of Babylon, the foremost of whom was Hammurabi. He succeeded in uniting Mesopotamia under his rule and established a code of laws, carved on a large stele which was found at SUSA. The Dynasty came to an end when the Hittites suddenly raided the city c. 1595 BC, during the reign of Samsuditana (*see* CHRONOLOGY, NEAR EAST).

**Babylonia.** The term applied to Southern Mesopotamia, comprising AKKAD in the north and SUMER in the south.

**Badarian culture.** From the season 1893–4 onwards, at a number of sites in Upper Egypt, W. M. Flinders PETRIE and others began to find large numbers of graves containing artifacts which belonged to a previously unknown people. Further digging at other Upper and Middle Egyptian sites led Egyptologists to date this people to the period before Egypt's Dynastic era and to divide this Predynastic Period into two phases: NAQADA CULTURE I and NAQADA CULTURE II. Later, an even earlier culture was discovered by G. Brunton and G. Caton-Thompson, which was termed Badarian after the large Predynastic site at el-Badari.

The results of a stratified dig at the Predynastic village of el-Hamamiyeh carried out by Caton-Thompson, proved the Badarian to predate the Naqada cultures. In the SEQUENCE DATING system, therefore, Badarian artifacts are placed before S.D.30. THERMOLUMINESCENCE

tests on Badarian pottery fragments have provided dates in the second half of the 5th millennium BC. This evidence conforms well with the view that the succeeding Naqada I culture, usually dated to the first half of the 4th millennium BC, is in part overlapped by the Badarian.

Badarian civilization is restricted to the immediate area of el-Badari and includes the sites of Deir Tasa, Mostagedda, Matmar, Qaw el-Kebir, and el-Hamamiyeh. The so-called Tasian culture, named after its find-site, was once thought to represent a separate earlier culture but is now generally accepted as being an early phase of Badarian. No remains of any kind of house have survived in Badarian settlements, but whether this means the Badarians lived in skin or matting tents or homes of perishable materials is open to debate. The presence of sticks and matting in some graves may indicate the former type of dwelling. Undoubtedly the climate was cold and damp: kilts or long skirts, made of linen or skins with the fur inwards, were worn, and the marshy lowland teemed with hippopotami and crocodiles.

Most Badarian graves are oval in shape, only the larger being rectangular and even they usually have rounded corners. Cemeteries lie to the east of settlements. The bodies, placed in hampers or wrapped in matting or skins, lay contracted, in the foetal position, generally with face to the west and head to the south. Massive girdles of blue-glazed steatite cylinder beads are characteristic of the period for male burials, but necklaces, bracelets, and anklets are also typical forms of jewelry. The materials used are generally coral, shell, pebble, bone, and soft stones, although some turquoise does occur. Both sexes wore ivory bangles but nose studs are very rare. Rectangular stone palettes were used for the grinding of green malachite, which was kept in ivory containers mixed with fat or castor oil so that it might be applied to the face or body.

A few female figurines are the earliest examples in Egypt of art in the round, but far more characteristic of the period are carved animals, animal heads, and birds, which surmount the handles of ornamental combs and spoons made from bone or ivory. Amulets in the form of hippopotami and gazelle heads make their first appearance here. Indeed, animals must have played an important part in the life of the Badarians. Cattle, sheep, and goats may have been domesticated; fish and birds formed a staple part of the diet, to judge from the quantity of fish and bird bones which have been found. The discovery in the cemeteries of the bodies of dogs, sheep, and oxen wrapped in matting or linen, like their human counterparts, suggests that already certain animals were revered.

Information on Badarian settlements has been supplemented by the discovery at Matmar of clay bins lined with matting, which were used as granaries. Husks and the remains of bread found in graves show that the grain was emmer (*triticum dicoccum*) and barley. Flint saw-edged knives were presumably used for harvesting, querns ground the grain, and hearths with cooking pots were found beside the granaries. The weaving of linen, basketmaking, and the production of leather articles seem to have been thriving industries. Bone awls and needles were used for piercing and sewing the leather. Although hunting was important and many flint arrows with winged and leaf-shaped heads have been found, no bow has ever been discovered. The flint industry in general, however, seems to have been rather poor, making use of worn nodules found lying about instead of fine-quality stone from the nearby cliffs. Copper was known but no tools larger than awls have been found.

Common to nearly every burial and characteristic of the whole period is the pottery, which falls into two categories: coarse and fine. In the former, bowls and deep pots are the most common. Fine ware has three main types: Polished Red, with a burnished red slip, Polished Black, and Black-topped Red, the latter probably so-colored by upturning the hot pot in a fire. The exceptional thinness of some of these vessels' walls and the quality of the burnishing has possibly never been surpassed in Egypt's subsequent history. The characteristic rippling effect was produced by combing the surface of the still soft clay with a toothed implement before burnishing and firing. Some vessels have interior plant and branch designs.

Although the Badarian culture was almost exclusive to a small area of Middle Egypt, it was not without outside contacts. Elephant ivory used for spoons must have come from the South, shells for jewelry from the Red Sea, turquoise beads probably came from Sinai, and copper for beads and small implements from the North or South. The few female figurines have their nearest parallel in the Beersheba culture of Palestine, but the original homeland of the Badarians is probably to be sought in the South, close to a source of Amazon stone: they produced large quantities of green-glazed stone in imitation of the latter, because they were no longer able to obtain it. Their use of flint nodules also suggests that their homeland lacked flint. These facts, in conjunction with their use of Red Sea shells and the ibex as an ornamental motif, and the presence of Black-topped Red ware in the Khartoum Neolithic culture, make it likely that the Badarians came from the area to the South of Egypt via the Red Sea and Wadi Hammamat.

**Baden culture.** The name given to a complex of related groups in the Carpathian basin in the 3rd millennium BC, contemporary with the Early Bronze Age in the Aegean.

Named after the *Königshöhle* (King's mound) in the town of Baden, not far from Vienna, it has also been referred to as the "Ossarn" or "Pecel" culture, and as the "Channeled Ware" or "Radial-decorated pottery" culture. It was in many areas a successor of the LENGYEL culture and a transitional stage has been identified in the area of Lake Balaton in Hungary. It is notable for being the first prehistoric culture of the Hungarian plain to unite both Eastern and Western halves, as it appears in the Tisza River basin as well as Pannonia. Colonization, both of the mountain fringes, and of the dryer sandy area between the major rivers, began to take place at this time.

The Baden culture shows evidence of contact both with Aegean Early Bronze Age groups and with the tribes of the South Russian steppes. The Aegean in-fluence is most marked in the pottery, where jugs and cups in fine black wares with rippled decoration make their appearance, and form the prototypes of many of the vessel forms of the Central European Bronze Age. Contact with the steppe areas is revealed in the small model carts, one of which was found at Budakalasz, just north of Budapest. This is the earliest evidence of wheeled vehicles in Europe, and may be compared on the one hand to contemporary models from under mounds on the Russian steppes, and on the other with finds of actual wheels from slightly later contexts in Northern Europe, belonging to the CORDED WARE CULTURE.

**Bahía.** A phase, dating from just before the time of Christ, which was uncovered on La Plata Island, Manabi, Ecuador. Its large pyramidal mounds, helmeted figurines, spouted jars, and incised pottery have been cited as evidence of contacts with the Nayarit coast of Mexico.

**Baia** (Baiae). A Roman bathing establishment, famous and fashionable in antiquity, on the Northwest coast of the Puteolian Gulf, Italy. Remains of the monumental baths, with three Hadrianic vaulted chambers, survive.

**Balawat.** The site of the ancient Imgur Bel, east of Mosul in Northern Iraq. The Temple of Mamu was discovered, together with three sets of gates (two now restored, in the British Museum, London, and one in the Baghdad Museum). These were made of wood and were decorated with bronze bands illustrating the campaigns of Assurnasirpal II and Shalmaneser III. The site seems to have been a country retreat of the Assyrian kings in the first half of the 9th century BC.

**Ballgame, Mesoamerica.** *Tlachtli* is the Aztec name for the sacred Mesoamerican ballgame. It was traditionally played in an I-shaped court with a playing alley between two walls and a wider playing area at each end. Rings were mounted in the middle of the side walls and the object of the game was to propel the ball, of solid rubber, through the ring on one side or the other. The ball could not be touched with the hands or feet, and normally the game was played by two opposing teams. Descriptions of the Aztec form of the game have been recorded by the early Spanish chroniclers who witnessed the competitions.

Various accoutrements were associated with the game. Ceramic figurines from the Maya site of LUBAANTUN show players wearing leather face masks and flaps to protect the hips. Stone yokes, palmate stones and hachas were also probably associated with the game (see YOKE, MESOAMERICA; PALMATE STONE). Special masonry courts do not seem to have been built before the Classic Period but the game was played in the Preclassic Period, as Preclassic bas-relief carvings of players, found in the valley of Oaxaca, show. The largest and best known of these specialized structures is the great ballcourt at CHICHEN ITZA, but there are others at MONTE ALBAN, EL TAJIN, Tula, Xochicalco, and many other Mayan and Mexican sites of Classic and Postclassic date.

The game had a religious significance, and was sometimes used as a form of divination. Sculptures on the walls of the courts at Chichen Itza and El Tajin have scenes of human sacrifices. Drawings of ballcourts appear also in the Mixtec historic codices, where the hero, Eight Deer, is depicted playing various opponents (*see* CODICES, MESOAMERICA).

**Ballista.** An arrow-shooting machine, worked by torsion, described by Greek sources and used, with various developments, throughout the Classical period. It was taken over by Roman legions, and became a standard piece of Roman military artillery.

**Bampur.** A site in Southeastern Iran. A series of prehistoric mounds are dominated by a medieval fort. A pottery sequence for the mounds has been established, dating from the second quarter of the 3rd millennium to *c.* 1900 BC. It shows links with pottery from Afghanistan and with Umm an-Nar on the Persian Gulf.

**Baptisterium.** Mortar and tile-lined basin used in the early church in the Roman period as a baptistery for novitiates. Occasionally a freestanding building (as at the Lateran, in Rome), it usually formed part of a church.

**Barcelona** (Barcino). An Augustan Roman colony in Spain, which reached its peak under the Flavian emperors.

**Barlovento.** A site on the lowland Gulf coast of Colombia. It has distinctive pottery, with wide-lined incised curvilinear designs, that dates from between 1500 and 1000 BC.

**Barrancoid subtradition.** A ceramic tradition that lasted from 700 BC to AD 1000. It spread from the lower Orinoco River drainage of Venezuela down to the coast and, subsequently, at the turn of the millennium, east and west to Guyana and Colombia.

**Barrow.**
*Long.* The term barrow means a mound. Long mounds cover many types of megalithic grave (*see* MEGALITH; CHAMBERED TOMB), but the term long barrow is used to refer to Neolithic burial monuments found principally in Britain (with analogous structures on the North European plain as far east as Poland) which cover collective burials in unchambered graves. The division between them and chambered tombs is not rigid, for some long barrows have megalithic elements, and the presence or absence of suitable building stone seems to have been the decisive factor influencing their respective distributions. Up to 300 ft. (91 m) long, long barrows were oval, rectangular, or trapezoidal in plan, and were built of earth, turf, chalk, gravel, or even small boulders, the material usually derived from flanking ditches. The great majority cover burials at one end. These were mostly inhumations (i.e., without cremation) of a few to over 50 people, of all ages and of both sexes, made either suc-

cessively or at the same time. Many bodies were disarticulated, suggesting also previous exposure of the corpses before burial. Cremation was more normal in Yorkshire long barrows. Burials were usually contained in some sort of mortuary structure, either like a wooden tent or formed of parallel banks with a roof. This may have been left freestanding for a long period before the erection of the mound, since this, once completed, denied further access, unlike in chambered tombs. Grave goods were few. Massive timber façades are found around many long barrows. These were used to revet (support) the mound, but in some cases may have served first as a freestanding enclosure around the mortuary structure. In Britain, the principal distribution is in Southern and Eastern England, with outliers in Southern and Eastern Scotland, complementary to that of chambered tombs.

*Round.* These burial mounds or tumuli (*see* TUMULUS) are the typical burial monuments of the Late Neolithic and Bronze Age in Europe north of the Mediterranean; characteristically, they cover a primary single burial in a simple grave, and as such may be distinguished from Neolithic round mounds covering collective burials in chambered tombs. They range in diameter from a few ft. to well over 100 ft. (30 m), and are highly varied in form and construction. Typically, the building material is derived from an encircling ditch and, in many cases, it is revetted by turf or timber walls. Varieties common in Southern England and the Netherlands include a small mound separated from the ditch by a broad "berm" (the so-called "bell" and "disc" barrows).

The primary burial was typically placed in the center of the mound, either on the old land surface, or in a pit cut in the subsoil. Wooden tent-like structures covered

A group of Early Bronze Age round barrows and, top left, a Neolithic long barrow, at Winterbourne Stoke, Wiltshire.

some graves, and inhumation and cremation were practiced. Many had rich grave goods. Successive or secondary burials were often placed around the primary grave, either at a similar level or, after the construction of the mound, within its structure. Round barrows were often arranged in groups or cemeteries, which could represent dynastic or kinship burial places, and they are usually taken to typify the appearance of more stratified societies after the earlier communities who practiced collective burial.

**Basilica.** The Roman name for a large aisled and columned hall, serving as marketplace and magistrates court. The earliest basilica of Rome was built by Cato in 184 BC. Many others followed, and this type of columned hall, often with a clerestory central aisle, was a common feature within fora throughout the Roman world. The basilica form was adopted by the early church as its monumental building type.

**Baths.** In Classical Greece only a very few buildings specifically for bathing are known, but examples exist at OLYMPIA, ATHENS, and from Hellenistic times at other centers. The bath building was, however, one of the most specifically Roman of constructions: most large private houses from the 2nd century BC onwards had their own bath suite, and there were public baths c. 100 BC at POMPEII. Such buildings combined "turkish bath" or "sauna bath" conditions, with massage and other rooms for relaxation and exercise, the main part being the hot bath (*caldarium*), the warms rooms (*tepidarium*), and the cold plunge (*frigidarium*). Imperial public baths became more and more grandiose: they were often laid out on a grand scale, and made use of concrete for vaulting. There were at least four large series of baths at Rome, provided by Titus, Trajan, Caracalla, and Diocletian. Many other provincial cities had similar buildings on the same scale, e.g., ARLES, AUGST, TRIER, and CARTHAGE.

**Beaker culture.** In the late 2nd millennium BC, when individual burial under round barrows (*see* BARROW) characterized much of Northern and Central Europe, particular assemblages of grave goods, consisting of decorated pottery and items of fighting equipment, such as arrowheads, wristguards, and daggers, made their appearance in many regions. Once believed to represent a group of people of common origin who dispersed across Europe from either Spain or Northern Hungary, the custom of making finely decorated drinking cups as status symbols for the male warriors with whom they were often buried can now be seen as an international practice which probably grew up over a wide area of Central Europe, and was imitated in the regions to which it was linked by trade.

Characteristic of the distribution of features of this "Beaker" complex is its occurrence in small groupings articulated by major river routes. While occasional individual finds of the typical zone-decorated bell-shaped beakers are found as far apart as Denmark and North Africa, the "core" area reaches from Czechoslovakia in the east, along the River Danube to the Rivers Rhine

and Rhône, and thence both northwards and southwards along these axes. It is well represented in Southern France and Spain, and also in the Low Countries, from where it spread to Britain, where the new style of fine pottery existed alongside other traditions of making cooking and storage pots. The style of decoration survived in this relatively peripheral Northwestern area long after it had gone out of fashion on the European continent: various regions of Britain were still producing their local varieties of beaker well into the 2nd millennium BC.

**Behistun.** Situated near modern Kermanshah, in IRAN, Behistun is the site of a famous trilingual inscription and rock relief cut by Darius I to record his victory over his enemies in 521 BC. The almost inaccessible inscription in Babylonian, Persian, and Elamite was copied by RAWLINSON, and it led to the decipherment of cuneiform writing. (*See also* ACHAEMENIDS; WRITING.)

**Beisan.** *See* BETH SHAN.

**Belgae.** A confederacy of Celtic tribes living in Northeast France to the north of Paris and to the south and west of the Ardennes Mountains. Caesar called their territory Belgium, and it formed the core of the Roman province of Gallia Belgica after their conquest by him in the mid-1st century BC. The Belgae had originally lived in the Low Countries but, under pressure from the expanding Germanic peoples, probably in the 2nd century BC, they had been forced to migrate southwards into present-day France. It may have been at the same time that some of the Belgae migrated to Southeastern England, where they are recognized archaeologically as the AYLESFORD-Swarling culture of the 1st century BC. Only a generation before Caesar, certain of the Belgic tribes on both sides of the English Channel were ruled by the same man, Diviciacus.

The close bonds between the Belgic tribes of England and France were recorded by Caesar, and manifested themselves in various ways: for example, the name Atrebates was used as a tribal name on both sides of the Channel, and the earliest coins (gold) were of the same types in both areas. Both areas shared types of wheel-thrown pottery, the same burial rite (cremation in urns), and a new kind of fortification known as the *Fécamp* type (after a site in Picardy), which was distinguished by a wide flat-bottomed ditch and sloping glacis-fronted rampart. In England urbanization developed quickly under the Belgic Dynasties and, by the time of the Roman Conquest in the 1st century AD, proto-states had come into being, one of them ruled by the renowned Cunobelin —Shakespeare's Cymbeline. (*See* URBANIZATION, PREHISTORIC EUROPE.)

**Bells, China.** Bells had an important ceremonial role in ancient China, and their music at the courts of princes is described in texts of the CHOU DYNASTY (1027–221 BC). The earliest type, made in the SHANG DYNASTY (c. 1600–1027 BC), were mounted mouth upwards and struck. Later bells were hung mouth downwards. The history of these bells has been a subject of recent archaeological research. Southern China has been shown to provide an important link between the bells of the Shang Dynasty and their revival in the Eastern Chou period.

**Belt hook.** An ornamental belt fastening found in Eastern Siberia and China from the 5th century BC. The belt had a ring at one end which fastened over the hook attached at the other end by a stud.

**Benin.** The city of Benin in Southern Nigeria is one of the best-known sites in Africa, due to the superb metalwork produced by the indigenous Edo craftsmen and brought to the notice of the Western world at the end of the 15th century AD by Portuguese maritime expansion. Although the uniqueness of the bronzes has been known for more than 400 years, our knowledge of the society that produced them and its underlying economy is very limited indeed. We still do not know when bronze casting began, nor where the necessary raw materials originated. We do know that bronze cannot be made without copper and that copper does not occur in Southern Nigeria. Benin must therefore have been engaged in extensive foreign trade from an early date.

Oral tradition suggests that the Edo peoples of Benin had established their distinctive political system and customs before the 14th century AD, and the limited archaeological evidence does not disprove this. Up until 1977 only four archaeologists had worked at Benin. The first scientific excavation was carried out in 1954, and an account of Benin archaeology was published in 1975. What have the various excavations added to the oral tradition? The beginnings of an archaeological sequence based on stratification, radiocarbon dates, and imported objects of European origin are now available and suggest that, by the 13th century AD, a substantial settlement was already in existence at Benin, although the region as a whole must have been occupied since at least 3000 BC.

The recent excavations have also provided a large corpus of pottery, which may be used in future as a basis for dating other archaeological occurrences. As well as pottery, the excavations recovered large numbers of beads, bronze- and ironwork, and fragments of cotton cloth that was probably also of local manufacture.

The CIRE PERDUE or "lost wax" method of casting was used to manufacture the famous bronzes, and it was probably introduced to Benin from the nearby, but less well known, state of Ife. Prior to the arrival of the Portuguese, due to the difficulty of obtaining the necessary raw materials, bronze casting was an exclusively palace art, producing sculptured heads for the royal shrines. The arrival of the Portuguese considerably increased the availability of brass and copper, so that the production of cast-bronze objects increased and, at the same time, non-African motifs were introduced. There is, however, no doubt that in origin the bronzes of Benin are of indigenous inspiration and craftsmanship.

**Bennett, Wendell** (1905–53). An American archaeologist who undertook major excavations in Peru from the 1920s to the 1950s. Many of the early sequences on the Peruvian coast, as well as in the central highlands, are based on his ceramic studies. His syntheses of the regional sequence of Peru were a major breakthrough in Andean archaeology.

**Beth Shan.** Present-day Beisan, site of the Biblical city where Saul's body was exposed. It is a huge TELL guarding the road to DAMASCUS and was excavated from 1921 to 1933. The earliest levels belonged to the middle of the 4th millennium BC. Several superimposed Egyptian fortresses of the 14th–12th century BC were excavated, together with some interesting shrines in the Late Bronze Age and Iron Age levels. (*See also* SYRIA–PALESTINE.)

**Beycesultan.** An inland site in Southwestern ANATOLIA, excavated in 1954–59, which produced a sequence of occupation from the Chalcolithic to the Late Bronze Age. Of particular interest were a range of Bronze Age shrines, arranged in pairs with horned altars and freestanding columns, and a series of 2nd-millennium BC palaces recalling Minoan palaces and containing buildings of the MEGARON type. It is thought that this was the capital of the 2nd-millennium BC state of Arzawa. (*See* the chronological table, p. 198.)

**Big Game Hunting tradition.** The first indigenous cultural complex in North America. It may have developed from an earlier, uncertainly-dated hunting culture, whose people would have used crude stone choppers and chopping tools and would have arrived in North America between 20,000 and 40,000 years ago in an interstadial (or break) in the Wisconsin Ice Age. Or, more probably, this culture derived from a different migration of people across the Bering land bridge sometime before 10,000 years ago. These later migrants would have brought with them a more developed toolkit, which may have been similar to that of the Upper Palaeolithic of Europe.

The tradition arose on the grasslands of North America, particularly the Great Plains, but also in New Mexico and Arizona, where present-day deserts would then have been grasslands, and in Eastern North America. The now extinct large mammals of the late Pleistocene were, if not the main source of food, at least that by which these people are known. At the "kill" sites of animals such as mammoths, bison, horses, and camels, various types of fluted projectile points have been found. They are generally characterized by being lanceolate in form, and fluted, and were probably attached to spears. The method of hunting might have been that of following single animals, wounding them, tiring them, and perhaps cornering them in marshes and lakes where they would have been most vulnerable. Although sites are only of this "kill" type, it must be presumed that these people also relied on gathering vegetable foods and killing small mammals, even though there is no evidence of this. In historical Stone Age societies the killing of large animals, although very important, is always a spasmodic activity.

The tradition lasted from about 10,000 BC to about 4000 BC in the Plains. With the increasing dryness of climatic conditions after 7000 BC the big game began to disappear, although it continued for 3 millennia in the Plains, where the specialized hunting of bison with Plano points continued. The earliest projectile points are those from New Mexico known as Clovis. Sandia projectile points may be of a similar date and are also from New Mexico. Folsom points developed from Clovis points: they are slightly finer than Clovis points, and are known from New Mexico, Colorado, and Wyoming. Plano points are known from a much wider area of the Plains, but are not fluted. In Eastern North America a relatively greater number of finds of similar projectile points are known, but there are fewer dated sites. Fluted points, similar to Clovis points, are, for instance, known from the Bull Brook site in Massachusetts, where they have been dated to 7000 BC. (*See* CLOVIS POINT; FOLSOM; PLANO POINT; SANDIA.

The Big Game Hunting tradition influenced and acted upon other developing cultures as it declined. In the far West, in Montana and Idaho, its limited appearance was replaced with less specialized hunting and gathering groups; in the Southwest the DESERT TRADITION replaced it after the disappearance of the game through the desiccation of the area.

**Bigo.** On the South bank of the Katonga River in Western Uganda in East Africa is a series of extensive earthworks that are comparable with the hillforts of Iron Age Europe. The largest and the only excavated site is at Bigo, where an extensive bank-and-ditch enclosure has been dated to the 15th century AD. In the center of the enclosure is a series of large mounds of unknown function that were constructed on top of the original settlement. The inhabitants kept large numbers of cattle, some goats, and also hunted wild pig and antelope. Oral tradition associates the earthworks with the legendary Dynasty of the Bachwezi, who ruled the kingdom of Kitara. The available archaeological evidence in no way contradicts the oral tradition, and suggests that the material culture at Bigo was not dissimilar to that of the cattle-owning Bahima who live in the area today.

**Birdstone.** A polished stone weight (also called bannerstone and boatstone) which occurs in the cultures of the ARCHAIC TRADITION (8000–1000 BC) and later cultures in the Eastern Woodlands of North America (*see* HOPEWELL; WOODLAND TRADITION). They were probably attached to throwing sticks or atlatls to add weight and leverage. The highly distinctive shapes of these objects include bird, boat, and bannerlike forms. The boatstones were probably tied to the throwing stick, while bannerstones were hafted.

**Biskupin.** An Iron Age defended village (one of many in this region) on a former island in Lake Biskupin in Polish Pomerania. It was inhabited by several hundred people from *c.* 550 to 400 BC. The waterlogged ground has preserved many of the structures in the village, which covered all of an oval island, an area of 1.7 ac. (6,900 m²). Its perimeter was reinforced by timber piles, inside which was an elaborate defensive wall of earth contained within a cellular timber structure. A single gate pierced

this wall, and from it there led a timber causeway to the shore of the lake. There were just over 100 wooden houses ranged side by side in 13 parallel rows; between them were streets paved with logs. All the houses were of identical design (based on a square plan) and size, 26 × 29½ ft. (8 × 9 m). Each house had an antechamber or veranda facing south, and a main room with a stone hearth; in many houses this room was divided into a larger and a smaller chamber. Some of the houses were used as workshops by weavers and bronze founders. The whole village was rebuilt twice within its 150-year life, and on at least one occasion, it was ransacked by Scythian marauders from the east (*see* SCYTHIANS).

*Bît hilani.* An architectural unit consisting of an open portico of one to three columns at the top of a short flight of steps. At one end of the portico there is a staircase to an upper story, and it leads to a long reception or throne room parallel to the façade, with smaller rooms beyond. This unit is first found at TELL ATCHANA in the middle of the 2nd millennium BC, and it is a feature of Syro-Hittite cities. The Assyrians also adopted and adapted it in their palaces.

**Bithynia.** Originally under Persian domination, Bithynia became a Roman province in the Northwestern part of Asia Minor. Its capital was Nicomedia, and important cities were APAMEA and Heracleia.

**Blade.** *See* STONE TECHNOLOGY.

**Boğazköy.** The Anatolian site of the Hittite capital of Hattusas, excavated by the Germans intermittently from 1906 until the present day. The original settlement, on the hill of Büyükkale, dates back to Chalcolithic times and a trading center was established there in Old Assyrian times (beginning of the 2nd millennium BC). Under the Hittites, during the second half of the 2nd millennium BC, a palace was built on Büyükkale, with the city spread out below over a huge area enclosed by walls; these were pierced by gateways decorated with reliefs, and by a postern passage (Yerkapi). Many huge temple complexes were built all over the site and there is a rockcut sanctuary at nearby Yazılıkaya, decorated with reliefs and dating to the 13th century BC. The large number of tablets excavated have thrown light on the history of the city, of the Hittites, and of the Near East.

**Bola.** A device, found in the New World, for grounding animals and flightless birds. It consists of two weighted balls joined by a line, and is flung in such a way as to wind itself round the legs of the animal and bring it to the ground.

**Bonampak.** A small, Late Classic Period Maya site in the state of Chiapas, about 25 mi. (40 km) from YAXCHILAN, along the Usumacinta River drainage. It is famous for the unique polychrome paintings on the walls and vaulting of a small, three-roomed building which has been preserved. These murals are the most complete graphic portrayal of Maya life known. The scenes show an assembly of nobles standing before a ruler, who in turn is showing a child to them; a battle scene; the arraignment and torture of prisoners (or slaves); a robing scene; a dance around what appears to be a human sacrifice; and an orchestra arrayed in fantastic headdresses and playing an assortment of wind and percussion instruments. As such, these rare paintings provide us with invaluable ethnographic data and insights into Maya social order, styles of dress, types of ceremonial processions, and daily activities.

**Bone.** From early prehistory the bones and horns or antlers of the animals man hunted or kept for food provided him with a vital source of raw material for constructing artifacts. Although tough and durable in its lifetime, bone is rarely well preserved on archaeological sites, so that its study is uneven. From early times the long or limb bones of larger animals were especially selected for a wide range of tools, from simple pins, gouges, and toggles, to points, harpoons, and hooks which required greater preparation. Early postglacial hunters in Scandinavia, for example, were skilled at making barbed harpoons of bone, as well as constructing cruder perforated mattocks. As crafts improved, bone was put to wider uses, and occurs by the Iron Age, for example, as an inlay material, and was fashioned into weaving or carding combs, and cheek pieces or bits for horses. Antler was used for a more restricted range of artifacts but was nonetheless widely employed. Palaeolithic hunters made antler points by cutting out a long strip with a burin from an antler, a technique which continued into the Mesolithic. Antlers were widely used in the Neolithic unaltered, as picks, or digging sticks, and are common on earthworks and flint mines, together with the shoulder blades of large animals used as shovels. Antler was also widely used in Europe to provide a "sleeve" around stone axes, a sort of shock absorber between blade and wooden haft. However, antler was used less than bone after the beginning of the Bronze Age.

**Borsippa.** The present-day Birs, site of the highest surviving ZIGGURAT remains (154 ft.; 47 m), built by Nebuchadnezzar and dedicated to Nabu. Its proximity to BABYLON led to its being identified with the Tower of Babel.

**Boscoreale.** The site of two villas in the suburbs of Rome, one of which produced the Boscoreale treasure: the second contained many important painted rooms, dating from *c.* 40 BC, arranged round a courtyard and peristyle.

**Botta, Paul Emile** (1802–70). The French Consul in Mosul, Northern Iraq, from 1842. He began excavating the TELL of Kuyunjik on the site of NINEVEH and then moved to KHORSABAD, where he and Flandin recorded the Assyrian buildings and reliefs he found.

**Boucher de Perthes, Jacques** (1788–1868). A customs official and amateur archaeologist living in Abbeville, France, in the 19th century. Boucher de Perthes collected stone tools from the Somme gravels, and published them in 1837 as "antediluvian" axes. Not until 1859 did his claims to have found evidence of very early man gain recognition.

**Bouleuterion.** The Greek name for the council hall: usually a rectangular or D-shaped hall with three sides or the curved side occupied by rows of seats. Athens' bouleuterion was built *c.* 500 BC. The form was taken over by the Romans for Senate buildings (CURIA).

**Breccia.** The term for deposits of stones and earth that have become concreted together, usually by calcium-charged water. Many caves occupied by early man, in the Dordogne, Southwest France, for example, have revealed layers of breccia crammed with bones, tools, and even art objects.

**Breweries.** Those of the 19th century have the third-longest casualty list of any type of industrial building, the first being WAREHOUSES and the second being small RAILWAY STATIONS. A few prestigious companies—Carlsberg in Copenhagen, Denmark, Guinness in Dublin, Ireland, Whitbread in London, England—have taken care of their old headquarters buildings, partly for family reasons and partly because the advertising value is high, but a large number of architecturally excellent local breweries have been jettisoned as brewing groups have become steadily larger and manufacturing more centralized. In a few instances an alternative use has been found for the redundant brewery premises. The Museum of Modern Art in Oxford, England, is in a former brewery building and so, more appropriately, is the Museum of Beer and Brewing at Plzeň, in Czechoslovakia. The famous Guinness Museum in Dublin is housed in the company's old laboratory block.

**Brick.** The chief building material throughout the Near East has always been mud brick and it is this fact which, more than any other, has contributed to our knowledge of the past (*see* TELL). The bricks were made of clay, molded into blocks, and variations in their shape and size can be used as dating criteria. *Riemchen* bricks, which are square in section, flat on one side and curved on the other, are distinctive of the URUK and JEMDET NASR periods and are succeeded by plano-convex bricks in EARLY DYNASTIC times in Mesopotamia. Generally the bricks were sun dried, but baked bricks were used as an outer skin for official buildings and temples and often bear stamped inscriptions. Decorative glazed bricks first appear in Assyrian times and the foremost example of their use is the Ishtar Gate in BABYLON.

**Brick- and tilemaking.** These industries have been very inadequately treated by archaeologists so far. Many small works have ceased production during the past 30 years: most were in rural areas or on the outskirts of towns and are still there to be surveyed, although some have been converted to other uses, particularly to the manufacture of breeze blocks and other concrete products. One of the old type of conical brick kilns survives at Nettlebed, Oxon., England, and at the site of the Pitfour Brickworks, Glencarse, Scotland, the remains of the grassed-over Hoffmann Kiln (1871), an early example, can still be seen. The largest brickmaking area in the world, near Bedford, England, mass-produces common bricks and has put most of the smaller firms in the country out of business. The great brickworks at Stewartby, with its model village begun in 1926, is a monument to the industry's economic transformation. Many 19th-century bricks and tiles show the name of the works, and it is interesting to note this when old buildings are being pulled down.

**Bristlecone pine.** *See* RADIOCARBON DATING.

**Britain in Prehistory.** Traces of man in Britain probably go back beyond 400,000 years ago, but, during the PALAEOLITHIC down to the end of the last glaciation some 10,000 years ago, they are not numerous. In the frequent cold phases of the ICE AGE the British Isles would have been uninhabitable, and sites belonging to the warmer phases are rarely undisturbed. In the Lower Palaeolithic, down to *c.* 100,000 years ago, flake tools of the CLACTONIAN culture were contemporary with and succeeded by handaxes of the ACHEULIAN culture. A wooden point at Clacton and a working floor at Hoxne, Suffolk, are notable discoveries. In the Middle Palaeolithic, industries of Mousterian tradition probably belonged to NEANDERTHAL MAN. Two phases of occupation in Britain in the Upper Palaeolithic (*c.* 30,000 BC and *c.* 12,000 BC) belong to warmer phases of the last glaciation, and hunting sites are known. Fully modern man (*Homo sapiens sapiens*) had evolved by *c.* 30,000 BC, and henceforth we are dealing with cultural not physical evolution. The end of the Ice Age ushers in the Mesolithic (*c.* 8000–*c.* 3500 BC), when the ice sheets retreated far to the north, making most of Britain habitable. Sea levels rose and Britain was an island by *c.* 6000 BC. Warmer temperatures brought the spread of forest—first birch pine and hazel, then oak, ash, elm, and lime—by *c.* 5000 BC. Much of our knowledge depends, as in the Palaeolithic, on finds of flint tools, typically axes and small points or insets known as microliths, but occasionally well preserved sites like Star Carr in Yorkshire reveal more. This was a winter camp for a small band subsisting on red deer and other forest animals and making barbed antler harpoons. Colonization of Ireland by 6000 BC, and of Scottish islands down to the 4th millennium BC suggests continuing exploration and population growth (*see* IRELAND IN PREHISTORY).

The Neolithic period (*c.* 3500–2000 BC) begins with the colonization of Britain by communities of mixed farmers from the European continent in search of land. Cattle, pigs, goats, and sheep were kept, and wheat and barley were grown. Settlement was widespread over the whole of Britain, and determined inroads were made on the forest cover to create fields and better grazing. By the later Neolithic in Southern England there were large areas of open grassland. A few sites with small rectangular houses are known, and in Southern England, as far north as the Midlands, there are many ditched and banked enclosures (known as camps from their interrupted ditches). Some of the population were buried in collective tombs, built in imposing mounds (*see* CHAMBERED TOMB; BARROW), which may have served as focuses for the scattered farming communities. Flint was mined from the chalk and hard rocks quarried to produce axes for forest clearance: these were distributed over long distances by exchange and trade. Pottery, plain and decorated, was made in simple shapes. From 3000 BC onwards, fine plain pottery was distributed from Cornwall to as far away as Wiltshire, though much was probably locally made. In the late Neolithic (*c.* 2500 BC onwards) tombs were still used but no longer constructed; some cremation cemeteries are known. Henges, ceremonial enclosures with ditches inside banks (*see* AVEBURY; HENGE), and cursuses, long parallel banks and ditches, were the principal monuments. The Dorset cursus was exceptionally long—about 20 ft. (6 m). The stone-built settlement at SKARA BRAE provides an unusually well preserved village.

The BEAKER CULTURE bridges the transition from the Neolithic to the Bronze Age (*c.* 2000–700/650 BC). It introduced from the continent a distinctive style of fine drinking cups, copper tools, and single burials under small round mounds. By the close of the Early Bronze Age (*c.* 1400 BC), bronze metallurgy was widespread: daggers, flat axes, spearheads and halberds were notable products. Settlements are virtually unknown, except in Southwest England. Round barrows are by contrast extremely numerous. A small percentage in Wessex and other parts of the South contain extremely rich graves, with objects in gold (produced since the Beaker culture), amber, shale, jet, and faience, as well as in bronze. This phenomenon (*see* WESSEX CULTURE) has been connected with an immigrant aristocracy, but can be better seen as the result of the enrichment of native society by the new contacts with Europe brought by metalworking. In the Middle Bronze Age (*c.* 1400–900 BC), cremation cemeteries became important. Settlements of small homesteads with fields are known in the Southwest, in Cornwall, and on Dartmoor. In the South, settlements of the Deverel–Rimbury culture have round houses in small enclosures, grain storage pits, and probably the earliest Celtic fields. Other small enclosures, perhaps used for stock, are also known. The production of metalwork continued, and palstaves, rapiers, and swords were notable innovations. In the Late Bronze Age (*c.* 900–650 BC), the evidence of metalwork is paramount, as burials were rare and few settlements are securely dated to this phase, although the HILLFORT was introduced then. Traditions of metalworking were by now regionalized: the South was more advanced, with the innovation of bronze alloyed with lead. Swords and socketed axes were characteristic products, and horse-gear and sheet bronze vessels are notable.

The metalwork of the end of the Bronze Age shows numerous contacts with the European continent, and iron tools dating from the 7th century BC mark the formal beginning of the Iron Age (*c.* 650 BC–AD 43). These contacts may be as much the result of trade as of

The White Horse, a tribal emblem cut into chalk through grass in the 1st century BC, at Uffington, Oxfordshire.

the immigration of a European aristocracy. In Eastern Scotland, however, it is claimed that immigrants from Northwest Europe introduced hillforts, iron tools, and new forms of bronzeworking (the Abernethy culture). Thereafter, it is doubtful whether there was any immigration in the Iron Age until the arrival of the Belgae, with the possible exception of the 5th-century introduction of the Arras culture into Yorkshire from Northeast France. A complex society emerged. Hillforts, large and small, were widespread and numerous, and probably served as tribal centers. Many kinds of agricultural and pastoral settlement are known (of which Little Woodbury is one); traces of Celtic fields are widespread on the chalk downland of the South; and settlement traces, including fields, are known from many river gravels. Pottery and other goods, such as iron bars (probably ingots), were widely distributed and traded. By the later centuries BC, specialist bronzeworkers produced a series of magnificently decorated sword sheaths, helmets, and shields. Belgic tribes immigrated into Southeast Britain from Northern France and Belgium from around 100 BC onwards. Coinage was introduced by them, and spread widely in the South. At this time, several large settlements in the South, such as Colchester and St. Albans, began to lose some of the character of the hillfort, and cremation cemeteries in the Southeast included some very rich burials. Trade with Roman Gaul flourished and, after Julius Caesar's incursions in 55 and 54 BC, various political alliances with Rome were maintained. By the time of the Roman Conquest in AD 43, a section of society in the South was already partly Romanized. By contrast, Southwest England, Wales, and the rest of Britain north of the Midlands were much less culturally developed.

**Britannia.** A Roman province formed after the military conquest of Britain in AD 43. The province, divided into *Inferior* and *Superior*, included all of Britain south of Hadrian's Wall. Its chief city was London (Londinium). Britain was abandoned by the Romans in AD 410.

**British Mountain culture.** The name given to a late Palaeolithic culture of the Northwest Arctic in Yukon, near the border of Canada and Alaska. The artifacts found share many of the traits of European and Asian Levallois–Mousterian stone toolkits, for instance percussion flaking, which produces flakes with large bulbs of percussion. It has not been definitely dated but may be up to 18,000 years old. The site at which the culture was first identified is Engigstciak. The stone tools found include end and side scrapers, flakes with notches, heavy chopping tools, and the flakes and disc cores from which many of the tools were made. These finds were associated with the bones of extinct bison and caribou, indicating that the climate was warmer than it is now, and thus that British Mountain may be one of the major ancestral complexes of later traditions in North America. This is partially suggested by the proximity of the area to the Bering land bridge, and also by the discovery of a fluted point of the type which may have developed into the CLOVIS POINT and other projectile points of the Plains. (*See also* PRE-ESKIMO ARCHAEOLOGY.)

**Bronze, Prehistoric Europe.** The metal used in the Copper Age, from 4000 to 3000 BC in Europe, was a pure, unalloyed copper with only accidental traces of other elements such as silver. As such, it was hard to cast—it was shaped mainly by hammering—and still relatively soft. The earliest alloys were not, however, with tin to make bronze, as tin is a rare metal which is only occasionally associated with ores of copper: instead, arsenical copper was produced by deliberate admixture of arsenic-rich minerals of the kinds which often accompany copper ores. The use of arsenical alloying had a long history in the Near East, and was introduced to Europe from the Caucasus in the 3rd millennium BC. Both arsenic and tin have the same effect, improving casting properties and making a harder metal.

Tin came into use around 2000 BC, and was based on two sets of sources: those of Bohemia, and those of Cornwall. In both areas it was obtained by panning, as the rocky matrix is very hard, and there were few attempts at mining before Roman times. Early bronzes have fluctuating amounts of tin, often only a few percent, but soon the optimum quantity of 10% was recognized and regularly attained. Early bronzes often still had a high arsenic content, as a result of the use of high-yielding gray ores (fahlerz) which have high impurity levels. Surprising alloys with nickel or even zinc are occasionally found for this reason, though arsenic and antimony are the most usual impurities in any quantity.

Towards the end of the Bronze Age, the deliberate addition of large amounts of lead was practiced, partly for reasons of economy and partly to improve the increasingly complex castings.

**Bronze Age, Europe.** Down to the late 3rd millennium BC, archaeologists often find it convenient to work in cultural units of up to 1,000 years. After this date, such units are noticeably shorter, being of half the length or less. This in itself is some indication of the quickening pattern of change in European societies. The appearance in museum storage cupboards of increasing quantities of objects in a new durable material, copper alloy, is only one symptom of the kinds of change which led early investigators to separate the Bronze Age as a major phase of cultural development.

Among other features which differentiate the 2nd millennium BC from preceding ones are possession of the domestic horse and advanced wheeled vehicles and boats; the colonization of sandy and upland areas; an emphasis on sheep for wool and cheese, and on barley as much as wheat; more effective and finer tools; the development of fortification and weaponry; the occurrence of richly-equipped individual graves often under round barrows (see BARROW); and possession of a range of manufactured and imported materials. Bronze contributed to the effectiveness of tools and the development of weaponry; it often symbolized status; and its movement testifies to an economy which could organize the transport of large quantities of desirable materials. On the other hand, the Bronze Age covers a diversity of types of society, from the tiny, largely stone-using chiefdoms of the earliest phases, through the city states of Mycenaean Greece, with their closely controlled palace economies, to the expansionist barbarian tribes who constructed the earliest hillforts (see HILLFORT).

Many of the features typical of the Bronze Age have their roots in the second half of the 3rd millennium BC, in the CORDED WARE CULTURE. It was then that the practice of individual burial under round mounds began; that the colonization of sandy areas started; that local

copper extraction first took place north of the Carpathian Mountains; and that extensive and continuing interregional contacts occurred, evidenced both in pottery styles and traded materials such as Grand Pressigny flint.

Partly complementary to this, partly continuing and intensifying this trend, the Bell Beaker "link-up" phase (see BEAKER CULTURE) during the centuries on either side of 2000 BC brought into contact the areas linked by Europe's major rivers, the Rhine, Rhône, upper Danube, upper and middle Elbe, bringing the Atlantic seaboard, the West Mediterranean, Southern and Central Germany, and Czechoslovakia into an "interaction sphere" with a common superculture and style. Thus the metal resources of the far West, especially the rich gray ores of Ireland, were brought in to complement Central and Southwest European ores. The Beaker style lingered in the West, in Britain and the Low Countries, long after it had disappeared elsewhere; down, in fact into the first (A) period of the Central European Bronze Age system as defined by Reinecke.

The main innovations which mark the Bronze Age proper are the use of tin-bronze alloys and large-scale extraction of copper and its deposition in hoards. These features begin in Central Europe with the ÚNĚTICE PERIOD, with its rich burials and massive hoards of tin bronzes, especially in the Saale area. It is paralleled in Britain by the WESSEX CULTURE, which lacks the really large hoards but has comparably rich graves, and in Spain—the center of another major metal industry—by the Argaric culture. These begin around 1800 BC. Meanwhile Denmark, without metal resources of its own, continued in a prolonged "Late Neolithic," enlivened by the production of spectacular flint imitations of the bronze daggers current elsewhere. The Central European industry continued to be the most advanced, followed by the British, while the Spanish industry was archaic and slow to change.

By 1600 BC further impulses are evident, marked by the emergence (or rather, re-emergence, since it was an important Copper Age industrial area) of Transylvania as a major production center and stylistic school. This industry benefited from the patronage of powerful local chiefs whose fortified centers have been excavated in Slovakia. Their innovations, especially in new methods of hafting tools and weapons, as well as in wire ornaments and pins, conventionally define the Middle (B and C) phases of the Central European Bronze Age. This period is characterized by a continuing high output of metal—now using basic chalcopyrite ores rather than the enriched gray ores of the Early Bronze Age—and the beginnings of a local industry in Scandinavia based upon imported metal. (Their "Early Bronze Age" in the scheme worked out by Montelius is thus Reinecke's "Middle Bronze Age"). Such a situation has important implications for a return trade in subsistence products—perhaps cheese or dried fish.

Apart from this development, the Middle Bronze Age phase is in many respects more important as a typological division than as an indication of any radical change of economy and society. Tumulus burial continued, with many examples surviving on soils now too poor to be useful as arable. Hoards were less commonly deposited, though finds of scrap metal show that copper was being recycled. In Iberia, the conservative Argaric industry continued. Desirable materials continued to be traded: for instance, the large amber beads found in Bavaria. It was at this time that the Mycenaean civilization reached its apogee in Greece (see GREECE, ARCHAEOLOGY OF).

From around 1200 BC on, things began to change. Mycenaean society collapsed, while a vigorous process of expansion began in Europe. More intensive methods of land use began, with tightly held areas of arable fields dominated by local hillforts. Technical developments allowed the use of sheet metal, both for vessels and for (largely decorative) armor, as well as more economical methods of using the increasingly scarce bronze to make hollow axheads. Spoked vehicles used in chariots came into use. Cremation in urns began to replace inhumation burial, and round barrows were only used to mark the graves of exceptional individuals. Especially close links grew up between the area north of the Alps and the Rhine and Rhône Rivers: this region was characterized by its rilled Urnfield pottery and its massive output of bronze weapons, especially swords (see URNFIELD PERIOD). The increasing population of the alpine foreland began to develop links across the Alps to Northern Italy, itself the scene of marked economic expansion. This "inner ring" of cultures increasingly integrated peripheral areas like the Low Countries, taking them away from their cross-channel links which had characterized earlier centuries. Perhaps in reaction, an "Atlantic" network, linked by the fishing activities of the maritime areas, sprang up from Iberia to Brittany and the British Isles, and thence to Scandinavia.

In Britain, new continental influences are seen in metalwork, especially ornaments of the kinds known in Denmark. Tools such as palstaves—now partly replaced in Central Europe by socketed forms—were produced in large numbers, as were rapiers—in contrast to the slashing swords of the Urnfielders. More important, however, were the marked changes in agriculture, indicated by fresh colonization and the laying out of large-scale field systems on the downlands.

Meanwhile, the quickening trade of the Mediterranean, linking the East Mediterranean, Archaic Greece, Early Etruscan Italy, the Italic civilizations of the Po valley, and the Greek and Punic colonies of the West Mediterranean, brought new influences to its European hinterland, via the Alps and the River Rhône, including the knowledge of iron. The palatial hillforts of Eastern France, Southern Germany, and Bohemia, however, were in many ways the culmination of "Urnfield" development; and beyond the iron-using Central European network, the Atlantic fringe survived into its final bronze-using phase, with its huge hoards of scrap metal evidencing the production not only of socketed axes and slashing swords, but also of cauldrons, horns, and complicated horse-gear. It was in this context that the early hillforts of the British Isles began to appear. (For the Near Eastern Bronze Age, see ANATOLIA; IRAN; MESOPOTAMIA; SYRIA–PALESTINE.)

**Bronze technology, China.** Bronze casting developed relatively late in China. It is first found in early SHANG DYNASTY contexts, as at Erh-li-t'ou, c. 1600 BC. Because the methods adopted in China are unlike those used in the rest of the world, it seems likely that bronze casting developed independently in China. Neither molds carved in stone, nor the CIRE PERDUE (lost wax) method, both used in Europe and Western Asia, were adopted in China; instead, bronzes were cast in ceramic piece molds assembled around a central core. Very complicated molds were used to produce the RITUAL VESSELS, some of the most astonishing products of ancient bronze casting. This laborious technique, which involves the careful fitting of numerous separate molds, was probably developed because the Chinese already had very advanced ceramic technology. A close connection is confirmed by the similarity between the stamped designs on early Shang ceramics and the patterns impressed in the earliest molds and cast on the first bronzes. This technique had a number of effects on the bronzes made. Most noticeable is the tendency for the vessels to be designed in sections following the structure of the molds. Another consequence was the use of complicated but flat decoration which could be easily incised in the mold, rather than the three-dimensional castings which would have been possible if the cire perdue method had been in use. A form of mass production, or at least batch production, was inevitable as the process was so complicated, in that a number of stages, which each required different skills, were necessary. It is likely that the already dense population of China allowed the adoption of this labor-intensive method. The scale of bronze-casting operations has been confirmed by excavations: large deposits of models and molds have been found at foundry sites, particularly at AN-YANG and at the later site of Hou-ma in Shansi province, and important sections of the cities were devoted to the workshops and living quarters of the bronze workers.

**Bruk.** A Scandinavian institution, especially common in Sweden, the bruk may be defined as a self-contained, manorial type of industrial village, with ironworking as the most usual occupation. They were established, often by the Crown, between 1500 and c. 1850. A number of them have architecturally distinguished buildings. Notable Swedish examples are Korsån, Dalarna (1840); Forsmann, Uppland (1570); Lövsta, Uppland (1600); and Munfors, Varmland (1670). In Finland, Högfors Bruk dates back to 1819, and Kauthua Bruk to c. 1790.

**Burial.** *See individual areas and tomb types.*

**Burin.** *See* STONE TECHNOLOGY.

**Byblos.** The Greek name for present-day Gebeil and ancient Gebal, site of the chief Phoenician port on the East Mediterranean coast north of Beirut, and the main center of trade with Egypt. The city was founded before 3000 BC, and was still important in Crusader times. It has been excavated by the French since 1921. A number of important temples, shrines, and tombs have been found and Egyptian objects in them have been useful in establishing relative chronologies. The famous Ahiram sarcophagus, bearing one of the earliest Phoenician inscriptions known to us, was found in Byblos and is now in Beirut Museum. The name Byblos is the origin of the word "Bible."

**Byzantines.** A civilization which can be dated from AD 330, when Constantine I transferred the capital of the Roman Empire to Byzantium, which was renamed Constantinople. The empire fell when the city was captured by the Turks in 1453, but Constantinople remained an artistic influence in Greece, the Balkans, and Russia long afterwards. Before the mid-5th century, Byzantine culture is almost indistinguishable from Roman, but under Justinian I (AD 527–565) it flowered into a distinctive civilization, owing debts to both Western and Eastern traditions. The court exhibited flamboyance, political complexity and intrigue, and elaborate ritual. Byzantine influence spread outside its heartland of Asia Minor, Greece, the Western Balkans, and parts of Sicily and South Italy, as far afield as Western Europe and Asia.

Byzantium was essentially a Christian church state, preserving its religion against the onslaught of ISLAM, despite the Arab encroachments on Palestine, Syria, and North Africa during the 6th and 7th centuries AD. Roman law and letters and Greek culture were preserved, and the fall of Constantinople in 1453 led to many manuscripts reaching the West, giving impetus to the revival of Classical learning associated with the Renaissance. During the medieval period Constantinople was a link between East and West, providing luxury goods and influencing art styles as far afield as England and Scandinavia. In Northwestern Europe it was known as *Mikelgaarde*, "The Great City."

No private houses of the Byzantine period have survived (though it has been suggested that some buildings now used as warehouses on the shores of the Golden Horn in Constantinople are late Byzantine), and the only secular structure remaining above ground in Constantinople is the 8th-century so-called "House of Justinian." A surviving palace built for the Palaeologue emperors is now known as the Tekfour Serai, and the earlier Great Palace was partly excavated and found to have fallen into disrepair by the 12th century. Byzantium was regarded as almost impregnable, and in the Middle Ages was only captured once (by the Latins in 1204). The defenses were, however, unambitious compared with those of the Islamic world, though the town walls built by Theodosius II in the 5th century AD (replacing the earlier walls of Constantine) still survive with many later repairs. The 5th-century Golden Gate is as much a triumphal entrance in the tradition of Roman triumphal arches as a defensive work. The water system of the city was very sophisticated.

The greatest contribution of the Byzantines is in the fields of architecture and art. Byzantine art is formal and hieratic—its message spiritual. Byzantine architects mastered the dome, and borrowed both from Roman and Iranian building traditions to develop the distinctive style that reached its peak in the building of Hagia Sophia in Constantinople (AD 532–537). Other major Byzantine churches are those of SS. Sergius and Bacchus (AD 526–537) and St. Eirene (AD 532), both in Constantinople, and that of St. John in Ephesus.

A gilt-bronze plaque of St. Theodore, typical of Byzantine bronzework of the 10th and 11th centuries AD.

Mosaics are perhaps the supreme achievement of Byzantine art. Byzantine mosaics were the descendants of those of Rome, but were used for decorating walls and ceilings rather than floors. The range of materials used for *tesserae* was greater, gilt glass in particular gave a sumptuous effect to backgrounds. Very few mosaics survive in Constantinople, but some of the finest are to be seen in Ravenna in Italy, where they reached their peak in the time of Justinian. The most notable Ravenna mosaics are those in the churches of St. Apollinare Nuovo, San Vitale, and St. Apollinare in Classe. Byzantine wall paintings, manuscripts, and ivories are also notable. Outstanding ivories include the Barberini ivory in the Louvre, Paris, and the secular Veroli Casket in the Victoria and Albert Museum, London. Among the minor arts were tapestries, which reached Europe—one of the finest comes from the tomb of Charlemagne, at Aachen. Silverwork (some of which was found in the SUTTON HOO ship burial in England) and pottery, which was often attractively glazed, are also notable. Enamels and other ornamental metalwork have also survived.

**Byzantium** (Constantinople). Byzantium was originally a Greek colony at the entrance to the Black Sea; a typical Roman town was then laid out over it. The most important remains date from the later Roman period, when it was renamed "Constantinople" and became Constantine's imperial capital. Remains of the imperial palace lie south of the former Greek city nucleus. The land walls, giving the city an area greater than that of Rome itself and built by Theodosius II (AD 408–450), are among the best-preserved ancient fortifications anywhere. A number of 4th-century churches are also known,

The interior of part of the walls of Constantinople (Byzantium), near the prison of Anemas. These ancient fortifications were built by Theodosius II (AD 408–450).

among them Constantine's Apostle Church, the Irene Church, and the Great Church, which later became Hahia Sophia, as rebuilt by Justinian in the 6th century.

**Cachi.** An archaeological complex, 3000–1750 BC, from the Ayacucho valley, Peru. It shows the first evidence of the vertical economic system in which products of the lower villages and camps (corn, beans, squash, gourd, chile, lucuma, coca) were exchanged for the potatoes, quinoa, and camelids of the seasonally nomadic herders of the higher elevations.

**Caesarea** (Cherchel). Originally a Carthaginian trading station and colony on the North African coast. Colonized by Claudius in AD 40, it rapidly became the chief city of Mauretania Caesariensis. Of this period, there remain traces of the city wall, a THEATER/AMPHITHEATER, a CIRCUS, BATHS, and a lighthouse. It was sacked by Moors and Vandals but refortified by Belisarius in the 6th century AD.

**Caesarea Philippi.** An old Jewish city in Palestine, captured by Alexander Jannaeus in 103 BC, and rebuilt by Herod in 22–10 BC. It became the administrative center of the province of Judaea in AD 6. The remains are extensive and include the city walls, a THEATER, AMPHITHEATER, and CIRCUS.

**Cajamarca.** An Inca town in the Peruvian highlands which was built to function as a provincial capital. It was here, in 1532, that the Inca Atahualpa received, and was captured by, the Spanish expeditionary force; an event which ended the Inca period and Andean prehistory. There was also a distinctive regional culture centered here during the Middle Horizon and Late Intermediate Periods (AD 200–1476), which produced attractive slip painted pottery.

**Calendar, Mesoamerica.** Thanks to data from native informants, recorded in the 16th century by Catholic clerics like Bishop Diego de LANDA, archaeologists have been able to decipher many of the calendrical inscriptions and much of the pictographic writing in the surviving manuscripts.

Many of the same basic principles underly variants of the calendar used by all Mesoamerican peoples. It is believed that the calendar was devised by the Olmecs and then diffused, and probably improved. Although it may have been developed at first as a guide to the timing of agricultural operations, it soon became very important for auguries. There were teams of gods who shouldered the responsibility, in strict rotation, for each day, month, year, or longer period. Thus, the fortunes of any day would depend on the characters, benevolent or otherwise, of a number of gods for different periods of time.

The essential features were a year of 18 months of 20 days and 5 intercalary days to make up the 365-day year. In addition to this solar year calendar, there was a ritual calendar year of 260 days, made up of 20 day/names and the numbers 1–13. Days and numbers ran concurrently, intermeshing like the cogs of two great wheels. Numbers were usually represented by bars and dots: a bar being equal to the number 5, and each dot equal to 1.

In Central Mexico, the years were named after the particular day number and day name on which the year began. These were always one of 4: Rabbit, Reed, Flint, and House. Each successive year would start with a day number one higher than the previous year up to the number 13, which would be succeeded by 1. For example, the Aztec year would start successively on perhaps 11 Flint, 12 House, 13 Rabbit, 1 Reed, 2 Flint, 3 House, and so on. This is important to archaeology because many events were recorded with their dates mentioned in this manner in the historical codices. But this system only fixes a year in a period of 52 years; after 52 years the 365-day solar calendar and the 260-day ritual calendar would both return to their original starting point, and never before. This 52-year period is known as the Sacred Cycle or Calendar Round. The completion of the cycle was important to the Aztecs, and probably other Meso-american peoples also, because they believed that the world would be destroyed on one of these cycle endings. In preparation for this sacred event all fires were put out; fasting was enjoined; and a watch was kept until the sun arose again, when new fires were lit and the reconstruction of temples and their substructures was often undertaken, the new temples being built on the old. Sometimes as many as six rebuildings took place, and the duration of use of a temple can sometimes be determined by the number of previous buildings under one mound, because it is known that rebuilding took place at 52-year intervals.

While most Mesoamerican peoples were satisfied to compute time within this 52-year cycle, and to place a given date accurately in the half-century span, the ancient Maya were considerably more demanding of their record keeping. The highest calendrical expertize was the Maya use of the Initial Series or Long Count system of counting. Like the others, the Maya used a 365-day year, which they called the *Haab*, and the ritual 260-day year. However, they also meticulously recorded how many days had passed, not just within the 52-year span, but since the very beginning of the calendar. This enormous record of time was recorded in units as shown below:

1 Day = 1 Kin
20 Kin = 1 Uinal = 20 days
18 Uinals = 1 Tun = 360 days
20 Tuns = 1 Katun = 7200 days
20 Katuns = 1 Baktun = 144,000 days
20 Baktuns = 1 Pictun = 2,880,000 days

The usual calendar inscription shows two vertical rows of hieroglyphs. At the top, going from left to right, are the Maya readings for the number of Baktuns, then Tuns, Uinals, and Kins. Each of these units is preceded by the proper bar-and-dot numeral as well.

Most of these Long Count dates were calculated from a hypothetical day, 4 Ahau 8 Cumhu, which occurred some 4 millennia ago. The date to which the calculations led was most often the dedicatory date of the stele or monument. These dates are known from carvings on stelae, stairways, lintels, and walls of buildings in most of the Maya Lowlands. Other examples of the dates are known from pottery, jade carvings, and codices. The earliest date on a Maya stele is from TIKAL, which reads the 5th day of the 8th month of the 14th Tun in the 12th Katun of Baktun 8. For simplicity, archaeologists write this in the form 8.12.14.8.5, which corresponds to the year AD 292. The date also marks the start of the Classic Period (i.e., c. AD 300). The last recorded Long Count date was about AD 900, and this marks the end of the period. During the Postclassic Period the Maya recorded their dates in an abbreviated form, using Katun endings. This has resulted in a problem of correlation with the Gregorian calendar.

**Californian Prehistory.** The earliest substantial archaeological findings of California date from before 5000 BC, and derive from a mixture of the Old Cordilleran tradition, with its Cascade type points, and the proto-DESERT TRADITION, with its flint knives. The area in which this characteristic culture arose includes most of the modern state of California, excluding the Lake Mojave desert, and other areas adjoining the Great Basin. In this area there were three basic modes of subsistence, all of which descended in use into the historic period. The first of these is the gathering of plant seeds and hunting, using small stone tools, in the desert areas of California. While this subtradition related directly to the antecedent Desert tradition, the earliest finds do not include seed-grinding implements, which therefore must have developed later. The second type of subsistence was an economy based on the gathering of the abundant acorns growing in the central Sacramento and San Joaquin valleys, and in other mountainous areas. Combined with this was the hunting of large game animals such as elk and deer. The third form is that of marine hunting. The food sources varied considerably, and ranged from the gathering of shellfish to the hunting of sea mammals. In general the widely varying environmental conditions led to a great diversity of types of subsistence. There was no agriculture in California until recent times.

Californian prehistory may be divided into three periods: the Early Period from 5000 to 2000 BC; the Middle Period from 2000 BC to AD 250, and the Late Period from AD 250 until the present day. While throwing sticks and darts were used in the earlier periods, bows and arrows came to replace them. Particularly characteristic were ground and polished stone implements, bowls, and effigies. No pottery was used until the Late Period, when it was introduced from the Southwest cultural area. The Early Period is known as the Milling Stone Horizon along the Southern Californian coast: numerous manos and metates (*see* METATE) have been recovered from such sites as Little Sycamore in Ventana County. However, full use was not yet made of marine food resources. In the Sacramento valley, Windmiller phase sites have yielded quantities of bone fish hooks as well as grinding tools, suggesting that fishing was as important as the gathering of plants and hunting. In the Middle Period sites are more widespread and larger, suggesting an increase in population. The site of Little Harbor on Santa Catalina Island, in the Southern coastal area, has yielded a date of

1900 BC. This midden (rubbish mound) has produced quantities of mussel and abalone shells as well as the bones of marine mammals such as dolphins. In general the Middle Period saw a greater utilization of marine resources, producing other great shell middens, such as the Emeryville Shell Mound on San Francisco Bay. In Central California the use of mortars became more common, and decorative rings of shell became a feature of burials. Population density may have reached a maximum in the early part of the Late Period. It was at this time that the bow and arrow replaced the throwing stick and dart. Steatite was used for making tobacco tubes, cooking bowls, and, in the Canaliño culture of the South coast, effigies of sea mammals such as whales.

The historical tribes of California were of several different linguistic groups, particularly the Penutian and Hokan. The major unifying characteristic of the approximately 30 tribes at the time of the first European contact was that they were well adapted to the varying ecological niches in California.

**Camare.** An assemblage of artifacts, including choppers, scrapers, leaf points, and other tools from the surface of the high terraces of the Rio Pedregal of Venezuela. It may be up to 15,000 years old.

**Camden, William** (1551–1623). The greatest of the group of antiquaries who achieved prominence in Britain in the 16th and early 17th centuries. Although he was preceded by others like Leland, and while many of his contemporaries like Speed and Stow made their own valuable contributions, Camden established his great reputation by his originality and scope. His monumental work, *Britannia*, represents the flowering of a true interest in the past of this country as represented archaeologically, rather than in unverifiable legends. Camden was interested in the past from boyhood, and after leaving Christ Church, Oxford, he traveled widely in England: a pursuit he continued in holidays from his teaching at Westminster School. He learned Anglo-Saxon and Welsh to assist in his studies. Encouraged by Ortelius in 1577, he began to systematize his topographical studies, and his first book, *Britannia*, written in Latin, was published in 1586. This was at first a slim volume with only one illustration, and was enlarged in successive editions in his lifetime as he widened his studies and travels. From the first its scope was impressive, covering all of the British Isles, from the Scillies to the Shetlands, and was concerned with the past from the ancient Britons to the Normans. It had a regional and topographical framework, based on the study of manuscripts, records, and visible antiquities. (He described, amongst other monuments, Silbury Hill, megaliths, and round barrows, though he had little conception of prehistory as such.) Its success was great, and subsequent studies by him concerned with more recent chronicling were less effective.

**Camelid domestication.** Four camelids are found in the Andes of Peru: vicuña (Lama vicunna), guanaco (Lama guanicui), llama (Lama glama), and alpaca (Lama pacoc). The first two are wild and the last two are domesticated. Reputedly they are all descended from a paleo-llama of the Pleistocene period, but there is little evidence yet to support this. It has also been suggested that llama and alpaca came from wild guanaco, domestication occurring between 2000 and 1000 BC. This is hard to prove from excavated bones, as all the four so-called species interbreed and have fertile offspring. (It would also be difficult to tell some hybrids from transitional forms, from wild to domesticated.) Some archaeological evidence is slowly accumulating to permit hypotheses on the problem of taming and domestication, but it is not yet sufficient for a solution to the problem. The evidence comes from three regions of the Central Andes of Peru: Lauricocha, Junin, and Ayacucho. In these regions cave excavations have yielded animal bones from *c.* 8000 to 1000 BC. It has been suggested that herding of llama began first in the Junin region and then spread north and south; however, a high proportion of young camelid bones uncovered from this period may merely indicate selective hunting or culling of a wild herd. Evidence for herding is also found in the presence of stone corrals in the Ayacucho region, *c.* 3000–2000 BC.

The camelids in the early period seem to have been used primarily for meat. Between 2000 and 1000 BC, evidence of herding camelids appears on the Central coast and some wool occurs, suggesting that by this time camelids were raised for wool as well as for meat. Robust llama bones do not occur until about the time of Christ or later, which may indicate that llama were not used as pack animals until then. Andean roads and tambos or corrals for pack animals do not appear until the MIDDLE HORIZON Period, AD 600–1000, thus apparently confirming the hypothesis that llama use for pack trains or pack animals is a late development. (*See also* DOMESTICATION, SOUTH AMERICA.)

**Camp.** A term used to describe the temporary fortifications erected by the Roman army when on campaign. Described in 143 BC by the Roman historian Polybius, it was square, and based on the centrally placed general's tent. There is a great resemblance between this description and surviving examples of the camps built by Scipio's men in Spain, at the seige of NUMANTIA in 133 BC. A slightly different type of camp, rectangular and split into thirds, is described by an anonymous writer in the 3rd century AD. Camps of this kind are known at MASADA, Herod's fortress in Israel, and at several places in North Britain and Wales, where their ramparts still survive as substantial earthworks.

**Campus Martius.** Flood plain of the River Tiber, below and to the northwest of the hills of Rome. In early times it held the Altar of Mars, and was an open space used for army exercises and for voting assemblies. Later it was built on, first with several republican buildings, and later with more monumental imperial structures, including Pompey's theater (52 BC), Augustus' Altar of Peace, the theaters of Marcellus and Balbus, the baths of Nero, and Domitian's stadium, now the Piazza Navona.

**Canaan, Canaanites.** *See* SYRIA–PALESTINE.

**Canals.** From the point of view of industrial archaeology, the most satisfactory canals are those which had the least commercial success: the narrow, shallow canals designed for horsedrawn barges and subsequently either abandoned or, where the cost has not been too great, maintained for pleasure-boating or for small-scale freight operations. Those canals which have met a real and continuing need have usually been enlarged, modernized and in some cases re-routed out of all recognition. British canals are for the most part unmodernized and constitute an archaeologist's paradise, whereas most American and Continental canals have been transformed during the present century.

Canals which have survived in something close to their original form include, in France, the Canal du Midi (1681), which connects the Atlantic with the Mediterranean; in Sweden, the Göta Canal (1810–32), which is an important part of the water link between Stockholm and Göteborg; in Britain, the Kennet and Avon Canal (1794–1810), linking Bristol with London; and, in Canada, the Rideau (1820s), built to improve military communications between Ottawa and the interior.

The United States has a number of conservation schemes involving parts of canals which history has left behind. A section of the Miami and Erie Canal, nearly 4 mi. (6 km) long, at Lockington, Ohio, now forms the Lockington Locks Historical Area. It contains seven locks and several turning basins, all built between 1833 and 1845.

**Canario.** A site on the Central coast of Peru, just inland from Ancon. It gave its name to a complex of artifacts and economic evidence that dates from between 5500 and 4200 BC. This archaeological phase has well made laurel-leaf bifacial points, scrapers, and woven textiles in association with wild plants and marine remains. The subsistence system seems to have been very successful, for some sites seem to have been occupied throughout the year, while others are hamlets with small ovoid posthole houses: an example of settled village life occurring before agriculture.

**Can Hasan.** A site near Karamen in ANATOLIA. Can Hasan III is an aceramic (pre-pottery) mound with about 7 building levels (*c.* 6500 BC). Levels 7–4 on the main mound are Late Neolithic, with dark burnished pottery, while painted pottery appears in Phase 3. Phase 2B3 was destroyed by fire in *c.* 4900 BC, and had rectangular or square houses built up against each other, with interior buttresses and access from the roof. Copper occurs in all the Chalcolithic levels and there is evidence of contacts with Cilicia. Clay and stone figurines also occur and extramural burial was practiced. There is a gap in the sequence between phases 2A (*c.* 4900–4500 BC) and 1 (*c.* 4300 BC), which belongs to a different Neolithic culture.

**Cantharus.** A Greek pottery drinking cup with wide handles and a pedestal base.

**Cape Gelidoniya.** The site of a Bronze Age (late 13th century BC) shipwreck near the Southern coast of Turkey, between Rhodes and Cyprus. The predominantly American team, which excavated the wreck in 1960 and salvaged the bronze ingots and tools it contained, was the first to include diving archaeologists and, as a result, many new techniques were developed.

**Capitolium.** The principal hill of Rome, and the one which formed its religious center. In the Temple of Jupiter Capitolius, built in 509 BC and restored and rebuilt at various times thereafter, resided the state cult of Rome. A number of other cities erected temples to Jupiter on a slightly elevated podium: such a temple, in imitation of the original, was known as a capitolium.

**Capua.** An Oscan settlement in Italy, taken over by the ETRUSCANS, who laid out a town of regular plan on the site. Later, it was one of the greatest cities of the Roman world. Its principal remains are its THEATER, AMPHITHEATER, BATHS, and a MITHRAEUM with painted frescoes.

**Carbon-14.** *See* RADIOCARBON DATING.

**Carcassonne.** The best-preserved example of a medieval fortified town in Europe. Situated in Southwest France, it was extensively restored in the 19th century. Part of the walls are 6th-century AD Visigothic, but the inner wall and citadel date from the 11th and 12th centuries and the outer from the 13th century. The walls were additionally fortified by gates, barbicans, and ditches.

**Carchemish.** A site at Jerablus, on the Syro–Turkish frontier at a crossing of the River Euphrates. It was excavated by the British from 1878 to 1881 and from 1911 to 1914, and consists of a large fortified citadel and two walled extensions with monumental gateways and processional ways decorated with reliefs and hieroglyphic Hittite inscriptions. The earliest levels go back to HALAF times (5th millennium BC), and there are some interesting Bronze Age burials.

**Carmel, Mount.** The site, near Haifa in Israel, of a series of limestone caves which have revealed important prehistoric finds. The earliest deposits are ACHEULIAN. Rich Mousterian levels above have revealed a series of burials, notably a cemetery in the Skhul cave, in which the occupants were intermediate between NEANDERTHAL MAN and modern man. The Upper Palaeolithic sequence ends with the NATUFIAN, in which there are indications of grain reaping and grinding.

**Carolingians.** A Dynasty of the Franks, named after Charlemagne (AD 742–814). It extends from Pepin the Short (d. AD 768) to Louis V (d. AD 987). During the Carolingian period there was a Classical revival, and Carolingian art and architecture reflects Roman models. The capital of the Carolingians was at Aachen, where remains of the period include the Palace Chapel. Also surviving are manuscripts (produced in centers such as

Aachen, Tours, and Rheims), ivories, and frescoes. Important buildings include the oratory of Theodulf, Germiny-des-Près (AD 806), the Abbey Church of Centula, Saint-Riquier (begun *c.* AD 790), and the Abbey Church at Corvey (AD 837–885).

**Carthage** (Carthago). A city on the North African coast, beginning as a Phoenician colony, coming into conflict with Rome in the 3rd and 2nd centuries BC, finally destroyed by her, and reconstructed as a Roman city. Little remains of the Phoenician city: the walls enclosed a massive area, including inner and outer harbors, the citadel (Byrsa), and the Tophet, the holy area of Tanit, the local deity.

Despite its importance as one of the greatest of Roman cities, remains of imperial Roman Carthage are slight and badly damaged. Temples and a porticus were built on the Byrsa hill, and an ODEUM, a THEATER, a CIRCUS, and an AMPHITHEATER, all within the city zone, are still visible. An aqueduct, built in Hadrian's reign, brought water from its source 82 mi. (132 km) away, and an elaborate system of storage cisterns existed throughout the city.

**Caryatid.** A Greek statue of a woman, used instead of a column to carry a lintel. The best known are those of the ERECHTHEUM at Athens.

**Casas Grandes.** A culture of Northern Chihuahua, Mexico, named after a site of the same name. The earliest occupation levels at Casas Grandes are dated to before AD 1000, and are characterized by MOGOLLON-type pottery and pithouse dwellings. After this period (the Viejo), comes the Medio Period, which is characterized by houses constructed of ADOBE or mud brick. The third period, the Tardio, dating after AD 1300, is heavily influenced by Mesoamerican traits: the earlier periods are directly related to the cultures of the Southwestern United States. In this last phase, Mesoamerican traits such as ballcourts, platform mounds, and spindle whorls appear. The pottery of the Tardio Period was polychrome and the multiroom buildings were constructed in several stories.

**Casting.** Three principal techniques of casting were successively developed in prehistoric Europe: one-piece stone molds for flat-faced objects; clay or stone piece molds that could be dismantled and reused; and one-off clay molds for complex shapes made in one piece around a wax or lead pattern (CIRE PERDUE or "lost wax" process). Every metal exploited in early Europe, except iron, was used for casting artifacts. (*See also* BRONZE TECHNOLOGY, CHINA.)

**Castle, Medieval.** One of the most distinctive products of the Middle Ages. Castles were fortified dwellings, built in response to the particular social organization and warfare. Although many different types of fortification are known in prehistoric Europe, castles were not developed until the establishment of the feudal system. This necessitated a strict stratification of society, in which land and other privileges were granted in return for military service. Warfare, whether on a local or a national basis, was essential to society—it found employment for landless younger sons, controlled the population, and offered hope of advancement to those fighting. Castles were passive elements in medieval warfare: they were the focus of sieges rather than bases from which to launch attacks.

Throughout, castles served both as houses for the nobility and as barracks. They were usually equipped for prolonged periods of isolation from the outside world. In medieval eyes, a fortified house was only a castle if it had a wall walk and battlements on its enclosing wall.

Castle architecture consisted essentially of three elements: a tower (keep or donjon), a residence for the noble, and a fortified enclosure wall. These, however, could be combined in various ways—the tower could be combined with the gatehouse, and could have accommodation within it for the lord. The main techniques in siege warfare were scaling (ascending the walls with ladders or in mobile timber towers) and sapping (the undermining of walls). Walls were breached with battering rams or siege engines designed to hurl missiles (the mangonel or trebuchet). Very high walls were built to counter scaling, and wall tops were furnished with overhangs from which missiles could be dropped on the attackers. To prevent siege engines being brought up to the walls, moats were constructed, and walls given a splayed plinth which also ricocheted stones bounced off it by the defenders from above. Sapping was most effective on the angles of walls, so round (or solid-based) towers were developed. Bastions also kept sappers at bay.

Gatehouses were furnished with bridges, which could be lifted, and double gates. Barbicans were often constructed to delay a direct rush. Elaborate systems of concentric walls were developed to provide covering fire and to protect the inner court (or bailey) and its buildings even after capture of the outer. Such elaborate systems of defense were as much to provide a psychological advantage to the castle occupants as a real one, for a simple tower was as easily defended as an elaborate castle of enceinte (walled castle). As the Middle Ages progressed, increasing attention was paid to symmetrical planning in castle architecture.

Inside, the keeps were designed rather like houses, but built upwards instead of outwards. It was usual for the ground floor to be a windowless store, while the main hall, entered by a wooden ladder, was on the first floor, with private apartments above.

In England and Normandy a distinctive form of castle was the motte and bailey, with a timber tower consolidated by an earth mound (the motte) and an encircling earthwork (the bailey). These seem to have been developed in response to the Norman Conquest of England, and few outlived the 12th century.

With the advent of firearms in the mid-14th century, castles became easy to capture, and warfare became more a matter of attack than defense. At the same time, a taste for comfort among the nobility led to the abandonment of these gaunt, draughty, and costly fortified residences for more comfortable and luxurious halls and palaces.

Among notable examples of castle building can be

One of the finest examples of medieval castle building: Harlech Castle in Wales, built by Edward I.

singled out Edward I's castles of Caernarvon, Harlech, and Conway (in Wales), the Tower of London, Warkworth, Kenilworth, and Dover (in England), Vincennes and Loches (in France), Lucera and Castel del Monte (in Italy), Eltz and Marksburg (in Germany), and Krak de Chevaliers (in Syria).

**Castra Castellana** (Falerii). An Etruscan city near Rome, originally the capital of the Faliscans, and reputedly founded by the Pelasgians from ARGOS. The city was captured by Rome in 240 BC, and the inhabitants moved to Falerii Novum, whose walls, with 50 towers and 9 gates, still survive.

**Catacombs.** The name for underground cemeteries, found in several places (e.g., Naples and Syracuse), but usually referring particularly to those in Rome. Various plans and layouts of these exist, but the tomb chambers are usually linked by a series of passages, the coffins themselves being placed in niches (*loculi*) in the walls.

**Çatal Hüyük.** A huge Neolithic site in the Konya plain of ANATOLIA. Thirteen levels were excavated by the British in the early 1960s and date from *c.* 6250 to 5400 BC, but a vast accumulation of earlier material remains to be dug and aceramic (pre-pottery) levels were not reached. The economy was based on agriculture (using irrigation), cattle breeding, trade, and industry. The

small rectangular houses were built up against each other and access was by ladder from the roof. The dead were buried under the sleeping platforms. The shrines were only distinguished from the houses by decoration: wall paintings, benches decorated with horn cores, bucrania (bull heads), and reliefs. Pottery was generally creamy-gray and burnished, and clay and stone figurines are numerous. There were active weaving and chipped stone industries, and lead and copper were used for trinkets. Most raw materials had to be obtained by trade and the Çatal Hüyük culture seems to have covered a large area. At the end of the Neolithic period the settlement was moved to Çatal Hüyük West which, although it has not been fully excavated, has produced some pottery.

**Catastrophists.** In the 18th century geologists, puzzled by the number of successive rock strata and their fossil content, visualized a series of upheavals or catastrophes destroying the existing fauna, which had to be replaced by a new set of creatures. Georges CUVIER was the last prominent advocate of catastrophism. One aspect of this philosophy, namely that new forms came from elsewhere, has never been completely abandoned.

**Cave art.** More than 100 caves in Europe have traces of painting or engraving left by Ice Age man. This art belongs to the latest part of the Old Stone Age, called the Upper Palaeolithic period, and is the earliest representational art in the world. France has revealed the largest number of cave art sites, and the next largest come from Spain. Other countries, such as Italy, have produced a few examples, and in Russia there is one painted cave.

Even within France the decorated caves are very localized, occurring mainly in the limestone of the Périgord and Pyrennean regions of the Southwest.

The most famous caves, such as those at ALTAMIRA, LASCAUX, Niaux, and Pech Merle, have numerous paintings, but more than half of the others have only engravings—fine lines incised on the limestone walls with a flint chisel called a burin. The painted caves also have engravings, and there are fine examples in some of the galleries of Lascaux, as well as in sites like Les Combarelles and Gabillou, all in the Dordogne. Some of the carving is more ambitious, and figures stand out in low relief. Occasionally, modeling in clay is found, and some small statuettes were even made of baked clay. Figures on the wall of a cave in the Rhône valley were smeared on the wall in bright red clay.

The painting is all done with two pigments: iron oxide, which occurs naturally in limestone, and gives reddish colors ranging from brown through orange almost to yellow; and manganese dioxide, also occurring naturally and giving a vivid black to purplish color. They were not apparently mixed, but do sometimes shade from one to the other. Sometimes the paint was applied with the fingers, sometimes probably blown on through a tube. A brush may have been used in some cases.

The subject matter is surprisingly restricted in view of the hundreds of known representations. This restriction remains even in the so-called mobiliary or portable art, small objects, sometimes utilitarian, found associated with open camps or cave settlements of the period across Europe. Essentially all the art consists of animals, symbols, and, very occasionally, humans. Landscapes, vegetation, sun, moon, or clouds, scenes of everyday life, or anything else in a clearly recognizable form are absent.

Altogether more than 20 species of animals have been depicted, but by far the most common are the horse and the bison, followed by red deer and ibex, and then by ox, mammoth, and reindeer. Of the symbols, a few are overtly sexual, representing vulvas and penises. Most of the remainder are obscure, but they can be somewhat arbitrarily divided into major and minor symbols. The minor ones include blobs, lines, and meanders, often arranged in groups or lines. Major symbols include big squares, compartmented and colored, bell shapes, "club" shapes, and barbed and other linear signs.

A recent theory suggests that the caves were sanctuaries set out according to a prescribed pattern. Certain pairings of animals, such as bison and horse, were required, and certain signs were confined to the more remote parts of the caves. The first decorated caves were discovered in the 1870s, but it was not until 1900 that their authenticity was generally accepted. Discoveries continue to be made and, since 1960, the pace of discovery has slightly increased, although the new finds are not quite as spectacular as some of the older ones.

**Çayönü.** A site near Diyarbekir in Southeastern ANATOLIA, not far from Ergani Maden, where native copper was obtained and worked. The site is at present being excavated by a Turkish-American team and dates suggested are *c.* 7500–6800 BC. So far, it has produced the earliest occurrences of copper, clay bricks, baked figurines, and pottery.

**Celadon.** Stonewares with a green glaze, made in China from the SUNG DYNASTY (AD 960–1279) onwards. The principal kilns, several of which have been excavated or surveyed, are in Yao-chou in Shensi province and Lin-ju in Honan province in the North, and in Li-shui and Lung-ch'üan in Chekiang province in the South. (*See* CERAMICS, CHINA.)

**Celts.** One of the great barbarian peoples of the ancient world, recorded by Greek and Roman writers as having lived to the north of the Mediterranean countries in the final centuries BC. Their existence was first attested *c.* 500 BC, but there is no doubt that they had been in existence long before that. Like the CIMMERIANS and SCYTHIANS, the early Celts were not a people in the modern political sense, for at no time did they ever constitute a nation or a single politically unified group. Three factors distinguished them from other peoples: their language, their beliefs, and, to a lesser (but still large) extent, their material culture. Their language belonged to the Indo-European family, and divided into two branches at an early date, probably in the 2nd or even possibly the 3rd millennium BC; these two branches, referred to as P- and Q-Celtic, are respectively represented by the Welsh and Irish Gaelic languages. In late prehistory both branches were probably still comprehensible to most Celts.

The original homelands of the Celts appear to have been on the Western and Central mainland of Europe: in France, Germany, Bohemia, Austria, and Switzerland. By the mid-1st millennium BC, they had also settled large parts of Iberia (Spain and Portugal), Britain, Ireland, the Low Countries south of the Rhine delta, and Italy north of the River Po. In the 4th and early 3rd centuries BC they spread southwards and eastwards into Central Italy (sacking Rome in 385 BC), Yugoslavia, and the Danubian countries. They advanced deep into Greece, sacking Delphi in 279 BC, and a large body of them crossed the Bosporus into Asia Minor in 278 BC and settled, a couple of generations later, around modern Ankara, becoming the people known as the Galatians in the New Testament. Most of the Celts later lost their ethnic identity through absorption into the Roman Empire or by being swamped by the southward expansion of the early Germanic peoples in the 1st centuries BC and AD. Those in Scotland and Ireland lived on beyond the Roman Empire to become the ancestors of the Scots and Irish; the inhabitants of Wales, barely touched by Romanization, later developed into the early Welsh kingdoms of the post-Roman period. The present inhabitants of Brittany are of British stock, their ancestors having migrated there from Cornwall and Wales in the 5th–7th centuries AD.

The political and social structure of Celtic society underwent profound changes during the course of the 1st millennium BC, largely as a result of developments in the Mediterranean world (*see* IRON AGE). Up to the end of the 5th century BC, it had been based on control of the key raw materials for large-scale industry, on certain highly valued commodities such as salt, which was mined at many localities (e.g., HALLSTATT and Dürrnberg, in Austria, and Halle in Germany—*hall* being the Celtic word for salt), and on long-distance trade of them. In many parts of mainland Europe, large centers of chiefdoms developed during the 6th and 5th centuries BC, such as the Asperg, the Heuneburg, and the Magdalenenberg in Southwest Germany, and Mont Lassois in Burgundy. Their chieftains were buried with great magnificence in enormous barrows close to these settlements, often with extremely fine imported goods from the Mediterranean world. The Vix burial, near Mont Lassois, contained the largest and finest Greek bronze vessel yet found anywhere: a bronze crater (for diluting wine with water), standing 5 ft. 4½ in. (1.64 m) high, and weighing 460 lb. (208.6 kg). With the collapse of long-distance trade with the Mediterranean civilizations at the close of the 5th century BC, these chiefdoms soon came to an end, and there followed a period of disruption and internecine warfare in which the Celts spread south- and eastwards into Central Italy and as far as Asia Minor. However, towards the end of the 2nd century BC a greater stability was once more established in many areas, and large tribal areas, kingdoms, and even proto-states came into existence in France, Switzerland, Southern Germany, and Southeastern England. Many of the defended settlements on hills (*see* HILLFORT) and new large settlements in lower-lying situations developed into large manufacturing and trading centers (*oppida*), often incorporating mints for coinage. This process of urbanization has continued uninterrupted until the present day in many regions, including such places as Geneva (Switzerland), Mont Beuvray (ancient Bibracte, the predecessor of the largest city in Roman Gaul, Autun), and Colchester (ancient Camulodunum, the seat of King Cunobelin—Shakespeare's Cymbeline—in England).

The Celts were renowned in the ancient world for their skill in warfare (and for the fact that warriors fought naked except for torcs—rings—around their necks), particularly in their use of the chariot drawn by two ponies; after battle they cut off the heads of their enemies and carried them off as trophies. There is also archaeological evidence that in some areas they rifled graves to retrieve the skulls. In Gaul and in Britain there was a separate group of men, the Druids, who were the religious leaders of Celtic society; their influence was exaggerated by Caesar for purposes of propaganda in his wars against the Gauls and the Britons. The Celts had many deities, which under Roman rule came to be identified with the Roman pantheon. The water deity was particularly revered, for the Celts placed a large number of fine goods into wells, peat bogs, lakes, and rivers (many of which have come to light in modern times), as well as in sacred groves in forests. One of these deposits was looted by the Romans and yielded an enormous treasure of precious metal which did much to replenish the coffers of Rome: the famous *aurum tolosanum* at Toulouse. On the mainland of Europe there were a large number of square, banked enclosures used for religious ceremonies, and even for human sacrifice, which was also widely practiced.

From the 5th century BC, the Celts developed the first sophisticated abstract ornamental art styles in Europe,

A bronze-faced shield with repoussé relief ornament and red glass settings, from Battersea, London, 1st century AD.

under the successive stimuli of Greco-Etruscan, Hellenistic, and early Roman imperial ornamental floral styles. They also drew on the animal styles of the Scythians and Persians, and on their own native traditions of the 6th century BC and earlier, in which ducks and birds had been favorite decorative motifs. Animal and human faces were interwoven with vegetal and abstract motifs, and from the 3rd century BC onwards this led to the development of particularly ambiguous decoration, which could be read either as pure pattern or as the faces of animals and human beings. This feature of Celtic art was especially developed in the ornamental work of the British Isles in the 1st centuries BC and AD.

**Cement and Concrete.** One of the most important industries to have developed within the past century. From an archaeological point of view, it can be studied on two different types of site: where the cement was made and where it was used in the structures for which it was destined. The modern type of rotating kiln works continuously and wears itself out fast under what is little more than a steel-framed asbestos shelter, and it is unlikely to provide future archaeologists with much information. Nine of the earlier and more solid type of static kilns (*c.* 1870) have been preserved near Coplay, Lehigh County, Penn., United States, and now form part of the Saylor Cement Kiln Park, the only thoroughgoing piece of cement-manufacturing conservation in the world. Several professional institutions, however, maintain good historical archives relating to cement and concrete. Two of the most important are the collections of the History of Concrete Committee of the American

Concrete Association and of the Cement and Concrete Association in London.

**Cempoala.** The principal city, located 24 mi. (39 km) northwest of the modern port of Veracruz, occupied by the TOTONACS at the time of the Spanish Conquest, although it paid tribute to the Aztecs. On his march to Tenochtitlan, Cortez rested his troops here for a few days and persuaded the Totonacs to rebel against the Aztecs. It was later the site of the defeat of Navaez by Cortez. Though the structures visible today belong to the Postclassic Period, there is evidence for occupation as early as the Preclassic Period. There is also some indication of Classic Period–Teotihuacan influence.

The principal buildings of the site include the *Templo Mayor*, another pyramid known as *Los Chimeneas* in the northeast corner of the site, and the circular temple of the wind god. To the east of the ceremonial center are a number of isolated structures, including one known as *Las Caritas*, taking its name from a number of miniature pottery heads arranged in panels on the walls. An unusual architectural feature of the site is the presence of circular or rectangular enclosures of low walls with stepped crenellations. Construction of the buildings was not of dressed stone, but of large water-worn stones set in mud and covered with a lime plaster made from burnt shell.

**Cenote.** A waterhole or natural well caused by the collapse of the limestone crust which covers most of the Yucatan Peninsula, Mexico, and which provided a major source of drinking water. Sometimes the cenotes reached considerable depths below the surface. Probably the best known is the so-called "Cenote of Sacrifice" at CHICHEN ITZA, into which victims and offerings were thrown as a sacrifice to the rain gods. It was about 65 ft. (20 m) from ground level to the surface of the water and an additional 65 ft. (20 m) to the bottom. The cliffs surrounding it were vertical or overhanging so there was little chance of survival. Recent scientific underwater exploration and dredging has produced artifacts made of gold, jade, pottery, balls of incense, and a number of human bones. Generally, however, the cenotes were the source of drinking water, and Precolumbian Mayan sites were often located nearby.

**Ceramics, China.** Together with LACQUER and SILK, PORCELAIN and stonewares are China's most characteristic products. At every period very advanced firing techniques were used in materials of exceptional quality, producing the longest and most exciting ceramic tradition in the world.

Pottery making did not begin exceptionally early in China, but it was rapidly exploited to a high level of excellence in the handmade painted pottery of the YANG-SHAO CULTURE (*c.* 4500 BC). From a technical point of view, the wheel-turned pots of the later Neolithic LUNG-SHAN CULTURE (*c.* 2500 BC), are more extraordinary. These were made of a black pottery, unpainted, but turned to an incredible thinness and constructed in exotic shapes.

The first steps in stoneware making were taken in the SHANG DYNASTY (*c.* 1600–1027 BC), with the introduction of felspathic glazes which required firing at temperatures of 1100°–1200°C. Changes in kiln design, stimulated perhaps by innovations in bronze casting, made such temperatures possible. By the Western CHOU DYNASTY (1027–771 BC), examples of this type of ceramic were so widely distributed in China that there must have been several kilns making such wares.

It was in the Southwestern provinces of Kiangsu, Cheking, and Anhui that the manufacture of such pots took root and, in the HAN DYNASTY (206 BC–AD 220), gave rise to a well established tradition of stonewares glazed with felspathic glazes which were fired in a reducing atmosphere. These were the precursors of the YÜEH WARE of the 3rd century AD, which was initially made in bronze forms as though it was intended to be a substitute for bronze. The period between the Han Dynasty (206 BC–AD 220) and the T'ANG DYNASTY (AD 618–906) was a crucial time for ceramic production. It saw the full development of the Yüeh wares and also a Northern green-glazed stoneware. At the same time, pots made of white clay containing kaolin, which from the Shang had been used intermittently, were now fired at a much higher temperature—the first steps towards the production of porcelain, a Chinese invention. The foundations of porcelain making were laid in the T'ang period, and it was finally produced in the SUNG DYNASTY (AD 960–1279). There were essentially two types of porcelain: a Northern creamy colored one known as TING WARE, and a Southern one from Kiangsi province with a bluish or YING–CH'ING glaze. The experiments of the T'ang period, not only in white ceramics, but also in green-glazed and black wares known as HUANG-TAO WARE, flowered under the Liao, Sung, and Chin Dynasties from the 10th to the 13th century AD (*see* LIAO DYNASTY; CHIN DYNASTY), in a great variety of types which each reflected the skills and available materials of the different areas.

Various kilns have been investigated, including the Northern kilns which made slip-decorated stonewares, namely TZ'U-CHOU WARE, and also those which made Ting ware, CHÜN WARE, and Northern CELADON. In the South, the Lung-ch'üan and KUAN WARE kilns have been surveyed, as well as those making black-glazed wares. The immense scale of production is evident from the large kilns and vast mounds of sherds and wasters found. This underlines a salient feature of Chinese ceramics: they were not and never could have been the achievement of individual potters working on their own. The technical demands were such that large numbers of people must always have been involved, organized in a batch-production system, if not on a factory basis.

The development of a semi-factory type of organization was inevitable when the porcelain kilns at Ching-te-chen, Kiangsi province, came to dominate ceramic production in the whole of China, and the local wares of the Sung Dynasty declined in importance. This happened in the YÜAN DYNASTY (AD 1279–1368), concurrently with the introduction of the painting of porcelain in underglaze blue. This important decorative innovation was probably made as a result of the demands of the Islamic market. Such export markets were very important to the Chinese. Indeed today, larger quantities of Yüan Dynasty porcelains are to be found in Iran, Turkey, and Syria than in

China, and ceramics of the T'ang and Sung Dynasties have been excavated in Indonesia, Malaysia, the Philippines, India, the Persian Gulf, and the coast of East Africa. Later porcelains of the Ming and Ch'ing Dynasties were as widely distributed, being particularly popular in Europe and the New World (*see* MING DYNASTY; CH'ING DYNASTY).

**Ceramics, Japan.** Since the mid-1950s archaeological methods have transformed our knowledge of Japanese ceramics of the historical period. The main results have been: (1) Proof of continued and very extensive production of pottery over widely separated areas of Japan from the 7th to the 15th century AD. (2) Confirmation of the great changes in pottery styles in the late 15th, 16th, and early 17th centuries as a result of Korean and other Asian influences and of the beginning of porcelain manufacture. (3) Evidence of the replacement of pottery by porcelain as everyday wares in the late 18th and early 19th centuries.

It is now known that unglazed pottery of the SUE WARE type (*see* GREAT TOMBS PERIOD) died out gradually in the Ōsaka area but was continued through both the NARA PERIOD and the Heian period (7th–12th century AD) in the Tokai region, especially at the Sanage kilns east of Nagoya. This area was the new center of Japanese pottery until the 16th century. Soft pottery glazed in two or three colors in the style of the T'ANG DYNASTY has been identified at over 200 kilns, mainly in Nara and Kyoto (8th and 9th centuries AD). These were formerly thought to be Chinese imports. In the provinces, especially at Sanage, simple green-glazed and ash-glazed wares were made from the mid- to late Heian, when Seto, to the northeast of Nagoya, began to make more refined shapes with brown, green, and yellow glazes. There were 600 kilns there and more than 1,000 at Tokoname, which provided glazed wares for all Japan in the Kamakura period (late 12th–14th century).

Large ash-glazed storage jars, formerly thought to have been restricted to "the six old kilns" (Tokoname, Seto, Bizen, Echizen, Tamba, Shigaraki), have now been shown to have been made locally all over Japan, on the Atsumi peninsular, for example (Kamakura period). From the late 15th century, pottery taste was changed by the demands of the Tea Ceremony. The new center was Mino to the north of Nagoya, where Black Seto, Yellow Seto, Oribe, and Shina types were made. The island of Kyushu became as important as older areas, with Korean immigrants developing more varied glazes, particularly in the Karatsu region. In nearby Arita porcelain was initiated by Koreans, and excavations at Nishi Arita have revealed blue-and-white bowls in pure Korean style (late 16th century). Work at Kutani in Kaga province has lent support to the "Old Kutani" label, and has established the presence of 17th-century porcelain kilns.

**Cerro Blanco.** A Chavinoid site located in the Nepena valley, on the Central coast of Peru. The principal feature of the temple complex consists of a platform arrangement with stone walls covered by carved and painted clay reliefs in the zoomorphic system of the early CHAVIN

style, representing a bird with outspread wings. The device of two bird profiles forming a frontal mask is employed: the head is a low platform, with the body, wings, and tail formed by low walled terraces at the sid and rear.

**Cerro Sechin.** One of the oldest sites related to the CHAVIN culture, *c.* 1200 BC, located on a granite hill at the confluence of two rivers in the lower Casma valley, Central coast of Peru. The site consists of numerous walled enclosures surrounding dwellings and a temple platform. The most important features are dressed and carved granite slabs which face the largest compound. These incised line carvings represent warriors and dignitaries in regalia with maces and trophy heads. Possibly the most ancient example of monumental stone carving in the Andes, the slabs are arranged in a post and fill-in system, with wall sections in between smaller squarish stones. The temple contained within the enclosure was built with conical ADOBE bricks, plastered and painted.

A detail of the carved granite slabs which face the largest compound at Cerro Sechin, Casma valley, Peru.

**Cerveteri** (Caere). One of the most important Etruscan cities in Italy, Cerveteri lies about 25 mi. (40 km) north of Rome. The earliest settlement of the site was of the VILLANOVAN CULTURE, but it flourished particularly from the 7th to the 5th century BC as one of the 12 major

Etruscan cities. Traces of its Etruscan past are slight, and the surviving remains are mainly those of the cemeteries.

**Cesena Treasure.** A hoard found about 20 mi. (32 km) from Ravenna in Italy, consisting of a collection of Ostrogothic jewelry. It comprised a gold chain, two gold necklace pendants, a gold finger ring, a large gold earring with garnets and pearls, a pair of gold knife mounts, two jeweled crosses flanked by fishes, a hairpin (gold with inlays), and an inlaid gold eagle brooch. The hoard dates from the beginning of the 6th century AD.

**Chacmool.** A Mesoamerican life-size stone sculpture in the round representing a reclining man with head turned to the side, knees drawn up, and hands supporting a shallow receptacle on the stomach area. The function of these sculptures is uncertain, but offerings were probably placed in the receptacle. They belong to the Postclassic Period and are common at Toltec sites, such as Tula and CHICHEN ITZA, as well as at some Postclassic Tarascan and Aztec sites.

**Chagar Bazar.** A site on a tributary of the River Khabur in Northern Syria, excavated by M. E. L. Mallowan from 1935 to 1937. Five levels (1–5), ranging from the beginning of the 3rd millennium BC to the middle of the 2nd millennium BC, were preceded by 10 prehistoric or protohistoric levels, of which levels 6–12 contained pottery of the HALAF type, and levels 13–15 of the Samarra type. Iron was found in level 5, and copper in level 12. (See the chronological table, p. 198.)

**Chalcolithic.** A term first used in the Near East at MERSIN to define the painted pottery cultures which succeeded the Neolithic. This period is characterized by increased trade and cultural exchanges; copper occurs but is mainly used for trinkets, and there is still a substantial stone industry. This term is not to be confused with the term "Copper Age," which is used by Anatolian and Caucasian archaeologists to describe 2nd-millennium BC cultures. (See the chronological table, p. 198; COPPER AGE, EUROPE.)

**Chaldaeans.** An Aramaean tribe, called after the Kaldu, which probably moved into Southern Mesopotamia in the 10th century BC (see ARAMAEANS). After a period of Assyrian domination, Marduk-apal-iddina (Merodach–Baladan of the Bible) made a bid for independence, carried out guerrilla warfare in the Marshes and ruled in BABYLON on two occasions at the end of the 8th century BC. In 626 BC the Chaldaeans, under Nabu-apal-usur (Nabopolassar), founded the Neo-Babylonian Dynasty, with Babylon as their capital. In 612 BC, with their allies the MEDES, they overthrew NINEVEH.

The reign of Nabu-kudurri-usur (Nebuchadnezzar, 604–562 BC) is marked by great architectural, literary, and scientific activity. He also drove the Egyptians from Syria, captured Jerusalem and deported the Jews to Babylonia. After his death there is a period of confusion. Nabu-na'id (Nabonidus, 555–539 BC) is an enigmatic

character, interested in history and religion, who spent 10 years in Arabia and left Babylon in the care of his son, Bel-shar-usur (Belshazzar). In 539 BC, Babylon was captured by the Achaemenid King Cyrus II, and this marks the end of the Dynasty.

It should be noted that the term "Chaldaean" is also applied to a present-day Christian community of Northern Iraq, while Chaldian is another name for the Urartians, the followers of the god Khaldis (see URARTU, URARTIANS).

**Chambered tomb.** In Europe chambered tombs are stone-built burial chambers set in mounds made of earth or stones. A variant is the rockcut tomb, with the chamber hewn out of soft rock, such as limestone or chalk (see SEINE–OISE–MARNE CULTURE). Chambered tombs belong generally to the Neolithic of Atlantic Western Europe, beyond the loess-lands of Central Europe, and are distributed from Iberia to Scandinavia, with outliers in the West Mediterranean. They vary greatly, both from region to region and within any one region. Chambers of round, rectangular, or trapezoidal plan were built of large boulders or of smaller stones, and were roofed by a large flat capstone or by drystone vaulting known as corbeling.

One or more were set in mounds, generally stone built, of various ground plans, from round to trapezoidal. In many cases these were connected to the façade by passages of varying length (see PASSAGE GRAVE), though in others there was direct access. The entrance was often elaborated architecturally into a forecourt. Geometric motifs, shallowly carved, decorate many chambers, pas-

An interior view, looking down the main passage towards the end chamber, of West Kennet Long Barrow, Wiltshire.

sages, and kerbs. In several areas (e.g., Britain, Denmark, Northern France) collective inhumations (i.e., noncremation) were contained in the chambers, and the assumption has been made of a similar function in other areas where bone is not preserved. The so-called court cairns of Ireland contained only cremations, not burnt *in situ*, and suggest that many chambered tombs were not merely used as mausoleums, but also as communal focuses for early farmers in their scattered settlements.

In China, chambered tombs date from the HAN DYNASTY (206 BC–AD 220). Each consisting of a main burial chamber, containing the coffin, with other rooms leading off it, they were either hollowed out of a cliff or constructed underground.

**Chanapata.** A culture of the CUZCO area in the Peruvian Andes, *c.* 1000–200 BC. The type-site, on a Cuzco hillside, was excavated in the early 1940s. Its pottery is dark-hued or red, with incised, punctated, and relief-modeled decoration, and a burnished or brushed finish. It has the technical characteristics of the Early Horizon Period, but not the stylistic features of the CHAVIN style.

**Chancay.** A distinctive black-on-white style of pottery associated with large effigy figurines, dolls, and fine lace-like textiles from the Central coast of Peru. It dates from the Late Intermediate Period, between AD 1000 and 1450–76.

**Chanchan.** One of the largest of the Precolumbian cities of Peru, the capital of the CHIMU Empire from AD 1000 until the Inca conquered the area in AD 1476. The major part of the site consists of ten large ADOBE compounds of about 1312 × 656 ft. (400 × 200 m), situated north of Trujillo on the North Peruvian coast. Within each of the high-walled enclosures were vast reception areas, residences of the elite, a burial platform, many storerooms and administrative units, kitchens, some low-class housing, and a large sunken garden area. The royal tombs have provided evidence that the compounds were not built simultaneously but in sequence, one for each ruler. The tombs have yielded quantities of fine black and red Chimu pottery, textiles, feather mantles, jewelry of gold, bronze, and silver, bronze weapons and tools, and carved items of wood. Recent excavations have also revealed relief-ornamented walls with repetitive figurative and geometric motifs, walls with white-painted murals, and vast irrigation systems associated with the capital. Economic and political control was exercised over the Chimu Empire from this capital. The population estimates for the huge compounds, together with lesser administrative, residential, and storage areas, are in the region of 40,000–200,000.

**Ch'ang-An.** An early capital of China near the present-day city of Sian, first used by the Western CHOU DYNASTY (1027–771 BC). Famous under the HAN DYNASTY (206 BC–AD 220) and the T'ANG DYNASTY (AD 678–906), it alternated with LO-YANG as the capital of a great empire. The T'ang city was immense, laid out in a grid pattern oriented north–south within formidable city walls. Some large buildings of this date, notably the Han-yüan palace, have been excavated, as have tombs of the T'ang imperial family which lie outside the city.

**Charcoal.** In antiquity, charcoal was widely used as a fuel in industrial processes in preference to wood, since no heat was wasted in the furnace in removing steam or in converting cellulose and lignin into elemental carbon. It was also used in making steel and black pigments.

**Chariot.** Chariots were used in many parts of the ancient world from prehistoric times. In the European Iron Age they were used in warfare and, occasionally, for very rich burials.

In the Near East, light horse-drawn chariots were introduced by the Indo-European aristocracy of the Hurrians and led to a new style of warfare necessitating the building of imposing earthworks round the cities of Syria-Palestine. Earlier, onager-drawn wheeled vehicles were used by the Sumerians but they can only have been of limited use. They are depicted on mosaics and in bronze and actual examples have been found at Ur and Kish.

In China, the chariot dates from the latter part of the SHANG DYNASTY, *c.* 1200 BC, and burials of complete chariots with horses and charioteers have been excavated. Significant features are the use of a wide, low box entered from the front; a wheel rim in two or more sections or felloes; and numerous spokes to the wheel. The Chinese chariot resembles those used at a slightly earlier date in the Caucasus, suggesting some direct contact between the two regions. Chariots were used for warfare in the Shang (*c.* 1200–1027 BC) and Western Chou (1027–771 BC) Dynasties. But when warfare extended into the swamps and mountains of Southern China their use became impracticable, except as conveyances for civil officials.

**Chase.** *See* METAL TECHNOLOGY, PREHISTORIC EUROPE.

**Chasséen culture.** The Middle Neolithic culture of virtually the whole of France. Named after the Camp de Chassey in Bourgogne, it appeared in the South before 3500 BC, and in the North before 3000 BC. Plain and decorated pottery gives an appearance of uniformity, but other elements were more sharply regionalized.

**Chavin.** The style or culture, *c.* 1200–300 BC, which is named after the site of CHAVIN DE HUANTAR in Peru. The art style spread from the North Peruvian Andes and dominated most of Peru during the EARLY HORIZON Period. It is characterized by religious motifs and its spread indicates considerable cultural and religious influence. The extent of political influence is not yet known, as there is no evidence of military fortifications. Principal architectural forms include monumental terraced platforms and sunken courts in ceremonial centers. Simplified elements of the complex iconography of the style appear in various forms in the different regions, on stone, shell, bone, pottery, gold, and silver objects, and woven and painted textiles. Mythical beings were shown in highly abbreviated forms, and in some cases single details from the more elaborate representations were used as an abstract geometrical form. Characteristic of the style is the balance achieved and the regular modular framework of bands of straight and curved lines. The pottery forms include plain bottles, single spouted stirrup bottles, pumpkin-shaped jars and straight-sided bowls. The decorative techniques employed include modeling, incising, dentate rocker stamp and textured surfaces on polished gray or black backgrounds. The Chavin-influenced style of the Northern coastal area is called the CUPISNIQUE. On the South coast at Paracas, contemporaneous religious motifs make an early appearance in association with an "occulate being," heavily influenced by the "Great Image" deity of Chavin de Huantar. Chavin represents the first Andean civilization. Its outstanding art style was never surpassed in the complexity of its iconography.

**Chavin de Huantar.** The name of the major ceremonial and urban site of the CHAVIN culture, which was a mecca of early Andean religion in the North Peruvian highlands. Surrounded by peaks in a small valley and extending 656 ft. (200 m) along the bank of the River Mosna, the principal temple consists of a pyramid, inside which are irregular stories of stone-lined galleries and chambers connected by stairways and ramps. The temple faces east across a sunken court. The three phases of its construction are evident in the façade of cut-stone blocks rising to a height of 56 ft. (17 m). A portico of incised columns, which stood before the third phase building (c. 800 BC), and a cornice of slabs incised with eagles and hawks were major features of the temple. Carving in the round was confined largely to animal and human heads, which had projecting tenons for insertion into the wall. Carvings of the three principal deities have been found: the Great Image, the Cayman, and the Staff God. The Great Image, a fanged figure depicted on the knife-shaped Lanzon stone, 13 ft. (4 m) high, was probably the only cult figure not moved from its original position, since it stands in an underground chamber on the central axis of the U-shaped temple of the first phase. The Staff God, portrayed full face on the Raimondi stone, appears throughout prehistoric Andean styles. The Cayman, portrayed on the Tello Obelisk, is, like the Staff God, in the more complex late style of post-800 BC. Elongations and substitutions of dense iconographic detail proliferate within the outlined main figures. Most common forms depicted in the sculpture are eagles and hawks, and a fine jaguar frieze marks the approach to the temple. Jaguars and serpents are less often represented in entirety, but elements of them occur on most pieces as substitutions of features.

Two types of ceremonial ceramics have been found in deposits in the Rocas and Ofrendas galleries, after which they are named. Probably the earlier style, Rocas ceramics have a solid appearance, similar to stone. Forms include bottles, with globular bodies and a small but thick stirrup spout, and bowls with vertical walls. Gray and black wares are decorated with incised, engraved, or modeled designs, to which are added fine engraved, polished, and dentate ornamentation contrasted with smooth burnished plain areas. Pieces of red pottery were found with broad incised designs, whose incisions had been filled with a black and a graphite-based pigment. Ofrendas pottery, of which there are four sub-groups, is very fine and more varied in style. Predominant forms are bottles, with elongated spouts, globular bodies, and flat bases; and bowls, usually with divergent walls and flat or rounded bases. The style of this pottery is based on an image of a figure with an enlarged head and two fangs, portrayed in relief decoration and by incision.

**Chemical analysis.** Although potentially useful in identifying the remains of many organic materials which have largely perished, the main use of chemical techniques in archaeology has been the microanalytical identification of trace elements characteristic of particular sources of raw materials such as OBSIDIAN. Spectrographic X-ray diffraction, and neutron activation techniques are commonly employed.

**Cheng-chou.** A site in Honan province on the Yellow River in China, where remains of an important SHANG DYNASTY (c. 1500–1200 BC) city have been excavated. A rectangular wall, 7,869 yd. (7,195 m) long, enclosed an area of around 1 sq. mi. (3 km²), divided into different quarters. An analysis of the stratigraphy and artifacts suggests that this city was occupied before the foundation of AN-YANG and ceased to be used, at least on a large scale, halfway through the An-yang period.

**Chibcha.** The Chibcha or Muisca, as they called themselves, are a highland tribe from the Bogota region of Colombia. Although their culture was described in glowing terms by travelers of the 16th century, archaeological evidence is of a scattered rural population who cultivated highland crops and traded salt and emeralds for cotton, gold, and luxury goods.

**Chichen Itza.** Originally a Late Classic Maya site in Yucatan, Mexico, with architecture closely related to the Puuc style: many such buildings still stand on the south side of the site today. In the 11th century AD, however, Chichen Itza was occupied by Toltec invaders, and it became their principal center in the Yucatan until 1180. The site is most notable for its fusion of Mayan and Toltec-Mexican architectural styles and artwork.

Much of the site's fame was due to the CENOTE of Sacrifice, a natural well sunk into the limestone crust of the earth, from which gold, jade, and human bones have been dredged. Chichen Itza has some of the best survivals of Toltec architecture in Mexico on the north side of the site, including the great ballcourt, the largest known in Mesoamerica, and a huge terraced pyramid, named the "Castillo" by the Spaniards. This is surmounted by a temple in Toltec style, but with Maya vaulting. The Temple of the Warriors, which is today partly restored, is an enlarged and improved copy of the Temple of Tlahuizpantecuhtli at Tula, where the TOLTECS originated. There are great colonnaded halls in the front and at the side, many of which, as well as the columns in the temple itself, are carved in bas relief with figures of Toltec warriors, while the entrance portals are giant feathered

View, from the Temple of the Warriors, of the Castillo at Chichen Itza, Yucatan, Mexico.

serpent columns. The remaining pure Maya buildings are in the southern part of the site, known as "Chichen Viejo." Among the more important are the Caracol, the Nunnery, and the House of the Three Lintels. The name "Nunnery" is a European misnomer, as the actual use of the building is unknown. The Caracol is a circular structure in Puuc style, which was apparently used as a Mayan astronomical observatory.

**Ch'i-chia culture.** Dating from *c.* 1700 BC, this culture is found in the Northwest of China in Kansu province. It is a descendant of the earlier painted pottery Neolithic cultures, and is characterized by the use of jars with loop handles and by copper tools.

**Chichimec.** The name given collectively to the various tribes which invaded the valley of Mexico from about the 7th to 12th century AD in periodic waves or migrations. The TOLTECS are believed to have been one of the first of these tribes and the AZTECS one of the last. Such Chichimec invasions may have been at least partly responsible for the destruction and burning of TEOTI-HUACAN. The Toltecs, following conquest, absorbed many of the civilized cultures in the valley region. Other Chichimec tribes followed the Toltecs and set up separate independent kingdoms, the most important being the Aztecs, who arrived in the Late Postclassic Period.

**Chien ware.** A brown-glazed Chinese stoneware made of a clay which turned a chocolate brown when fired. By careful control of the kiln temperatures, streaking and iridescent patches were formed on the glaze to make the "hare's fur" and "oil spot" glaze. Chien ware was manufactured in the SUNG DYNASTY (AD 960–1279) in Fukien province, where large deposits of kiln wastes have been found at Chien-yang-hsien.

**Chihua.** A well represented archaeological phase of 4300–3000 BC, in the Ayacucho basin of Peru. The people seem to have practiced TRANSHUMANCE and it was during this period that agriculture may have been introduced to the region. Plants used included potatoes, coca, squash, gourds, common beans, lucuma, quinoa, and, near the end of the period, corn (maize). Guinea pigs were also domesticated. In contrast to the Peruvian coast, the beginning of agriculture in the highlands preceded settled village life.

**Chilca.** A coastal valley, a few miles south of Lima, Peru, which was the scene of intensive archaeological investigation in the 1950s and 1960s. One of the best-known sites—usually called Chilca Monument I—was an ENCANTO-type village, with a mainly maritime economy and dated 3750–2500 BC. At this site the remains of conical brush houses, associated with wild foodstuffs, marine resources, and only a few domesticated plants were found.

**Childe, Vere Gordon** (1892–1957). The dominant European prehistorian for 30 years, Childe introduced the concept of the archaeological culture. Through his Marxist beliefs, his profound knowledge of Western Eurasian archaeology, and his belief (now disputed) that Near Eastern civilizations provided the stimuli for developments elsewhere, he considerably advanced the study of European prehistory.

**Chimu.** The kingdom of the LATE INTERMEDIATE PERIOD (AD 1000–1478) on the North coast of Peru, formerly the homeland of the MOCHICA culture. Documentary history is meager but some reconstruction of the major events and structures of the state is possible. The Chimu state ruled adjacent coastal valleys. The capital was CHANCHAN, a vast settlement of giant rectangular enclosures. Associated with the Chimu expansion was a modeled mold-made black ware, although red pottery also occurs. The professional gold- and silversmiths produced some of the most expert and attractive metal cult objects and ornaments known in the New World.

**China.**

*Palaeolithic.* Man first occupied China in the early Pleistocene period, about a million years ago. The site of Lan-t'ien in Central China, which belongs to this time, has produced a series of stone tools, as well as the jaws and skull of an early form of HOMO ERECTUS, with a brain size of approximately 778 cc, intermediate between man and ape. It is possible that the southernmost, subtropical part of China was occupied earlier still by some kind of AUSTRALOPITHECUS, and some experts believe that a fossil giant apelike creature called *Gigantopithecus* was a relative of man living in China.

The best-known Palaeolithic men from China were from Chou-k'ou-tien, 25 mi. (40 km) southwest of Peking. Fossil remains of some 30 individuals have been found, including about a dozen skulls. All these remains disappeared during World War II, but some more remains, including a skull and lower jaw, have been found since. These fossil men are regarded as late *Homo erectus*

Map of China and the Far East, showing archaeological sites and kiln sites.

and probably belong to a long timespan around 0.5 million years ago. They were similar in size to smaller modern races, and are the earliest fossil men known with brains regularly more than 1,000 cc in size. They made simple stone tools, often of the type called chopping tools, somewhat reminiscent of the CLACTONIAN of Europe, and they had FIRE. The extent to which they hunted big game, and to which they habitually lived in the caves, is not reliably known.

Neanderthal-type and Upper Palaeolithic man are known from China, but we have few details of the dating of these or their archaeological association. The people of the Late (Upper) Palaeolithic, as from the Upper Cave at Chou-k'ou-tien (about 18,000 years ago), seem to have been of a Mongoloid type.

*Neolithic and Dynastic.* The most important single characteristic of China, which has emerged from archaeological investigations, is its extraordinary independence from other ancient civilizations. This is particularly obvious in the technologies of bronze and iron casting, ceramics, SILK, LACQUER, and JADE. At the same time, it is clear that the early Neolithic cultures of China (*see* CH'ING-LIEN-KANG CULTURE; TA-WEN-K'OU CULTURE), including the YANG-SHAO CULTURE (*c.* 4500 BC), originated from the sophisticated hunting and gathering societies of the Far East, in particular those in the South and perhaps in Thailand.

Once the early Dynasties were established in China (*see* SHANG DYNASTY; CHOU DYNASTY), its distinctive character developed apace. The Chinese use of ideographic characters was already established in the Shang ORACLE BONES, and the RITUAL VESSELS show a range of religious practices and beliefs. Some contact with the KARASUK CULTURE of South Siberia can be traced, but its significance is minimal. China only began to reach out into Central Asia, and towards Vietnam and Korea, under the HAN DYNASTY (206 BC–AD 220), when wars with the nomadic tribe of the HSIUNG-NU led to Chinese conquest of large tracts of land. From this arose the trade along the SILK ROUTE, which was as important to Byzantium as it was to China. This trade was at its height under the T'ANG DYNASTY (AD 618–906), and added to the exotic character of the capital city, CH'ANG-AN.

**Chinampa.** The term used for the very fertile land made by large baskets being floated into shallow lake waters and filled with earth for agriculture. This results in artificial floating plots of land rooted in place by trees. Much of the Aztec city of TENOCHTITLAN utilized such reclaimed land.

**Chincha.** The kingdom of Chincha was a small state comprising several valleys on the South coast of Peru, which flourished during the LATE INTERMEDIATE PERIOD, *c.* AD 1000–1478. The main city was La Centinela, which included pyramids, platforms, and courts surrounded by storerooms and dwellings of the nobility. Chincha prospered through trade with the adjacent highlands and Northern coastal areas.

**Chin Dynasty.** A Chinese Dynasty (AD 1115–1234)

founded by the Jürchen tribes, who were formerly vassals of the Khitans or LIAO DYNASTY (AD 916–1125). They overran most of North China and captured the Sung capital of K'ai-feng in AD 1126, forcing the Chinese to move their capital south to Hang-chou. The Chin adopted the Chinese administrative system and culture and continued the manufacture of many types of Chinese ceramics. The main sites of this period so far excavated are tombs.

**Ch'in Dynasty.** The ruling house (221–206 BC) that unified China into a single empire. Examples of the standard weights and measures imposed on the whole of China have been excavated, but most spectacular are a large group of life-size pottery figures of warriors and horses found in an area adjacent to the tomb of the first Ch'in emperor.

**Ch'ing Dynasty.** The last ruling house of China (AD 1644–1911), although in fact Manchu in origin. Few sites of this period have been excavated, apart from some elaborately constructed tombs. In general, finds from such tombs—jades, ceramics, and textiles—are less fine than those which have survived above ground, as it was a period of industrial production and export to Europe and other areas of the world on a large scale. Most of the surviving buildings in China date from this period and are at present being surveyed and restored.

**Ch'ing-lien-kang culture.** An Eastern Neolithic culture of China (*c.* 4000–3000 BC) found in the provinces of Southern Shantung, Kiangsu, and Northern Chekiang. The excavated painted pottery, which includes bowls decorated with flower-like designs, has certain affinities with the pottery from the Western Neolithic YANG-SHAO CULTURE. In most other respects this culture belongs to an Eastern group, including the TA-WEN-K'OU CULTURE and the LIANG-CHU CULTURE. With the use of pottery vessels on high pierced stands, fine flat polished axes, and decorative pendants in JADE, it is an important precursor of the later Neolithic LUNG-SHAN CULTURE.

**Chiripa.** An early village site in the Southern Titicaca area of Bolivia, excavated in the 1950s. Late Chiripa pottery of the Early Horizon Period (1800–200 BC) is decorated with cream on red color zones, separated by incised lines.

**Chiusi** (Clusius). An important Etruscan settlement on Lake Trasimene in Italy, whose principal remains are those of grave chambers. It later became a Roman ally and colony.

**Chivateros.** An ancient quarry site of the coastal lomas (areas of fog vegetation), a few miles north of Lima. Excavations revealed upper preceramic tool complexes that date from between 9,000 and 11,000 years ago; these overlie a red zone, with some flint chips and possible artifacts.

**Choga Zambil** (or Zanbil). A site near SUSA, in IRAN,

with the remains of the Elamite city of Dur-Untash, founded in the 13th century BC. The city was laid out on a vast scale but never completed. There are several palaces and a large ZIGGURAT, built in stages with access to the upper parts by means of vaulted stairways. Most of the sculptural decoration was later removed to Susa but there is early evidence of the use of GLASS and glazes.

**Cholula.** Situated near the modern city of Puebla in Mexico, Cholula was occupied continuously by a succession of peoples belonging to different cultures from the Late Preclassic Period to the Spanish Conquest.

The visible remains are a huge mound, 118 ft. (36 m) tall, on which a Christian church now stands, overlooking a large courtyard. Recent investigations have explored the principal mound, and tunnels have been driven through the structure, revealing some five different phases of construction of different, and successively larger, temple pyramids. The presence of a style of TALUD-TABLERO architecture indicates TEOTIHUACAN influence at the site during the Early Classic Period. Some Tajin-like carvings point also to Veracruz influence during the same period. During Postclassic times, the site was an important religious center which attracted pilgrims from all over Mesoamerica.

**Chou Dynasty.** The successors in China to the SHANG DYNASTY. Their long rule (1027–221 BC), is customarily divided into two sections, the Western Chou (1027–771 BC) and the Eastern Chou (770–221 BC), so-named by the different locations of the capitals of the two periods. There is no conclusive archaeological evidence to document the life of the Chou before they conquered the Shang in 1027 BC, although they are mentioned briefly in the inscriptions on the ORACLE BONES. Their first capital was established near Sian and a number of sites have been excavated in the area, but none as spectacular as the Shang cities at AN-YANG or CHENG-CHOU. The rest of the Chou kingdom was divided into feudal principalities, and inscriptions on the many bronze RITUAL VESSELS excavated give details of these arrangements of political dependencies.

Although the territory under Chinese influence expanded, as first agriculture and then roads, cities, and trades were developed in new areas, the authority of the Chou king began to decline in the 8th century BC, under pressure from the nomads from without and the increasingly independent princes within. During the second part of the Eastern Chou Dynasty, the independent states divided China among them. Both cities and tombs from this time have been excavated.

Changes in methods of warfare were also very significant. The disappearance of the CHARIOT, and the introduction of the sword and the CROSSBOW are recorded in the burial goods of the time. Also significant was the increase in the numbers of warriors and casualty figures were sometimes in the hundreds of thousands.

**Chou-k'ou-tien.** See CHINA.

**Chronology, Near East.** The regular Nile floods led to the early establishment of an Egyptian year of 365 days. The discovery of inscribed monuments and calendars of the Egyptians associated with dated astronomical observations has meant that a firm Egyptian chronology could be drawn up, and this has served as a framework for all the other Near Eastern chronologies. Inscribed Egyptian objects found in Near Eastern contexts have enabled these to be dated. In Mesopotamia we have year names, king lists, and eponym lists which give us a series of sequences but these are often damaged or incomplete, and it is not always possible to put them in the right order. The main problem is the date of the 1st Dynasty of BABYLON, which is based on observations of the planet Venus, which give 1651, 1595, 1587, and 1531 BC as possible dates for the end of the Dynasty. These have led scholars to establish rival high, middle, and low chronologies, although the middle date of 1595 BC is now generally preferred and is used here. For periods or areas for which no textual evidence is available, relative chronologies have to be established and these are mostly based on pottery sequences, though the yearly replastering of walls, found in some cultures, gives valuable information about the length of time a building was in use. RADIOCARBON DATING (C14) for organic matter and THERMOLUMINESCENCE dating for the firing of pottery are useful if the samples have not been contaminated; but they are not accurate enough for fine dating, and recent problems have arisen in connection with the radiocarbon method, so that dates now have to be calibrated to agree with dendrochronological dates (*see* DENDROCHRONOLOGY).

**Ch'ü-chia-ling culture.** A Neolithic culture of Central China, principally in Hupei province, *c.* 3000 BC. It follows the YANG-SHAO CULTURE and precedes the LUNG-SHAN CULTURE. In the cultivation of rice it differed from the Northern wheat- and millet-growing cultures. The pottery includes painted items, and among the implements are found flat polished axes.

**Chullpa Pampa.** A site, about 19 mi. (30 km) south of Cochabamba in Southern Bolivia, dating from just before the time of Christ. It has a distinctive pottery style, with flat-bottomed beakers made of gray and red ceramic.

**Chultun.** A bottle-shaped underground cistern, found primarily in the Maya subarea of Mexico, and probably used for water storage. At some sites in the Southern Maya Lowlands, chultuns may also have been used for food storage.

**Chün ware.** A stoneware with a pale blue opalescent or a translucent green glaze, made principally in the Sung and Yüan Dynasties (11th-14th century AD) at the kilns near Lin-ju-hsien and at Kung-hsien in Honan province in China. (*See* CERAMICS, CHINA; SUNG DYNASTY; YÜAN DYNASTY.)

**Chuquitana.** A late preceramic site, also referred to as "El Paraiso," located on the coast on the Chillon River north of Lima, Peru. It comprised eight complexes of approximately 25 rooms, each built of stone. They were simple irregular structures on terraces, with small stairways and platforms, and rooms were of similar size throughout, with repetitive architectural motifs. Excavation indicates that the complexes were rebuilt five or six times by filling in earlier rooms and using them as platforms for new rooms. The site was occupied between 1800 and 1600 BC. Artifacts included implements and objects in shell, stone, bone, and wood, woven cotton textiles, and polished dried clay figurines.

**Ch'u state.** An independent state in Central China, south of the Yangtze River, during the second half of the CHOU DYNASTY, 8th century BC, and a great military threat to the Northern Chinese states. After a temporary break in the bronze-casting tradition inherited from the SHANG DYNASTY, bronze casting was revived and exceptionally fine inlaid bronzes, weapons, and mirrors were made in the area (*see* MIRROR). The region was particularly famous for LACQUER and SILK. Most of the excavated sites are situated near the great Tung-t'ing Lake, and have therefore been continuously waterlogged, ensuring the survival of large quantities of organic materials. Among the most extraordinary remains are birds and animals in lacquer-painted wood, which served as drum supports, and fantastic monsters with protruding tongues and antlers. The latter are the outcome of the popular beliefs in the area in which shamans were used to intercede with the spirits.

**Cimmerians.** A group of tribes who caused havoc in Anatolia during the second quarter of the 1st millennium BC. They were previously settled in South Russia and their early history is uncertain, but they may have been responsible for the Catacomb and Kuban cultures (*c.* 1700 BC onwards). They may also have been split into two groups by the bearers of the Timber Grave (Srubna) culture in the 13th century BC: a Westward group, later defined as Thraco-Cimmerian, which disappeared in *c.* 500 BC, and an Eastern Colchidic-Koban group. It is these Eastern Cimmerians who emerge into history in the late 8th century BC, when the Scythian advance drove them through the Caucasus into URARTU, where they defeated Argishti II in 707 BC. They then moved into Cilicia, where Sargon of Assyria defeated them in 706 BC. The Cimmerians therefore swept westwards into Phrygia, and caused the suicide of King Midas in 696 BC. Defeated by the Assyrians in 679 BC, they in turn defeated the Lydians and killed Gyges in *c.* 652 BC, and raided the Ionian settlements. They were finally crushed by the Scythians in *c.* 630 BC.

**Circus.** A long, narrow U-shaped arena, used for chariot racing in the Roman world. The audience was arranged in banked seats around the track. Races were run round a central island, which held a turning post at each end. The best-known circus is the Circus Maximus at Rome, originally built by Tarquinius Priscus, but enlarged at various times until the late Roman period.

*Cire perdue* (lost wax). A method of casting bronze or copper objects. The object is modeled in wax over a clay core; an outer mold of clay is built over this and pinned in position to the inner core by chaplets. The whole is then heated, the wax is allowed to run out, and the space left is filled with molten metal. The outer mold is then broken off and the inner core is also sometimes removed. This process was used in early metal casting and is found in the *Sammelfund* hoard from URUK (*c.* 3000 BC), and in the Early Dynastic quadriga from Tell Agrab in the DIYALA—both from Mesopotamia. The 13th-century BC lifesize statue of Napir-Asu, wife of Untash-Gal of ELAM, was cast in two halves by this method. *Cire perdue* was also practiced in prehistoric Europe, and in Classical Greece and Rome.

**Cist tomb.** A form of burial common in Siberia, Northern China, Korea, and Japan in which the grave is lined with stones and covered with further slabs, alternatively known as a slab tomb. (*See* TOMB ARCHAEOLOGY IN CHINA.)

**Clactonian.** Named in 1926 by S. H. Warren, this is regarded by some prehistorians as a distinct tradition, contemporary with the ACHEULIAN handax tradition, but with a different set of tools. It is named after Clacton, Essex, England, but Clactonian is also well known from the lower levels at Swanscombe, England, both sites being about 0.25 million years old. Recently, human remains have been found with the Clactonian at Bilzingsleben in Central Germany.

**Classic Period, Mesoamerica.** *See* MESOAMERICA.

**Cleaver.** *See* STONE TECHNOLOGY.

**Climate and Archaeology.** Climate changed dramatically in many areas in the prehistoric period, and there is good reason to believe that its effect was often of vital importance to man. Since the end of the last Ice Age, the changes have been relatively minor, but the alternation of glacial and interglacial periods implies major shifts of climate (*see* ICE AGE).

A common method of climatic reconstruction is from pollen analysis and associated vegetational remains (*see* PALAEOBOTANY). The pollen is extracted from successive layers of an organic deposit, and it is often possible to see how a deciduous forest dominated by trees like oak replaced pinewoods, which had replaced tundra scrub vegetation. Individual plants can be informative, such as the warm-indicating Montpellier maple, found in last interglacial deposits in Southern Britain, or the water fern *Azolla filiculoides*, which became extinct before the last interglacial in Europe.

Animal remains are also indicators of climate. Some molluscs, whose shells survive as fossils, are adapted to climates warmer than those of the region where they are found, and thus indicate warm climate periods. Similarly, mammals like the hippopotamus seem to indicate warm climate. Reindeer, musk-ox, and several other species suggest colder climate when found in temperate regions.

Evidence of ice advance is perhaps the most dramatic indicator of cold climate, but a whole range of features associated with permafrost (permanently frozen ground) such as ice wedges and polygonal soils (surface patterns in permafrost areas), give good evidence of colder climate well outside the area glaciated. The wind-blown dust called loess, of which thick layers are found across Europe, is also claimed to indicate cold dry climate. Certainly fluctuations in rainfall and aridity seem to have occurred in Africa, but the details are still disputed.

One of the most precise indications of former temperatures comes from a new technique of calculating the amount of Oxygen 16 and Oxygen 18 (isotopes of oxygen) from DEEP SEA CORES. This can indicate the temperature in which shell creatures lived, recorded chemically in the shells. It has been widely applied to temperatures in the oceans, but the temperature changes on land may have been somewhat greater.

*Cloisonné. See* METAL TECHNOLOGY, PREHISTORIC EUROPE.

**Clovis point.** The earliest projectile point of the BIG GAME HUNTING TRADITION of North America. Named after a town in Western New Mexico, these large lanceolate stone spear points have the following characteristics: they were percussion flaked, fluted near the base, with their widest points towards the base. The base of a Clovis point is concave, and the edge of the base has usually been blunted through grinding, probably to ensure that the thongs, attaching the point to the projectile, were not cut. The projectile is assumed to have been a spear because of its size. The length of the points varies from 2 to 4 in. (7 to 12 cm), and their width at the widest point is $1-1\frac{1}{2}$ in. (3–4 cm). It is from these points that the later, more sophisticated points, such as the FOLSOM point, developed. Clovis points have been dated to *c.* 9220 BC in the Blackwater Draw site in New Mexico. They were used to hunt now extinct mammals such as the mammoth and the giant bison.

**Coal.** The only country to have tackled the archaeology of the coal industry with thoroughness and determination is East Germany. In the Oelsnitz-Erzgebirge area, near Karl Marx Stadt, a group of pits has been selected to illustrate the development of mining techniques in the hard-coal industry. These include the surface installations at the Gottessegen pit (1860), the Hedwig pit (1885), the Albert Funk pits (1920), and the Karl Liebknecht pit (1922–25). The Oelsnitz district had a worldwide reputation for its pioneering work in the field of pithead winding gear. At Zwickau, the Hoffnungs pit (1844–1906) has also been preserved as a "central monument." It was one of the first big pits in Germany and the first to operate its haulage gear by electricity.

Nothing similar has been attempted in West Germany, although the important Mining Museum at Bochum documents the history of the industry in its own way, and preserves, as an outstation, the superb Art Nouveau machinery hall and other disused surface buildings at Dortmund-Bövinghausen.

In Britain, only isolated attempts have been made to preserve the on-site evidence of an industry that was the basis of 19th-century industrialization. Historic surface installations have been destroyed in a thoroughly irresponsible fashion and, outside the Northeast, little trouble has been taken to safeguard representative miners' cottages and other material evidence of the living and working conditions of the population of mining areas. A notable exception to the general apathy and neglect is to be found at the disused colliery at Prestongrange, East Lothian, Scotland, where the Cornish beam pumping engine of 1874 and its surroundings have been made the basis of a conservation scheme illustrating the history of coal mining in Scotland.

The most dramatic and permanent evidence of American mining, whether of coal, copper, or iron, is its destruction of the environment. In Hallan County, Ky., more than 3 million ac. (1 million ha) (the size of Connecticut) have already been ravaged by opencast coal mining, and 10,000 mi. (16,093 km) of rivers and streams have been contaminated.

**Coalbrookdale.** The part of Shropshire, England, on the River Severn, which is claimed, with considerable justice, to be the birthplace of the Industrial Revolution. Abraham Darby pioneered the smelting of iron with coke here in 1709. The furnace survives as part of the Ironbridge Gorge Museum.

**Cochise.** A culture in the South and West of the United States. In the Southwest it is the earliest manifestation of the DESERT TRADITION, and in California it is related to the cultures which suceeded that tradition. Cochise is divided into three periods. The first, the Sulfur Spring phase, dates from 7000 to 5000 BC. Subsistence depended on hunting animals such as horses, mammoths, antelope, and bison with percussion flaked projectile points: these were sometimes leaf shaped and sometimes barbed. Grinding tools were also found at Sulfur Spring, although they were of simple form. The Chiricahua phase dates from 5000 to 2000 BC, and is important because the first finds of maize date from it. These come from Bat cave in New Mexico, where they have been dated to the 3rd millennium BC. Although the earliest maize is very primitive, in the upper levels of Bat cave maize has been found which had been genetically improved. This would either have happened through the importation of new strains from Mexico, or through local selection. During the San Pedro phase, 2000–1 BC, the Desert tradition aspects of the culture begin to give way to the Southwestern elements of the MOGOLLON culture. In particular, pottery begins to appear towards the end of the San Pedro phase, and grinding tools for seeds—the mano and METATE—become more important and more highly developed. Centers of population become larger and more settled. This transition from hunting and gathering as a basis of subsistence, to farming, is best seen in the Mogollon subarea of the Southwest.

**Codices, Mesoamerica.** Only a small number of Precolumbian pictographic manuscripts have survived the wholesale destruction of such writings, believed by the church to have been connected with the old religion of the Indians. Almost always, Mesoamerican codices consisted of a long strip of paper made from bark or maguey fiber, or from deerskin treated with gypsum to provide a smooth surface for drawing. They were up to 40 ft. (12 m) long and about 10 in. (25.4 cm) wide, folded backwards and forwards like a screen, and both sides carried drawings.

Only three Precolumbian MAYA codices have survived, all of which contain calendrical and astronomical information, such as eclipse tables, and pictures of various gods. There is a group of MIXTEC codices which are purely historical. Many of these deal with the life of a character named Eight Deer Tiger Claw, a king of the Mixtec city of Tilantongo. Various attempts to interpret these have been made, notably by Alfonso Caso. They are less sophisticated than the Maya codices, being entirely in a pictographic form of writing. The third group, known as the Borgia group, is very similar to the Mixtec codices insofar as style of the pictographs is concerned, but they are calendrical and ritual, giving information about the deities presiding over the various months of the year and other ritual matter connected with the individual days. Both these groups date from the Postclassic period.

There are a number of post-Conquest codices. Perhaps the most interesting is the *Codex Mendoza*, commissioned by the first viceroy of Mexico for the Spanish Emperor Charles V to give him an idea of his new dominion, but now in the Bodleian Library in Oxford. This document is in three parts: the first is historical, giving the names and conquests of the Aztec rulers and their dates; the second is a tribute list, copied from the *Metricula de Tributos*; and the third is ethnographical, giving an account of the daily life and customs of the Aztecs. The whole document is pictographic, but interleaved with each page is a commentary on the pictures in Spanish.

## Coins, Europe.

*Greek and Roman.* The first use of coinage as a trading medium is attributed to the Lydians of Asia Minor, *c.* 630 BC. The first coins were almost exactly equivalent in bullion value (usually electrum, a compound of gold and silver) to the goods exchanged. Each Greek city issued its own coinage, the lead being taken by Aegina, which was the main trader with Asia Minor. Usually the various cities struck their coins with a die pattern on one side only, bearing an oblique reference to the city's protective deity by a portrayal of his or her symbol. Early developments include striking the same pattern on both sides of the coin, then, *c.* 530 BC, a series of reverse types were introduced, and the reverse often added some written characters to show the coin's origin. Two "standards" of coinage were in force: the Aeginetan and the Euboeic.

From the Hellenistic period onwards, only the largest states still issued coins independently, among them Rome, whose first coins possibly date from *c.* 290 BC. Soon the common denomination of bronze coinage (as) was issued, and, *c.* 211 BC, the silver denarius (equal to 10 asses) appeared. This fixed the main types of Roman coinage for some years. Coins were normally issued by senatorial decree, but increasingly they bore some sign of an annually-appointed magistrate, who supervised the mint until it was taken over by Augustus' imperial freedmen and slaves *c.* 4 BC. The history of changes in the coinage is complex: it was completely altered by Augustus, and extensive revisions were carried out under Nero, Caracalla, and many later Roman emperors, when inflation was beginning to wreck the Roman economy.

Throughout the imperial period, the Roman emperors kept close control of the mints, established at many places; the coins always bore the head of the emperor or one of his family on the obverse, and on the reverse there was a succession of different subjects, often commemorating specific events. From the archaeological point of view, it is the latter which makes coins of most use, since their date of minting is almost always ascertainable. They thus determine the date of the stratigraphical layer in which they are found, and hence of the other objects in that layer.

*Celtic.* During the 2nd and 1st centuries BC and in Britain up to the mid-1st century AD, a new form of currency was made by the CELTS from Southern England to the lower Danube River. Gold, silver, and copper coins were issued, though with varying emphasis in different areas. Thus, in Austria and the Danubian countries they were mostly silver, in Bohemia mostly gold with some silver, in Southern Germany and Switzerland gold alone, and in Gaul and England all three metals, although, apart from in early 1st-century AD Southeast England, all three were hardly ever issued together. This last case seems, however, to reflect an earlier pattern of currency usage in which several metals were used simultaneously. Like earlier forms of currency, Celtic coinage was probably of the "special-purpose" variety, valid only for certain socially prescribed transactions (*see* CURRENCY, PREHISTORIC EUROPE). The designs of Celtic coins are often miniature masterpieces of stylized art, depicting the heads of rulers, and a variety of animals (especially boars and horses), motifs, and scenes; the later coins were often inscribed with names (generally abbreviated). However, the standard of workmanship exhibited by Celtic coins is rarely as high as that of Classical Greek and Roman issues. The latter provided many prototypes for Celtic coin designs: the gold staters of Phillip II and Alexander III of Macedon (359–336 and 336–323 BC) were widely imitated by the Celts, who over the years gradually broke down the designs of the prototypes and reformulated them into abstract patterns of often bewildering complexity.

*Medieval.* Roman coins continued to influence European money during and after the MIGRATION PERIOD. In the East, the coinage of Byzantium continued the traditions of late Roman currency, and influenced the coinages of Eastern Europe and Western Asia. In the West, on founding their kingdoms, the barbarian invaders imitated Roman currency. In Italy, Spain, and Gaul gold tremisses (a denomination worth ⅓ solidus) were struck until the 8th century AD.

From the 8th century onwards, gold coinage was replaced in most of Western Europe by the silver penny or

Examples of medieval coins: top, pennies of William I (left) and Edward I (right) of England; center, the obverse and reverse of a French denier of Richard the Lionheart; bottom, a 13th-century bracteate of Augsburg, Germany.

**Cologne** (Colonia Agrippinensis). Formerly the capital of a German tribe called the Ubii, the city was given the status of a Roman colony in AD 50. As capital of Germania Inferior it was an important harbor on the River Rhine, a crossing point for trade and traffic. Remains of the city walls with the bizarrely decorated "Romerturm," the Govenor's Palace, and the earliest Roman church, under the cathedral, survive.

**Column.** True columns in the ancient world appeared only in Egypt, Classical Greece, and the Roman Empire. Among the earliest stone columns in Egypt are engaged examples in the step pyramid complex at Saqqara. They are drum-built, fluted and have curious pendant leaf capitals. From the fluted shaft probably developed the so-called proto-Doric column with 8 or 16 fluted faces, common in Middle Kingdom private rock-cut tombs. Unlike its Greek successor, the Egyptian column stood on a circular base. Since most elements of Egyptian architecture were based on plant prototypes the three main column types which evolved were the palmiform, the lotiform, and the papyriform.

The monolithic palm column had a cylindrical shaft with a capital composed of a bundle of nine palm leaves secured by five bands. The drum-built lotus column had a ribbed shaft composed of a cluster of four or six stalks held together at the top by five bands. The capital imitated a closed, or occasionally an open, lotus bud. The six or eight clustered stalks in a drum-built papyrus column were triangular in section and tapered towards the base, where basal leaves were always depicted. In the earliest examples the capital was a bud. From the papyriform column developed the monostyle papyrus column, in which the clustered stalks of the shaft became a single smooth-faced cylinder and the bud capital a smooth-sided inverted bell shape. The campaniform papyrus column had an open papyrus umbel as capital and a smooth-faced cylindrical shaft.

In the Late Period composite columns, possibly developed from the campaniform papyrus column, have a cylindrical shaft, basal leaves, and a capital made of many layers of decorative floral and plant elements. Twenty-seven varieties of composite column have been identified. In temples devoted to the worship of the goddess Hathor, capitals were in the form of the soundboxes of a sistrum (an Egyptian musical instrument) bearing Hathor's face. Unique tent-pole columns, in the form of a smooth cylindrical shaft with a bell-shaped capital, occur in the Festival Hall of Tuthmosis III at Karnak.

In Mesopotamia, the lack of wood precluded the use of wooden supports so that columns have never been a feature of the architecture, though some brick-built examples do occasionally occur and can be decorated to imitate date-palm trunks. In other areas of the Near East wooden posts were used, as they are today, in domestic architecture. Columns, sometimes of stone or with stone capitals and bases, were integral parts of the APADANA, BÎT HILANI and MEGARON.

In Classical Greek architecture, columns were characterized by three main styles: the Doric, the Ionic, and the Corinthian; all employ a distinctive type of column.

denier, derived from the Roman denarius. This remained the principal coin in Europe until the 13th century, when the expansion of trade and the rapid growth of towns necessitated a larger denomination. The new unit favored was the silver groat, worth four pennies and known by various names such as gros, groschen, or grossone. In the 13th century gold reappeared in European currency, one of the most universally accepted currencies being the florins of Florence, struck first in 1252.

Medieval coins were issued from a great diversity of mints; royal, ecclesiastical, feudal, and urban. They are characterized by wafer-thin flans, which were struck by hand or "hammered" until the gradual adoption of the machine press from the 16th century onwards. However, the types tend to be monotonous, and rarely show the artistry or originality of Greek and Roman coin designs.

**Colchester** (Camulodunum). A Roman city on the site of the most important pre-Roman tribal center, which became a colony founded by Claudius in Britain soon after its conquest. It was destroyed by Boudicca in an uprising in AD 60, but rebuilt. Remains of the city walls and gates, and the Temple of Claudius survive.

The Doric column is smooth or fluted, usually tapering towards its top, and is surmounted by a plain, rather squashed-looking capital. The Ionic column is fluted, it also tapers (though only slightly) from bottom to top, and in proportion is usually more slender than the Doric. The capital is square or triangular, with a volute spiral at each corner. The Corinthian order has a fluted column, with a richly decorated capital, usually bearing representations of acanthus leaves or naturalistic carvings. This order was largely taken over by the Romans for use in temples and public buildings.

**Commagene** (or Kommagene). The Classical name for the area between the Taurus Mountains and the River Euphrates, between CARCHEMISH and Malatya. The earlier history of this area is unknown, although OBSIDIAN was exported from Nemrut Dağ from *c.* 8000 BC onwards. It appears at Kummuh in Assyrian annals from 866 BC, generally as an ally, but was finally annexed as a province and the population deported to Southern Mesopotamia in 708 BC. In about 80 BC, an independent kingdom was once more established in the area under a local Dynasty. There is a fine relief at Arsameia showing King Mithradates Kallinikos shaking hands with Heracles (*c.* 50 BC), and on the top of the mountain of Nemrut Dağ there is a tumulus with three terraced courts, two of which are surrounded by colossal statues, a fire altar, and reliefs, while the third is a processional way. The complex dates to 62 or 61 BC.

**Computers.** These were developed in a generally usable form after World War II, and they were first applied to archaeological problems by American ethnologists working out tribal groupings from lists of cultural items. These operations involved the sorting of matrices—lists of attributes and the extent to which they occurred together. This is a common archaeological problem, basically one of clustering similar entities, and it is fundamental to any kind of typology or higher classification. The ability of the computer to handle very large numbers of observations makes its use essential in avoiding arbitrary personal biases when dealing with quantities of material. It is a major tool, therefore, wherever the problem is one of forming groups.

Another kind of structure which may be sought in masses of data is that of linear arrangement. This is most often caused by continuous change through time, for instance as old types fall out of popularity and new ones come in. A sequence can thus be constructed by linking assemblages which hold types in common. This method of ordering graves was in fact worked out by Sir Flinders PETRIE in the early years of the century, and calculated laboriously by hand. The use of the computer makes this analysis simple.

More sophisticated programs are available for various kinds of spatial analysis, and principal components or factor analysis has also been applied to archaeological problems. But a more humble, though equally useful, role for the computer is simply to keep track of the many thousands of items in museums and produced on excavations, and to provide sorted indexes.

**Conchapata.** A site on the outskirts of Ayacucho in Peru, dating from *c.* AD 600. A distinctive polychrome style of pottery, representing TIAHUANACO gods on large beaker-shaped urns, was found there.

**Constantinople.** *See* BYZANTIUM.

**Copan.** The great Maya ruins of Copan are in extreme Western Honduras, not far from the Guatemalan frontier. The setting is the Copan valley, a tributary of the Motagua; and, at an elevation of *c.* 2,000 ft. (610 m), the environment, although tropical forest, is not the lowland jungle typical of most sites of the Classic Maya civilization. Copan is at the southeastern edge of the Classic Maya domain, but is one of the largest and most impressive sites of that civilization.

The earliest levels at the site date from the Late Preclassic Period (*c.* 300 BC–AD 250). The earliest stele date known from the site is AD 465, and it is probable that Copan was an important politico-religious and trading center at this time. Its heyday came in the Late Classic Period, especially in the 8th century AD, when many of its finest temples, palaces, and monuments were dedicated. Notable for this period is the famed Hieroglyphic Stairway, the largest single hieroglyphic text in the Maya area. Other texts and sculptures at the site suggest that Copan was a very important intellectual and astronomical center in the Late Classic. The stone used in the construction and monuments of Copan is andesite tufa, a relatively soft greenish-gray rock that is easily carved. Perhaps because of this, much of the Copan sculpture is in the full-round, rather than the bas-relief characteristic of the limestone carvings of most Maya sites. Copan ceramics are in the tradition of regions to the east and southeast, in Honduras and Salvador.

The main Copan center covers an area of 247 ac. (100 ha), and is situated in the center of the Copan valley bottoms. These valley flats and surrounding hillslopes, an area *c.* 7 × 2 mi. (12 × 4 km), are thickly dotted with small mound structures, presumably the remains of the residential units of the supporting population, which must have numbered at least 10,000 persons during the Late Classic Period.

Stelae dedication and public building ceased at Copan in the 9th century AD, with the last stele dated at AD 800. Thereafter, the site was used only occasionally, as a burial place or for short-term occupation.

**Copper.** Ores of copper are found in mountainous areas where metal-rich vapors have penetrated into cracks from deep in the earth's crust to produce veins of copper minerals. The primary ores are usually sulphides (chalcopyrite), but the weathering which occurs at the surface of a vein produces simpler minerals such as Cuprite, Malachite, and Azurite, and the "gray ores" such as Enargite, Tennantite, and Tetrahedrite.

**Copper Age, Europe.** The period, sometimes referred to as the Chalcolithic or Eneolithic, when simple copper metallurgy was known, though before the discovery of alloying with tin to make bronze. It lasted for almost 1,000 years in Southeast Europe, from 3500 BC.

**Copper mining, Industrial.** Until the 18th century, the mine at Falun, Sweden—the Stora Kopparberg—produced more copper than anywhere else in the world. Here, as in many other mining centers, the archaeology consists to a great extent of enormous holes in the ground, but the company has preserved a number of 18th- and 19th-century buildings around the pit as industrial monuments. By the early 20th century, the main centers of world production were in the Western United States and Canada. At Butte, Mont., where copper was first mined in 1864, considerable evidence of the early days survives, much of it in the World Museum of Mining, which has a good collection of 19th-century buildings. Copper production at Hancock, Mich., ceased in 1931, but some of the surface machinery has been restored and tours of the underground workings are regularly arranged.

On the Keweenaw Peninsula, Mich., an historic area has been established on part of the land once owned by the Calumet and Hecla Copper Mine. Known as Coppertown, it occupies the complex of 1880–1900 buildings which were the nucleus of the mining operations, and serves as a "theme center" for tourists wishing to explore the Keweenaw copper country.

**Copts.** Christianity came to Egypt in the 4th century AD. In the following century a native Christian culture evolved with a distinctive art that eventually was to influence Europe. The Copts were essentially a peasant people, a fact reflected in their art, with its stiff, childish figures and bright colors. It borrowed widely from Syria, Sassanian Persia, and the Egyptian past, sometimes using Christianized symbols from ancient Egyptian religions. From Hellenistic art it adopted interlace and many motifs. A few wall paintings and stone carvings survive from the 5th to 8th centuries, and Coptic textiles, mostly tapestries in wool or linen, are to be found in museums and private collections all over the world.

Egypt was conquered by the Arabs in AD 641, and Islamic art became increasingly influential, until the two styles merged almost indistinguishably between the 9th and 12th centuries. Although the Coptic Church survived, it made little contribution to art from this period on.

Due to the export of Coptic textiles and sculptures, many motifs spread to ISLAM, to the Christian kingdoms

Part of Stora kopparberg, the old copper mine at Falun, Sweden.

of the Sudan and Egypt, and to Italy, England, and Ireland. Coptic influence can be seen in British sculptures, such as the Northumbrian crosses of Ruthwell and Bewcastle, and in manuscripts, such as the Book of Kells. Coptic bronze bowls have been found in Anglo-Saxon graves, and Coptic glass in Christian Celtic contexts. In Italy, Coptic influence is apparent in the frescoes of St. Maria Antiqua in Rome.

**Corded Ware culture.** In the latter half of the 3rd millennium BC, the cultures of the North European plain, which had formerly buried their dead communally in megaliths, began the practice of individual burial under round barrows (*see* BARROW; MEGALITH). Characteristic objects buried with adult males included pottery vessels, richly decorated with impressions of twisted cord, and stone "battle axes" of fine rocks with drilled shaftholes.

This complex of local groups is thus known as the Corded Ware, or Corded Ware/Battle Ax culture. The burials are of special importance archaeologically because of the few traces of settlement sites which survive, probably because communities were mostly small and houses relatively insubstantial. This, along with the occasional finds of horse bones, has seemed to indicate that these groups were nomadic herdsmen; although impressions of cereals on the pottery show that crops were grown. The many finds of burials on poorer land indicate the pressure to find new arable land, which was not able to withstand prolonged cultivation, and thus rapidly took on the character of heathland on which so many of the barrows have been preserved down to the present day. This explains the often complementary distribution of round barrows and megalithic monuments—not as contemporary ethnic groupings but as successive phases of agricultural expansion, whose tombs have been preserved in different areas.

It was during the Corded Ware period that wheeled vehicles first reached Northern Europe. Finds of actual wooden wheels, made of solid wood in three pieces, have been made in Holland and Denmark. The better transport and more open conditions of this period led to greater contact between the scattered settlements of the North European plain.

**Core.** *See* STONE TECHNOLOGY.

**Coricancha.** The principal Sun Temple of the Inca in their capital of CUZCO, Peru. It was founded *c*. AD 1438 on the site of their first settlement. Coricancha is a QUECHUA word, meaning "Enclosure of Gold." Within the enclosure, the temple consisted of a principal building, with an apsidal end and four small sanctuaries, surrounding three sides of a courtyard. Constructed of the finest fitted masonry, the shrines were richly adorned with plates of gold and silver. In the largest shrine the image of the Sun was kept, while large niches displayed mummies or idols of the past rulers. Large and small niches were used to display cult objects. A garden to the Sun for housing sacrificial animals was attached

to the temple and contained many gold and silver images of fauna and flora.

**Corinth.** One of the main cities of Classical Greece, lying within the Peloponnese, but important because it controlled the isthmus. It was destroyed by the Romans in 146 BC, but fragments remain, including the city walls and a Temple of Apollo. Most of the surviving remains are of the Roman city which replaced it: the marketplace, surrounded by temples, halls, and other large buildings leading down to the harbor.

**Corinthian Pottery.** Greek pottery made at Corinth from the late 7th century BC until the mid-6th century BC. Its painted decoration is influenced by Eastern "naturalistic" designs of animals, maenads, and satyrs.

**Cortaillod culture.** The first main Neolithic culture of Western Switzerland, named after the type-site on Lake Neuchâtel. It lasted from before 3000 to after 2500 BC, and is known from many well preserved lakeside settlements, which have yielded numerous organic artifacts which do not normally survive.

**Cosa.** A Latin colony of Rome, founded in 273 BC near Ansedonia. Its remains are the well preserved city walls, the FORUM, capitol, BATHS, and temples. It was abandoned in the 1st century BC.

**Cotzumahualpa.** Santa Lucia Cotzumahualpa, on the Pacific slopes of Guatemala, was the home of a localized culture belonging to the Late Classic Period. It has only slight resemblances to the cultures of Central Mexico, and even less to the Maya. The site is famous for its unique Cotzumahualpa style of stone sculpture, depicting scenes of deities gazing upward, skulls, serpent heads, and human sacrifice—often all being enclosed within cartouches. The style may have connections with Nahua-speaking immigrants who had fled Central Mexico. The site is dated to the Late Classic Period because of the frequency of San Juan PLUMBATE pottery. However, recent work suggests that some of the sculptures may be as early as the Late Preclassic Period.

**Cozumel.** An island located about 12 mi. (20 km) off the East coast of the Yucatan Peninsula. During 1972 and 1973, an archaeological team sponsored by the Peabody Museum, Harvard University, the University of Arizona, and the National Geographic Society, with the cooperation and authorization of the Instituto Nacional de Antropologia e Historia, carried out intensive surveys and controlled excavations on the island. Preliminary results indicate the importance of Cozumel.

The archaeological remains date from 300 BC (the Late Preclassic or Formative Period) to the time of the Spanish Conquest in the 16th century AD. At least one (San Gervasio) of the more than 30 sites on the island is comparable in size to the largest sites on the East coast of Quintana Roo, and Cozumel appears to have played a significant role in Yucatan prehistory, especially during the Late Postclassic or Decadent Period (AD 1250–1521) of ancient Maya culture, and perhaps as far back as AD 800.

During the Late Postclassic Period, Cozumel was a major link in the long-distance trading network which the ancient Maya operated between Honduras and the Guatemalan Highlands to the south, around the Yucatan Peninsula, to Tabasco, Campeche, and Veracruz in the west. Using very large dugout canoes, rowed perhaps by dozens of men, the ancient Maya traded large quantities of cacao beans (the money of the time), cotton, salt, honey, and volcanic stones such as OBSIDIAN, in addition to more exotic luxury items such as copper and JADE. Slaves were also moved along this trade route. Cozumel was important in this huge commercial network because of its strategic location and large supply of readily obtainable fresh water. Its influence and wealth was also enhanced by the presence there of the shrine of the Maya goddess of the moon, Ix Chel, to which pilgrims from all over the Maya area came to worship.

**Crater.** A Greek pottery bowl with a wide-open mouth and double handle, used for mixing wine.

**Crete.** A Mediterranean island lying south of Greece, where the first flowering of Greek Bronze Age culture took place (c. 2600–2000 BC). Strongly influenced by Eastern ideas, with THOLOS-type tombs, this was followed by the first palace period (Middle Minoan: 2000–1700 BC), and the second palace period (1700–1400 BC), during which the population of the island greatly increased and large palaces and settlements were built (see KNOSSOS; GREECE, ARCHAEOLOGY OF; MINOAN ARCHAEOLOGY). About 1400 BC the palace civilization was destroyed, possibly by an earthquake or tidal wave from the eruption of THERA, but despite the shift of emphasis to MYCENAE, on the Greek mainland, because of its position on trade routes from the East, Crete remained an important trade center. The island was, however, outside the mainstream of Greek history: it became notorious as the base of pirates, and was captured as a province by the Romans in 68–67 BC.

**Cromagnon.** A type of fossil man found in the Upper Palaeolithic of Europe. Unlike NEANDERTHAL MAN, the remains are hardly different from modern man, and may be our ancestors. The name derives from Cromagnon, on the edge of Les Eyzies village in the Dordogne region of France, where the first such remains were found in 1868.

**Crossbow.** Invented by the Chinese in the late CHOU DYNASTY (c. 400 BC) for the defense of their cities, the best-preserved examples of the crossbow have been excavated in the area of the CH'U STATE. It was the Chinese consummate skill in bronze casting which enabled them to make the accurate trigger of several interlocking parts on which the effectiveness of this weapon depended. It does not appear in archaeological contexts in other parts of the world until it was developed in medieval Europe.

**Ctesiphon.** A capital city founded by the Parthians. It was also chosen by Ardashir as capital of the Sassanian Empire, and Shapur I (AD 241–272) built a huge palace there. The latter is one of the outstanding achievements of mud-brick architecture, with a central *iwan* (an audience hall open at one end) some 100 ft. (30 m) high and 140 ft. (43 m) long.

**Cuicuilco.** This important Late Preclassic site, located just south of Mexico City near the modern National University of Mexico, is marked by an unusual, round platform, nearly 390 ft. (119 m) in diameter, which rises 90 ft. (27 m) above the ground. This pyramid construction, with ramps running up two sides, is one of the earliest known of this form from Mexico, and was covered by a lava flow from a nearby volcano in about AD 300. The cataclysm apparently forced total abandonment of the center, one of the largest and most important in this region during the Late Preclassic Period.

**Cumae.** The oldest of the Greek colonies in Italy, founded in the mid-8th century BC in the Bay of Naples. It later came under Samnite, and then Roman, control. Cumae was famous in Roman times as the home of the Sibylline Oracle. Remains survive of temples to Jupiter and Apollo, both now churches, and of the Roman town, on level ground below the acropolis.

**Cuneiform.** *See* WRITING.

**Cupisnique.** A coastal manifestation of the CHAVIN style. It occurs on the North Central Peruvian coast, and dates from between 900 and 200 BC. It gave rise to three styles: Salinar, Gallinazo, and Vicus.

**Curia.** The senate building for council meetings, found in many Roman towns. It had the Greek BOULEUTERION as its precursor, and was laid out with tiers of seats round a large D-shaped or rectangular room.

**Currency, Prehistoric Europe.** A great variety of objects had been used as currency in all parts of the world before and after the development of the coinage system, but archaeological studies of currency have focused particularly on prehistoric Europe.

Currency is normally divided into two kinds: special- and general-purpose currencies. The latter is like our own, and can be used to procure most goods and services. Special-purpose currencies, however, could only be used for certain socially prescribed transactions, and are characteristic of archaic and "primitive" societies. Such currencies are only under exceptional circumstances convertible, in that, for example, gold coinage could only normally be used for gift exchange or for bride price, and never, except in a dire crisis, be exchanged for subsistence goods; similarly, bronze coinage could not be converted into gold, however large an amount of it one amassed. Greek and Roman documentary sources indicate that their own coinages, and the Celtic ones too, were of the special-purpose variety.

Currency, moreover, is not always actually exchanged,

but may also, or alternatively, be used as units of account or for gauging the relative values of things or even of people. Although gold, silver, and finally copper coinages were introduced into many parts of Europe in the centuries after 500 BC, other forms of currency had undoubtedly been in use from a considerably earlier date. The earliest objects to be used as currency may have been stone axheads, and copper and gold trinkets. Later forms were the copper "ingot torcs" of the Central European Early Bronze Age, the gold and bronze plain "bracelets" used throughout Europe in the Middle and Late Bronze Age, and the iron sword-shaped "currency-bars" of the later Iron Age in Western England. From the 4th millennium onwards, currency was hoarded, often in large quantities, and was exchanged in precisely measured amounts by weight.

**Cusichaca.** A large Inca site in an excellent state of preservation, located in the Urubamba valley at Quente in the Department of Cuzco, Peru. Within the site area are the towns of Patallacta and Pulpituyoc. Six other contemporaneous satellite sites include the fort of Huillca Raccay and Huayna Quente, which was a small ceremonial center.

**Cuvier, Baron Georges** (1769–1832). The greatest early 19th-century expert on fossil bones (he was nicknamed "the Pope of Bones"), and one of the most influential proponents of "catastrophism" (*see* CATASTROPHISTS). He made major contributions to geology and to the identification of fossil species, but he and his followers never accepted the antiquity of man.

**Cuzco.** The political and religious capital of the INCA Empire. Although previously occupied, the site was first settled by the Inca in the Late Intermediate Period, *c.* AD 1200. After 1438 the Inca Pachacuti planned and built a city metropolis representing the four great quarters of the empire. The inner city consisted of great palaces located around the Huacapata (Holy Place) and covering an area between two small rivers, 6,562 × 1,312–1,968 ft. (2,000 × 400–600 m). The palaces were occupied by members of the Inca elite and were administrative, religious, and academic centers. Amongst the most important structures were the Sunturhuasi, a tower which stood in the square, and the Sun Temple, CORICANCHA. Structures were arranged in wards separated by paved streets with water channels running along them. Many palaces were built of finely fitted, dressed masonry in the rectangular masonry style, while the compound enclosure walls were sometimes constructed in the polygonal masonry style. Outside the nuclear area, all the provinces of the empire were represented in buildings constructed of stone and ADOBE. The canons of the Inca architectural style—inclined walls and trapezoidal forms for features such as doorways, windows, and niches, and fine pitched roofs thatched with ichu grass—were rigorously adherred to inside and outside the city. The enormous fortress of Sacsahuaman, which dominated and overlooked the city, was built largely by Topa Inca, son of the Inca Pachacuti.

**Cyprus.** An island lying at the east end of the Mediterranean Sea. There is evidence of prehistoric settlement there and it was influenced by the Bronze Age cultures of CRETE and MYCENAE. Initially, its most important center was Enkomi, but this was later replaced by the Classical city of Salamis. Cyprus had a chequered history, passing under Phoenician, Assyrian, and then Egyptian domination. The Persians conquered it in 525 BC, and they in turn were ousted by the Greeks, but the island was finally taken over by the Ptolemys of Egypt. Annexed by Rome in 58 BC, it was attached to the mainland province of Cilicia.

**Cyrene.** The city of Cyrene, lying halfway between Egypt and Tunisia on the African coast, was founded by Greek colonists from THERA, *c.* 650 BC. The fertility of its soil ensured the success of the colony, and by Roman times it was one of the greatest of the African cities. There remain many remnants of both its Greek and Roman past, including temples, BATHS, and a THEATER.

**Dacia.** A Roman province north of the Danube, roughly present-day Romania. Its capture by Trajan between AD 101 and 105 is commemorated on Trajan's Column in Rome. It was chiefly valuable for the gold and silver mines, which had been used since prehistoric times by the indigenous peoples. The main cities of the province were Sarmizegethusa and Apulum.

**Dagger-ax** (or *ko*). A Chinese bronze weapon in use from the SHANG DYNASTY (*c.* 1500 BC) to the HAN DYNASTY (206 BC–AD 220). The earliest forms consisted of a broad dagger-like weapon mounted at right angles to a wooden shaft through which the tang projected. Later forms had a slender blade which was extended down the shaft at right angles to the main point to prevent it snapping.

**Daima.** On the Southern flood plain of Lake Chad, in the Bornu province of Nigeria, is a series of large mounds which are the remains of early farming villages. The largest mound, near the village of Daima, is 35 ft. (11 m) high and was occupied from about 600 BC to AD 1200. For the first five centuries the Daima people only had polished stone axes and tools of worked bone, together with stone grinders and querns (*see* QUERN). Pottery, including a fine red burnished ware, is present from the time of the first occupation, and after the beginning of the Christian era iron tools become common. Somewhat higher up (and therefore later) in the sequence there is evidence for bronze casting. The economy was based on the husbandry of cattle and small stock such as sheep or goats and, although there is only indirect evidence, it is likely that cereal crops were cultivated.

**Dalmatia.** A Roman province lying on the east coast of the Adriatic: roughly co-extensive with present-day Yugoslavia. Roman expansion into this area began in the mid-2nd century BC, but it was only pacified in AD 9. Its major city was Salona (SPLIT).

**Damascus.** A huge oasis at the inland end of a pass

through the Anti-Lebanon, and present-day capital of Syria. The medieval town is built on the low TELL which represents the accumulation of earlier débris, including the Biblical town, and excavation is therefore impossible. It was an important Nabataean trading center at the time of St. Paul.

**Dar Tichitt.** The earliest evidence for the development of farming on the Southern fringes of the Sahara Desert is from a series of Neolithic sites at Dar Tichitt in Southern Mauritania. Excavations have shown that the first village settlements of the Naghez phase, 1200–1000 BC, were composed of circular compounds connected by wide paths. Although cattle and goats were herded, fishing, some hunting, and the gathering of wild grasses formed an important part of the economy. Stone axes, arrowheads, and gouges, as well as pottery, were in use. During the Chebka phase, 1000–700 BC, a decrease in rainfall caused the lakes to dry up so that fishing was no longer possible, but animal husbandry continued and, although wild grasses were still collected, there is evidence for the deliberate cultivation of millet. The architecture of the village remained unchanged during the Chekba phase except for the addition of protective walls and fortified entrance gates. The last, Akanjeir phase, 700–300 BC, saw a further climatic deterioration which caused the end of permanent settlement in the Tichitt valley.

**Darwin, Charles** (1809–82). Darwin is generally regarded as the founder of modern evolutionary biology and of the theory of the origin of species by means of natural selection. In his book, *The Descent of Man* (1871), he speculated that our closest relatives in the animal world were the chimpanzee and gorilla, and that Africa was our likely homeland, a view now favored by most scientists.

**Dating in archaeology.** One of the main preoccupations of archaeologists is the construction of timescales (chronology) to provide a firm basis for interpretation. This is because, unlike historians working from written documents, archaeologists rarely work with materials that can be directly dated with precision and with a minimum of problems. Since our evidence of the past of man from archaeological sources is so incomplete, new discoveries constantly force revision of the chronologies that have been built up by painstaking work on the known material. Archaeologists have devised a number of methods for the chronological ordering of ancient artifacts: typology, seriation, stratigraphy, and cross-dating by association. The development of many scientific techniques of dating artifacts and the deposits in which they are found has proved an immense boon to archaeology, despite the complications that frequently arise in attempting to apply them (*see* SCIENCE IN ARCHAEOLOGY). The impact on the study of prehistory of such techniques as RADIOCARBON DATING and DENDROCHRONOLOGY has been far greater than merely getting the dating right and reducing guesswork to a minimum. The application of these two techniques has led, for example, to the realiza-

tion in this decade that later prehistoric Europe depended far less in its social and technical development on stimulation from the civilizations of the Near East than has hitherto been assumed. They have also led to the demonstration that monumental funerary architecture was developed not only independently but at an even earlier date in Western Europe than in the Near East.

Typology depends on the study and classification of artifacts according to their design. By comparing similar artifacts with each other, they can be grouped together and classified into types; this procedure is variously called morphology and taxonomy. Comparison of similar types often leads in turn to the definition of a type series in a more or less simple linear order; this is known as a typological series. Study of the contexts in which we find objects of the types constituting such a series enables archaeologists to determine which are the typologically earliest and latest forms. This is the essence of the typological method: it was developed by the 19th-century Swedish archaeologist, Oscar Montelius, and is often therefore called the Montelian method. So great was his success in applying the method to the study of prehistoric European artifacts that his system of classification still forms the foundation for much of the work carried out today, a century after it was conceived.

The method of seriation was devised by the great Egyptologist Sir Flinders PETRIE in the late 19th century, in the study and chronological ordering of Predynastic tombs in Egypt. For long neglected by archaeologists, seriation has come to be widely applied in the past two decades—principally as a result of the development of electronic computers, which greatly facilitate its application. The method is based on the ordering of "closed" finds (assemblages) of artifacts—groups of objects buried together (e.g., in graves or hoards) or associated with one another in archaeological layers on the sites of ancient settlements. In essence the method is similar to typology, except that whole groups of artifacts are arranged in chronological series rather than individual objects. Its application is more difficult and generally requires the aid of computers, since the analysis requires comparison of perhaps hundreds of assemblages each containing tens of artifact types, which leads to an enormous number of potential permutations that only an electronic computer can work out in a reasonable length of time.

STRATIGRAPHY, the recording and study of layers (stratification) on the sites of ancient settlements, depends on the simple principle of superimposition, namely that the lowest layers were deposited before the uppermost, and that objects or structures found within them are respectively earlier and later than each other. Sites occupied continuously over long periods in antiquity and up to recent times gradually rose higher and higher, owing first to the absence of garbage collection and the consequent deposition of all waste materials within the confines of the settlement; and second to the practice, before the advent of high-rise buildings with their need for deep foundations, of erecting new structures on the demolished remains of the old. The stratification of such sites can be enormously complex, but study of it can give very precise chronologies for the various types of objects used within ancient settlements. The method was borrowed from the infant study of geology in the late 18th and early 19th centuries, and, together with the theory of evolution of life (which provided the inspiration for typology), led to the collapse of the Biblical model of the history of the earth and of mankind in the middle of the last century.

The transference of the dating of one kind of artifact to another kind of unknown date deposited with it forms the basis of the method of cross-dating by association. While, like typology, seriation, and stratigraphy, it is of great value in the construction of relative chronologies (the ordering of types and assemblages in their correct sequence), the principal use of this method has been to build up systems of absolute dating by reference to the historically dated civilizations. However, whereas this method has proved, since the application of scientific techniques in recent years, to be very reliable in cases such as the Late Bronze Age and Iron Age of Europe (1st millennium BC), where links between literate and illiterate societies are well documented, it has proved less reliable in earlier periods, where the links are more tenuous. In the latter cases, it is now seen that many of the alleged similarities between types of artifacts from literate and illiterate societies, that were used to construct absolute chronologies, were more apparent than real, for the application of scientific techniques of dating has shown the allegedly similar types to be of completely different dates.

Indeed, the introduction of many new scientific methods of dating has revolutionized the study of prehistory, and has considerably eased the work of archaeologists. This has led them to concentrate far more of their attention on constructing models of the development of technology and society in early times.

**Dead Sea Scrolls.** *See* QUMRAN.

**Deep Sea Cores.** In contrast to the situation on dry land, sedimentation is often continuous on the ocean floors, and consists of a silty ooze with numerous shells of foraminifera and other tiny sea creatures. In some cases many feet have accumulated in the last million years. Cores through these sediments are currently analyzed in terms of the changing species at different levels, as well as changing levels of the isotopes of oxygen: Oxygen 16 and 18 both give an indication of changing temperature and therefore of date.

**Deir el-Medina.** The site of a pharaonic workmen's village on the Nile's west bank at THEBES, situated between the Valleys of the Kings and Queens. It was thoroughly excavated and fully published during the 1920s and 1930s by the French Egyptologist, Bernard Bruyère. Its inhabitants were stone cutters, masons, plasterers, scribes, draughtsmen, and artists who excavated and adorned royal and private tombs in the Theban necropolis from the early 18th Dynasty until the end of the New Kingdom. Founded on a virgin site and eventually abandoned, Deir el-Medina provides a

A limestone stele from Deir el-Medina, 19th Dynasty, *c.* 1230 BC. It shows the chief workman Neferhotep, son of Nebnefer, adoring the deified King Amenophis I and his mother, Queen Aahmes-Nefertari.

complete picture of the everyday life of a small enclosed community of skilled workers and their families over a period of nearly 500 years.

The original wall built by Tuthmosis I enclosed a village of about 60 mud-brick houses, built side by side and back to back along one main street running north–south. Each comprised a reception room, living room, bedroom, kitchen, and cellar. Son followed father into a profession and the houses, too, stayed in one family for generations: many detailed family trees have been constructed. The workmen built and adorned their own tombs above the village as finely as those they worked upon for a living; these too were used by whole families.

A great deal of information has come from writing tablets and the limestone flakes or ostraca (inscribed pieces of pottery or sherds) on which the literate villagers scrawled their lists or thoughts. We know of their religious beliefs, methods of shift working, staple diet, sense of humor, scandals, code of justice, and even their excuses for nonattendance at work. The community was kept in seclusion, cut off from the outside world, so that their knowledge of tombs' locations might be kept secret: everything from laundry to the collection of firewood was done for them. But because even necessities like water and food had to be brought in, any breakdown in the commissariat caused hardship. Strikes because of nondelivery of rations are known from the troubled 20th Dynasty, and eventually the villagers began to rob the very tombs they had helped to create.

**Delos.** A small island in the Aegean, central among the Cyclades, and regarded by the Greeks as sacred to Apollo. The island was the central treasury of a league of maritime island states which joined forces against the Persians in the 5th century BC, and it was dominated by Athens until 314 BC. It was later captured by Rome, and made an Athenian colony. The principal remains are those of the sanctuary and its surrounding courts, but there also are extensive remains of Hellenistic living quarters, theaters, agoras, docks, and warehouses largely dating from the 3rd and 2nd centuries BC.

**Delphi.** Situated at the foot of Mount Parnassus, Delphi was supposed by the Greeks to lie at the center of the earth. It was a sanctuary of Apollo and had an oracle which was frequently consulted by all Greek city states at the start of a new enterprise. Extensive remains of the sanctuary, including the large Temple of Apollo, the theater, and stadium have been excavated, and are laid out to view. Many Greek cities built their own monuments and treasuries within the sanctuary area.

**Dendrochronology.** The growth of tree rings varies with climatic and environmental conditions, but is constant for any one year for any one species in one ecological area. It is therefore possible to obtain absolute dates for archaeological sites from the study of tree rings in charcoal and wood samples. The size of tree rings from samples in archaeological contexts can be correlated with a control series, if, that is, a control series of wood samples can be built up stretching back from the present day. This technique of dating, sometimes called tree-ring dating, has been particularly successfully used in the Southwestern United States. (*See also* RADIOCARBON DATING.)

**Desert tradition.** A group of prehistoric cultures in Western North America, dating from *c.* 9000 BC. This tradition arose in the area of the Great Basin, centering on Nevada, but including parts of Utah, Wyoming, Idaho, Oregon, and California; its subsistence base depended on the collection of small seeds, berries, bullrush rhizomes, and nuts, and on the hunting of all forms of animal life. Because of the dryness of the area, fragile artifacts, such as baskets, have been preserved; other characteristic finds include grinding and milling stones and small projectile points. The tradition spread to surrounding dry areas and remained in the form established at around 7000 BC until the 19th century AD in the original area, the Great Basin.

One of the earliest sites of the Desert tradition is Danger cave in Western Utah. The earliest levels, dated 9500–9000 BC, did not, however, yield artifacts from the Desert tradition. The few crude stone implements found may have belonged to hunters, perhaps in the Old Cordilleran tradition. In Zone II at Danger cave (8000–7000 BC), more typical artifacts were found. These include fragments of twined basketry and stones for milling seeds, and notched projectile points. In Zone III (5000–3000 BC) coiled basketry techniques first appear. The Leonard Rocks shelter in Nevada, with an earlier level dating from 9200 to 5000 BC, has produced a slightly different version of the Desert tradition assemblage. In Oregon, at the Fort Rock cave, artifacts dating back to 7000 BC have been found: these included twined sandals. The Lake Mojave phase of Southern California was succeeded by the Pinto Basin phase, (*c.* 7000–1000 BC) which is more closely related to the Desert tradition than to the Old Cordilleran. The diagnostic feature of Pinto Basin assemblages is a dart point with a concave base. In New Mexico and Arizona the Desert tradition begins with the Cochise culture dating, perhaps, to 7350 BC. As elsewhere the characteristic artifacts are the mano and METATE and other milling tools, as well as, in the Sulfur Spring phase, stemmed percussion flaked leaf points. The Desert tradition merges into the Southwestern tradition with the establishment of agriculture. Elsewhere the tradition continued until much later. In Southern California it continued until about AD 1000, when the present-day Yuma and Shoshone Indians may have moved into the area. In the other areas historical peoples, such as the Utes and Paiutes of the Uto-Aztecan language group, used toolkits similar to those which had developed over 9000 years. It is reasonable to use the analogy of the Paiutes to suggest how the ancient peoples of the area may have lived. They were organized in small bands until the 19th century, perhaps containing around 25 people. Usually this group consisted of a grandfather and his children and grandchildren. The band, while not being truly nomadic, moved around from valley to valley in search of seasonal plant and animal foods; they had few possessions except milling stones and baskets. (*See also* COCHISE.)

**Diaguita culture.** Named after a tribe from the North coast of Chile, the Diaguita culture dates from AD 1000 to 1500.

**Dilmun** (or Tilmun). The Sumerian name of the island of Bahrein. Recent Danish excavations have shown it to have been an important trading center during the 3rd millennium BC, and texts mention it in connection with trade with MAGAN AND MELUHHA. (*See also* PERSIAN GULF.)

**Dimple Based pottery.** Dating from the 4th century AD and associated with the first Iron Age communities in East Africa, Dimple Based pottery comprises decorated pots, bowls, and beakers, usually with a well beveled rim and a thumb impression on the center of the base. Distribution is restricted to Kenya, Uganda, Eastern Zaire, and Tanzania, although derivative forms, known as Chaneled ware, occur in Malawi, Zambia, and Rhodesia.

**Diyala.** One of the main tributaries of the River Tigris, just east of Baghdad, where four sites were excavated by the Oriental Institute of the University of Chicago from 1929 to 1938. Tell Asmar was the site of ancient Eshnunna and consisted of several tells (*see* TELL). A palace, an audience hall, a temple of the late 3rd and early 2nd millennia BC, and an Akkadian palace, in which a temple treasure had been hidden, were excavated. The temple itself was dedicated to Abu and the excavations revealed 20 levels going back to the end of the 4th millennium BC. Twelve statues were found in the Early Dynastic II temple.

Khafajah also consisted of several mounds and three temples were excavated. The Oval Temple was built in Early Dynastic III, and its enclosure resembles that at UBAID. The contemporary Sin Temple was traced back to the end of the 4th millennium BC through 10 building levels. The third temple was dedicated to Nintu. Ischali, dated to the beginning of the 2nd millennium BC, and part of the town plan was recovered. Yet another temple sequence was discovered at Tell Agrab. The sites are important in that attention was also given to recovering house plans, a pottery sequence was established for this part of Mesopotamia, and many objects were found, some of which illustrate advances in bronze technology (*see* CIRE PERDUE). A dam has recently been built on the Diyala, and rescue excavations have been carried out at several sites of different periods.

**Docks and harbors.** Detailed descriptions of harbors, together with reliable information about any of the old equipment, such as cranes, disused rail links, and warehouses which still survive, are needed from the historian and archaeologist. Such descriptions, at their best, are concerned with what cannot be seen, the substructures, as well as what is in front of the visitor's eyes. The real interest of the Digue Centrale at Cherbourg, France (1788–1853), for example, lies below the waterline.

Regrettably few docks have been deliberately preserved as such. Two interesting exceptions are the shipbuilding dock (1822) at Motala, on the Göta Canal in Sweden, and the dry dock in Bristol, England, which was made for the construction of Brunel's *Great Britain* (1841–42) and now accommodates the old ship in her retirement. The popularity of pleasure-boating has been responsible much more than any official action or historical interest for the conservation of many small harbors, which would otherwise have rotted away and silted up.

**Dolmen.** An enclosure for a burial in a jar of the YAYOI PERIOD in Japan. It consisted of a single large stone slab supported on a ring of stones. It can be related to a CIST TOMB, for in Korea such dolmens often enclosed cists (tombs of stone slabs). The term is also used in European archaeology to denote a standing stone. (*See* MEGALITH.)

**Domestication of plants and animals, archaeology of.** The definition of domestication has caused controversy among archaeologists. In modern conditions, a sharp line can be drawn between animals and plants which are husbanded for food, and those which live wild and may in some cases be hunted or gathered for sport or variety. This line is less easy to draw in the past, when, for instance, larger areas of uncleared woodland would have supported extensive wild populations of wild pig and cattle. Similarly, we can no longer think of "hunters" as randomly killing off whatever game was available: conservation and even herd management are likely to have been extensively practiced where one species was a staple food.

Nevertheless, there are certain cases, as in the introduction of sheep and cereal grains to Europe from the Near East, where human interference with the natural way of life of a species clearly went far beyond the kind of manipulation attempted by the hunters and collectors of the preceding millennia. In addition, the use of the secondary products (milk, wool, etc.) of some animals marks a new stage in their exploitation, though this probably occurred some time after their first use as household animals. "Domestication" is a useful shorthand for the new kinds of relationships between man and certain species of animals and plants which occurred in the postglacial period, often but not inevitably accompanied by genetic changes affecting size and diversity and and possession of advantageous characteristics from the human point of view.

While it is a necessary condition of domestication that the animals should breed or be capable of breeding in captivity, and that plants should be propagated by human agency, the idea of deliberate selection is not an essential part of the definition, and indeed such conscious breeding of specialized strains is probably restricted to large-scale urban economies.

**Domestication, South America.**
*Animals.* Unlike the Old World, few animals were available for domestication in South America and consequently more dependence was placed on plants for food. Species of animals domesticated include camelids (*see* CAMELID DOMESTICATION): alpaca, raised for its wool, and llama, raised for meat, an inferior quality of wool, and as a pack animal; the guinea pig or cavy, raised in homes since preceramic times for meat; the dog, which from INCA times appears as both a pet and a scavenger (the Inca dog was a medium-sized breed, short-haired and short-legged); and the muscovy, a large duck which was raised for meat.

*Plants.* The list of South American domesticates is too long to include here, but it should be noted that the quantity and range of these is extremely important to the cultures which depended on them for food, narcotics, fibers, dyes, resins, soaps, containers, and construction purposes. Although its precise origins in the preceramic period are not known, one of the most important Andean domesticates is the potato (*Solanum tuberosum*), which in the 16th century was spread to Northern Italy and subsequently to the rest of the world. The sweet potato (*Ipomoea batata*) has also become very important in the Western world. Three other Andean crops for which there is archaeological evidence are coca (the stimulant *Erythroylon*), Lucuma (*Lucuma bifera*), cultivated *c.* 4000 BC in the Central Andes, and quinoa (*Chenopodium quinoa*), cultivated *c.* 5000 BC, also in the Central Andes: none of these ever became important in Old World subsistence systems. Beans, cotton, guava, peppers, galactia, and peanuts occur on the Peruvian coast by 2000 BC, but some of these may have been cultivated earlier in the highlands and tropical forest areas, as may also have pepino, avocado, squash, pineapple, anu, and oca, which appear in the last millennium BC on the coast. The New World trilogy of domesticates, corn (*Zea Mays*), beans, and squash, occur over much of Northern South America. The earliest evidence of corn is from Ayacucho, *c.* 3000 BC; beans (common and lima) date from *c.* 6000–5000 BC, and gourds and squash from *c.* 3000 BC.

**Dorestad** (Duurstede). The trading center of the Frisians, from which they controlled the old Rhine, the Vecht, and the Lek. Excavations on the site were carried out mainly in the 1920s, when it was found to cover about 33 ac (13 ha) and to have been enclosed by an earthwork defense. Pippin, King of the Franks, established a fortress on the site in AD 689, and the settlement grew up around it. It possessed an important mint.

**Dornach.** A model workers' suburb at Mulhouse, France. One of the major 19th-century housing projects, it was constructed during the 1850s and 1860s on the initiative of the Industrial Society of Mulhouse, a group of local textile manufacturers, with a subsidy from the Government. By 1867, 1,400 houses had been built, each providing a separate apartment for four families. A good deal of internal modernization and rearrangement has been carried out during the present century, but Dornach still looks much as it did 100 years ago.

**Dorset.** The Dorset subtradition of the ESKIMOS of the Canadian Arctic developed from the pre-Eskimo Arctic Small Tool tradition between 500 BC and AD 500. A typical site of the late Dorset subtradition is known as Port aux Choix 2 in Western Newfoundland. The site consists of about 40 house pits with rectangular floors dug beneath ground level. Pits for storage and fire were lined with stones, but the rest of the houses were less substantially built of skin stretched over wooden frames. Subsistence depended largely on the hunting of seals, but other bones—of birds, caribou, and fish—have been found. The site was probably a summer camp to which the Eskimo went to hunt seals as they migrated north. Also in evidence at Port aux Choix 2 is a stone tool assemblage related to the Arctic Small Tool tradition. Among the most common tool types were points with two notches for hafting, spear points, and end scrapers.

**Dougga** (Thygga). A Numidian settlement, a dependency of CARTHAGE until the 3rd century AD. Its remains are some of the most extensive in North Africa, comprising a FORUM and capitol, the Temple of Mercury, a CIRCUS, a THEATER, and a system of water cisterns.

**Dura Europos.** A site on the middle Euphrates River, at the junction of a north-south route along the river with a desert road westwards towards Palmyra. It was exca-

vated by French and American expeditions from 1920 to 1937. The city was founded by the SELEUCIDS at the end of the 4th century BC, and fell to the SASSANIANS in AD 256. Within an irregular *enceinte* (enclosure), the city was laid out on a grid system. Its mixed population worshiped many deities and temples to the Palmyrene gods, to Artemis, Atargatis, Zeus Dolichenos, Megistos, and Mithras, Christian sanctuaries, and a synagogue were excavated. Many frescoes, reliefs, papyri, and scrolls were found.

**Dur Kurigalzu.** *See* KASSITES.

**Dur Sharrukin.** *See* KHORSABAD.

**Dzibilchaltún.** Located about 7 mi. (11 km) north of Merida, on the Northern Yucatan Peninsula, this Mayan site has only recently been investigated (by the National Geographic Society and Tulane University). These studies have revealed it to be one of the largest Mayan cities ever built, covering an area of nearly 50 sq. mi. (129 km²), and containing a population of over 50,000. Equally important, the site has a continuous archaeological record running from its origin, *c.* 1500 BC, until the Late Postclassic Period, one of the longest documented from the Maya subarea. The central zone of Dzibilchaltún is marked by the restored Temple of the Seven Dolls, named from clay figurines found buried beneath the floor of the structure. A large number of ceremonial structures, including pyramids, platforms, and causeways, are also present in the central precinct, as well as a CENOTE.

**Early Dynastic.** This period of Mesopotamian chronology begins *c.* 2900 BC and ends with the founding of the Dynasty of AKKAD, *c.* 2334 BC, and for this reason it is also known as the Pre-Sargonid period. It is the time when the Sumerian city states flourished under their separate dynastic rulers, the foremost being Mesanepada of UR, Lugalzagesi of Umma, Mebaragesi of KISH, and Urnanshe, Eannatum, Lugalanda, and Urukagina of LAGASH. The term "Early Dynastic" was first coined by Henri Frankfort, who divided it into three phases (I, II, and III) based on different styles of cylinder SEALS and on his DIYALA excavations. In more recent literature, the terms Mesilim, Imdugud/Sukurru, and 1st Dynasty of Ur have been used to identify subdivisions. The remarkably homogeneous civilization was obviously farreaching, for MARI and TELL CHUERA in Syria both fell within its orbit. (*See* the chronological table, p. 198.)

**Early Horizon.** A time division in Central Andean chronology, *c.* 1200–300 BC, used to refer to the unifying influence of the CHAVIN culture, its style, and its immediate derivatives. Also included are those cultures which do not show strong influences but are contemporaneous. (*See also* ANDEAN CHRONOLOGY.)

**Early Intermediate Period.** A term used to refer to a period of time characterized by regional diversification, in the Central Andes *c.* 200 BC–AD 600. Archaeological

Stone statues near Hangaroa, Easter Island, recently re-erected on their stone foundation platforms.

evidence indicates that the main characteristics of the cultures of the period included: nationalism; full population; first large-scale irrigation works in coastal valleys, and possibly terrace works in the highland valleys; interregional warfare and the construction of forts; intensive craft specialization, social class distinctions, and the rise of the first great Peruvian cities. (*See also* ANDEAN CHRONOLOGY.)

**Easter Island.** For a small volcanic island no more than 15½ mi. (25 km) long, situated 2,485 mi. (4,000 km) from the coast of South America and 1,242 mi. (2,000 km) from its nearest inhabited Polynesian neighbors, Easter Island had a remarkable prehistory. Although discovered by Europeans in 1722, few records of its inhabitants were made until after 1862, when the population was decimated by slave raiders from Peru. By 1877 the population had dropped to 110 from a prehistoric peak of 3,000 or more, and the continuity of oral tradition was irrevocably lost. Virtually all reliable information about the island's prehistory comes therefore from archaeology and linguistics.

Easter Island was settled by Polynesians early in the 1st millennium AD. They had a horticultural economy with domesticated chickens and a range of plant foods of Southeast Asian origin, such as yam, taro, and banana, although one important plant, the sweet potato, was of Andean origin. By AD 700, the islanders were building large stone platforms, some of cut stone, and between 1000 and 1700 these platforms supported rows of huge stone statues, some with separate top knots. The statues were shaped by stone tools (the islanders had no metal) from quarries in the volcano of Rano Raraku, and the largest ever erected on a platform was 37 ft. (11.5 m) high with its top knot, and weighed about 98 tons (88,904 kg). One 66-ft. (20-m) giant still lies unfinished in the quarry. There are about 300 platforms on the island, and about 600 statues: the largest platform had a row of 15 statues.

By about 1700 the warrior chiefdoms of the island were evidently engaged in internecine warfare, and all the statues were toppled from their pedestals. In this final phase, the platforms were used for human burial in stone chambers inserted into the stonework. The reasons for this period of decay are unknown.

Other important archaeological features of Easter Island include a village of stone houses with corbeled roofs at Orongo, and many petroglyphs, some (especially at Orongo) showing birdman figures clutching eggs. These refer to a ceremony in which young men swam from Orongo to an offshore island each year to collect the eggs of the sooty tern: the first to find a newly laid egg swam back with it to his master, who enjoyed a special ceremonial status for a year.

**Eastern Chin Dynasty.** A ruling house of Chinese origin controlling Southeastern China at a time (AD 337–420) when Northern China was under the rule of Turkic tribes. Numerous tombs of the period have been excavated. They consist of a chamber with slightly bowed walls to support a dome and have an approach ramp. From the known dates of some of these tombs the YÜEH WARE found in them have been accurately dated.

**East Rudolf.** A key area for research into earliest man. The Rudolf basin lies in Northern Kenya and extends into Ethiopia. East of Lake Rudolf, now renamed Lake Turkana, are sediments rich in fossils, and volcanic layers of the 1–3 million-year time range. In addition to very early stone tools, a series of skulls of probable human ancestors has been found.

**Ebla.** *See* TELL MARDIKH.

**Ecology.** In archaeology, ecology seeks to reconstruct the past environment of man and his impact upon it. A wide variety of approaches is now being brought to bear on this problem. In the field of PALAEOBOTANY, analysis of pollen frequencies in peat bogs and acidic soils (palynology) has enabled not only the detailed reconstruction of vegetational, and hence by inference climatic, changes during the past 12,000 years, since the end of the Pleistocene epoch, but also the detection of man's endeavors in the fields of forest clearance and cultivation. Pollen analysis, however, has the disadvantage of reflecting changes in vegetation over wide areas, since pollen is often carried great distances by the wind, and it has a further disadvantage in that pollen is only preserved in acidic environments. The analysis of assemblages of land snails in buried soils is particularly advantageous in this respect, since their shells are best preserved in calcareous soils (derived, for example, from chalk and limestone subsoils), and since it gives an indication of the nature of the landscape in the immediate vicinity of the deposits in which they are found. Pedology (the science of soils) has shed important light on man's use and misuse of soils in antiquity, and has shown, for example, that the heathlands in many parts of Europe were induced by the overworking of soils by early agriculturalists who failed to refertilize them by crop rotation or manuring.

**Effigy pipe.** A small stone tobacco pipe, particularly from the HOPEWELL culture of the Eastern Woodlands of the United States. They were often carved in the form of birds or animals, and are found in the tombs of Hopewell Mounds, 300 BC to AD 200. They consist of a flat base, usually curved, with a mouthpiece at one end. On top of the curved base is an animal or bird facing the mouthpiece, with a bowl for the tobacco in its back. The animals depicted in these fine small sculptures include manatees, rodents, snakes, and birds of prey. They were always carved in one piece. In other areas and periods in the United States, larger stone effigy pipes were carved in a variety of zoomorphic and human forms, perhaps the most famous of which is the human effigy pipe from the Adena Mound, Ohio.

**Egypt.**

*Dynastic Period.* The historical Dynastic Period in Egypt began *c.* 3100 BC, when the two Predynastic kingdoms of Upper and Lower Egypt were united by a legendary king, Menes, possibly to be identified with the historical King Narmer. By convention, Egypt's subsequent history is divided into 30 Dynasties (meaning ruling houses), followed by a Greek Period when the country was ruled by the Ptolemys, descendants of Alexander the Great's general. The Ptolemaic Period and Egypt's independence were brought to an end in 30 BC, when Queen Cleopatra VII died and the country was absorbed into the Roman Empire.

Most information about the Archaic Period (*c.* 3100–2686 BC), composed of the 1st and 2nd Dynasties, has come from excavations at Saqqara, Abydos, and Hierakonpolis. It was then that the most distinctive features of pharaonic civilization emerged. The 3rd to 6th Dynasties (*c.* 2686–2181 BC), forming the Old Kingdom, marked the great age of pyramid building and an early peak in artistic and intellectual achievement. Excavations in the MASTABA fields around the pyramids at Giza, Abusir, Saqqara, Meidum, and Dahshur have thrown much light on everyday life over 45 centuries ago. A weakening of the central authority after the close of the 6th Dynasty allowed the country to break up into independent princedoms which

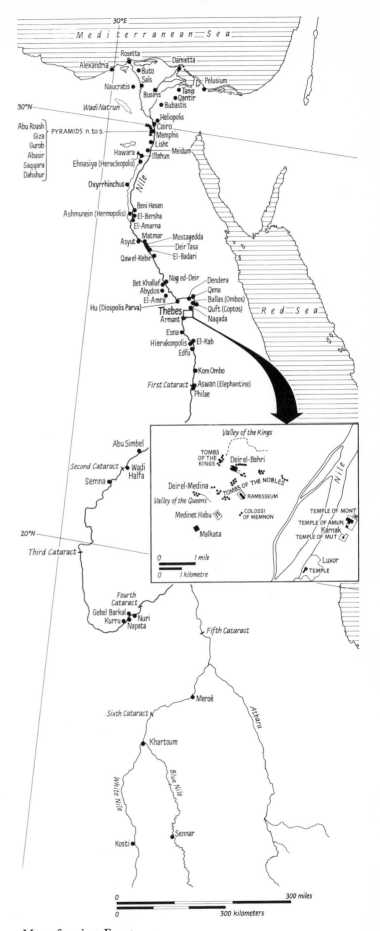

Map of ancient Egypt.

gradually polarized around the rulers of Herakleopolis in the North (9th to 10th Dynasties) and THEBES in the South (11th Dynasty). So few royal monuments remain from this troubled First Intermediate Period that it is the burials of the common people which have provided the most insight into the state of the country. Order and prosperity were restored around 2040 BC, when Mentuhotep II of Thebes reunited Egypt once more.

The succeeding Middle Kingdom (*c.* 2040–1633 BC), composed of the 11th to 13th Dynasties, marked another highpoint in pharaonic civilization. New standards of excellence were attained in art and craftsmanship, attested by the excavation of rich burials of princesses, court ladies, and high officials in the Fayum area and at Thebes. The extent of Egyptian influence has been shown by finds in Crete, the Levant, Asia Minor, and Nubia. During the 13th Dynasty, nomadic Semitic peoples who had infiltrated the Delta became strong enough to set up their own rulers as pharaohs and eventually subject the native Egyptian kings. These foreign Hyksos pharaohs, who formed the 15th Dynasty (*c.* 1650–1567 BC) were opposed in the South by the Theban 17th Dynasty (*c.* 1650–1567 BC), one of whose princes, Ahmose, eventually expelled the Hyksos from Egypt around 1567 BC, ended the Second Intermediate Period, and established the 18th Dynasty.

The New Kingdom (*c.* 1567–945 BC), composed of the 18th to 21st Dynasties, saw Egypt emerge as one of the most powerful and wealthy empires in the Near East, her Northern boundary at the River Euphrates' headwaters, her Southern beyond the Nile's 4th cataract. The site of Tell el-Amarna, built on virgin ground and abandoned after one generation, and the workmen's village at DEIR EL-MEDINA have provided valuable information about the everyday life of the period. Excavations in the Theban necropolis have uncovered intact burials (*see* TUTANKHAMUN'S TOMB), fine reliefs, and wall paintings which attest artistic excellence and give details of funerary beliefs and customs. Huge temples cleared at Abydos, Memphis, Abu Simbel, and Thebes (the latter including Karnak, Luxor, the Ramesseum, Deir el-Bahri, and Medinet Habu) testify to Egypt's might. But first the HITTITES and then the SEA PEOPLE abroad, and an ever-weakening government and economy at home, led to decline.

At the end of the succeeding Third Intermediate or Libyan Period (*c.* 945–750 BC), comprising the 22nd to 24th Dynasties, Egypt was so weak that Egyptianized Nubian kings from the Sudan conquered the country and formed the 25th Dynasty (*c.* 750–656 BC). This period marked an artistic renaissance based on Old Kingdom models, a revival which continued under the native Egyptian kings of the 26th Dynasty (*c.* 664–525 BC), the Saite Period. But an expansionist policy abroad brought conflict first with the Assyrians and then with the Babylonians, and in 525 BC Egypt was invaded by Cambyses and made a Persian satrapy. Although the native 28th to 30th Dynasties (*c.* 404–343 BC) managed to throw off the Persian yoke for a generation, it was not until 332 BC that Alexander the Great restored Egypt's independence.

*Hellenistic and Roman Period.* After Alexander the Great, who established the great city of Alexandria, control of Egypt passed to the Ptolemys, by whom there was a largely unsuccessful attempt to Hellenize Egypt, the only result being that the originally Hellenistic Ptolemys became more and more Egyptian. Egypt was treated as the property of the emperors under the Roman Empire, and it was largely exploited and neglected. There is therefore little trace of Roman presence in Egypt apart from the military one. (For Egypt in the Predynastic Period, *see* BADARIAN CULTURE; NAQADA CULTURE I; NAQADA CULTURE II.)

**Elam, Elamites.** Present-day Khuzistan in Southwestern Iran, on the border of Iraq. It is fertile and well watered and was settled (*see* MESOPOTAMIA) in the 8th millennium BC. Its chief city was SUSA, and recent excavations have shown that its flourishing Proto-Elamite culture was based on an extensive trade network with the East (*see also* TEPE YAHYA) and that many cultural advances, including writing, appeared very early. Indirect trade relations with Egypt at the end of the 3rd millennium BC are also documented. The riches and fertility of Elam have attracted tribes from the neighboring highlands throughout its history, and it has always been closely linked to Southern Mesopotamia. The golden age of Elamite civilization, *c.* 1300–1100 BC, reached its peak under Untash-Gal (*c.* 1265–1245 BC), the builder of CHOGA ZAMBIL, while two massive raids into Mesopotamia brought about the downfall of the Kassite Dynasty in 1157 BC. The period is remarkable for its advances in GLASS technology and bronze casting (*see* CIRE PERDUE). In the titles of Elamite and Achaemenid kings, Elam is linked to Anshan, identified as the site of Tall-i Malyan, which is at present being excavated (1977).

**Electricity.** Public electric lighting dates from the 1880s. One of the earliest monuments is Deptford Power Station, London (1889), where most of the original buildings survive. Throughout the 1890s, small power stations were built in most cities to provide light and also current for tramways. Two such power stations can still be seen in Bristol, England (on Temple Back [1893], and on Phillip Street). Many of the stations erected by the private supply companies during the 1920s and 1930s were architecturally distinguished buildings, and some are still in use, to provide extra capacity at peak times. Concrete cooling towers date from the mid-1920s— examples from this period can be seen at Lister Drive Station, Liverpool, England; but wooden towers of the same vintage, or even earlier, are still in existence. The first pylons carrying national grid lines, with a high-voltage AC supply, were erected in the early 1930s and many of them continue in service.

The buildings connected with the American, but not the European, pioneers of electricity and of the communication systems based on it have been well cared for by the conservationists. The Edison National Historic Site, at West Orange, N.J., contains Edison's workroom, laboratories, and house. Alexander Graham Bell's house, at Brantford, Ont., Canada, from which the first long-distance telephone call was made, is preserved as a museum. Folsom, Calif., preserves the power station from which electricity was sent more than 25 mi. (40 km) for the first time. What is believed to be part of the world's first telephone exchange (1878) is on the ground floor of the Metropolitan Building, New Haven, Conn.

**Eleusis.** An important town in Greece, famous for the mysteries celebrated in honour of Demeter and Persephone. The sanctuary was in use from the Bronze Age onwards, but its most famous monument, the telesterion (a hall with rockcut seats), was built in the late 6th century BC. There are considerable remains of Greek and Roman additions to the sanctuary.

**El Inga.** A preceramic site in Ecuador, located 17 mi. (27 km) from Quito at a height of 9,100 ft (2,774 m) in the Rio Inga gorge. A group of heavily eroded hummocks appears to have been an OBSIDIAN workshop and hunting campsite. The estimated date of 10,000 BC is based on similarity of the obsidian tools to the FOLSOM and Clovis points of North America (*see* CLOVIS POINT). There were also "fish-tail" stemmed points similar in shape to those in FELL'S CAVE. Excavation revealed that the artifacts lay in an unploughed part of the midden (rubbish mound) in an 8–12 in.(20–30 cm) thick occupation layer. The variety of point styles and tool types suggest that several cultures may be represented, covering over 5,000 years of intermittent occupation.

**Ellora.** A cave temple site in Maharashtra state, India, with examples of Buddhist, Jain, and Hindu temples containing fine sculptures. Its most spectacular sight is the freestanding Hindu Kailaśa temple, hewn from the hillside. The principal excavations date from the 6th–8th century AD. (*See also* INDIA.)

**El Tajin.** A Mayan site situated about 125 mi. (201 km) northeast of the city of Veracruz, Mexico, among small but thickly wooded hills. The famous Pyramid of the Niches is located there, and was known long before any archaeological work was undertaken. The earliest mention of the site was in 1785, but scientific research began only in 1935, with the clearing of the site.

In addition to the Pyramid of the Niches, there are several sizable mounds and plazas, only a few of which have been cleared or excavated, as well as two famous ballcourts. To the north of this area, on somewhat higher ground, is another part of the site known as Tahin Chico. This contains a number of chambered buildings on low substructures and also a remarkable one with large columns.

Most, if not all of El Tajin proper belongs to the Classic Maya Period. Pottery shows that the city was much influenced by TEOTIHUACAN and CHOLULA, but there are also indications of contact with the Huasteca further to the north. On the other hand, some pottery from Tajin Chico suggests a later, Postclassic Toltec affinity.

The Pyramid of the Niches, as the name implies, has 365 square niches built into the sides, corresponding to the 365 heads on the Temple of QUETZALCOATL at Teotihuacan. Figurines, representing gods of the day, were perhaps placed into each niche. On the walls of the Tajin ballcourts there are elaborately carved scenes of the ritual game in progress, ending with a sacrificial scene of the losers (*see* BALLGAME, MESOAMERICA). The carving is done in bas-relief in a double-border style usually attributed to the TOTONACS.

**Emery, Walter Brian** (1903–71). A British Egyptologist, noted for his careful surveying and study of prospective sites, which enabled him to make spectacular discoveries. In publishing his excavations, he used G. A. Reisner's painstaking methods as a model but added further refinements of his own. As a very young man he was in charge of the expedition to Armant which discovered the galleries of the Bucheum, burial place of the sacred Buchis bull. During the Nubian Survey of 1929–34, he uncovered astoundingly rich burials at Ballana and Qustol belonging to Nubian X-Group kings, queens, and nobility of the 4th to 6th century AD, hidden under mounds which some archaeologists had considered to be natural formations.

From 1935 onwards Emery worked virtually exclusively at Saqqara, excavating many Archaic Period mastabas (*see* MASTABA). His most important discovery, however, was a row of splendid 1st-Dynasty tombs all attributable to kings or nobles of that Dynasty, often surrounded by subsidiary burials, like those around contemporary tombs at Abydos. From these large mastabas came fine stone vessels, copper implements, and tableware, the remains of wooden figures, ivory gaming sets, numerous jar sealings, inscribed labels, pottery vessels, and the earliest known papyrus, unfortunately uninscribed. One tomb, that attributed to Hor-aha, had attached to it model buildings and a brick-built solar boat grave. The publications of these tombs are models of their kind and invaluable for students of the development of Archaic Period funerary architecture.

A brief spell in Nubia produced much material and information from the fortress of Buhen and its environs. Work was also begun at Qasr Ibrim which later was to produce some of the most important discoveries of the Nubian campaign. Emery's return to Saqqara yielded a catacomb of sacred ibis mummies, another of sacred hawks, a third devoted to the burial of sacred baboons, and the Iseum, burial place of the sacred cows who were mothers of the sacred Apis bulls (*see* SERAPEUM). Due to Emery's death, none of these discoveries, nor the mass of Late Dynastic material uncovered, has been fully published.

**Enameling, Medieval.** A process closely connected with glassworking. Powdered glass is heated until it fuses into an opaque mass. Enameling was employed by the pre-Roman CELTS in Europe, and it was popular in Roman times, a factory for its production being known at Namur, France. In the MIGRATION PERIOD, a type of enamelwork, known as *champlevé*, was popular. In this, the areas to be set with enamel were cut away, leaving cavities, so that the surface of the enamel was flush with the surface of the metal. Fine enamelwork was produced by the Early Christian Celts in Britain and Ireland. Enameling continued to be popular in the late Middle Ages, an important center for its production being Limoges in France (*see* LIMOGES ENAMEL).

**Encanto.** A cultural phase which marks a new adaptation, from the LOMAS to the exploitation of maritime resources, in settled communities along the coast of Central Peru, *c.* 3750–2500 BC. Stone artifacts include milling stones, small percussion-flaked projectile points, and simple scrapers, but bone and wooden tools were increasingly used. (*See also* PACIFIC LITTORAL TRADITION.)

**Environment.** The problems of ancient environments range in scale from, for instance, reconstructing a leatherworker's hut in early medieval York, with its festering heaps of skins and their rich fauna of flies, larvae, and fungi, to the reconstitution of the complete landscape around a Palaeolithic settlement, with its much altered geomorphology and partly extinct animal and plant species. For any period of the Palaeolithic, geological information is essential, since the succession of ice advances and the climatic changes beyond the ice caps resulted in radical changes in the environment: sea levels changed by as much as 328 ft (100 m); lake levels rose and fell; and whole rivers were diverted by ice and deposits up to hundreds of feet thick were laid down by ice, water, and wind. Faunal and vegetational zones shifted to such an extent that the remains of Palaeolithic hunters in the Thames or Somme River valleys, for example, may be associated in different periods either with the bones of the hippopotamus, or with those of the reindeer and woolly mammoth.

After the end of the last glaciation some 10,000 years ago, the warmer temperatures allowed woodland animals and plants to recolonize the former tundras. Fast-moving pioneer species arrived first, and birch woods flourished until oak, elm, and linden established themselves to give more shade and replace them with denser forest, which supported fewer deer and wild cattle for the hunters.

The pace of environmental change quickened dramatically with the introduction of agriculture from 7,000 years ago onwards: forests were cut down, and cultivation led to soil degradation and erosion. New species were introduced, both as crops and weeds, and the relentless growth of population ensured that man's activities made an ever-increasing impact on the landscape.

**Ephesus.** A city on the West coast of Asia Minor, originally an Ionic city of which only a few fragments survive. The city walls are Hellenistic, but the majority of the remains date from the Roman period, when the city was one of the most important in Asia. Still preserved are market buildings, gymnasia, BATHS, a STADIUM, and a THEATER.

**Epigraphy, Greek and Roman.** Epigraphy is the study of inscriptions written on stone or metal or scratched on pottery or tile. It does not normally include the study of texts painted on ceramics, or written on papyrus or wood,

which are regarded as within the studies of ceramics and papyrology respectively. Epigraphy deals both with the form of the inscriptions, and with their content: study of the form enables assessment of the development of language and the alphabet; their content is, however, usually more important for the light thrown on the social, political, religious, and economic life of the ancient world. Of the more important Greek texts surviving from antiquity are the tribute lists of the Athenian league of maritime states, the law code of Gortyn in Crete, the bilingual autobiography of Augustus, and the edict of Diocletian specifying maximum prices for standard foods. Most important among inscriptions in Latin are the public *acta*, embodying laws, and the consular *fasti*, which list the principal magistrates for various periods of Roman history, thus providing a framework for dating many other inscriptions. Most are much humbler than these, and provide first-hand illustration of many aspects of legal, civil, financial, military, and personal life in the ancient world.

**Erbil.** The great Assyrian city of Arab'ilu lies buried beneath the modern city, which lies on the summit of a huge TELL. The important prehistoric site of Qalinj Agha has recently been excavated in the suburbs of Erbil.

**Erechtheum.** A temple dedicated to Erechtheus, legendary king of the city, on the Acropolis at Athens. Built in 421–407 BC, it is remarkable for its decorative details—notably the western porch, with its caryatid pillars—and for the complexity of its plan.

**Eridu.** Present-day Abu Shahrein is the site of a Sumerian city which stood on a lagoon. By the end of the 3rd millennium BC, desiccation had led to its decline, but it remained important throughout Mesopotamian history as a religious center and sanctuary of Ea-Enki. According to tradition it was the oldest city in history and excavation has shown it to be the seat of the earliest-known culture in Southern Mesopotamia. A succession of mud-brick shrines was built here (levels XIX–XV), with the first on virgin soil. These are associated with painted pottery known as "Eridu" ware or Ubaid 1, with geometric designs which later developed into the Hajji Muhammad or Ubaid 2 style (levels XIV–XIII), and then into the Early Ubaid style (Ubaid 3), which is also associated with temples (levels XII–VIII). Later temples continued to be built on the same site, which is partially covered by a corner of the late 2nd-millennium BC ZIGGURAT. (*See* the chronological table, p. 198.)

**Ertebølle culture.** Named after a locality in Denmark, the Ertebølle culture is commonly associated with giant mounds of shells and other refuse called "kjokken moddings" or kitchen middens. Although usually classified as Late Mesolithic hunters, these people had pottery and may have been in contact with the first farmers.

**Eshnunna.** *See* DIYALA.

**Eskimos.** The Eskimo tradition evolved between 2000 and 100 BC among peoples living around the Bering Straits in Alaska; it then spread out into the Canadian Arctic and Greenland. It was not, therefore, imported as a whole into America. Instead it gradually evolved from the earlier pre-Eskimo cultures, such as the earlier Arctic Small Tool tradition and the Aleutian Core and Blade industry, while receiving new impetus from the Mesolithic and Neolithic cultures of Siberia (*see* PRE-ESKIMO ARCHAEOLOGY).

The distinctive features of Eskimo culture are those brought about by the climate: the persistence of ice, the long periods of darkness in the Arctic, and below freezing temperatures. The culture of the Eskimos is traditionally based on hunting, with the hunting of sea animals becoming increasingly important. Seals, whales, and walruses were the principal food sources from the sea, although various fish and birds were also hunted. Caribou was the principal land animal hunted, and some historical Eskimo populations were dependent on it. The material culture of the Eskimos is consistent from early prehistoric times until the 20th century. Houses, for the winter months, were often partially underground: these were constructed of whalebones and driftwood and covered with turf and stone. Alternatively, especially in the Canadian Arctic, igloos were constructed of ice. The summer dwellings usually consisted of skin tents.

Skins were used for clothing and, when stretched over wooden frames, also for boats—the *kayak* or closed boat, and the *umiak* or open boat. However, the archaeological record depends on the tools used to hunt the animals from which the skins were taken. The harpoon in particular, with all its various bone, stone, and ivory parts, is significant both because it is the article most often found, and because it was the most important subsistence tool of the Eskimo. Harpoons were made of the following parts: a wooden shaft; a bone or ivory foreshaft set into a socket of bone or ivory on the wooden shaft; a detachable point to the foreshaft; an icepick of ivory set into the butt of the shaft; and a finger rest of bone or ivory in the middle of the shaft. These bone and ivory parts have been found in large quantities on Eskimo sites of all periods, and it is small stylistic and functional changes which have enabled the various cultures and subcultures to be distinguished.

The Eskimo tradition has been divided into four major subtraditions which clarify the early prehistory of cul-

tures still existing today. The Pacific-Aleut subtradition is that which covers the very separate area of the Aleutian Islands and the Eskimo areas of the South Alaskan coast. Two major subtraditions occurred in the Bering Sea and Alaskan Arctic area, and then spread eastwards. The first of these is termed the Choris-Norton-Near Ipiutak and was centered on the Bering Sea and Bering Straits area. The other subtradition, the Northern Maritime, centered on the Northern Arctic coast of Alaska. The last subtradition, known as the DORSET, is restricted only to the Eastern Arctic, where it was later replaced by the Northern Maritime tradition as it moved eastwards.

The Pacific-Aleut subtradition is the most separate of the four. It has been estimated that the Aleut language separated from the rest of the Eskimo language at around 2600 BC; it became so distinct that for a long time it was assumed to be of a different language group. This local development of the Eskimo tradition diverged from the other subtraditions in part because of the isolation of the population on the Aleutian Islands, and Pacific Coast. The environmental conditions there were milder, and so the material remains are, of course, different. Additionally other cultures influenced the Pacific-Aleut subtradition more than any others. The Northwest Coast peoples, for instance, of Southeastern Alaska, intermingled with Eskimo populations. Additionally the Aleutian Islands, once part of the Bering land bridge, probably continued to receive Asian influences. The crucial sites in this subtradition are the Chaluka Midden and Kachemak Bay sites. The Chaluka Midden, in the Aleutians, is dated to around 1000 BC, and lies at the point between pre-Eskimo and Eskimo cultures. The Kachemak Bay sites, in Cook Inlet on the Alaskan mainland, show the development of the subtradition from around 750 BC to the present day. The villages of Kachemak Bay were of partially underground dwellings: among the non-Eskimo traits of these sites was an emphasis on woodworking, demonstrated by the number of woodworking tools found, and the introduction of weaving in later times. Eskimo characteristics include stone oil lamps, slate blades, barbed bone darts and various bone needles, pins, and awls. The subsistence of Kachemak Bay was largely based on sea hunting and fishing, although land game was hunted and berries were collected.

While the Pacific-Aleut subtradition is the least characteristic of the Eskimo traditions, the most typical is the Northern Maritime. This has five phases: the OKVIK, Old Bering Sea, Birnirk, Punuk, and Thule. The THULE CULTURE is that which spread from Alaska to the

An Old Bering Sea walrus ivory harpoon head with a stone point, from Alaska, 4⅝ in. (11.9 cm) long, *c.* AD 100.

Canadian Arctic and Greenland to form the historical Eskimo culture. All the cultures preceding Thule are only known in Alaska, around the Bering Sea and North Arctic Coast. The Okvik is dated *c*. 300 BC, and Thule *c*. AD 1000. One of the most distinctive aspects of the Northern Maritime subtradition is the art style of the earliest cultures—the Okvik and Old Bering Sea. These include all over linear and curvilinear designs traced with dots and lines. The third tradition, the Choris-Norton-Near Ipiutak, dates from about 1000 BC to the middle of the 1st millennium AD (*see* IPIUTAK). Although the sites from the subtradition are sometimes situated in areas of the Northern Maritime tradition, it has certain distinctive features. In particular Siberian influences were strong. The Norton culture of *c*. 500 BC produced a pottery which was coarse, thick, and tempered with sand and fibers. It was either plain or decorated with simple stamped designs. Another distinguishing characteristic of the Norton culture is the absence of an art style and engraving on ivory in general. The fourth subtradition, the Dorset, lasted from about 800 BC to AD 1000 in the Canadian Arctic, particularly in Baffin Island, Hudson's Bay, and the Melville peninsula. It was afterwards replaced by the Thule culture of the Northern Maritime subtradition.

**Ethnohistory.** In areas where prehistoric and non-literate cultures have survived into historical times, it is possible to reconstruct history before contact with literate populations through the study of myth and oral traditions, collected ethnographically. In some parts of the world, such as Central America, the aboriginal written records are used in conjunction with early European records, archaeological investigations, and oral tradition to reconstruct prehistoric life. This is known as ethnohistory.

**Etowah.** A large site in Georgia in the MISSISSIPPIAN TRADITION of the Southeastern United States, dating from Temple Mound II period, AD 1200–1700. It consists of a fortified farming village along the banks of the Etowah River with three temple mounds. The biggest of these was about 70 ft. (21 m) high, 380 ft. square (35 m²) at the base, and probably contained more than 4 million cu. ft. (113,267 m³) of earth. The tops of these temple mounds were either used as temples, as the name suggests, or for priests' houses. From Etowah and other Georgia sites come the most important figurative sculpture of Eastern North America. Stone figures of men were carved, probably gods; they were about 15–30 in. (38–76 cm) high and were portrayed sitting. Like the temple mounds themselves, they are probably the result of Mexican influence and may represent Mexican-derived deities. The pottery of Etowah is of several types: some was decorated with complicated stamped devices, some with incisions, and a third group was decorated with negative stamps.

**Etruscans.** A pre-Roman people of Central Italy who for a time challenged the Romans for the political leadership of the area north of Rome. In *c*. 500 BC, they were at the peak of their power, and a collection of confederate cities dominated an empire reaching from Campania in the South to the Po valley in the North. These separate states were, however, gradually taken over by Rome.

The origin of the Etruscans is a subject of debate. Their language, in which about 10,000 inscriptions are known, belongs to an old Mediterranean linguistic substratum, but is largely undeciphered. Whether this language was introduced by invaders, or whether it was indigenous to this part of Italy is not known. There is no appreciable culture break between the Villanovans of Northern Italy of early Iron Age date and the Etruscans, except perhaps in the change from cremation to inhumation (burial without burning) as a burial rite. In the field of religion, however, there are aspects of Etruscan worship which seem to betray Eastern influences and customs.

Although there is uncertainty over their origins, it has been established that by the late 7th century BC the Etruscans had attained a unity of culture and language. Their archaeological remains are mainly those of tombs, sculpture, and painted frescoes. No major Etruscan city has been excavated, but city walls—the so-called terrace walls—at VEII and at Luni survive. What is known of Etruscan architecture comes mainly from tombs, which from the 7th century BC onwards were fashioned in the shape of houses. In Southern Etruria, these took the form of rockcut chambers (at Caere, Tarquinia), sometimes with carved façades. In the North, rectangular chambers were more the norm (e.g., at Populonia and Vetulonia). Temples were of wood, and their superstructures decorated with terra-cotta ornament.

Etruscan art, as displayed in wall (usually tomb) paintings and coffin portraits, is influenced by Greek and Oriental motifs: among the earliest examples are the Orientalizing paintings on graves at Caere and Veii, followed later by the brightly colored series of scenes at Chiusi, Orvieto, Veii, and at Tarquinii, where the artists have portrayed the dead man at his everyday pursuits, mixed in with demonic scenes.

In the field of metalwork, too, the Etruscan craftsmen were outstanding, and their products were exported widely within the Mediterranean world. The Capitoline Wolf and the Chimera of Arretium are prime examples of the statuettes and statues of exceptionally fine workmanship in bronze that they produced; the traditions for this type of modeling were grounded in the use of terracotta, the usual medium for smaller pieces of sculpture. The most common objects made were busts or masks, representing the face of a dead man and left as grave goods in his tomb.

**Europe (Eastern) in Prehistory.** The study of prehistory began early in the more central parts of Eastern Europe, and dates to the beginning of the 18th century, when a number of rich private collectors, such as Prince Szechenyi, who founded the Hungarian National Museum in 1801, began systematically to assemble and publish their prehistoric antiquities. In Southeast Europe, archaeology was slower to develop because of the Turkish occupation, but when this ended at the beginning of this century, foreign excavations began to reveal the great richness of the prehistoric civilizations of the Balkans. Nationalist interest also resulted in programs of excavation, such as that of Vassits at Vinča (Yugoslavia) in 1910 (*see* VINČA CULTURE). Scholars based in Athens extended their interests northwards into Macedonia, as this region was freed from the Turks. Although interrupted by two world wars, progress in archaeological knowledge has been rapid: in the 1920s, writers from Eastern Europe, such as Albin Stocky in Czechoslovakia, were in the forefront of synthesis and wrote major studies of European prehistory; while today, the modern socialist states have recognized the importance of archaeological research, and funded many large excavations.

For the Palaeolithic period, Eastern Europe is important especially for the excellently preserved sites under great depths of loess, which allow whole settlements to be uncovered in their entirety, with the outlines of huts and other features of these encampments. Well known examples are at Předmost, Czechoslovakia, and Kostienki, Russia. The painstaking excavation of these open sites has done much to complement the picture worked out in Western Europe based on cave sequences, and has also revealed the great richness of mammoth-hunting cultures during the last glacial period (around 20,000 years ago), especially in their small sculptures of ivory and bone.

In the Neolithic period, Eastern Europe, and especially the Southeast, achieved a particular prominence because of its proximity to the Near East, which explains the early date at which village-based agriculture arrived in this area—in Greece at around 6000 BC and in Hungary by 5000 BC, some 1,000 to 2,000 years before agriculture appeared in Northwestern Europe. The cultures at this period show a strong relationship to ancestral areas in Western Turkey, especially in the use of painted pottery and figurines. The characteristic sites in Southeast Europe at this period are tells, with a deep accumulation of deposits resulting from a continuous occupation over millennia with many rebuildings of mud-brick structures. One such is the site of KARANOVO in Bulgaria, the scene of a major program of postwar exavations, which has provided a standard sequence for the Neolithic and Bronze Ages of this area, and has offered the solution to many of the problems of linking the well-investigated Central European sequence with centers of early Near Eastern civilization such as TROY. Such deep sites occur commonly in Greece, Bulgaria, Romania, Yugoslavia, and sporadically in Hungary.

It was from Hungary that the main spread of the LINEAR POTTERY CULTURE took place, some time in the mid-5th millennium, as a result of adaptation to Central European conditions. This culture spread not only westwards up the Danube but also eastwards around the northern edge of the Carpathians, to reach as far as European Russia. A rather slower movement of eastward expansion is shown by the TRIPOLYE CULTURE, from the early 4th millennium onwards, reaching round the northern shore of the Black Sea, and carrying the tradition of intricately painted pottery eastward into the forest steppes at the same time that related cultures in the Balkans were making their experiments in the production of simple copper objects.

This simple copperworking was possible because of the abundance of weathered ores of copper adjacent to the long-settled parts of Southeast Europe, in the Carpathian and Balkan mountains. The ores were mined and smelted to produce raw material for shafthole axes and a variety of ornaments, the oldest in Europe and among the oldest in the world. Gold was also obtained by panning and worked into simple decorations.

It was as a result of developments in the steppe area proper, in the later 4th and 3rd millennia, that the Southeast European tell cultures disappeared. The domestication of the horse in the dryer areas allowed the use of the steppes as pastureland, and so began the pattern of contacts by pastoralist groups around the shores of the Black Sea, reaching as far as the ancient civilizations of the Caucasus and Iran—a pattern which continued down to the time of the SCYTHIANS and beyond. These new contacts not only changed the old-established cultures of Southeast Europe, but brought the techniques fundamental to the technology of the Bronze Age.

These continuing eastward contacts are a noteworthy feature of the later prehistory of Eastern Europe, and manifest themselves for instance in the characteristically eastward-looking art of the Thracians and Dacians, which was important in imparting an exotic element to early Celtic art. The vulnerability of Eastern Europe to mounted raiders was perhaps also responsible for the relative lack of development of centralized proto-urban communities, which were a feature of Western Europe during the later part of the Iron Age.

Much of the information about these developments has come from excavations conducted in recent years by the local museums and academies of sciences in the various socialist states of Eastern Europe. Although the differences are not now so marked as they were 10 or 20 years ago, there is still an official Marxist line of interpretation of prehistory, stemming from the writings of Friedrich Engels. Engels took over some of the theories concerning earlier states of society of L. H. Morgan, a 19th-century American banker and ethnographer; and it is thus not uncommon to find references to ideas, such as that of "matriarchal society," in the work of Eastern European authors which are no longer accepted in the West. Recent theoretical works, however, have not stressed this division, but instead have shown an interesting parallelism in their use of cybernetic and statistical models.

**Europe (Western) in Prehistory.** In Western Europe the Neolithic period marks the introduction of farming, pottery making, and long-distance trade in finished products, the beginnings of villages, of regular formal burial of the dead in certain sections of society, and of the construction of earthworks and stone and timber monumental architecture. It also marks the extinction over large tracts of Europe, excluding Northern Scandinavia, of HUNTING AND GATHERING as the major mode of existence of most of the indigenous inhabitants, and the

81

arrival of substantial new populations from Eastern Europe and the Eastern Mediterranean.

The first signs of an established Neolithic mode of existence in Western Europe occur in the 7th millennium BC; by 3000 BC all but Northern Scandinavia was populated by farming communities. Two main stands of Neolithic colonization can be detected in Western Europe. The first, coming by way of the Mediterranean, is known by the generic title of the IMPRESSED WARE group, after its characteristic pottery decorated by impressing cockle shells into the fabric: this group became established along the coasts and on the islands of the West Mediterranean by c. 6000 BC. The second came from the Middle Danubian basin across the easily farmed light loess-soils of Central and Southern Germany towards the Low Countries and Northern France, arriving there soon after 5000 BC; this, the Danubian, or LINEAR POTTERY CULTURE, seems to have practiced a form of shifting agriculture, caused by rapid exhaustion of the light soils through lack of manuring and crop rotation, and was based on enormous settlements of long rectangular timber-framed buildings in which people and animals lived at opposite ends. During the 5th millennium BC, these two strands led to the formation of a number of regional groups (see CHASSÉEN CULTURE; MICHELSBERG CULTURE, and WINDMILL HILL CULTURE), including the first farmers in the British Isles. During the 4th and 3rd millennia BC, large mounds (mostly elongated in Northwest Europe, and round in the Southwest) containing mortuary chambers, often built of large stones (see MEGALITH), were constructed, and in Brittany and the British Isles circles and avenues of large stones spaced at regular intervals were erected. These monuments continued to be constructed and used into the mid-2nd millennium BC, the most famous of the circles being STONEHENGE in England. Many of these avenues and circles may have been used and constructed according to strict mathematical and astronomical canons.

In the mid-3rd millennium BC there appear the first signs of metallurgy in Western Europe, heralding the Copper Age, in which copper was used for trinkets, small implements, and small daggers, and gold for ornaments. Metallurgy may have been independently invented in Spain and Portugal, and disseminated from there to France, the British Isles, the Low Countries, and Switzerland by the BEAKER CULTURE, whose distinctive pottery, developed from indigenous wares in Southern Iberia, was made throughout Western Europe in the late 3rd millennium BC alongside indigenous forms of vessels. In Italy, knowledge of metallurgy may have spread from Greece, and in Germany and the Eastern Alps from Eastern Europe. The Beaker people and a further intrusive population, from Eastern Europe, the CORDED WARE CULTURE or Battle Ax people, mingled with each other and with the local peoples to produce a new population in Central Europe, which are the ancestors of all subsequent peoples in prehistory between the Rivers Rhine and Vistula. Both these peoples introduced the new rite of single burial to Western Europe, where communal burial had previously been practiced. The Early Bronze Age (early to mid-2nd millennium BC) witnessed the flourishing of various societies, probably arising from their control of the long-distance trade in raw materials for metallurgy and in other scarce and highly prized materials (e.g., amber and jet), and from their specialist skills in making finished products. Two such societies stand out: the Aunjetitz or ÚNĚTICE CULTURE in Brittany, Bohemia, and Saxony, and the WESSEX CULTURE in Southern England. The final and most elaborate phases of Stonehenge were the product of the Wessex culture.

These rich, chieftain-dominated societies were eclipsed in the third quarter of the 2nd millennium BC, but by then a number of large-scale bronze industries had become established throughout Western Europe, including those areas like Denmark where none of the necessary raw materials occurs naturally. In the area of the Northern Alps, Southern Germany, and Bohemia, there developed, from about 1200 BC, the so-called Urnfield people, who were the immediate ancestors of the CELTS (see URNFIELD PERIOD). The Urnfield people, who cremated their dead and buried them in urns in cemeteries, were the first to use lead in bronze to give easier complex castings, to use the investment method (CIRE PERDUE) of moldmaking, and to make large metal vessels and defensive metal armor in Western Europe. It is probable that, early in the 1st millennium BC, Urnfield people spread outwards from their Central European homelands into France, Spain, and Northern Italy. During these centuries ironworking became established in Italy, and led to the development of the VILLANOVAN CULTURE, from which Etruscan civilization was later to develop. In the late 8th and 7th centuries BC, iron quickly replaced bronze as the metal used for the manufacture of weapons and edge tools, and this led to the collapse of the old bronze industries throughout Western Europe. By the middle of the 1st millennium BC, Celtic-speaking peoples had spread over all of Western Europe except parts of Spain, Italy south of the Po, Scandinavia, and North Germany. From the late 2nd millennium BC, large fortified centers, many on hills (see HILLFORT), began to develop, and were to form the first urban centers in Western Europe in the late 1st millennium BC (see URBANIZATION, PREHISTORIC EUROPE).

During the Iron Age, Western Europe enters the pages of written history, and by the 1st century BC, even before their conquest by Rome, many parts of Celtic Europe knew the use of writing, employing first Greek script and later, after the mid-1st century BC, the Roman alphabet. From the 5th century BC, peoples and their tribal names gradually become known to us through contemporary writings. Iron Age material culture north of the Rivers Po and Ebro, and south of the English Channel and the North European plain is normally divided into two phases, dated c. 700–450 and 450–1 BC, and named after two localities in the alpine zone where important finds were made in the middle of the 19th century: respectively HALLSTATT (Austria), the site of a large early Celtic salt mine with a richly furnished cemetery; and La Tène (Switzerland), the site of a riverside settlement, destroyed in a catastrophic flash flood about 100 BC, on the right bank of an old course of the

Thielle (Zihl) River shortly before it debouches into Lake Neuchâtel.

**Evans, Sir Arthur** (1851–1941). The son of another famous archaeologist, Sir John Evans, Arthur had a varied career as a journalist and war correspondent in the Balkans before beginning work at the site of Knossos, which he revealed as the capital of the first Bronze Age civilization, that of Minoan Crete. He was Keeper of the Ashmolean Museum, Oxford. (*See* CRETE; KNOSSOS; MINOAN ARCHAEOLOGY.)

**Excavation.** The technique by which the archaeologist retrieves the material remains of man's past activities buried beneath the surface of the ground. It originated in the Renaissance period, when people began to realize that ancient works of art often lay buried and could be reached by quarrying the sites of ancient cities such as Rome. Gradually, careful excavation has become dominant, and it is no longer carried out just to satisfy the collector's thirst for ever-more attractive objects to display in their houses or (increasingly over the past two centuries) in public galleries or museums.

The principal role of excavation nowadays is to find out answers to specific sets of problems or questions. Although it is often thought to occupy the greatest part of the archaeologist's time and energy, excavation is really but one stage of his research into man's past. However, the sites of so many ancient settlements are now being destroyed each year by plowing, quarrying, and the construction of freeways, houses, factories, offices, dams, etc., that there has grown up a specialized branch of archaeology, known as salvage archaeology, whose sole purpose is to record as many of these threatened sites as is possible before they are lost for ever.

An aerial view of a round barrow under excavation, with radiating sections, at Earls Farm Down, Wiltshire.

The purpose of excavation is not only to find things but also to record them in the positions (and the deposits) in which they are found, and to interpret their stratigraphic relationships to each other. The standards of excavation (of both the digging itself and the recording of the work) have become higher as archaeology has developed, and continue to improve year by year. Thus, early in the last century several burial mounds would be excavated in a day, whereas nowadays the time required to investigate a single mound may be several months or even years. Until this century, very little care was taken, except by some notable pioneers such as Thomas JEFFERSON, who excavated in his native Virginia, and General Pitt-Rivers, who conducted a long series of meticulous excavations on his private estate near Salisbury in Southern England in the 19th century. In our own time, standards of work have been revolutionized by such outstanding people as Gerhard Bersu, who worked in Germany, Switzerland, and Britain, and the Englishman Sir Mortimer WHEELER who, in a series of brilliant excavations ranging from Wales to India from the 1920s onwards, was able to demonstrate the value of careful, well organized excavation to all archaeologists. His pupils, such as Dame Kathleen Kenyon, have so propagated his standards that they are now regarded as the minimal acceptable level of work in many parts of the world.

Once he has selected a site for excavation, the archaeologist carefully collects together a team of people and the equipment they need to carry out the work of excavation at the site successfully. Although many of his helpers may have no particular skills, some of the team are specialists, and their number and variety will depend on the nature and location of the site he is to dig, and not least on his financial resources, for few archaeological projects are sufficiently well funded for the archaeologist to take with him all he would like. If he is working not far from his base, he may be able to call on the advice of certain specialists only as the need arises, rather than have them with him the whole time; alternatively, he may collect samples of materials (e.g., soil, charred grain) for them to work on in the laboratory instead of in the field. But whether or not specialists are available in the field, large numbers of samples, in addition to the artifacts that are found, are taken away from the site for further examination and analysis in the laboratory, once the excavation is finished.

Before the excavation actually begins, a careful survey of the surface configuration of the site is made, either on the ground or, increasingly nowadays, by AIR PHOTOGRAPHY. Many sites are also surveyed at this stage with scientific instruments, such as resistivity meters or proton magnetometers, to give an indication in advance of the kinds of features (walls, kilns, filled-in pits, and ditches) that lie buried (*see* SURVEYING).

Although excavation occupies a place in archaeology very similar to that of dissection in zoology, and is conducted with commensurate skill and care, it differs in one important respect. Archaeological sites differ from one another to a far greater extent than do individual members of a single species of animals; moreover, unlike animals, they cannot be replicated by breeding.

Therefore, once excavated, an ancient settlement cannot be re-examined by the archaeologist, and he thus cannot afford to make the same number of mistakes as a zoologist, who can usually obtain another specimen if necessary. Since the archaeologist can never start his excavation again, the options open to him are much more limited and he must therefore think far more carefully at every stage of his work as to how he should make the next move. (Since the detailed picture resulting from the excavation of an ancient site cannot thus be checked, archaeology is more prone than other disciplines to dishonesty, to the determined hoaxer or forger.) This state of affairs has naturally led to a constant re-examination of the ways in which archaeologists set about the task of excavation. Over the years a number of methods and techniques have been devised to extract the maximum amount of information from a site, and to conduct the excavation of different types of site.

Essentially, excavation proceeds by uncovering, recording in the three dimensions, and removing layers, deposits, and structures in the reverse order to which they accumulated and were laid down and built. Different layers and deposits in the ground are recognized by differences in the color, texture, and general character of the soil. According to circumstance, the soil may be carefully sifted by sieving through ever finer meshes (sometimes to a fineness of one millimeter) to recover the smallest remains (e.g., splinters of bone, seeds, and tiny artifacts such as microliths—very small stone tools) and by flotation—washing the soil so that seeds and other remains of lighter density than the soil float to the surface of a pan of water. Whereas the archaeologist makes use of these techniques and of such fine implements as camel-hair brushes and manual dental tools in excavation, he also utilizes coarser ones, from builders' pointing trowels, picks, shovels, and spades to mechanical earth removers like those utilized in freeway construction: his choice of tool varies according to the task confronting him at any particular moment.

Since the archaeologist is concerned with establishing the three-dimensional relationships of the components of a site, he constantly photographs his work and prepares plans and section drawings. "Section" is the technical term for the faces of the walls of archaeological trenches and of baulks (narrow walls of unexcavated ground) left across the excavation area to facilitate the study of the vertical relationships of the features (walls, filled-in pits, layers, floors, etc.) being excavated. He also keeps detailed records of the features he uncovers—their positions and stratigraphic relationships, their nature, and the artifacts and other remains that they contain. The finds and samples that are taken for laboratory examination and analysis are carefully stored and kept in separate containers (clearly labeled to indicate precisely where they were found).

The layout of the excavator's trenches depends on a number of factors, the two principal ones being the nature of the site itself, and whether or not total excavation is intended. Partial excavations are designed either to "sample" a site (i.e., as an exploratory exercise to discover what lies buried there), or to investigate a specific part of it, such as a temple or a group of artisans' houses within an ancient town. In sample excavations, the trenches will normally be few in number and quite small in size (only a few feet across). However, in the second kind of partial excavation, as in total excavation, the layout of the trenches depends in large measure on the size of the area under investigation, and on the surface and likely underground character of the site. If the surface is more or less level, then either a single very large trench is opened up, or a grid of smaller ones with baulks left between them. Round mounds (e.g., burial mounds) up to around 100 ft. (30 m) in diameter are normally excavated in segments like the slices of a cake, leaving a series of baulks radiating from the center.

Once the excavation is completed, there begins the arduous task of analysis of the recovered material and of the information recorded in the excavator's notebooks, plans, drawings, and photographs. This process generally takes far longer than the excavation itself, indeed often several years, and culminates in the publication of a report on the work.

**Experimental archaeology.** This is now recognized to be of considerable value in understanding certain aspects of the past, and is increasingly practiced by European archaeologists in an attempt to advance their knowledge of past conditions. One of the earliest examples was General Pitt-Rivers' observations of the rate and duration of ditch silting on his excavations at Cranborne Chase, Dorset, England, in the 19th century. There are now several more controlled experiments on the weathering of earthworks, which are producing quantified results on silting and stratigraphy. Another illuminating line of experiment has been with storage pits sunk into the ground in chalk and other subsoils: sealed pits may have been capable of storing grain for food for several years, though decay is accelerated each time a pit is opened. Other valuable experiments have been conducted in metalworking and housebuilding. It is harder to recreate and observe whole systems at work. Danish archaeologists provided useful data by practicing "slash and burn" agriculture in natural woodland in Jutland, and showed the improved yields resulting from the enrichment of poor soils by potash. Experimental prehistoric farms have been set up in England (e.g., at Butser in Hampshire) and Scandinavia, but it is hard to recreate accurately past environments, stock, and crops, and the pests and diseases which once plagued them, and in these aspects ethnographic studies may be of greater value.

**Faience.** The term applied by archaeologists to the kind of glazed frit used to make beads, usually tinted blue by the addition of copper minerals, which became common during the Early Bronze Age. It was very common in Egypt. Opinion is divided as to whether European finds (from Hungary to the British Isles) were locally made or represent imports from Egypt.

**Fara.** The site of the ancient Sumerian city of Shuruppak, in Southern Mesopotamia, excavated by Robert

KOLDEWEY and Walter ANDRAE (1902–3) and by Erich SCHMIDT (1931). The latest surviving occupation level dates to the first half of the 3rd millennium BC, and important tablets and seal impressions have been found which date to EARLY DYNASTIC periods II–III (also called *Fara Zeit* by the Germans). This site should not be confused with TELL FARA in Palestine.

**Farming.** *See* AGRICULTURE, EUROPE.

**Fell's cave.** A stratified cave in Patagonia, excavated in the 1930s. The deepest strata contained bones of extinct mammals that had been killed and eaten by men. Artifacts included "fish-tail" stemmed points. The site provided evidence of human occupation at the tip of South America by the end of the last continental glaciation, 9000–8000 BC.

**Fibula.** For 2,000 years, from *c.* 1200 BC, the fibula, a metal brooch which worked like a safety-pin, was the favorite European clothes fastener. It was often elaborately decorated and was sometimes inlaid with glass and semiprecious stones.

**Fiesole** (Faesulae). An Etruscan city near Florence, with important Roman remains. Largely built by Sulla in the 1st century BC, the city preserves traces of an Etruscan temple dating from the 3rd century BC.

**Figurines and fertility symbols, Prehistoric Europe.** Small figurines made of bone, wood, clay, and other materials occur throughout prehistory from the Upper Palaeolithic onwards, though they seem to be less common from the Bronze Age. The human figure is widely represented, usually in female form. Examples range from the Venus of Willendorf of the Palaeolithic of Central Europe, to the clay figurines of the Neolithic and Chalcolithic (*see* COPPER AGE, EUROPE) of Eastern Europe. Animals were also represented, and range from those carved in amber in the early Mesolithic of Scandinavia to the catlike clay heads of the VINČA CULTURE.

The interpretation of the meaning and function of these figurines is very difficult. The explicitly sexual features of Palaeolithic examples have often been linked with an interest in fertility, and Neolithic and Chalcolithic female figurines have been connected with the idea of a widespread cult of a universal "Mother Goddess," believed also to be shown in some Megalithic art (*see* MEGALITH). Though models of shrines are known from Chalcolithic Eastern Europe, a widespread unified system of beliefs is uncertain: diverse local traditions may be more plausible. Some figurines may only be children's dolls. More obvious fertility symbols are the carved phalli known from several sites, while in the Neolithic and Bronze Age rock carvings of Scandinavia and Italy rampant male humans and animals are a frequent theme, reflecting an understandable concern with fertility.

**Fire.** The use of fire was one of the major landmarks in man's adaptation to the cooler environments of the globe.

A limestone fertility figurine, *c.* 4 in. (10 cm) high, from Willendorf, Austria, dating from nearly 30,000 years ago.

It seems to have begun some 400,000 to 800,000 years ago in Europe or Asia. But ability to make fire efficiently and at will rather than merely catching it from natural sources may date from less than 200,000 years ago.

**Fishing.** *See* HUNTING AND GATHERING.

**Fission Track dating.** One of the newer and less familiar dating techniques, based on the breakdown of uranium. It involves counting the tracks left by electrons (or β-particles) emitted in the breakdown of Uranium 238. Volcanic rocks commonly contain uranium, and the number of tracks visible microscopically in the rock, relative to the amount of uranium, gives a date for the formation of the rock. It has proved useful in checking POTASSIUM-ARGON DATING at sites like that of OLDUVAI GORGE in Tanzania.

**Flake.** *See* STONE TECHNOLOGY.

**Flint.** Nodules of flint occur commonly as seams in the upper and middle chalk of Northwest Europe. Flint was one of the favorite raw materials of Stone Age man, because it was easy to chip and thus make tools. In the Neolithic period flint was mined and traded.

**Flotation.** During an excavation, items of interest are recovered in two ways: either by direct retrieval in the trench (spotted and picked up by the digger), or else by various mechanical means of sorting through the earth after it has been dug out. This usually involves some form of screening or sieving, but also other sorting procedures, depending on the kind of material sought. Objects of differing sizes and specific gravities fall at different rates, while some organic materials may actually float on certain liquids, and even on water.

One of the simplest ways of recovering seeds from the contents of a pit or house floor is to place a sample in water and skim off the floating fraction: it will often be found to contain carbonized grain or other seeds. This method is too haphazard for scientific use, however, and various machines have been devised which make use of upward currents of water and the presence of a frothing agent to assist the flotation of organic remains. In this way large amounts of earth can be scanned for the presence of evidence vitally important in the reconstruction of prehistoric and later subsistence.

Smaller samples may be taken to be searched for other remains, such as those of molluscs or beetles, both of which give valuable indications of contemporary environments. Paraffin is sometimes used in floating off delicate insect remains.

**Folsom.** A site in New Mexico where the remains of 23 extinct giant bison were found associated with distinctive fluted stone points, now known as Folsom points, in the BIG GAME HUNTING TRADITION of North America. At another site in New Mexico, Blackwater Draw, the Folsom layer has been dated to 8340 BC by radiocarbon. Folsom points are slightly different from the CLOVIS POINT: they are smaller, with their widest dimension near the middle rather than towards the base; the base is more concave than that of Clovis points, and the edges of Folsom points were retouched. The best-known site from which a Folsom type assemblage has been recovered is the Linenmeier site in Colorado. Other artifacts found there include unfluted projectile points, scrapers of various kinds, and core choppers.

**Food and drink industries.** Changes of scale and of hygiene standards have caused most pre-1920 food and drink factories either to close or to be modernized and enlarged out of all recognition, and archaeologists working in this field have a more than usually difficult task. The great Chicago meat-packing plants and stockyards are no more, although the entrance portico survives; the early milk-processing plants of Gail Borden and the canning factories of H. J. Heinz have been transformed or relocated; the 19th-century California salmon canneries have long since vanished. Local BREWERIES have been closed by the score as the movement towards centralization and standardization has gathered force. In many countries—Bulgaria and Australia are

good examples—wine is produced from large, highly mechanized vineyards and factory-type processing plants. A few items, however, have survived and are now cherished: Denmark's first commerical milk-processing factory (1882) at Ølgod has been restored, together with its original machinery; in France, the Espelosin wine museum, at Rochecorbon, is where such a museum should be, in the buildings of a fully productive vineyard; and in Leningrad, on the Moscow Prospekt, one can still find the early 19th-century slaughterhouse, an impressive building with three fine porches, each with a bronze oxhead in the center. The archaeologist's main work lies, however, with the relics of the small enterprises which were typical until World War I—the local bakeries, slaughterhouses, creameries, and canneries.

**Ford, James** (1911–68). An American archaeologist who conducted an important archaeological survey in the Virú valley of coastal Peru in the 1940s. His ceramic typology, seriation, and stratigraphic testing established the coastal archaeological sequence for the first time.

**Fortification, Greek and Roman.** The origins of fortification in the Greek and Roman world are to be sought in the massive defenses, themselves probably influenced by Eastern Mediterranean civilizations, at the major cities of the Greek Bronze Age. The defensible hilltops (ACROPOLIS) of ATHENS and TIRYNS and the whole of the city of MYCENAE were strongly walled. This tradition of settlement in and around a protected acropolis lasted well into the 8th and 7th centuries BC. In Italy, there was no comparable Bronze Age culture of the 2nd millennium BC, and the eventual Roman tradition of fortification began with Early Iron Age defenses of the Apennine and Villanovan cultures in the 10th and 9th centuries BC (see VILLANOVAN CULTURE).

In mainland Greece, from the 8th century BC onwards, there was at first little progress in defensive technique, other than patching up earlier Bronze Age defenses built of massive irregular blocks (the so-called "Cyclopean" style of masonry). It was only when parent cities in Greece sent out colonists to Asia Minor and Sicily that the new settlers were presented with the layout and siting of completely new cities, often in hostile surroundings. For the first time it became necessary to enclose the whole of the city, as at Byzantium and Syracuse, within rudimentary defenses which, despite the presence in those areas of civilizations, like the Phrygian and Carthaginian, with highly developed siegecraft, still relied heavily on simple walls and the maximum use of natural defenses.

The rise of the Persian Empire in the 7th century BC compelled first the cities of Asia Minor, then the island kingdoms, and finally those of mainland Greece to build adequate walls round the whole settlements. Such walls, by contrast with archaic defenses in the "Cyclopean" style, were usually built of carefully faced rectangular or polygonal stone blocks. Two-story towers were also employed, and gateways enfiladed.

The Peloponnesian Wars of the 5th century BC in Greece saw an increase in fortification, both in cities and in small outpost forts to control territorial possessions.

Wall circuits on Peloponnesian and Athenian sites were brought to a high peak of complexity with an increase in towers and other defensive features. At this time, too, more ambitious projects were undertaken, for example the "Long Walls" of Athens and Megara, which linked city to harbor.

Further development of defensive architecture in Greece after the 4th century BC came as a result of the advanced siege techniques employed by the Carthaginians in Sicily and the Macedonians in mainland Greece. Hellenistic fortifications of these later centuries began to include defensive features as countermeasures against the battering ram, siege tower, and catapult, and eventually enabled defenders not only to absorb attacks, but also to launch counterattacks with machines mounted on the walls or in towers similar to those traditionally used by a besieging army. With this complex series of defensive features, the most highly developed of Greek fortifications achieved a state of stalemate.

Roman defensive architecture stemmed from Etruscan and Greek elements. Etruscan cities in Italy were usually built on defensible hills, and probably had some form of walls in the 7th and 6th centuries BC, but the best-known Etruscan defenses are the terrace walls of VEII and the walls and tower of Luni, both of which belong to the 4th century BC.

Rome herself was invaded and sacked by Gallic tribesmen in 386 BC, and as a result a new defensive wall of expansive proportions (the so-called Servian Wall) was built of tufa blocks to unite the seven hills of the city as a single unit. The construction of this massive wall signaled the beginning of a phase of wall building among Italian towns, some of which received large extensive circuits (Cora, Coas), while others became smaller rectangular "castra" (OSTIA, Minturnae).

Development of this type of monumental fortification continued into the 1st century BC, with the increasing addition of new defensive features—arched gates, gatehouses, and provision of catapults mounted on the walls. Typical walls of this period are those of ALBA FUCENS, now built with rubble concrete, and replacing an earlier circuit.

With the advent of Augustus and Rome's acquisition of imperial territory, a military hand becomes far more evident upon the style of Roman fortifications. The standard form of Roman camp or fort was a rectangle within which each soldier had his regular place. When arranging new colonies for veteran soldiers, therefore, Augustus' architects often planned their new cities in the style of Roman forts, thus accentuating the prevalent fashion for rectangular town planning. Cities such as Aosta, Turin, and Ljubljana, lying in the areas newly acquired by Rome, still reflect the four-square nature of their original plan.

The construction of fortifications in more peaceful parts of the Roman world, except for purposes of prestige, came to an end with Augustus in AD 14. For the next 250 years, only cities in fringe provinces like Britain, or those otherwise near to the frontiers of the Roman world, could expect to be provided with walls. Military fortifications were concentrated instead on the frontiers of the empire, where the army kept strict control of traffic from their forts, whose rectangular shape is familiar in all parts of the empire.

The final phase of fortification came in the late 3rd and 4th centuries AD. Barbarians broke through the frontiers in many areas and threatened cities unwalled and unaccustomed to such harassment. Defenses were hastily constructed and new forts built. The new style of construction found the defended area of cities more constricted, and the walls themselves far more massive than before, with external towers and few, heavily defended, gates. Rome herself gained a new circuit of walls under Aurelian (AD 270–275): this was built in brick-faced concrete, and heightened by late 5th-century emperors. With this new style of wall, the majority of which had to be built in the Western part of the empire, many late Roman cities probably differed little in aspect from the strongly walled early medieval cities. Indeed, at cities such as Carcassone and Le Mans in France, the 4th-century Roman walls were used, with very little addition, until well into the medieval period. (*See also* HILLFORT.)

**Fort Ridgely.** A frontier post in Minnesota, established by the U.S. War Department in 1853 in its fight against the Sioux Indians. The site was soon abandoned, but because of its historical importance it was excavated from 1939 onwards in order to reconstruct some of the buildings. As well as much evidence of the type of farriery, tools, household utensils, and military articles in use, it also enabled the accurate dating of local Indian sites. For instance, the material which immediately preceded white occupation at the fort was found to be of the same type as that recovered from undated burial mounds in the vicinity. Evidence was also found at Fort Ridgely to show that, before the arrival of the white man in the area, the Indians were using trade flintlock guns at the same time as they were making stone arrowheads.

**Forum.** The central area in a Roman town, sited at the crossing point of the two main roads, called *cardo* and *decumanus*, on which the street system was always aligned. The open place was surrounded by public buildings of all sorts—temples, basilicas, the market (*macellum*), the senate house, shops, triumphal arches, and columns. In Rome, the Forum was the central point from the time of the republic onwards and various emperors built fora of their own: Caesar, Augustus, Vespasian, Nerva, and Trajan, whose forum was massively planned and laid out symmetrically. Most provincial fora included a temple (sometimes the CAPITOLIUM), a peristyle courtyard, a BASILICA, and possibly a CURIA, where the town council met.

**Franks.** A loose confederacy of small tribes which grew up during the first two centuries AD between the Rivers Weser and Rhine. Many settled within the Roman Empire and often served as federate troops in the Roman army policing the frontier. From the earliest Frankish cemeteries, such as Vermand, Haillot, and Eprave, the remains chronicle the growth of the Franks during the

A garnet brooch from the grave of Queen Arnegunde at St. Denis, near Paris.

late 4th to 6th century AD, from Romanized federates to an important barbarian people who expanded into Gaul and defeated the Roman ruler Syagrius in AD 486, prior to establishing a Frankish kingdom. Eventually the Franks and surviving Gallo-Romans fused into a unified culture under the Merovingians in the 6th century AD.

Most of the early Frankish remains are Roman in character, such as the *francisca* or throwing ax. Distinctive *cloisonné* jewelry developed in the early 6th century, in particular bird and fish brooches and later disc brooches reminiscent of types found in Anglo-Saxon England. At Tournai, the richly furnished burial of the Frankish King Childeric (d. AD 482) was unearthed in 1653. The finds included gold and garnet inlaid swords, gold buckles, belt mounts, a heavy gold torc (neck ring), and a purse with 100 gold coins. Most have been lost, except for a cast of his ring, some sword mounts, and some cicada mounts from his robe, and only exist as drawings.

The Franks adopted Christianity under Clovis, who was probably converted in AD 503. A gold chalice and portable altar from Gourdon with colored inlay which combines both barbarian and Classical taste, survive from his reign. A double cathedral at Trier is known from excavations, and the Baptistry of St. Jean at Poitiers, a 5th-century building with alterations from the 7th century, is still extant. A pair of graves of a woman and a young boy, presumably members of the royal house, were unearthed in 1959 in Cologne Cathedral. Both dated from the mid-6th century AD, and were richly furnished. The woman's grave included a rich array of gold jewelry, and that of the boy contained full warrior's equipment. At St. Denis, near Paris, the grave of Queen Arnegunde, wife of Chlotar I (AD 558–561), has been discovered. The queen probably died *c*. AD 570, and in

her grave furnishings was a ring inscribed with her name, a pair of buckles, and some strap ends decorated with interlaced ornament.

Relatively little work has been done on Frankish settlements, but an important Merovingian village was excavated at Brebières, near Douai, between 1965 and 1968, dating from the 6th and 7th centuries AD. The dwellings were all sunken-floor huts, and the copious finds included an unusual amount of GLASS. After the 6th century AD, documentary evidence for the Franks is fuller, and archaeology less important, though outside influences on the developing Merovingian world can be traced through finds.

The last of the Frankish rulers was Pepin, who was succeeded at the end of the 8th century by Charlemagne, the founder of the Carolingian Empire (*see* CAROLINGIANS).

**Fraser River.** The archaeology of the Fraser River delta in British Columbia, Canada, provides the sequence for the early prehistory of the NORTHWEST COAST TRADITION. Three periods have been identified: Early, 1000 BC–AD 1; Intermediate, AD 1–1250; and Late from 1250 to the present day. The Locarno Beach phase of the Early Period saw the hunting of sea mammals established as the major means of subsistence: harpoon points, of bone or antler, and ground slate, rather than flaked stone, have been found. Small adzes and chisels were made of nephrite, but there were no large woodworking implements. It may be that skin boats, rather than wooden ones, were used at this point. The Northwest Coast feature of three-dimensional sculpture was already present, as demonstrated by the recovery of small stone labrets and a single throwing-stick hook in the form of a human head. In the Marpole phase, 300 BC–AD 400, of the Intermediate Period this assemblage was refined and added to. Flaked stone points became more common and better made, and ground stone implements, such as crescent-shaped knives, were more finely formed. The discovery of heavy tools for woodworking, such as large stone adzes and hammers, suggests that dugout canoes were made. Plank houses, of the type known from the ethnographical record, were probably erected in the village, which now covered several acres. The most significant development in the Marpole phase was the production of stone sculpture, particularly in the form of stone bowls held by seated figures. Made of steatite or sandstone, the heads were already carved in characteristic Northwest Coast style, with raised eyebrows and incised eyes. These may have been used in shamans' rituals, or else for initiation ceremonies.

**Frauds.** Artifacts of almost every archaeological period have been copied by forgers and claimed as genuine. The list of frauds ranges from Palaeolithic decorated bone plaques to Bronze Age goldwork and Iron Age coins. Art was faked from at least the later Middle Ages, and coins and fossils began to be copied from the 18th century onwards. The case of Piltdown man was a celebrated fraud from the earlier part of this century: the skull was claimed to be an early hominid fossil, but it is now known to consist of the jaw of a modern orangutang and the cranium of a modern man.

A more recent fraud was the faking of Middle Palaeolithic flint tools in the Netherlands. Most copies are of types already well known, but more ambitious frauds have sought to create new types of object or artifact, as in the Piltdown case. The falsification of whole sites has been much rarer, because of the greater difficulties, but has nonetheless been tried: a cave in the Dordogne region of France may be painted with wholly spurious "Palaeolithic" art; a German archaeologist faked a new type of Neolithic cremation grave in the Wetterau in the early years of the century; while the mystery of the site of Glozel in Southern France is still not fully unraveled. The motives of forgers are not only commercial: some try to win recognition for its own sake while others, like the 19th-century eccentric "Fossil Willy" or "Flint Jack," are inspired by a mischievous desire to fool the expert. Scientific aids can now be combined with archaeological expertise to make the detection of frauds easier (*see* SCIENCE IN ARCHAEOLOGY).

**Fréjus** (Forum Iuli). A market town on the Gallic Mediterranean coast, founded by Caesar. Remains of the city walls, AMPHITHEATER, and harbor can still be seen.

**Fuegian tradition.** A coastal tradition of the Alacaluf tribes, often called the Shell Knife culture, which existed in Tierra del Fuego from *c.* 2000 BC to historic times.

**Funerary monuments, Greek and Roman.** The most important cult monuments which survive from the Aegean Bronze Age are the graves. These took several forms—the shaft graves of MYCENAE of the 16th century BC, the chamber tomb, probably covered by a tumulus of earth, and the THOLOS-type "beehive tomb," used for royal burials. All such inhumation (non-cremation) burials were accompanied by grave goods, often of astonishing richness.

From the 11th century BC onwards, graves were less monumental in style, and were either cremation or inhumation burials with a tumulus heaped over them. From the large Dipylon cemetery at Athens, which lay just outside the city and lined one of the principal routes to it, come the earliest graves of the archaic period, which contained large pots of geometric style. From the 7th century BC onwards, the site of a grave was marked with a stone (STELE). At first these were plain, then they began to bear an idealized representation of the dead person and perhaps the personification of a protective deity. Propertied families might have their own grave plot enclosed with walls and many types of stelae. Demetrius of Phaleron (317–307 BC) banned the use of grave reliefs and thereby brought the Attic series of elaborately carved reliefs to an end: later graves were marked by a simple stone.

Hellenistic grave monuments, however, continued to be produced: they often borrowed themes and forms from temple architecture, as for example the Mausoleum at HALICARNASSUS. From the early 3rd century BC, the richest graves had a forechamber with a temple-like façade, and throughout the period there was a mixture of tumuli, underground chambers, rockcut tombs, and façades, the complete repertoire of which was taken over by the Romans.

Etruscan cemeteries lay in isolated areas round the towns, and different areas produced very different types of tombs. The grave was thought of as the home of the dead, and reflected the commonest house types of the Etruscan period: the ceilings were decked out as roofs and painted scenes recall the everyday life of the dead person (*see* PAINTING).

Roman burial practice took over both Hellenistic and Etruscan forms—rockcut tombs, sometimes with ornamental façades, and occasionally a family tomb containing several sarcophagi. TUMULUS graves, probably with Etruscan antecedents, were also used, and mausoleums, the tholos type of grave monument, but on a smaller scale than Mausolus' original. Augustus had a tumulus for his family grave, and this type of tomb was often crowned with a tholos to give it added prominence.

Cemeteries were common along the roads leading into cities in both Greece and Rome, and the collections of grave monuments—from elaborate tombs to simple grave slabs bearing a crudely figured relief—must have stretched, as they do between Rome and Beneventum along the Via Appia, for quite some distance. At Rome the so-called Columbarium was a communal cemetery, where urns containing cremated remains could be lodged in niches. In the 2nd century AD there was a general change of fashion from cremation to inhumation, and the CATACOMBS (grave chambers with niches for bodies and family groups) were cut out to take a large number of burials.

**Funnel-necked Beaker culture.** A complex culture which represents the first agriculturalists in Scandinavia and the North European plain, appearing from 3500 BC onwards to the north of the earlier occupied loess-lands of Central Europe. It is named after its characteristic pottery, which is often found in megalithic tombs in Northern Germany (*see* MEGALITH).

**Fustát.** The old city of Cairo, founded in AD 641, and burnt to the ground in 1168. It was first excavated between 1912 and 1925 by the Islamic Museum in Cairo, which concentrated on the area east of the Mosque of 'Amr. Between 1930 and 1964 various Egyptian Islamic scholars worked on the site, mainly in the area between the earlier excavations and the Mosque of 'Amr. The present series of excavations began in 1964, and has produced a great deal of important information about the way Fustát was laid out, the relationships between industrial and housing areas of the city, and the construction and function of water supplies and sanitation systems. Careful excavation of the low levels of this much disturbed site and of the numerous pits has offered more reliable dating for a wider range of artifacts than had hitherto been possible, including considerable quantities of GLASS and very early Islamic pottery types. Chinese sherds have also been recovered. The most notable find so far is the earliest datable piece of luster glass (AD 773).

**Gallery grave.** A generic term for megalithic monuments with a long narrow rectangular chamber, and a short antechamber at the end or at the side. Some may also have been covered with mounds. They belong to the later part of the Neolithic period in Western Europe, and many contain multiple burials.

**Gallinazo.** A pottery style and "culture" of the first phase of the EARLY INTERMEDIATE PERIOD from 200 BC to AD 200, found on the North Central coast of Peru. The pottery features resist (i.e. negative) painting.

**Garagay.** An INITIAL PERIOD site occupied into the EARLY HORIZON Period, located near Lima airport, Peru. The site is of the U-shaped ceremonial formation common in this period. On the central mound, a sunken plaza is surrounded on three sides by platforms, which on the Southeast side contain a series of pits for offerings. The central mound was built in three consecutive phases, estimated to be between *c.* 1800 and 300 BC. CHAVIN-like clay figurines, painted in several colors, and pottery are among the artifacts excavated.

**Gasworks.** The construction during the 1950s and 1960s of national and international grid systems to supply natural gas involved the closure of hundreds of local gasworks and the demolition of most of their buildings, including the retort houses. A high proportion of the gasholders, however, have survived, since they still have a function, and these are well worth studying and dating. The earliest surviving gasholder (*c.* 1830) is at Fulham, London, England. Point Breeze Works (1854), Philadelphia, Penn., United States, which is still in use, preserves an exceptional proportion of a 19th-century gasworks. The estate gasworks (1832) at Petworth, England, is a remarkably complete survival of a private plant.

**Gathering.** *See* HUNTING AND GATHERING.

**Gaul** (Gallia). A Roman province formed by present-day France and parts of Germany and Switzerland. Before Caesar, Roman influence was confined to the Mediterranean coastal strip, with a few native settlements (e.g., Glanum), but after the conquests of Caesar in the Northern part, and the development by Augustus of the Southern area, many new cities and colonies were founded. Gaul contained many Roman cities, among the best known of which are Nîmes, AUTUN, ARLES, ORANGE, TRIER, and FRÉJUS. But most provincial towns in France lie on the site of a Roman predecessor, and there are remains at Le Mans, Senlis, Beauvais, and Périgueux.

**Gauls.** *See* CELTS.

**Gaviota.** The final preceramic phase, 2000–1750 BC, of the Central Peruvian coast. It features a sedentary agricultural village life and the first construction of large ceremonial centers.

**Gaza.** *See* TELL EL AJJUL.

**Gela.** A Cretan and Rhodian colony on the coast of Sicily, founded *c.* 690 BC.

**Gems.** Modern usage employs the term "gemstone" for a deeply engraved semiprecious or precious stone, used to give an impression to seals, but precious stones were also common in antiquity as ornaments and charms. Engraved stones (intaglios) are first found in the Middle Minoan period in CRETE, but the technique of working stones fell out of use until the 7th century BC. In the 6th century BC, the "scarab" form of seal was introduced from Egypt, and the form (with a rounded beetle-type back) was developed into the Classical Greek gemstone technique. Roman gems were usually flat stones to be mounted in a ring, and their engravings show portraits of a wide variety of mythological scenes. The most popular stones were quartzes—agate, carnelian, jasper, and sard. For jewelry itself, the most popular stones were semiprecious—garnets, amethysts and lapis lazuli—but emeralds and sapphires were known, as was JADE in the Far East. Paste and glass imitations were common. (*See also* JEWELRY, EUROPE.)

**Geological dating.** *See* DATING IN ARCHAEOLOGY; GEOLOGY AND ARCHAEOLOGY.

**Geology and Archaeology.** Geology is closely related to archaeology in several ways. An understanding of the timescale over which man developed is mainly provided by geology. The primates (monkeys, lemurs, and apes, as well as man) emerged over the last 70 million years (the Cenozoic era), while man himself seems to have evolved during the Pleistocene period, the last 2 million years or so of geological time.

A variety of methods are used by geologists to construct their timescale. STRATIGRAPHY involves tracing layers of a particular rock type and recording the order of superposition of these layers. Geologists also try to understand the mode of deposition. The correlation of different stratigraphic columns is traditionally done by the use of fossils.

The newer method, which has greatly strengthened earlier conclusions about the geological sequence, is absolute dating. This involves dating the layers, or at least samples from them, in years. Most of these methods are based on the radioactive breakdown of isotopes. Pioneer dating used the long lived isotopes Uranium 235 and Uranium 238. Today, by far the most valuable method is POTASSIUM-ARGON DATING, which measures the progress of the breakdown of radioactive potassium, which is present in most volcanic rocks, into argon. For very recent periods (the last 50,000 years) the breakdown of radiocarbon can be used (*see* RADIOCARBON DATING).

An important new discovery has been that not only is contemporary magnetism recorded in volcanic and other rocks, but that at some periods in the past the earth's magnetic field has been completely reversed (*see* MAGNETIC REVERSALS). This seems to have happened at least eight times in the past 4 million years, a discovery that has proved useful in correlating different sequences of time.

A typical Geometric neck-amphora of the second half of the 8th century BC, from Athens.

**Geometric.** An archaeological term generally used to describe the style of the earliest period of Greek art, current between 1100 and 700 BC. It is derived from the triangular, circular, meander, and otherwise linear decoration on Greek pottery of this period.

**Gerasa** (Jerash). Founded by the Seleucids, Gerasa became a major Roman city in Judea. There are extensive remains of the city's layout: a colonnaded street, FORUM, STADIUM, triumphal arch, THEATER, temples to Athena and Zeus, and several early Christian churches.

**Geyre** (Aphrodisias). A Carian and Roman city in Asia Minor. Remains survive of a THEATER, a temple dedicated to Aphrodite, an ODEUM, STADIUM, BATHS, a porticus, and late Roman defenses.

**Gezer.** A Biblical city situated at Tell Jazar, west of Jerusalem. Occupation dates back to the 4th millennium BC. The Early Bronze period II-IV settlement was walled. The city was particularly prosperous during the 2nd millennium BC; it is mentioned in Egyptian texts from the 15th century BC onwards, and continued to be inhabited until Crusader times. (*See also* SYRIA–PALESTINE.)

**Ghana.** The ancient kingdom of Ghana, in Africa, was centered on the site of Kumbi Saleh, which lies some 200 mi. (322 km) north of Bamako in the modern republic of Mali. From the period between AD 500 and 1200, Ghana monopolized the gold trade from West Africa to Europe. Strategically situated at the Southern end of the trans-Saharan caravan routes and the North-ern end of the trading routes from the gold-producing areas of West Africa, Ghana was the first of the several West African trading states to exploit successfully the gold monopoly. In exchange for gold, Ghana received salt, and North African and European trade goods.

Although excavations have been carried out at Kumbi Saleh, most of the information concerning ancient Ghana comes from the writings of North African and other Arabic writers. Al Fazari, writing soon after AD 800 talks of the "land of gold," and by AD 830 Al Kwarizimi had shown the position of Ghana on his map. It is, however, the work of Al Bakri of Cordoba, writing in AD 1067, who is the source of most of our information. Al Bakri did not himself visit Ghana but collected information from many of the traders who did. He describes how the king and his court lived in a town built of traditional materials, whereas the more successful Muslim traders built in stone on an adjacent site. The traders were assured of safety and hospitality provided they observed the laws of, and paid taxes to, the king of Ghana. Kumbi Saleh was a city of some 15,000 people and Al Bakri graphically describes the pomp and circumstance of the royal court, the tax structure of the kingdom, and the size and power of the army, which numbered "200,000 in the field, more than 40,000 of them being armed with bows and arrows." The collapse of the Ghana Empire at the beginning of the 13th century was, like that of most other empires, due to outgrowing its own strength. Power and wealth passed to the successor kingdom of Mali.

A visitor to the site of Kumbi Saleh today sees little of the former glory of the capital. The stone-built town of the Muslim traders consists of a number of low mounds and the town of the king and court has left no visible trace and has yet to be precisely located. Excavations carried out on the low mounds showed the remains of a densely inhabited and partially stone-built town of Mediterranean design. The houses were of two stories with warehouses on the ground floor and living quarters above. Many spindle whorls were found and imported glassware and fine pottery were recovered.

**Ghassul.** A Chalcolithic site in the Jordan valley, with four main occupation levels. The site has given its name to the late 4th-millennium BC culture of Palestine.

**Ghazna.** An Islamic site in Afghanistan, excavated in 1957 and 1958. The most important buildings uncovered were the palace and the so-called "house of lusters." The palace, founded during the reign of either Ibrāhīm (AD 1059–1099) or his son Mas'ūd (1099–1115) and finally destroyed by the Mongols, followed the traditional Iranian plan. In the "house of lusters" much luster-painted pottery was found. Ghazna is also important for the relief sculptures bearing vegetal and, more unusually, figural designs, and for the wealth of ceramics, shedding light on the pottery industry of Eastern Islam during the Ghaznavid and Ghurid periods.

**Ghost towns.** The relics of the 19th-century gold and silver booms in the American and Canadian West. They can be divided into four groups: first, mining towns, like

Tombstone, Ariz., and Jacksonville, Ore., which started as mining camps, but which have been kept alive by the introduction of new industries. They usually contain some of the original buildings. Second, there are partly ghost towns, such as Telluride, Colo., where many of the early buildings survive unoccupied, although part of the town is inhabited and still earns a living from mining; third, mining towns which are true ghosts, completely deserted, although buildings still line their streets. Bodie, Calif., and Gold Road, Ariz., are of this type. Fourth, there are mining towns, such as Beartown, Mont., and Silver Reef, Ut., which have disappeared and whose sites only remain.

**Glaciation.** *See* ICE AGE.

**Glanum** (St. Rémy de Provence). A settlement in Southern Gaul, originally founded by the Greek colonists of Marseilles. Remains of houses and, possibly, a BOULEUTERION of the 2nd century BC have been excavated. Of the later Roman town, little remains apart from a truncated monumental arch and a mausoleum, perhaps dating from the mid-1st century BC.

**Glass.** It would appear that glass was a Mesopotamian invention, for the scarcity of precious stones led to the development of the technique of glazing stones, especially steatite, as early as the 4th millennium BC. Kassite glass imitations of LAPIS LAZULI cylinder SEALS appear from the 14th century BC onwards, together with multicolored glass vessels from MESOPOTAMIA. Glass rods decorated temple doors at CHOGA ZAMBIL (13th century BC).

*Egyptian, Greek, and Roman.* Glass was known and used in Egypt, whence it passed to Bronze Age Crete. Egypt remained an important center for production throughout the Classical Greek and Roman periods, but Asia Minor and Southern Gaul also shared the market. Early vessels were molded, but the invention of glass blowing in the 1st century BC made glass vessels much cheaper, and local centers of production grew up. There was still a market, however, for luxury goods: millefiori bowls, made of polychrome glass, and layered glass, where the outer layer is carved like a cameo (e.g., the Portland Vase) or with complex and intricate layered patterns (so-called *diatrete* glass).

*Medieval.* The traditions of Roman glassmaking continued in Northern Europe during and after the barbarian migrations. Roman-style soda-lime glass was produced in the main glassmaking centers of the Rhineland and Northern Gaul until at least the 9th century AD. The range of forms can be established from pagan graves, at first in many parts of Northern Europe, later mainly in Scandinavia. The forms of glass vessels changed as a result of barbarian taste. Drinking vessels such as palm cups, stemmed beakers, drinking horns, bell, bag, and claw beakers (the last named after the applied "claws" on the sides of the vessels) predominated. Decoration tended to be simple, notably trailing or simple molding. In the 10th century AD the alkali was increasingly potash from wood ash, rather than soda lime. In Italy, where

more ambitious decorative methods such as cutting, engraving, and gilding or painting were sometimes used, glass production continued virtually unbroken from Roman times until the growth of the Venetian glass industry. At Torcello, near Venice, a 6th–7th-century glassworks excavated in 1961–62 showed that furnace design and the method of operation remained identical from Roman to medieval times. The Venetian glass industry probably evolved in the late 10th century, though no glass can be ascribed to Venice with any certainty before the 14th century. In the late 15th century Venetian glass grew to prominence, often richly decorated with trailing, gilding, and enameling. Plain glass was also produced. Venetian products apparently reached the Low Countries and England by the late 14th century. From the 10th century, vessel glass is rarely found on excavated sites in Northern Europe, glass production apparently being concentrated on windows, both "clear" and colored. From the 12th century, window glass became increasingly popular in churches, castles, palaces, and the homes of the rich. Most vessel glass in Northwestern Europe was locally made, in secular and monastic workshops, and is occasionally found in excavations. From the 5th century onwards some glass was imported into Northwestern Europe from the East—there is glass from Coptic Egypt at Tintagel in England, for example—and imports include some Islamic vessels.

In the Near East glass production continued in Egypt, Syria-Palestine, Iraq, and Iran in the post-Roman period. The Roman type of soda lime glass continued up to the 7th century AD, mainly in bluish-green, though some new forms appeared. Decoration consisted of trailing, mold-blown patterns, cutting, and engraving. In the Sassanian world facet and relief cutting of colorless glass was frequent. After the Arab Conquest of the 7th and 8th centuries AD, new techniques appeared, notably the common use of applied bosses and trails, often coupled with modeling, particularly on vessels with animal shapes. Shapes of vessels changed, glass vessels being made less for the kitchen and dinner table and more for ceremonial and personal use. During the 9th and 10th centuries, Iraq and Iran became famous for their fine cut glass. Luster painting was employed in Egypt from the 6th century, while gilding and enameling became popular in the Islamic world from the 12th century. Islamic glasses with both gilding and enameling were produced in the 13th and 14th centuries, and are regarded as the finest of their kind ever produced. Enameled glass ceased to be produced in Syria and Egypt soon after 1400, and Islamic glass production went into decline.

*Industrial.* In general, the history of glass objects has been well documented by historians and archaeologists, but the history of glass as a building material has been covered very inadequately. The two great world museums of glass, the Corning Museum in New York and Pilkington's Museum of Glass at St. Helen's, England, focus on collectors' glass. On-site factory evidence of early sheet-glass manufacture is very scanty. At the Ravenhead glassworks, St. Helen's, two bays of the original 1773 casting hall survive, with traces of what may have been annealing furnaces, but most of the glass-manufacturing monuments throughout the world, like the Catcliffe glass cone near Sheffield, England, relate to the production of bottles, glasses, and ornaments. The archaeologist's chief source of information is buildings, e.g., in England, the Palm House at Kew (1844–46), and the east and south fronts (1689–1702) of Hampton Court Palace, with their original crown-glass; and, in Italy, the glass-roofed shopping arcade (1865) in Milan.

**Globular amphora culture.** This appeared during the late 3rd millennium BC, when the eastern wing of the European FUNNEL-NECKED BEAKER CULTURE became differentiated from the western part. It is especially characterized by individual burials in stone cists, accompanied by a standardized form of vessel described as a "globular amphora," since it probably contained an offering of drink.

**Glottochronology.** The study of language groups in order to determine the absolute dating of the moment of division between subgroups. This provides archaeologists with approximate dates for the origination of subcultures diverging from each other. For instance, in Alaska the great difference between the Aleut language and other Eskimo languages is thought to have been a result of the cultural isolation of the Aleuts from the 3rd millennium BC onwards.

**Gold.**
*Europe.* Gold was much prized in antiquity, as today, both for its appearance and for its property of remaining untarnished. Large quantities of alluvial gold had accumulated in rivers draining gold-rich regions, and it was not technologically difficult to obtain—though relatively restricted in its occurrence. As in more recent times, Transylvania and Ireland were among the most important source areas.

Gold is, in fact, a rather easy metal to work in comparison with copper and, because of its inertness, it did not have to be smelted from ores. It is highly malleable and can be made into a wide variety of shapes by hammering, as well as being beaten into gold foil which could be used to cover a core of other materials. Patterns could then be produced upon it by incision, either with a simple tracer to score straight lines or by a rocker to produce curves. Such uses were common in the Bronze Age: for instance, in the crescentic collars known as *lunulae* from Early Bronze Age Ireland.

More complex ornaments could be produced by melting: pure gold melts at a similar temperature to copper, but a gold/copper alloy melts at nearly 200° below either. This allows fine wire or small droplets of gold to be soldered onto a backplate, producing filigree and granulation work. The wire drawing might be achieved through different shapes of perforation, thus giving decorative cross sections: or the wire itself might be twisted. These more complex operations were chiefly developed in the specialist workshops associated with palaces or courts; and the workmanship of objects discovered by Heinrich SCHLIEMANN at TROY show the achievements of the Bronze Age smiths.

*Near East.* The most probable sources for gold in the ancient Near East would have been Egypt, an Eastern source which may have been situated in Southeastern Iran, and alluvial gold from Anatolia (especially Lydia, Cilicia, Armenia, and Transcaucasia). Electrum, an alloy of gold and silver, occurs frequently in the Royal Tombs at UR.

*Mesoamerica.* While fabulous tales of gold of the Indies and the search for it were an important motive for the Conquest of Mexico, it was only in the Postclassic Period that the working of gold, and indeed any metal, finally reached Mesoamerica from Colombia, Ecuador, and Peru. The concept and techniques of metallurgy probably came partly through Panama and Costa Rica, and partly via coastal trade up the Western shore of Mexico to the TARASCANS.

The Mixtecs were undoubtedly the best Mesoamerican goldworkers, and the most famous hoard of Precolumbian gold was discovered in Tomb 7 at MONTE ALBAN, where MIXTEC ornaments and jewelry of all kinds, made by the CIRE PERDU (or "lost wax") technique, were found with other grave goods. Much of the exquisite Postclassic Aztec goldworks taken by Cortez were manufactured by skilled Mixtec craftsmen. Large gold discs with *repoussé* designs, illustrating the conquest of the MAYA on the Yucatan by the TOLTECS, have also been dredged from the CENOTE of Sacrifice at CHICHEN ITZA.

**Gold mining, Industrial.** The industrial archaeology of gold mining is widespread in North, South, and Central America, South Africa, Australia, and the Soviet Union. Only in the United States, Canada, and Australia, however, has any considerable amount of archaeological work been carried out at gold-mining sites, with a view to safeguarding and interpreting this part of the national heritage. The available material is often extensive. At Skagway, Alaska, a goldrush town of the 1890s, the Historic District preserves 100 buildings of the boom period; and in the Dawson area of Y.T., Canada, there is a 70-mi. (113 km) system of pipes, ditches, and flumes, constructed in 1907 to provide a water supply for the gold mines. The Western United States contains an abundance of 19th-century buildings and other evidence of the old diggings, in various stages of decrepitude.

**Gordion** (or Gordium). The capital of the kingdom of PHRYGIA in Western Anatolia, situated at a crossing of the River Sangarius (Sankarya). It was excavated at the beginning of the century, and again by an American team from 1949 onwards. On the city mound a monumental gateway, palaces on the MEGARON plan, houses, and fortifications of the 8th century BC have been brought to light. The burial tumuli (mounds) surrounding the site have also been investigated. They date from the 8th to the mid-6th century BC, and the dead were buried in a wooden chamber covered with stones and earth. The largest is about 984 ft. (300 m) in diameter and 174 ft. (53 m) high, and the burial chamber was found intact and well preserved. It contained 9 tables, 2 screens, 3 bronze cauldrons, 166 smaller bronze vessels, and 145 fibulae (brooches), and it has been ascribed to King

Midas, who committed suicide in 696 BC, at the time of the Cimmerian invasion.

**Gortyn.** The most important city of Classical Greek and Roman CRETE. Paramount among finds from the extensive excavations is the law code, an inscription dating to *c.* 450 BC, but which embodies many older laws and provides a prime source for the study of legal rights in the pre-Hellenistic Greek age.

**Gournia.** A small Minoan settlement in CRETE, with remains of the civilian town and a palace at its center. It contains two narrow curved streets, many small houses, and an open square, south of the palace.

**Gravettian.** The name proposed by Garrod in 1938 to replace Breuil's later AURIGNACIAN stage of the Upper Palaeolithic in Europe, of which Gravette points were a typical feature. French workers now normally use the term Later Perigordian for this group of cultures of 20,000 to 25,000 BC. Cultures of Central and Eastern Europe of the same time and later have sometimes been grouped as East Gravettian, but are often now regarded as separate culture groups.

**Great Silla Dynasty.** The first unification of the Korean peninsula under a single rule (AD 668–935). Buddhism flourished and the archaeological remains include Buddhist temples. Simultaneously, the size of burials diminished from large mounds to small tombs with a stone square chamber, or simply an urn containing ashes in the Buddhist fashion. The T'ANG DYNASTY of China exerted considerable influence; for example, the plan of the capital, Kyong-ju, was copied from that of the T'ang Dynasty capital CH'ANG-AN.

**Great Tombs period** (or Kofun). This Japanese period (4th–7th century AD), is known for the round tombs covered by a mound, with a square platform added to the side making a keyhole shape. Towards the end of the period such tombs were very large; typically, each was surrounded by a moat, and earthenware figures and models (Haniwa) were placed in a series of concentric rings around the tomb. Inside the tomb was a chamber of stone slabs, probably adopted from the CIST TOMB of Northeast Asia. The elaborate burial goods included bronze mirrors, long swords of Chinese type, and, during a brief period, fine polished stone ornaments, including MAGATAMA. The pottery buried was the high-fired SUE WARE. Few habitation sites of this period have been excavated, so the way of life has to be conjectured mainly from the tomb models.

**Greece, archaeology of.**
*Prehistoric.* For the Neolithic period in Greece (*c.* 6000–3000 BC), the main archaeological evidence comes from the Sesklo culture of Thessaly, with its undefended hilltop settlement sites. These have round or rectangular huts and the megaron type of house makes its first appearance (*see* HOUSE, EUROPE).

In the sub-Neolithic period (*c.* 2900–2500 BC), the key find-site is Dimini, also in Thessaly, where new pottery types and decorations suggest a clear break from the Sesklo culture. Sporadic finds of bronze and gold suggest the ending of the Neolithic, which came properly with the Early Helladic, from 2500 to *c.* 1900 BC.

The Early Helladic period, divided into three separate periods, is characterized by new influences from Anatolia, which brought copper and bronze, and trading links with Eastern civilizations. Settlements could be sizable, and were sometimes defended (e.g., those at Aegina and Lerna). Houses were rectangular or had curved sides: at TIRYNS, a strong round tower suggests a ruler's fortified house. The THOLOS type of tomb makes its first appearance.

The Middle Helladic period (1900–1600 BC) is a short one. Invaders, who were the precursors of the Mycenaean Greeks, destroyed Early Helladic settlements, and gained control over almost the whole of the Greek mainland. Most of the settlement sites remained those of the Early Helladic period, but house plans and pottery types differ considerably from those of the earlier culture. A period of settled prosperity, however, allowed the gradual development and flowering of the mainland Greek Mycenaean civilization, in the shadow of the Minoan civilization in Crete.

*Minoan Civilization.* The Early Minoan period in Crete, running roughly parallel to the Early Helladic period on the mainland (*c.* 2600–2000 BC) saw the beginning of trade and contact with the East, particularly with Anatolia and Egypt. Crete's position on the natural route between Greece and the East made her the first point of contact for new ideas and objects.

It was not until the Middle Minoan period (2000–1700 BC) that Cretan civilization flowered, with the establishment of palaces for rulers at KNOSSOS and PHAESTUS and settlements round them. Through trade and commerce, there were widespread contacts with Egypt and the Greek mainland; it is even possible that at this time parts of the Greek mainland were dependencies of Crete.

In the second palace period, which lasted from the latest part of the Middle Minoan until the Late Minoan II period (1700–1400 BC), the first known script appeared—LINEAR A (17th century BC). Then followed the expansion of the city of Knossos (at its greatest, with perhaps 50,000 inhabitants), and the development of several palaces and towns, the most famous of which are Phaestus, MALLIA, and GOURNIA. From the 16th century BC onwards, the Minoans were faced with the developing power of mainland Greece and the Mycenaean civilization, and contacts were established between them on islands like THERA, lying between the two.

The 15th century BC saw the first Mycenaean influences on Crete, with the arrival of the second script, LINEAR B, an import from the mainland. This apparently followed the destruction of the palace of Knossos, *c.* 1500 BC, which may have been the result of an earthquake at Thera. However, occupation of Knossos is attested until *c.* 1375 BC.

*Mycenaean Civilization.* The flourishing period of Bronze Age civilization in mainland Greece came in the Late Helladic period (divided into periods I, II, and III),

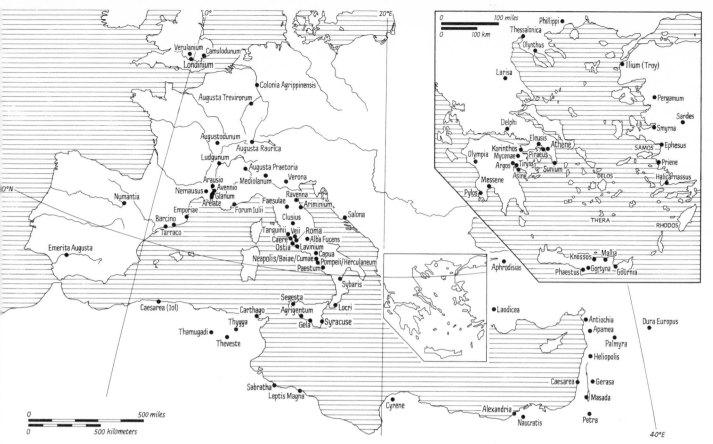

Map of the ancient Greek and Roman world.

beginning c. 1580 BC. The most important center of this new culture, a mixture of the old Middle Helladic cultures and Minoan influences, was MYCENAE, where the first indications of the beginning of new influences are the shaft graves, whose contents of metalwork and jewelry show that there were new wealthy settlers of importance. During the two centuries from c. 1400 BC (L.H. III), Mycenaean civilization reached its peak. Many settlements were walled at this time with large "cyclopean" defenses: those of Mycenae and TIRYNS are the best preserved. Palaces, too, were built, as at Mycenae, Tiryns, and PYLOS. These were highly decorated with frescoes, as were the Minoan examples, and excavation has revealed that they centered on a throne room. Finds of clay tablets, bearing a linear scipt (Linear B) which has been deciphered and is a form of Greek, show the civilization to have been highly organized.

In about 1200 BC, there were a series of destructions of undetermined origin, after which the Mycenaean centers went into a slow decline: Mycenae itself was finally destroyed c. 1120 BC, when Greece was overrun by a people called the Dorians, who invaded and settled in the Peloponnese and Crete. They may have enslaved the former inhabitants, but many fled to the region of ATHENS, which managed to retain its independence.

*Preclassical Greece.* The new invaders left little archaeological trace: they were warlike, but seemingly without any great cultural tradition, so much so that the first few centuries of the 1st millennium BC in Greece have been called the "Dark Age" of Greek history.

During this period, contact with the East produced a new (the present) Greek alphabet, and an adventuresome breed of Greek traders who were foremost in the movement to colonize new areas. Mother cities in Greece, anxious for space, sent out groups of colonists to the Black Sea, Italy, Sicily, Spain, Southern France, and Africa from about 750 to 550 BC. During this period, when trade was of prime importance, archaeological finds of Greek artifacts are found throughout the Mediterranean world.

The Preclassical age in Greece was one of political and social development in the various city states. From the archaeological viewpoint, these early settlements have left little trace, other than in their monumental architecture (temples), which developed from the 7th century BC. Houses of this date, probably of simple form, have been built over by later Classical, Hellenistic, and sometimes Roman developments. Most important for understanding the cultural life of the period is the study of the art, as seen in sculpture and in vase painting in particular, and the artifacts—bronze and metalwork. Until the 5th century BC, recognized as the peak of Classical Greek achievement, many influences were at work on the mainland of Greece. The Peloponnese, still Dorian, lagged behind Athens and Attica, whose seafaring increased contact with the Aegean islands and the East. It was Athens which recognized the growing power of the Persian kingdoms and organized Greek defense against the Persian invasions of the early 5th century BC, famous for the battles of Marathon and Thermopylae.

*The 5th century BC.* The 5th century BC was one of great achievement throughout Greece, but nowhere more so than at Athens. That city had suffered heavily in the

95

Persian invasions (490–480 BC) and was largely rebuilt during the course of the 5th century BC, from which period some of her most famous monuments, notably the group of temples on the Acropolis, derive. The period was one of brilliance at Athens not only in its monumental and artistic achievement, considerable though it was, but also in the political and literary sphere: this was the era of Themistocles and Pericles, and the playwrights Aeschylus, Sophocles, and Euripides; later, though marred by the jealous rivalry of Sparta, which led to the ultimately self-destructive Peloponnesian Wars, Athens produced the writers Aristophanes and Thucydides, the war's great historian.

*The 4th century BC and after.* The Peloponnesian Wars between Athens and Sparta heralded a period of struggle for supremacy between the warring Greek states, always in the shadow of Persian power. The final gain was made by the Macedonian King Philip II, who won control of the Greek states towards the middle of the 4th century BC. Despite nearly a century of warring between themselves, the period had been for the Greeks one of the utmost achievement in the political, social, and artistic fields. Reunited, if somewhat uneasily, under Macedonian rule, first of Philip, then of Alexander, the Greek cities now settled to a further period of enterprise which, because of the pioneering spirit of Alexander himself, spread Greek Hellenistic culture far and wide.

Inevitably the successors of Alexander found themselves increasingly threatened by the power of Rome, and in the 2nd century BC, Rome inflicted a series of defeats on the Macedonians and their allies: confederacies of Greek states attempted for a time to remain independent, but in 146 BC, with the destruction of Corinth, Rome became the master of Greece. As one of her most peaceful provinces, Greece contributed much to the Roman Empire, and Rome was content to leave Greece largely undisturbed. In this way, Greek and Hellenistic culture still flowered, spurring the Romans on to some of their greatest artistic and cultural triumphs.

**Grime's Graves.** One of Europe's largest flint mines, covering at least 35 ac. (14 ha), situated near Thetford in Norfolk, England. It was operational from *c.* 2300 to 1700 BC, and consists of hundreds of shafts and pits, sunk up to 39 ft. (12 m) into the solid chalk subsoil to quarry flint seams, for the manufacture of axes and other tools.

**Grubenhaüser.** A term applied to the characteristic huts of the Germanic peoples during the MIGRATION PERIOD, which have sunken floors, usually subrectangular, and a superstructure supported on two, four, or six posts. They are found in the Low Countries, Britain, and France, often alongside rectangular buildings of more orthodox post construction. Many may have served as workshops.

**Guitarrero cave.** An important stratified cave from the Calleyon de Huaylas on the Western flanks of the Andes in Central Peru. The earliest stratified deposits date from between *c.* 12,500 and 6000 years ago, and the later layers include evidence of the domesticated lima bean and common bean.

**Gumelnitsa culture.** Named after the type-site in Romania, this was one of the most flourishing of the painted-pottery cultures of the late 4th millennium BC, and is widely represented by TELL settlements in Romania, Bulgaria, and Northern Greece. The sixth level at KARANOVO belongs to this culture. It was one of the pioneers of simple copper metallurgy in Europe.

**Guti.** An obscure tribe from the Zagros Mountains, which invaded Mesopotamia *c.* 2200 BC and brought about the downfall of the Dynasty of AKKAD. Many towns must have maintained their independence, such as LAGASH under its ruler Gudea, and they joined forces under Utu-hegal of URUK to eject the Guti in about 2120 BC. A style of cylinder seal has been ascribed to the Guti, but other SEALS of the period bear witness to the beginnings of a Sumerian revival.

**Gymnasium.** An area within or outside a Greek city, used as a sports ground. It normally incorporated a running track and a PALAESTRA, as well as bathrooms, dressing rooms, and rooms for various ballgames and exercises.

**Hacılar.** A site in Southwestern Anatolia. The earliest seven levels are aceramic (pre-pottery) Neolithic and date from the first half of the 7th millennium BC. The houses consisted of small, mud-plastered rooms and larger ones with red burnished lime plaster floors. Hearths, ovens, and bins stood in the courtyard. Some skulls have been found but no burials. Later occupation of the mound dates from the second quarter of the 6th millennium BC to the first quarter of the 5th, in 13 levels, with a distinctive pottery which is painted in the later levels. Clay statuettes have been found in several levels, particularly in level VI. Level II was destroyed by the bearers of a new culture with a new type of painted pottery and anthropomorphic vessels. The cemetery was outside the settlement and was not excavated, but it has since been looted. Many of the so-called Hacılar figures and pots which have appeared on the market as a result have been found to be forgeries.

**Hadrian's Wall.** The best known of Roman frontier works, built in Northern Britain on the orders of the Emperor Hadrian in AD 122–127. Its history is complex, but in its completed form it comprised a stone-walled ditch facing north, and a military zone behind it protected by an earthwork to the south. This protected zone ran for 80 Roman mi. (about 73 mi.—117 km) from Bowness on Solway (west of Carlisle) to Wallsend (east of Newcastle). Along its length were small forts (milecastles) and turrets, as well as 17 Roman forts.

**Halaf.** A site on the River Khabur, excavated by the Germans from 1911 to 1913 and from 1927 to 1929. It gave its name to the Halaf period of the 6th and early 5th millennia BC, with its characteristic painted pottery (*see* MESOPOTAMIA). The site was then abandoned for some 2,000 years but was subsequently rebuilt within rectangular fortifications. On the acropolis were temples and palaces, among them the "Tempel-Palast" of Kapara, son of Hadianu, which was decorated with crude reliefs and huge statues, while others were found elsewhere on the site. The date of this level is disputed, but it must be somewhere between the 12th and 9th centuries BC. The next level is Assyrian, when the city was called Guzana and was ruled by governors. (*See* the chronological table, p. 198.)

**Halicarnassus** (Bodrum). A Greek city in Asia Minor, the birthplace of the great historian Herodotus. It formed part of the Delian league, but its most illustrious period was as the capital city of Mausolus, who ruled Caria from 377 to 353 BC. He built walls and public buildings, but the most famous is the Mausoleum—one of the seven wonders of the ancient world—his funerary temple, of which nothing now remains but fragments preserved in the British Museum in London.

A reconstruction of the Mausoleum at Halicarnassus. Built of white marble, it was originally *c.* 134 ft. (41 m) high.

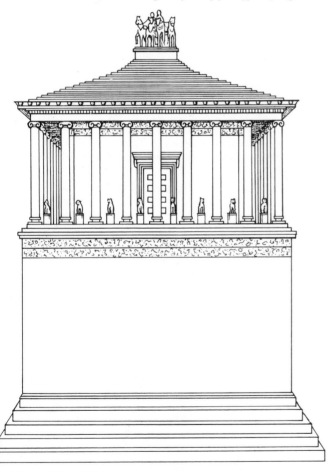

**Hallstatt.** Situated in the Austrian Alps, Hallstatt was the principal Central European salt mine from about 700 to 500 BC, and gives its name to the earlier phase of

the Celtic Iron Age. This wealthy, hierarchical community imported goods from far afield (e.g., Scandinavian amber, Italian wine and glass), and placed exceptionally fine objects in its graves.

**Hama.** A huge TELL in the modern Syrian city of Hama, the ancient Hamath, was excavated by the Danes and remains of the 5th millennium BC have been uncovered, together with a long sequence of occupation. It was particularly important at the end of the 2nd millennium BC, when it became the capital of an Aramaean kingdom. (*See also* SYRIA-PALESTINE; the chronological table, p. 198.)

**Hamangia culture.** Named after the type-site near the mouth of the Danube in Romania, this culture was once thought, on account of the impressed decoration on its pottery, to be a member of the 5th-millennium BC impressed pottery cultures of the Mediterranean, but it has now been radiocarbon dated to the early 4th millennium BC. It was later absorbed by the GUMELNITSA CULTURE.

**Hammerstone.** *See* STONE TECHNOLOGY.

**Han Dynasty.** After the collapse of the brief rule of the CH'IN DYNASTY, the Han Dynasty (206 BC–AD 220) took over the control of a now-unified China. The Dynasty is divided into two main periods by the brief usurpation of Wang Meng (AD 8–23): the Western Han (206 BC–AD 8), with the capital at CH'ANG-AN, and the Eastern Han (AD 25–220), with the capital at LO-YANG. Areas of these two cities have been investigated and partially excavated. Under one of the early Han emperors, Wu-ti (141–87 BC), the Chinese were drawn into wars with the nomads on their borders, principally the HSIUNG-NU, and in this way came to control much of Central Asia. Exports from China, including textiles and decorative bronzes similar to those found at NOIN ULA, have also been excavated at sites along the SILK ROUTE. In exchange for the large quantities of silk which China exported, and which found its way as far as the Roman world, China imported horses from regions such as Ferghana in Western Asia. Many tombs of the period have been excavated. In the early part of the Dynasty the SHAFT TOMB predominated, as at MA-WANG-TUI, but the CHAMBERED TOMB appeared at about this time, as at MAN-CH'ENG, and had spread widely by the second half of the Dynasty.

The great prosperity of the early Han period is reflected in the rich grave goods, which included bronzes, JADE objects, textiles, LACQUER, and ceramics. However, by the Eastern Han period, the economic predicament of China was so acute that edicts were passed to prevent the burial of precious materials. Their place was taken by substitutes in earthenware, which were often lead-glazed; among the most interesting are models of buildings and figures. This preoccupation with daily life, rather than with the RITUAL VESSELS that had been buried earlier, reflects the progressive secularization of the state, which was by now ruled by a civil bureaucracy.

**Hang-t'u.** The Chinese technical term for *pisé* or compressed earth. It was widely used as a form of construction from the late Neolithic period and SHANG DYNASTY (*c.* 1600–1027 BC) notably at AN-YANG.

**Haniwa.** Earthenware cylinders, or representations of horses, animals, and houses placed in concentric rings around the tombs of the Kofun (GREAT TOMBS PERIOD—4th–7th century AD) in Japan.

**Harappa.** One of the twin capitals of the Indus civilization (2300–1750 BC), situated on the banks of the River Ravi in the Punjab, Pakistan. Excavations begun here in the 1920s were continued by Sir Mortimer WHEELER in 1946. A brick-walled town with pre-Harappan material precedes the city of the mature civilization. It is larger than MOHENJO-DARO, its citadel rising to 50 ft. (15 m), with massive 40-ft. thick (12 m) mud-brick walls faced with baked brick. To the north of the citadel lie the granaries, a series of working floors and a complex of small, one-roomed workmen's huts. South of the town are a rare Indus inhumation cemetery, dating towards the end of the Indus period, and a cemetery of dismembered burials with non-Indus pottery, dating from the period of reoccupation, possibly by Aryans. (*See also* INDIA.)

**Harmal.** *See* TELL HARMAL.

**Harran.** A city in Northern Mesopotamia mentioned in Hittite, Old Testament, and Assyrian texts. Its main deity was the moon god Sin, and the Chaldaean King Nabonidus rebuilt the temple in the 6th century BC. The mound of Sultantepe has been excavated and important texts and stelae were found there. The site was also important throughout the early Islamic period. In 1951, the gateway of the citadel was partially excavated, followed, in 1956 and 1959, by the Great Mosque. This appears to have been built by Marwān II (AD 744–750), though additions were made in about 830 and major alterations took place under Saladin between 1171 and 1184.

**Hasanlu.** The site of an Iron Age citadel in Iran, near the present-day frontier with Iraq and Turkey, south of Lake Urmia, excavated by the Americans since 1959. The citadel dates from the 10th century BC and is built on accumulated débris of the 6th to 3rd millennium BC. It was violently destroyed in *c.* 800 BC and, in the ruins of one of the burnt buildings, a skeleton was found holding a superb gold bowl decorated with mythical scenes. Objects of gold, silver, electrum (an alloy of gold and silver), glass, and ivory were found and several buildings, palaces, and temples were excavated.

**Hassuna.** A prehistoric site near Mosul, which has given its name to one of the earliest cultures in the area. (*See* MESOPOTAMIA; the chronological table, p. 198.)

**Hatra.** An important caravan city in Parthian times, situated in the desert southwest of Mosul in Northern Iraq, and relying on cisterns for its water supply. Within the circular fortifications are a huge palace of the *iwan* type (with an audience hall open at one end) and several temples, which have recently been excavated by the Iraqis. All are decorated with numerous reliefs and statues in Parthian style, carved from local marble, and depicting religious subjects, deities, rulers, and both male and female dignitaries. The city was destroyed by the SASSANIANS in *c.* AD 241.

**Hatshepsut.** An Egyptian queen of the 18th Dynasty, the daughter of Tuthmosis I and widow of Tuthmosis II, who reigned as pharaoh for 21 years (*c.* 1503–1482 BC) during the minority of her stepson Tuthmosis III. Her reign was marked by peace, prosperity, and artistic achievement: her funerary temple at Deir el-Bahri on the west bank at THEBES is one of the most original and beautiful in Egypt.

**Hattusas.** *See* BOĞAZKÖY.

**Hazor.** A very large site in the Jordan valley. The TELL was inhabited from the Bronze Age until Hellenistic times and the city expanded onto the surrounding plateau, which was fortified in Middle Bronze Period II. Important religious and secular buildings were found. (*See* ISRAEL, ISRAELITES; SYRIA–PALESTINE.)

**Hebrews.** *See* SYRIA–PALESTINE.

**Helgö.** A MIGRATION PERIOD trading and industrial post on an island in Lake Malaren, Sweden. The excavations since 1954 have shown that Helgö had trade contacts with Britain and the Continent, as well as with the Baltic-Bothnean area, during most of the 1st millennium AD. Important finds included a workshop for making brooches, dress pins, and clasp buttons, and a Buddha figurine, presumably imported from Northern India.

**Heliopolis** (Baalbek). A Roman colony founded in 16 BC on an ancient Arabian religious site in Syria. It has extensive remains of the Temple of Jupiter Hadad, its surrounding courtyards, and ancilliary temples.

**Henge.** The term, derived from STONEHENGE ("hanging stone"), applied to a class of late Neolithic/Early Bronze Age ritual monuments in Britain, of which Stonehenge is a rather unusual example. Others lack the elaborate trilithons, for instance, but all have the basic features of a circular bank with opposed entrances. Their purpose is unknown.

**Herculaneum.** A small town about 5 mi. (8 km) south of Naples, buried by volcanic ash and destroyed in the eruption of Vesuvius in AD 63. Excavations since the 18th century have opened a large portion of the town, whose planned regular layout is in complete contrast with that of POMPEII. Herculaneum was a quieter, wealthier, and less gaudy place than Pompeii: its houses were more modern, and tastefully decorated. The weight of volcanic deposits on the town has damaged buildings more than at Pompeii, but there are still remarkable survivals of furniture and artifacts.

**Herzfeld, Ernst** (1879–1948). A German orientalist and excavator of Samarra (1911–14) and PERSEPOLIS (1931–34).

**Hetepheres' reburial.** On February 9, 1925, the tripod of a photographer working for the joint Harvard-Boston Expedition at Giza struck a patch of plaster which was found to be masking a cutting packed with small dressed blocks of limestone. Twelve steps were uncovered leading into a rockcut tunnel, which in turn penetrated the wall of a vertical shaft. The mouth of the shaft had been filled with rough limestone so that it looked like the natural surface of the rock. The stairway opened into an old quarry, which lay east of the Great Pyramid among the MASTABA tombs of the family of Khufu (Cheops), the pyramid's builder. It appeared that originally the northernmost of the three small pyramids of Khufu's queens was intended to stand on the site of the shaft, for a sloping passage which would have led to a burial chamber had been begun but abandoned. Moreover in Khufu's chief queen's pyramid 92 ft. (28 m) west of the shaft, the passage leading to the burial chamber is parallel to the abandoned one. Work in the quarry was also stopped at the same time as the queen's pyramid's substructure was resited. It was clear that the shaft marked a secret burial which might well have escaped plunderers because its position was not marked by a superstructure.

Work was begun on the removal of the limestone blocks filling the shaft. At a depth of 29 ft. (9 m) a niche was uncovered, containing the remains of a sacrifice comprising the skull and three legs of an ox wrapped in matting, two beer jugs, some charcoal, and some chips of basalt. The basalt chips showed that the shaft was filled during or after the laying of the basalt pavement of Khufu's pyramid temple. It was known that the shaft was already in existence before the queen's pyramids were built because it was under the building surface on which they stood. It certainly predated the northern queen's pyramid which, as shown, was resited so as not to uncover the secret shaft. At 39 ft. (12 m), broken pottery, remains of a well known funerary ritual, were found; at 56 ft. (17 m), fragments of copper and, at 72 ft. (22 m), more fragmentary pottery were found. The shaft was now much deeper than any normal burial shaft of the period, but it was not until a depth of 82 ft. (25 m) was reached that courses of well laid masonry were uncovered in one of the shaft's walls. After two courses were removed the line of a chamber roof came into view.

It later became clear that the chamber was unfinished: a cutting in the east wall had been filled with limestone blocks, another in the west wall had been similarly blocked and plastered over. The plaster still bore the mason's thumb print. A hole in the floor at the northwest corner was filled with rubbish. G. A. Reisner's assistants had eyes only for the glitter of gold which lay on every side. The chamber had been filled with furniture and boxes of wood, most of which had shriveled, disintegrated, or been attacked by fungus. The contents had spilled out, the metal bindings or inlays of the wooden objects had collapsed onto the contents, and the metal, stone, or pottery objects standing on the perished wooden

pieces had fallen onto the heap. A large alabaster sarcophagus lay amid all this ruin, but it could not be opened until the decayed inlaid panels, gold-cased wooden poles, and canopy beams lying on its lid were removed. These, however, could not be reached until the floor was cleared. In some places the debris lay up to 3 ft. (1 m) deep. This task of clearing the debris was to take 10 months, 321 working days in all, which produced 1701 foolscap pages of notes and 1057 large photographs.

The very large mastabas to the east of the Great Pyramid surrounding the shaft belonged to members of the royal family: here were buried Khufu's sons Kawab, Hordadef, Khufukaf, and his daughter-in-law Meresankh, to name but a few of the royal children. This led Reisner at first to hope that the secret burial or reburial might belong to a king; the name of Sneferu had been noticed on an inscribed panel. But it soon became clear that the contents of the chamber belonged to a woman and the inscribed tomb goods revealed the owner to be Hetepheres, wife of Sneferu and Khufu's mother. It was also obvious that the grave goods had been intended originally for a larger room and were placed in the cache in reverse order to what might be expected. In addition, chamber and shaft were unfinished and pieces of plaster were mixed up with the contents of boxes, which did not, moreover, correspond to their labels, as though all had been swept up and pushed into the nearest container. Most strangely, the sarcophagus could only have come down the narrow shaft in a vertical position. Yet the burial was intact. But when the sarcophagus was opened in March 1927 it was empty. There must once have been a body, as an alabaster canopic chest, its four compartments still containing the remains of the queen's embalmed viscera, was later found in a plastered recess.

Hetepheres would have been interred originally at Dahshur, near her husband's pyramid. Obviously this burial had been plundered within a few years of her death, during her son's reign. But elaborate and secret reburial would only make sense if her body had survived the robbing of her tomb, which clearly it had not. That Khufu believed his mother's body had survived seems evident from the sacrifice made near the top of the shaft to her KA. The only explanation can be that no-one dared to tell the king that his mother's body was destroyed and her spirit doomed to roam eternally without a home, and so the reburial went ahead as though the mummy had survived. This reburial of an empty sarcophagus remained undetected for 4,300 years until the 20th century.

Fortunately for Egyptology G. A. Reisner, the field director of the Giza Expedition, was noted for his scrupulous attention to detail and his exemplary recording. As a result of his own and his picked team's care, at the end of nearly a year's painstaking work every last fragment from the floor of the burial chamber had been recorded and its position noted before its consolidation, if necessary, and its removal. So detailed was this work that it was possible later to reconstruct exactly the personal possessions and funerary goods which had accompanied the queen. She had two wooden armchairs, one of which, with lion's legs, was completely encased

An aerial view of Maiden Castle, Dorset, a hillfort with banks and ditches, and elaborate gateway fortifications.

in sheet gold and had an inlaid back panel. Of the justly famous carrying chair, only the gold inlaid inscription strips had survived, but a complete reconstruction with modern wood was possible. A lion-legged bed would have been used inside a tent, formed from gold- and copper-encased wooden poles and beams hung with material to make a canopy. An empty wooden box nearby probably once held these curtains. The smaller objects were no less spectacular: they included fine alabaster toilet vessels, a copper ewer and basin, gold eating utensils, gold razors, and the contents of the queen's jewelry box. The latter comprised 20 silver bracelets (usually referred to as anklets) inlaid with semiprecious stones in the design of a butterfly.

These objects comprise the only Old Kingdom royal grave goods found in anything like an intact state and give some indication of the excellence reached by craftsmen of the period.

**Heuneburg.** In the 6th century BC, the Heuneburg, a HILLFORT above the River Danube, was the center of the dominant Celtic chiefdom in Southwest Germany. Imports from Scandinavia, Greece and its colonies, and even China, and the presence of a Greek bastioned rampart of sun-dried brick, demonstrate its wealth and wide political contacts.

**Hieratic.** *See* HIEROGLYPHS.

**Hieroglyphs.** A form of pictorial script evolved *c*. 3100 BC for writing the ancient Egyptian language. Hieroglyphs are essentially a monumental script intended to be incised into hard materials or painted on a large scale. Hieratic, a more cursive form of hieroglyphs, evolved at the same time as an adaptation of hieroglyphs for a new medium: papyrus, ink, and brush. The third form of script employed by the Egyptians, from about 700 BC, was the even more cursive demotic (*see* ROSETTA STONE).

**Hillfort.** A prehistoric European settlement situated on a hilltop and often surrounded by elaborate fortifications. In size, hillforts ranged from less than one acre to several hundred acres. They are found throughout much of Europe, except Russia and Scandinavia, and are particularly characteristic of early Celtic society. The earliest are of Neolithic date, but they do not become common until the 1st millennium BC (Bronze Age onwards); thereafter they declined in importance, except in Northern and Western Britain and in Ireland, where they continued to be inhabited until late in the 1st millennium AD.

Hillforts were the centers of chiefdoms, and served as permanent settlements in which industrial activities (e.g., metalworking) were carried on, and commodities (e.g., grain) were stored in massive quantities for trade or redistribution. In them we may detect the beginnings of urbanization, particularly late in the 1st millennium BC, when they developed into administrative and market centers (*see* URBANIZATION, PREHISTORIC EUROPE). Their inhabitants also worked the land and kept herds of animals: field systems and ranch boundaries survive around many hillforts, and agricultural and pastoral implements (e.g., plowshares and sheepshears) are commonly found within them. Hillforts and low-lying fortified settlements were called *oppida*, i.e., fortified towns, by Classical writers; but some Celtic towns (e.g., Alesia and Bibracte in France) were described as *urbes* by Caesar, a term normally reserved for Rome itself, indicating how advanced these places were.

The fortifications took the form of ditches and banks, walls or palisades of wood and rough stone, sometimes in several concentric rings. A sophisticated and very strong form of wall was devised in the 1st century BC to withstand siege warfare, the *murus gallicus*. The wall was built of stone with internal timberwork, held together with massive iron nails which gave great strength to the whole structure.

**Hittites.** An Indo-European people who moved into Central ANATOLIA towards the end of the 3rd millennium BC and settled in the bend of the Halys River (Kızıl Irmak) and the surrounding area. They probably established their first capital at Kushara, which has not yet been identified. The first known rulers of the Old Kingdom are Labarnas and his son Hattusilis I, who was probably responsible for transferring the capital to Hattusas (BOĞAZKÖY) and for beginning a policy of expansion to the south and west, which Mursilis I continued, even overthrowing BABYLON in *c.* 1595 BC.

The HURRIANS caused trouble during the next reign, that of Hantilis, but Telepinus restored order and strengthened the frontiers of a reduced kingdom. There follows an obscure period before the founding of a new Dynasty by Tudhalyas II, the first king of the Hittite Empire. He attacked ALEPPO in the 15th century BC, but his successors came into conflict with the North Syrian kingdom of Mitanni (*see* HURRIANS). In *c.* 1380 BC, Suppiluliumas came to the throne and raided as far south as DAMASCUS. Northern Syria was divided between Mitanni, Egypt, and Assyria and this lack of unity enabled the Hittites to gain control of the area in 1340 BC. Egyptian interests in Syria were thus threatened and, in 1286–1285 BC, at Qadesh, the Hittites under Muwatallis met the Egyptians under Ramesses II in one of the great recorded battles of antiquity: the result seems to have been indecisive, though the Egyptians claimed victory and depicted the battle in several reliefs.

The Hittite Empire disappeared in the tide of SEA PEOPLE which swept through the Near East at the end of the 13th century BC, but Hittite culture survived for five centuries in the Neo-Hittite kingdoms of Southeastern Anatolia and North Syria, and it is the inhabitants of these states who are the Biblical Hittites. Malatya, KARATEPE, CARCHEMISH, Sakcegözü, Marash, SINJERLI, TELL AHMAR, and HAMA have all produced examples of Neo-Hittite art, but the hieroglyphic inscriptions are not in the Hittite of Boğazköy but in Luwian (*see* LUWIANS). The ARAMAEANS annexed some of these states in the first centuries of the 1st millennium BC, and the remainder fell to the Assyrians in the 8th century BC.

**Hohokam.** A subarea of the Southwestern cultural area of the United States. The areas which the culture occupied, in Arizona and the neighboring Mexican state of Sonora, are dry desert. Occupation was confined to riverine places where irrigation could be used for agriculture. The stimulus towards agriculture originally came from the MOGOLLON peoples further to the north, although the cultures developed separately. The early Hohokam culture is exemplified by the site of Snaketown in the Gila valley of Southern Arizona. Irrigation began in the Pioneer period (100 BC–AD 500), and canals became very long: one at Snaketown leaves the River Gila 10 mi. (16 km) from the site. Other essential Hohokam traits became established at this time: the typical red-on-buff pottery appears in the second half of the Pioneer period.

The tradition of making small crude painted pottery figurines was established then, as was that of making carved stone palettes and vessels in the form of animals. The dead were cremated throughout the Hohokam, beginning in the Pioneer period, while house structure changed throughout the sequence. In the Pioneer period there were large but shallow pithouses with wattle-and-daub walls; in the Colonial period (AD 500–900), the shape of the houses changed from square to oblong; in the Sedentary period (900–1200) they become oval in outline. Ballcourts, of the Mesoamerican type, were constructed from the Colonial period onwards. The earliest is that at Snaketown, and it is also the largest, measuring 394 ft. (120 m) long. In the Sedentary and Classic (1200–1400) periods they were generally smaller and oriented in a north-south rather than east-west direction. Another Mesoamerican feature of later Hohokam periods was the construction of platform mounds. One such is at the Gatlin site: at its greatest extent it measured 95 × 72 ft. (29 × 22 m) at its base. The Classic period is marked by various changes brought about by the arrival of ANASAZI peoples. They made a red, white, and black polychrome pottery, and buried their dead rather than cremated them. They also built large, defensive, rectangular ADOBE structures. The largest building at Los Muertos had walls more than 7 ft. (2 m) thick at its base, perhaps for defense against Apache intruders. After the Classic period, many of the sites were abandoned and presumably much of the Hohokam and Anasazi population moved away. However, it is likely that the Pima and Papago, the modern inhabitants of the area, are descended from the Hohokam who remained behind.

**Homeric archaeology.** Study of the poems attributed to Homer, the *Iliad* and the *Odyssey*, has suggested that they could have been epic poems recited and composed orally within a tradition handed down over several generations. However, it has long been recognized that not all the events and artifacts (e.g., the weapons) described in the poems were contemporary: there seem to be echoes from the Bronze Age (Mycenaean period), but also references to artifacts and objects not known to the Greeks until the 8th century BC. The study of Homeric archaeology is the attempt to match the description of an object, building, social structure, or custom within the poems with its antecedent as known and understood from the archaeological record of the preceding centuries. Prime examples of portions of the poems which seem to refer to the Mycenaean age are the "long spears" and the "large shields" of the Greek heroes: pictorial representations of Bronze Age date show large spears and shields which, by the 8th and 7th centuries BC, had been superseded by the (relatively) lighter-armed hoplite. On a larger scale, the catalogue of Greek allies in the Trojan War (*Iliad* 2) presents a picture, not of Greece at about 800 BC, but of Mycenaean Greece, archaeological evidence for which has only appeared in the last 100 years, and certainly would not have been known to Homer. The latest chronological "strand" in the poems appears to be the sitting statue (reminiscent of archaic Greek sculpture) in *Iliad* 6: 302, or the mention of the Phalanx (*Iliad*

13:131). (*See also* GREECE, ARCHAEOLOGY OF; MYCENAE; MYCENAEAN ARCHAEOLOGY.)

*Homo erectus.* The fossil species ancestral to *Homo sapiens.* Based on Java man (formerly *Pithecanthropus; see* JAPAN AND THE FAR EAST, PALAEOLITHIC) and PEKING MAN (*Sinanthropus*), it is also known in Europe and Africa. Body size was similar to that of today, but brain size was *c.* 775–1,225 cc and teeth were bigger.

*Homo habilis.* The name given to fossil human remains from OLDUVAI GORGE, Tanzania. It has been regarded as a possible ancestor of HOMO ERECTUS or HOMO SAPIENS. Other experts believe it should be included in the species *Australopithecus africanus* or *Homo erectus*, or be regarded as transitional from one to the other.

*Homo sapiens.* The contemporary species of man, with a worldwide distribution. The fossils of CROMAGNON belong to an earlier stage of *Homo sapiens*, and in the classification currently favored both the classic NEANDERTHAL MAN and the earlier Neanderthal man are grouped as a more archaic stage of *Homo sapiens*.

**Hopewell.** A culture in Eastern North America, which succeeded the ADENA culture in the Burial Mound II Period (300 BC–AD 200). The complex of burial mounds became more highly developed, particularly in the central Adena-Hopewell area of Ohio. Some of the earthworks may have been used for defensive purposes, but most were conical mounds associated with elongated mounds in a variety of shapes. Some, such as the Edwin Harness group in Ohio, enclosed areas of up to 100 ac. (40 ha). The mortuary buildings were wooden, as in the Adena culture, although they were more complex, with a series of rooms. The grave goods are much more varied and plentiful. They include copper and mica cutouts in the shape of heads, serpents, and geometric designs, polished stone ear ornaments, birdstones, effigy pipes, engraved bones, and caches of flint and obsidian points (*see* BIRDSTONE; EFFIGY PIPE). Additional grave goods included fresh water pearls and, occasionally, pottery: the tradition of carving small flat incised stone tablets continued. However most burials were cremations, and the rich tomb burials were confined to a small section of the population. Bodies were cremated after all the flesh had disappeared or been removed, and cremation took place in clay-lined pits. The ashes were then placed in mortuary houses within enclosures. Copperworking was conducted in the same manner as by the Adena people, and, in addition to copper, small quantities of beaten gold and silver have been found in Hopewell sites. Axes and adzes were either of polished stone, without grooves, or else of copper or iron from meteorites. Hopewell pottery is firmly within the WOODLAND TRADITION, being mostly cord marked on the surface. In addition there is a class of Hopewell pottery, perhaps for ceremonial use, which is covered with incised geometric and curvilinear designs enclosing zones of rocker-stamped decoration. The design of these pots, as well as of the stone tablets, reflects a continuation of the Adena culture motifs

Great Serpent Mound, Adams County, Ohio, Hopewell or Adena culture. The length of the serpent is 700 ft. (213 m).

of abstract birds and serpents. The settlement patterns of the Hopewell people are little known; however, it is most likely that they lived in semipermanent villages without mounds or banked enclosures. The latter were probably used as ceremonial centers or as the ritual and political centers for surrounding areas.

Agriculture became more firmly established by the Hopewell, and charred remains of maize have been found in Ohio. The Hopewell culture spread out from Ohio in a relatively short period of time, as is demonstrated by the wide range of imported raw materials: conch shells were traded from the Gulf Coast, mica from the Appalachians, and copper from the Great Lakes. The Hopewell culture underwent a rapid decline in the last part of Burial Mound II Period, and the luxury trade items disappear. The next phase is called the Intrusive Mound culture, since graves were placed within other graves dug into Hopewellian mounds. No new mounds were erected in this period, and the quality and variety of grave goods decline. However the Intrusive Mound culture remains firmly within the Woodland tradition.

**House, Europe.**
*Prehistoric.* Man constructed windbreaks from early in his history, and simple huts supported by stakes, and in some cases by mammoth tusks, are known from the Palaeolithic and Mesolithic. Houses as such, however, are generally considered to appear with the more settled life of the Neolithic farming communities. Though villages are known, in many areas and in many periods little survives of houses apart from a few postholes or

stone wall-footings, and construction must have been unfavorable to long-term survival. Some of the finest houses of prehistoric Europe date from the early Neolithic, and belong to the LINEAR POTTERY CULTURE and its successors (see RÖESSEN CULTURE; LENGYEL). Massive timber longhouses up to 164 ft. (50 m) long were built, at first supported by three internal rows of posts as well as by posts in the walls; later, more weight was taken by the side walls. These may have housed extended family groups, but the typical house of most of prehistory is considered to be a single family unit. Well preserved houses of the Neolithic and Bronze Age in Switzerland (see CORTAILLOD CULTURE) were supported on a lighter post frame than longhouses, and walls, floors, and roofs were built of planks. Clay models from the Neolithic of Eastern Europe show internal fittings, which can also be seen in the stone-built Neolithic houses of Orkney. Round houses appeared in the Bronze Age and were common in the Iron Age. A pitched roof was supported by a central post, and the walls were of wattle and daub.

*Greek and Roman.* The oldest house type in Greece is the so-called "megaron"—a rectangular room with its entrance on one of the shorter sides, and often with a portico and a central hearth. It was from this shape of house that the Classical Greek temple developed. Houses of megaron type are known from the Neolithic Sesklo and Dimini cultures, but there were then also other types of rectangular house in current use. The Early Helladic period saw further developments: at TIRYNS, ASINE, and Lerna there were houses with apsidal shapes. At Tiryns the ruler's house was a strongly built round tower.

In the Middle Helladic period, new house types appeared—oval and apsidal buildings—but the megaron form persisted, and was adopted in the Mycenaean period to become the central portion, the throne room of the Mycenaean palace. In this, perhaps its best-developed form, the megaron had a columned forehall or portico, a vestibule, and then a rectangular room, with, at Tiryns and Pylos, a central hearth and a throne. Houses of lesser importance were irregular, small rectangular units, often with several rooms grouped round a courtyard.

After these spectacular developments, the house form of Dark Age Greece reverted to earlier types. The megaron reappeared, but may have had religious significance, although, as the earliest temples and temple models were "houses of the god," they may accurately represent the typical house of the period. Clay models (from Argos and Perachora) suggest that houses of the GEOMETRIC period had tiled roofs, but flat roofs were also used.

Simplicity of plan and ostensible lack of comfort remained the keynote for houses until the 4th and 5th centuries BC. At LARISA there is a more complex building, an "old palace," which is a pair of megaron-type buildings set side by side, with rooms forming a pair of wings. The main evidence for house building comes from Olynthus, in Northern Greece, where, in the late 5th century BC, an extensive new quarter to the town was laid out. Although the interior arrangements varied considerably, the houses were laid out in blocks of ten. The most common form is that of a house hinged round a central passage (*pastas*), with a courtyard on one side and a series of rooms on the other.

In later houses, the central space becomes a rectangular courtyard surrounded by columns—typical of the form of Mediterranean house adopted in the Roman period for luxury villas. Hellenistic houses of this type are found at Delos. The rooms give onto the central space, which is reached by a short entrance passage from the street.

In the Hellenistic period houses became more opulent, and while in the 4th and 5th centuries there were few buildings which could be classed as palaces (a courtyard house at Larisa, successor to the "old palace," is perhaps the only exception), at Pella and Palatitsa in Macedonia large houses with suites of rooms grouped round a central courtyard have been found. These peristyle houses or palaces have their predecessors in the rest houses which grew up near sanctuaries (for example, at Troizen and at the Leonidaion at Olympia): the successors are the houses (such as Casa del Fauno) at POMPEII.

The earliest houses in Italy were round huts of Neolithic date: in the Bronze Age, the *palefitte*, platform houses, were characteristic of the Terra Mare culture, and in the VILLANOVAN CULTURE of the Early Iron Age (11th–8th century BC), houses of round, oval, and rectangular form were in use. The oldest settlement of the Palatine Hill in Rome dates from the 8th century BC and consists of a series of sunken-floored huts with timber posts holding clay walls and a thatched roof.

In the Etruscan period a form of house with multiple rooms was introduced: these have not been found in the ground, but house models and rockcut tombs, clearly built in the shape of houses, display the development. From this period may have sprung the typical Italian *domus*, with a central ATRIUM (courtyard) acting as a light well, and giving onto all the main rooms, of which the principal one was the *tablinum*. The earliest appearance of this developed form of the *domus* is in the Casa del Chirirgo at Pompeii (4th–3rd century BC). Later houses of the new type (e.g., Casa di Sallustio at Pompeii) have an atrium with an *impluvium* for catching rainwater. The atrium became a peristyle, and the complexity of these spacious town houses is well seen at Pompeii, where the so-called Casa di Pansa has a double atrium, one of which is a peristyle courtyard, on a central axis.

But not all town houses were as sumptuously appointed, and where space was at a premium, in the rectangular blocks between town or city streets, many-storied apartments grew up. Living quarters might be built over shops at ground level, as at OSTIA or Pompeii, and be relatively spacious, though little archaeological evidence survives for the first floor upwards. The impressions given by Roman poets (Martial and Juvenal) is of squalor, discomfort, and danger from fire in these apartments. Their height was limited by Augustus, and the use of brick and concrete rather than timber and wattle improved the standards of safety from the late 1st century AD onwards.

The development of the imperial palace in Rome grew up on the Palatine Hill (hence *palatium* = palace) where the remains of Augustus' relatively simple house were greatly enlarged by succeeding emperors. Tiberius and Caligula carried out extensions, but Nero envisaged a *domus Transitoria*, linking the Palatine to the Esquiline Hill and his "Golden House." Domitian's palace, built on the southwest of the Palatine remained the emperor's official residence until late Roman times: this added a basilica, a peristyle courtyard, and a hippodrome to the complex of rooms already built round the nucleus of Augustus' house. Later emperors built imperial residences in many of the provinces: perhaps the most unusual is the retirement palace of Diocletian at SPLIT, where, within the walls of what appears to be a Roman fort, were spacious suites of rooms looking out over the Adriatic Sea. (*For the medieval period, see* GRUBENHAÜSER.)

**Hsin-tien culture.** Found in Northwest China in Kansu province and in Sinkiang in *c.* 1500 BC, this culture was based on farming and the use of handmade pottery and copper tools. The pottery was often painted with rudimentary scrolls, a feature that must have descended from the PAN-SHAN urns.

**Hsiung-nu.** A nomadic tribe living in the Northwest of China, 2nd century BC to 2nd century AD, which provided a considerable threat to the HAN DYNASTY ruling China. They wore bronze plaques decorated with animals as harness and belt ornaments. Important Hsiung-nu graves have been excavated at NOIN ULA.

**Huaca Prieta de Chicama.** A late preceramic shell mound, 50 ft. (15 m) deep and measuring 400 × 150 ft. (122 × 46 m). It is located on a peninsular overlooking the sea in the Chicama valley, Peru. The stratified occupations were excavated in the 1940s. The earliest date obtained was 2125 BC, and from then onwards the site was constantly occupied until the INITIAL PERIOD. Remains include a permanent village of semisubterranean houses with cobble stones lining the walls, domesticated plants, bone, wood, shell and stone tools, baskets, early twined and knotted textiles, and, in the later levels, woven cloth. Early evidence of art occurs in twined and knotted textiles and gourd containers. Human, animal, bird, snake, and fish motifs occur in conventionalized designs. Geometric designs also occur.

**Huamanga.** The archaeological phase, AD 900–1100, in Ayacucho, Peru, which follows the downfall of the HUARI Empire. It is characterized by crude polychrome pottery. The ruins of the great Huari towns or smaller fortified sites were often reoccupied during this period.

**Huang-tao ware.** A Chinese stoneware, glazed in black or brown and splashed with an opalescent bluish or gray contrasting glaze. Manufactured during the T'ANG DYNASTY (AD 618–906), kilns where it was made have been found in Honan province.

**Huanuco Viejo.** A major Inca administrative capital, *c.* AD 1480, of a province in the highlands of Peru, near modern Huanuco. The subject of major inter-disciplinary projects combining ethnohistorical and archaeological data, excavations are providing important data on the function of Inca buildings and the social organization of the center.

**Huari** (or Wari). An empire was named after this huge site, which covered 25 ac. (10 ha) in the center of the Ayacucho basin, and dates from AD 600 to 1000. At its apogee, *c.* AD 850, probably as many as 100,000 people—including many full-time specialist workmen—lived in this capital of an empire that included most of Peru and was contemporary with the smaller TIAHUANACO Empire of Northern Bolivia and Southern Peru. Beautiful polychrome pottery, often with human or supernatural motifs, characterizes this period. Administrative centers were built in the characteristic form of rectangular compounds laid out in a grid pattern.

**Huastecs.** A people who occupied the Northern part of Veracruz, Mexico, and parts of Tamaulipas, San Luis Potosi, and Hidalgo. In the 16th century AD they spoke a dialect of the Maya language, from which culture they had separated in the Preclassic Period. A stratified series of ceramics from the region shows, in its lowest levels, pottery very comparable to Preclassic Maya pottery and Early-Middle Preclassic pottery of Oaxaca and the valley of Mexico. Classic Period pottery shows affinities with TEOTIHUACAN; and the Postclassic with Toltec and Aztec ceramics. They also developed a unique regional style of black-on-white painted pottery.

The Huastecs are probably best known for their unusual stone sculptures of standing male and female figures wearing conical headgear, with a large semicircular "halo" behind. The designs on these "halos" often resemble sunrays. One remarkable sculpture, however, the "Youth of Tamuin," is more natural in treatment. It represents a young man with artificial cranial deformation, his naked body marked with tattoos, and wearing an "alter-ego" figure on his back.

Ceremonial buildings were raised on circular or D-shaped substructures, though less frequently they made rectangular mounds or platforms. At Tamuin, the Huastecs' most important site, there is a large low platform covered with smooth lime plaster; another platform has the remains of a temple on it, an unusual feature of which is a walkway leading to two altars. In this building there is a painting, in Toltec style, showing seated and walking figures in elaborate feathered costumes with the insignia of the god QUETZALCOATL. While Huastec sites are very numerous, they are not usually large and few have been excavated.

As a largely peripheral culture, the Huastecs' contribution to Mesoamerica was probably in their sculptural style and in their elaborate carved openwork shell ornaments and gorgets. They probably worshiped Quetzalcoatl, and may even have invented him.

**Human Evolution.** Since the time of Charles DARWIN, scientists concerned with human origins have explored the idea that man had a common ancestor with the apes some millions of years ago, and that after the time of the

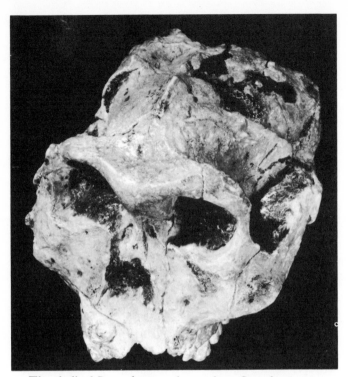

The skull of *Paranthropus robustus*, from Swartkrans.

split between the human and ape lines a series of gradual transformations led to modern man. Proposed in the 19th century with hardly any relevant fossil material available, the idea has been extensively supported by discoveries over recent decades.

The fossils discovered span the whole of the Pleistocene and Pliocene periods, as well as the later Miocene. Since it is very questionable that they should all be called "men," even though they seem to be closer to the human family than to the apes, they are usually called hominids (from Hominidae, the human family in Linnean or normal biological classification). The main groups of fossil hominids, starting with the most recent, are: CROMAGNON man or modern-type HOMO SAPIENS of Europe and elsewhere; NEANDERTHAL MAN and "Pre-Neanderthal" man; HOMO ERECTUS (Java and PEKING MAN and related types); the australopithecines (including *Australopithecus africanus* of Sterkfontein [*see* AUSTRALOPITHECUS], *Paranthropus robustus* of Swartkrans and HOMO HABILIS of OLDUVAL GORGE); and finally *Ramapithecus*, the Miocene form.

Experts have long debated whether all these fossil populations belonged to a single line of species leading to man, or whether branching had occurred, leading to extinct cousin species. The problem with branching is that it would require the populations to be isolated from each other for a long time, possibly even millions of years, while they developed in different directions under the influence of natural selection, and became reproductively isolated. Yet, as far as we know, man has but one role, namely that of an unspecialized toolmaker and meateater: his mobility and wide distribution made isolation even for short periods very unlikely.

Accordingly, the idea that every new fossil hominid found should be placed in a different species (and by the

1950s over 40 had been claimed) produced an absurd picture which no modern biologists accept. On the other hand, the simpler model that only one hominid species ever existed at a time also seems to be wrong, for there is one case where a separate hominid lineage seems to exist. This is the form called *Paranthropus robustus* or the robust australopithecine, which survived contemporary with *Homo erectus* down to about a million years ago.

Assuming that just this one branching lineage exists, the story of human evolution is relatively simple. In the late Miocene we have the early hominid called *Ramapithecus*, found in India, Pakistan, East Africa, Turkey, Greece, and possibly Hungary. Little is known about the body, posture, or brain in this form, but the teeth are already unlike those of apes, having no trace of the dagger-like canines.

Next, between 6 million and 2 million years ago, we find a small-bodied, upright-walking hominid with a small brain (300 to 800 cc) and teeth unlike those of apes. The average of about seven brain sizes measurable comes to *c.* 460 cc, larger than the chimpanzee (*c.* 350 cc), but much smaller than modern man (1,350 cc). Because of the smaller body size, however, the ratio of the brain to the body weight is almost the same as in modern man (about 1:50). This hominid is usually called *Australopithecus africanus* or *Homo africanus*.

Next we find, 2–1.5 million years ago, forms intermediate between *africanus* and *Homo erectus*, the next species recognized. These hominids may have been a little bigger bodied and were certainly bigger brained than *africanus*. Five specimens average *c.* 650 cc brain size. They have sometimes been called *Homo habilis*. There is some evidence that the hand structure was approaching our own.

The next main stage, 1.5–0.5 million years ago, was *Homo erectus*, based especially on the fossils found in Java from 1890 onwards. They have a brain size averaging *c.* 900 cc, based on 10 skulls. As the name implies, *erectus* was certainly an upright walker; we have examples of his pelvis and femur, and he was not much smaller than ourselves. The only way in which *erectus* was smaller than *africanus* was in his teeth, which were slightly smaller all round and thus beginning to approach the small tooth-size range found in modern man.

A fine sample of late *Homo erectus* is known from Chou-k'ou-tien near Peking (*see* CHINA). Here, brain size averages over 1051 cc and falls within the modern human range. The robust hominids survived down to the time of *Homo erectus*, who had a brain nearly twice as big. The difference was probably one of culture: the robust species is not known to have made tools, or hunted, or eaten meat; in fact his big molar teeth, probably for grinding abrasive foods, suggest a vegetarian diet. The human lineage clearly hunted, ate meat, and made tools; his teeth were like ours, though they were relatively bigger at the front.

Fossils since *Homo erectus* are often classified as *Homo sapiens* and include many Neanderthal types. Like *Homo erectus*, most early *sapiens* fossils, such as Steinheim and Tautavel, have big brow ridges and a heavy facial structure. But the brow ridges are a little smaller, and by the time of the classic Neanderthals, some 50,000 years ago, they were smaller again, though more obvious since the forehead was higher.

True Neanderthal man of Europe, living some 80,000 to 40,000 years ago, had a large brain: he was the first to equal or surpass the modern average. He also had relatively large front teeth and a protruding face and nose. For a long time a debate has raged over whether he could have been the ancestor of modern man. Once it was fashionable to believe that all Neanderthal-like people from Europe, Asia, and Africa died out without issue, and indeed that modern-type man lived alongside them somewhere. This view is now generally rejected. The alternatives are that some Neanderthals, especially in Western Asia, evolved into modern man, and replaced European Neanderthals by spreading across Europe, and the simpler view that, in Europe and elsewhere, Neanderthals evolved into Cromagnon man.

Some Cromagnon men living between 40,000 and 20,000 years ago still had the prominent brow ridges and large teeth of the Neanderthals, but in a lesser degree. This is known from the Czechoslovak sites of Brno, Pavlov, and Předmost. But most Cromagnon men were very like ourselves, and it is generally accepted that modern European (Caucasoid) peoples are descended from the Cromagnons; but the ancestry of the Mongoloid and Negroid peoples is still much debated.

Modern Europeans tend to be shorter and surprisingly smaller brained than the Cromagnons. The only evolutionary change of any significance in the last 10,000 years has been the trend to "overbite," i.e., modern people have upper incisors overlapping their lower incisors, while in the Cromagnons they met edge to edge.

**Hunting and Gathering.** A way of life believed to have lasted for over 2 million years during the Palaeolithic and Mesolithic periods. It also survived down to recent times over considerable areas, for example, in Australia until the Europeans came, in much of Southern Africa until the Portuguese and Bantu came, and over much of America, until the Europeans settled, and Siberia.

Pioneers of prehistoric research in the 19th century, such as Henry Christy and John Lubbock, suggested that the study of present-day hunters could cast light on early man, and that comparisons should be made wherever possible. At the present time a majority of prehistorians still take the view that such "ethnographic" evidence is valuable, but can be misleading.

The hunting and gathering way of life seems to have been universal before farming. Typically, non-agricultural peoples have an economy in which the hunting of animals is performed by the male and the gathering of food, mostly vegetable, is done by the women and children. The monogamous family, typical of such peoples, follows from the desirability of sharing the products of the food quest, and of the necessity for carefully rearing children with a long dependency period.

In practice the contribution of the two sources of food is rarely equal. In the equatorial belt it is common for gathered vegetable food to make up more than twice as much of the bulk as hunted meat; but it is not necessarily such a large proportion of the protein. By contrast, in high latitudes it is common for vegetable food to make up less than a tenth of the diet. In these circumstances women are less productive, and often less numerous than men due to selective infanticide. Coastal people often obtain a lot of food by fishing, as do groups with access to lakes and rivers with fish.

It seems likely that hunting began no earlier than the earliest toolmaking 2–3 million years ago, while gathering is much older. According to one theory, stone tools with sharp edges were first needed when hunting began, to slit open the prey. Before this, hunting would have been unproductive, because humans cannot tear open their kills.

Big game hunting is known to have been practiced some 300,000 years ago and possibly over a million years ago. Once hunters had mastered the art, it seems that they became ambitious quite soon—aided perhaps by bigger body size, and eventually by quite sophisticated spears with sharpened tips.

Very little is known about how early man hunted. No pitfalls or traps have ever been found, but an elephant has been found with a spear through it, and a number of animal bones have been found with spear wounds. At Solutré, in France, there is evidence that horses were killed by forcing them over a cliff.

Very commonly, one animal species was hunted more intensively than the others: in Europe it was most often the red deer, horse, and reindeer. Bovines, rhinoceroses, and elephants of various species also figure prominently in the list of animals most often hunted. In Africa antelopes were commonly hunted.

The main advances in hunting seem to have come at the end of the Ice Age. The barbed spear or harpoon was invented about 15,000 years ago, and a spearthrower was used to propel it. The value of this device is indicated most strongly by the way it was adopted on every continent, from Australia to America via Africa and Eurasia. An alternative to carved bone or antler barbs was the inset of small flint blades as barbs.

The bow and arrow were invented by 11,000 years ago, and these must have increased the killing power of the hunters greatly. About the same time we find the first fish hooks, as well as fish gorges and so-called bird darts. These devices were all probably designed to be baited and swallowed by fish or birds.

The Mesolithic hunters, who had to cope with the forests which spread northwards across Europe at the end of the last Ice Age, are believed to have switched to a style of hunting in which fish, fowl, and small mammals played an increasing part. From the sites of Mesolithic man, excellently preserved in peat bogs across Northern Europe, we find nets, hooks, wicker fish traps, and a host of other devices thought to have been used in catching food animals.

Whereas the Ice Age hunters of reindeer and horse in Europe probably got most of their food from herd animals, as some arctic peoples do today, the Mesolithic hunters of the temperate forests probably got a much higher proportion from vegetable sources. Unfortunately, archaeologists have only the slenderest chance of learning about these plant foods. Most commonly found remains are hazelnut shells, which fossilize quite readily. They are found in sites of the last interglacial temperate period, as well as in many postglacial sites. Pips of the hackberry are also found on many early sites. Presumably nuts and seeds were eaten on a large scale.

A number of coastal settlements are known from the Mesolithic, typically indicated by shell middens—piles of shellfish and fish bones. The fact that they are not often found from earlier periods may indicate that sea level during the Ice Ages was usually hundreds of feet below present levels, and thus coastal sites would have since been drowned or destroyed.

**Hurrians.** An Asianic-speaking people who may have originated in Armenia. Their names have been found in texts dating back to Akkadian times, but they settled in large numbers in Northern Syria and Mesopotamia from the end of the 3rd millennium BC onwards (*see* TELL ATCHANA), and by *c*. 1600 BC they had established a series of kingdoms in the area. The name Mitanni has come to be applied to an Indo-Iranian element in the population, which seems to have formed an aristocracy and is probably responsible for the introduction of the horse and the chariot into the Near East. The kingdom of Mitanni seems to have been a federation of these Hurrian states under the rule of the kings of Washukanni (perhaps TELL FAKHERIYAH), of whom the best known is Saustatar (15th century BC). It came into conflict with HITTITES, Egyptians, and ASSYRIANS and, in the middle of the 14th century BC, the kingdom fell to the Hittites and the Assyrians. A distinctive type of pottery, known as NUZI ware, is found on a number of Hurrian sites, including Tell Atchana. Recent Iraqi excavations at Tell el Fukhar have brought to light tablets of the same date as those from nearby Nuzi.

**Hüyük.** *See* TELL, TEPE, or HÜYÜK.

**Hydria.** A form of Greek jar, used for carrying water. It has a bulbous body, round neck, single strap handle, and two side handles.

**Hyksos.** *See* EGYPT; SYRIA–PALESTINE.

**Hypocaust.** A Roman form of warm-air heating, usually found in bath houses, but in colder provincial climates also used for heating living quarters. Warm air, heated in an outside stokehole, circulated under the raised floor and also often entered the room through vents above floor level.

**Ice Age.** The idea of an Ice Age in the geological sequence is usually credited to Jean Louis Agassiz, a Swiss naturalist, who suggested it *c*. 1837. A number of earlier workers had suggested that traces of former glaciers and ice sheets indicated that these had once been more extensive than today; but it was Agassiz who conceived of a worldwide cold period when areas as far apart as North America and Germany had been glaciated. Today, many lines of evidence confirm that such a period did exist in the last few million years at the end of the geological sequence. Indeed, earlier Ice Ages are known, spaced out at intervals of over 200 million years.

Traditionally, archaeologists have accepted the idea, proposed by Albrecht Penck in 1909, that there were four Ice Ages (called in Europe, Gunz, Mindel, Riss, and Würm) separated by warmer interglacial periods. This complex made up the Pleistocene period, following the Pliocene period of warmer climate. Now we know that the situation is much more complex than that. Even in the last 700,000 years there were at least 7 cold periods, well separated by warm climate, and before that at least 6 more. But we must make a distinction between cold periods and glacial advances. In most of the 13 cold periods mentioned above, there is evidence of colder climate only from biological or chemical indications. The evidence for separate ice advances exists for no more than 4 or 5 periods.

Ice Ages manifested themselves differently in different areas. In high mountains, the permanent snowline came down to a much lower altitude and glaciers descended further down the valleys and even into the plains. The rivers flowing out of the mountains developed "terraces" of coarse rubble in their river plains, to be cut through as the river eroded down during the next warm period. It was from such terraces that Penck's sequence for the Northern Alps was created.

The great ice sheets of Antarctica and Greenland seem to have first formed over 2 million years ago, but the formation of a comparable ice sheet over North America and Scandinavia came later. In Europe only three main periods of ice advance are well documented: all fall in the last 0.5 million years. Outside the actual ice mass. there would have been an extensive belt of tundra stretching equatorwards to the boreal forests, which would have been pushed far southwards in Europe and North America.

**Igbo Ikwu.** To the east of the River Niger, some 25 mi. (40 km) south of Onitisha in the small town of Igbo Ikwu, Nigeria, a number of bronze objects were accidentally discovered in 1938. It was not until 1959 that a professional archaeologist, Professor Thurstan Shaw from the University of Ibadan in Nigeria, excavated a series of very rich Iron Age deposits in the area of the original finds. Shaw discovered the wood-lined burial chamber of a royal person who had been buried with items of regalia, including a crown, bead necklaces and a ceremonial staff topped with a cast bronze leopard's head. Adjacent to the burial chamber was a muniment house that contained vessels and other objects of bronze, pottery, ivory, and wood. The most spectacular find was a bronze vessel which had been cast in one piece and built on a stand adorned with an interlaced rope of bronze. An iron sword in a bronze scabbard was also discovered. Magnificent as the Igbo Ikwu finds are, they raise many problems. Three radiocarbon analyses suggest a date in the middle of the 9th century AD, but such an early date is unacceptable to many archaeologists because of the associated imported goods in the muniment house. The solution to the

107

problem of the date of the Igbo Ikwu site will therefore have to wait until further excavation has been carried out.

**Impressed pottery cultures.** The groups of related cultures found along the Southeastern coast of China. They are so-named after the pottery with impressed designs, the product of groups of people living a semi-settled life in which fishing played a large part. Although some bronze weapons and a few vessels have been found, they used little metal. However, the bronze decoration of the CHOU DYNASTY, in the heart of China, where bronze was extensively utilized, influenced the designs stamped on the pottery of the coastal cultures; and, in its turn, the repetitive nature of the pottery designs also influenced bronze decoration.

**Impressed ware.** Communities of early mixed farmers established themselves from the 6th millennium BC onwards in Southern Italy and Sicily, Northwest Italy, Southern France, Eastern Spain, and the West Mediterranean islands. They are recognized especially by their "impressed" ware pottery: in simple forms, it is profusely decorated with impressions made with the fingernail, the fingertip, shells, and other tools.

**Inca.** During the LATE INTERMEDIATE PERIOD, the Inca emerged from amongst a number of local groups in the Cuzco area of Peru as the dominant influence. After 1438, by means of military conquest over other Andean provinces, they imposed a remarkably uniform political system, architectural, art, and ceramic style upon a large number of diverse cultural groups. Through a rigid administrative system new towns were built, peoples were resettled where necessary, and control was exercised over the natural resources and products of a large and extremely varied empire, which by the 16th century covered 2,175 mi. (3,500 km) from north to south and an average of 199 mi. (320 km) from the west coast inland. The Incas were non-literate, and therefore details of their imperial system and the ways of life under their rule must be reconstructed by combining ethnohistorical and administrative records with archaeological data.

For the Early Inca Period, c. AD 1100–1438, the records are incomplete, but antecedents to the Inca ceramic style have been found in KILLKE settlements in the Cuzco area. Origin myths suggest the ways in which the Inca Dynasty was founded, their arrival at Cuzco, and the beginnings of imperial domination. From AD 1438, the records are more complete. Pachacuti Inca (1438–71) consolidated further conquests and the administrative government was established and developed. His son Topa Inca (1471–93) extended the frontiers into Bolivia and Chile, and made further political refinements. Despite some civil unrest, the empire continued to expand under Huayna Capac (1493–1525), until the arrival of the Spanish in 1532, and the capture and ransom of Atahualpa Inca effectively terminated the Inca domination of the Andean area.

The empire was divided into four provinces, and administered through an elitist social hierarchy of pyramidal form. At the apex stood the Sapa Inca, the title given to the political, religious, and military supreme ruler. The Apus, or council, and the provincial governors were drawn from the Inca nobility, while native leaders indoctrinated into Inca ideologies operated at the local level. Some of the pre-Inca native boundaries were

The Inca administrative center of Tambo Colorado, c. AD 1476–1532, in the Pisco valley, Peru.

maintained, while other groups were redefined, exchanged or resettled within the empire according to the requirements of the administration. These requirements included the levying of manpower for political, economic, military, or religious purposes, the manufacture and distribution of various products, and especially the collection and redistribution of foodstuffs. Under Inca rule, many new building works were undertaken for a variety of purposes. The location and layout of the towns, engineering works, etc., reflected the social hierarchy and local and imperial requirements, expressed in terms of a highly standardized and functional architectural style.

The keynotes of Inca technology were efficient organization, usually in workshops or factory sites, and a high degree of proficiency. The textiles, metal products, and ceramics were all extremely functional, and although very fine and distinctive, the Inca organizational system permitted little individual creativity. As with the architectural style, forms and motifs are standardized and repetitive. The Inca drew upon traditional expertise in order to ensure the highest standards—thus CHIMU goldsmiths were brought to Cuzco and their techniques formed the basis for the imperial gold metallurgy. The pottery is handmade, and usually decorated with slip paint in the Cuzco polychrome tradition of small, repetitive geometric designs. The range of forms is limited, and both elegant and functional. Provincial styles, based on diverse local traditions, can be identified by fabric and decorative techniques, although they are strongly influenced by the prestigious Cuzco ceramics.

As with other aspects of the state, religion was organized to serve unifying political purposes. Local native deities were respected, provided that the primary importance of the Sun, as the divine ancestor of the Inca Dynasty, was acknowledged. The cult of the Sun is linked to the great importance of astronomical and calendrical observations to a people whose organization was based on an agricultural economy. However, Viracocha, the creator god, was conceded first place in the hierarchy of deities amongst the Inca elite. (*See* CUZCO; MACHU PICCHU; HUANUCO VIEJO; CUSICHACA; TAMBO COLORADO.)

## India.

*Palaeolithic.* The Indian subcontinent has produced almost no fossil men, but it has revealed a fine sample of hominid remains from a time long preceding the first men, and possibly ancestral to them. They belong to the genus *Ramapithecus* and come from the Siwalik beds, some 8-12 million years old and up to 1.2 mi. (2 km) thick. As recently as 1976 a new lower jaw of *Ramapithecus* was found at Gandakas in Pakistan. On the basis of the jaw fragments of *Ramapithecus*, he seems to have already lost the dagger-like canine teeth always found in apes and to have had a shorter rounded tooth row, as found in man.

The Palaeolithic in India is not known to be very ancient, but this may turn out to be due to inadequate data on sites over 0.5 million years old. The earliest stone tools may be those from the "boulder conglomerate"

formation of the Punjab region. Sometimes called Soan or Pre-Soan, they are mainly pebble tools and large flakes a little reminiscent of the CLACTONIAN of Europe and the Oldowan of Africa (*see* OLDUVAI GORGE).

It is known that handaxes and cleavers like those of the African ACHEULIAN were also widely made in India, and there are tools like "Levallois flakes" and "scrapers," which resemble and may be contemporary with those of the Mousterian of Europe. Blade tools like those of the Upper PALAEOLITHIC of Europe were also made, and preliminary results from RADIOCARBON DATING suggest a similar age (back to 25,000 years ago or earlier). Some of these finds are from caves. At the close of the Palaeolithic, tiny bladelet tools like those of the European MESOLITHIC were being used.

*Neolithic.* In recent years evidence has come to light in several parts of India and Pakistan for the transitional stage between the hunting and gathering economies of the Mesolithic and fully settled agriculture. Excavations at Gumla, Sarai Khola, and Jalilpur in Pakistan reveal Neolithic settlements, probably datable to the 4th millennium BC, which may belong to this stage. Neolithic sites occur in Kashmir (Burzahom), the Ganges valley (Chirand), and particularly in the Southern peninsula. Here, there is evidence of a mainly cattle-raising people, living in hilltop or plateau villages of wattle-and-daub or mud huts. They buried their dead within the village: the children in large jars, the adults extended in graves and accompanied by funerary offerings. They used ground stone axes and microlithic (very small stone) blade tools.

*Indus Civilization.* Settled mixed farming seems to have been introduced into India from Iran and Baluchistan, where 4th-millennium BC settlements closely resemble early farming sites in the Indus Valley. The latter, including the type-site of HARAPPA, after which the civilization is often called, are the immediate antecedents of mature Indus civilization sites. They contain many elements, such as artifact types and monumental architecture, that foreshadow the full civilization and are found over a similar area to the latter, whose main distribution covers the alluvial plain of the Indus and its tributaries, with outlying sites along the West coast and in the extreme East.

Radiocarbon dates for the mature Indus civilization suggest a timespan of *c.* 2300-1750 BC. This supports the evidence, in the form both of seals and other typical artifacts and of Mesopotamian literary references, of trade between the Harappan civilization and Sargonid Sumer, with Bahrain acting as an entrepot. The Indus civilization also maintained a trading network in less civilized areas, obtaining various raw materials from other parts of India, Afghanistan, Iran, and Arabia. Within the civilization itself, a well organized system of craft production and distribution ensured the widespread enjoyment of the products of localized specialists or source areas. Cloth impressions on the reverse of many of the well known Indus seals indicate that they may have been employed in some such mercantile context. The presence of weights and measures of standard sizes furthers the impression of efficient organization.

This is nowhere more apparent than in the layout of Harappan towns and cities. All conform to a general plan: an open grid-plan residential area of carefully laid out main streets and smaller side streets with houses of various sizes, from single-roomed dwellings to mansions laid out around courtyards. One of the most surprising features is the emphasis on cleanliness: almost all the houses have a bathroom, linked by chutes to the city drains which run down the center of the main streets. To the west of the lower town lies the citadel, a raised fortified area containing what appear to be administrative buildings, possibly the residence of the ruling oligarchy (whose nature remains a mystery), and including enormous granaries, which imply a high level of state control of production. Most of the architecture is of dried or baked mud brick, with timber employed in roofing. (*See* MOHENJO-DARO; HARAPPA.) One site which departs from the norm is the coastal town of Lothal on the Gulf of Cambay, where a dock and massive brick wharf are known. This port underlines the importance of trade to the Harappans.

The economy was one of mixed farming, in which wheat and barley, supplemented by legumes, dates, sessamum and mustard, were the staple diet. Cotton for cloth was also grown. Sheep, goats, and fowl were the main domestic animals, and possibly also cattle, buffalo, and pigs. The occurrence of the bones of elephants and their popularity as a motif on seals suggest that they, too, may have been domesticated. The diet was supplemented by hunted deer and tortoise.

Although copper was known and used for everyday tools, these were generally rather primitive and not common, doubtless due to the expense of importing copper. The most common tools were chert blades struck from a prepared core. Beads are frequently found, particularly of etched carnelian, and they were also exported. The pottery is mainly wheelmade red-slipped ware, with a variety of black-painted decorative motifs, especially animals and plants. The frequent occurrence of light-hearted little representations in terra-cotta of people, birds, carts, and animals, possibly children's toys, helps to counteract the gloomy impression given by the dull uniformity and standardization of most material aspects.

Around 1800–1700 BC, the Indus civilization suddenly collapsed: the upper levels at Harappa are a disorderly jumble of scrappy huts, while at Mohenjo-Daro the streets are lined with corpses. Many theories explain this decline: deforestation for the firing of mud bricks upsetting the delicate balance of nature; a change in the course of the Indus leading to flooding or drought; plague; or the advance of the Aryan hordes. The latter seems a likely contributing factor; further work may confirm or destroy these hypotheses.

*Post-Harappan cultures.* After the end of the Indus civilization, in both Kathiawar and the Sind, once outposts of the Harappans, the material culture continued little changed throughout the 2nd millennium, but the highly organized way of life disappeared: for example, town planning ceased. Minor developments occurred, especially in the appearance of new pottery styles and the beginning of the cultivation of rice and millet. Around 1000 BC, iron made its first appearance. Ahar and Gilund in the Banas valley, Nagda and Navdatoli in Malwa, and other sites in these areas enjoyed a similar way of life during this period, living in wattle-and-daub huts, practicing mixed farming and making stone and copper tools and a variety of ceramics, including the ubiquitous Black-and-Red ware. The cultures were probably indigenous, with Aryan immigrants. In the Deccan, this period is represented by many excavated sites, including Nevasa, Prakash, and Inamgaon, where extensive excavations are still in progress. They share many elements with these post-Harappan cultures, including copper tools, wattle-and-daub dwellings, and various pottery types, like Black-and-Red ware, while other elements, particularly stonework, continue the traditions of the South Indian Neolithic.

*Iron Age.* The Peninsular Iron Age, which marks no sharp break in the culture sequence, is characterized by the so-called "Megalithic" grave culture, which comprises a number of different tomb types, some, though not all, of which include the use of massive boulders or slabs. The main tomb types found are cists, often with a porthole, pits, urnfields and rockcut chambers; legged sarcophagi occur in many of the cists. Despite the diversity of tomb types, the culture is uniform in the use of stone circles and cairns to mark the majority of graves, of Black-and-Red ware as the chief ceramic type, of iron tools and weapons, and of the rite of burial involving the dismemberment of bodies after exposure. Little dating evidence has come to light but the culture must fall some time in the period after the first appearance of iron in South India around 1100–1000 BC, continuing through the Roman period, when a few Roman-style artifacts are found associated with some of the megaliths. The absence of settlement evidence leaves this culture rather a mystery.

Literary and archaeological evidence combine to suggest the appearance of waves of Aryan invaders in Iran and Northern India between *c.* 1800 and 1000 BC. It is uncertain whether they were responsible for the downfall of the Indus civilization; however, flimsy structures of reused brick at Harappa, associated with a hybrid pottery type, probably indicates their presence here in the later 2nd millennium. Further east in the Ganges-Jamuna plains, the Painted Gray ware culture seems to be the archaeological manifestation of the Aryans *c.* 1000 to 600 BC, supporting the change of geographical focus seen in later Aryan literature. These later Aryans used iron, lived in wattle-and-daub huts with mud floors, used plows, and added rice to the earlier mixed economy of wheat, barley, cattle, and horses. Prior to Aryan settlement in this area, it was occupied by native cultures dating back to the Indus civilization and before, represented archaeologically by Black-and-Red ware in the Central Ganges valley and Central India, and by ocher-colored pottery in the Upper Ganges—Jamuna plains, which was also associated with hoards of copper artifacts, including antennae-hilted swords, flat and anthropomorphic axes, harpoons, and chisels.

*Ganges Cities.* By the 6th–7th century BC, the villages of the Ganges-Jamuna and the Central Ganges valley were becoming true city states. These were enlarged by territorial warfare, which culminated in the formation of the Mauryan Empire in the 4th century BC under Chandragupta Maurya, who reconquered the Northern areas lost to Alexander the Great in 327 BC, and pushed his borders as far South as the Deccan. Literary evidence from this period describes fortified cities with monumental buildings—like the pillared hall in the Mauryan capital at Patna, happily preserved, along with part of the box timber rampart fortifying the city. Archaeological evidence for this period consists mainly of the characteristic gleaming Northern Black Polished ware, iron and copper tools, seals inscribed in early script, silver and copper coins, supplemented by scanty structural remains of wells and mud ramparts. However, traditional tales of the Buddha, who lived in the 6th century BC, are supported by finds at his birthplace, Lumbini, at the scene of his enlightenment, at Bodh Gaya, and of his first sermon, at Sarnath, and important sites from his life, both in the form of contemporary archaeological material and in pillars erected by the third Mauryan emperor, Aśoka, who was a Buddhist convert and made a pilgrimage to the principal Buddhist holy places in 249 BC. Rock edicts at various spots in his empire proclaim his faith and moral code. He is reputed to have built 84,000 Buddhist stupas (funerary domes with a surrounding decorated stone railing), evidence of which survives at Sanchi in Central India, where a stone-faced stupa of the 1st century BC covers Aśoka's brick stupa. Bharhut, also in Central India, has the remains of a 2nd-century BC stupa, while at Amaravati further south construction continued until the 3rd century AD. All these stupas are decorated with sculptured scenes of events in the life of Buddha. Amaravati shows representations of the Buddha in human form, a departure from the earlier prohibition. This was a development which occurred simultaneously in the native art of Mathura, a subtle blend of Indian and foreign elements, and in Gandhara, where successive influences from the West had inspired a distinctive art style. Many decorative elements of the stupas, the Aśokan pillars, and Mauryan art and architecture show Persian and Achaemenid influence. Gandhara, the Northwest frontier province, was, from the 6th century BC, part of the Persian Empire and it acted as a medium through which Western ideas were transmitted to India, and even foreign craftsmen themselves are thought to have been active in India at this time. After Alexander the Great's conquest of Persia and North India, Indo-Greek settlement continued foreign traditions in Gandhara, especially in the cities of TAXILA and Charsada, where neat chessboard town planning shows Greek influence.

Rome continued the trade with India begun by the Greeks and Persians. Luxury items at Taxila bear witness to the importance of Roman trade in North India. In the 2nd and 3rd centuries AD, the Afghan site of Begram near Kabul was an important entrepot on the trade route between China and the West, bypassing the hostile Parthian Empire that straddled the more direct route: a magnificent hoard of pieces from China, India, and the West witness its importance. Trade with South India, especially in spices, became important after the Roman discovery of the use of monsoon for a direct sea crossing, in the 1st century BC. (*See* ARIKAMEDU.)

This period also saw the beginning of rockcut cave temples in Central and Southern India. The ghats of South India are of laterite, a stone which is soft initially but which becomes hard after exposure to air, so the region is particularly suited to this architectural type. Rockcut architecture is generally imitative of freestanding wooden buildings, and in the early cave temples details of carpentry are faithfully reproduced. The cave temples fall into two groups, earlier Buddhist caves, *c.* 2nd century BC to 2nd century AD, and later Buddhist, Jain, and Hindu caves (5th to 8th century AD). The earliest examples followed their wooden prototypes closely and included a pegged-on wooden façade. In later examples the latter is of stone, and the architecture and sculpture is more elaborate and less in the wooden tradition. (*See* AJANTA; ELLORA.)

**Indo-Europeans.** Linguistically related peoples who make up the greater part of the population of Europe today. A series of migrations brought Indo-Europeans into the Near East, probably from the North and/or East. The earliest attested are the LUWIANS, the HITTITES, and related peoples who entered ANATOLIA at the end of the 3rd millennium BC. An Indo-Iranian aristocracy appears at the head of the linguistically unrelated HURRIANS in Northern Syria and MESOPOTAMIA during the first centuries of the 2nd millennium BC; it seems to have been responsible for the introduction of horseriding and chariots into the Near East. (*See* SYRIA–PALESTINE; CORDED WARE CULTURES.)

**Industrial archaeology.** The discovery, recording, and study of the physical remains of yesterday's ways of making and selling things, and of transporting goods and people. This evidence may be readily visible (e.g., old railway stations, canals, textile mills, or quarries), or it may only be revealed as a result of excavation (e.g., the sites of former potteries, glassworks, and ironworks). It may be of any age.

**Industrial housing.** An essential part of the archaeology of industry. It ranges from on-site accommodation provided for lock-keepers, to the mansions of industrial millionaires, and from the slum tenements of Lille in France, to the garden-city provision of PULLMAN, near Chicago in the United States. What has survived from the 19th century is chiefly that part of the old stock of working-class housing which was suitable for modernization, and those employers' and managers' residences which could be adapted to today's needs and which were not in the way of urban redevelopment schemes. In the United States, mansions at Newport, R.I., are an interesting reflection of American capitalism in its unfettered days: they include "The Breakers" (1895), built by Cornelius Vanderbilt for $5 million. Another survival from American capitalism in its heyday is "La Cuesta Encantada," built by the newspaper magnate, William Randolph Hearst, at San Simeon, Calif., and now furnished just as it was in his lifetime and preserved as an historic monument. The outstanding European example of the same kind and period is the Villa Hügel (late 1860s), the former residence of the Krupp family, at Essen, West Germany, which is now also a museum.

Many of the housing estates built by 19th-century industrialists for their workers were ahead of their time in spaciousness, construction, and amenities, and for this reason they have had a better-than-average chance of survival. Outstanding among early housing projects of this kind in Britain are those at NEW LANARK, Scotland (c. 1799); Cronkbourne Village, Kirk Braddon, Isle of Man (1846–50); the Railway Village at Swindon (1840s); and Saltaire, near Bradford (1850–70). Outstanding in France is DORNACH, at Mulhouse, built mainly in the 1850s and 1860s. Belgium has the miners' colony at LE GRAND HORNU (1819–40). The Ruhr industrialists undertook extensive building of workers' settlements, sometimes of the garden-city type, between 1860 and 1914, notably in the areas of Essen, Oberhausen, and Dortmund. Many of these houses and apartment blocks were destroyed or damaged during World War II, and others have been demolished recently, in a fit of enthusiasm for new multistory blocks. The best American examples of this kind of paternalistic housing are George Westinghouse's new town of WILMERDING, near Pittsburgh, Penn. (1869 onwards) and George Pullman's town of Pullman (1880–84) near Chicago.

**Industry, Greek and Roman.** The emergence of industries in Greece, as distinct from craftsmen, came with the growth of the money system in the 6th century BC, when carpenters, potters, smiths, and leatherworkers were able to set up *ergasteria*—workshops, staffed by slaves or free workers under the charge of foremen. In the Hellenistic period such enterprises multiplied, and food production too was organized on the same lines: similar techniques were adopted by the Ptolemys in Egypt, who brought much of the production of Egypt under state control.

Roman industry was essentially the same as Greek, with the owner's factory staffed by slaves and manufacturing a specialized product. Some, for example the *terra sigillata* potteries of Gaul, exported to all areas of the empire, but gradually local entrepreneurs were able to produce goods of similar quality to satisfy local markets. The later Roman period was one, however, in which the economy was theoretically far more planned: in particular, government factories supplying essentials for the army were set up in many areas, and the numbers of smaller industries dwindled.

**Ingapirca.** An Inca period settlement near Cuenca, Ecuador. The main feature of the site is an oval enclosure with a single entrance and a central back-to-back structure.

**Ingot.** *See* CURRENCY, PREHISTORIC EUROPE; CAPE GELIDONIYA; METAL TECHNOLOGY, PREHISTORIC EUROPE.

**Initial Period.** This period marks the introduction of pottery into the Central Andean area, between c. 1900 and 1200 BC. The settled maritime and herding life styles of the preceramic period antedated full agriculture, but the traits and trait complexes postulated as the Central Andean or Peruvian cultural tradition had coalesced by this period. These included the cultivation of most plants of the area, including maize, and the domestication of the llama and the guinea pig; the basic clothing types of slit-necked shirts, shawls, and carrying bags; settled communities and monumental U-shaped ceremonial complexes constructed by communal labor; stone and clay reliefs to embellish public buildings; and crafts, including weaving, ceramics, shell, wood, and stone carving. Metallurgy was absent. The art motifs which were to persist were already common to a number of sites. Symmetrical, repetitive, and opposed designs of fish, serpents, birds, humans, and felines were already part of the artistic tradition.

**Ipiutak.** An Eskimo site, dating from AD 350, on Point Hope on the Chukchi Sea in Northern Alaska. Discovered in 1939, Ipiutak is particularly important for its demonstration of the continuing influence of Siberian cultures on the Eskimo tradition. The site consists of more than 500 house sites spread over several beach ridges. The houses had underground floors and were rectangular with rounded corners. The floors were covered in gravel or poles, with the fireplace in the center of the building, and the roofs were flat with a central smoke hole. A cemetery was found with burials placed in log coffins, the bodies in an articulated extended position, sometimes with grave goods, which featured linked chains, snow goggles, skulls, and small animals carved in ivory. Other burials were placed in wooden graves, probably on the surface of the ground: it was these which had the most elaborate grave goods, including ivory attachments to masks decorated with animal motifs. This lively animal art style may have derived from Siberian influences.

The Ipiutak people were both sea and land hunters. As well as the usual Eskimo complex of harpoons, quantities of small stone points have been found, suggesting that the hunting of caribou was also important to their economy. This might indicate a knowledge of the interior of the country, as might the fact that they used bark bowls. The Eskimos of Ipiutak were also expert stoneworkers, making ground stone labrets and adze blades. They did not make pottery. The Ipiutak culture was probably a development from the Choris-Norton-Near Ipiutak subtradition, intermingled with Northern Maritime and Siberian influences. (*See also* ESKIMOS.)

**Iran.** The modern name, derived from "Aryan," for ancient Persia. The country is limited to the north and south by the Caspian Sea and the Persian Gulf. To the west, the Zagros Mountains form a natural frontier with Iraq, but the Northwestern frontier in the Caucasus and the Southwestern in Khuzistan are not so well defined, and nor are the Eastern boundaries. A Central desert depression is bordered by mountain ranges, and it is in these that various cultures have developed, often in isolation, but often also linked by the trade routes from the East which passed south of the Caspian and

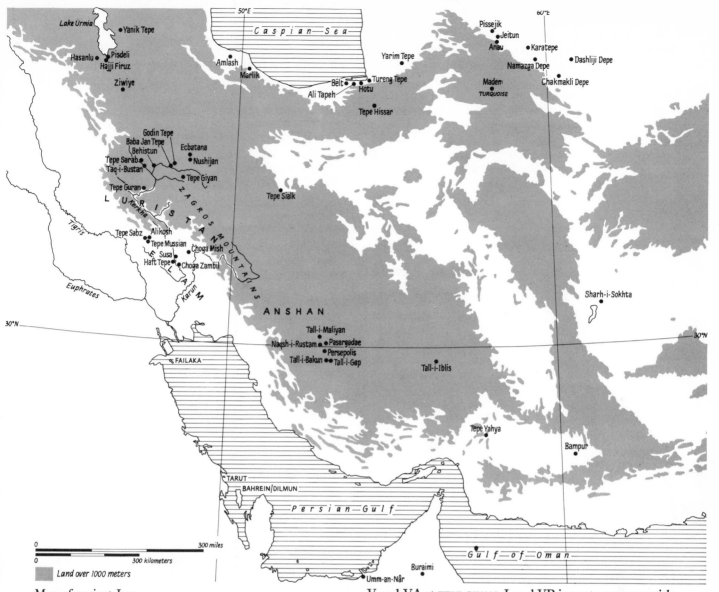

Map of ancient Iran.

north of the Gulf. Incursions of nomads from the North, on both sides of the Caspian, provided a North-South direction to these contacts.

The early cultures of the Western Zagros and of Khuzistan are dealt with in connection with MESO-POTAMIA, since they were often antecedents of lowland cultures. The sites of Ganjdareh E and Asiab in the Kermanshah area in the Central Zagros produce evidence of early seasonal settlements of the 9th and 8th millennia BC. In Ganjdareh D were found mud-brick cubicles with plastered floors (destroyed *c.* 7000 BC), the earliest dated pottery in the Near East, a niche containing two animal skulls, human figurines, and some burials below the floors. Ganjdareh C–A illustrates further developments, but Alikosh in nearby Khuzistan was still without pottery. The settlers at Tepe Guran in LURISTAN (*c.* 6500–5500 BC) lived first in huts and then in mud-brick houses with *terrazzo* floors; they herded domesticated flocks and used both plain and painted pottery. Tepe Sarab, near Kermanshah, has produced female figurines. After a period of transition, the sequence continues with levels

V and VA at TEPE GIYAN. Level VB is contemporary with Early UBAID and with the Dalma culture, which continues until *c.* 4000 BC and is found as far afield as Yanik Tepe in Azerbaijan and is characterized by painted and impressed pottery. By Giyan VC the Late Ubaid stage of development is reached.

Further north in Azerbaijan, on the main East-West trade route, are the mounds of Hajji Firuz and Yanik Tepe, representatives of a culture which began in the middle of the 6th millennium BC. Some irrigation agriculture and domesticated animals formed the basis of the economy, houses were square or rectangular, intra-mural burial was practiced, and some of the pottery was painted. It was succeeded by the Dalma culture, mentioned above. At the Southeast corner of the Caspian there are cave sites (Ali Tappeh, *c.* 10,500 BC onwards, Hotu, Belt).

By the middle of the 6th millennium BC, farming villages of the Jeitun culture appear in Southwest Turkmenistan and in the Gurgan plain at Yarim Tepe and Tureng Tepe. The economy was based on irrigation agriculture supplemented by hunting in the early stages. The houses are detached and square with a prominent hearth or oven. A shrine with animal paintings was found at Pessejik. The Jeitun culture was succeeded by the Chakmakli Depe and Anau IA cultures of the last quarter of the 6th millennium BC, with imported copper tools, houses with buttresses, and attractive painted pottery. These, in turn, were succeeded by the Namazga I culture, with some large sites (Namazga and Kara Depe). The village of Dashliji is particularly representative and a shrine at Anau IB is decorated with geometric wall paintings. Intramural burials appear briefly. The Namazga II/Anau II culture follows in c. 4500 BC, well represented by the sites of Yalangach and Mullali, which are fortified with round towers, and show an increasing use of metal. Further developments appear in Namazga III.

In Central Iran, northeast of Shiraz, there are two painted pottery cultures represented by Tal-i-Jarri B and Tal-i-Mushki. The sites of Tal-i-Bakun, Tal-i-Gap, Tal-i-Iblis, and TEPE YAHYA near Kerman all belong to the second half of the 5th millennium. The economy was based on mixed farming but the presence of turquoise from Maden near Nishapour indicates trade, which local supplies of chlorite and copper would have helped to encourage. Near Kashan, the Sialk culture flourished from c. 5500 BC, centered on TEPE SIALK, and earlier cultures are being revealed by excavations (e.g., Tepe Zaghe, Tepe Sang-i-Chakmak).

With the end of the 4th millennium and the beginning of writing (Tepe Sialk, Tepe Yahya, SUSA), we enter the historical periods, but with the exception of ELAM, which has itself produced texts and which is also mentioned in Mesopotamian documents, little is known about the history of Iran during the 3rd and 2nd millennia BC. The 3rd millennium BC is illustrated by such excavated sites as Susa, Shahr-i Sokhta, Tepe Yahya, TEPE HISSAR (periods II-III), Godin Tepe, Yanik Tepe, HASANLU (period VII), BAMPUR, and Tureng Tepe. Hasanlu VI, Godin Tepe III, and Haft Tepe document the first part of the 2nd millennium, while CHOGA ZAMBIL, Hasanlu V, and Marlik, where an important treasure was found, represent the Early Iron Age.

From c. 1000 BC, most of Iran gradually emerges into history with the advent of the MANNAEANS and of the Indo-Aryan MEDES and Persians. From then on Iranian Dynasties played a dominant role in the Ancient Near East, which was ruled successively by the ACHAEMENIDS, the Greek SELEUCIDS, the PARTHIANS and the SASSANIANS. (See also the chronological table, p. 198.)

**Iraq.** See MESOPOTAMIA.

**Ireland in Prehistory.** Irish prehistory is much shorter than British prehistory (see BRITAIN IN PREHISTORY), for undoubted traces of man are not older than the postglacial period. To make up for this shorter span, Ireland is the richest country in Europe in field antiquities, for land use since prehistory has been less destructive than elsewhere. In addition, old laws and legends written down by early medieval monks probably reflect much of the ways of prehistoric Celtic society, which was never altered in Ireland by a Roman presence. There is no formal date to end Irish prehistory, and to all intents and purposes the Iron Age lingered on in the earlier centuries AD, until Ireland was Christianized in the 5th century AD.

The earliest traces of man in Ireland belong to the Mesolithic period, and date to before 6000 BC. During the Ice Age (down to about 8000 BC), Ireland was probably uninhabitable or inaccessible. Mesolithic sites are numerous, particularly in the Northeast and on the East coast, though this probably reflects the bias of archaeological exploration. More were probably destroyed by rising sea level. Flint implements were less distinctive than in Britain, as a conspicuous series of microliths (tiny blades) is lacking, but retouched leaf-shaped flakes, notched scrapers and axes were typical. In addition axes were ground and pecked out of hard stone other than flint. Subsistence appears to have been based on the coastal resources, and those of the inland rivers, such as the Bann. Shell middens (rubbish mounds) are known from sites like Rough Island, Co. Down, and inland sites, like Newferry, Co. Antrim, appear to represent fishing camps. Upland sites are not known in any quantity, unlike in Britain.

Mesolithic sites persisted well into the 4th millennium BC, and some were contemporary with the earliest intrusive Neolithic sites, the first of which is currently Ballynagilly, Co. Tyrone, dated from c. 3700 BC onwards. Northern and Eastern Ireland provide the clearest evidence in the British Isles for a gradual rather than an abrupt transition from hunting and gathering to farming: late Mesolithic communities adopted domestic animals and pottery before being finally absorbed into Neolithic communities. From the later 4th millennium BC forest clearance was widespread, and individual sites like Ballynagilly show centuries of attack on the forest. In addition to cereals, oxen, sheep, and goats may have been introduced, though pigs were certainly a native species. Traces of field walls have been recovered in Co. Mayo dating from the middle of the 3rd millennium BC, towards the end of the Neolithic period, and renewed clearance dates from the end of the 3rd millennium; however, the spread of blanket peat from this period may be linked to the intensity of previous Neolithic land use. Small settlements with rectangular houses are known, as at Lough Gur, Co. Limerick, but enclosures, as at Lyles Hill, Co. Antrim, were rare. Flint was not mined, but porcellanite, a hard rock found in Co. Antrim, was widely used for axes, which were distributed as far as Scotland. Chambered tombs were numerous. Portal dolmens in the Irish Sea and the more elaborate court cairns of the North may have been earlier than both passage graves and wedge-shaped graves, the latter found far to the west and south of court cairns. Cremation was more usual than inhumation, and passage graves were typically arranged in large groups, often around one outstanding monument (see NEWGRANGE). Stone circles were numerous, and may date to the late Neolithic or Early Bronze Age, but henges were not constructed in Ireland (see CHAMBERED TOMB; HENGE; PASSAGE GRAVE).

As in Britain, the BEAKER CULTURE bridges the transition in Ireland from the Neolithic period to the Bronze

Age (c. 2000–600/500 BC), though it was not so widespread. It introduced copperworking, notably flat axes and daggers, goldworking (sheet ornaments such as the so-called sun discs and *lunulae*), and the burial rite of single inhumation. By the full Early Bronze Age (lasting until c. 1400 BC), a developed and distinctive tradition of bronzeworking had emerged, producing daggers, flat axes, and halberds which were exported to Europe. Ireland was rich in tin, which was widely sought. Its copper sulphide ores, more complex to work than oxide ores, were exploited, testifying to considerable metallurgical skill. Few settlements are known: burials were made in round barrows (more restricted in type than in Britain—*see* BARROW), cairns, or in cists (made with stone slabs) unmarked by a mound. Metalworking continued to develop in the Middle Bronze Age (until c. 900 BC), with palstaves, rapiers, and the first swords being typical products. Some bronze shields probably date to this phase. Impressive goldwork was produced, notably twisted torcs (neck rings). In the Late Bronze Age (until 600–500 BC) Ireland, like highland areas of Britain, was less developed than Southern England in terms of metalworking. Palstaves and winged axes persisted, but there is a notable series of trumpets, sheet bronze buckets, and cauldrons, with associated "flesh hooks," and swords and spears were locally made, while the magnificent gold collar from Glenisheen, Co. Clare, shows the development of earlier skills. Spear patterns from Co. Derry and a leather shield from Co. Longford are unusual finds. Crannogs, or small settlements set on artificial islands in lakes or marshes, are known at Ballinderry, Co. Offaly, and Knocknalappa, Co. Clare. This type of settlement persisted until well into the Christian era in Ireland. The earliest ringforts (earthen *rath* and stone-built *cashel*), as at Cush, Co. Limerick, probably date from at least this period, and continued for a long time.

Iron was never common in the Irish Iron Age, although it was used for swords, knives, spearheads, and axes, amongst other tools; the earliest examples may be two socketed axes. Some 7th- and 6th-century BC bronze swords show contacts with Europe, and the little-known chronology of the Iron Age is in fact best based on the splendid series of decorated bronzework. Fine Celtic ornament on sheaths, horse-gear, and dishes probably dates from the late centuries BC and the early centuries AD. Fine goldwork continued, as for example in the torc from Broighter, Co. Londonderry. Agricola contemplated an invasion and some trade with Roman Britain took place, although, in the 3rd and 4th centuries AD, Irish raiders became a serious problem in Western Britain. The use of crannogs and ringforts continued, and many of the larger hillforts probably date to the Iron Age. Few other settlements or field systems are securely dated within its span.

An unusual picture of a late prehistoric society is preserved in the oral traditions of laws, legends, and other knowledge recorded by early medieval monks, which goes a long way to improving our rather poor knowledge of the Irish Iron Age. Society was stratified, with an aristocracy at its head and vassals at its base.

The ties of kinship and social obligations to leaders were paramount. Legends suggest the heroic character of the age, with social eminence going to the prosperous, the skillful, and above all to the brave.

**Iron.** Iron was first systematically worked by the HITTITES in Asia Minor. Early in the 1st millennium BC iron industries were established in Greece and Italy, and by 500 BC iron had replaced bronze for the manufacture of tools and weapons throughout Europe. However, even in the late 2nd millennium it was occasionally used to make jewelry in Europe, and long before its adoption by the population at large it had been made into tools by smiths for the working of bronze. In time, iron came to be used for many artifacts, e.g. cauldrons, vehicle-fittings, horse-harness, and even currency. By lengthy forging in charcoal-fuelled hearths, iron was often converted into high-quality steels, and by varying their carbon content steels were forged together to make sword-blades of exceptional resilience.

Iron was never intentionally cast in early times outside China, for in Western Eurasia, Africa, and America no furnaces for maintaining the high temperatures necessary for melting iron (over 1,500° C) were devised, and coal, which is a more suitable material than charcoal for producing such temperatures, was only occasionally exploited. Early iron was mostly smelted from the easily worked ores of haematite ($Fe_2O_3$), limonite ($Fe_2O_3H_2O$), and siderite ($FeCO_3$). Pure iron is rare, occurring in two forms, telluric and meteoric, which were both occasionally used in ancient times.

## Iron Age.

*Near East.* Iron first makes its appearance in the Near East towards the middle of the 3rd millennium BC, at ALACA HÜYÜK, CHAGAR BAZAR, and Tell Asmar. Its qualities were not appreciated, however, until the advent of the Iron Age at the end of the 2nd millennium BC. In Palestine, an iron dagger and knife, dating from the 12th century BC, appear in Philistine tombs at TELL FARA.

*Europe.* Following the collapse of the Hittite Empire (where iron technology had been developed but kept a closely guarded monopoly) under the onslaught of the SEA PEOPLE c. 1200 BC, iron technology spread quickly throughout Western Eurasia. It became established in Greece and Italy shortly after 1000 BC, replacing bronze for the manufacture of tools and offensive weapons. In the 7th and 6th centuries BC, the new industry became dominant throughout Europe; although small iron objects had been made in Central Europe for some time, and there is now quite widespread evidence of the use of steel tools for bronzeworking well before iron was adopted to make tools and weapons. Bronze was, however, still used on quite a large scale, particularly for personal ornaments, decorative fittings, and metal vessels.

In some areas of Europe, such as the British Isles and Southern Scandinavia, the establishment of iron industries led to a collapse of the wealth that had been generated by the large-scale use of bronze, and the effects of this were felt for centuries. Other areas, however, where high-grade iron, copper, and mineral salt abounded, such as Austria, Southern Germany, and Iberia, seem to have prospered even more greatly. This was probably largely due to their closer proximity to the Mediterranean world, where immense trading networks were created to satisfy the need for scarce and highly valued raw materials in the Near East and in Greece. The impact which the Mediterranean world had on temperate Europe in the earlier Iron Age is witnessed by the expansion in the late 9th century BC of the Phoenician network into the Western Mediterranean and its establishment of ports of trade ("colonies") at CARTHAGE (Tunisia), Tartessos (Spain), and elsewhere; the establishment of Greek colonies along the coasts of Sicily (e.g., SYRACUSE), Italy (e.g., Tarentum), and Southern France (Massilia, modern Marseilles); the appearance of Greek imports in France, Germany, Switzerland, and even in Belgium and Bohemia, in the 6th and 5th centuries BC; the rise in Central Italy of the VILLANOVAN CULTURE and

A Celtic bronze helmet, with abstract patterns on its neckguard, from North Britain, 1st century AD.

its successor, the Etruscan civilization, which had close links with Central Europe from the 1st millennium until the 4th century BC; and the development, from the 5th century BC, of the highly original abstract decorative styles of the Celts out of Greek and Etruscan floral decorative work. Without this extensive network, it is doubtful whether 5th-century BC Athens would ever have shone so brilliantly. Indeed, it is no coincidence that the beginning of the decline of Athens at the close of the Peloponnesian War (431–404 BC) marks the disappearance of Greek imports from Celtic Central Europe, and that less than two decades later the Celtic tribes began their southward expansion into Central Italy, where they sacked Rome in 385 BC, and eastward expansion into the Danubian countries towards Greece, in an attempt to lessen the impact of the loss of Greek trade. Celtic society in Western Europe was profoundly shaken. The power structure that had flowered and prospered in the 6th and 5th centuries BC in Burgundy

(the Vix culture), Champagne (the Marnian culture), the Rhineland-Palatinate and Saarland (the Hunsrück-Eifel culture), Southwest Germany, Bohemia, the Salzkammergut of Austria (e.g., the important salt mines at HALLSTATT, and at the Dürrnberg near Hallein), and the Italian foothills of the Alps (the Golasecca culture), collapsed in the early 4th century BC. There then followed a period of internecine warfare in these and other Celtic areas, in which weapons were the focus of the highest skills in metalworking, and in which regional schools of sword-scabbard ornamental styles were developed to a high standard of originality and elegance, from the middle Danubian basin to Northern Ireland. In Britain, great stress was laid on the manufacture of bronze-faced shields, which are amongst the finest achievements of prehistoric metalworking in Europe. In this period of disruption, lasting throughout Celtic Europe until the late 2nd century BC, and in Northern and Western France, Northern and Western Britain, and Ireland until much later (in Ireland until the late 1st millennium AD), there developed a world in which power was based on military strength; this is reflected in the oral traditions of Ireland, written down by Irish monks in the mid- to late 1st millennium AD.

From the 3rd century BC, the growth of Roman power exerted a profound influence on Europe, leading to the progressive extinction of Celtic societies by AD 100 (except in Scotland and Ireland), of the Punic Empire in the West Mediterranean, based on the Phoenician foundation, Carthage, and of Greek states and Macedonia in the Third Punic War (149–146 BC), of the Iberian peoples by the end of the 2nd century BC, and to the halting of the southward expansion, in the 1st century BC, of the early Germanic peoples at the Danube and Rhine Rivers. Long-distance trade with Rome led to the growth of urban centers in many Celtic societies which, in the late 2nd and 1st centuries BC, reformulated into new tribes, kingdoms, and even proto-states.

The material culture of the European Iron Age is generally divided into two phases, named after the sites of Hallstatt (Austria) and La Tène (Switzerland), where important discoveries were made in the middle of the last century. The Hallstatt phase (c. 700–450 BC) saw the introduction and consolidation of the use of iron on a large scale, while the succeeding La Tène phase (450–1 BC) witnessed the development of an extraordinarily vigorous succession of abstract and animal art styles by the Celts and the beginnings of urbanization (see URBANIZATION, PREHISTORIC EUROPE). The origins of many of the modern cities and towns of Europe (e.g., Geneva, Bern, Basle, Toulouse, Paris, London, Colchester) lie in Celtic settlements of the pre-Roman period. (See also INDIA.)

**Ironbridge.** The site, in Britain, of the world's first iron bridge (1779). It ceased to be used by vehicles in 1934 but continues to serve as a footbridge, and extensive civil engineering work has recently been carried out to safeguard the abutments. The components were cast at COALBROOKDALE, which required an enlargement of Darby's original furnace there.

The iron bridge, 1779, at Ironbridge, Shropshire, England.

**Iron technology, China.** Iron was first used in China (*c.* 1200 BC) in its meteoric form. Treated like a semi-precious stone, it was mounted in bronze fittings for ceremonial weapons. Iron was first properly worked in China as cast iron in the 7th or early 6th century BC, in remarkable contrast with Europe, where this technique was not evolved until nearly 1,000 years later. To cast iron the ore must be smelted at an extremely high temperature (1835° C), so that the metal can be poured in liquid form. The sophisticated kilns in which Chinese ceramics were already being fired to high temperatures laid the foundation for this development (*see* CERAMICS, CHINA). Iron in its cast form was used primarily for farming implements or tools. Wrought iron was developed some centuries later, by the HAN DYNASTY (206 BC–AD 220). The control of the carbon content was sufficiently well advanced for fine swords to be made of steel.

**Ironworking, Industrial.** Until the beginning of the 19th century, the demand for iron, even in wartime, was by modern standards very small, and the remains of 17th- and 18th-century ironworks reflect this. The scale of operations before the Industrial Revolution is well illustrated by the mid-17th-century Saugus ironworks in Mass., United States, the site of which was excavated in the late 1940s, prior to the reconstruction of the complex during the 1950s. The restored buildings of the early 19th-century ironmaking community at Hopewell Village, near Elverson, Penn., show the same self-contained village atmosphere in which most industry was carried on. A similar picture is provided at Allaire, N.J., where the Allaire State Park contains the restored Howell Works (1830).

The best preservation of monuments relating to the iron industry is probably to be found in Sweden, where modern firms have shown an exceptional degree of responsibility in caring for old forges and furnaces. A number of 18th-century forges have survived in Germany, with their water-driven tilt hammers. There is one in a good state of repair at Essen-Margarethenttal,

117

in West Germany, and at Essen-Wöcklum a 17th-century charcoal ironworks, the Luisenhütte, rebuilt in 1833-34 and 1854, has been restored and opened to the public. Much conservation work has also been undertaken in East Germany.

The British ironworking monuments of the 18th and 19th centuries have not, in general, received the care and respect they deserve. The Darby furnaces at Coalbrookdale, where iron was first smelted with coke, in 1709, were excavated and restored by an industrial firm, not by the Government. Very little official attention has ever been given to another site of world importance, Funtley, near Portsmouth, where Henry Cort pioneered the puddling process for making wrought iron (1784).

**Iroquois.** In New England and Southeastern Canada, the WOODLAND TRADITION survived into historical times. In the Lower Great Lakes region and New York State the most important culture is that of the prehistoric Iroquois, which dates from the middle of this millennium. The village sites were built away from waterways and were sometimes fortified. Subsistence was derived from hunting and the simple farming of maize, and perhaps beans and squash. Projectile points for arrows were of flaked stone, and ungrooved axes, curved adzes, hammerstones and simple maize grinding tools were other important implements. Pottery was used for cooking and storage vessels and for tobacco pipes, which were also sometimes made of ground stone. Typical pots were globular, with raised rims and heightened corners which were sometimes formed into collars. They were unpainted, but the rims and collars were often decorated with incisions and dots. The pottery pipes were of "trumpet" form, with thick rims decorated with incised lines. The dead were buried in cemeteries, usually with little or no grave goods: the burials of the historical Iroquois, on the other hand, were more lavish.

**Islam.** The rise of Islam was the direct result of the unity which the Muslim religious movement gave to the Arab lands. Mahomet was born *c.* AD 570, and, following

An Islamic plate, 9th century AD.

the Hegira or migration to Medina, the latter became the center of both the Islamic religion and state. The Arabs, unlike many other religious groups, did not force their beliefs on the peoples they conquered, but their culture had an important impact on the lands they ruled. By a series of conquests, the Islamic world had come to embrace North Africa, Iberia, Arabia, Armenia, and Persia, and stretched from the Indus to the Atlantic coast of Spain, by the 8th century AD. After the initial period of expansion the capital became Damascus, where an outstanding court flourished under the Umayyad caliphs in the early 8th century. Thereafter the Islamic world went into decline, and by the 10th century the Muslim world ceased to exist as a political unity. Apart from their religion, the Muslims developed a distinctive style of art and architecture whose influence spread outside the Islamic world.

**Israel, Israelites.** Semitic desert nomads who probably moved into the region to which they have given their name in the middle of the 13th century BC. Destructions at LACHISH, Beth-el, Tell Beit Mirsim, and HAZOR have been attributed to them, although the relevant level at JERICHO seems to have been eroded away. They settled mainly in the hill country and the Canaanites remained in control of the coast, which they later had to share with the PHILISTINES.

The Old Testament has left us a record of the history of the Israelites, but few of the events or people mentioned can be tied in with archaeological discoveries. There is nothing which can specifically be ascribed to David (*c.* 1010–955 BC), but the Temple of Solomon (*c.* 955–935 BC) has been identified in JERUSALEM and contemporary levels have been found at Hazor and MEGIDDO. The palace of Omri (885–874 BC) and the store of ivories collected by Ahab (874–853 BC) have both been found at SAMARIA. There is written material from Tell Qasile, Samaria, ARAD, and Lachish, and in the Siloan tunnel in Jerusalem. Jehu (841–814 BC), the son of Omri, is represented on the "Black Obelisk" of Shalmaneser III of Assyria, and Assyrian reliefs and annals document their incursions into the area. Nebuchadnezzar's capture of Jerusalem in 587 BC is also chronicled.

In 538 BC, Cyrus II allowed the Israelites to return from their exile in BABYLON, and the walls of Jerusalem, rebuilt by Nehemiah in the 5th century BC, have been identified. The finds at QUMRAN illustrate the struggle of Jewish patriots against the Romans. (*See* SYRIA-PALESTINE.)

**Italy, archaeology of.** The earliest traces of settlement in Italy were in the Palaeolithic and Neolithic periods. The Terramare culture and the Villanovan culture of the Iron Age followed. Before ROME, Italy was inhabited by various peoples: Illyrian immigrants in the East, Volsci and Umbrians in the Central mountains, Ligurians, Etruscans, and others, including Latins, in the West. Greeks, too, colonized parts of the South and the Western coasts. However, by the 6th century BC, Rome, a settlement of the Latins, was growing in strength, perhaps at times under Etruscan domination, for some of the early kings of Rome were recorded by tradition as ETRUSCANS. The story of Italy from this point onwards is that of the emergence of Rome as a dominant power. Although it became the strongest and the most successful of the Italian settlements, Italy itself was never really united under Rome's rule as a cohesive unit: it retained (and still retains) its strong regional characteristics, and even in the Roman period these were not suppressed by the might of Roman domination.

**Izapa.** A large and important Middle-Late Preclassic site, located on the Pacific coastal plateau of Chiapas, Mexico. It is best known for its distinctive and elaborate style of stone carving, which included stelae, and altar stones. Some scholars see cultural connections between the Olmec and Maya linked through Izapa. Certainly the Izapa style, which is now becoming known, had a striking impact on nearby regions during the Late Preclassic and Protoclassic Periods.

**Izumi, Seiichi** (1918–70). A Japanese archaeologist who worked in Peru in the 1960s. He excavated at KOTOSH on the Higueras River, near Huanuco, in Central Peru.

**Jabal Sais.** An early 8th-century AD site in Syria, southeast of Damascus, dating from AD 707–715. Excavated in 1962–3, the architectural remains consisted of a fortified palace of Umayyad type, a small mosque, and a bath house with an audience hall.

**Jade.** The name given to two quite distinct minerals, nephrite and jadeite. In both, the crystals are interlocked and felted together. They are therefore both, as a result of this structure, too hard to be worked with steel, and have to be ground with abrasives. Nephrite is a silicate containing calcium, magnesium, and aluminium, with or without iron, and thus belongs to the group known as emphiboles. It varies in color from pale gray or white to a very dark green. Jadeite is a silicate of sodium and aluminium and thus belongs to a group known as pyroxenes. The colors of this mineral are more extreme, including white, apple green, violet, and yellow. Jade, in the form of polished axes, was traded in the Neolithic period in Europe but it is chiefly known from archaeological contexts in China and Mesoamerica.

*China.* In China, so far as is known, there are no sources of jade. The main sources of nephrite were Baikal, and the oases of Yarkand, and Kashgar. Jadeite was not used in China before the 18th century AD, at which time it began to be imported from Burma. From as early as the Neolithic period, jade was evidently highly prized in China and was worked into rings for ritual or ceremonial purposes. From this the jade working industry of the SHANG DYNASTY (c. 1600–1027 BC) developed. Discs and rings persisted and to these were added ceremonial weapons and small animal amulets. Later types of jade included girdle pendants and grave jades. The latter are first found in the CHOU DYNASTY (1027–221 BC) as eye covers, veil ornaments, and body plugs, all of which can be considered the predecessors of the jade suits of the HAN DYNASTY (206 BC–AD 220), such as those excavated at MAN-CH'ENG. It was believed that

jade thus used would preserve the bodies of the dead. In later periods jade was used for personal ornaments, miniature sculpture, and for precious vessels.

*Mesoamerica.* In the form of jadeite, jade was probably one of the most highly prized raw materials in Mesoamerica. The OLMECS and MAYA made fine carved jade figurines, plaques, jewelry, and ceremonial axes. Some of the most spectacular pieces which are known today include the large jade sculpture of the Mayan sun god from ALTUN HA, Belize; a jade mosaic mask from the tomb of the Temple of the Inscriptions at PALENQUE; and a mosaic mask in the form of a large bat from MONTE ALBAN. The significance of this stone probably lay in its green color. Its importance is witnessed through the widespread custom of placing a small piece of jade in the mouth of the dead, as a passport to the next world.

**Jaina.** The island of Jaina, 20 mi. (32 km) north of Campeche, Yucatan, was an important Late Classic Period Maya burial zone. Within the graves of the Jaina cemeteries have been found numerous lifelike ceramic figurines. These naturalistic portraits in clay depict Classic Maya life, dress, ornamentation, hairstyles, and gestures. Some are hand-modeled and solid, while others, more standardized, are hollow and moldmade.

**Jamestown.** The first permanent English settlement in Virginia in North America, Jamestown was also the capital of Virginia until 1699. The excavations from 1934 to 1941 provide an excellent example of the use of both documentation and archaeology to reconstruct the history of an important site. The location of Jamestown was well known before the excavations began, because the remains of the old church were still standing, and because various brick walls were reported in the vicinity during the 19th century.

A greal deal of general cultural knowledge was gained, as well as much information about street and building plans. The large ceramic collections show that the people of Jamestown had trading links with Spain, Italy, Mexico, Holland, and England. Because of the quality of library documentation about Jamestown, it has been possible to use dated finds as cross-references for objects found in other, particularly Indian, sites. The discovery of glassworks, dating from 1608–9 and 1621–24, enabled glass beads, traded to Indians, to be dated when found on Indian sites. Several brick and tile kilns were also found at Jamestown, thus destroying the previous assumption that these were traded from England as ballast in ships. It was also assumed that the inhabitants lived very meagerly in cottage-type dwellings: in fact, their houses were not at all crude, and had brick floors, wine cellars, ornamental plasterwork, and glass windows.

**Japan and the Far East, Palaeolithic.** Java is the earliest-known region in Asia to have been occupied. The earlier fossils of Java man (HOMO ERECTUS) are probably well over a million years old. The later and better known Java men of Sangiran and Trinil are probably about 700,000 years old. No stone tools are known with any of these human fossils, but they may be present in beds of the same age. The Indonesian islands were probably occupied from this time onwards, but the archaeological evidence is weak. One theory is that early man in Indonesia was the ancestor of the present-day Australian aborigine.

Southeast Asia was evidently occupied at the same time as Indonesia: the site of Kota Tampan is claimed to have stone tools of great antiquity. Certainly, it seems that man must have got to Indonesia by this route, but the details are poorly established.

Occupation of Japan is thought to go back well before 100,000 years ago, but this is not accurately fixed. At the end of the last Ice Age much more archaeological evidence of man is known, and ground stone tools and tiny blade tools have been found. Pottery seems to have been invented by about 12,000 years ago: this is accordingly some of the earliest-known pottery and a rare example of it preceding farming.

**Jaywa.** A preceramic phase, from 7100 to 5800 BC, in the Ayacucho basin of the Central Andes of Peru. The people were nomadic groups of hunters and gatherers who used a distinctive toolkit of stemmed and pentagonal projectile points.

**Jefferson, Thomas** (1743–1826). The third President of the United States, Thomas Jefferson was the first person, in North America or elsewhere, to undertake, in 1784, excavations of a prehistoric site as a means to understanding the people who had built it. In particular he wanted to find out why the burial mounds, on his land in Virginia, had been built. One mound he excavated carefully with trenches, noting that skeletons had been placed in the ground and covered over. This process had been repeated many times to produce, finally, a mound 12 ft. (4 m) high. In observing the different levels, he was anticipating the stratigraphical method which became common practice in Europe and America only at the end of the 19th century.

**Jemdet Nasr.** A small site northeast of Babylon, which has given its name to one of the periods in Mesopotamian chronology (also known as Protoliterate C and D), c. 3100–2900 BC. The period is chiefly characterized by pictographic tablets (see WRITING), by pottery with painted designs or a plum red slip which is usually burnished, and by plain pottery with beveled rims. Cylinder SEALS are squat and plain and the drill is frequently used in the designs.

**Jericho.** A repeatedly excavated site in the Jordan valley, in a fertile oasis on a main East-West route. It was first occupied in Mesolithic times (late 10th millennium BC). In the 8th millennium BC, a Pre-pottery Neolithic culture (PPN) fortified the city and built a round tower, 29 ft. (9 m) in diameter. Plastered skulls with shells replacing the eyes were also found. Pottery appears in the second half of the 6th millennium BC, after a break in occupation. Jericho seems to have been uninhabited in Chalcolithic times but was frequently rebuilt during

the Early Bronze Age (3rd millennium BC). Amorite nomads settled there at the end of the 3rd millennium BC, and many of their tombs have been excavated. During the Middle Bronze Age, the city was heavily fortified, with a glacis of beaten earth on the slopes of the TELL. Many tombs have been found from that period. The later levels of the tell, including Joshua's Jericho, have been eroded. (See SYRIA–PALESTINE.)

**Jerusalem.** Continuous occupation of the site has made excavation difficult but, naturally enough, it has been frequently undertaken from the middle of the 19th century until the present day. The original 4th-millennium BC site seems to have been on the eastern ridge. The settlement was walled in the Middle Bronze Age, and the Jebusites held it when it was finally captured by David in c. 1000 BC. The city was enlarged under Solomon to include the new Temple, thus forming an elongated city along the eastern ridge and on terraces on the slopes. In 587 BC, the city was captured by Nebuchadnezzar and the population was exiled to BABYLON. In 538 BC, Cyrus II allowed some of the exiles to return and the Temple was rebuilt; the walls were rebuilt along the crest of the hill under Nehemiah, c. 445–433 BC. The western ridge was only occupied in Herodian times.

Jerusalem became a Hellenistic city under Antiochus IV, and was Romanized in the 1st century BC. The Jewish revolt of AD 70 inspired Titus to destroy the city, and a military Roman colony grew up under Hadrian. Under Constantine, however, it gained new importance as a Christian center, with the construction of a series of new churches. Jerusalem was destroyed once more in AD 614, by the Persians. (See ISRAEL; SYRIA–PALESTINE.)

**Jerwan.** The site in Northern Iraq, of a 919-ft. (280 m) long stone aqueduct, built by the Assyrian King Sennacherib to carry a canal across a valley.

**Jewelry, Europe.**
*Prehistoric.* Animal claws and teeth, shells, and amber were mainly used as jewelry in prehistoric Europe until the introduction of metallurgy, when, progressively, copper, gold, silver, bronze, iron, glass, and sometimes coral, faience, and jet came into use. Jewelry was worn on all parts of the body at various dates: neckrings (torcs), pins, brooches, and armlets were favored most.
*Greek and Roman.* Craftsmanship in precious metals was known in antiquity from the earliest times. The most important was goldworking, and smiths achieved a high degree of sophistication in beaten gold ornament and in filligree work from the 2nd millennium onwards. Silver and electrum were also used, however, as were complicated inlays of niello and enamel. All forms of ornament were common—brooches, earrings, bracelets, pendants, buckles, and belt fittings, but the ring was perhaps the most important: it could be either an intaglio (a seal ring), a votive offering, an indication of class (whether slave or free), or a marriage bond.

The most famous early jewelry comes from TROY II (c. 2300 BC) and heralds the Greek Bronze Age craftsmanship in CRETE and MYCENAE. Finds from the shaft graves at Mycenae are prime examples of the jeweler's art. In this, as in many cultural achievements, there was a break after the Mycenaean period, with a new beginning in the 8th century BC, first with decoration very much inspired by Eastern motifs and influences, later improving and reaching the complexity of Hellenistic workmanship.

In Italy, Etruscan jewelry is of high quality, but early finds from Rome, at the beginning of the republic, are scarce. But with the expansion of the empire and the takeover of gold and silver mines in Dacia and Spain, gold and silver ornaments became more common and enhanced the luxury of Roman life. (*See also* GEMS.)

**Jobo, El.** An archaeological complex, featuring leaf points, from the middle terraces of the Rio Pedregal in Western Venezuela. A date of 13,000 to 7000 BC has been determined by the discovery of similar tools at TAIMA-TAIMA and other excavated sites.

**Jomon Period.** Lasting from *c.* 12,000 to 400 BC, this Japanese culture is characterized by a hunting, fishing, and gathering economy with pottery but not metal. It thus conforms to the general pattern of the North Eurasian Neolithic period. One of the earliest dates in the world for the making of pottery has been established, by RADIOCARBON DATING, at *c.* 12,700 BC for level III in Fukin Cave, Kyushu. Jomon Japan seems to have been remarkably isolated, particularly from its great neighbor, China, and it may have had more in common with the islands of the Pacific. Hundreds of sites have been studied, including many shell mounds and settlements, which, from the quantity and size of the pottery, appear to have been semipermanent. A fundamental difference is observed between Eastern and Western Japan: the West produced pottery decorated with rotary stamps, while in the East pottery was decorated with shells. In an otherwise very stable society, the only major change was a distinct growth in the late Jomon (2500–1000 BC) of a true maritime economy with emphasis on ocean fishing, and the toggle harpoon for catching sea mammals was also invented at this time.

An earthenware spouted bowl, diameter 7 in. (17.8 cm), of the late Jomon Period, *c.* 2500–1000 B.C.

**Judea.** A Roman province in Palestine, annexed by Pompey in 64 BC. It was ruled at first by Herod the Great as a client king, but later by Roman procurators, of whom Pontius Pilate is the best known. Its chief city was Jerusalem, but there were many other spacious towns in the province, of which important remains survive (e.g., CAESAREA and JERICHO).

**Ju ware.** A very small group of pale blue or lavender glazed stonewares. They were made in the North of China in the 12th century AD, probably for the court. (*See* CERAMICS, CHINA.)

*Ka.* In ancient Egypt, the *ka* was the vital life force or double created with each person at birth but not released to exist separately until death, when it was thought to inhabit the *ka* statue in the tomb chapel. It was the *ka* to whom food offerings were made, and *ka* priests were appointed especially to attend to their daily provision.

**Kalambo Falls.** Situated at the south end of Lake Tanganyika, on the borders of Zambia and Tanzania, the archaeological levels at Kalambo Falls span over 100,000 years, from ACHEULIAN at the bottom through to Iron Age at the top. Peat deposits have revealed a quantity of prehistoric wooden tools there.

**Kaminaljuyu.** Located on the outskirts of modern Guatemala City, in the Guatemalan Highlands, Kaminaljuyu was one of the most important centers of ceremonial activity in Mesoamerica during the Preclassic and Classic Periods. A number of excavations at the site, first by the Carnegie Institution of Washington and more recently by Pennsylvania State University, have revealed that the site was occupied by the Maya. During the Late Preclassic Period an elaborate tomb was constructed within one of the numerous adobe (mud brick) platform mounds, and the remains of a priest or dignitary were deposited. Lavish grave goods by the hundred were added, along with a number of slain adult and child retainers. Sculptures during the Preclassic Period included mushroom-shaped stones, possibly representing an hallucinogenic mushroom cult, as well as religious stelae and carved boulder-like monuments.

During the Classic Period, however, marked cultural changes appeared at this highland center. Unusually, pronounced TEOTIHUACAN influences appear from Central Mexico. Teotihuacan-style pottery and the distinctive TALUD-TABLERO temple pyramid style of architecture were soon dominant at the site, suggesting an actual invasion and probable socio-political takeover of the locale, possibly because of its nearby OBSIDIAN sources or its proximity to the Maya Lowland centers.

**Kanesh.** *See* KÜLTEPE.

**Karanovo.** A multi-period TELL near Nova Zagora in Central Bulgaria, which covers a timespan from 5500 BC down to 2000 BC. Its 40 ft. (12 m) of deposits have been divided into seven phases, covering the Neolithic, Copper Age and Early Bronze Age.

**Karasuk culture.** Dating from around the 13th century BC, the Karasuk developed from the ANDROVONOVO CULTURE in South Siberia, when a gradual change was made from settled communities to seasonal transhumance. Most remains are burials in slab tombs under a low mound (*see* CIST TOMB). Important artifacts include small curved knives closely related to those found at AN-YANG in China.

**Karatepe.** A Neo-Hittite site in Southeastern Anatolia, excavated by a Turkish and German team. The citadel was the summer residence of King Asitawada *c.* 700 BC. It was adorned with interesting reliefs and with the longest known hieroglyphic Hittite inscription, which is accompanied by a version in Phoenician. (*See also* HITTITES.)

**Karnak.** *See* THEBES.

**Kassites.** A tribe which moved into Mesopotamia from the Zagros Mountains of Iran in the 2nd millennium BC. Kassite names first appear in texts of the early 18th century BC, and it would appear that the Kassites were probably of Caucasian stock, led by an Indo-Aryan aristocracy who taught them horsebreeding and riding, which they introduced into Mesopotamia. After the Hittite raid of *c.* 1595 BC, which brought about the downfall of the 1st Dynasty of BABYLON, the Kassites established a Dynasty. The main source of information for the period is the Amarna correspondence (*see* AKKADIAN), written especially during the reigns of Burnaburiash II and Kurigalzu II, which illuminate foreign relations in the 14th century BC, but throw little light on internal organization. The Kassites seem to have adopted the language and culture of Mesopotamia. There are important Kassite levels at NIPPUR, UR, and URUK. The capital, Dur Kurigalzu, has also been excavated and a palace with wall paintings, a ZIGGURAT, which is still an impressive ruin near Baghdad, and a temple were partially uncovered. The Kassites used distinctive boundary stones called *kudurru*. They were overthrown by the Elamites in 1157 BC.

**Key Marco.** A late prehistoric site of Southern Florida on the Gulf Coast of America, dating from the first half of the present millennium. A large cross section of the material culture of these people has been recovered because of the wet nature of the lagoon swamps. The Indians lived in thatch houses built on stilts along lagoon shores; subsistence depended principally on the collection of shellfish, fishing, and hunting. Weapons included spearthrowers and swords armed with sharks' teeth, and fishing was carried out either with shell nets, or else with fish hooks of bone with wooden shanks. The most unusual items recovered were realistic wooden sculptures. Among them were several naturalistic carvings of animals, including the heads of a deer, a wolf, and a bird. They are all very sensitively carved and much of the painting, for instance on the deer's head, has survived. Other more prosaic items, such as stools, trays, bowls, and dugout canoes were also made of wood, using a

A deerhead mask in carved wood, originally painted, from Key Marco, Florida, $3\frac{3}{8}$ in. (8.5 cm) high, AD 800–1400.

variety of adzes and cutting tools with shell and antler blades. Many other perishable items have survived, including rush and bark matting, basketry, and untempered pottery.

**Khafajah.** *See* DIYALA.

**Khmer.** The Khmer Empire of Cambodia was one of the most impressive civilizations of Southeast Asia, well known in particular for its spectacular and monumental religious architecture. In the late 6th century AD, the nascent Khmer state of Chenla annexed the declining Funan Empire of South Cambodia and, under Iśaravarman (AD 611–635), extended it westwards. The latter emperor founded a fine capital at Isanapura, with impressive brick towers. The 7th century AD saw great artistic developments, within a Hindu and Buddhist context, and the perfection of hydraulic engineering techniques that were of the first importance in the later, Angkor, period, but political difficulties led to the breakdown of the empire in the 8th century AD.

In AD 800 renewed vigor was injected into the declining empire by Jayavarman II. He established three capitals in the region of the Tonlé Sap Lake, near Angkor, an area both easily defensible and fertile. Indravarman I (AD 877–889) exploited this area to the full by constructing a vast irrigation system: upon this abundance depended the densely settled and highly centralized Angkorian Khmer Empire. Under Yasovarman I the capital shifted to Angkor, temple architecture flourished and the empire was greatly extended. It reached its furthest extent under Suryavarman II (1113–1150), who built the famous and vast temple complex at ANGKOR WAT. Jayavarman VII (1181–1219) undertook the construction of the great capital city of ANGKOR THOM, whose ruins still stand. His vast expenditure on public building and works exhausted the state, and it fell into decline, being finally overrun by the Thais in 1444.

**Khorsabad.** The site of the ancient city of Dur Sharrukin, capital of Sargon II of Assyria. The city was square, with a citadel dominated by a high platform astride the northwest wall, on which were built the palace, temples, and a ZIGGURAT, with a fortress on the southern wall. The city was never completed and was abandoned after Sargon's death.

**Kian ware.** Black-glazed Chinese stoneware, usually bowls, decorated with leaves, medallions, birds, and plants. It was made in the SUNG DYNASTY (AD 960–1279) at Chi-chou in Kiangsi province. (*See* CERAMICS, CHINA.)

**Kidder, A. V.** (1885–1963). A Harvard-trained archaeologist working in the Southwest of the United States during the first quarter of the 20th century. His stratigraphical excavations were important pioneering works during the "Classificatory-Historical" period of North American archaeology. His most important excavations were at the Pueblo of Pecos in the Upper Pecos valley of New Mexico. These sites consist of a series of successive rooms combined with large middens (rubbish mounds) up to 20 ft. (6 m) deep. In order to establish the nature of the stratigraphical sequence, test profiles were made in the middens to determine the different types of pottery from each level. He paid particular attention to ensuring that the excavations used for establishing pottery sequences were uncontaminated by intrusions. The pottery from each location was tabulated in a diagram showing the numbers of sherds of each type of pottery from each level and location. It was the first time that this way of presenting data was used: his report, *The Pottery of Pecos*, was published in 1931. (*See* NORTH AMERICAN ARCHAEOLOGY, HISTORY OF.)

**Killke.** A culture and pottery style, *c.* AD 1000–1438, which immediately preceded the Inca Period in the Cuzco basin and its environs in Peru. The name derives from a hillslope site southwest of Cuzco. Killke sites were located on hills, or on slopes above the valley floor, but outside the Cuzco basin sites occupied defensive positions.

**Kiln.** The kiln was used in antiquity from prehistoric times, primarily for firing pottery. It was usually a clay dome within which the pots were stacked upside down on a shelf. An opening for draught was left at the top, and a flue provided at the side. Fuel was piled within and around the kiln, and when the heat was at its greatest, the openings were shut down to preserve the temperatures and fire the pots inside. A temperature of between 800° and 1000° C could be achieved by this method. Ovens providing less heat were also used for baking in the same fashion, as well as for drying grain.

**Kintampo Neolithic.** The distribution of Kintampo Neolithic sites is restricted to the savanna woodland and forest margin in the basin of the Black Volta River in the Northwest of Ghana, Africa. Dating from the middle of the 2nd millennium BC, the Kintampo culture is important because it provides the first evidence for animal husbandry in West Africa. Two sites are particularly important: Ntereso, which is located in dry savanna woodland on a ridge above the Volta River, to the west of Tamale; and Kintampo rock shelter, which is situated on the forest fringe in the well watered sandstone uplands to the north of Kumasi. Both sites have yielded comb-decorated pottery, stone celts (axes), shale and sandstone arm rings, finely worked stone points and "cigars," artifacts unique to Ghana. The cigars are of hard baked clay, occasionally of shale, of flat oval section some 4–8 in. (10–20 cm) long and carefully scored over both faces. Their function is not known, although many suggestions have been made, varying from bark cloth hammers to food grinders. Goats and cattle, both of small dwarf varieties, were herded and at Ntereso fish and freshwater oysters formed an important part of the diet. Several different fishing methods were in use as bone hooks, harpoons, and net sinkers were present in the archaeological deposits. Although domestic animals were herded, hunting still formed part of the economy as several different antelope species have been recovered from both Ntereso and Kintampo rock shelter 6.

**Kish.** The ancient city is spread over a series of tells (*see* TELL) a little to the east of Babylon and was inhabited throughout Mesopotamian history. According to tradition, it was the seat of four early Dynasties. It was first excavated by the French under Henri de Genouillac in 1912, then by a mixed English, American, and French team from 1923 to 1933, and most recently by an American team. A Sumerian palace was found, together with an Early Dynastic cemetery. On other mounds were found an Old Babylonian settlement and a ZIGGURAT, Neo-Babylonian forts, temples, and tombs, a Parthian fort and buildings, and a Sassanian palace and buildings. There were also two further ziggurats, and a deep sounding revealed a cemetery, in which there were Early Dynastic II burials with two- and four-wheeled chariots. Material from the lowest JEMDET NASR and Neolithic levels was scanty.

**Kiva.** The circular ceremonial structures of the Southwestern United States, particularly of the Pueblo peoples. The word means "old house" in Hopi. Originally kivas may have derived from the circular pithouses of the Basketmaker culture, 100 BC–AD 700. (*See* ANASAZI.)

**Knossos.** The most important settlement of prehistoric CRETE, Knossos preserves remains of a Bronze Age palace dating from the 16th–15th century BC. The palace is grouped round a central courtyard with steps leading to the ceremonial rooms of the west wing. On the ground floor of this same wing is the throne room, while the living quarters are in the east wing. The palace is notable for its important frescoes and stucco reliefs, and for its architectural achievements, with its complex differences of levels between the various parts.

The throne room at Knossos. This was the audience chamber of the palace, and would have been richly decorated.

The excavation of Knossos, by Sir Arthur EVANS in 1900–9, laid the foundations for Minoan studies and revealed the complexity of the Cretan Bronze Age civilization. (*See also* GREECE, ARCHAEOLOGY OF; MINOAN ARCHAEOLOGY.)

**Knowth.** One of the largest of a group of passage graves on the River Boyne in Co. Meath, Ireland (*see* NEW-GRANGE; PASSAGE GRAVE). It consists of a massive oval cairn, measuring 295 × 262 ft. (90 × 80 m), and containing two chambers (one cross-shaped) set back to back, each approached by a long passage. Dating from *c.* 2800 BC, it contained cremated human remains.

**Kofun culture.** *See* GREAT TOMBS PERIOD.

**Koldewey, Robert Johann** (1855–1925). A German architect and archaeologist chiefly famous for the excavation of BABYLON (1899–1917).

**Kommagene.** *See* COMMAGENE.

**Koryo Dynasty.** Throughout most of this period (AD 918–1392) Korea was threatened by the nomadic tribes which ruled China as the LIAO DYNASTY, the CHIN DYNASTY, and the YÜAN DYNASTY. In adversity the Koreans turned to Buddhism and built many temples near the capital Kaesong, 45 mi. (72 km) north of Seoul. The Koryo period is best known for exquisite CELADON objects (copied from Chinese YÜEH WARE) made at Kanjin

in the extreme Southwest and Pusan on the West coast. The kilns have been investigated and are known to have been built on the slopes of hills.

**Kotosh.** A site consisting of nine groups of structures, mainly on two mounds, on the lowest terrace of the Higueras River near Huanuco, Peru. Excavated in the 1950s, the mounds were made of deposits derived from stratified stone buildings belonging to several periods, *c.* 2000–500 BC. Buildings were constructed on top of each other by filling in the previous platform levels with stones, which has resulted in the excellent preservation of stone buildings of the earliest occupations. The most important of these, the Temple of the Crossed Hands, derives its name from a clay plaster relief sculpture of crossed hands located under a niche. The building, entered through a single doorway, has low platforms constructed before large and small niches symmetrically arranged around its internal walls. A radiocarbon date of 1800 BC postdates the temple and is associated with the first appearance of pottery. Primitive pots are decorated with crudely incised horizontal lines below the rim. The third period, called "Kotosh-Kotosh," had a distinctive pottery style which seems ancestral to that at CHAVIN. Artifacts found at most levels have their predecessors in previous periods, but the Chavin style appears to be intrusive here, *c.* 1000 BC.

**Kuan ware.** A fine Chinese stoneware with a dark body under a thick bluish cracked glaze, made near Hangchou after the court was established here in AD 1135. (*See* CERAMICS, CHINA.)

**Kültepe.** A village in Central Anatolia, and the site of the large mound of Karahüyük. The city on the main mound, with temples and palaces, may have been called Nesa. At its foot lay a settlement which was the center of the Assyrian merchant colony or *karum* of Kanesh, which flourished during the 19th century BC and has produced tens of thousands of cuneiform tablets, known as "Cappadocian." These relate to the day-to-day activities and business transactions of the colony, and, owing to the mention of Assyrian rulers and eponyms, they can be fairly closely dated. From them, it is known that textiles and metal were traded. Documents relating to Anitta and his father Pithana, kings of Kushara at this period, have also been found. Earlier levels contain quantities of "Cappadocian" painted pottery and a MEGARON. There was also an important later Phrygian occupation.

**Kuntur Wasi.** A Chavinoid site of the EARLY HORIZON Period, *c.* 800 BC, in Northern Peru. It has a stone-faced, triple-terraced pyramid, surmounted by a temple or temples which are now largely destroyed. Stone statues, heads, carved slabs, and lintels are found on and around the pyramid. Among others, a bird with feline attributes and a full round sculpted head are like the sculptures found at CHAVIN DE HUANTAR.

**Kurgan.** A form of burial in South Siberia and Russia, consisting of a stone-lined burial chamber beneath a mound.

**Labret.** The term used in North American archaeology and ethnology to describe the lip plugs that were used in many areas as articles of adornment. The plug, of stone, wood, or bone, was inserted in the lower lip. Sometimes a succession of lip plugs would be worn, each one larger than its predecessor, thus gradually increasing the size of the hole. In historical times the size of the labrets signified the eminence of the wearer, as, for instance, among the women of high rank of the Northwest coast.

**Lachish.** Present-day Tell Duweir, in Palestine, was excavated by the British during the 1930s and produced evidence of Chalcolithic and Early Bronze Age cave dwelling, after which the caves were used for burials and the settlement was founded. Only the later levels on the TELL were excavated, together with three phases of a temple built at the foot of a massive Middle Bronze Age bank around the town. The Assyrian King Sennacherib depicted the capture of the town on stone reliefs at NINEVEH, and the town fell to the Babylonians in 588 BC. (*See* SYRIA-PALESTINE; ISRAEL, ISRAELITES.)

**Lacquer.** The sap of the lacquer tree (*Rhus Vernicifera*), indigenous to Southern and Central China. It can be painted in layers on almost any surface, and in China was commonly used to decorate vessels on a hemp or wooden base. Lacquer-painted items in perfect condition have been excavated from Han Dynasty tombs in Hupei and Hunan provinces.

**Lagash.** A Sumerian city state in Southern Mesopotamia. French excavations have been centered on the mound of Telloh since 1877, but it now seems that this was the religious center of Girsu rather than the city site itself. The latter has been identified with Al Hibba, and is at present being excavated by an American team. A mass of sculpture and tablets has thrown light on the two main periods at Telloh—the EARLY DYNASTIC and the Neo-Sumerian periods. During the latter the ruler, Gudea, undertook extensive rebuilding of the temples and had dozens of statues made of himself; some important Sumerian literary texts of this period also survive. His father, Ur-Ningirsu, built an enigmatic structure which was originally thought to have been a hypogeum, but it has now been identified as a hydraulic construction. (*See also* SUMERIAN.)

**Lagoa Santa caves.** A series of caves in Eastern Brazil where, in 1842, a distinctive long-headed skeleton was reported to have been found associated with extinct and modern animals. Investigations in the 1950s produced stemmed points and other tools in strata about 9000 years old, while recent (1974) investigations have produced charcoal dated to *c.* 20,000 years ago.

**Landa, Bishop Diego de** (1524–79). Bishop Diego de Landa was born in Spain and joined the Franciscans at the age of 16. He was later sent to the Yucatan, Mexico, where, from 1552 to 1562, he held various ecclesiastical appointments and engaged in missionary activities. During this time he made copious notes on information obtained from native informants on the history and customs of the Maya before the Conquest. In 1562 he returned to Spain to stand trial on a charge of maltreating the natives. For his defense he incorporated his notes in a book which became the famous *Relacion de las Cosas de Yucatan*, now the primary source for the interpretation of Maya archaeology. Especially important was his section on the calendar, in which he recorded the day and month names and a rudimentary explanation of the Katun. All subsequent research on the calendar stems from this section.

**Lan-t'ien man.** *See* CHINA.

**Laodicea.** A city founded in Syria by Seleucus I, one of the greatest cities of the Seleucid kingdom. Laodicea became a Roman city when the kingdom was taken over by the empire, but in AD 194 it was largely improved by Septimus Severus, who made it the capital of Syria and relegated Antioch to village status.

**Lapis lazuli.** A distinctive blue stone used for cylinder SEALS or for decorative purposes such as jewelry, particularly during the first half of the 3rd millennium BC in Mesopotamia. As it was mined in antiquity only in Badakhshan in Afghanistan, its occurrence is useful as an indication of trade.

**Larco-Hoyle, Rafael** (1912–58). A prominent Peruvian amateur archaeologist, who conducted excavations in

Northern coastal Peru and established the cultural sequence for that region.

**Larisa.** A prehistoric Greek city on the West coast of Asia Minor, later an Aeolian settlement. Remains of the city walls, a late archaic temple, and the large palace area survive.

**Larsa.** The seat of an Amorite Dynasty during the first quarter of the 2nd millennium BC in Southern Mesopotamia.

**Lascaux.** Discovered in 1940 by four boys, Lascaux, in Southwest France, is the site of possibly the most famous of the prehistoric painted caves. It is also the most controversial, as it has been closed to the public since 1960, when it was noticed that the spread of an alga, *Palmellococcus*, was causing the deterioration of the paintings. The bulls are the largest figures in the cave, but deer and horses are also commonly represented, and there are fine engravings as well. (*See also* CAVE ART.)

A painted cow kicking up her heels and small galloping horses, from the cave at Lascaux.

**Lashkari Bāzār.** A site in Afghanistan, excavated during five seasons from 1949 to 1951. The focus of the work was the palace founded by Maḥmūd (AD 998–1030) and finally destroyed by the Mongols. Following the traditional Iranian plan, it was decorated with wall paintings, the most important surviving one being a depiction of Maḥmūd's Turkish guard. The pottery of the site has been published in detail and forms an important body of evidence for the history of Islamic ceramics.

**Late Horizon.** A division of time of Central Andean chronology AD 1438/76–1532, which coincides with the Inca Empire's expansion from Cuzco, the greatest unifying force in South American archaeology. This period lasted until the Spanish Conquest in 1532.

**Late Intermediate Period.** A term used to refer to a period of time of regional diversification in the Central Andes, *c.* AD 1000–1438/78. New styles, cultures, and kingdoms arose after the breakdown of the unifying forces of the MIDDLE HORIZON Period. Warfare and secularization of urban centers are characteristic of this period. Ethnohistorical accounts record some traditions of the people and of cultures of immediately pre-Inca times. On the Peruvian coast, the rectangular enclosure plan introduced during the previous period became the predominant planning and architectural form in urban centers. From north to south, the cultures and styles were CHIMU, CHANCAY, Pachacamac, CHINCHA, and Ica. In the Peruvian highlands, from north to south, small states included those of CAJAMARCA, Chanca, KILLKE, Lucre, Colla, and Lupaca. Constant fighting over land and water rights resulted in a defensive settlement pattern in the highlands until the onset of the Inca period.

**La Tène.** *See* CELTS; IRON AGE.

**La Venta.** One of the most important Olmec sites, located in the Tabasco Lowlands of Mexico on a small, island-like area of raised land in the Tonala River. The site is marked by a 110-ft. (33.5 m) tall earthen pyramid, the tallest in any of the Olmec sites, as well as other earthen constructions, mostly built along a north-south alignment. La Venta has produced a wide array of typical Olmec Preclassic sculptures, including the colossal stone heads and altars. RADIOCARBON DATING places Olmec occupation there between 1000 and 600 BC. (*See* OLMECS.)

**Layard, Sir Austen Henry** (1817–94). The British excavator of NIMRUD, NINEVEH, and ASSUR in the 1840s, and author of *Nineveh and its remains* (1849).

**Lead.** In antiquity, galena (lead sulphide, Pbs) was the main source of lead in the Old World, although anglesite (lead sulphate, $PbSO_4$) and cerussite (lead carbonate, $PbCO_3$) were also exploited. Lead was principally used to make patterns for investment casting, to "wetten" bronze and so ease its casting, in making glazes, and, alloyed with tin, to make soft solder for joining metals and pewter for tablewares.

**Leakey, L. S. B.** (1903–72). Born at Kabete, Kenya, on August 7, 1903, Louis Leakey was the leading African prehistorian of his time. He grew up among the Kikuyu, to whom he was known as "the black man with the white face." He was a first-class fieldworker, an uncompromising and provocative academic, a man of tremendous energy, great conviction, and unusual intellectual ability.

Best known for his discoveries at OLDUVAI GORGE, Leakey contributed to the advancement of knowledge on many fronts. He is unique in this century for the discoveries he made about the biological and cultural evolution of man. His first East African Archaeological Research Expedition in 1926–27 and the subsequent field seasons between 1928 and 1935 laid the foundations for all that has later been learned of the archaeology and palaeontology of East Africa. The breadth of his interest and knowledge was remarkable, and his published papers numbered more than 200, covering the subjects of biography, geology, zoology, human palaeontology, ethnography, and politics.

**Leather.** This is rarely preserved on archaeological sites, although its uses were as varied in the past as today. Before textiles, it must have served as man's clothing, while in the Bronze Age, its uses included shield backing, sheaths, and, as untreated hide, coffin sheets. Leather-working tools are found on sites of many periods.

**Lebanon.** *See* PHOENICIA, PHOENICIANS; SYRIA–PALESTINE.

**Lecythus.** A Greek pot used to contain oil. It is a thin, bottle-shaped vessel with a single handle and narrow neck.

**Le Grand Hornu.** An industrial village, near Mons, Belgium, built in 1819–40 by the coalowner, Henri de Gorge-Legrand, to the design of Bruno Renard. The centerpiece of the plan is a huge colonnaded oval, with workshops, stores and offices round the circumference and a cast-iron statue of Legrand in the center. Coal mining in the area, the Borinage, ceased during the 1950s

An aerial view of the workshops, workers' housing, and the owner's house at Le Grand Hornu, Belgium.

and the workshop complex, much dilapidated, was subsequently bought by a private architect, who has restored it at great expense and now uses it as his professional headquarters. It is one of Europe's major industrial monuments.

**Lengyel.** A culture, named after a type-site in Western Hungary, which spans the greater part of the 4th millennium BC. Its characteristic pottery is found along the Middle Danube, in Moravia, and up into Southern Poland. It is parallel in time to the RÖESSEN CULTURE in the West, both being descendents of the LINEAR POTTERY CULTURE.

**Leptis Magna.** The original settlement on the coast of North Africa was of Phoenician date, but it became a colony under the Roman Empire, and was the birthplace of Septimius Severus. The oldest nucleus of the town comprises the THEATER and the FORUM and CURIA (1st century AD). BATHS were added in Hadrianic times, but the major period of building was under Septimius Severus, who built a harbor, forum, BASILICA, and a colonnaded street. In addition, Leptis possesses an AMPHITHEATER and the so-called Hunting Baths, decorated with frescoes of hunting scenes.

**Levallois technique.** *See* STONE TECHNOLOGY.

**Liang-chu culture.** A Chinese Neolithic culture found in Central Southern China, principally in Chekiang province, *c.* 3000 BC. It belongs to a group of associated cultures, characterized by painted pottery, which succeeded the YANG-SHAO CULTURE and preceded the LUNG-SHAN CULTURE.

**Liao Dynasty.** The Khitan tribes which occupied Manchuria and parts of Mongolia established the Liao Dynasty (AD 916–1125) in China. With the collapse of the T'ANG DYNASTY, they overran part of China and adopted some Chinese institutions and practices. Elaborate chambered tombs on the Chinese pattern have been excavated: particularly interesting are such architectural details as the bracket systems intended to support tiled roofs. The ceramics found in these tombs continue the Chinese tradition of lead-glazed earthenware.

**Limoges enamel.** From the 12th to the 14th centuries AD, Limoges in France led Europe in the production of *champlevé* enameled copperwork, decorated with figure and heraldic subjects. Boxes, candlesticks, bowls, and ecclesiastical objects were all exported. It declined in importance in the 14th century, with the rise in popularity of enameled silver and gold, but became important again in the 15th century for its copperwork with painted enamel. (*See also* ENAMELING, MEDIEVAL.)

**Linear A.** A form of pictographic writing developed in CRETE in the 2nd millennium BC (1900–1500 BC). Linear A, slightly different from Linear B, but clearly its antecedent, is as yet undeciphered, but the documents recorded in the script are records (accounts?) on clay tablets, religious dedications, and graffiti. (*See also* GREECE, ARCHAEOLOGY OF; MINOAN ARCHAEOLOGY.)

**Linear B.** A pictographic script first found at KNOSSOS in CRETE, but now known to have been more widespread on the Greek mainland, and presumably the script (and language) of Mycenaean Greece, dating from the 13th century BC. In 1952, decipherment by Michael Ventris revealed that it was a form of Greek, written in syllables, following a form of the Cretan Linear A script. Documents in Linear B are mainly accounts on clay tablets dealing with foodstuffs and supplies for the Mycenaean palaces, though a group of tablets from Pylos speaks of defensive preparations against an unnamed attacker. (*See also* GREECE, ARCHAEOLOGY OF; MYCENAEAN ARCHAEOLOGY.)

**Linear Pottery culture.** Named after the curvilinear incised patterns which make its pottery so recognizable, this culture represents the first agricultural communities in Central Europe, which spread rapidly across the loesslands from the middle Danube to the middle Rhine in the centuries following 4500 BC. Its settlements are closely related to rivers and streams, and consist of massive, often trapezoid-shaped, longhouses.

**Llano.** The Llano complex is the earliest dated culture from the plains of New Mexico, which were grasslands in 10,000–9000 BC. The assemblage includes Clovis-type lanceolate flaked stone projectile points, bone tools, hammerstones, small points, and scrapers. Most of the sites where the Llano complex have been found are between Clovis and Portales in New Mexico. The best known of these sites is Blackwater Draw, which in prehistoric times was a marshy lake. In time it became filled up with refuse and sediment, in which the remains of early hunters of the BIG GAME HUNTING TRADITION have been found. The deposits are 12 ft. (4 m) thick: in the lowest level Llano assemblages have been found, and above that FOLSOM and Plano points, each in different layers. (*See* CLOVIS POINT; PLANO POINT.)

**Locks.** The first locks were developed by the medieval river improvers. The earliest type, the flash lock, consisted either of vertical boards slipped behind a swinging horizontal beam, or of a pair of gates which could be opened to allow a boat to pass over and through the weir formed where water was impounded for a mill. A variant of the flash lock, the staunch, employed a gate which lifted to allow a boat through. Survivals of flash locks and staunches are to be found at a number of places in the eastern half of Britain.

The pound lock, the modern type, consists of lifting or swinging gates enclosing a "pound" of water long enough to take a boat. The boat can then be raised or lowered within the lock and released at either the higher or lower level, as required. Pioneered in Italy—in the late 14th century—the first pound locks had turf sides. One, the Sheffield Lock, survives on the Kennet Navigation, in Berks., England. Series or flights of locks are found where great differences in level occur within a short distance. One of the most spectacular of such flights can be seen at Devizes, England, where the Kennet and Avon Canal climbs through 29 locks, set close together. In Sweden, the flight of locks on the Göta Canal at Borenshult is impressive. Boats are lifted or lowered 49 ft. (15 m), the lock gates being operated entirely by hand.

**Loftus, Sir William Kennet** (1821?–58). A British geologist and excavator. He worked at URUK, SUSA, UR, LARSA, NINEVEH, NIMRUD, and other sites in MESOPOTAMIA.

**Lo-lang.** A colony established in Korea by HAN DYNASTY China. It was set up when an alliance between the peoples of the area and the HSIUNG-NU provoked the Emperor Wu-ti to send troops to the region in 108 BC. Great administrative buildings were constructed, and hundreds of tombs were clustered around them, many of which have been excavated. The immense quantities of high quality Chinese goods—ceramics, metalwork, and LACQUER, together with the traditional Chinese wooden coffins—demonstrate the close links which the expatriate Chinese maintained with their own country. The colony was destroyed in AD 313 by Koguryo warriors. (*See* THREE KINGDOMS.)

**Lomas.** As a result of the climatic shift at the end of the Pleistocene, the Peruvian coast was covered with areas of this type of vegetation which could live off the moisture from the fog in the air. A "culture" was developed in these areas by hunters, who transferred the basis of their economy to exploitation of this vegetation. Around 4000 BC, there was a further climatic change and much of the lomas dried up, the area becoming a desert. Lomas sites were abandoned and resettlement took place on the coast, where maritime resources were exploited.

**London** (Londinium). The capital city, on the Thames in England, of the Roman province of BRITANNIA. Remains of the city walls, baths, possibly the governor's palace, and the waterfront and harbors have been excavated.

**Los Millares.** An important CHALCOLITHIC (Copper Age) site, which lies on a promontory formed by the Andarax and another river, several miles inland from the coastal town of Almeria in Southeast Spain. It consists of a settlement, with outlying forts, and a large cemetery of passage graves. The settlement lies within a 12-ac. (5 ha) area defined by a stretch of stone wall 8 ft. (2 m) thick, with circular bastions built at irregular intervals. It contains many houses within it: though poorly investigated, these include circular huts against the wall and rectangular houses elsewhere. Four stone-built circular forts lay on a ridge over half a mile (0.8 km) southwest. The largest was some 100 ft. (30 m) in diameter, with double concentric stone walls linked to each other, and furnished on the outside with bastions. Scattered over a similar distance to the west were about 80 passage graves, set in round stone mounds of an average diameter of about 49 ft. (15 m). A few were wholly megalithic, other round chambers had megalithic walls and drystone

vaulted roofs, while others again had vaulted round chambers and even side chambers built entirely of dry-stone walling. The short passages, drystone or megalithic, were often compartmented, and some chambers were plastered and painted. The monuments contained many rich artifacts, including copper tools, painted pottery, figurines, and objects made of imported African ivory and ostrich-shell. The site as a whole serves to typify a "Millaran culture" of the mid-3rd millennium BC in Southern Spain and Portugal.

**Lo-yang.** A Chinese city still to be found on the banks of the Lo River, a tributary of the Yellow River in Honan province, and one of the capital cities of ancient China. It must have been an important center as early as the Neolithic period and the SHANG DYNASTY (*c.* 1600–1027 BC), as significant remains of these periods have been excavated in the region. It was first established formally as a capital city in 770 BC, when the CHOU DYNASTY were forced to move eastwards from CH'ANG-AN under pressure from the nomads. After the collapse of the Western HAN DYNASTY, too, the capital of the Eastern Han was established at Lo-yang. Important tombs of all periods have been excavated near the city, and special attention has been paid to reconstructing the city plan as it was when recorded in a text of the NORTHERN WEI DYNASTY.

**Lubaantun.** A small, Classic Period Maya center, located in Southern Belize, Lubaantun appears to have been constructed and flourished entirely within the Late Classic Period. Recent research by Cambridge University, England, has revealed that the site had a sizable population and a flourishing regional market system in Belize, despite the lack of evidence of the Classic Maya "stele cult," so prominent at other Lowland centers of the same date.

**Lung-shan culture.** A major late Neolithic culture in China, *c.* 2500 BC, which postdates the painted pottery Neolithic cultures. In the central area, namely Honan province, it lies stratigraphically over the YANG-SHAO CULTURE and below the deposits of the SHANG DYNASTY. The most important area occupied by this culture is, however, Shantung province, where it clearly inherited features from the TA-WEN-K'OU CULTURE and the CH'ING-LIEN-KANG CULTURE which preceded it.

It is clear from the ax forms that forest clearance no longer played the prominent part that it had in earlier times, and that agriculture was pursued on a more permanent basis. In consequence, settlements increased in size and came to be fortified. The division of the settlements into different quarters, and buried deposits of JADE objects in ritual or ornamental forms, suggest social stratification. Differences in burial practices, particularly in the burial posture, emphasize the clear distinctions between this predominantly Eastern culture and the earlier Western Neolithic cultures.

The most striking artifacts made by the Lung-shan peoples are the very thin, wheel-turned black pots. In shape, the pieces are often very exotic, with high pierced stands and complicated constructed forms. Both these

Luristan

pots and the use of jade are characteristically Eastern features and are less commonly found in Central China.

**Luristan.** A province on the Western frontier of Iran, where well watered plains are intersected by the Zagros Mountains. Excavations at TEPE GIYAN and Tepe Djamshidi have shown that there was a metal industry in the area from the 4th millennium BC onwards. From the 9th to the 7th century BC, decorated bronze weapons, horse bits, and trappings, whetstone handles, pins, standards, and vessels were made in the area, but the famous "Luristan Bronzes" in museum collections had been looted from cemeteries. Iron was also worked at an early date. Early tombs, containing plain bronzes, have been excavated in the neighborhood of Ilam, while excavations at Baba Jan have uncovered a stone-built settlement of the period of the decorated bronzes, two of which were found in a datable context.

**Luwians** (or Luvians). INDO-EUROPEANS who invaded Anatolia in the 3rd millennium BC and established themselves in the province of Assuwa (to the west of the HITTITES). Hieroglyphic Hittite and Lycian are, in fact, both dialects of Luwian. Rock monuments of the 2nd millennium BC, at Karabel near Izmir, near Manisa, and at Eflatun Pınar and Fasıllar, are connected with springs and may have a religious significance.

**Lycia, Lycians.** A kingdom which appeared in Southwestern Anatolia during the 1st millennium BC. The capital was at Xanthos, which has been excavated by the French. The Lycians spoke an Indo-European dialect of Luwian.

**Lydia, Lydians.** One of the kingdoms which appeared in Western Anatolia during the 1st millennium BC. Its capital was at Sardis, which has been excavated by the Americans since 1958. Gyges (680–652 BC), whose kingdom was overrun by the CIMMERIANS, is mentioned by the Assyrians. At the end of the 7th century BC, the Lydians invented minted coinage and their kingdom became a powerful state. Croesus (560–546 BC) was ruler when the ACHAEMENIDS captured Sardis and made it the terminal of their Royal Road from SUSA. Sardis was captured by Alexander the Great in 334 BC and became a Greek city.

**Lynchet.** An artifical terrace formed on a hillslope in the course of agricultural clearance and plowing. The term is usually only applied to terraces of this type in Southern England.

**Lyons** (Ludgunum). A Roman colony founded in 43 BC and, from the time of Augustus, the capital of Gaul. Its principal remains are a THEATER, a small ODEUM nearby, and a Temple of Cybele.

**Luxor.** *See* THEBES.

**Macellum.** A Roman marketplace, usually a courtyard of shops with a central round or octagonal building.

130

Examples are known from Rome and from several provincial and Italian towns.

**Machalilla.** An early ceramic site, *c.* 2000 BC, on the coast of Ecuador. It may be connected with VALDIVIA, on the basis of its fine incised decorated pottery.

**Ma-chia culture.** A phase of the Western branch of the early Neolithic YANG-SHAO CULTURE of China. The main excavated site is Ma-chia-yao in Lin-t'ao-hsien, but further habitation and burial sites are known. RADIOCARBON DATING places the culture at about 3000 BC.

**Machu Picchu.** A major INCA citadel, located in a mountain saddle between two peaks at a height of 9,000 ft. (2,743 m), 2,000 ft. (610 m) above the Urubamba

Machu Picchu, an important Inca citadel, which was built on a high ridge in the Southwest Andes, Peru.

River, Southwest Andes, Peru. Rediscovered in 1911 by the American explorer, Hiram Bingham, Machu Picchu, with its well preserved and reconstructed architecture, has since become a major tourist attraction. Naturally defended by its topographical situation, the town is built on about 100 ac. (40 ha) of terraces around a central plaza. The plan is notable for the number of shrines and buildings of unusual design. The architecture is distinguished for qualities of engineering skill and fine stone masonry. Structures are arranged around courts in enclosures and with patios on terraces. The majority of structures are single or back-to-back one-roomed buildings, with niches symmetrically arranged on the inside walls. Following the canons of Inca architecture, the walls are inclined and features such as doors, niches, and windows are trapezoidal in form. The temples are open-fronted structures, and cave shrines in the "Torreon" and in the nearby "Temple of the Moon" are lined with fine masonry and niches. Outstanding examples of sculpture include the Intihuatana stone (meaning the stone to which the sun was tied) and other boulders carved *in situ*, with planes and abstract forms. Stairways provide access between terraces and groups of buildings and stone-lined water channels distribute water through 16 finely carved fountains beside the main thoroughfare.

**Madinat az-Zahrā.** A site near Cordova in Spain, founded in AD 936 by the Caliph 'Abd al-Raḥmān III, and destroyed in AD 1010. Excavations have revealed the remains of the royal palace, including a small mosque, and a great deal of finely carved stucco wall decoration.

**Madinat Sulṭān.** A site in Libya, where the foundations of the main mosque, parts of the southwest fort, and other sites in the city center have been excavated.

**Magan and Meluhha.** Distant lands with which Mesopotamia traded. In the 3rd and 2nd millennia BC the names seem to have been applied to the Gulf of Oman and the Indus Valley (*see* INDIA) but in 1st-millennium literary texts they describe Ethiopia. In the earlier periods they were the source of timber, gold, copper, ivory, and semiprecious stones. (*See* PERSIAN GULF.)

**Magatama.** Comma-shaped beads in glass or finely polished stone found in 4th–7th-century AD tombs in Korea and Japan.

**Magdalenian.** The last of the classic cultures of the Upper Palaeolithic cave sequence of Southwest France. RADIOCARBON DATING suggests a timespan of 18,000 to 11,000 years ago. Sites are rich in stone tools and decorated stone and bonework, while barbed antler harpoons are typical of the later stages. Reindeer was the principal quarry, but salmon may also have been important.

**Magellan Periods.** On the basis of excavations in Fell's and Palli Aike caves in Patagonia, a chronological sequence covering the entire period from 8000 BC to AD 1000 has been constructed. The sequence is divided into five phases, which describe a series of hunting and marine adaptations. (*See* FELL'S CAVE.)

**Maglemosan.** The first Mesolithic culture to be recognized in Northern Europe. The name comes from "Magle Mose" or Great Bog, where Mullerup, the first recognized site, is situated. A wide variety of game was hunted by these people, and all kinds of equipment, such as nets and fish hooks, have survived.

**Magnetic reversals.** During the 1960s it was discovered that volcanic lava flows, which like kilns and fired clay record the magnetism at the time they were hot, retained measurable magnetization in a reversed direction. Evidently, at these times compass needles would have pointed the opposite way. It is now known that over the last 4 million years magnetic direction changed at least 10 times. It switched to normal, as we know it, 700,000 years ago. These reversals have proved an important dating aid to archaeology.

**Maikop.** A site, to the east of the Black Sea, where a tumulus has been excavated to reveal a burial of *c.* 2300 BC, containing silver vessels decorated with animal scenes, copper weapons, and jewelry. Above the burial there had been a canopy, with ornamental discs and plaques and supported by gold and silver rods and by four gold figures of bulls.

**Malambo.** A village site on a lagoon south of Barranquilla on the Gulf coast of Colombia. Distinctive pottery, with incised, punctated, and "adorno" (*appliqué*) modeled decoration, which dates from 1120 BC to AD 100 was found there; and pottery griddles indicate that manioc or casava was grown, as these plants are not edible until cooked.

**Mallia.** A Cretan village, east of KNOSSOS, the site of a Minoan palace and a small town. The palace dates from the Early Minoan period, but the visible remains are of the latest palace period. (*See also* CRETE; GREECE, ARCHAEOLOGY OF; MINOAN ARCHAEOLOGY.)

**Maltai.** A site some 37 mi. (60 km) north of Mosul in Iraq, decorated with rock reliefs of the Assyrian King Sennacherib and a procession of deities.

**Man.** *See* HUMAN EVOLUTION.

**Man-ch'eng.** The site in Hopei province, China, where the tombs of Liu Sheng (*c.* 113 BC), Prince of Chungshan, and his wife Tou Wan were recently excavated. The numerous grave goods, 2800 items, JADE objects, inlaid and gilded vessels, and fine weapons were excellently preserved in the rockcut chambered tombs behind sealed doors (*see* CHAMBERED TOMB). Jade suits, in which the bodies of the prince and his wife had been encased, were the most remarkable finds. These were composed of numerous jade plaques, graded in size to fit the contours of the body, and fastened with knots of gold wire at each of the four corners of the plaques. It was believed that jade would preserve the body.

**Mannaeans.** These were probably a non Indo-European tribe which settled in Western Iran, south of Lake Urmia, at the beginning of the 1st millennium BC. Both the Assyrians and the Urartians campaigned against them. The sites of HASANLU and ZIWIYE were in Mannaean territory.

**Mano.** *See* METATE.

**Marajó.** An island at the mouth of the River Amazon in Brazil, where sites with a sequence from 1000 BC to the Portuguese Conquest in AD 1500 have been excavated.

**Maranga.** A site and culture of the Rimac valley, Lima, Peru, dated *c*. 200 BC–AD 800.

**Marathon.** The plain of Marathon, on the North coast of Attica, is famous for the battle between the Persians and Athenians in 490 BC, and for news of the battle taken by Pheidippides from Marathon by road. The tomb of the Athenians who fell (the Soros) is preserved as a tall mound.

**Marble.** In Classical times polished stone was used for sculpture and decoration, and for architecture from the 7th century BC onwards. The most used were the fine white marbles of Greece—Pentelic (of which the PARTHENON at ATHENS is built) and Hymettian—and also the marbles of Naxos and Paros. Colored marbles were used as decoration in Hellenistic architecture. Roman marble, principally from the Carrara quarries at Luna, became popular from the 1st century BC onwards, when there was an increasing tendency to use expensive marble only for the façades of brick-work buildings.

**Marcavalle.** An EARLY HORIZON Period pottery style of the Department of Cuzco, Peru, overlapping with and from which the Chanapata style derived. It is a phase *c*. 1200 BC, defined from a site near the town of Cuzco.

**Marchiori.** An archaeological ceramic complex from the mouth of the Amazon River, with unusual geometric incised and painted motifs on a white background, and dating from 2500 BC.

**Mari.** Present-day Tell Hariri, on the River Euphrates near Abu Kemal. Excavations by the French since 1933 have revealed an extensive EARLY DYNASTIC walled city, with a large palace and temples rich in sculpture. This was succeeded by a palace and temples dating from the end of the 3rd and beginning of the 2nd millennium BC, decorated with wall paintings. The vast correspondence of the kings of Mari, Iasmah-Adad (1796–1780 BC), son of Shamshi-Adad of ASSYRIA, and Zimrilim (1779–1759 BC), throw light on the political situation in the Near East, on the day-to-day activities in the state and palace, and on commercial enterprises. The city was destroyed by Hammurabi of BABLYON in 1759 BC.

**Masada.** The royal citadel of Herod, west of the Dead Sea, and the last outpost of the Zealots against Rome in the 1st century AD. Most of the buildings were erected between 37 and 31 BC.

**Mastaba.** A form of ancient Egyptian freestanding tomb built on open terrain, especially during the Old Kingdom but also during the Middle and New Kingdoms. The superstructure, built over a burial chamber usually reached by a shaft or staircase, has a rectangular ground plan and outer walls with a slight batter: the Arabic name comes from the general resemblance to a bench. The earliest mastabas had solid superstructures, but later they contained a whole series of rooms. Most often tombs for courtiers, mastabas were usually built in regular streets around the pyramid of the reigning king.

**Mausoleum.** *See* HALICARNASSUS.

**Ma-wang-tui.** A site in the neighborhood of Ch'angsha, Hunan province, in Central China. The tombs of the Marquis of Tai (d. 186 BC), his wife, and his son were excavated here between 1970 and 1974. The wife was buried in a SHAFT TOMB lined with kaolin and a layer of charcoal, which had preserved the contents in a most remarkable way: even the corpse was intact. The other spectacular finds included lacquer-painted wooden coffins, a vast array of lacquered wooden vessels, figures, and musical instruments, and a banner painted on silk. The other two tombs were much less well preserved, although important historical and philosophical texts were found in the tomb of the son.

**Maya.** The Maya area, named after native peoples of that language family, consists of Guatemala, the whole of the Yucatan peninsula, and neighboring portions of the Mexican states of Tabasco and Chiapas, on the west, and Belize and portions of Honduras and Salvador, on the east. The principal Maya languages, while not mutually intelligible, are closely related, indicating a common origin in the remote past. The principal divisions are those of the Lowlands (Yucatec, Chol, Chorti) and Highlands of Guatemala (Mam, Quiche).

*History.* The probable ancestors of the Maya can be traced back to the Early Preclassic Period (*c*. 2000–1000 BC), a time at which they were living as simple village farmers in both Highlands and Lowlands. In the Middle Preclassic Period (1000–300 BC) an increasing complexity can be inferred for ancient Maya society in their construction of mound platforms for temples and palaces. This trend continued throughout the Late Preclassic Period (300 BC–AD 250), with the establishment of large politico-religious centers and other indications of a rapidly developing non-egalitarian society. For both Highlands and Lowlands the Late Preclassic was a time of population growth, and by the end of this period the Highland Maya center of KAMINALJUYU (on the site of present-day Guatemala City) was a true urban zone and one of the largest communities of Mesoamerica.

The Early Classic Period (AD 250–600) was marked by a strong Central Mexican (TEOTIHUACAN) presence at

Temple 2 (on the left) and a group of small oratories at the Classic Period Maya site of Tikal, Guatemala.

Kaminaljuyu. This is seen in public architecture at that site, in ceramics, and in various indications of trading contacts. This same Teotihuacan influence was carried down into the Maya Lowlands, from Kaminaljuyu, where some of the earliest hieroglyphic texts at TIKAL attest the arrival of a Kaminaljuyu noble, of Teotihuacan ancestry, who married into the Tikal royal lineage and founded a new Dynasty. Teotihuacan-Kaminaljuyu influence is also seen in Tikal sculptures and ceramics at this time. Toward the end of the Early Classic Period, Teotihuacan influence waned at both Kaminaljuyu and Tikal. In the Lowlands this was followed by the 6th-century hiatus, a period of almost 100 years during which there was little architectural activity at Tikal and other sites and during which stelae dedication virtually ceased. The causes of the hiatus may lie in the breakdown of a centralized Maya polity, based at Tikal, which had been supported by the Kaminaljuyu and Teotihuacan alliances.

In the first two centuries of the Late Classic Period (AD 600–800), the Lowland Maya made a vigorous comeback from the hiatus. Tikal flourished, numerous other centers were revived and enlarged, and new ones were founded. PALENQUE, PIEDRAS NEGRAS, COPAN, QUIRIGUA, Naranjo, Calakmul, and Cobá are among the most famous of the Lowland sites, but there are hundreds of others. During the last two centuries of the Late Classic Period, sometimes referred to as the "Epiclassic" (AD 800–1000), Maya civilization of the Southern Lowlands declined and eventually disappeared. This collapse in some ways resembled the earlier hiatus, except that this time there was no recovery, and after AD 900 most of the Southern Lowlands were completely depopulated. This collapse of Maya civilization is one of the great mysteries of archaeology. The causes were probably complex, multiple, and interlocked, involving agricultural failures, overproduction, and foreign pressures from Central Mexico. In the Northern Lowlands the decline began somewhat later than in the South and does not appear to have been so severe. Here, the Classic Period comes to an end with the invasion of Mexican TOLTECS, who established themselves at CHICHEN ITZA in c. AD 1000. In the Highlands there was no collapse or abandonment, although Toltec influences begin to appear toward the end of the Late Classic.

In the Lowlands, the Chichen Itza Toltecs dominated the North in the first half of the Postclassic Period (AD 1000–1200); after this there was a Maya Renaissance of sorts at MAYAPAN; however, Mayapan succumbed to civil wars in the 15th century. When the Spanish arrived in AD 1520–40, there were a number of small towns in the North but no truly major cities in the old tradition. The Southern Lowlands remained essentially unpopulated throughout the Postclassic Period. In the Highlands the Spaniards found a number of small kingdoms.

133

*Archaeology.* A typical Maya center, or city, consisted of terraced platforms and pyramids arranged around open plazas. These platforms and pyramids were topped by buildings utilized as temples and palaces. Construction was usually of dressed limestone blocks set in true lime mortar, and the centers of the platforms and pyramids were made of rock and earth rubble. A principal architectural device was the corbeled vault or false arch, which sustained the roofs of temple and palace buildings. It had no keystone and depended for stability on setting the stones in a solid matrix of concrete, and cantilevering each course of stones a little further out than the previous course. The two sides of the arch were then continued upwards until the gap between the two sides could be bridged by a capstone. Quite obviously, the Maya centers and great buildings were intended to be viewed from the outside and from below, designed to impress the beholder. Towering ornamented roof combs were placed on the tops of buildings or, in some regions, equally impressive effects were gained through high flying façades. Architectural ornamentation was achieved with carving and stucco relief. There is notable regional stylistic variation in architecture, and this includes the PETEN style of the South and the Rio Bec, Chenes, and Puuc styles of the North. Architecture in the Highlands was less flamboyant: the corbeled vault was rare or absent there, and construction was frequently in ADOBE or adobe and stone with no mortar.

Hieroglyphic writing and calendrics were highly developed among the Lowland Maya, particularly in the South. Stelae or monuments were set up at certain intervals. These bore dates in a Maya calendrical system of great complexity, and also historical and dynastic information. The earliest dates, in the latter part of the 3rd century AD, mark the division between the archaeological Preclassic and Classic Periods; and the latest dates, occurring late in the 9th century, were inscribed as the Classic Maya were entering their collapse. Maya calendrics also served as a basis for divination, as well as for history. The Maya maintained several calendars: the Long Count or dating system, a 260-day divinatory one, a true 365-day solar year, and a 584-day Venus calendar (*see* CALENDAR, MESOAMERICA). Such calendrical scholarship was based on an astronomical tradition of some antiquity, and there are indications that certain sites and buildings were used as observatories. Perhaps one-quarter of Maya hieroglyphs can be deciphered. These glyphs, which are fanciful depictions of men, animals, and demons, probably were in part ideographic and in part phonetic.

**Mayapan.** Bishop Diego de LANDA and other early Spanish writers mentioned the city of Mayapan, which became the capital of a united Maya state in the Yucatan in the 14th century AD. Traces of building material in the Puuc Maya style indicate an occupation in the Classic Period, but native tradition says it was "founded" in the Katun, covering the years 1262–83. The so-called "founding" refers to the settlement there of a group of colonists from CHICHEN ITZA. Buildings are essentially in the Toltec Chichen Itza style, with a center comprising a replica of the Castillo and a number of colonnaded halls and other temples. The workmanship, however, was shabby and degenerate in contrast to Chichen Itza. Stones were only roughly shaped, and irregularities were made good with plaster, a sad departure from the magnificent masonry of Chichen Itza. Mayapan art and sculpture, too, were degenerate. Between the center, which was surrounded by a low wall, and an outer perimeter wall over 1 mi. (1.6 km) long, was a closely packed area of dwelling houses. These were scattered at random as in a modern Maya village, in contrast to the careful planning of Central Mexican cities, and each dwelling stood in its own little plot surrounded by a low dry stone wall.

**Medes.** Indo-Aryans who settled in the Western and Northern parts of the Iranian plateau, with their capital at Ecbatana (Hamadan), in *c.* 1000 BC, and who appear in Assyrian records from the 9th century BC onwards. In 612 BC the Medes, allied with the CHALDAEANS, sacked NINEVEH and brought about the collapse of the Assyrian Empire. They were rivals of the Achaemenid Persians until the two ruling houses were united in marriage and Cyrus II, the son of this marriage, asserted Achaemenid supremacy. Median sites have been excavated at Tepe Nush-i-Jan (8th to 6th century BC), Baba-Jan Tepe, and Godin Tepe II. (*See* IRAN.)

**Megalith.** A term derived from the Greek words for "large" and "stone," which can be applied to any large stone in an archaeological context. The largest megaliths of STONEHENGE weigh over 20 tons (18,144 kg). Single stones set upright are common (known in French as *menhirs*) and arrangements in circles and linear alignments date from the Late Neolithic and Early Bronze Age in Europe. The term is most often applied to the many stone-built collective tombs of Neolithic Atlantic Europe, from Iberia to Scandinavia. The kerbs, passages, chambers, and capstones of these monuments were frequently built with suitable large boulders (*see* CHAMBERED TOMB; in French and Spanish, *dolmen* is used as a similar general term). Long barrows sometimes contain elements of megalithic construction, but were, in effect, the equivalent of megalithic monuments in areas without suitable stone (*see* BARROW). These monuments were generally used to house collective burials, and may also have had the function of communal focuses for widely scattered early farming communities. Their independent origin in Western Europe has been demonstrated by RADIOCARBON DATING, for examples in Brittany dated to *c.* 4000 BC are earlier than analogous tombs in the Eastern or Central Mediterranean. The timber longhouse of the LINEAR POTTERY CULTURE and its successors may have inspired their appearance in many areas, though megaliths are mostly absent from the loess-lands of these cultures.

**Megaron.** This basic unit of Greek architecture has antecedents in ANATOLIA, in levels of Early Bronze Age III date. In TROY, BEYCESULTAN, and KÜLTEPE we find rooms containing a central hearth surrounded by wooden columns, with sleeping platforms in the portico. (*See also* HOUSE, EUROPE.)

**Megiddo.** A Biblical city identified with Tell al-Mutasallim in the Jezreel valley, excavated by the Oriental Institute of the University of Chicago between 1925 and 1939. The aim was to remove one layer after another, but only the top five strata, from *c*. 1000 to 350 BC, were entirely cleared; the stratigraphy is somewhat confused, since cities are not built up in horizontal levels. Soundings revealed a total of 20 levels, beginning with the Chalcolithic period in the 4th millennium BC. Interesting Bronze Age shrines, a number of tombs, and ivories were found. (*See* ISRAEL, ISRAELITES; SYRIA–PALESTINE.)

**Meillacoid subtradition.** A ceramic complex, with incised cross-hatching and *appliqué* decoration, which occurs mainly in Haiti, *c*. AD 850 to 1000.

**Meluhha.** *See* MAGAN AND MELUHHA.

**Memphis.** The ancient Egyptian Northern capital city and the seat of the creator god Ptah, on the west bank of the Nile opposite Cairo. It was founded, according to legend, by Menes, the first king of the 1st Dynasty, in *c*. 3100 BC (*see* EGYPT). Excavations have recently uncovered some Middle Kingdom burials, an 18th-Dynasty temple, and the embalming place of the Apis bulls, but little else remains of the city. It was not originally called Memphis: the name came from that of Pepy I's pyramid in the Memphite necropolis at Saqqara.

Saqqara was the burial ground for Memphis from the 1st Dynasty until Roman times, a period of over 3,000 years. Hundreds of tombs have been uncovered but many more await excavation. Recently, the oldest existing mummy was found there, and the lost tomb of King Horemheb was rediscovered. In North Saqqara lie the line of large Archaic mastabas uncovered by W. B. EMERY and, near them, the Iseum, the newly found burial place of the mothers of the Apis bulls (*see* MASTABA; SERAPEUM). Apart from the splendidly decorated Old Kingdom mastaba tombs of noblemen, the best-known monuments at Saqqara are the Step Pyramid of Djoser, the Pyramid of Wenis (*see* PYRAMID), and the Serapeum.

**Mentuhotep II.** An Egyptian king of the Theban 11th Dynasty, who reunited Egypt in about 2040 BC after the troubled First Intermediate Period. His funerary temple at Deir el-Bahri (*see* WINLOCK, HERBERT EUSTIS), on the west bank at THEBES, may have influenced the design of that of Queen HATSHEPSUT, built later on the same site. Meket-Re was an important official during his reign.

**Merida** (Emerita Augusta). A Roman colony in Spain, founded by Augustus in 25 BC. Many Roman buildings survive in part: the THEATER (built by Agrippa), AMPHITHEATER, temples, and aqueducts. The Roman bridge of 64 arches over the Guadlquivir is still in use.

**Meroe.** The former kingdom of Meroe, which flourished between 500 BC and AD 400, lies 1000 mi. (1609 km) south of the Mediterranean on the east bank of the River Nile, in what is today the Republic of the Sudan. Like Egypt, Meroe was dependent on the Nile. The economy was

Representations of rams lining the approach to a Meroitic temple at Naqa, Sudan.

based on farming, fishing, hunting, mining, and extensive trading activities. At first a culturally Egyptianized kingdom, Meroe acquired during the course of development a unique and essentially African character.

The heartland of the Meroitic kingdom lay in the triangle of land at the confluence of the Nile and the Atbara. Our knowledge of Meroe is based on the excavations of J. Garstang between 1909 and 1914 and those of P. L. Shinnie between 1961 and 1971. Extensive ruins occur some 500 yd. (457 m) from the river. Most prominent is the Amun Temple and the walled enclosure of the Royal City. Within the enclosure are many buildings of different periods and functions, varying from important temple complexes to simple domestic buildings. An unusual feature is a large brick-lined tank with an elaborate system of water channels, which may have been a swimming bath. Adjacent to the Royal enclosure are the ruins of the commercial town and the six large slag heaps for which Meroe is famous. These bear witness to what was probably the main industry of the inhabitants of Meroe, that of ironworking. Whether the knowledge of ironworking in Africa spread from Meroe or from elsewhere is still an open question, but the evidence at present available suggests that ironworking first spread into sub-Saharan Africa from Carthage rather than from Meroe. Further to the East, on the southern margin of the town, are several large cemeteries.

Upstream from the capital is the important town and temple complex of Wad ben Naqa. Lying a day's journey to the east of the Nile is the site of Naqa, another major center, where the reliefs of the so-called Lion Temple contain a wealth of information on Meroitic custom and dress. Ten mi. (16 km) to the northeast of Naqa is the town of Musawwarat es Sofra, which relied for its water supply on elaborate engineering work. The extent of the

Meroitic kingdom is still not well defined, but we do know that trading links extended far afield—certainly to the Classical world of the Mediterranean and the Near East and probably to India.

**Merovingians.** A Dynasty of the FRANKS named after its founder, Merovech (5th century AD). The Merovingians ruled France from the time of Clovis (AD 481–511) to that of Charles Martel (*c.* AD 688–741). The term Merovingian is used to describe Frankish archaeology of the 6th to mid-8th century AD.

**Mersin.** The huge TELL of Yümük Tepe, south of the Taurus Mountains in Cilicia, was excavated by the British under John Garstang in the 1930s. Nine Neolithic levels (XXXIII–XXVII) contained predominantly the same dark burnished wares as were found on the Anatolian plateau. Painted pottery was found throughout the Early Chalcolithic levels (XXIV–XX), and after the destruction of Level XX there was Late HALAF pottery (XIX–XVII), though contact with the plateau was maintained. There are few architectural remains, but in level XVI (*c.* 4500–*c.* 4200 BC), which was destroyed by fire, a fortress was partially excavated. The pottery is burnished and is cream, red, black, or polychrome and has some affinities with pottery from the plateau. Metal tools were also found. The Late Chalcolithic is illustrated by levels XVb–XIIa and UBAID-type pottery becomes common. The Early Bronze Age is poorly represented but the site was inhabited until *c.* AD 1500. (*See* the chronological table, p. 198.)

**Mesoamerica.**

*Introduction.* Mesoamerica (or Middle America) is a culture area which traditionally has been defined as stretching roughly from the Rio Sota de la Marina and the Rio Sinaloa in Mexico to Honduras, Salvador, and the Nicoya Peninsula of Costa Rica in the South. World famous sites such as TEOTIHUACAN, Tula (*see* TOLTECS), EL TAJIN, MONTE ALBAN, CHICHEN ITZA, UXMAL, TIKAL, and COPAN are located within its borders. Between *c.* 10,000 BC (and probably much earlier) and the time of the Spanish Conquest in the 16th century AD, it was the scene of continual cultural development which climaxed with the rise of the Aztec Empire just prior to the arrival of the Spaniards. The development from nomadic hunters and gatherers to complex civilizations such as those of the OLMECS, MAYA, Teotihuacan, the Toltecs, and the AZTECS has attracted the attention of a huge number of archaeologists, with the result that, in terms of archaeological knowledge, Mesoamerica is one of the best-known areas in the world. In particular, it has been the focus in recent years of many archaeological studies which have used its data to test hypotheses about the development of a complex society and the rise of the pre-industrial city.

In the past, archaeological studies in Mesoamerica have tended to confine their focuses to individual sites, limited regions, or single cultures or civilizations. However, it is becoming clear to most Mesoamerican scholars, especially those who view Mesoamerican developments from an evolutionary point of view, that an area-wide focus is necessary in order to appreciate many developments in Mesoamerica, especially after the growth of civilization. In fact, some archaeologists have argued for the existence of a single Mesoamerican civilization rather than a series of separate ones.

The chronological terminology currently in use in Mesoamerica belongs to the older regional viewpoint and grew out of research on the Maya Lowlands. Basically it divides the time from 1500 BC to the time of the Spanish Conquest into three periods: the Preclassic (1500 BC–AD 300), Classic (AD 300–900), and Postclassic (AD 900–1521). Unfortunately, this scheme has been extended over all of Mesoamerica. In recent years, as our knowledge of the area has grown incredibly, it has become an increasing burden to archaeologists and has begun to obscure more area-wide relationships than it has clarified. Thus, here, the Precolumbian period in Mesoamerica has been divided into five numbered phases.

*Phase I (10,000–1500 BC).* Phase I marks the time prior to the beginning of complex society, which saw the rise of both agriculture and settled village life. There is some evidence for the presence of ancient hunters and gatherers before the end of the Pleistocene Ice Age. While there are clouded indications that early man may have been present prior to about 10,000 BC, the first secure dates come just after this time. Scattered projectile points dating to the early part of the phase are found throughout the area, while a kill site of extinct mammoths has been uncovered at Iztapan in the valley of Mexico.

Recent field research in the Tehuacan valley, a semi-arid highland valley to the south of present-day Mexico City, has given archaeologists a new and clearer picture of the cultural developments during this long phase. Contrary to previously held ideas, research has shown that the domestication of plants (maize, beans, and squash), perhaps prior to 5000 BC, did not cause a cultural revolution; rather there was a slow evolution in Mesoamerica over thousands of years from migratory bands of hunters and gatherers to sedentary villages (by *c.* 2000 BC). The earliest pottery dates to about the mid-3rd millennium BC.

*Phase II (1500–200 BC).* Institutionalized ceremonialism and the rise of a priestly elite followed settled village life. On the Gulf Coast, the first civilization in Mesoamerica, the Olmec, emerged as early as 1200 BC. There are three large, well known Olmec sites on or near the coast. They are SAN LORENZO, LA VENTA, and TRES ZAPOTES. They appear to have had their heyday between 1200 and 600 BC, although occupation at these sites continued for centuries after this period. Olmec civilization is characterized by a highly distinctive religion and an art style which features motifs such as jaguars, huge carved basalt stone heads, monumental ceremonial construction, and fine portable sculpture, often in jade—elements or traits which a few scholars see as evidence of transpacific influence from China or other areas.

Olmec influence, certainly of both a religious and economic nature, if not political as well, spread to many parts of Mesoamerica, particularly to the adjacent High-

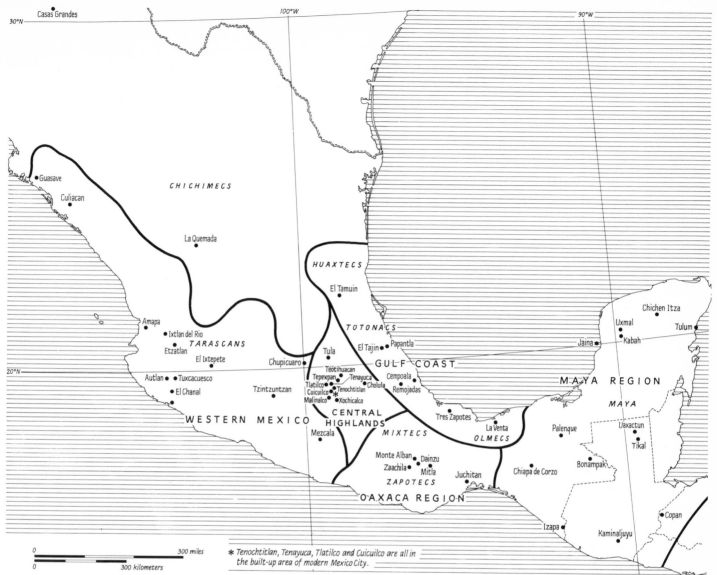

Map of ancient Mesoamerica.

Within the map labels (as visible): Casas Grandes · Guasave · Culiacan · La Quemada · CHICHIMECS · Amapa · Ixtlan del Rio · TARASCANS · Etzatlan · El Ixtepete · Chupicuaro · HUAXTECS · El Tamuin · TOTONACS · Tula · El Tajin · Papantla · GULF COAST · Autlan · Tuxcacuesco · Teotihuacan · Tepexpan · Tlatilco · Tenayuca · Cholula · Cempoala · MAYA REGION · Chichen Itza · Uxmal · Tulum · Kabah · Jaina · El Chanal · Tzintzuntzan · Cuicuilco · Tenochtitlan · Xochicalco · Malinalco · Remojadas · WESTERN MEXICO · CENTRAL HIGHLANDS · Mezcala · MIXTECS · Tres Zapotes · La Venta · OLMECS · Palenque · Uaxactun · MAYA · Monte Alban · Dainzu · Zaachila · Mitla · Juchitan · Chiapa de Corzo · Bonampak · Tikal · ZAPOTECS · OAXACA REGION · Izapa · Kaminaljuyu · Copan

* Tenochtitlan, Tenayuca, Tlatilco and Cuicuilco are all in the built-up area of modern Mexico City.

0 — 300 miles
0 — 300 kilometers

lands, Central Mexico, and the Highlands of Guatemala. Olmec influences can even be found in the Southern Mesoamerican frontier in Honduras, Costa Rica, and Salvador.

Olmec contacts with nearby highland Oaxaca seem to have stimulated cultural growth there. Perhaps even prior to Olmec influence, this region appears to have begun to evolve the beginnings of a complex society based on its long history of plant domestication, relatively early beginnings of settled village life, and rudimentary irrigation. Within a few centuries of Olmec contact, Oaxaca, with its vastly greater resources and potentially richer agricultural base (with irrigation), appears to have begun to gain the upper hand in this relationship. By 600 BC at the latest, it had become the dominant partner and Olmec civilization began to decline.

In the valley of Oaxaca, the site of MONTE ALBAN predominated, and here are found the first hieroglyphic texts in Mesoamerica. Until the rise of TEOTIHUACAN, it may have been the dominant site in Mesoamerica.

The Olmecs also stimulated more gradual cultural developments in Central Mexico, which matured to produce the first great urban empire in the area. The rise of this empire, based at the city of Teotihuacan, marks the start of Phase III of Precolumbian development.

*Phase III (200 BC–AD 700).* Teotihuacan is located about 31 mi. (50 km) northeast of present-day Mexico City. The combination of location, environment, and resources was the key factor in Teotihuacan's development. It was located on a potentially important trade route to the South, its valley was eminently suitable for irrigation, and it was situated next to a major OBSIDIAN source. Through the systemic reinforcement of these factors, the population and size of Teotihuacan grew rapidly. Recent surveys indicate that, by AD 200, the site occupied an area of 12 mi. (20 km) and may have had a population exceeding 125,000. Some of its largest and most impressive structures, such as the Pyramid of the Sun, were erected during Teotihuacan's heyday, which lasted until AD 700–750, when the site apparently was burned and sacked.

Phase III also was the time of the rise of Classic Maya civilization in the Lowlands of Guatemala and adjacent areas (which are often called the Southern Lowlands). The architecture and monumental art of the Classic Maya, as seen at the great sites like TIKAL, PALENQUE,

137

YAXCHILAN, or COPAN, represent some of the first artistic expressions in Precolumbian America. By the 3rd century AD, all the major features of Classic Maya civilization were present, including ceremonial centers with large temple complexes, a dominant theocratic elite, a distinctive art style, polychrome pottery, hieroglyphic inscriptions, and a sophisticated astronomical/mathematical system. Some of these features arose indigenously, while others diffused from the adjacent Highlands, where they may have arisen much earlier under stimulus from the Olmecs.

The ceremonial centers, with their resident priests and helpers, were supported by the peasants who resided in a scattered pattern around the centers. They practiced a shifting agricultural system known as slash and burn, and raised crops such as maize, beans, and squash. As the Early Classic Period (AD 300–600) developed, these centers expanded as the population grew, and there was a trend toward nucleation of settlement and the rise of urban centers in the Classic Period.

*Phase IV (AD 700–1300).* This phase of Precolumbian development opens with the destruction of the great city of Teotihuacan. After more than eight centuries of growth and power, Teotihuacan was burned and largely abandoned by AD 750. The exact causes of its decline are not clear, although the immediate cause apparently was an invasion by peoples from the North.

The decline and collapse of Teotihuacan and its empire left a huge power vacuum in Mesoamerica which a number of local cultures attempted to fill. However, it took more than 200 years before the TOLTECS, based at the city of Tula, to the northwest of Teotihuacan, were able to replicate Teotihuacan's dominant position.

Among the important centers at the beginning of this phase were CHOLULA, Tula, and Xochicalco in Central Mexico, EL TAJIN on the Gulf Coast, and a number of Late Classic Maya cities. However, the late Classic Maya fluorescence was particularly shortlived because, by about AD 800, the Classic Maya civilization completely collapsed and most Southern Lowland centers were virtually abandoned.

The causes of the collapse appear to have been multiple. The tropical rainforest environment seems to have been unable to support the growth of large urban centers, given the technology of the ancient Maya, and severe internal strains emerged which the Maya priests seem to have exacerbated rather than alleviated. At about the same time, the Classic Maya civilization had to face an external threat from the Putun, a non-Classic Maya people who began to expand, in the 8th century AD, from their Tabascan homeland.

By the 10th century AD, the Toltecs and the Putun, particularly the former, began to emerge as major Mesoamerican powers. The Toltecs were more militaristic, with greater secular orientation than their predecessors. From their capital at Tula they spread their influence throughout much of Mesoamerica. They traded with regions on both the Northern and Southern frontier of Mesoamerica and they conquered sites as far away as CHICHEN ITZA in the Northern Lowlands of Yucatan. West and Northwest Mexico also emerged as important

regions and metallurgy was just one of the contributions which West Mexico made to the mainstream of Mesoamerican development at this time.

In Southern Mesoamerica the Putun became a leading economic and political power. These people were a mercantile-oriented group who were canoeists and seafarers without equals. They expanded out from their Gulf Coast homeland into the borders surrounding the Classic Maya civilization in the Southern Lowlands, into the Guatemalan Highlands, into the Northern Lowlands of Yucatan, and along the East coast of the peninsula. They were involved in the downfall of the Classic Maya civilization, the contemporaneous florescence of the Puuc region in the Northern Lowlands, and the establishment of a long-distance trade route which linked Honduras and Central America with Yucatan and the Gulf Coast region. In addition, they apparently were close allies of the Toltecs in Yucatan.

Both the Toltecs and the Putun helped usher in major cultural changes in Phase IV, as Mesoamerican civilization became relatively more secular in emphasis. Militarism and the growth of a merchant class were two of the vehicles of this change. However, the influence of the Putun continued into the next phase, while Tula and the Toltec Empire collapsed sometime in the 13th century AD.

*Phase V (AD 1300–1521).* This final phase of Precolumbian development is marked for the most part by the rise of regional powers throughout the area until near its close, when the Aztecs consolidated their power and began forming their empire. The League of MAYAPAN in Yucatan, and Quiche in the Guatemalan Highlands, the Totonac on the Gulf Coast, the MIXTEC in Oaxaca, and the Tarascans in West Mexico are some examples of the new regional powers which dominated most of the phase. In addition, the Putun continued their control of the long-distance sea trade from Tabasco to Honduras.

The most significant development of the time was the growth of the Aztec Empire. The AZTECS were a group of nomads who entered the politically fragmented basin of Mexico in the 14th century AD. Banished to an unwanted island in Lake Texcoco, this warlike people slowly consolidated influence and power through a series of alliances and wars until they were able to emerge as a major power in Central Mexico by the start of the 15th century AD. Under the Emperor Ahuitzotl at the end of the century, the Aztecs expanded their empire to the farther reaches of Mesoamerica.

The Aztec capital of Tenochtitlan grew in size and sophistication as Aztec power and influence expanded. At the time of the Spanish Conquest, it may have held anywhere from 100,000 to 300,000 inhabitants. Thousands of people traded in its great markets while tribute from all over the empire flowed into the hands of the Aztec nobility. Aqueducts brought fresh water from the mainland, while a vast system of chinampas or floating gardens in adjacent parts of the lake helped provide some of the food to support the huge resident population (*see* CHINAMPA).

Unfortunately, it will never be known how great or complex the Aztec Empire might have become, because just at the beginning of its florescence the Spanish conquistadores arrived and put an end to the native civilization of Mesoamerica. Within two years of his landing in Mesoamerica in 1519, Hernando Cortes conquered the Aztec Empire and brought about its rapid destruction. He achieved this through his own military skill, support gained from local allies such as the Tlaxcalans, the fluid nature of the rapidly changing Aztec society, and the belief of the Aztec Emperor Moctezuma II that Cortes might be the great god QUETZALCOATL, or his representative, returning from the East. Within several more decades most of Mesoamerica lay under Spanish control.

**Mesolithic** (or Middle Stone Age). One of the five divisions most commonly recognized in prehistory: PALAEOLITHIC, Mesolithic, NEOLITHIC, BRONZE AGE, IRON AGE. It is used mainly in Europe for the prehistoric hunters who lived after the last ICE AGE. But in Western Asia it is sometimes used for the societies in transition to a farming economy. It must not be confused with the "Middle Stone Age" of Africa, which refers to a much earlier, pre-blade tool, stage.

It was in 1866, only a year after John Lubbock had proposed the division of the Stone Age into Palaeolithic and Neolithic, that Hodder Westropp proposed a Mesolithic period to be sandwiched between them, fulfilling a common desire of archaeologists to have their ages neatly subdivided into threes. Like later prehistorians, Westropp conceived the Mesolithic as a transitional period between the Palaeolithic and Neolithic.

Not until the 1920s did Mesolithic come to have its modern meaning, under the influence of prehistorians like V. Gordon Childe and Grahame Clark. Clearly, most Mesolithic cultures did not evolve into the early Neolithic farming cultures in Europe, though they may have influenced them considerably. The most important changes during this stage were the replacement of the tundra and steppe of the glacial period with birch and pine woodlands, giving way eventually to deciduous forest, where the oak flourished. The large herds of reindeer, bison, horse, and other herbivores became scarcer and were replaced by red deer and roe deer, and eventually, when the forest reached a climax of density, there were almost no large mammals except a few wild boar.

At the same time sea level was changing. In the closing stages of the Ice Age, sea level was so low that much of the continental shelf was exposed. Even in the first 2,000 years of postglacial time there was still dry land over much of the Southern North Sea area, and "Doggerland" was certainly occupied by early man. By 5000 BC all this land was drowned and the sea invaded low-lying areas like Holland and the Fens. Mesolithic man came to occupy a shrinking world.

One of the most typical features of the Mesolithic is the manufacture of axes by flaking on both surfaces and removing a sharpening flake or "tranchet" by a side blow on one end. Obviously a likely use for such axes would be in felling small trees, or in hollowing out logs as canoes. Several such canoes, as well as paddles, have been found.

Also typical are little triangular flint points and other geometric shapes, made by the microburin technique. Sometimes found in groups, they were probably rows of barbs set in spearheads of wood or bone. They seem to have replaced bone and antler points with carved barbs.

**Mesopotamia.** The alluvial plain created by the Rivers Tigris and Euphrates and their tributaries the Khabur, the lower and upper Zab, the DIYALA, the Kerkha, and the Karun. This is roughly the area covered by modern Iraq and it is bordered to the north by the mountains of Armenia and Kurdistan, to the west by the Syrian desert and to the east by the Zagros mountain range. In the South there are extensive marshes. The area has few natural resources: minerals and many raw materials have to be imported and agriculture depends almost entirely on irrigation.

From *c.* 10,000 BC, settlements are found first at Shanidar and later also at Zawi Chemi and Karim Shahir. At Ali Kosh/Bus Mordeh, in Khuzistan (*c.* 8000?–6500 BC), we have the first evidence of domesticated sheep, some farming and some clay buildings, and imported OBSIDIAN. A third phase is illustrated again by Ali Kosh, and by Jarmo in the North—both pre-pottery Neolithic with multiroomed houses. Obsidian at both sites, and a bead of native copper and others of turquoise at Ali Kosh, indicate trade.

Pottery appears in the top levels at Jarmo, at Tamerkhan near Mandali, at Ali Agha in ASSYRIA, and at Ali Kosh/Muhammad Jafar (*c.* 6000–5600? BC). At this period the first lowland settlements appear in the plains of Northern Iraq at Umm Dabaghiyah and in surrounding tells, at Telul et-Talathat and at Tell Sotto. Pottery is abundant, mostly unpainted and some of it imported. Cattle are now domesticated and the architecture is based on an orderly arrangement of cubicles. The antecedents of the Umm Dabaghiyah culture have yet to be found and its relationship to the succeeding HASSUNA culture is not clear. The relationship of the Hassuna, Samarra, and HALAF cultures is also uncertain since they were once thought to be consecutive, but new evidence seems to point to their being contemporary and interrelating regional cultures. All three are mainly distinguished by their pottery. The main Hassuna sites are Tell Hassuna itself and Yarim Tepe I, southwest and west of Mosul, characterized by painted, incised, and painted and incised pottery. To the south lie the Samarran sites of TELL ES-SAWWAN near Samarra, which was walled, Choga Mami near Mandali, and Tell Shemshara in the Northern Zagros Mountains, with an early monochrome phase and a later polychrome phase. Some of the designs are naturalistic but most are geometric. TELL ARPACHIYAH and Yarim Tepe II are the most important representatives of the Northern Halaf culture, which has three phases of very fine and closely decorated painted pottery. The earliest known settlement in the South is at ERIDU and its distinctive painted pottery also occurs in the neighborhood and at UR (UBAID I). A different pottery sequence has been found at Choga Mami in Khuzistan, and both probably date to the end of the 6th millennium BC.

From *c.* 5000 BC onwards, a number of sites in the Khuzistan plain, including Jaffarabad and Choga Mish,

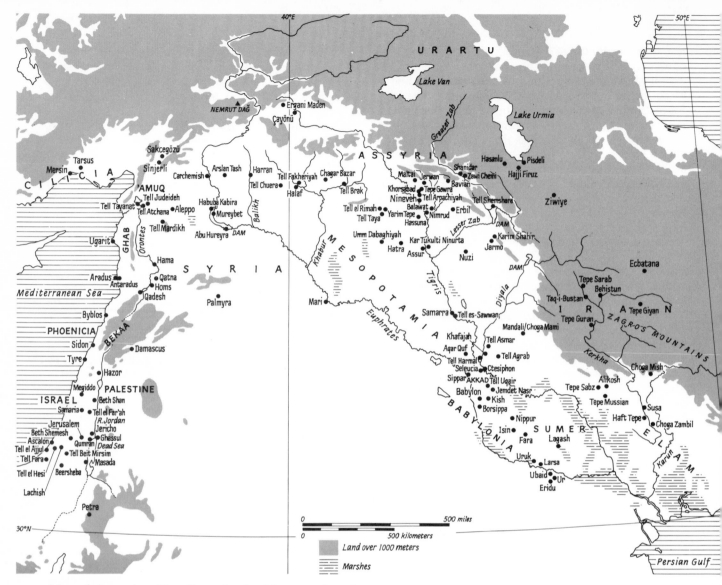

Map of the ancient Near East, showing Mesopotamia and Syria-Palestine.

produce pottery belonging to the Tepe Sabz culture, with close links with lowland Mesopotamia. This was succeeded by the Khazineh culture, contemporary with the Hajji Muhammad phase in Southern Mesopotamia (Ubaid 2) which is found from Ras el-Amiyah, near Kish, to Eridu. In Khuzistan, animal designs on pottery appear alongside the geometric at Memeh. The Early Ubaid phase in Southern Mesopotamia (Ubaid 3), characterized not only by pottery but also by clay sickles and nails, is succeeded in c. 4200 BC by the Late Ubaid or Ubaid 4 phase, which shows a decline in the quality of the pottery but a tremendous increase in quantity, since it is found, with regional variations, from Cilicia and Northern Syria, throughout Mesopotamia and into IRAN, and as far afield as Saudi Arabia, where it occurs not only on the coast of the PERSIAN GULF but even more than 40 mi. (65 km) inland. Lizard-headed figurines, cast copper objects, and, in the North, stone stamp SEALS, appear and so do the gray and red URUK wares, which predominate in the next period and which also occur in the North (Grai Resh and Habuba Kabira). In the

North, however, a different culture predominates, known from its type-site at TEPE GAWRA as Gawran. An interesting sequence is also represented at NINEVEH.

Towards the end of the 4th millennium BC, monumental architecture and the discovery of the wheel and of writing herald a new age. These innovations have been attributed to the arrival of the Sumerians, but others maintain that they are the culmination of a long local development. Urban communities sprang up throughout the South in the JEMDET NASR or Proto-Literate period. Rival city states were established in the EARLY DYNASTIC period and discoveries at Ur, at LAGASH, and in the Diyala have revealed a highly developed and very rich culture. The extensive 3rd-millennium BC remains at Tell Taya, west of Mosul, are evidence of urban development in the North, and MARI and TELL CHUERA in Syria fell within the orbit of this culture.

During the second half of the 3rd millennium BC, the Semitic Akkadians united Mesopotamia politically for the first time. The GUTI invasion from the east brought about the downfall of the Akkadians and after a period of chaos the Sumerians again achieved predominance in what is known as the Neo-Sumerian or Ur III period (see UR). More Semitic incursions led to the settlement of the ARAMAEANS and the establishment of the Isin-Larsa and Old Babylonian Dynasties at the beginning of the 2nd millennium BC. Hammurabi of BABYLON (1792–1750 BC) again sought to unite Mesopotamia, but in the North the city of ASSUR was becoming increasingly rich and powerful, in what is known as the Old Assyrian period, as a result of its trading ventures, which had led to the establishment of merchant colonies as far afield as Anatolia. A Hittite raid destroyed Babylon in c. 1595 BC (see CHRONOLOGY, NEAR EAST), and although the raid was an isolated event, it brought about the fall of the 1st Dynasty of Babylon. The KASSITES, another tribe from the East, then seized power in the South and established their capital at Dur Kurigalzu.

From c. 1200 BC onwards the history of the South becomes obscure, but we know that the Kassites were overthrown by the Elamites in c. 1157 BC. Meanwhile, in the North, the rulers of Assur had been consolidating their power at the expense of the Hurrian state of Mitanni. There was then a period of decline in Assyrian fortunes which only revived at the end of the 10th century BC, and from then on, until 612 BC, the Assyrian Empire dominated the Near Eastern scene. In that year, however, a coalition of Chaldaean kings from Babylon and MEDES from Iran brought about the fall of NINEVEH, and a Neo-Babylonian Dynasty then ruled Mesopotamia until 539 BC, when Babylon, in its turn, fell to the Achaemenid king, Cyrus II. From then on, Mesopotamia was dominated by foreign rulers, and ACHAEMENIDS, SELEUCIDS, PARTHIANS, and SASSANIANS succeeded one another until the Arab Conquest. (See also the chronological table, p. 198.)

**Messene.** A Greek city in the Southwest Peloponnese, founded in 369 BC. Its city walls, which date from the foundation, are one of the best-preserved examples of Hellenistic fortification. Excavations round the marketplace have revealed remains of Hellenistic and Roman date: a THEATER, assembly hall, and a Temple of Artemis.

**Metal analysis.** Even in the early 19th century, when the "Three Age System" (Stone, Bronze, and Iron) was being worked out, archaeologists were aware that prehistoric man had used the copper-tin alloy, bronze. But because older methods of "wet" chemical analysis demanded the destruction of large samples, little progress was made beyond the additional identification of an initial phase in which pure copper was used. Since 1950, however, the routine application of microchemical methods has produced a wealth of quantitative data about ancient metal compositions, including the identification of a widely used ancient alloy of copper and arsenic.

The main method used so far has been a spectrographic technique, in which a tiny sample is burnt in an arc to produce an optical spectrum characteristic of its elemental composition. Some 20,000 analyses of ancient copper objects have been carried out by a German team based in Stuttgart. Eleven elements are routinely sought: tin, lead, arsenic, antimony, silver, bismuth, nickel, gold, zinc, cobalt, and iron. Work along similar lines has been carried out in Russia, at Moscow and Baku; while a team

in Vienna has attempted to link locally found prehistoric copper and bronze objects to the compositions typical of the various alpine copper ores.

While attempts to identify sources for metal objects have not generally met with success, much information has been accumulated on the kinds of metal composition used at different periods. In the COPPER AGE, very pure copper was in use, probably native ore or smelted malachite. In its later phases, deliberate alloying with arsenic became common, and this persisted into the BRONZE AGE in areas without tin. Bronze Age ores were usually sulphides, with traces of sulphur and iron, and very often the use of gray enriched ores can be identified by high arsenic and antimony contents.

Work now in progress involves the use of X-ray diffraction techniques, and greater attention to the way in which different elements separate in casting. (See also ARSENIC; BRONZE, PREHISTORIC EUROPE; COPPER; GOLD; IRON; LEAD; TIN.)

**Metal technology, Prehistoric Europe.** The principal metals used in prehistoric Europe were copper, gold, iron, silver, lead, and tin; the last two were mainly exploited to make copper alloys. Gold and tin were extracted as grains and nuggets from river deposits. Copper, iron, and lead were obtained by smelting ores quarried from surface outcrops or even mines—enormous copper mines were worked in Central Europe during the BRONZE AGE. Silver was normally extracted as an impurity of lead. Furnaces were normally small, clay-lined circular depressions in the ground, sometimes with shallow domed covers. The metals were often refined to over 99% purity, and were transported as ingots which, in Southern Europe, as in the Near East, were shaped like animal hides.

Metal artifacts were made by hot and cold working and by casting, although iron was never intentionally cast in Europe in prehistoric times. Open, piece, and investment molds, of stone or fired clay, were successively introduced for casting: the metal was poured from open crucibles made of quartz-tempered clay. Stone, bronze, and steel tools were introduced in succession for working and decorating metal. The main techniques of joining metals were riveting, casting-on (burning-on), soldering, and, for iron only, welding. The principal decorative techniques were the scribing, chasing, and engraving of grooves, and the beating-up of sheet metal from the back in *repoussé* relief; granulation, filigree work, and inlays of glass, enamel, and other substances (e.g., coral) in *champlevé* and *cloisonné* technique came into use in the late 1st millennium BC. Copper, gold, silver, and tin were all used in plating metal. (See also [for Europe] BRONZE, PREHISTORIC EUROPE; CASTING; COPPER; COPPER AGE, EUROPE; GOLD; LEAD; IRON; IRON AGE; MINING, EUROPE; TIN. For other areas and periods see BRONZE TECHNOLOGY, CHINA; CIRE PERDUE; IRON TECHNOLOGY, CHINA; RITUAL VESSELS, CHINA; SHANG DYNASTY.)

**Metate.** A term for the bench- and trough-like QUERN which was used for grinding foodstuffs, particularly maize, in aboriginal America. The hand counterpart to the metate is called a mano. They were often made of volcanic rocks in Mesoamerica.

**Metope.** A plain or decorated panel of a Classical temple, between the triglyphs, part of the solid lintel above the columns.

**Miao-ti-kou.** An important site of the Neolithic YANG-SHAO CULTURE in China. Like the other major site of this culture, PAN-P'O-TS'UN, it appears to have been occupied periodically, suggesting that a slash-and-burn type of agriculture was practiced. The very fine pottery from the site is decorated with designs based on arcs and dots. This appears to be an abstraction derived from the fish decoration seen on pottery from Pan-p'o-ts'un.

**Michelsberg culture.** A 3rd-millennium BC Neolithic culture, closely related to the FUNNEL-NECKED BEAKER CULTURE, which occupied the Rhineland and the Low Countries in succession to the RÖESSEN CULTURE. One of its innovations was the use of deep mines for flint, such as those at Spiennes in Belgium, or Rijkholt in Holland, where axes were made.

**Microlith.** *See* STONE TECHNOLOGY.

**Middle East, Palaeolithic.** The earliest traces of man in the Middle East (Southwest Asia) are from Ubeidiyah in the Jordan valley, where an assemblage similar to that found at OLDUVAI GORGE has been found under a series of ACHEULIAN-type assemblages. The first occupation here is thus probably over a million years old. Man was probably present at a very early date in Turkey, and occupation, with traces of fire, is known from the Petralona cave at the head of the Aegean Sea, dating from some 700,000 years ago.

As late as the beginning of the last glacial period, some 100,000 to 60,000 years ago, handaxes of the Acheulian type were still being made in the East Mediterranean caves. A fossil skull from the Zuttiyeh cave may belong to this time. A number of different types of Mousterian tools, some like those of Europe, are found from Israel to Iraq. They are associated with Neanderthal-type men: some, as at Shanidar, are like European Neanderthals, others, from Mount Carmel and Jebel Qafseh, are closer to modern man. At the moment experts are unsure whether this is because the advanced forms, as from the Skhul cave on Mount Carmel, are later in date (*see* CARMEL, MOUNT; NEANDERTHAL MAN).

The Upper Palaeolithic in the Middle East begins at about the same time as in most parts of Europe, but is still not well understood in detail. The latest culture of the last Ice Age period in the East Mediterranean is called NATUFIAN. A large number of burials dating from this time are known from a cemetery at the Wad cave of Mount Carmel. The Natufians seem to have had the equipment for reaping and grinding corn, and some of the earliest evidence for food production comes from the Shanidar site in Northern Iraq, where indications of domestic sheep and wheat were found.

**Middle Horizon.** A division of time, *c.* AD 700–1000, in Central Andean chronology, used to refer to the first imperialistic domination of the area under the unifying forces of the TIAHUANACO and HUARI cultures.

**Migration Period.** A term used to cover the late 4th to early 6th century AD in Western Europe, when barbarians from beyond the Roman frontiers settled within many of the former provinces. The term is often extended to cover the period from the 3rd century AD to the accession of Charlemagne in AD 800.

Pressure from the barbarians was first felt in the Roman Empire in the 3rd century AD. Weakened by internal disputes and a rapid succession of usurpers, the empire fell prey to the attacks of pirates and civil unrest in Gaul, where *bagaudae* (dissatisfied peasants) carried out guerrilla attacks on provincial administration. The pressures were resisted until the 4th century AD, when tribes and larger confederacies of people moved across the frontiers searching for new lands to settle and plunder. The causes of the migrations are not fully understood, but a taste for Roman goods acquired through trade and barbarian service in the Roman army, a population explosion, and a failure of food supplies were contributory factors.

The folk movements started when the nomadic or seminomadic peoples from the Western plains of Russia displaced the Huns, who in turn pressed upon a loose confederacy known as the Goths, of whom the Ostrogoths occupied the Crimea and the Visigoths the Danube basin. Moving from these homelands (to which they had migrated from Scandinavia many centuries before) they met and defeated the Roman army at Adrianople (on the border between modern Bulgaria and Turkey) in AD 378, before pressing on to Constantinople. Their advance was briefly held back by the Emperor Theodosius, but they sacked Rome in AD 410 and moved into Gaul and Spain. In the wake of the Goths came the Huns, who overran Central Europe and advanced on Rome, only to be turned back at the gates in AD 452.

From the Germanic areas of Northern Europe came a further but less mobile group of settlers. Some of these people had settled on the German frontier and had become familiar with Rome through service as mercenaries. Of these the FRANKS settled in France, eventually forming the Merovingian kingdom, and in Germany south of the Rhine. Angles, Saxons, and others settled in England, merging to form the ANGLO-SAXONS. Spain was settled by Visigoths, the extreme south of Spain and Africa by Vandals, Italy by Lombards and Central Europe by Slavs. The extent to which civilization was destroyed by the incoming barbarians varied regionally. In France Gallo-Roman life continued for some time and many Roman institutions were adopted by the Franks, who occupied many towns and used Roman-style currency and titles. The Goths in Italy tried to imitate the Romans, by issuing Roman-style coins and having aspirations to found their own imperial Dynasty. In Gaul, Italy, and Spain Latin survived, to provide the roots from which the "Romance" languages of French, Italian, and Spanish developed. Gradually the barbarian

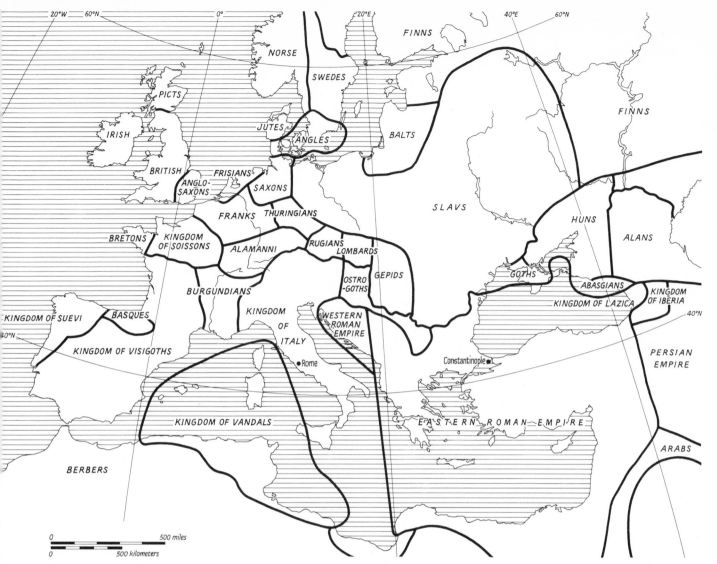

Map of Europe in AD 476, showing the areas settled by the barbarian tribes during the Migration Period.

peoples were converted to Christianity.

Jewelry is the chief product characteristic of the Migration Period. The most distinctive types are decorated in *cloisonné* work, with inlays set in cells or *cloisons* against a metal background, not infrequently gold. Semiprecious stones, particularly garnets, were used for inlays, along with enamels and GLASS. This resulted in a brightly colored finish, often termed polychrome work. Eagle-shaped brooches are typical products. Although different styles are detectable, the art of the barbarians was not naturalistic but depended on animal forms used as ornament, and purely abstract design.

**Milan** (Mediolanum). Milan was the principal road center of North Italy, brought under Roman control in 194 BC. It was of great importance in Roman imperial times, particularly in the late empire, when it was second only to Rome within Italy and the site of an imperial palace. Visible remains are the trace of its Augustan and later walls, the THEATER, AMPHITHEATER, CIRCUS, Constantinian BATHS, and several early churches, of which the most notable is S. Lorenzo.

**Milestones.** Roman roads were marked with milestones—cylindrical blocks of stone usually about 6 ft. (1.8 m) high—recording the distance from a central point within the province or a local center. They bear the title of the emperor or the consuls under whose direction the road was laid out or repaired.

**Mimbres.** A subculture of the ANASAZI cultural sequence in the MOGOLLON area of the Southwestern United States. It is named after a river of New Mexico and dates from AD 1000–1200. The Mimbres people were farmers growing maize and gathering foods such as beans and acorns, and hunting deer, antelope, and rabbits. Mimbres black-on-white pottery is, rightly, often considered to be the finest aesthetic product of the prehistoric Southwest. The bowls used in burials were decorated with a variety of patterns: one of the themes is a series of stylized naturalistic representations of animals such as rabbits, bears, and insects, and also of humans.

**Ming Dynasty.** One of the major late Dynasties of China (AD 1368–1644), succeeding the Mongol YÜAN DYNASTY (AD 1280–1368). It is famous above all for

143

painting and the decorative arts, PORCELAIN, LACQUER, *cloisonné*, and textiles. Among the most important excavations relating to this period is that of the tomb of the Emperor Wan-li (AD 1573–1620) at the site of the Ming tombs near Peking. Of this group only this tomb has been fully explored, revealing a vast, solidly built sequence of underground chambers. Inside, most of the grave goods were found intact, including spectacular jewelry and textiles, and more ordinary porcelain and JADE objects. Peking was laid out in its present form under the Yung-lo emperor (AD 1403–1423), although many of the surviving buildings were restored in the CH'ING DYNASTY.

## Mining, Europe.

*Stone.* It was the colonization of the North European Plain and the introduction of the plow in the 3rd millennium BC which first necessitated mining for flint, in order to produce supplies of stone to make axes for clearing forest. Across Northern Europe, from Britain to Russia, mines were sunk through the soft chalk to satisfy this demand.

In Britain, the major mines were on the South Downs of Sussex, to the north of Worthing. Cissbury, Blackpatch, and Findon each have a complex of shafts going down 33–49 ft. (10–15 m), perhaps a thousand or so in all. Smaller establishments are known from the Wiltshire and Oxfordshire chalk, with another major industrial complex at GRIME'S GRAVES in Norfolk.

Belgium and Holland have many sites of this kind in their chalk regions, including the famous mines of Spiennes and Obourg in Belgium—the latter is well known because of the find of a prehistoric miner, still clutching his antler pick, killed by a roof fall.

Similar mines occur in Jutland, but there is then a gap further east, since the chalk is largely masked by thick glacial deposits on the North European plain. In consequence, there was a huge center of industrial activity in the Holy Cross Mountains of Little Poland, where one site alone is roughly twice the size of Grime's Graves.

*Metal.* One of the most exciting finds of recent years has been the discovery in Southeast Europe of the actual mines used to obtain the supplies of copper which supported Europe's first metallurgical industry. In Bulgaria and Yugoslavia shafts, dated by finds of 4th-millennium BC pottery, have been traced in the neighborhood of prehistoric settlements, and many more may yet be found.

The Yugoslav example is at Rudna Glave, near Bor in the Northeast of the country, and was discovered in the course of open-cast mining. It consists of vertical shafts running up to 82 ft. (25 m) into the limestone along veins of malachite. The Bulgarian ones are less spectacular, but show a similar kind of activity. Other possible sites of this kind, not yet proved by finds of pottery, are indicated by the existence of waisted stone mauls, originally hafted with withies and used for breaking up the stone to extract the ore. These are known in Spania Dolina, near Banska Bistrica in Czechoslovakia, and also in Britain (e.g., at Alderley Edge in Cheshire) and Ireland.

More complex than these, however, are the famous Late Bronze Age (late 2nd millennium BC) mines in the region of the Mitteberg in the Salzkammergut in Austria. These are complex multiple shafts, designed to allow miners to penetrate deep into the hillside, in search of chalcopyrite, by allowing the circulation of fresh air. Fires lit at appropriate places in ventilation shafts allowed miners to work hundreds of feet from the surface.

The first systematic mining in Classical times was carried out at the silver mines of Laurium in Athens: the work was done by slaves, and concessions were let to Athenian citizens. Rome developed and controlled mines in the provinces—principally Spain, Britain, and Dacia (present-day Romania). Remains of the arrangements for drainage (water wheels) and for treating and washing out the ore produced have been recognized.

**Minoan archaeology.** The flourishing period of Bronze Age civilization (Minoan) in CRETE lasted from *c.* 3000 to 1000 BC, incorporating the subdivisions first suggested by Sir Arthur EVANS: those of Early, Middle, and Late Minoan periods (*see also* GREECE, ARCHAEOLOGY OF). The main differences between these periods are shown by the different forms and decorations of pottery. Pottery of the Early Minoan period is in few forms, with burnished patterns or simple linear painted designs, which by the Middle Minoan period have become more complex, with designs in two or more colors on slip-coated pots. The introduction of the first potters' wheel, *c.* 2000 BC, enabled the production of finer pottery, which reached its peak of achievement *c.* 1700 BC. In the Late Minoan period new fashions evolved, with complexities of patterning of dark on light vases which, in the latest stages, developed into various forms of plant and marine designs. The two main periods of palace building were the Middle Minoan I–II, and Middle Minoan III–Late Minoan IIIA, separated by a period of destruction. In the latter period, the palaces were arranged round courtyards and stood two or more stories high, the lower parts built of stone, the upper of mud brick. There was much use of stone or timber columns, either straight or tapering from top to bottom. Palace walls were highly decorated, with painted frescoes and stucco reliefs showing naturalistic motifs and ritual and ceremonial scenes, including those connected with the religious ceremonies. These centered on a goddess whose attributes included a snake and a double ax, and whose festivities may have included bull-leaping, also represented in frescoes and vase paintings. The Middle Minoan period was also one in which craftsmanship in metalworking in gold and bronze, in jewelry manufacture, and faience was of an exceptionally high order.

**Mirror.** In China, mirrors were thought to have magical powers to influence the spirits, and were therefore frequently buried in tombs from the late CHOU DYNASTY (1072–221 BC) until the T'ANG DYNASTY (AD 618–906). Made of bronze, they were cast with elaborate decoration on the reverse of a highly polished convex surface. Mirrors never completely disappeared in China, and they also exercised an important influence in Japan.

In the Greek and Roman world, mirrors were normally disks of polished metal (tin and bronze), decorated with engraved patterns and figures. They usually had handles, which were possibly of bone or ivory.

Some remarkably fine bronze mirrors have survived from Celtic Britain, carrying abstract designs typical of the art of this period (c. 100 BC–AD 100), known as "Insular art".

**Mississippian tradition.** The name given to the group of cultures which arose in the central and lower Mississippi valley, in the United States, after AD 700. It stands in contrast to the WOODLAND TRADITION because of the appearance of three new traits. The first is the building of rectangular, flat-topped mounds used as the bases for temples. These platforms were sometimes arranged around plazas in a Mesoamerican fashion. Burial mounds, although they do not disappear, become a much less prominent feature of Mississippian sites than they had been during the Woodland tradition. Pottery changes radically in Mississippian cultures: pulverized shell, rather than grit, was often used for temper. New pottery shapes and forms, such as the OLLA, and new types of decoration, such as burnishing and painting, appear. Maize becomes the predominant crop. However Woodland pottery, as well as burial mounds and other Woodland tradition traits, remains common, particularly in the areas of the Eastern Woodlands furthest away from the central Mississippi valley. The new traits definitely derive from Mesoamerica, but it is not clear how they arrived in the Mississippi valley.

The two periods of which the Mississippian tradition is the central feature are Temple Mound I period, AD 700–1200, and Temple Mound II period, AD 1200–1700. The main features of this tradition spread out from the central area between St. Louis and Memphis, in Temple Mound I period, to Georgia and Wisconsin. In the central area the best-known site is Cahokia in Illinois: this was a prominent political and religious center with large flat-topped temple mounds built of earth and clay. The Old Village subculture of Cahokia is known much higher up the Mississippi valley at Aztalan in Wisconsin. Aztalan consists of a large palisaded mound enclosing two pyramid-shaped mounds. The people of Cahokia were maize farmers living in wattle-and-daub houses. Another important early Mississippian site is that at Macon, Ga. Both Macon and Aztalan were fortified, suggesting that they were constructed, perhaps by immigrants, in hostile territory. The various mounds and other buildings at Macon were surrounded by two earthworks. One of the buildings was circular with 50 seats, 3 of which were placed on an eagle effigy altar, perhaps suggesting its use as a council chamber. The Mississippian tradition reached its peak during Temple Mound II period. The great mound at Cahokia was enlarged to a height of 98 ft. (30 m), and the sides of the base were increased to 656×984 ft. (200×300 m). The site of Etowah in Georgia also reached its largest extent in this period, and showed influences from the Tennessee variants of the Mississippian tradition, which included

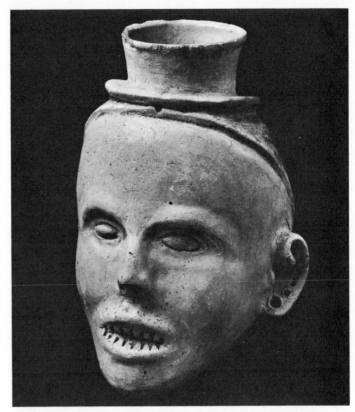

A Mississippian Tradition pottery vessel in the form of a human head, from Arkansas, AD 1200–1500.

the production of stone effigy figures. Moundville, Ala., the second largest site after Cahokia, was much less influenced by Northern Woodlands traits than Etowah. One of the major features of these large sites, which include the Spiro Mound in Oklahoma, are a series of ritual objects from what has been termed the Southern Cult. These include carved shell gorgets and embossed sheets of copper; some of the designs represent anthropomorphic eagles, others show eyes, arrows, and representations of death in the form of bones and skulls.

It is probable that when the first Spanish explorers appeared—such as de Soto in the 16th century, the great political centers at Cahokia, Etowah, and Moundville were still important. However, with the introduction of European diseases and the consequent decrease in population, the Mississippian tradition went into decline. Historical tribes can be associated with some of the late phases of the tradition. In the early 18th century the Natchez of Louisiana and Mississippi still possessed a ceremonial center and a hierarchical class system with an aristocracy. In other parts of the Eastern Woodlands, for instance in the Northeast of the United States, historical tribes such as the Iroquois retained earlier elements of the Woodland tradition, including, perhaps, Hopewellian pottery types (see HOPEWELL).

**Mithraeum.** A small Roman temple, used for worship in the Eastern cult of Mithras. The building was a long narrow room, without windows or at best dimly lit, within which the participants sat on benches and underwent ritual ordeals. The worship of Mithras was very popular with the Roman army, and many fort sites have

Mithraea nearby, but they are known from civilian centers, too.

**Mitla.** An important Postclassic Zapotec site, located about 25 mi. (40 km) southwest of Oaxaca City, Mexico, Mitla is composed of five clusters of columned, flat-roofed palace structures and is fortified by a hilltop stronghold nearby. A Colonial period church is built into one of the palaces. The buildings are beautifully decorated with long panels of geometric mosaics in elaborate step-and-fret designs. The site was supposedly the residence of the Zapotec high priest. (*See also* ZAPOTECS.)

A detail of the relief mosaic decoration which adorns the buildings at Mitla, Oaxaca, Mexico.

**Mito.** The earliest preceramic occupation, *c.* 2000–1800 BC, associated with the Crossed Hands and Nichitos temples at the site of Kotosh, in the Higueras valley on the east slopes of the Andes, Central Peru.

**Mixtec.** The term Mixtec refers to the people of the Mixtec, or Mixteca, region of Oaxaca, Mexico. The culture of the Mixtecs flourished in the Mixteca Alta, not far from the earlier Zapotec sites, like MONTE ALBAN (*see* ZAPOTECS). In later, Postclassic, times there seems to have been a blending of Mixtec and Zapotec cultures to some degree, and the Mixtec are known to have reused some Zapotec tombs. The best example of this is the fabulous Tomb 7 of Monte Alban, which was originally built by the Zapotecs, but was later used to inter a Mixtec official, along with hundreds of gold, silver, crystal, pearl, coral, jade, and shell offerings. Mixtec Postclassic metallurgy was some of the finest produced in the New World, and there were also skilled artisans in many other

different materials. Although the Zapotec and Mixtec cultures mingled, and at times were allies against common enemies like the AZTECS, the two Oaxacan cultures developed independently.

**Moche sequence.** The Moche valley pottery sequence, in which five pottery phases are identified by the details of spout formation on stirrup-necked bottles, can be used for relative dating of the spread and chronology of MOCHICA sites, *c.* 300 BC to AD 700, from their homeland in the Moche and Chicama valleys, Peru.

**Mochica** (or Moche). The Mochica culture, AD 200–700, spread from the Moche valley, Peru, and it represents the earliest significant civilization from the North coast. In the third phase there is evidence of militaristic expansion into neighboring valleys, and in the fourth phase it reached the ultimate extent of this expansion. Impressive religious and urban centers, which mark this expansion, featured huge pyramids with colorfully painted murals, for example the Huaca del Sol and Huaca de la Luna, south of Trujillo. The Mochica grave pottery, mainly effigy bottles, was realistically modeled, depicting a range of subjects, and was mass-produced from molds. Scenes are also painted in dark pigment on a cream ground, around the bottles and inside the bowls. Ceramics and textiles were mass-produced by specialists. Metallurgy had already reached a high technical standard and included the use of alloys, gilding, and casting methods. Vast irrigation schemes were another important achievement of the Mochica.

**Models in archaeology.** Devices used by archaeologists to aid the interpretation of data. Models consist of hypothetical reconstructions of dynamic processes partly based on material remains and partly testing the validity of interpretations of material culture.

**Mogollon.** A major cultural and geographical area of the prehistoric Southwestern United States. In Southern New Mexico and Eastern Arizona, Mogollon sites consist of groups of houses formed into small villages subsisting on a mixture of agriculture, and hunting and gathering. Mogollon may be divided into five periods. The first (100 BC–AD 500) developed from the COCHISE culture from which the first usage of maize in the United States is known. In Bat cave in New Mexico, primitive strains of maize have been found dating to the 3rd millennium BC. In the upper levels of the same site domesticated maize was also found, and it is likely that beans, *Phaseolus vulgaris*, were cultivated from the beginning of the 1st millennium BC. It is probable that the Mogollon mountains, after which the subarea is named, were the early center of farming in the Southwest: from there it spread to the ANASAZI and other cultural traditions. The first Mogollon period is also the first period of sedentary life: dwellings were in the form of pithouses, dug out of the ground and covered with roofs of earth and stone on timber struts. In Mogollon II (AD 500–600), III (600–900), and IV (900–1000), this tradition continued. In Mogollon V (1000–1400), houses began to be built in the Pueblo style of architecture, with buildings above ground with multiple interconnecting rooms of stone and masonry. The earlier pithouses varied in shape from circular or oval forms to rectangles in the later periods, when entrance was generally through passages. Food was stored in bell-shaped pits outside the buildings, and in underfloor pits inside.

Mogollon dead were always disposed of by primary burial (without later disturbance). The graves were usually placed in houses which had been abandoned, or between houses. In Mogollon V bodies were also placed beneath rooms still in use. Grave goods included ornaments of shell and turquoise, as well as perishable articles such as mats; the most common grave good is, however, pottery.

The earliest Mogollon pottery is a plain red-and-buff ware. In the latter part of Mogollon I, these wares are more often polished than not, and also decorated with incised designs. In Mogollon II the tradition of painting red designs on brown pottery is established, while in Mogollon III rectangular designs in this red-on-brown technique become common, and white slipped pottery also appears. From Mogollon IV the MIMBRES black-on-white developed with a variety of highly complicated geometric curvilinear and rectilinear designs painted in black on the white slipped pottery. In Mogollon V the fine polychrome Mimbres pottery appears. A variety of animal and human forms were painted in a stylized geometric fashion on the bottom of bowls used for burial. In general the later periods of Mogollon are less well known than Anasazi, which came to influence Mogollon, as seen particularly in the pottery styles. Other Mogollon artifacts include a large variety of heavy implements, such as manos, metates, and mortars and pestles, all used for grinding maize (see METATE). Mogollon projectile points were typically triangular, becoming narrower in Mogollon V, when grooved stone axes also became common. Because of the dryness of the area, many perishable objects have been preserved, including blankets, basketry, and sandals. Cotton was first used in Mogollon.

**Mohenjo-Daro.** One of the two main cities of the Indus civilization in Pakistan, which flourished c. 2300–1750 BC, situated on the right bank of the Indus, 400 mi. (644 km) southwest of HARAPPA. Excavations were conducted here in the 1920s and by Sir Mortimer WHEELER after 1947. No information could be recovered relative to the earliest phases, as the high water table prevented deep excavation: it also caused flooding, which may be partially responsible for the ultimate abandonment of the site. The 35-ft. (11 m) citadel to the west of the town contains a number of buildings at the south end, including, a pillared hall with brick piers and a small room with a male statue, possibly a temple. At the north end of the citadel is a great brick bath with steps leading down into it, possibly for ritual ablutions. There is also a fine brick granary with narrow ventilation shafts. Round the citadel are traces of the baked brick defenses. (See also INDIA.)

The great bath at Mohenjo-Daro, in the Indus Valley.

**Molinology.** The description and study of watermills and windmills. (*See also* WINDMILL.)

**Momil.** A site on the Sinu River, on the Gulf coast in Western Colombia, which has revealed two ceramic periods. Momil I dates from 1000 to 500 BC and Momil II from 500 BC to the time of Christ.

**Monte Alban.** An important elite center located high on an eminence in the valley of Oaxaca, Mexico, Monte Alban was inhabited from at least the Middle Preclassic Period. The so-called Temple of the Danzantes, a structure decorated with dancing (?) bas-relief figures on large stone slabs, was raised in this early period. Some of these nude male figures have Olmec-like features. The large center, with plazas, platforms, a ballcourt, and temple structures, was primarily built up and expanded in the Classic Period. Most archaeologists believe the site was constructed by the ZAPOTECS, but some faint MAYA and TEOTIHUACAN influences can also be detected. Subterranean vaulted and frescoed tombs have been discovered all over the site, and the grave offerings, many of JADE, suggest the wealth of the Monte Alban lords. The site was abandoned, for an unknown reason, about AD 900. Later cultures, like the MIXTEC, reused the site as a sacred burial ground.

**Mosaic.** Greek mosaics dating from the 5th century BC were simple pebble floors, originally with limited decoration, but becoming more complex and sophisticated

A detail of the mosaic of the Battle of the Issus, *c.* 300 BC, showing Darius III, King of Persia (336–330 BC).

under the Macedonian kings, and the mosaic floors at Motya and Pella represent the first advances in this technique. Mosaics were popular throughout the Hellenistic world, PERGAMUM, DELOS, and ALEXANDRIA producing the best and most complex examples. The techniques of wall, architectural, and floor mosaics are known from POMPEII and ROME, where the earliest forms are usually of single colors, but gather momentum and complexity throughout the Roman provinces from the end of the 1st century BC onwards. Good examples come from TIVOLI (Tibur), AQUILEIA, and OSTIA, and some of the best late Roman mosaics in polychrome techniques come from Africa, Antioch, the Piazza Armerina in Sicily, and the Northwestern provinces, including Britain.

**Mousterian.** *See* PALAEOLITHIC.

**Mycenae.** Mycenae lies in the northeast portion of the plain of Argos. It was famous in Homer as the home of Agamemnon, the leader of the Greek heroes at Troy (*see* HOMERIC ARCHAEOLOGY). It was inhabited in the Early Helladic period (2500–1900 BC), but taken over *c.* 1900 BC by Greek-speaking invaders; by the beginning of the 15th century BC it had increased considerably in wealth and importance, as is shown in particular by the finds from the shaft graves. The Late Helladic, however, was Mycenae's greatest period. The defensive walls in "Cyclopean" style and the palace which crowns the city's hill were constructed then, and considerable extensions were carried out *c.* 1250 BC, when the famous Lion Gate was built. The walls enclosed not only the earlier grave circles, but also many official and public buildings, a granary, and buildings which contained a large number of cult statues and may, therefore, have formed a temple. Near the city are the Treasury of Atreus and the Tomb of Clytemnestra, two of the best-preserved and constructed THOLOS tombs.

The city remained prosperous until the second half of the 13th century BC. Destruction occurred several times thereafter, but the most serious was *c.* 1200 BC, traditionally attributed to the Dorians (*see* GREECE, ARCHAEOLOGY OF). The population declined, and though there was some settlement in the archaic Greek and Classical periods, Mycenae ceased to have any real importance.

**Mycenaean archaeology.** The culture of the Mycenaean period in Greece (broadly the Late Helladic period) is a distinctive mingling of Middle Helladic and Cretan (Minoan) influences. The early part of this period (1580–1400 BC) is characterized by the finds from Mycenae's shaft graves, whose golden ornaments and bronze swords show the intricacies of pattern and technical excellence of the metalwork and jewelry. Pottery of the period is of high quality, with a variety of plant and other naturalistic decorations. Burial was by inhumation (i.e., without cremation); chamber tombs came into use, and THOLOS tombs were reserved for royalty.

The golden age was the later period, *c.* 1400–1120 BC. In architecture, this phase is distinguished by the construction of defensive citadels and palaces. Fortification walls are made from massive irregular and well-jointed

The Lion Gate at Mycenae, c. 1250 BC, forming the main entrance to the citadel through the "Cyclopean" walls.

blocks ("Cyclopean" masonry), examples of which survive at TIRYNS, although there are traces at other sites (e.g., the ACROPOLIS at ATHENS). In addition to the palace at MYCENAE, there are excavated examples at Tiryns and PYLOS, all of which have the megaron-type throne room (*see* HOUSE, EUROPE) at their center. The megaron and other rooms within the palaces were decorated with painted and stuccoed frescoes, similar to those of the Minoan civilization, but with the occasional addition of more warlike scenes. Some traces of architectural decoration survive (e.g., on the façade of the Treasury of Atreus at Mycenae), but the palaces were mostly built of rubble masonry covered with plaster.

Objects in common use included gold jewelry, and ivory carvings in a variety of shapes. Arms and armor, which included helmets, breastplates, swords, and spearheads, were of bronze. Pottery, found widely distributed over the Mediterranean world, is of uniform shape and style: the decoration is formal, and a number of shapes were particularly popular, among which the CRATER, the bowl with a high stem (Kylix), and the stirrup jar are prominent.

Most remarkable of the discoveries connected with the Mycenaean civilization are the clay tablets bearing scripts known as LINEAR B, clearly the language of the Mycenaean world which was developed from the Cretan LINEAR A.

**Mylasa** (Milas). A town in Asia Minor, possibly founded by Mausolus, ruler of Caria (377–353 BC). The Hellenistic and Roman site contains important buildings: a Corinthian-style Temple of Zeus in a sharply terraced enclosure, a (Roman) Temple of Augustus and Rome, a ceremonial arch, and a mausoleum of Antonine date.

**Nabataeans.** A Semitic people who established a kingdom in Edom, on the trade route from the Red Sea to the Mediterranean, in the 4th century BC. Their capital was PETRA, but at the height of their power they also controlled Bosra and DAMASCUS. A temple has been excavated at Khirbet Tannur, there is another in the Wadi Rum, and there are also a number of watch towers and an elaborate hydraulic network. The Nabataean kingdom was annexed by the Romans in AD 106 as "Provincia Arabia Petraea."

**Naples** (Neapolis). Founded *c.* 600 BC by Greek settlers, Naples soon established its importance in the Campania plain, and was conquered by Rome in 327 BC. Little remains to show its Classical splendor, revealed in small fragments of buildings, temples, and houses under the modern city.

**Naqada culture I.** A Predynastic culture of ancient Egypt. Evidence of it was first discovered by W. M. Flinders PETRIE at Naqada and it is from this find-site that the Middle and Late Periods of Predynastic Egypt are termed Naqada I and II by most Egyptologists. Although the great site for the period is Naqada, Petrie did not undertake stratified excavation and so great reliance must be placed on the results of excavations at two relatively unimportant sites, el-Hamamiyeh and Armant, which both indicate continuity between the BADARIAN CULTURE and Naqada I. The Badarian civilization apparently overlapped the beginning of Naqada I and should therefore be allotted sequence dates well into the 30s (*see* SEQUENCE DATING). THERMOLUMINESCENCE tests have produced a date in the middle of the 4th millennium BC. Apart from Naqada itself, cemeteries have been excavated at Hu (Diospolis Parva), Mahasna, and el-Amra, the latter giving rise to the name Amratian.

At el-Hamamiyeh, above the disturbed post-Badarian stratum, the remains of small circular huts, made from clay with the imprint of reeds or straw on the inside, have been found. No superstructure or roofing has survived and the lack of any doorway or opening in the wall suggests that entry was made from a high point. Wooden posts and postholes at el-Mahasna are probably all that remain of a kind of windbreak. According to Petrie, the southern settlement at Naqada was a fortified town with rectangular houses built of bricks, but it is doubtful if it can be dated back to Naqada I. Graves are similar to those of the Badarians: burials were still in the foetal position, usually with the head to the south and the face to the west.

Green malachite face paint was still ground on stone palettes, the earlier one geometric in form, like those of the Badarians, the later in the shape of animals, such as the Nile turtle, hippopotamus, antelope, and birds, including the double bird which occurs for the first time.

An Amratian pot with a schematic drawing of a boat, Naqada Culture I, mid-4th millennium BC.

The long ivory hair pins, their tops either in the form of a knob or a bird, are new. Ivory, shell, and bone bangles continue, as do soft stone bead necklaces and female figurines.

Pottery continues in two types, fine ware and coarse, although the latter is rare. The fine ware (mostly bowls, beakers, and vases) has two main forms, Polished Red and Black-topped Red, the latter in considerable quantity at first but decreasing later, to which is added a new type, White Cross-lined. For this, white or cream is used on the Polished Red or occasionally on the Black-topped Red. Scenes rarely depict men and animals but the patterns are mostly geometric. Locally made examples imitate in stone Badarian ivory cosmetic containers. Rare basalt vases with a splayed foot must be Mesopotamian imports.

The Naqada I flint industry, instead of using crude surface nodules, employed best-quality mined flints to produce characteristic large double-edged knives with finely serrated edges and fish-tailed knives. Disk-shaped stone mace heads which characterize the culture may have developed from rare flat-topped Badarian mace heads. Although they have very small holes, if slung on a leather thong they could have had a practical rather than a symbolic use as has often been suggested. Copper objects are rare and very small; gold is completely absent, although it may be due to an accident of survival. It has even been suggested that the historic name for Naqada, meaning in Egyptian "golden", has significance: perhaps Naqada received its name from its gold trade. This would certainly have helped to pay for the turquoise, lapis lazuli, exotic stone vessels, and other luxuries which came from well beyond the sphere of the Naqada I culture, whose boundaries lay in the South just beyond the First Cataract and in the North at Asyut.

**Naqada culture II.** There is no real evidence that there was any invasion of Egypt by an Asiatic people at the end of the Naqada I period: all the new features in Naqada II can be accounted for by direct imports and by increasing cultural contact with the rest of the Near East and, in particular, with MESOPOTAMIA. Presumably it was now that the strong Semitic element in the Egyptian language came about: the Hamitic element is due to the Badarians. The presence of rock drawings of foreign boats in the Eastern Desert is no longer thought to reflect a foreign incursion by that route. However the Naqada II culture was more widespread than its predecessor: no less than three cemeteries and a surface station have been found in the Fayum area. In the South, cemeteries extend into Lower Nubia.

From rather slight evidence at Naqada and el-Badari, a model house from el-Amra, and the discovery of some brick-lined tombs, it is deduced that houses were rectangular, built from mud bricks, with one roofed room and a forecourt. The poor were still buried in oval graves in a loosely contracted position but the more elaborate graves were rectangular and often lined and roofed with wood or matting. Towards the end of Naqada II, important people were interred in a recess at one side of the

The body of a Predynastic man from Gebelein, Naqada culture II, *c.* 3300 BC.

chamber and the rest of the space was used for the storage of grave goods. As wooden coffins became more common, the custom of wrapping bodies in matting died out, but linen and knitted woollen material have been found.

In Naqada II, beads and amulets increase greatly in number, being frequently made of hard stones such as lapis lazuli. This material, together with OBSIDIAN and silver, must have been imported, yet some quite large objects made from silver have been found, including an adze, the figure of a hawk, a dagger, and a knife. Gold, however, is still rare. Copper objects are much more common: daggers, knives, harpoons, needles, finger rings, beads, and what might be toilet utensils have been found, but copper adzes and axes were probably imports from a more advanced metalworking culture.

Basalt, breccia, alabaster, serpentine, schist, porphyry, and, especially, limestone were used increasingly to produce bowls, and squat, cylindrical, and barrel-shaped vessels. Clearly the manufacture of fine stone vessels, made easier by the use of the stone borer, had become a specialized industry. Several shapes are common to Egypt and Mesopotamia, but it is obvious from which direction the influence came: the footed cylinder must have had an Asiatic origin. Stone and pottery vessels in the form of animals and birds show close connections with the JEMDET NASR culture of Mesopotamia, but the bulk of Naqada II pottery develops from that of Naqada I. Coarse ware, with few shapes and obviously mass-produced for domestic purposes, increases but Black-topped Red and Polished Red wares become increasingly

rare. The clay used seems to have been of finer quality than before and was baked to a buff or pink color. Directly onto this pale background were painted, in dark red, scenes of birds, animals, plants, and boats carrying cabins, shrines, and standards. The shapes for this Decorated ware are mostly shouldered or bellied narrow-mouthed vessels, some with lug handles. The slow wheel may have been in use to make them. Decorated ware and two other new types, Wavy-handled (with scalloped handles) and spouted Fancy wares, were strongly influenced by the pottery of Uruk and Jemdet Nasr in Mesopotamia (a Jemdet Nasr cylinder seal was actually found in one burial at Naqada) and by that of the Early Bronze Age people in Palestine; Black Incised ware must have been imported from the Sudan. The famous wall painting in a tomb at Hierakonpolis echoes Decorated ware scenes with its boats and animals, but the theme of heraldic opposition of animals with a tamer between them is new. This composition is completely Asiatic in origin and is repeated on contemporary Naqada II knife handles.

The Naqada II flint industry, however, although highly developed, is firmly based on that of Naqada I. Most characteristic of the period are the thin ripple-flaked blades made by detaching flakes regularly from both edges of the surface to give the effect of fluting. Fish-tailed knives continue but the shape changes from the Naqada I U-shape to a distinctive V-shape. Chisel-headed arrowheads and hard stone pearshaped mace heads only indicate the efficiency of the Naqada II stone worker, not the advent of a new warlike people as has sometimes been suggested.

Artificial irrigation may have been introduced in the Naqada II period to counteract increasing desiccation.

Such a system would only be effective if developed and maintained over Upper Egypt as a whole under unified leadership. At the end of the period this unified leadership was able to subdue Lower Egypt and create a single kingdom in Egypt. Unfortunately it is impossible to judge how long before the beginning of the Dynastic Period the unification of Upper Egypt took place. What is clear, however, is that, although during the Naqada II period Egypt was strongly influenced by other Near Eastern cultures, the final impetus which led her, united, into the literate historic Dynastic Period was purely Egyptian in its origin.

**Nara period.** A Japanese period (AD 710–794) named after the new capital of Nara, or Heijo as it was then known, to which the court moved from Fujiwara. It was a time when the control of the emperor was firmly established over the whole country. The products of official workshops were diffused through regional headquarters and the Buddhist temples, as the bureaucracy promoted local craftsmanship and the use of provincial materials. Temples were built in all regions as symbols of prestige. The might of imperial power is reflected in the great temples of Tōdai-ji, Saidai-ji, Shin-yakushi-ji, and the Daian-ji.

**Natufian.** An East Mediterranean culture, dating from the close of the last Ice Age, some 12,000 to 9,000 years ago. One important site is the Wad cave at Mount Carmel, where a large cemetery of the period has been uncovered. Querns, for grinding, and sickles were part of the equipment of these people, who were evidently hunters of gazelles, but may also have been growing or at least gathering crops. (*See also* CARMEL, MOUNT; SYRIA-PALESTINE.)

**Naucratis.** An early Greek trading post at the mouth of the Nile. Abundant finds of Greek pottery, dating from the 7th century BC, show when Greek interest began. It is mentioned by Herodotus, and remained the chief point of contact between Egypt and Greece until the Hellenistic period and the rise of ALEXANDRIA.

**Navajos.** One of the Indian peoples of the Southwestern United States of the Athabascan language group. Most of the other Athabascan-speaking peoples live in the Northwestern subarctic areas of Canada, and were originally nomadic hunters and food gatherers. It is likely that their intrusion into the Southwest helped bring about the abandonment of Pueblos in the ANASAZI subarea: they were probably aided in this by various groups of Apache Indians, also Athabascans, moving into the Southwest at this time.

**Nazca.** During the EARLY INTERMEDIATE PERIOD (*c.* 200 BC–AD 600), the Nazca culture developed on the South coast of Peru. Settlements were modest in size, perhaps because of the limiting influence of the extremely dry environment on population growth. Ceramics form the basis of the chronological subdivisions of the culture. The pottery is handmade and technologically sophisticated, with 14 slip colors. Designs are zoomorphic, and

the most common shapes are usually globular, frequently with two spouts connected by a horizontal strap handle. On the coastal plain, configurations of lines cover a large area. They are made by clearing away surface stones to expose the underlying sand. Some of the lines are perfectly straight or of abstract form, while others can be dated by their similarity to motifs found on the pottery, e.g., killer whales, monkeys, and spiders. They are on a very large scale and difficult to observe from ground level. Their purpose is unresolved, but Maria Reicht has been responsible for documenting the lines and awakening wide interest in them.

**Neanderthal man.** During blasting in 1856, parts of a skeleton were found in the Feldhof cave in the Neander valley near Wuppertal, West Germany. Since then, a series of skulls of long, low form and with big brow ridges has been recognized as resembling the original Neanderthal discovery, and they are believed to belong mainly to the time 100,000 to 40,000 years ago. Opinions are still divided on whether Neanderthal evolved into modern man.

**Neolithic.**

*Africa.* At about 12,500 BC, in many parts of Africa the toolkits of the prehistoric hunters undergo considerable change, marked by a drastic diminution in the size of the blades on which the stone tools are made, coupled with an increase in the proportion of bone tools used. Bored stones, harpoons, and complex composite tools also appear for the first time in the prehistoric record. The skeletal remains of the Neolithic or Late Stone Age hunters are indistinguishable from those of modern man, and it is reasonable to suppose that, both materially and spiritually, the way of life differed little from modern hunting peoples such as the Southern African Bushmen.

The Late Stone Age peoples were well adapted to their environment and in many parts of the continent practiced a mobile economy, making effective use of plant and animal resources. It is to this period that much of the surviving African ROCK ART can be dated, and many of the paintings contain detailed scenes of everyday life. In much of Southern Africa and in parts of Eastern and Central Africa, a Late Stone Age way of life continued until well into the 19th century AD. The persistence of such a lifestyle long after the development of formal farming societies well illustrates how successfully the Late Stone Age peoples had adapted to their respective environments. Many economic practices were highly specialized either in the choice of the plant or animal exploited or in the time of year such exploitation was carried out or both. Such specialized economic activity has resulted in equally specialized toolkits, so that during the Late Stone Age the toolkits studied by archaeologists are highly variable, being different both between sites and regions, the overriding common attribute being the microlithic (or tiny blade) nature of the stone component of the toolkit and certain specialized technological features.

*Europe.* Agriculture, the hallmark of the Neolithic in Europe, was first introduced to Southeast Europe around 6000 BC, and it spread slowly across the continent to reach the British Isles some 3,000 years later. The development of the Neolithic was thus dominated by the process of colonization, first on a continental scale and then filling up smaller areas of unoccupied land.

The first settlers were of Anatolian origin, and Neolithic culture in Greece is very similar in character to that of the Near East at this time: mud-brick villages, often occupied on the same spot for hundreds of years and so forming tells (see TELL), using painted pottery, and cultivating cereals and legumes while keeping sheep as the main livestock. The introduction of village-based agriculture into the fertile basins and plains of the Balkans marked a fundamental change in the economy and culture of these regions, and caused a substantial increase in their population.

In a more gradual way, which caused less change in the established pattern, the Neolithic arts spread westwards around the Mediterranean fringe, being carried by coastal contact among the fishing and gathering populations living in caves and camps along the littoral. The more sophisticated techniques of pottery decoration were lost in this process, and the characteristic wares are decorated by impressions, especially of the edges of shells (see IMPRESSED WARE). The keeping of sheep was perhaps more important than cereal growing to these groups, who continued to use marine resources as a significant part of their diet. Sites are rarely found far inland: they occur in Italy, Southern France, North Africa, and Spain, as well as on the larger islands of the West Mediterranean. This group of cultures lasted for over 1,000 years.

While this spread probably took place among existing populations, the main onset of the Neolithic in Central Europe was due to actual movements of people into areas relatively underused by their Mesolithic predecessors. Moving up the River Danube into Hungary, peripheral groups of the Southeastern painted pottery cultures underwent a transformation in their economy and material culture, producing a pattern more appropriate to the Central European forests. Cattle became more common than sheep as stock animals, while timber architecture took over from construction techniques based on mud. As in the Mediterranean, these pioneer groups produced simpler kinds of pottery: instead of painted designs, decorative effects were achieved by incised lines, usually in flowing ribbon-like designs—hence the term *linearbandkeramik* (see LINEAR POTTERY CULTURE). The successful adaptation to new conditions was marked by an explosive spread of this cultural pattern in the mid-5th millennium BC. In a highly selective fashion, occupying only those areas with high quality soils along rivers in well drained lowland areas, this culture spread out from the Carpathian basin to occupy small areas of land in Bohemia, the middle Elbe River (one of the largest concentrations), the upper Danube River, Franconia, the Rhineland, and then across into the Low Countries and the Paris basin; and in the opposite direction into Silesia, Little Poland, Kujavia, and the Ukraine. From France to Russia, therefore, a surprisingly uniform pattern of culture stretched for 1,243 mi.

(2,000 km) between the alpine mountain chains and the North European plain.

At the same time as this wave of colonization was taking place across Central Europe, important changes were taking place in the Southeast. Population growth had by now produced a dense network of substantial tell sites in the plains of the Balkans, and these areas became centers of innovation and trading activity. Their pottery was often spectacularly fine, being decorated in paints prepared from a variety of minerals, and fired under carefully controlled conditions. It was used not only to produce containers, but also many kinds of imaginative statuettes and figurines of cult significance. Shell ornaments, traded from the Aegean coasts, were widely used. This new technical proficiency and trading intensity was the milieu in which the first extensive use of copper developed, at first merely hammering naturally occurring pure copper, and then smelting the extensive deposits of brightly colored oxide and carbonate ores which occur in the Balkans.

The exploration of upland around the plains, and the continuing colonization of some of the remoter valleys, brought new contacts between groups hitherto separated by mountains. Thus the middle Danube basin was linked to the Adriatic coast via the Bosna and Neretva Rivers; while links across the Adriatic produced a parallel series of cultures in Southern Italy, whose attractive painted wares rivaled those of the Balkans. The numerous villages of this period, enclosed by ditches, show up well on air photographs of Apulia. Elsewhere in the Mediterranean at this time there were few radical developments from the Impressed ware pattern, and many of the known sites are still in caves. Copper was not yet used.

On the Central European loess-lands, the initial cultural uniformity of the groups using incised linear ornament began to break down into more local styles. In the Eastern part of the distribution there was more influence from the Southwestern region, including some importation and reworking of copper objects in the sphere of the LENGYEL culture; while in the Western half there was a large measure of continuity into the RÖESSEN CULTURE, which did, however, begin to explore the areas beyond the loess-lands.

During the course of the 4th millennium BC, important changes began to take place on the periphery: small groups began to move into areas hitherto occupied only by bands of hunters, fishers, and collectors—for instance, in the lake region around the Alps, and on a larger scale in the North European plain and Southern Scandinavia. In North Italy, these groups made square-mouthed pots which give them their archaeological name; in Northern Europe, funnel-necked beakers characterize the earliest settlers (see FUNNEL-NECKED BEAKER CULTURE). Large areas of France were occupied by comparable groups belonging to the CHASSÉEN CULTURE, and, in Spain, by groups like the Almerian. Some of the innovations of these marginal groups spread back among older-established groups, especially in the West, producing the MICHELSBERG CULTURE of the Rhineland. It was from the adjacent coastlands of Northern France and the Low Countries that Britain was first colonized at this time.

A somewhat quickened pace of development can also be discerned in the Mediterranean towards the beginning of the 3rd millennium BC, becoming more marked by its end. The intensity of sea traffic increased, and short distances were regularly traversed. The importance of islands is strikingly exemplified by Malta, whose fertile and easily cut limestone provided raw material for elaborate community shrines, which grew increasingly complex as the millennium wore on. Large permanent communities, by now aware of the need for self-defense, had by this time arisen on the shores of the mainland. In Southern Spain, the extensive walled settlement of LOS MILLARES, with its cemetery of corbeled tombs, shows evidence of the production of simple copper weapons and tools.

In Northern Europe, as in Spain, funerary architecture showed striking developments in the 3rd millennium BC, making use of large boulders to produce megalithic structures for communal burials, which are among the most impressive monuments of prehistory. These testify to the first opening-up of Northwest Europe, and some remained in use for up to 1,000 years, before a further wave of expansion produced the changes associated with the single grave "corded" cultures which preceded the Early Bronze Age.

**"New archaeology".** The main proponent of the "new archaeology" in North America is L. R. Binford who, in *New Perspectives in Archaeology* (edited with S. R. Binford) in 1968, stressed the following ideas: first, the use of new techniques, such as the computer, for statistical and matrix analyses of data, and the concept of the ecosystem for the understanding of the economic and subsistence bases of prehistoric societies; second, an evolutionary view of culture; and third, the use of models of cultures, viewed as systems, incorporating the evolutionary view of culture. A close relationship between archaeology and anthropology is postulated by him so that, effectively, archaeology is seen as an aspect of anthropology. With the use of new techniques, including RADIOCARBON DATING, the systematic study of settlement patterns and the use of ethnographic analogies, the aim of archaeology is set out as the total recreation of prehistoric life. This includes speculative reconstruction of social and religious life, the determination of subsistence patterns, the pattern of ecological and climatic changes, and the calculation of absolute dates.

**Newgrange.** One of the largest of a group of passage graves on the River Boyne in Co. Meath, Ireland (*see* PASSAGE GRAVE). It consists of a massive stone cairn with kerb, *c.* 262 ft. (80 m) in diameter, with a megalithic passage 62 ft. (19 m) long leading to a cross-shaped megalithic chamber surmounted by a corbeled roof. Dating from *c.* 2500 BC, it contained cremated human remains.

**New Lanark.** The first textile mill in this Scottish town was built in 1785, and in 1799 the enterprise was sold to the philanthropist, Robert Owen. He transformed it into an industrial community, with a school, meeting hall and blocks of tenement housing. Considerable restoration was carried out during the 1960s.

**New Zealand.** The North and South Islands of New Zealand, together with the smaller Stewart Island, cover over 96,525 sq. mi. (250,000 km²) and stretch for 808 mi. (1300 km) between 34° and 47° South latitudes. Their size and temperate climate make them unique in Polynesia, which is for the most part tropical and composed of tiny islands, and the first settlers necessarily had to make major cultural adaptations in the new land. Settlement of New Zealand took place in about AD 900, possibly from the Cook or Society Islands. The Maoris were the only prehistoric settlers of the country, and are Polynesians.

The first settlers were unable to plant their tropical crops because of the climate, and only the sweet potato managed to survive very well. Domesticated dogs were also present, and a native fern rhizome provided the mainstay of the diet, together with fish, sea mammals, and shellfish. The early settlers of the Archaic Phase (*c.* AD 900–1350) lived in seasonal camps, mainly by fishing and gathering. Large land birds (moas) were also present, but they became extinct by about 1400. Sweet potato horticulture had only a minor significance, so far as is known. Very finely made stone adzes and bone fish-hooks, similar to those found in the Marquesas, Society, and Cook Islands, were also made in this phase. The South Island, virtually outside the range of horticulture, maintained this fishing and gathering way of life with a decreasing population until European discovery by Cook in 1769 (Tasman's visit of 1642 was not accompanied by a landing).

After 1300 the focus of cultural development is centered in the North Island. The warm coastal regions of the North supported the vast majority of New Zealand's 100,000 or so inhabitants in 1769, and sweet potato horticulture was then of considerable importance. The potatoes were stored in underground rectangular or bell-shaped pits during the cool winters, and this plant, together with the fern rhizome and plentiful shellfish, supported a dense population after 1350. This later phase of New Zealand prehistory (*c.* 1350–1769) is referred to as the Classic, and it is confined to the North Island and the Northern fringes of the South Island.

During the Classic, new types of artifact (adzes and weapons especially) appeared in the North Island, and settlements were normally defended by earthworks. These fortified villages, called *pa*, now dot the coastal landscapes of the North Island, and an estimated 4,000–6,000 still survive. They enclose between 0.25 and 123 ac. (0.1 and 50 ha), and the largest comprise the terraced outer slopes of extinct volcanoes. Smaller forts with ditches and banks were built on ridges, promontories, or on flat land, and palisaded villages were also constructed on artificial deposits in lakes and swamps. Narrow entrances and raised stages for defenders are attested archaeologically. Weapons were the spear and handclub (*patu*): the Maoris did not use the sling or bow, although these were known to other Polynesians.

Maori society in 1769 was characterized by well developed genealogical ranking, and by a vivid artistic tradition exemplified in canoe and house carving, and in the working of greenstone for handclubs and the distorted human figure pendants known as *tiki*. European influence, both good and bad, as well as endemic warfare using muskets, unfortunately broke down much of the old tribal system in the early 19th century, but modern Maori society is actively preserving many aspects of its historic art and social organization.

The Chatham Islands, located 559 mi. (900 km) to the east of Christchurch, were probably settled from New Zealand, but environmental conditions ruled out horticulture. The Chatham Islanders (called Moriorios) maintained a rather separate lifestyle until they were absorbed by Maori settlers in the 19th century.

**Nîmes** (Nemausus). A town in Southern Gaul, originally a Celtic settlement. It became a Roman colony in 16 BC, and its walls and gates were the gift of Augustus. Besides these, its visible remains comprise the *Maison Carrée* (a Classical temple), the AMPHITHEATER, the sacred precinct and springs of the city's patron goddess, and, a little way outside the present city, the PONT DU GARD, which forms part of its AQUEDUCT.

**Nimrud.** The Assyrian capital of Kalhu (Calah of the Old Testament), founded in 883 BC over the ruins of an earlier city built by Shalmaneser I in the 13th century BC, by the River Tigris, south of modern Mosul in Northern Mesopotamia. Sir Austen Henry LAYARD worked on the acropolis between 1845 and 1851, chiefly in the ZIGGURAT area and in the Northwest Palace of Assurnaṣirpal II, and found many statues and reliefs. Hormuzd Rassam worked on the Nabu and other temples in 1853 and 1878 and Sir William Kennet LOFTUS dug in the Southeast or Burnt Palace in 1854 and 1855 and found a large number of ivories. From 1949 to 1963 a British expedition returned to the site. Excavations on the acropolis mound established architectural plans for its buildings. In addition a large complex, known as Fort Shalmaneser, built in the middle of the 9th century BC, was excavated at the southeast corner of the city wall. More reliefs, statues, and portal figures were found and many of them bore interesting inscriptions. Among the tablets were military reports, which throw light on the Assyrian political scene. In storerooms in Fort Shalmaneser, several thousand ivory panels and objects, mostly used to decorate furniture, were found and can be dated from the 9th to the 7th century BC.

**Nineveh.** The Assyrian capital from the end of the 8th century BC. The city of Ninua, with its principle shrine dedicated to Ishtar of Nineveh, stood on the River Tigris near modern Mosul in Northern Mesopotamia. The city was walled and contained two large mounds, Kuyunjik and Nebi Yunus, but the latter has barely been touched because of the presence of a modern village and cemetery. During the 19th century, BOTTA, PLACE, LAYARD, LOFTUS, Rassam, George Smith Thompson, and King excavated the site and found the Southwest Palace of Sennacherib, the Palace of Assurbanipal,

and the temples of Nabu and Ishtar, hundreds of reliefs, many portal figures, and Assurbanipal's library of tablets, containing scientific, literary, and religious texts from many periods. Further British excavations from 1927 to 1932 sought to throw light on the earlier history of Nineveh, and a deep sounding showed that only 18 ft. (5.5 m) accounted for Assyrian and later levels, while the remaining 72 ft. (22 m) produced a type of pottery called Ninevite 5 (contemporary with Early Dynastic I in Southern Mesopotamia), preceded by levels going back to the early 4th millennium BC. The city was destroyed by the MEDES in 612 BC.

**Nippur.** A sacred city of the Sumerians in Southern Mesopotamia between the Rivers Tigris and Euphrates. American excavations have been conducted on the huge site from 1889 to 1900 and periodically since 1948. All levels from the EARLY DYNASTIC to the Parthian are well represented and the Kassite is particularly well documented. A large number of tablets have been found, among them Kassite administrative archives and the business archives of the Murashu family (455–403 BC). The ZIGGURAT and Temple of Enlil has been partially excavated: it had been converted into a Parthian fortress. A sounding below it produced URUK pottery of the 4th millennium BC. A sequence of Early Dynastic temples, dedicated to the goddess Inanna, has recently been excavated.

**Nishāpūr.** A site in the Iranian province of Khurāsān. Trial digs in the area of the old city were made on Tepe Alp Arslan, North and South Horn, and at the East Kilns, while Qanat Tepe, Village Tepe, Sabz Pushan, and Tepe Madraseh were subjected to more extensive excavation. None of these sites was occupied prior to the very end of the 8th century AD, and most were extinguished by the Mongol invasions in 1221. Nīshāpūr is archaeologically important for the large quantities of ceramics, glass fragments, and a small but important body of metalwork found.

**Noin Ula.** A site in the mountains north of Ulan Bator, Mongolia. A group of large shaft tombs, some at least 33 ft. (10 m) deep with double wooden coffins, excavated here are thought to be the royal tombs of the HSIUNG-NU. Textiles found in them include items imported from China. These graves represent the introduction of a new type of culture, influenced by Chinese customs, superseding the cist tombs of the Lake Baikal region. (*See* CIST TOMB; SHAFT TOMB.)

**Nok culture.** We know very little about the Nok culture, which is associated with the first iron-smelting people of West Africa. Excavations at Taruga, on the Southern part of the Jos plateau in Northern Nigeria, have yielded a number of terra-cotta figurines, iron slag, and several radiocarbon dates of *c.* 300 BC. Several hundred other figurines have been recovered during tin-mining operations there. Some art historians consider the Nok figurines to be ancestral to the medieval sculpture of the Yoruba and Ibo, but this connection is not certain.

**Noricum**. A Roman province roughly co-extensive with present-day Austria. In Roman times its principal cities were Virunum (near Klagenfurt) and Ovilava (Wels).

**North America in Prehistory**. People first moved across the Bering land bridge, from Siberia into Alaska, during the Wisconsin glaciation. The ice fields covering the Northern part of the world contained sufficient water to reduce the sea level and make this possible. These first American inhabitants were probably bands of hunters who arrived some time before 20,000 BC. America was the last continent to be inhabited, and, unlike Asia, Africa, and Europe, its first inhabitants were all HOMO SAPIENS, or modern man. From their first arrival until

about 6000 BC, subsistence depended to a large extent on the hunting of Pleistocene game. When that disappeared a series of different cultures arose in the different ecological areas of America. Each of those cultures adapted to the possibility of hunting local animals and collecting plants as the climatic conditions changed. From *c.* 5000 BC, in Mexico, specialized plant gathering activities lead to the cultivation of maize, squash, and beans. Similar activities began in the 2nd millennium BC in the Southwestern United States and spread to other areas. Agriculture spread from the Southwest up the Mississippi valley and throughout the Eastern half of the United States. However, the prehistoric and early historical cultures of the far North, the Northwest, and California never became agricultural and always relied on hunting and gathering.

Map of North America.

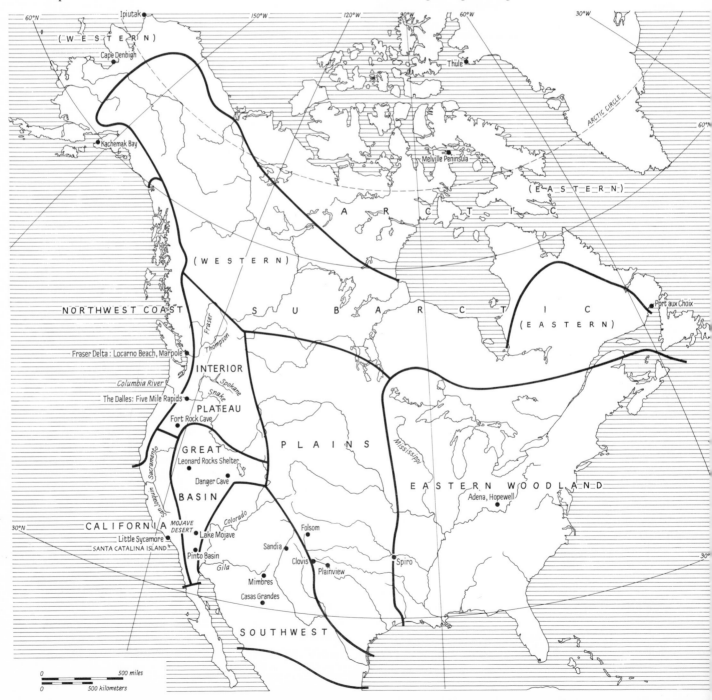

Of the several hundred tribes contacted by Europeans between 1500 and 1850, most belonged to 13 different language groups. The language groups do not, however, always correspond to the general cultural areas of North America, nor to the prehistoric cultures from which they came. The Eastern Woodlands, the area south of a line from the mouth of the St. Lawrence to the Great Lakes and the mouth of the Mississippi, were inhabited by people of the Algonquian and Iroquoian language groups in the Northeast, and by the Muskogeans in the Southeast. The Great Plains were largely inhabited by people of Siouan languages, and in the South also by Caddoans and Athabascans. The Southwest was inhabited by Athabascan, Hokan, and Uto-Aztecan groups, and the Great Basin by people of the Ut-Aztecan language group. California was occupied by Athabascan, Hokan, and Penutian groups; the Interior plateau by Salish and Klamath-Sahaptin peoples; the Northwest coast by Salish and Wakashan groups; and the sub-Arctic by Athabascan and Algonquian peoples. Eskimo-Aleut peoples inhabited the Arctic Coast. Although these are the groupings which prevailed at the time of the first White contact with Indians, and are therefore not necessarily the prehistoric languages of the areas for much of their history, they provide an indication of which peoples lived where. In North American archaeology, ethnographical analogy, with modern Indian groups, provides a means of reconstructing a more complete history.

**North American archaeology, history of.** The first American archaeologist may be said to have been Thomas JEFFERSON, the third President of the United States. In 1784, he began to excavate mounds on his land in Virginia to find out why they had been built. Until 1840, however, most archaeology and most archaeological publications were speculative, although a few people described mounds and artifacts accurately, even though they speculated that their makers were non-American. Winthrop Sargent, for instance, published some Hopewellian artifacts in the *Transactions of the American Philosophical Society* for 1799. The American Antiquarian Society was founded in Massachusetts in 1812; one of its first volumes of transactions was Caleb Atwater's *Description of the Antiquities Discovered in the State of Ohio and other Western States.* Atwater subscribed to the prevalent theories of the time, believing that the mounds he described had been built by Hindus who, having migrated to North America from India, later moved on to Mexico.

The next period of American archaeology, which lasted up until World War I, concentrated on the description of archaeological sites and artifacts, and on their classification. The earliest works, such as that by Squier and Davis, *Ancient Monuments of the Mississippi Valley*, published by the newly founded Smithsonian Institution in 1848, contained a mixture of straight narrative and speculation. These theories about the building of mounds by non-Indian immigrants were only laid to rest with the publication of Cyrus Thomas's *Report of the Mound Explorations of the Bureau of Ethnology* in 1894. A general attempt was made by H. R.

Schoolcraft in his *Archives of Aboriginal Knowledge*, 1851–60, to classify all known information about both ancient and modern Indian society. Various new journals were founded, including the *American Antiquarian*, 1878, and the *American Anthropologist*, 1888, to open up outlets for the description and classification of finds. Museums such as the Peabody Museum, founded in Cambridge, Mass., in 1866, were set up to receive the physical remains of ancient cultures. Another feature of this period was that as the people of the United States moved westwards, so did the archaeologists, beginning work on the archaeology of California, the Southwestern United States and the Arctic. However, the most important feature of the period was the lack of historical depth given to finds, since stratigraphical methods had not been adopted. One of the few early attempts at STRATIGRAPHY was made by W. H. Dall in his publication *On Succession in Shell Heaps of the Aleutian Islands.* There was, therefore, a continual controversy over the possible age of the first Indian inhabitation of America. Although various finds were said to come from Pleistocene contexts, there was not yet any proof that there had been people in America during the last Ice Age.

The salient feature of the next period, 1914–39, was the classification of sites and artifacts in relationship to timescales derived from stratigraphical excavation. The introduction of stratigraphy, the excavation of a site layer by layer, also meant that it became possible to relate cultures of the same area through the cross referencing of finds. One of the first important stratigraphical explorations was that of N. C. Nelson in the Southwestern United States. His findings, entitled *Pueblo Ruins of the Galisteo Basin*, were published in 1914. The relative dating of Pueblo sites was worked out on the basis of stratigraphical findings of pottery types. The second decade of this century was particularly important in the history of Southwestern archaeology, with the work of A. V. KIDDER on Pecos Pueblo and that of A. L. Kroeber on the Zuñi. Another important development was the first definite evidence of the human occupation of America during the Pleistocene. J. D. Figgins found at FOLSOM, New Mexico, in 1926, stone tools in association with mammals 10,000–15,000 years old.

With the new emphasis on chronology came interest in the excavation of sites with historical documentation: this line of approach produced books such as W. D. Strong's *An Introduction to Nebraska Archaeology.* In the same period more attention was being given to synthesizing the archaeology of particular areas, for instance in A. V. Kidder's *An Introduction to Southwestern Archaeology*, 1924. Finally, attempts were made to conceptualize these developments; one such attempt was that of H. S. Gladwyn's, *A Method for the Designation of Cultures and their Variations*, 1934. In this work the development of culture was visualized as a tree with the roots forming the beginnings of a sequence, the trunk the main development, and the branches as subsidiary phases of the culture.

From about 1939 onwards the questions asked in American archaeology broadened. In particular, archaeologists started to be interested in cultural contexts, as well as in the geographical and temporal ordering of cultures. Archaeologists, such as F. C. Cole and Thorne Duel in *Rediscovering Illinois*, emphasized the possible aboriginal uses of artifacts as well as their development *per se*. W. W. Taylor, in *A Theory of Archaeology*, attacked A. V. Kidder and others for not trying to reconstruct every aspect of prehistoric life. From this time onwards archaeologists asked fundamental questions about the trade or religion of prehistoric peoples as well as, for instance, the way in which a pottery typology developed. The primary emphasis of this "NEW ARCHAEOLOGY" was on the ecological and ethnographical contexts of prehistoric cultures. This had already been done, to some extent, with A. L. Kroeber's *Cultural and Natural areas of North America*, 1939. In archaeology this developed into a theory of ecosystems which provides a basis for the understanding of subsistence and economic life.

Many new scientific techniques have played a part: for instance, RADIOCARBON DATING and THERMOLUMINESCENCE help provide accurate absolute dates. Plant remains have begun to be recovered by the technique known as FLOTATION, in which debris is floated on water to separate organic particles and so identify food sources. The use of computers has helped in the sorting out of statistical data. In general, archaeology has become more involved with testing theories in the manner of the deductive reasoning of natural sciences. In the reconstruction of prehistoric life, ethnographical analogies from anthropological literature and ethnological collections have become important. The greatest proponent of the "new archaeology" is L. R. Binford.

**Northern Wei Dynasty.** The rule of the Toba tribe in Northern China (AD 386–534). They were important patrons of Buddhism but in other respects, including burial, continued Chinese practices.

**Northwest Coast tradition.** The prehistory of the Northern Californian coast, Oregon, Washington, British Columbia, and Southeastern Alaska is a unified whole, with its origins probably lying in the FRASER RIVER delta dating from about 1000 BC. The area, from then until this century, is characterized by the following traits: subsistence was based on the hunting and gathering of the abundant riverine and marine food sources; mollusks were collected in the early periods in great quantities; salmon, halibut, and olachen were caught; and sea mammals, such as the whale, seal, and sea otter, were hunted. The wood resources of the area, including redwood, cedar, and firs, were very important in the material culture of these coastal areas. At the time of the first European contact in the 18th century, great ocean-going canoes were built, rectangular plank houses were erected, and innumerable ritual and household items were carved.

Although the ethnographical pattern from the 18th to the 20th century is well known, the prehistory is still little understood. The two possible early prehistoric traditions which contributed to the Northwest Coast culture are the ESKIMOS and the OLD CORDILLERAN TRADITION. Leaf-shaped projectile points, characteristic of the Old Cordilleran tradition, have been found in many of the earliest known contexts. On the East coast of Vancouver Island, for instance, they have been dated to 6300 BC. It is also probable that the Northwest Coast received some of its traits, such as wooden slat armor, directly from Asia. Harpoons and other hunting and fishing equipment are the most common archaeological finds. Harpoons were of two forms: either they were of the toggle type, fitted over the end of the harpoon shaft; or else they were barbed and socketed into the shaft. Bone and antler points were also used in unbarbed forms. Flaked projectile points, either with or without stems or barbs, were used, and ground slate points and knives were made. For woodworking, ground stone tools, with wedges made of bone or antler, and ground stone hammerstones were used. Carving was an important aspect of both the prehistoric and historic Northwest Coast culture, and stone forms, particularly in archaeological contexts, are important. Bowls in the form of seated human figures, clubs carved with human faces, and various ornaments were made. The rendering of animals was particularly important in this art.

Most of the later features of the Northwest Coast culture were probably present in rudimentary form at around 1000 BC in the Fraser River delta. Similar cultures have been found on other parts of the coast. On Gunther Island, off the North California coast, bone wedges, stone hammers, and stone bowls have been recovered which date from the 1st millennium AD. On the Oregon coast, at the Nearts Sand Spit site, a wooden plank house of typical Northwest Coast form, dating from AD 1400 to 1800, was excavated. In the coastal areas of British Columbia, a large number of burial mounds have been located: the body was placed in a central stone cairn, but usually without grave goods, and so it has been almost impossible to date these sites. (*See also* OZETTE.)

**Northwest microblade tradition.** An interior sub-Arctic cultural sequence of Alaska, the Yukon, and the Northwest Territories of Canada. It probably dates from around 6500 BC and lasted until *c*. 3500 BC. In Western Canada it survived until *c*. 1000 BC. Characteristic of the tradition are numerous small stone blades, made from conical or tongue-shaped cores, burins, crude bifacial knives, and lanceolate projectile points. Although there is a long gap between the latest dates for the Northwest microblade tradition and the beginning of the Denetasiro tradition, it is likely that one leads onto the other. In Southwest Yukon, the last phase of the microblade tradition is Taye Lake, 2000–1000 BC, in which microblades and burins were still being made, although they were less important than they had been in earlier phases. In addition, polished stone adzes, for woodworking, were beginning to appear. In the first Denetasiro phase, the Aishihik, dating from AD 300, grooved adzes and other woodworking tools were important, whereas the microblade tradition had disappeared. Nevertheless the Taye Lake and related phases may have gradually evolved into the Aishihik. If this is so, then the Athabascan population of the interior Western sub-Arctic may have started arriving in North America considerably earlier than the

ESKIMOS. The Athabascans, the historical tribes of the Denetasiro tradition, were specialized fishers, hunters, and trappers in the forests of the Northwest whose culture changed very little between AD 300 and 1900.

**Northwest Riverine tradition.** Sometimes called the Plateau tradition, this is the series of cultures which reached maturity in the interior of Oregon, Washington, and British Columbia, and in Idaho at the beginning of this millennium. In this area, bounded by mountains and with the Columbia-Snake, Fraser-Thompson, and Klamath Rivers running through it, the OLD CORDILLERAN TRADITION had arisen. Many of its traits, such as pebble choppers and leaf-shaped flaked stone projectile points, continued into the Northwest Riverine tradition. To this assemblage were added stone hammers, stone bowls, tubular pipes, stone clubs, and various fine stone carvings. The pattern of life which was established remained the same until the arrival of the Europeans at the beginning of the 19th century. Tribes such as the Shushwap and Wishram followed a migratory pattern: in winter they lived in villages beside rivers, from which they hunted deer. Salmon abounded in the rivers and were fished, in historic and prehistoric times, from the river villages and from temporary fishing camps. Other temporary camps were set up for berry and root collecting. The ethnographical material culture differs little from that found archaeologically on sites such as Vantage on the Columbia River. This included stone hammers, pestles, fishing implements, and digging sticks. House types varied in the Plateau area. On the Spokane River, pole structures above ground were probably made with mat-like roofs, but in the Dalles region partially subterranean structures of planks were built. This pithouse form dates back to *c.* AD 500.

**Novgorod.** A very important medieval trading city on the River Volkhov in the USSR. Extensive excavations have been carried out since 1932, especially between 1951 and 1962, under the direction of Artiskhovsky and Kolchin. Over 1,000 timber buildings have been found, associated with corduroy streets of split tree trunks, frequently replaced. A stratification of 28 street levels covered the period from the 10th to the 15th century AD. Novgorod was the first site for which dendrochronological dating provided a reliable chronological framework (*See* DENDROCHRONOLOGY).

Numerous texts on birch bark consisted of notes of debts, expenditure on purchases, private letters, complaints by peasants to their overlords, and other communications. As these were in colloquial speech, they have shed much light on the language of the period. Other discoveries included woodwork, leatherwork, the remains of workshops, and a variety of imports from as far afield as Byzantium and Sweden.

**Numantia.** A Bronze Age, HALLSTATT, and Celtic site on the upper Duero River in Spain, the scene of heroic Celtiberian resistance to Rome in 133 BC. Excavations have uncovered the settlement, the siege works, and 13 Roman camps dating from this period.

**Numidia.** A kingdom, formed by the "nomads," lying west of Carthaginian territory on the North coast of Africa. Later it was converted into a Roman province, whose chief city was Cirta, and remains exist at Lambaesis, Timgad, and Theveste.

**Nuzi.** The ancient name for Yorgan Tepe near Kirkuk (ancient Arrapha) in Northern Mesopotamia, excavated by the Americans from 1927 to 1931 after a few Old Assyrian tablets had been found on the site. The earliest level found (XII) is Chalcolithic. During the second half of the 2nd millennium BC, the city was known as Gasur (VI-III). In level II a temple and a palace decorated with wall paintings were excavated, together with a large quantity of tablets, indicating that Nuzi was part of the kingdom of Mitanni (*see* HURRIANS) in the middle of the 2nd millennium BC. The site has also given its name to a distinctive type of pottery (Nuzi ware), which can also be dated to the middle of the 2nd millennium BC and which is found at other Northern sites (e.g., TELL BRAK, Tell Billa, and TELL ATCHANA), and is perhaps associated with the Hurrians.

**Obsidian.** A generally dark colored, vitreous lava or volcanic rock.

*Near East and Europe.* Much sought and widely traded in prehistory for making cutting tools, recent research has isolated various sources used in antiquity in the Near East—one group in Central and one in Eastern ANATOLIA—and has established that obsidian trade began as early as the Upper Palaeolithic and only ended with the introduction of metal tools in Chalcolithic times. It also occurs in the Carpathian Mountains, on the island of Melos in the Cyclades, and on the Lipari Islands off Sicily.

*Mesoamerica.* This volcanic glass was used extensively throughout Mesoamerica from the earliest times until the Spanish Conquest. As a cutting material, it was chipped to make all kinds of razor-sharp tools and weapons. TEOTIHUACAN, with its rich deposits of obsidian nearby and its 400 workshops for the refining of the material, may well owe its prominent position in Mesoamerican history to the successful commercial exploitation of this stone.

Apart from the purely utilitarian purposes mentioned above, obsidian was used for decoration, and also had a ritual significance not yet understood. At TIKAL and UAXACTUN it has been found in votive caches, in the form of wide flakes with incised designs representing Maya deities. In the Aztec period, beautifully ground labrets (lip jewelry—*see* LABRET) and miniature ear spools (or earrings) have been found. Pendants and breast ornaments of this material were made in Jalisco, and a number of mirrors were made, possibly for use by astronomers and magicians.

Obsidian is also important for archaeology, because trace element analyses of the stone provide positive identification of its source locality. Consequently, it is possible today to identify, and quantify, examples of the trade in obsidian over extensive areas of Mesoamerica.

**Odeum.** A small Greek and Roman theater-like building, probably used for concerts and speeches. The earliest is that constructed by the Greek, Pericles, at Eleusis in 445 BC, but Roman examples exist at POMPEII, LYONS, Pula, and many other sites.

**Oil industry.** Apart from a devastated landscape, the archaeology of oil consists of what remains of obsolete oil-field equipment and refineries. Early production was mostly in the United States, where oil was discovered at Titusville in 1859. The world's first well was drilled there in the same year, and the Drake Well Memorial Park contains a replica of the first derrick and engine house. A very early oil refinery has been preserved in excellent condition on Oljeön Island (Oil Island), near Engelsberg, Sweden. Wood-fired, it dates from 1876 and is a simple plant of a type common in the United States a decade earlier, but no longer represented there. Parts of a later type are preserved at Newhall, Calif. This, the first successful Western refinery, was opened in 1876, several years after the first extraction of oil in the state, to produce kerosene and lubricating oils.

**Okvik.** An Eskimo site on Punuk Island, off St. Lawrence Island in Northwestern Alaska. The site, discovered in 1931, dates from c. 300 BC. It is well known for the appearance of artifacts in the art style which developed through the succeeding Old Bering Sea and Punuk phases of the Northern Maritime subtradition. The style was used to decorate ivory tools, such as harpoons, and also figurines with designs of straight and curving lines incised into the ivory, perhaps with metal tools. The most famous example is probably the Okvik "madonna," a figurine of a woman, holding a child, whose face is carved with an agonized expression. (*See also* ESKIMOS.)

**Old Cordilleran tradition.** The name given to the earliest cultures of the Northwest and Pacific areas of the United States. The first material identified as being from this tradition comes from the valleys of the Cascade Mountains in Oregon and Washington. The type-site is Five Mile Rapids, on the Columbia River in Oregon, where a succession of cultures has been identified dating from 7800 to 5700 BC. At the earliest levels an assemblage of leaf-shaped points, chopper tools, BOLAS, and burins has been found. The diagnostic features of the tradition are the flaked stone points which are known as Cascade points. They are bifacial and pointed at both ends. At the Five Mile Rapids site there is a gradual change in the sequence from tools and faunal remains, characteristic of subsistence based entirely on nomadic hunting, to one in which settled communities concentrated on salmon fishing. Other sites in the Pacific Northwest have been identified, by Cascade points, as being part of the same tradition. The Yale site on the FRASER RIVER in British Columbia has produced them at a level dating to c. 7000 BC. A similar date has been calculated for Ash cave in Washington, where leaf-shaped points have been found.

The origins of the Old Cordilleran tradition are uncertain. It has been suggested that the assemblages of the Five Mile Rapids site may have begun to evolve in the area at around 9000 BC, thus making them contemporaneous with the beginning of other traditions, particularly the BIG GAME HUNTING TRADITION. It has also been suggested that the fluted points of the Big Game Hunting tradition evolved from the Cascade point, but this is only a hypothesis.

In California, the earliest sites have yielded leaf-shaped points. The most important of these early complexes is the Lake Mojave in Southern California. Between 9000 and 7000 BC the area was wet and the lakes were filled with water. As well as leaf-shaped points, used for hunting the game which then abounded there, other types have been found, but they are localized in occurrence. The Lake Mojave point, kite-shaped with a long stem and short point, is the most typical. Other finds include choppers, drills, and scrapers. While the Lake Mojave culture was not typical of the Old Cordilleran tradition, it is more like that tradition, because of the leaf shape of the points, than the DESERT TRADITION or the Big Game Hunting tradition. The diversification of artifacts associated with the Old Cordilleran tradition was probably due to the increasing aridity of the area in the early part of the period 9000–7000 BC. In each subarea, cultures developed from the same base to accommodate the relatively fast changes in ecology and, therefore, in technology required. (*See also* NORTHWEST RIVERINE TRADITION.)

**Old South American Hunting tradition.** Dating from between 10,000 and 7000 BC, this tradition is characterized by its "fish-tailed" fluted stone projectile points and leaf-shaped lanceolate points, whose origin may be related to North American pressure flaked points of the Clovis (*see* CLOVIS POINT) and FOLSOM types. It gave rise to the Andean Hunting and Collecting tradition.

**Olduvai Gorge.** A gorge some 30 mi. (48 km) long, cut through sediments of the last 2 million years, situated in Tanzania between the Serengeti game park on the West and the volcanic belt of the Great Rift valley of Eastern Africa. No site in the world has produced a longer sequence of stone tool assemblages and of hominid (man-like) fossils.

The lowest level, Bed I, included a lava flow and a series of lake silts and ash falls, dating from c. 1.75 million years ago. This bed had a fine fossil skull, originally called *Zinjanthropus boisei* and belonging to the robust type, as well as several of the type HOMO HABILIS (so-called because he probably made and used tools). Bed II, a little later in date, had more skulls of *habilis*, while Upper Bed II, possibly about a million years old, had a fine skull of *erectus* type (*see* HUMAN EVOLUTION) and some evidence from teeth of the survival of the robust type. Bed IV, dating from perhaps a little over 0.5 million years ago had an *erectus* skull and pelvis, but no more trace of the robust form. Finally, after the cutting of the gorge, some minor beds, Ndutu and Naisiusiu, were formed on its side. A complete *Homo sapiens* skeleton was found buried here: it is about 17,000 years old. Altogether some 40 hominid pieces have been found, some of which are complete enough to reconstruct the size of the brain: the robust skull was 530 cc in capacity; three *habilis* skulls averaged about 640 cc; the *erectus* skulls were 1067 and 727 cc, compared to a size of *c.* 1400 cc for modern humans.

Stone tools were found throughout the sequence from about 1.75 million years ago onwards. In the lower beds handaxes (bifacial tools) were absent, and only simple flaked cobbles called pebble tools were found. Later, during Bed II times, handaxes were introduced, and these ACHEULIAN-type assemblages were found through Bed IV to the top of the gorge. In the latest beds, Middle Stone Age and Kenya Capsian tools were found.

**Oliviense.** A flake industry occurring on terraces in the Caleta Olivia and Bahia Solano region of Southern Argentina. Originally believed to be of Late Pleistocene date, these assemblages may actually represent fairly recent flake-manufacturing sites.

**Olla.** A term, particularly used in American archaeology, for globular pottery jars with flaring necks and rims.

**Ollantaytambo.** An important Inca town and fort located at the junction of the Tulymayo River with the Urubamba valley. Some very fine masonry construction is found in the hillside fort, for which stone was brought from a quarry high on the opposite side of the river. The town, located beside the Tulumayo, is laid out in a regular grid pattern with buildings facing onto courts in enclosures.

One of the colossal stone heads, *c.* 8 ft. (2. 4m) high, constructed by the Olmecs at La Venta, Mexico.

**Olmecs.** The traditional name for the Preclassic culture of Southern Veracruz and Tabasco, Mexico, also called either Tenocelome or La Venta culture. It should not be confused with the historic Olmecs, who were a later group and may have helped destroy TEOTIHUACAN, and whose tyranny was responsible for the migration of many Mesoamerican peoples. The major Olmec sites of LA VENTA and SAN LORENZO were occupied from about 1000 BC, or earlier, but other Olmec centers, such as TRES ZAPOTES, continued to the Late Preclassic Period.

The Olmecs were among the leaders, if not the original pioneers, of the revolutionary changes which took place in the Preclassic Period, when ceremonial centers evolved from simple agricultural villages and hierarchical government began. Many archaeologists view the Olmec as the first true civilization of the New World.

The ceremonial center of La Venta consisted of an earthen pyramid, a prototype for later Mesoamerican structures of stone and unique in that it was fluted rather than square; a plaza; and a number of mounds, one of which covered a massive tomb with substantial walls and a roof of columnar basalt. Olmec artifacts include colossal stone heads, rectangular altars, and, at Tres Zapotes, dated stelae. Among smaller objects were nude jade figurines showing characteristic snarling mouths, elongated heads, and slanting eyes. Ceremonial stone axes were carved with fierce faces which could be interpreted as either men with drooping lips or as snarling jaguars. There is a link between this jaguar, or demi-god, and sculptures found at Potrero Nuevo showing the procreative union of a woman and a jaguar. Doubtless this represented a mythical union with a divine jaguar from which the incipient hierarchy claimed descent, and through which they established their authority.

Olmec influence and art style were widely diffused. The Danzantes figures at MONTE ALBAN; the jaguar-like masks on Temple E-VII-sub at UAXACTUN; the baby-face figurines of LUBAANTUN in Belize; and jade figurines from many other areas bear witness to this culture's marked influence. The Initial Series dates on the stele from Tres Zapotes suggests that the Olmecs may also have been the Preclassic inventors of the Mesoamerican CALENDAR. Their numerous other cultural and technological advances suggest that the Olmecs were the mother culture of later Mesoamerican civilizations.

**Olympia.** The principal sanctuary of Zeus in Greece, and the site of the Olympic Games. The sanctuary may have its origins in the Greek Bronze Age, but it was built up early in the archaic period: in the 7th century BC a Temple of Hera was built, and the Temple of Zeus dates from the 5th century BC. Many buildings of various dates adorn the sanctuary: small treasuries of the various Greek states, a circular building of Philip of Macedon, and the buildings associated with athletes and the games—a GYMNASIUM, PALAESTRA, BOULEUTERION, and the Leonidaeon, the participants' hostel, as well as the running track itself. Excavations have revealed many votive objects and small bronzes, as well as the various phases of development of the site. A particularly interesting discovery is a workshop, possibly that of the Greek sculptor Phidias, who made the bronze statue of Athene at Athens and the statue of Zeus at Olympia.

**Olynthus.** A Greek town lying on the peninsula of Chalcidice, captured and destroyed by Philip of Macedon, and then abandoned. Excavations have revealed the main development of the town, which occurred between 432 and 348 BC. Almost all the road system and a large number of private houses have been examined. Its streets are laid out to form rectangular house blocks, occupied by multiple units of differing layouts.

**Oracle bones.** The shoulder bones of oxen or the shells of tortoises used in China for divination. The practice originated in the LUNG-SHAN CULTURE and was used extensively in the SHANG DYNASTY (c. 1600–1027 BC). Depressions were made in the bone and then a red-hot implement was applied which caused the bone to crack. The divination consisted of an interpretation of these cracks. The later Shang bones were inscribed with a description of the occasion of the divination, and are the earliest examples of the fully developed form of Chinese characters.

**Orange** (Arausio). An Augustan Roman colony in Gaul, famed both for the well preserved remains of its THEATER, and for the fragments of a Roman property map of the area carved on marble.

**Ordos.** A region lying inside the loop of the Yellow River where it turns northwards in Mongolia. From the 8th century BC it was inhabited by nomadic tribes, among them the HSIUNG-NU, providing a threat to the CHOU DYNASTY and HAN DYNASTY. Broad daggers and curved knives related to those of the TAGAR CULTURE have been found there. Similarly associated with Siberian cultures and ultimately the SCYTHIANS are pole finials, harness ornaments, and belt plaques decorated with animals in profile.

**Ortoire.** A phase dated to c. 800 BC, recognized on a site in Trinidad, and distinguished by crude chipped stone tools, netsinkers and grinding stones.

**Oseberg ship.** The most important of the Viking ship burials. It was discovered in 1903 in South Norway and excavated in 1904 from a mound 120 ft. (36.6 m) in diameter composed of peat, which had preserved the richly carved timbers of the ship and its contents in a remarkable state. It contained the bodies of two women, and was dated by the finds to the period AD 850–900. The ship was old when it was buried—the carving on it indicates a date around AD 800. The finds from the ship included three beds, blankets, pillows, eiderdowns, chests, barrels, a wall hanging, two looms, a four-wheeled carriage, four sledges, two tents, a chair, and numerous small finds which shed much light on the everyday life of the VIKINGS.

**Ostia.** Rome's harbor town at the mouth of the River Tiber. Towards the end of the 4th century BC, a rectangular fort was constructed on the site, and this secured Rome's interest in the trade routes through Ostia. The town grew until 78 BC, when it was destroyed in the Roman civil wars, but it was rebuilt by Sulla, retaining the old FORUM and CAPITOLIUM. Sulla added a defensive wall on the side of the town unprotected by the Tiber.

Excavations have revealed a large part of the republican and imperial town. In addition to the Temple of Rome and Augustus, the forum, capitol, and BASILICA, there are BATHS, a THEATER, and the associated *piazza delle corporazioni*, with its mosaics showing the various merchants of the town in the early empire. There are remains of buildings associated directly with the trade of the port: the *statio mensorum*, the official control of weights and measures, warehouses for wine and oil, and headquarters buildings for traders' unions, as well as shops particularly associated with the fish trade.

Within the town there were many private houses and temples: houses, normally tile built, range from the atrium-peristyle type to multistoried apartment blocks. Temples display a wide variety of cults: Roman (Volcanus, Hercules, Bona Dea, and Silvanus), Classical (Jupiter, Venus, Ceres, Spes, and Fortuna), and Oriental (Isis, Magna Mater, and especially Mithras, 19 of whose Mithraea [*see* MITHRAEUM] have been found). There was also a Christian basilica and several small chapels.

Perhaps the most important Roman achievement at Ostia was the construction of the harbor itself. Originally in the mouth of the Tiber, it began to prove inaccessible because of silting. A new harbor was therefore built by the Emperor Claudius on the open shore of the Mediterranean, involving the shifting of massive amounts of earth and the construction of two large breakwaters for protection. Trajan later added another basin of hexagonal shape.

**Ottonians.** The successors of the CAROLINGIANS, whose art was initially a conscious revival of the Carolingian. The Ottonian Empire is named after the Ottonian emperors (who were called Otto) and the period spans the years AD 936–1024. The influence of the Byzantines (Otto II married a Byzantine princess) led to a hieratic quality in some art, particularly manuscript painting, associated with very bright colors. Ottonian architecture is characterized by fortress-like basilicas with massive walls, groups of towers, and tiny windows.

**Oxus Treasure.** A large hoard discovered in 1877 on the River Oxus, near the present-day frontier between Russia and Afghanistan. It consists of Achaemenid and Persian gold and silver objects of the 5th and 4th centuries BC, and includes figurines, models of chariots, vessels, a sword sheath, ornamental plaques and jewelry, and a cylinder seal and seal rings.

**Ozyrrhinchus.** An important town in middle Egypt, about 186 mi (300 km) south of Alexandria, where a Greek colony was planted under the Ptolemys. Surviving remains are those of several temples, Christian churches, a large THEATER, and a GYMNASIUM. Ozyrr-hinchus is chiefly famous for an important find of papyri, mostly of Roman date, which comprises hitherto lost portions of ancient authors, as well as letters and other official documents.

**Ozark.** A cultural area named after the Ozark hills of Arkansas, Oklahoma, and Missouri. An Archaic culture, called the Grove phase and dating from before 5000 BC, was probably ancestral to the Bluff-Dweller sites of the Ozark area. These were occupied into the present millennium, and consist of rock shelters and caves, as well as open village sites. Because of the dryness of the cave sites, extensive remains of their material culture have been found. Baskets of twilled weave were used for flour sieves and containers, and pitch-lined baskets of twined weave were used for liquids. Subsistence depended on a mixture of hunting and gathering and farming, with maize, beans, squash, gourds, and sunflowers grown. Fish were caught with pebble-weighted nets, and elk, bison, deer, and turkey were hunted with spears and spearthrowers. Farming was carried out with bone hoes and antler and wooden digging sticks. Pottery was used for cooking. The bases of many of the pots have impressions of baskets marked into them, suggesting that they were supported on baskets while being made.

**Ozette.** A Makah Indian village site on the Pacific coast of Washington State, in the United States. In the 18th century it was one of the five main villages of the Makah, and the main center for hunting whales and seals on the Washington coast. The village was gradually abandoned by the Makah between 1900 and 1930, having been occupied continuously for thousands of years. The midden (rubbish mound) deposits of the village provide one of the few continuous records of a prehistoric culture in the NORTHWEST COAST TRADITION. In the 15th century, a mud flow descended on the village, covering several houses; thus both the houses and their contents have been well preserved. Large numbers of wooden storage boxes have been recovered, sometimes still containing wooden dishes, baskets, mussel-shell harpoons, and whalebone and wooden clubs.

**Paccaicasas.** The earliest assemblage of tools found in the four lowest strata of PIKIMACHAY CAVE in the center of the Ayacucho valley in the Central highlands of Peru. Choppers, bifacial tools, and waste flakes were found in association with bones of several extinct species which showed signs of butchery techniques. Radiocarbon dates range from 18,000 to 12,000 BC, providing the earliest evidence for man in South America.

**Pachacamac.** The HUARI influence on the Lima ceramics of the Central coast of Peru produced this style of polychrome pottery, c. AD 800–1000. The type-site, located south of Lima, was famous for its oracle.

**Pacific Littoral tradition.** A tradition which developed, c. 4000–1800 BC, on the Peruvian coast. Settled communities lived off a rich maritime diet and cultivated cotton and gourds to provide materials for the fishing industry. Bone, wood, shell, and stone were worked, twined and knotted textiles were made, an early art style developed and temple platforms were built in the earliest ceremonial centers.

**Paestum.** A Greek colony founded in the first half of the 7th century BC in Italy. It is chiefly famed for the series of four almost complete Doric temples of the 6th and 5th centuries BC, though other remains, including defenses, houses, a FORUM, an AMPHITHEATER, and other temple areas, have also been excavated.

**Painting, Classical world.**
*Greek.* The walls of Minoan and Mycenaean palaces (e.g. KNOSSOS; MYCENAE) often bore elaborate painted and stucco decoration which perhaps originated in the "Camares" style of polychrome naturalistic vase painting. The technique of these frescoes is clearly related to and derived from the Egyptians, but the motifs are unmistakably Cretan and Mycenaean: in CRETE itself naturalistic themes and figures (of gods?) predominate, whereas in the Mycenaean palaces, despite themes which also appeared in Crete (processions of women and bull-leaping), there are also chariot processions and hunting scenes. Pottery painting in Mycenae also evolved to include figured scenes.

Little is known of Greek painting from the end of the Mycenaean period until the first appearance of new forms of decoration on pottery of the Protogeometric period. The difference between this and Mycenaean art is marked. GEOMETRIC pottery of the archaic period carries a variety of abstract designs, usually in horizontal bands. The introduction of the human figure (e.g., in the so-called "Dipylon" vases found in Athens' largest cemetery) brought a fresh theme: human, animal, and plant motifs were reintroduced and began to displace the abstract circles, squares, triangles, swastikas, and lozenges of the purest Geometric style.

Eastern influences inspired the next developments: stylized birds, plants, animals, and mythological monsters first began to appear on Rhodian and Corinthian vases, but these were soon copied by Athens and Sparta. Painting of this "Orientalizing" period in the 8th century BC began to make use of polychrome designs, reaching its full development in the 7th century BC, in particular with the Corinthian school of vase painters. Scenes developed from small-scale single figure (or animal) motifs on small-scale vessels, to the use of the human figure, usually in silhouette, on a quite complex design. Both Geometric and Corinthian styles make use in the main of a buff ground, on which the figures are painted in the early period in black only, but in the later period also in red and purple, with occasional use (in some areas) of yellows and blues.

It is important to remember that, though little trace now survives, most sculptures were also painted, and buildings (especially temples) were decorated with painted motifs. In Aetolia at Thermon, remains of painted clay metopes, probably of the 7th century BC, have been found. These paintings, in a place where later temples employed sculptures, show that the development of monumental art to some extent was running hand in hand with that of pottery in this early period.

The 6th century BC ushered in a period of consolidation. At the end of the 7th century BC the black-figured technique was introduced: black figures with incised lines to show muscles and falls of drapery. In *c.* 530 BC this arrangement was reversed, with red figures against a black background and details picked out by brushwork. Mural painting was also developed in this century, and, though little of it survives, the designs on vases perhaps show the influence of frescoes. Though the early part of the 6th century BC saw great competition between Corinthian and Athenian schools of painters, by the end of the century the Attic black-figured designs predominated.

From the early 5th century BC, the highest point of Athenian vase painting, a number of names and signed works by individual painters are known. At this period, varied expressions and three-quarter profiles appear in figured painting, but the greatest advances evidently came in the murals on various public buildings in ATHENS and elsewhere—the leading exponent of which was Polygnotus, whose work is known only from descriptions by ancient authors.

By the beginning of the 4th century BC, the Athenian schools of vase painting had been overtaken by the Italiote vases produced in Southern Italy, which carried

A 6th-century BC Corinthian oinochoe, with animal motifs typical of the "Orientalizing" period of Greek painting.

on very much the same designs, with subjects from mythology or Greek drama. But the century was famous for its painters, although their works are only known now by their titles, and from Roman copies of the originals. These copies show the expertize which had been gained in the late 4th century BC in the effects of color, perspective, facial expression, and tone; one of the most famous is the portrayal of Alexander and Darius at the Battle of the Issus, a late 4th-century BC painting of which a mosaic copy was found at HERCULANEUM. Much of the further development of figured portrait, still life, interior, and landscape scenes in the Hellenistic world is seen in the art of the Roman world, and in particular at Herculaneum and POMPEII. The majority of the fresco and mosaic work at both sites is probably derivative of earlier Greek models, if not actual copies of Greek originals. (*See also* GREECE ARCHAEOLOGY OF.)

*Roman and Etruscan.* The majority of known Etruscan paintings were made on the walls of chamber tombs in cemeteries and date from the end of the 7th to the 1st century BC. In the archaic period, the paintings are sometimes purely decorative and episodes from Greek mythology are rare. The tomb walls are normally painted with scenes from life: mostly banquet scenes, hunting, sports, and dancing. The animal scenes of the earliest paintings are attributable to Oriental influences, and the inclusion of figures, as much of the development until the end of the 5th century BC, can be traced to Greek contact, either Ionian or Attic. From the 4th century BC, the subjects change: the afterlife is depicted as a world full of hideous monsters. Portraiture is popular in particular in the 3rd century BC, but is again combined with mythological and grotesque scenes.

The origins of Roman painting, on the other hand, are to be found in the Hellenistic world. Roman pictorial art is hardly mentioned in antiquity, and Pliny records that the difference between Roman and Greek painting was that the Greeks painted pictures, but the Romans painted walls: painting for Romans was an ornament to architecture, though some elements of native (Etruscan type?) tradition may have survived in tomb paintings or in the images of ancestors which were carried in funeral processions.

There are abundant examples of Roman mural decoration from *c.* 200 BC to AD 79 at Pompeii. In the 19th century, these were classified into four typical styles. In the first style (from the 2nd century BC), which originated in the Hellenistic world, the walls are painted as if they were faced with marble. The second style shows figured scenes, usually within a simple architectural frame (e.g., the paintings of the Villa of the Mysteries), and dates from 80 BC onwards. The third style (*c.* 20 BC–AD 20) also embodies architectural decoration, but includes within it large areas of color and pictures—often copies of famous Hellenistic originals—as if in frames and hung on them. The fourth style is one of architectural fantasy, with perspectives appearing to reach beyond the walls of the room. Within this framework there is still room for small paintings—landscapes or miniatures—sometimes in an impressionistic style. Wall and ceiling painting of later date is known from

A Roman mummy portrait, painted on wood, from Egypt, 2nd century AD.

—are very different and are often used to portray symbolic themes, which may also have been drawn from Greek mythology. Most of the surviving examples of Roman Christian painting can be seen as a continuation of Roman art, with the addition of specifically Christian motifs and symbols. The figured scenes are impressionistic, almost line drawings rather than paintings, and some works are the forerunners of Byzantine iconography (*see* BYZANTINES).

**Palaeobotany.** The study of the history of plant life and, consequently, of the earth's climate. In archaeology, palaeobotany has proved of particular value in assessing the early environment of man, his impact upon it, and his exploitation and husbanding of plants for food and as raw materials for the manufacture of artifacts. By the analysis of pollen frequencies in peat bogs and acidic soils (palynology), palaeobotanists have been able to reconstruct in detail the history of the climate in Northern latitudes since the end of the Pleistocene, and they are now engaged in the reconstruction of climatic sequences for the interglacial periods. The study of seeds from archaeological deposits, and of other plant remains preserved in arid or waterlogged conditions, has shed a great deal of light on man's domestication of plants, and on his diet at various dates in the past.

**Palaeolithic.** One of the fundamental divisions of prehistory used by archaeologists. The term was first introduced in 1865 by John Lubbock in his book *Prehistoric Times*, and was simply a translation of "Old Stone Age" into a Greek form ($\pi\alpha\lambda\alpha\iota\sigma$ = old; $\lambda\iota\theta\sigma s$ = stone). It contrasted with the Neolithic or New Stone Age, and together they made up the Stone Age, which preceded the Bronze and Iron Ages. In its original form the Palaeolithic was characterized by chipped stone tools as opposed to polished stone tools, and it was associated with a set of animals which included extinct forms like the mammoth and woolly rhinoceros, as well as species which migrated from Europe like the reindeer, musk ox, and hippopotamus.

Over the last century the Palaeolithic has assumed a slightly different meaning: it is the period of hunting cultures as opposed to the Neolithic farming cultures. Also, the introduction of the term Mesolithic has led to the restriction of Palaeolithic to cultures which existed before the end of the last Ice Age. For Europe, Palaeolithic has come to mean the period of hunters of the Ice Ages—more formally called the Pleistocene epoch of geological time. In America and Australia the term is not often used, and in Africa and the Far East there is a tendency to prefer other terms.

Traditionally the Palaeolithic is subdivided into Upper, Middle, and Lower Palaeolithic. The Upper Palaeolithic (the latest in time) is still generally believed to be a significant division, though few modern prehistorians regard it as a geological-style epoch in the way that its creator Gabriel de Mortillet did in the 19th century and as the term "Upper" suggests. Instead, archaeologists recognize it by the blade tools which predominate in Upper Palaeolithic assemblages.

numerous places, notably OSTIA, and is now being found in many parts of the imperial Roman world.

A remarkable series of Roman portraits has been preserved on mummies in Egypt from the 1st century AD onwards: the range continues into the 4th century AD, and most of the portraits, painted on wood, are excellent lifelike pictures.

*Early Christian.* The majority of early Christian paintings are found as wall decorations in the CATACOMBS in Rome and elsewhere, the stylistic characteristics of which suggest that this painting began in the early 3rd century AD, forming the basis for Byzantine art of the late 5th and early 6th centuries AD. Some of the decorative motifs, the arrangements of the figures, and the layout of the scenes are reminiscent of Pompeian styles, but the subjects portrayed—Christ, the Virgin Mary, Old and New Testament scenes, the apostles, and saints

RADIOCARBON DATING suggests that these assemblages go back to somewhere between 35,000 and 45,000 years ago, but there is a great deal of uncertainty about these dates. The Upper Palaeolithic differs from the preceding period in having bone tools of well defined types, and all across Europe there is evidence of engraving or painting of art objects. Above all the Upper Palaeolithic, in Europe at least, is associated with modern-type man, and not with Neanderthal and other archaic types. On radiocarbon evidence the Upper Palaeolithic ends about 10,000 years ago, i.e., at the end of the last Ice Age.

The Palaeolithic is usually taken to begin when stone tools were first made. This varies from continent to continent and is more difficult to date, as there has been disagreement about the authenticity of some of the earliest-claimed stone tools.

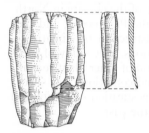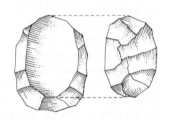

Left: the prepared core technique of flint flaking. The core of flint (left) has flakes removed from round its edge and from over one surface. The Levallois flake (right) is then removed from the prepared surface of the core by a blow on the faceted platform (at top). Right: an advance on the prepared core technique produced the blade core and blades.

Stone toolmaking in East Africa, north of Lake Rudolf, seems to have begun about 2.5 million years ago, according to the POTASSIUM-ARGON DATING method. In Asia it seems to be later than 2 million years, but this is not well established. There is also much uncertainty surrounding the date of the earliest stone tools in Europe. A single stone tool from Sandalja in North Yugoslavia is about 1.3 million years old. A site close to Monte Carlo, called Vallonet, has a few stone tools and is dated to about 900,000 years ago. Sites in Southern Spain may be earlier than this. Stone toolmaking did not become widespread in Europe until some 350,000 to 250,000 years ago.

The remaining dividing line in the Palaeolithic, between the Lower and Middle divisions, is much the most unsatisfactory. It is often located at the beginning of the last glaciation at the time of the Mousterian (after the site of Le Moustier in France) epoch named by 19th-century prehistorians. This may be somewhere between 120,000 and 70,000 years ago.

The Mousterian is associated with NEANDERTHAL MAN, but whether he was the only type of man at this time is disputed. We have relatively few examples of fossil man in the Lower Palaeolithic, but in Europe they seem to belong to an early form of Neanderthal man. Elsewhere, fossils resembling Java and PEKING MAN (HOMO ERECTUS) are found, and the very earliest fossils associated with

stone tools are of the type found in Bed I at OLDUVAI GORGE (HOMO HABILIS).

For the first million years or so, stone tools were simple and without much variety. Typically they were of the kind called choppers and chopping tools (though their function can only be guessed), lumps of stone with a few flakes knocked off one end to produce a rudimentary sharp edge; the term pebble tool is also used. Subsequently, over a wide area of Africa, Southern Asia, and Western Europe, the stone tool assemblages include tools we call handaxes, flaked extensively over both surfaces. These assemblages are often called ACHEULIAN.

A further advance is detectable when the technique of preparing the core or nucleus was developed, which allowed the flint worker to remove a flake of more or less the shape he desired, and with a sharp edge all round. The blades of the Upper Palaeolithic are a refinement of this technique. Some prehistorians like to begin the Middle Palaeolithic with such a prepared core (so-called Levallois) technique, but in some areas it begins very early, while in many Mousterian assemblages it was still not used as recently as 50,000 years ago. After 200,000 years ago assemblages with prepared core flakes and retouched flakes of various kinds (called "tools" by prehistorians) become more common. Man also began to live regularly in caves.

These give way in the Upper Palaeolithic to assemblages dominated by blades and blade tools, in particular backed points and knives, scrapers made on blades, and a special chisel-like tool called a burin. How widely over Asia and Africa such an Upper Palaeolithic exists is still not fully known.

**Palaestra.** A quadrangular courtyard for exercise and sport surrounded by a peristyle. Among the Greeks it formed part of the GYMNASIUM, but the Romans gave it a separate identity, either linking it with baths, or using it as a practice ground for gladiators.

**Palenque.** A Classic Period Maya center in Northern Chiapas, Mexico, known to travelers and archaeologists since the end of the 18th century. Inscribed monuments were erected from AD 630 until AD 810, after which the site was apparently abandoned. It is noteworthy for the delicacy of the bas-relief sculpture in the Temple of the Sun and the Temple of the Foliated Cross, and for the beautiful modeling in stucco on the piers of the palace. Unfortunately, much of this has been destroyed. The palace was built around four small courtyards and was unique in also having a three-story tower, possibly used as an astronomical observatory.

The most spectacular discovery at Palenque, and perhaps in all Mesoamerica, was that by the archaeologist Alberto Ruz of a tomb in the substructure of the Temple of the Inscriptions. Ruz noticed a paving stone with holes for lifting inside the temple. When he removed this, he found a rubble-filled stairway which led down to the tomb of a great ruler. The bones lay full-length in a sarcophagus sealed with a richly carved lid, and were accompanied by a rich assortment of jade objects, including a mask made entirely of a mosaic of jades. This

The palace at Palenque, Chiapas, Mexico.

find is as important in Mesoamerica as that of the tomb of Tutankhamun in Egypt.

**Palestine.** *See* SYRIA-PALESTINE.

**Palmate stone.** A large spatulate stone object, about 2 ft. (61 cm) long, believed to be a ceremonial representation of a device worn by ballgame players in Mesoamerica. It rested on a yoke which fitted around the waist and projected upward to protect the chest. Those worn in the game would probably have been made of stiff leather or wood. Examples found so far all seem to be of Totonac origin, and are elaborately carved on both sides. It is not known whether they were trophies, some form of religious symbolism, or used for burial purposes. They date primarily to the Classic Period.

**Palmyra.** A Syrian city on the caravan route from the Eastern Mediterranean to the River Euphrates. It came under Roman influence in the 1st century BC, but was annexed to the empire some years later. Its principal remains are the temple to Baal, dedicated in AD 32, and its AGORA. Several late Roman buildings also survive, notably the headquarters building of the fort emplanted by Diocletian, and Christian churches of the time of Justinian.

**Pampa Grande.** A major urban settlement in the Lambayeque valley, Peru. This was a Moche Period V site (*see* MOCHE SEQUENCE), dated *c.* 1000 BC, of which a large part was occupied for a relatively short time. Ruins at the site cover a roughly triangular area of about 1.5 sq. mi. (4 km²).

**Pannonia.** A Roman province, roughly coextensive with Southwestern Hungary.

**Pan-p'o-ts'un.** One of the most important excavated sites of the Chinese Neolithic YANG-SHAO CULTURE (*c.* 4500 BC). It was a large settlement of 12 ac. (5 ha), probably occupied on a repetitive rather than a continuous basis by a people who practiced a slash-and-burn form of agriculture and kept domesticated animals. The site is near a river and fish designs feature prominently on the painted handmade pottery characteristic of this culture. In date Pan-p'o-ts'un precedes the other major excavated site of MIAO-TI-KOU.

**Pan-shan.** A phase of the Chinese Neolithic YANG-SHAO CULTURE, found in the West, in Kansu province, and particularly in the MA-CHIA CULTURE. Later in date than the main Ma-chia phase, it is placed at *c.* 2500 BC. It is famous for large urns painted in spirals and lozenges in purple, brown, red, and black, found both in burial and on habitation sites.

**Pantheon.** Built by Agrippa in 27–5 BC, and rebuilt by

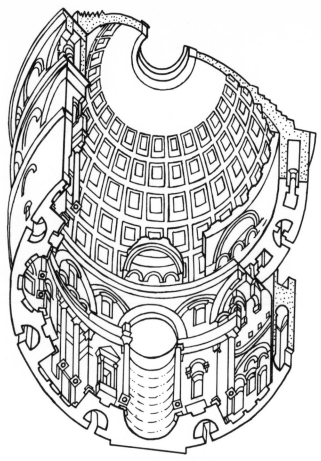

An axonometric view of the Pantheon, Rome, *c.* AD 120.

Hadrian *c.* AD 120, the Pantheon was one of the most remarkable buildings of Rome. A rotunda roofed by a
dome, and fronted by a portico and entrance hall, it is
built of brick-faced concrete, and its height is equal to
its internal diameter—*c.* 145 ft. (44 m). The sophistication of the construction of the domed coffered ceiling
makes this the most important building in the development of Roman architecture. (*See* ARCHITECTURE, ROMAN.)

**Papermaking.** The archaeology of the papermaking industry is complicated, since many old-established mills
have manufactured a variety of products during their
working life. Ørholm Mill, on the Mølleaa, near Copenhagen, Denmark, for example, began producing gunpowder in the 17th century. During the 18th century, it
turned successively to starch, iron, copper, scythes, and
cutlers, before beginning nearly a century and a half of
papermaking (1794–1933). It is now used for other
industrial purposes, not involving waterpower.

The mid-18th-century papermill of Richard de Bas,
at Ambert, Puy-de-Dôme, France, has been preserved as
a working museum. It contains a remarkable set of
water-driven wooden beaters for preparing the rags.
Finland has a number of sites of the same kind. The
papermill buildings at Möllby, near Turku, were put up
in 1820 and are still intact, although they are now used
by a fish-canning company.

With the development of new techniques using wood
as a raw material, the scale of papermaking was transformed and plant became rapidly obsolete. For this

reason, the modern paper industry preserves relatively
few monuments of its past. An interesting exception is
the E. B. Eddy Digester Tower (*c.* 1900) at Hull, Quebec,
Canada, which is now maintained as a national historic
monument. Built as a digester for pulpwood chips, it is
the only remaining structure on Canada's original
sulphite plant site.

**Paracas.** A large ceremonial area on the South coast of
Peru, dating from 900 to 200 BC, which has produced
resin painted polychrome pottery with distinctive paint-
filled incisions of Chavinoid deities. The iconography
includes felines, foxes, birds, demons, and humans.
Many of the vessels are the characteristic CHAVIN stirrup-
mouthed jars, while the double spout and bridge and
whistling jars also occur. The area is also noted for the
superb quality of textiles found in mummy bundles,
which have been preserved in the underground burial
chambers of Cavernas and Necropolis.

**Parthenon.** The monumental Temple of Athena on the
ACROPOLIS at ATHENS, built by Ictinus in 447–432 BC. It
is remarkable both for the quality of its decorated pediments and metopes (the "Elgin marbles," now in the
British Museum, London) and also for the exquisite proportions of all its features.

**Parthia, Parthians.** The name Parthia was originally
derived from the Greek name for the satrapy of Parthava,
east of the Caspian sea, which was captured from the
SELEUCIDS and settled by the Iranian tribe of the Parni,
under their ruler Arsaces, in the middle of the 3rd century BC. With the weakening of the Seleucid Empire, the
Parthians were able to expand and under Mithradates I
(*c.* 171–138 BC) their territories stretched from BABYLON
to Bactria. The silk road to China (*see* SILK ROUTE) was
opened under Mithradates II (124/3–87 BC), who also
came into contact with the Romans under Sulla on the
River Euphrates in the West. Frontier disputes led to the
ill-fated Roman expeditions under Crassus in 53 BC and
under Anthony in 36 BC, and proved the supremacy of
the Parthian mounted archers. For centuries the Romans
and the Persians continued to fight for control of
Armenia. These wars, and dynastic troubles at home
finally weakened the Parthian Empire and the Arsacid
Dynasty was overthrown by the SASSANIANS in *c.* AD 225.

Since the Parthians were originally nomadic, they
adopted the art of the countries they dominated and,
under their rule, Eastern and Western influences became
increasingly fused. The earliest Parthian remains come
from Nisa in South Russia. There was a great interchange
of religious ideas, and Zoroastrianism, various forms of
Mazda worship, Mithraism, and Gnostic systems
flourished. Many religious and funerary monuments
survive, especially at PALMYRA and on Nemrut Dağ in
COMMAGENE, while temples and synagogues dedicated to
a variety of deities have been found at DURA EUROPOS.
HATRA also has many temples and a great deal of sculpture survives, while palaces are planned round a central
*iwan*—an audience hall open at one end. Other Parthian
remains have been excavated at NIPPUR and URUK.

Wall paintings have been found at Kuh-i-Khawja, and painted stucco decoration at Qal'eh-i Yazdigird in Iran.

**Pasargadae.** *See* ACHAEMENIDS.

**Passage grave.** A generic term for megalithic monuments with a distinct chamber, often of elaborate form, approached by a passage. These were set in variously shaped mounds: round, oval, and long. They belong to the Neolithic period of Atlantic Western Europe from Spain to Scandinavia, and many were used for communal burial.

**Pasyryk.** A site in the Altai Mountains, South Siberia, where eight burials surmounted by mounds (or kurgans) were found dating from the 4th to the 2nd century BC. The intense frost had preserved their contents, including wooden chariots with their horses, textiles, and furniture. The bodies of the dead had survived sufficiently for the designs of tattooing on the skin to be reconstructed. A full range of representations of animals and birds in profile has been found in metal, felt appliqués, and tattooed designs.

A 5th-century BC appliqué swan, in felt, from Pasyryk.

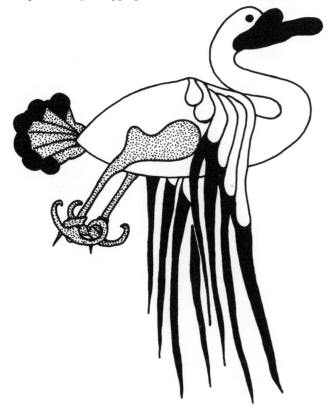

**Patayan.** Sometimes called Hakataya, this is the culture of the lower Colorado River in Western Arizona. The people, of Yuman speech, have occupied the area for at least 1500 years: the tribes include the Hazasupai, Mojave, and Walapai. They farmed the alluvial flood plains of the Colorado, and hunted and gathered wild

foods in the neighboring mountains. Patayan I period (AD 100–1000) is marked by the first appearance of pottery and agriculture, and the sites of this period are mostly confined to the Southern part of the region. Patayan II period (AD 1000–1500) pottery was spread over a much wider area—as far north as Southern Nevada. It was influenced by the HOHOKAM, and comprises vessels decorated with red-on-buff designs and stucco finishing.

**Pebble tool.** *See* STONE TECHNOLOGY.

**Peking man.** In the 1920s and 1930s, massive excavations at Chou-k'ou-tien, 25 mi. (40 km) southwest of Peking, recovered remains of over 40 fossil humans, some of which may date from over 0.5 million years ago. They are now attributed to the species HOMO ERECTUS. The original finds were lost during World War II, but a few new discoveries have been made since then.

**Pella.** A town lying about 25 mi. (40 km) north of Salonica, the capital of Macedonia from the turn of the 4th century BC until 168 BC. Excavations have now revealed the layout and mosaic floors of the palace of the Macedonian kings.

**Pergamum.** A town in Northwestern Asia Minor, important in the 3rd century BC, when it became the capital of the Attalid Dynasty of Hellenistic rulers. The site is a fine example of Hellenistic town planning, with buildings terraced up to the palace and the acropolis. Substantial portions also survive of the subsequent Roman town.

**Peristyle.** An architectural term to describe a columned hall enclosing a courtyard, e.g., an ATRIUM, STOA, or PALAESTRA.

**Persepolis.** The modern Takht-i Jamshid, near Shiraz in IRAN, site of the Achaemenid palace begun by Darius, *c.* 518 BC, and completed by Artaxerxes I. The palace seems to have been used for ceremonial purposes rather than as a dwelling. It was built on an artificial terrace and consisted of huge columned APADANA, halls and courts, ceremonial gates, and stairways, all lavishly carved with reliefs. The columns were topped with ornamental capitals decorated with animals. It seems that tribute was brought here to the king from the vassal satrapies at a ceremony which may have coincided with the New Year. The palace was built by teams of workmen and craftsmen from all parts of the empire. It was captured and burnt by Alexander the Great in 330 BC.

**Persia.** *See* IRAN.

**Persian Gulf** (Arabian Gulf). Until recently no ancient remains were known from this area, but Danish excavations on Bahrein (DILMUN), finds of UBAID pottery at various points along the coast, and of 3rd-millennium BC pottery at Umm an-Nar and in Buraimi oasis (Abu Dhabi) have led to increased archaeological activity in the area. Investigations have been carried out on the islands of Falaika and Tarut. MAGAN, which is mentioned with Dilmun and the more distant Meluhha, is generally supposed to have been on the Gulf of Oman.

**Peten.** The modern political district of Northern Guatemala. This tropical rain forest region, bordered by Mexico to the north and west, and by Belize on the east, largely comprises an area which Mesoamerican archaeologists call the Southern Maya Lowlands. It was in the Peten that the Maya civilization first emerged, at sites like TIKAL, PIEDRAS NEGRAS, and UAXACTUN, and finally collapsed, *c.* AD 900.

**Petra.** The capital of the NABATAEANS on the main route between the Dead Sea and the Red Sea. It is set in an amphitheater of mountains and the main access is through a cleft in the rock called the Siq. The buildings, temples, and tombs are mostly cut in the multicolored sandstone and are very Baroque in appearance. The water supply was obtained through an elaborate system of dams, waterworks, and cisterns.

**Petrie, Sir William Matthew Flinders** (1853–1942). A British Egyptologist, considered to have instituted modern scientific archaeology in Egypt by establishing basic principles for excavation which are still adhered to by modern archaeologists. He ensured that exhaustive records were made at the site where each object was found and later incorporated the information into a corpus. His insistence on the corpus method of recording enabled him to propound the SEQUENCE DATING system, which is still the basis for dating Predynastic artifacts. While excavating Predynastic cemeteries opposite Quft (Coptos), he found local workmen to be exceptionally gifted excavators, being careful, honest, hardworking, and interested in their work. In all subsequent excavations in Egypt, Petrie insisted on using these Quftis (men of Quft); this practice of employing Quftis became a tradition and even today most excavators in Egypt rely on a nucleus of Quftis in their workforce.

The work that Petrie did in the Predynastic cemeteries at Naqada was so basic to the study of Egypt's prehistory that the Middle and Late Predynastic Periods are usually termed Naqada I and Naqada II. His earliest work in Egypt, published as *Pyramids and Temples of Giza* (1883), embodied the first modern survey of the Giza pyramids using scientific methods and, until recently, it remained the standard work on the subject. In digging at over 39 sites all over Egypt during a period of nearly 50 years, Petrie made many major contributions to Egyptian archaeology. He discovered the lost Greek colony city of NAUCRATIS, excavated the workmen's village at Kahun, recovered much Archaic Period material from the royal tombs of the first two Dynasties at Abydos, discovered royal jewelry of the Middle Kingdom at el-Lahun, and cleared AKHENATEN's capital city at el-Amarna. (*See also* NAQADA CULTURE I; NAQADA CULTURE II.)

**Petrological analysis.** The use of stone as the primary raw material for toolmaking, and almost the only cutting agency known in the Stone Age, means that it is frequently available for study by archaeologists. The source from which the stone comes is of considerable interest, as it may indicate patterns of trade, or, at earlier times, the routes over which hunters trekked during their seasonal cycle or when colonizing new territory.

Unfortunately, different types of flint, the most common raw material used in Europe, are hard to tell apart, and modern techniques of trace analysis and microscopic study are being used to this end. OBSIDIAN, a rare volcanic glass, found for example in the Mediterranean area, was extensively used and traded in the NEOLITHIC period and occasionally earlier. Much success has been achieved in characterizing different types of obsidian from different sources, and thus reconstructing trade patterns.

The most common type of petrological analysis has been on polished axes. A small slice can be removed by sawing, and this is then studied by petrologists, for example in thin section under the microscope. As a result several ax factories, where the blocks of stone were roughed out for transport, have been identified in Britain, and the distribution of their products has been traced.

**Phaestus.** A Cretan Bronze Age palace site at the west end of the central plain. The ruins of the Minoan palace are extensive, and show roughly the same sequence of phases as at KNOSSOS and other palace sites. One remarkable find is the Phaestus disk, a stone engraved with (LINEAR A?) characters in a helix arrangement.

**Philistines.** One of the SEA PEOPLE who invaded Palestine at the beginning of the 12th century BC, gave it their name, settled on the coast, and then gradually spread inland. They seem to have adopted the culture of the Canaanites, but introduced a new type of pottery decorated with metopes and bird designs which recalls Late Helladic pottery of the 13th century BC from the Aegean. It is found in most coastal towns which have been excavated. Philistine tombs were found at TELL FARA and these contained iron weapons and pottery coffins with anthropoid lids.

**Phillippi.** A city of Macedonia founded by Phillip II in 356 BC. Its Roman remains are impressive: it retains a circuit of walls, an ACROPOLIS, a FORUM with GYMNASIUM, MACELLUM, BATHS, and THEATER and, in addition, a series of early Christian basilical churches.

**Phoenicia, Phoenicians.** Semitic inhabitants of the coastal towns of the Levant, who established merchant colonies throughout the Mediterranean and handled a large proportion of trade in the 1st millennium BC. Local conditions made the Phoenicians turn to trade, for the coastal strip was too narrow to feed the population of the cities. On the other hand, the nearby cedars and the murex shell dyes provided items for trade, and Egyptians and Akkadians sent expeditions to obtain wood from the 3rd millennium BC onwards, while the dyeing of textiles became a Phoenician monopoly (Tyrian purple). They also developed a form of WRITING, which facilitated their business transactions, and incidentally spread its use throughout the Mediterranean world: the alphabet.

The Phoenicians sailed from the island of Aradus (Ruad), from Antaradus (Tartus) on the mainland opposite, from BYBLOS, SIDON, TYRE, and other small ports along the coast. Their colonies in the West, known as Punic, also boasted good harbors, many of which are still in use today: Mogador on the Moroccan coast, Cadiz in Spain, Valletta in Malta, Bizerta, Utica and CARTHAGE in Tunisia, Cagliari in Sardinia, Palermo and Modica in Sicily. Many Phoenician and Punic towns are inaccessibly buried under modern cities and this has meant that few architectural remains have survived, apart from tombs. An exception is the Punic city of Kerkouane on Cap Bon in Tunisia, where small, carefully planned houses are in the course of excavation by a Tunisian team (1977). The art of the Phoenicians was hybrid and, depending on the period, it shows Egyptian, Assyrian, or Greek influences. Bronze bowls and ivories show this particularly clearly for the early periods. According to tradition, the Phoenicians circumnavigated Africa c. 600 BC, sailed to Britain under Himilco c. 450 BC, sailed to the Gulf of Guinea and back under Hanno c. 425 BC, and sent expeditions into the Sahara.

**Phrygia, Phrygians.** Originally a tribe from Thrace or Macedonia, which moved into ANATOLIA with the SEA PEOPLE, c. 1200 BC. They first appear archaeologically and historically in the 8th century BC, when they founded a kingdom in Central Anatolia with their capital at GORDION. In addition, there are rockcut monuments at Yazılıkaya, near Eskishehir, and at Afyonkarahisar, and interesting terra-cottas from Pazarlı. Phrygian pottery is found at many sites on the plateau and has affinities with Greek Cycladic pottery. Phrygians were well known for their metalwork and their writing resembled Greek. Though the Phrygian kingdom was destroyed by the CIMMERIANS at the beginning of the 7th century BC, their art lived on for a couple of centuries and the rockcut monuments date to this period. Their dynastic rulers were called Midas and Gordios, and the Phrygians have therefore been linked with the Mushki, who appear in Assyrian texts from c. 1170 to c. 709 BC, and who were ruled by kings called Mita.

**Picts.** A people who occupied Northeast Scotland in the post-Roman period. They first appear in history as one of the groups of Northern barbarians who threatened HADRIAN'S WALL—their name means "Painted People" in Latin, though they called themselves *Cruithne*. Their mysterious symbolic art survives as carvings on stones which are widespread in Northern Scotland. Many unsuccessful attempts have been made to interpret the symbols. Their language is known only from a few personal names, placenames, and brief inscriptions, which suggest that it was a mixture of Celtic and some older speech. It has been suggested that the Picts were descended from the prehistoric Abernethy culture, their ancestors having migrated from Germany to Scotland in the Late Bronze Age.

Apart from their art, the Picts have few features to

The Pictish Churchyard Cross at Aberlemno, Angus, Scotland, dating from the 8th century AD.

distinguish them from the contemporary Christian CELTS, apparently occupying hillforts and sharing much in common with their neighbors and sworn enemies, the Scots. They were distinguished metalsmiths, however, and in 1958, on St. Ninian's Isle off the coast of Shetland, a hoard of Pictish silverwork was found which had been buried c. AD 800, perhaps in the face of a Viking attack. It consisted of a hanging bowl (which was probably Northumbrian), other bowls, penannular (in the form of an almost complete ring) brooches, a sword pommel, a pronged implement, a spoon, and chapes, as well as "pepper pot"-shaped objects, perhaps from a sword harness, all richly decorated. It is the richest hoard of metalwork ever to come from Christian Celtic lands.

Picts and Scots were united under Kenneth mac Alpin, King of the Scots, around AD 842, and thereafter Pictish culture disappeared.

**Piedras Negras.** A Classic Lowland Maya site located on steep, irregular terraces in the Usumacinta River valley, Guatemala. The ruins at the site are made up of ballcourts (*see* BALLGAME, MESOAMERICA), temple pyramids, courtyards, and what some have termed ceremonial "sweatbaths." Some of the finest carved stone monuments, in the form of hieroglyphic inscriptions on lintels, stelae, and walls, come from Piedras Negras and the nearby site of YAXCHILAN.

**Piki.** An archaeological phase, occurring in the Ayacucho basin in the Central Andes of Peru. Artifacts belonging to the Piki complex (5800–4550 BC) were recovered from 18 surface sites and 7 excavated caves, which produced 24 living floors. These sites are located in all the environmental zones of the region. Important faunal remains, human faeces, and plant remains were also found. Wet-season camps increased in size and were occupied for longer periods as domesticated foodstuffs and guinea pigs were introduced into the subsistence pattern.

**Pikimachay cave.** An important stratified cave in the Ayacucho basin of Central highland Peru. It has yielded the longest stratigraphy in the New World. The earliest remains are perhaps 25,000 years old and goat herders were still living in the cave when excavations began in 1970.

**Piltdown man.** *See* FRAUDS.

**Piraeus.** The harbor town, some 4 mi. (6 km) southwest of Athens. It was fortified in the 5th century BC, and linked to Athens by long walls which ensured a safe corridor to the sea for Athenian trade and supplies. There were three main harbors, and the city was regularly laid out: few traces remain, but parts of the walls and a Hellenistic THEATER are visible. (*See also* ATHENS.)

**Pisac.** Inca remains sited on a mountain of this name, overlooking the Urubamba Vilcanota valley in Peru. Located at the top, in a saddle, the most prestigious group is of finely fitted masonry and is called Intihua-

The Inca remains on the mountain of Pisac, overlooking the Urumbamba Vilcanota valley, Peru.

tana. This is a small ceremonial center, which has adjacent to it several settlements, storehouses, terraces, lookouts, and controlled access.

**Pit Grave culture.** A culture (the Russian *Yamnaya Kultura*) which appears on the Ukrainian steppes in the 3rd millennium BC, where it is represented by fortified villages and burials in pits under barrows (*see* BARROW). Small model carts show that wheeled vehicles were known, and the horse was domesticated. These pastoralist groups may have been proto-Indo-Europeans.

**Place, Victor** (1818–75). A French Consul in Mosul and the excavator of KHORSABAD (1852–54). Almost all his finds were lost while they were being shipped down the River Tigris on rafts.

**Plains Village tradition.** The name given to the group of cultures which arose on the Northeastern Plains of the United States between AD 1000 and 1800, particularly in Kansas, Nebraska, and South Dakota. Contemporaneous with the MISSISSIPPIAN TRADITION of the Eastern Woodlands, the Plains Village tradition represents a fusion of that tradition with the Plains variant of the WOODLAND TRADITION. The cultural traits of the early Plains Village tradition are: subsistence dependent on hunting, and established farming along rivers, including the cultivation of beans, squash, and maize; small settlements consisting of earth-covered timber houses; and pottery which relates to Mississippian traits, such as incised decoration and rim adornment. The Mississippian traits, however, fused with the earlier Hopewellian ones in a new environment, and were not merely transferred to a new area (*see* HOPEWELL). Cultures such as the Nebraska, the Smoky Hill, and the Upper Republican exemplify the period

with timber houses constructed with four central posts. The fireplace was in the center of these dwellings, with the smoke ascending through a central hole in the roof, and storage pits were grouped beneath the floor. Mass burial was normal in this period. Many tools were made of bone, bison scapulae being used as digging implements. Bone wrist guards were made in the Upper Republican phase and decorated with incised lines. The Nebraska phase pipe, often made of pottery, was usually curved and sometimes was in the form of an animal or human effigy (see EFFIGY PIPE). The Upper Republican pipe was more usually made of stone and set at a right angle. In pottery types the degree of influence from the two main traditions varied: the Upper Republican pottery possesses stronger Woodland traits, such as cord roughened exteriors, while the Nebraska pottery is smooth finished.

In the period leading up to the arrival of Europeans, the cultural sequence and traits are less well established. In the 15th century, however, the Upper Republican settlements were abandoned, perhaps because of the movement of nomadic invaders from the Western Plains. It may be that for this reason some of the large village sites of the subsequent Lower Loup phase were fortified. The Lower Loup, in Eastern Nebraska, may have been the cultural ancestor of the historical Pawnee tribe. In general, it is possible to say that only the historical Arikara, Mandan, and Hidatsa tribes are descended from the Plains Village cultures, although the sequence has not been fully traced.

**Plano point.** The name given to the projectile points developed from the Clovis and Folsom points of the BIG GAME HUNTING TRADITION, after 8000 BC, in North America (see CLOVIS POINT; FOLSOM). Plano points are unfluted, large lanceolate stone forms made by pressure flaking techniques, rather than by the percussion techniques used for earlier ones. They have been found over a wide area of what, in early prehistoric times, would have been the Plains Grasslands of Western North America. There are two main types of Plano points. The first is called Plainview, after a bison kill-site in Texas: these points have concave bases and thinned ends for hafting, and they date from 7800 to 5100 BC. There is no absolute distinction between Plainview points and the second group, which are known as Parallel flaked points. However the latter, best exemplified by the Agate Basin culture of Wyoming, are much longer, slenderer, and more finely made than Plainview points, and they have flat or concave bases.

**Playa Hermosa.** A site, on the Central Peruvian coast, north of Lima, which has yielded an assemblage of pre-ceramic period tools, textiles, and marine resources, and evidence of cultivated corn, lima beans, and chili peppers, for the period c. 2300–2100 BC.

**Plumbate.** A type of very distinctive, finely made Pre-columbian pottery from Mesoamerica, which had a high percentage of iron compounds: upon firing, the ceramic surface acquired a hard, lustrous vitrified surface, often with a metallic shine. There were two types: San Juan Plumbate, which is associated with the Classic Period and the Highland Maya; and Tohil Plumbate, associated with the Postclassic Period. (See also COTZUMAHUALPA.)

**Pollen analysis.** See PALAEOBOTANY.

**Pompeii.** A Roman town lying at the foot of Vesuvius, in Italy, and covered by volcanic ash in the eruption of AD 79. The town was originally a market center and port, and consideration of the town plan has suggested how it grew from the small nucleus of the original settlement, perhaps as early as the 8th century BC, to its full extent of 160 ac. (65 ha) in Roman imperial times. The site was discovered in 1748 and subsequent excavation has now uncovered over two-thirds of the town. Most important in the town's history was the phase of Samnite occupation from the 5th century BC, marked towards the beginning of the 3rd century BC by strong Hellenistic influences—particularly on the main forum and public buildings (theater and baths)—and by the use of Hellenistic designs on wall paintings in private houses.

In 89 BC Pompeii was besieged by the Roman general Sulla and, together with the rest of surrounding Campania, it became subject to Rome and a new suburb (a military colony) was laid out next to the old town. Private houses and their decoration now became more Roman in style, and it is from the many extant examples of wall painting at Pompeii that the four main styles of Roman wall decoration of the period 200 BC–AD 80 have been distinguished. An earthquake in AD 62 left parts of the city in ruins, and meant that there was much rebuilding in Roman imperial style before the final disaster.

**Pont du Gard.** A Roman aqueduct in the form of a three-storied arched bridge over the River Gard near NÎMES in France. It is c. 300 yd. (274 m) long, and the concrete-lined water channel stands 160 ft. (49 m) above the river.

**Porcelain.** A ceramic ware made from kaolin and felspar and fired to a temperature of 1350°C. At this temperature, the glaze fuses with the body to make a fine translucent vessel. Porcelain was developed by the Chinese from a long tradition of making stonewares of a white clay. The earliest proto-porcelains were made in the T'ANG DYNASTY (AD 618–906), and true porcelain was made in the SUNG DYNASTY (AD 960–1279). It was so much valued by the rest of the world that Chinese porcelain was exported to Indonesia, Africa, the Middle East, and Europe. (See CERAMICS, CHINA.)

**Postclassic Period, Mesoamerica.** See MESOAMERICA.

**Potassium-argon dating.** A method, developed in 1946, which has replaced uranium dating as the principal technique for dating geological sequences. It is based on the breakdown of radioactive potassium (Potassium 40) into Argon 40, a gas trapped in the rocks in which it forms. It takes 1,300 million years for half the Potassium 40 to disappear.

## Pottery, Europe.

*Prehistoric.* Although it is now known that there was a long Neolithic period before the use of pottery was known, there is a clear relationship between the use of ceramic containers and the more sedentary patterns of life which became common in the postglacial period. Living in mud-brick structures and cooking their food in hearths and ovens, early Neolithic villages in Anatolia and surrounding areas were familiar, by the 7th millennium BC, with the properties of baked clay and its use for linings and refractory structures. From here it was only a short step to the manufacture of portable containers of fictile materials; and pottery came with the other Neolithic arts as part of the package which arrived in Europe.

Such pottery was not made on the wheel, but usually built up in coils; though it may also have been formed from lumps or slabs. Such products could be very thin walled and finely finished, and in addition could easily be decorated by the addition of mineral-rich slips or paints—finely suspended particles of clay applied to the surface.

While pottery could never have been made in every household, because of the limited distribution of good potting clays, for much of prehistory it was produced on a domestic basis, with certain villages specializing in its production. When made in primitive conditions, with rapidly fluctuating firing temperatures, the fabric has to be fairly open to avoid cracking, and hence fillers such as grit or crushed sherds were often added. To make such vessels less porous, the surface would often be polished with a pebble when the pot was "leather hard" before firing, producing a burnished effect.

During the European Bronze and Iron Ages, that is, the last two millennia BC, pottery continued to be made for the most part by the techniques of coil- and ring building. The potter's wheel was introduced in the 1st millennium BC, though in many areas only a slow wheel or tournette was used for a long time, simply to give a finer finish to coil- and ring-built vessels. But, by the 1st century BC, pottery was being thrown on fast wheels throughout most of Europe except the Germanic North, Ireland, and parts of Britain. As in the Neolithic, Bronze and Iron Age pottery acted as a medium for artistic expression, and an enormous variety of shapes and patterns was devised, exploiting a wide range of decorative techniques.

During these two millennia pots were commonly used for a quite new purpose, as containers for the cremated remains of the dead. Although most pottery was probably produced on a small scale, during the late 1st millennium large ceramic industries gradually became established in many parts of barbarian Europe, particularly after the introduction of the fast wheel. From Neolithic times down to the end of prehistory, pottery was often widely distributed in Europe, sometimes much more than a 100 mi. (161 km) from its place of manufacture. However, in many cases this may have been due to its use as containers for other materials: for example, the wide distribution of Late Iron Age graphite wares in Central Europe is likely to have re-

A handmade vase in black fabric, with simple burnished patterns, from Champagne, France, 4th century BC.

sulted from their use as containers for salt, which was then a highly prized and widely traded commodity.

*Greek.* The earliest pottery in Neolithic Greece (from *c.* 6000 BC) is handmade with a burnished surface. It is found throughout the Greek world, and on the mainland it was often painted with white spiral or linear decoration. Early Bronze Age pottery in Crete was influenced both from Eastern trading contacts and by the introduction of the wheel. The "Camares"-style ware of *c.* 1900–1700 BC has white-and-red painted decorations of linear or stylized plant form on a black ground. Minoan pottery of 1600–1400 BC reversed this decorative scheme, with black-on-white decoration, and naturalistic designs, including floral and marine subjects. Mycenaean pottery displays reddish brown decoration on a buff ground, taking its main inspiration from the designs and decoration on Late Minoan vases, with some new shapes, including the open handled kylix and the "palace style" jar. The designs later became more and more stylized, until they were reduced in the "sub-Mycenaean" period to GEOMETRIC decoration.

Pottery of the archaic period (the Protogeometric style) was made chiefly at Athens and in Attica and was decorated with neat compass-drawn circles, bands of color and pattern on a buff ground: this style of pottery has been attributed to the Dorians, who invaded Greece in the 12th century BC (*see* GREECE, ARCHAEOLOGY OF). It grew by degrees into Geometric pottery, with meander and zigzag patterns, but, by the 8th century BC, these were giving way to figured scenes.

Closer contact during the 8th century BC with Eastern influences brought a period in which an "Orientalizing" style flourished (*see also* PAINTING), featuring animal and figured scenes and stylized floral decoration. Experimental attempts at polychrome designs, outline drawing, and incised lines now appear, but by the end of the 7th century BC, the Athenian school of potters had gained a substantial hold of the markets with their black-figured style, in which most of the design is in black paint on a red ground, glazed hard in firing. The area of decorative pattern is cut down, and the body of the vase bears a figured (usually mythological) subject.

A further technique was introduced in about 530 BC, in which the design was left in red, and the background filled with black paint (red-figured technique). Parallel with this, a form of white ground pottery, with at first black and later polychrome designs, was mainly used in funerary deposits.

Classical Greek vases were made in a number of standard forms: storage jars (amphorae), mixing bowls (craters), jugs (hydria, oinochoë), drinking cups (cantharus, rhyton, kylix), small jars (aryballos, pyxis), and ritual or ceremonial vessels. Many of these were traditional forms, but few were used by the Romans.

Towards the end of the 4th century BC, the production of Attic red-figured vases ceased, and vases with relief decoration began to appear. Pottery in general was modeled on metalwork during the Hellenistic period, and the black fabric traditional from Athens was changed to a bright orange red in production centers in Asia Minor. This style was adopted by the Romans and influenced Arretine ware and its successors, Gallic and local TERRA SIGILLATA.

*Italian and Roman.* Pottery of the Neolithic and Bronze Ages in Italy is characteristically handmade ware, of dark fabric, but occasionally with light painted decoration. This ware continued in use into the Iron Age in a variety of local forms, only being wheelmade from about the 7th century BC in Etruria, with incised and later relief decoration. About 700 BC, painted pottery very closely derived from contemporary Greek wares is found at some centers—notably at Caere, where a remarkable series of large jars (hydrae) are best explained as the work of expatriate Ionian potters. By the end of the 6th century BC, Greek imported pottery had captured most of the Italian market, though local imitations are also found.

A school of red-figured potters became established in Southern Italy at the end of the 5th century BC. Modifications, such as the introduction of relief-figured vases and lighter painted designs, became more common, and the full impact of the East Greek red-buff relief-figured wares was only absorbed *c.* 30 BC, with the opening of the Arretine factories in Northern Italy.

With the production of Arretine ware, the forms of which were based ultimately on metalwork, Roman pottery was standardized for several centuries. Arretine, a fine red-glazed pottery bearing figured scenes of great

sophistication, was in production from 30 BC to the middle of the 1st century AD, when it was overtaken by mass production of similar sorts of pottery at several centers (*see* TERRA SIGILLATA).

*Medieval.* Islamic potters were unsurpassed in medieval Europe. In Roman times Near Eastern potters had produced glazed quartz fritwares, and in Iran, Mesopotamia, and Syria alkaline glazed pottery had been made since Achaemenid times (550–330 BC). Lead glazes were also found in the Eastern provinces of the Roman Empire. These traditions continued until around AD 800, when contacts with T'ang China provided new impetus through their white porcelains and stonewares. From the 12th to the 14th centuries AD, Sung white wares were influential and from the 15th century onwards Ming blue-and-white wares provided inspiration. Islamic pottery was used for secular purposes, and due to a Muslim prohibition on precious metals for vessels, clay dishes were decorated with metallic pigments to give a metallic effect. Ornament consisted of geometric and floral patterns, some with Arabic inscriptions.

Byzantine pottery was at first uninspired, but glazed earthenware, modeled on Islamic, gained popularity in the 8th and 9th centuries AD, when vessels of precious metals became too costly. The Byzantines favored whitish fabrics and canary-yellow or green glazes. Molded decoration, after the manner of Roman *sigillata*, was sometimes employed. Centers of pottery production were Constantinople and Corinth. Under the Macedonians (AD 867–1057), polychrome ware was developed, with vitreous colors employed on a white clay ground, sometimes covered with a transparent glaze. This is

A medieval glazed jug from England, dating from the late 13th century AD.

among the finest Byzantine pottery. From the 10th century *sgraffito* ware was developed, a type of pottery popular in the Islamic world: a pattern incised onto the vessel revealed a different colored clay underneath, a technique borrowed from metalworking. Colored *sgraffito* ware was popular at the time of the Crusades.

Europe lost the art of glazing pottery in the 5th century AD, but it was reintroduced to Italy in the 8th and 9th centuries, where the earliest examples were made in Rome and are known as Forum ware. Around the same time red-painted wares appear in Italy, and both glazed and red-painted wares spread to France, where they are found in the late 8th century. In England glazed pottery (Stamford ware) appears in the 9th century, and it appears in the Low Countries around the same time. In Germany lead-glazed pottery never proved very popular, but red-painted wares were mass-produced in the Badorf and Pingsdorf kilns. From the 12th century onwards, proto-stonewares replaced the products of Pingsdorf in Germany, and stoneware proper evolved in the 14th century. In France, the Saintonge region produced characteristic parrot-beaked jugs in whitish wares with bright green glazes; these, and the Saintonge polychrome wares, with patterns of a quasi-heraldic nature done in different colors on a light ground, were widely exported, as were richly decorated jugs from Rouen. In England, medieval pottery reached its peak in the late 13th–early 14th century, when the most distinctive products were glazed jugs, sometimes with rich applied decoration of human and animal figures. Cooking pots were unglazed. From the 14th century onwards ornament was less varied, and forms of vessels tended to copy those of metal. Jugs remained the main products, wood being used for plates and cups. Other types of vessels included storage jars, urinals, and richly decorated ewers, usually in animal shapes, known as aquamaniles. In Italy tin-glazed earthenware was developed in the late medieval period, and gave rise to *maiolica*, which reached its peak in the Italian Renaissance.

**Pottery, South America.** Pottery was first made *c.* 3000 BC in Northwest South America, and after 2000 BC in the Central Andes. It has played a critical role as an indication of cultural change and distribution because of its durability and variability. For this reason chronologies of areas in which pottery occurs are based on its forms and decorative traits. The technical excellence of the pottery was achieved without the use of the pottery wheel or glazes. Ceremonial and utility wares, pottery figurines and objects were widely produced and decorative techniques included a range of modeling, *appliqué*, and incising methods as well as slip (liquid clay) painting, post-fired resin painting, resist (negative) painting, and burnished finishes. Reduced and oxidized firing techniques were used, controlling the level of oxygen present in the process to influence the characteristics of the final product.

*(Pottery from other parts of the world can be found under the country or culture concerned and the type or name of the ware. See especially* CERAMICS, CHINA; CERAMICS, JAPAN.*)*

**Preceramic Period.** A period of South American chronology. The first inhabitants of South America were hunters, whose only surviving artifacts are stone tools. Preceramic chronologies are based on the variations in the traits of the stone assemblages. Better preservation at later sites indicates that hunters and gatherers used stone, wood, and bone tools, and stone bowls, gourds, baskets, and leather bags as containers. On the Peruvian coast, the Pacific Littoral tradition developed to the point where large ceremonial buildings were constructed before ceramics were introduced. In some areas, notably in Patagonia, ceramics were never made.

**Preclassic Period, Mesoamerica.** *See* MESOAMERICA.

**Pre-Eskimo archaeology.** If man entered the New World across the Bering Strait 20,000–40,000 years ago, the earliest traces of human occupation of America should be in Alaska, although the first camp sites are now likely to be covered by sea. The earliest-known culture is probably that called BRITISH MOUNTAIN CULTURE, which is located near the Yukon Arctic coast close to the Canadian-Alaskan border. There, at Engigstciak on the Firth River, a series of artifacts, perhaps developed from the Upper Palaeolithic of Eastern Siberia, have been found. The crude implements and chopping tools from the British Mountain complex are not directly associated with other early cultures, and are not well dated. However other finds of projectile points have been made in the Western Arctic. A few fluted stone points, similar to the Clovis points of the BIG GAME HUNTING TRADITION, have been found. Plano points have also been recovered and dated to 8000–4000 BC (*see* CLOVIS POINT; PLANO POINT). Another culture well represented in the Western Arctic is the OLD CORDILLERAN TRADITION, with its bipointed leaf-shaped points. These may have been either the forerunners of the Old Cordilleran tradition or representatives of it.

Later cultures, 6000–2000 BC, have more coherent sequences with increasing specialization of toolkits. In the sub-Arctic forests of Southwestern Yukon the first phase of the Northwest microblade tradition, called Little Arm, 5500–4000 BC, is located. Caribou and elk were hunted, using the characteristic lanceolate projectile points, but in the succeeding phases the toolkits become more specialized and the tools smaller. Diagnostic of the Northwest microblade tradition were the tongue-shaped cores, from which small blades were struck. The Arctic Small Tool tradition, 4000–1000 BC, spread from Alaska across the Arctic to Greenland and it is also characterized by small tools, made from fine pressure flaked blades. Many of the tools were retained in later Eskimo cultures, and it is therefore the first complex with some continuity with the Eskimo tradition. The type-site is Iyatayet on Cape Denbigh on the Western coast of Alaska, where the people used harpoons, fitted with blades, to hunt walrus, and latterly made arrowheads to tip arrows in the pursuit of caribou. Because no pithouses have been found it is assumed that the people of Cape Denbigh did not winter on the coast but moved inland. Unlike the later inhabitants of the area they made neither pottery nor stone lamps.

The final culture of Pre-Eskimo archaeology is the Aleutian Core and Blade industry. The Aleutian Islands once formed part of the land bridge between Asia and Alaska. On the island of Anangula, large blades and burins have been found, perhaps dating to 10,000 BC. It may be that elements of this culture persisted until 1000 BC, since large thick blades of that date have been found on the Island of Umnak. The historical population of the Aleutian Islands was separated from that of the mainland, and this isolation may date back to the Pre-Eskimo period, thus perhaps accounting for the persistence of this industry.

**Prehistory, study of.** Prehistory embraces the entire span of human development before written records. It begins and ends at different times in different continents. In Africa it began over 2 million years ago, in Asia over 1 million years ago, and in most parts of Western and Central Europe not much before 0.5 million years ago. Prehistoric man arrived in other areas later still: in European Russia not much before 100,000 years ago, in Australia not much before 40,000 years ago, and in America possibly not before 20,000 years ago.

Prehistory ended in Iraq *c.* 3400 BC, when Sumer became a literate civilization. In Greece it was around 1000 to 600 BC, and in Italy several centuries later. In most of Northern and Western Europe, prehistory lasted until the Roman Empire or later. In Australia it lasted until the 18th century AD, and in parts of New Guinea until the 20th century.

The study of prehistory involves the excavation, or at least the collection, of material traces of prehistoric man. The most common of these are artifacts like stone tools or pottery. Archaeologists also recover traces of structures, which can be as simple as a few stones supporting a former post of a hut, or as impressive as the banks of a massive fort like Maiden Castle in Dorset, England, which is easily visible without excavation.

A standard method of study is typology, wherein artifacts are arranged, without necessarily any knowledge of their function, in a developmental sequence. The prehistorian tries to understand the societies he uncovers in terms of their economy, their adaptation to their environment, and their place in the evolution of culture.

**Priene.** A small Hellenistic Greek town in Asia Minor, important as an almost completely excavated settlement of the 4th century BC. It is crowned by an ACROPOLIS, and the city walls are 1½ mi. (3 km) long. The street system is laid out on a rectangular grid, with house blocks, private houses, and public buildings: the AGORA, BOULEUTERION, PRYTANEIUM, STADIUM, GYMNASIUM, THEATER, and various temples.

**Prytaneium.** A building for the accommodation of the prytaneis, the administrative officials who at Athens and other Greek cities were chosen by lot to arrange state business of all kinds. The prytaneium, perhaps with its origin in the palaces of the tyrants or kings, combined official with residential functions. At Athens, it had a central courtyard with rooms round it; the so-called THOLOS, a round building serving as an office, was built nearby. Many cities followed the "democratic" Athenian pattern and had similar buildings.

**Ptah.** An ancient Egyptian creator god, who was worshiped from the earliest times and throughout the Dynastic Period. His chief cult center was at MEMPHIS. From the 1st Dynasty onwards, the sacred Apis bull (*see* SERAPEUM) was considered to be the earthly manifestation of Ptah, and was quartered near the latter's great temple at Memphis.

**Pucara.** A large ceremonial site in the Northern Lake Titicaca basin of Bolivia, dating from *c.* 200 BC to AD 600. It has a horseshoe-shaped enclosure made of huge dressed stone blocks, subterranean burial vaults, and stone sculpture.

**Pueblo.** *See* ANASAZI.

**Pueblo Bonito.** A large Pueblo site in the Chaco Canyon area of New Mexico. It is the largest of 12 sites in the Chaco Canyon, each of which consist of interjoining

Pueblo Bonito, the largest site in the Chaco Canyon, New Mexico, and dated to AD 919–1067.

apartment houses. Pueblo Bonito was built in the shape of a D: it is 525 ft. (160 m) long and covers 2.4 ac. (1 ha). In the middle of the D is an open space, and around its edge are a series of kivas, or round ceremonial chambers (*see* KIVA). The windows and doors face into the courtyard as a defensive measure against marauding Athabascan groups in search of water. The site has been dated by DENDROCHRONOLOGY to AD 919–1067. Along the outside walls, the buildings rise up four stories, each level constructed with wooden beam floors. Much of the site remains, including some of the floors.

**Puerto Hormiga.** A small site from the Caribbean Gulf coast, Colombia, which has yielded stratified deposits containing pottery. Sand-tempered pottery with wide-lined incising and *appliqué* decoration occurs in the upper levels, above layers with predominantly fiber-tempered pottery. The next to oldest level has been dated at 3090 BC, the earliest date for pottery in the New World. Typologically, the pottery from Valdivia in Ecuador, *c.* 2700–1500 BC, the pottery from Rancho Peludo in Venezuela, *c.* 2820 BC, the Stalling Island fiber-tempered pottery of Florida and Georgia, *c.* 2500–2000 BC, as well as other early pottery could well be derived from the kind of pottery occurring in the earliest levels of Puerto Hormiga.

**Pullman.** A landmark in both town planning and industrial archaeology. This company town, outside Chicago, Ill., United States, built 1880–84, was conceived by George Pullman, inventor of the sleeping car, and designed by the celebrated Chicago architect, Solon Beman. The successful integration of housing, factory, and community buildings made Pullman unique in 19th-century America and very rarely paralleled since. Much of what was created is still to be seen.

**Putnam F. W.** (1839–1915). Curator of the Peabody Museum, Harvard, from 1875 to 1909, and Professor of American Archaeology and Ethnology at Harvard University. He is important both as an archaeologist, who classified and described finds, and as an administrator and archaeological sponsor. He was particularly interested in the mounds of the Ohio valley, and also in evidence for the early antiquity of man in America. He organized excavations at the Turner and Great Serpent mounds, and arranged that the latter should be bought for the Peabody Museum in order that it should not be destroyed. He is most important for his insistence on scientific techniques: surveying, digging, drawing cross-sections of excavations, and plotting finds.

**Pylos.** A site on the Southwestern tip of the Peloponnese, the center of an area with extensive Mycenaean finds. At Ano Englianos, some miles to the north of the present town, the remains of a Mycenaean palace and township have been found. The destruction by fire of the latest phases of this palace baked a hoard of clay tablets written in LINEAR B, which record the business of the palace in its last days. (*See also* GREECE, ARCHAEOLOGY OF; MYCENAEAN ARCHAEOLOGY.)

**Pyramid.** Although the most famous Egyptian pyramids are the three at Giza, opposite Cairo, which were among the ancient wonders of the world, there are over 80 in Egypt and ancient Nubia (now the Sudan). Pyramids were exclusively royal burial places, built especially during the Old Kingdom (*see* EGYPT), but also during the Middle Kingdom. In Nubia they were used as tombs during the 25th Dynasty.

The earliest pyramid, indeed the earliest monumental stone building in Egypt, is the stepped structure at Saqqara, constructed by Imhotep for his Pharaoh Djoser during the 3rd Dynasty, *c.* 2650 BC. This prototype does not seem to have been originally conceived as a pyramid, but evolved when a rectangular-shaped MASTABA (the typical royal tomb of the first two Dynasties) was squared and then had five smaller square mastabas, each decreasing in area, set on top of it. Although the steps were cased in fine quality limestone, there was no attempt to fill them in. The appearance of six steps gave the Step Pyramid its name.

The earliest pyramid was the 3rd-Dynasty Step Pyramid of Djoser at Saqqara (above). This eventually gave rise to the true pyramid, such as the magnificent 4th-Dynasty Great Pyramid of Cheops at Giza (shown below with the Sphinx of Chephren).

After Djoser, each subsequent king of the 3rd Dynasty began to build a pyramid but because, in general, only their substructures were completed, these tombs were lost until they were excavated in modern times: the step pyramid of Sekhemkhat was only found in 1953. Huni, the last king of the Dynasty, has left a pyramid at Meidum, but it was completed by his successor, Sneferu, who built two pyramids of his own at Dahshur, the northern of which is the first true pyramid. Thereafter nearly every king of the 4th, 5th, and 6th Dynasties built himself a pyramid tomb, which stood at the center of a complex composed of queens' pyramids, a pyramid temple and a valley temple joined by a causeway, and surrounded by streets of courtiers' mastaba tombs. But after the massive structures built at Giza by Sneferu's son and grandson, Khufu and Khafre, pyramids became smaller and more poorly built. The pyramid of Wenis, the last king of the 5th Dynasty, was the first to contain the so-called Pyramid Texts, which were to appear in all 6th-Dynasty pyramids.

Since true pyramids can only be built on open ground, the princes of the 11th Dynasty at THEBES adapted the form to the local terrain when they capped their rockcut tombs with brick-built pyramidal superstructures. The kings of the 12th Dynasty constructed true pyramids once more, but they were of brick and in the Fayum area, at Lisht, Hawara, el-Lahun, and Dahshur, near their new capital city. All the Old Kingdom pyramids lay further north in a line running from Dahshur, through Meidum, Saqqara, Abusir, and Giza to Abu Roash. The Theban princes of the 17th Dynasty once more capped their rockcut tombs with brick pyramids but the pyramid was never used again after that as a royal tomb in Egypt. Much later, in the Sudan, the Egyptianized Nubian kings, who formed Egypt's 25th Dynasty (*c.* 750–656 BC), were buried under sharply angled pyramids, clearly inspired by those in the north.

**Qaluyu.** A site and cultural phase of the EARLY HORIZON Period, in the Northern Titicaca area of Peru. The site covers several acres and the pottery style is decorated either by incisions or with simple painted geometric motifs in red on cream.

**Qandahar.** A site in Afghanistan of particular interest for its Classical associations. Excavations were begun there in 1974 and much Islamic material has come to light. Pottery of the Timurid period (late 14th–15th century AD) is particularly important for the valuable type series it has provided.

**Qaṣr al-Ḥair.** Two archaeological sites in the Syrian desert, Qaṣr al-Ḥair al-Gharbī (the western one), and Qaṣr al-Ḥair al-Sharqī (the eastern one). The former was excavated between 1936 and 1938. In addition to Roman hydraulic installations, parts of a Ghassanid monastery, a *khān* (caravanserai) with a small mosque, a fortified palace, a bath house, and the remains of an extensive garden and garden barrage were found. These Islamic remains date from the reign of Hishām (AD 724–743); they were abandoned in the middle of the 8th century, and briefly reoccupied in the 12th and 13th centuries. Notable amongst the finds were pieces of stucco with vegetal designs, wall paintings, and some human figures of stone.

Excavations during the 1960s at Qaṣr al-Ḥair al-Sharqī revealed the sequence of development of the site and its various functions. The plan had been conceived in the Omayyad period and completed in the Abbasid period, and it consisted of an administrative center with areas for minor industry, trading, and storage. The town had been founded for political, military, and commercial purposes, and the building previously thought to be a palace was reidentified as a caravanserai.

**Qatna.** A site at Mishrife near Homs in Syria. It is a huge square site with ramparts and an upper town, which is fortified and has a glacis (bank). It was excavated by the French who found late 3rd- and 2nd-millennium BC shrines, a ruined palace, and tombs of the second half of the 3rd millennium BC. (*See* SYRIA-PALESTINE.)

**Quechua** (or Quichua). The name of a prehistoric Andean province and people who spoke this language, which also became the official Inca language. Quechua was used for the purposes of government and for all communications between the provinces under Inca rule.

**Quern.** The name (Old English in derivation) for a rubbing stone or grinder. The "saddle" quern consists of a concave lower stone, in which a smaller stone was rubbed to grind corn and other substances. The "rotary" quern consists of two circular stone discs, the upper of which is rotated by hand. This was introduced late in European prehistory. (*See also* METATE.)

**Quetzalcoatl.** There is much confusion about the name Quetzalcoatl because it is not only the name of a god, but also of an apparently historical person, as well as the official title of a high priest among the AZTECS. The literal meaning is Quetzal bird-snake, and, by association, feathered serpent.

The historical individual was Ce Acatl Topoltzin Quetzalcoatl, which means One Reed Prince Feathered Serpent. He was the son of a Tolteca-Chichimeca leader named Mixcoatl, Cloud Serpent, and of a Culhua princess, Chimalma, who died at his birth in a year One Reed, which corresponds to AD 843. He was brought up by grandparents and the priests at Xochicalco. He became the ruler of the TOLTECS in the year AD 883, and his reign began a period of material prosperity for the Toltecs. In his capacity of High Priest he introduced the practice of auto-sacrifice, or blood letting from the tongue and/or ears. He incurred the hostility of the adherents of the more barbarous worship of Tezcatlipoca by his efforts to curb the excesses of human sacrifice. Finally, he was driven into exile in AD 897.

There is a legendary account of this event in which the actors are the gods themselves. According to the story, Tezcatlipoca made Quetzalcoatl drunk, during which state he committed incest. With returning sobriety he realized his sin and as a penance went into exile towards the East with his followers. There is little doubt that this legend refers to the departure of the historic Ce Acatl Topoltzin Quetzalcoatl and his followers from Tula to the Yucatan. It was to have great importance, not only for the MAYA, but also for the Cortez expedition because, according to the legend, the god Quetzalcoatl promised to return. Centuries later Moctezuma, hearing of the arrival of the Spaniards, believed this to be the long promised return of the god Quetzalcoatl. Accordingly, instead of resisting the invasion, he sent to Cortez the ceremonial regalia of Quetzalcoatl as gifts and adopted a vacillating policy towards him.

**Quiani.** A shell mound, about 2.4 mi. (4 km) south of Arica on the Northern Chilean coast. Excavation has revealed a complex characterized by shell fishhooks and leaf points in the lowest levels, dating from *c.* 4000 BC. BOLA stones and crude choppers appear in the upper layers, *c.* 250 BC.

**Quipu.** A string and knot device used by the Inca of Peru for recording statistical information. The positions and formations of the knots tied on the strings, which hang from a cord, provided decimalized numerical information on topics identified by the color of the string. Although the Incas did not have writing, the quipus could also be used as aids in recording historical and liturgical information accumulated by the government.

**Quirigua.** An important Classic Period Maya site in the Motagua River valley of Guatemala, famous for the tallest sandstone stelae known. Giant boulder sculptures of mythical monsters and animals are also located there. The site is not far from the larger Maya site of COPAN, to which Quirigua may have owed political allegiance.

**Quishqui Puncu.** A preceramic site from the Calleyon de Huaylas in Peru that has yielded artifacts and fine leaf points which date from *c.* 4000 BC. Stratigraphy of the site was not well defined and sherds are often mixed with the stone tools, so that exact definition of the preceramic phase is not clear.

**Qumran.** The site of the discovery, in caves in 1947, of the first Dead Sea Scrolls. This led to the excavation of the headquarters of a religious community and of a large cemetery at Khirbet Qumran, both of the Greco-Roman period. (*See* ISRAEL; SYRIA-PALESTINE.)

**Radiocarbon dating.** Radiocarbon dating is, for the archaeologist, the most important byproduct of nuclear science. Its method was first demonstrated in 1946 by the American physicist, Willard Libby. Carbon contains a number of radioactive isotopes and one—carbon-14, or radiocarbon—is used for dating. This is produced in the upper atmosphere by cosmic rays, is oxidized to carbon dioxide, and mixes with non-radioactive carbon dioxide in the atmosphere. Carbon-14 is then absorbed by plants in the process of photosynthesis of carbon dioxide and passes into all living matter. It is therefore present in all organic material, which can be dated because, after the death of an organic substance, no new carbon is absorbed, and the radioactive isotope decays at a known rate. Thus the amount of radiocarbon left in a sample can be compared with its constant percentage in the carbon of living matter by counting the number of radioactive emissions. The decay is counted in "half lives," one half life (the figure generally used is $5730 \pm 40$ years) being the time it takes for the carbon-14 to decay to one half its original amount. Dates are usually given BP (before the present), the present being AD 1950.

Materials best for dating are wood (preferably as charcoal, whose chemical structure does not change during deposition), peat, seeds, hair, textiles, skin, and leather. Bone and antler can also be used but are often contaminated by the surrounding earth from which they may have absorbed fresh carbon. A few grams of organic material are generally sufficient for dating, except when the sample contains a very small percentage of carbon (e.g. uncharred bone and antler) when as much as $3\frac{1}{2}$ oz. (100 g) may be needed.

*The bristlecone pine.* It is now known that the production of carbon-14 has fluctuated in the past, possibly due to changes in the earth's magnetic field which may have affected the amount of cosmic radiation reaching the earth's atmosphere. It is also possible that the size of the carbon exchange reservoir may have been inconstant, e.g., during the Ice Age, when large amounts of carbon were locked up in the frozen water. The burning of fossil fuel (coal and oil) since the Industrial Revolution in the 18th century has reduced radioactivity in atmospheric carbon, whereas atomic weapon testing since World War II has introduced extra amounts of radiocarbon. Accurate dating by the radiocarbon method must therefore allow for these anomalies so that radiocarbon years correspond with calendar years.

DENDROCHRONOLOGY (or tree-ring dating) has so far proved the most promising method of correcting the more recent carbon-14 dates. When radiocarbon dates are compared with independently dated material, e.g. from Dynastic Egypt, discrepancies occur. Carbon-14 dates usually appear slightly younger than the historical dates. Tree rings (a tree grows a new ring every year) have therefore been used to correct radiocarbon dates of some samples where no historical dates exist, particularly those of the bristlecone pine (*Pinus aristata*), which grows at high altitudes in the mountains of California and lives to a great age—often thousands of years—due to unusual environmental conditions. Samples from these trees can be dated by tree-ring and radiocarbon dating and the difference between them calculated. The consequent gap between calendrical and radiocarbon dates appears to increase with the age of the sample.

Calibration of carbon-14 dates with bristlecone pine tree-ring dates has not, however, been universally accepted by the practitioners of radiocarbon dating.

**Raetia.** A Roman province lying north of the Alps in Europe, incorporating parts of Switzerland and Bavaria. Its capital was Augusta Vindelicorum (Augsburg).

**Railways.** In comparison with other branches of industrial archaeology, railways, windmills, and canals have received much enthusiasm and informed attention. Railway museums are numerous and popular, while railway societies and books and magazines on railway history proliferate throughout the world. Railway archaeology, on the other hand, has not infrequently lost its way, so that the fundamental reason for study and conservation—to increase our awareness and understanding of the past—tends to be forgotten, and preservation for its own sake becomes the goal. What is needed is a process of recording, interpretation, and, in a few exceptional instances, conservation, which illustrates the technical achievements, social implications, and follies of a century and a half of railways—a railway archaeology which provides answers to the question "Why?" as well as to "What?"

So far as the civil engineering work is concerned, the main point of archaeology is to increase the sense of wonder and admiration: how were these mammoth tasks carried out in such a short time with the equipment and materials then available? The list of even major triumphs is a long one: the Ormaizteguí viaduct (1864) on the main line from Madrid to Irún in Spain; the Oslo–Bergen line in Norway (1883–1909), with 28 of its 190 mi. (45 of its 305 km) in tunnels; the three-tiered viaduct (1845–51) over the Göltzchtal between Reichenbach and Plauen in East Germany; Brunel's Royal Albert Bridge (1859) over the Tamar at Saltash in England; the zigzag tunnel at Field, B.C., Canada. All these are fortunately still in use: it is extremely unlikely that they could ever be preserved as mere monuments.

**Railway stations.** One of the most interesting and most mishandled branches of industrial archaeology. All over the world, the typical railway station has been, from the

The railway station at Drevja, Norway. Built in 1864, it is the oldest railway station in Norway.

beginning, the modest example serving a rural area or a small town, but the category of station most likely to attract the attention of both preservationists and archaeologists is the grand building in a major city. There are exceptions: Mount Clare Station, Baltimore, United States (1830), the oldest surviving station in the world, is lovingly preserved as the centerpiece of the Baltimore and Ohio Museum.

**Ramesses II.** An Egyptian king of the 19th Dynasty, who reigned from *c.* 1304 to 1237 BC. After a series of campaigns in Syria and Palestine, he concluded a peace treaty, whose text is still extant, with his chief enemy, the king of the HITTITES, and later married one of his daughters. Among his numerous building works are the Ramesseum (his funerary temple at THEBES) and the rock-cut temples of Abu Simbel. Although a large number of inscribed objects bearing his name have been uncovered at TANIS, they were probably carried there at a later date from his Delta capital at Pi-Ramessu.

**Ras Shamra.** *See* UGARIT.

**Ravenna.** A city on the Adriatic in Northern Italy, almost surrounded by marshlands. It became a Roman city in 49 BC, and was the base of the Adriatic fleet. It was selected by the late Roman Emperor Honorius as his capital because of its security, and retains many remains of early Christian churches from the early 5th century AD and later.

**Rawlinson, General Sir Henry Creswicke** (1810–95). A British Consul in Baghdad. He copied the BEHISTUN inscription, which he deciphered and published with translation and notes in 1844 (*see* WRITING). He encouraged archaeological research and excavation in Mesopotamia.

**Rayy.** An early Islamic city of great importance and prosperity in Iran, south of Tehran. A short season of excavation was undertaken in 1934. A number of soundings were made, and large quantities of ceramics and other small objects of medieval date were found.

**Recuay.** A pottery style occurring in the Calleyon de Huaylas on the Western slopes of the Andes of Central Peru in AD 1–600. The pottery is decorated with red and/or gray motifs of interlocking fish, serpents, felines, and condors on a white slip.

*Repoussé. See* METAL TECHNOLOGY, PREHISTORIC EUROPE.

**Resistivity.** *See* SURVEYING.

**Rhodes.** An Ionian island, prosperous in Classical times because it was sited on the trade routes from Greece to Egypt and the East. Of the principal city, famed in antiquity for its beauty, there remain substantial traces of city walls, temples, a STADIUM, and an ODEUM. Nothing now survives of the colossus, which once stood astride the entrance to the harbor, and fell down in an earth-quake in 227–6 BC.

**Rimini** (Ariminium). A harbor town on the Adriatic Sea, founded by the Umbrians and taken over by Rome. Within the walls, one of the earliest of Roman triumphal arches was set up in 27 BC. The bridge over the River Ariminium (Marecchia) is still in use.

**Ring fort.** *See* IRELAND IN PREHISTORY.

**Rio Claro.** An early stratified site in the state of São Paulo in Eastern Brazil. The sequence begins with crude choppers dating from *c.* 20,000 years ago, and ends with large stemmed points, dating from *c.* 6000 BC.

**Rio Seco.** A large preceramic site, *c.* 2500 BC, on the North Central coast of Peru. It has two large pyramids, and many rectangular ground level and subterranean structures.

**Ritual vessels, China.** Although ritual vessels are found in many parts of the ancient world (the rhytons—or libation vessels—of the Greek Bronze Age are justly famous) they were particularly important in China, where they were used for sacrifices of food and wine offered to the ancestors. Found in tombs in the Shang and Chou Dynasties, they constituted the majority of the items made of bronze. The vessels were cast in ceramic piece molds around a central core. This technique had an important influence on the range of shapes which could be made, as the details of the early vessels were clearly dictated by the sections of the molds. As it was easy to incise decoration in the piece molds, very elaborate designs are found on the bronzes, particularly those of the SHANG DYNASTY (*c.* 1600–1027 BC). The most important design at that early date was the T'ao-t'ieh mask. Dragons, fish, snakes, and animals such as deer and water buffalo were also important elements of the decoration. During the Western Chou period (1027–771 BC) the designs became increasingly fantastic and extravagant, and then more abstract and repetitive. The bronzes of this period are particularly interesting for the long inscriptions on them recording political events associated with the casting.

A very high level of cast decoration was reached in the early Eastern Chou period (6th–5th century BC). By the end of the CHOU DYNASTY, however, there was less concern with cast decoration, and more with inlays in copper, silver, gold, and precious stones. During the HAN DYNASTY (206 BC–AD 220) ritual vessels gradually ceased to be of major importance.

**Rock art.** Painting and engraving on rock surfaces occur throughout the African continent. In contrast to the painted caves of Europe, the African art takes the form either of paintings in rock shelters, not in caves, or engraving on open rock outcrops or boulders. Areas where rock art is particularly common are the Tibesti and Hoggar mountains of the Central Sahara, the Eastern highlands of Ethiopia, Central Tanzania, and

parts of Kenya, the Matapo hills in Rhodesia, and many parts of the Republic of South Africa, particularly the cave sandstone areas of the Cape Province and the Natal Drakensberg.

Subject-matter varies between the different regions. In Southern Africa, antelopes and human figures predominate, with the eland being particularly important. In Rhodesia a greater variety of subjects occur—human figures, antelope, giraffe, rhinoceros, and elephant. In East Africa the subject-matter is more limited, and the paintings are less sophisticated. In Ethiopia the portrayal of cattle is particularly common in both the paintings and the engravings. The art of the Sahara is markedly different from that of sub-Saharan Africa. Pastoral scenes with sheep, goats, and cattle are widespread and influences from the Mediterranean and the Nile valley are clearly seen.

Recent evidence has dramatically extended the age range of the rock art. Much of the surviving evidence, particularly in Southern Africa, dates to the past few hundred years and indeed often to the second half of the 19th century. Excavated evidence, however, suggests that some of the art is considerably older. In Morocco, at the Grotte de Taforalt, a date of 11,000 BC is associated with painted evidence, and dates of 7000 BC apply to a number of painted gravestones in the Cape Province of South Africa. The best-dated occurrence of rock art comes from the Apollo II cave in Namibia (Southwest Africa), where a number of painted stone slabs have been recovered from levels dated to 25,000 BC. (*See also* CAVE ART.)

**Röessen culture.** The successor of the Western branch of the Neolithic LINEAR POTTERY CULTURE, with which it has many features in common. Its main distribution was in the Rhineland, and it is parallel to the LENGYEL culture in Czechoslovakia and the middle Danube.

**Rome.** The capital city of the Roman world, lying on the River Tiber about 16 mi. (26 km) from its mouth. The extent of the city took in several hills: the Capitol, Palatine, Aventine, Caelian, Oppian, Pincian, Quirinal, Viminal, and Esquiline. The site was a marshy one, and it was drained by a network of sewers, of which the Cloaca Maxima was the main outlet into the Tiber. Rome came to importance because it was the only crossing point of the Tiber by ford for a great distance.

Various authors gave different legendary foundation dates, none of which can be substantiated. The Romans themselves reckoned their years from a foundation date in 754/3 BC, with dates *a.u.c.* (*ab urbe condita*). The earliest archaeological trace of settlement is of Bronze Age date, *c.* 1500 BC. Settlement from the 10th century BC is attested on the Palatine Hill, and there is evidence for separate communities of Iron Age people on the various hills until about the early 6th century BC, when there was one large community. The first FORUM and early temples were now laid out, its center at the site of the later Forum, and the Capitol was from the first regarded as the religious citadel.

In 509 BC the Temple of Jupiter was founded on the

Capitol but, because of the size and thoroughness of later building, remains of this early period are fragmentary. The wall of Servius was built *c.* 378 BC, and a bridge replaced the Tiber ford.

Building activity was keen from the 4th century BC onwards: the first of many aqueducts was built in Rome in 312 BC, and temples, bridges, and basilicas were constructed, many of which were kept in repair or replaced in later periods. The largest complexes of republican buildings are the temple areas of the Piazza Argentina, and the Forum Boarium, and it is clear that, in the 2nd century BC, Rome was being built on a grand scale after the manner of a Hellenistic city.

The 1st century BC was a period of great progress. In the Forum area, the Tabularium planned by Sulla was the first attempt to unite different areas of the city, and Pompey built a new series of buildings in the Campus Martius, including a large porticus and theater. Julius Caesar added a new forum and started to build a basilica next to the main Forum. Under imperial rule, however, Rome's monuments grew steadily. Augustus built a new forum, although his palace was a modest building. Under his rule, much of the Campus Martius was constructed, including his own mausoleum, the Pantheon, and the Baths of Agrippa. Tiberius enlarged the imperial palace and built the new Praetorian Camp to house the imperial guard. A CIRCUS built by Gaius in the Vatican area was the scene of early Christian martyrdoms, later marked by memorials, one of which was traditionally the site of St. Peter's death. Claudius built new aqueducts, and Nero's Golden House, his new palace on the Oppian Hill, was later covered by Trajan's Baths. The Flavian emperors added the Forum of Vespasian, the Baths of Titus, and, perhaps the most monumental of all, the Colosseum, on the site of a lake. Later emperors, Nerva, Trajan, and Hadrian, added more monumental buildings: the Forum Transitorium, Trajan's Forum and Column, and Agrippa's Pantheon was rebuilt by Hadrian.

In the face of this spate of building in the 1st and 2nd centuries AD, there was little space in Rome for additional monumental schemes. Later building is on a grand scale, but localized. Examples are the Baths of Caracalla, of Diocletian, and of Constantine, the additions to the imperial palace on the Palatine by Severan emperors, and the great Basilica of Maxentius. The city's limits had to be extended first by Sulla (1st century BC), and then by Claudius (1st century AD), Vespasian (AD 69–79), and Hadrian (AD 118–138), and in its final form was ringed by a massive defensive wall by Aurelian (AD 270–275).

**Rosetta Stone.** In 1799, French soldiers demolishing a house at Rosetta in the Western Egyptian delta, in order to build Fort St. Julien, found an inscribed black basalt slab built into a wall. Lieutenant Bouchard, their officer, realized the importance of their discovery and added the so-called Rosetta Stone to the other antiquities collected by Napoleon's expedition. When the British defeated the French in Egypt, the Rosetta Stone was ceded to them by an article of the Treaty of Alexandria in 1801. It was incorporated into the Egyptian Collection of the British Museum, London, in 1802.

Its importance lay in the fact that, although the inscription was written in three scripts (HIEROGLYPHS, demotic, and ancient Greek), it displayed only two languages: both hieroglyphs and demotic were scripts used to write the language of ancient Egypt. Moreover, the Greek section stated that the text was a copy of a decree passed in 196 BC, during the reign of Ptolemy V Epiphanes, which was to be recorded in the language of the Greeks, of the common people (i.e., demotic), and of the priests (i.e., hieroglyphs). Thus, the Greek text was merely a translation of the two Egyptian scripts.

Until this time scarcely any progress had been made in the decipherment of hieroglyphs, but it was the Rosetta Stone's inscription, together with another bilingual text on an obelisk from Philae, which allowed scholars to make the breakthrough. Thomas Young, an Englishman, was the first to point the way towards the final decipherment, but it was the brilliant French scholar, J. F. Champollion, who followed through the suggestions made by Young and is therefore credited as the decipherer of the hieroglyphic script.

**Russia in Prehistory.** Palaeolithic occupation of Russia is mainly confined to the last 100,000 years, although the area south of the Caucasus was undoubtedly settled earlier. NEANDERTHAL MAN lived in Southern European Russia, especially in the Caucasus and Crimean area. It is claimed that he also colonized the far North, up to the Pechora River, close to the Arctic circle. Human remains have been found at Kiik Koba and Staroselje in the Crimea, and at Teshik Tash in Soviet Central Asia.

Upper Palaeolithic sites, dating from between 30,000 and 10,000 years ago, are much more widespread. Unlike those in Western Europe, the majority are open-air sites, and the hunters mostly pursued the mammoth. Russian prehistorians have made a major effort to uncover house plans and certainly some of these, although based on only the slenderest indications, do seem to be genuine. The most typical plans are oval houses and, towards the end of the Ice Age, long houses measuring *c.* 656 ft. (200 m).

A number of burials, often covered with red ocher, headdresses, and other ornaments are known. The most spectacular and interesting are from a site called Sungir, to the northeast of Moscow. It was possible to reconstruct most of the clothing from the rows of beads found over the burials, which had formerly been sewn to cloaks, trousers, and poncho-like shirts.

Small carved art objects are abundantly represented in the Russian Palaeolithic, especially the so-called "venus figurines"—female figurines which have large distended breasts and stomachs as in pregnancy, minimal facial features, and tapering legs. One painted cave is known: Kapovo cave in the South Urals.

From the Neolithic period two zones in Russia had extensive settled populations, while the development of nomadism was an important feature of a third. In the Southwest, adjoining Turkey and Iran, civilizations of Near Eastern type developed in the Caucasian and the Southern Caspian areas. To the north of these lay the steppe and desert belt, which had few inhabitants until the 2nd millennium BC, when pastoral nomadism became possible with the use of the horse. To the north again, the thin line of deciduous forest around 55° N provided an area for colonization by agriculturalists from the 3rd millennium BC onwards; while beyond this, scattered communities of hunters and fishermen lived in the marshes and dense coniferous forest, or pursued the reindeer of the tundra. In the postglacial period, agriculture spread into Russia by three routes: from Iran to Southern Turkestan (Jeitun culture); from Southeast Europe into the Ukraine (TRIPOLYE CULTURE); and from the North European plain (Fatyanovo culture).

During the 3rd and 2nd millennia BC, the steppe areas of the Ukraine and further east were colonized by pastoral groups able to make use of these dryer areas; their distribution is marked by barrows or *kurgans*, beneath which the dead were buried in pits (yamno=PIT GRAVE CULTURE). Other groupings of steppe tribes, burying their dead in underground log-lined chambers, were the ancestors of the SCYTHIANS. These Indo-European-speaking pastoralists dominated the steppes down to historic times. (*See also* SIBERIA.)

**Sabratha.** First a Phoenician, and then a Roman port in Africa. Excavations have revealed the FORUM, BASILICA, BATHS, and temples, as well as the harbor quarter with cramped housing, and a new suburb laid out in the 2nd century AD. The town declined in the 5th century AD, but was briefly rebuilt in Byzantine times: one of its 6th-century AD churches has outstanding mosaic floors.

**Sacsahuaman.** A monumental fortress, built by the Incas in the 15th century AD, and located on a hill behind CUZCO, Peru.

The great Inca fortress of Sacsahuaman, which overlooks the city of Cuzco, Peru.

**Sahagun, Father Bernardino de** (16th century). Father Bernardino de Sahagun, who was part Indian and an important writer of the 16th century in the New World, is most famous for his book, *General History of Things of New Spain*, with its detailed accounts of the Aztec way of life.

**St. Albans** (Verulanium). One of the leading cities of Roman Britain, mainly built and laid out at the end of the 1st and the beginning of the 2nd centuries AD. Traces of the city walls and gates, houses, and a THEATER survive.

**Saladero.** A distinctive ceramic complex of the Orinoco River of Venezuela, dated between 1000 and 700 BC. The people responsible for this tradition were forced out of the Orinoco just before the time of Christ by the Barrancoid group, and moved into the lesser Antilles, Trinidad, and the Virgin Islands. Here, the Saladoid subtradition becomes the basis for later ceramic developments.

**Salinar.** A phase, *c.* 200 BC–AD 200, from the North Central coast of Peru, characterized by oxidized red pottery, often with incised and white painted designs. It seems to be transitional between the earlier Chavinoid style of CUPISNIQUE and the later MOCHICA style.

**Salin Styles I–III.** Terms applied to ornamental styles of art current in Northern Europe from the 5th to the 9th century AD, characterized by zoomorphic symbols. The styles are named after B. Salin, who first distinguished them in his *Die altgermanische Thierornamentik* (1904). Style I is characterized by disjointed animals, while in Style II, which replaced it in the late 6th century AD, attenuated bodies form interlacing lizards (it is also called the "Ribbon Style"). Style III, the first of

the Viking styles which replaced Style II at the end of the 8th century, has more complicated ornament involving a motif known as the "gripping beast."

**Salt industry.** The archaeology of the salt industry tends to be spectacular and very suitable for presentation to tourists. Austria and Southern Germany are particularly rich in old underground workings which are safe and attractive to visitors. Notable Austrian examples are at Solbad Hall (Tyrol), HALLSTATT (Upper Austria—see for an account of prehistoric mining), and Hallein (Salzburg). France offers salt archaeology of a different kind. At Arc-et-Senans, near Besançon, the Saline de Chaux preserves the elegant remains of an ideal city (c. 1770) based on the saltworks. Salt is still produced by the open-pan method on the Mediterranean coast, between Sète and Agde, and in Lorraine the great salt deposits have been exploited since Roman times.

**Samaria.** A city on the main North-South route through Palestine. It was founded in the 9th century BC, and was occupied continuously until it was destroyed in AD 614. A Crusader church was later built there. The Palace of Omri and Ahab has been found, together with a group of ivories, and also 63 ostraca (inscribed pieces of pottery, or sherds) belonging to the reign of Jeroboan II. (See ISRAEL, ISRAELITES; SYRIA-PALESTINE.)

**Sambaquí tradition.** A tradition, from north of Rio de Janeiro, Brazil, known from shell mounds along the coast. Artifacts include stone axes, adzes, and choppers, as well as shell tools and polished stone effigies, c. 5000–1000 BC.

**Samian ware.** *See* TERRA SIGILLATA.

**Samos.** An Aegean island off Western Asia Minor whose principal city flourished in the 6th century BC under Polycrates, its tyrant. It was later part of the Delian league of Aegean states, and was eclipsed by Rhodes in Hellenistic times. The principal remains are its Temple of Hera and her sanctuary, and a remarkable aqueduct tunnel about ¾ mi. (1 km) long.

**San Agustín.** A site in the Andes of Southeast Colombia. It has many large mounds, deep tombs, monumental stone sculptures of gods, demons, and humans, and incised and modeled pottery. Gold ornaments from large underground burial chambers have also been found. It probably dates from 500 BC to the time of Christ.

**Sandia.** Sandia cave, in the Sandia Mountains in New Mexico, is the type-site for an archaeological complex of a similar age to the LLANO complex. Although the earlier Sandia or Folsom levels of Sandia cave have not been dated by the radiocarbon method, by analogy with other remains of the BIG GAME HUNTING TRADITION they can be dated to approximately 10,000–9000 BC. In the earliest levels of Sandia cave, a series of stone artifacts have been found which are different from those of the Llano complex. These include Sandia points of types I and II.

Type I is a lanceolate blade, without fluting, and without the concave base of Clovis or Folsom points. Their particular distinctive feature is a shoulder to one side of the base of the blade, suggesting that they may have been used as knives as well as points for spears. Type II has a rounded base. The Sandia complex is outside the main Big Game Hunting tradition, which is identified through the sequence of Clovis, Folsom, and Plano points. (See CLOVIS POINT; FOLSOM; PLANO POINT.)

**Sangoan.** First discovered in 1920 at Sango Bay on the West shore of Lake Victoria in Uganda, Sangoan tool assemblages have been reported from East and West Africa, the basin of the Zaire River, Angola, and parts of Zambia and Rhodesia. The dating and distribution is ill defined and many claimed occurrences are of doubtful validity. The term is therefore best restricted to the sites in Eastern Zaire and parts of Uganda and Kenya, where a date between 100,000 and 20,000 BP (before the present—see RADIOCARBON DATING) is likely.

The tool types include handaxes, scrapers, heavy duty picks, small specialized tools, and very finely flaked lanceolate points which must have been hafted and used as spearpoints.

It has been argued that the Sangoan is an adaptation to a forest environment and that many of the tools were used for woodworking. No undisturbed living sites are known and we know nothing of the physical appearance of the people or the economy practiced.

**San Lorenzo.** An important Preclassic Olmec site, located in Southern Veracruz, Mexico, along the Coatzacoalcos River basin. The site has been recently investigated by Yale University, and has the longest stratigraphic history of any known Olmec center. It was actually constructed on an artificial raised mass of land, built by the Olmecs to support a number of earthen pyramid constructions, plazas, and mounds, all laid out along a north-south axis. Numerous huge stone sculptures have been uncovered. By 1250 BC (the Chicharras phase), the Olmec culture was emerging at this site, but most of the pure Olmec monuments and structures date from between 1150 and 900 BC, making San Lorenzo one of the earliest Olmec centers. It was abandoned by the Olmecs c. 700 BC. In addition to San Lorenzo itself, there are a number of other minor, satellite Olmec sites nearby. (See OLMECS.)

**San Pedro culture.** This culture comes from the Atacama region of Northern Chile, and polychrome *kero* or beaker-shaped vessels have been found in its graves. Two phases can be distinguished, which seem to be contemporaneous with the TIAHUANACO culture in Bolivia, AD 500–1000.

**Saqqara.** *See* MEMPHIS.

**Sardes.** The capital city of Lydia, Sardes was the political center of Asia Minor under Persian rule before the Hellenistic period. It belonged to various ruling Hellenistic Dynasties, and became a Roman city in 133 BC.

Excavation began in 1910, and the palace of the Lydian kings, among then Croesus, has been revealed, as have the Temple of Artemis and the remains of its 3rd-century synagogue.

**Sarmatians.** Nomadic tribes related to the SCYTHIANS, from the steppes of Central Asia, who appeared in South Russia in the 4th century BC. Metalwork with jeweled inlays and gold openwork plaques, now preserved in the Hermitage Museum in Leningrad, have been attributed to them. Royal Sarmatian tombs in South Russia and Eastern Europe, from the 3rd century BC onwards, contain rich objects (e.g., Novocherkassk on the Don).

**Sassanians.** The Iranian successors of the Parthians, who ruled from AD 224 to 651. Their empire extended from India to Syria, where they came into conflict with the Romans. Shapur I defeated the Emperor Valerian in AD 260. There are rock reliefs at Naqsh-i-Rustam, Firuzabad, Naqsh-i-Bahram, Sar Meshed, Taq-i-Bustan, and Darab, and palaces and temples at Firuzabad, Ctesiphon, Bishapur, Takht-i-Suleiman, and Sarvistan. Sassanian metalwork has survived in the form of bowls and dishes with *repoussé* designs in gold and silver. There are also fine stamp SEALS and textiles.

**Sauveterrian.** The MESOLITHIC hunting culture which succeeds the Azilian (an epi-Palaeolithic culture) and precedes the TARDENOISIAN, dating from some 9,000 years ago. Based on the site of Sauveterre-la-Lemance in Lot-et-Garonne, Southwest France, it is characterized by "geometric" microliths (tiny flint barbs), which are also found in Britain and other parts of Western Europe.

**Sawmilling.** The archaeology of this industry tends to be exceptionally impermanent, especially in the major logging and lumber areas of the world, where sawmills and settlements have been abandoned and moved on as felling progressed. In Scandinavia, however, a deliberate attempt has been made to protect such sites. In Finland, a sawmill of *c.* 1900 is preserved at Svartå Bruk, and there are others of the same vintage at Trollböle, near Ekenäs, and at Grabbskog. Canada, where timber has always been of great economic importance, has devoted much attention to the history of the industry. An outstanding example of this is the Balaclava Mill, Dacre, Ont., which worked from 1857 to 1968. This water-powered complex in a lumber-town setting was rebuilt to the original plan in 1936. All the original machinery remains. A less ambitious example of conservation is the Avery Sawmill, at Deep Bight, Trinity Bay, Nfld. It is probably the only survivor of the once numerous water-driven sawmills in the province.

**Schliemann, Heinrich** (1822–90). A German archaeologist. His lifelong ambition was to find and excavate the remains of Homer's Troy, which he believed must still exist. He had a successful career as an international financier, making most of his considerable wealth in the California goldrush. In 1870, after a tour round the world, he began excavating the Hissarlik hill in the extreme

Northwest of Asia Minor, continuing at intervals until his death in 1890, where he achieved his ambition and indeed discovered Troy. He also excavated at MYCENAE in 1874–8, and at TIRYNS in 1884–5. His excavations caused controversy at the time, but he is now regarded as a pioneer of scientific archaeology. (*See also* TROY.)

**Schmidt, Erich** (1897–1964). An American archaeologist. He was the excavator of TEPE HISSAR (1931–33), FARA (1931), and PERSEPOLIS (1934–39).

**Science in archaeology.** For over two centuries, scientific techniques have been applied to the study of ancient materials in order to shed additional light on the past of man to that which is produced by the application of the methods of work that are central to archaeology. Late in the 18th century, a London scientist melted down a series of ancient British bronzes and subjected them to wet methods of CHEMICAL ANALYSIS in order to determine their composition. Since then, the number of scientific techniques of examination, analysis, and identification applied in archaeology have grown enormously, so that they now run into three figures. Every scientific discipline, from zoology to nuclear physics and theoretical astronomy, now contributes to our expanding knowledge of man's past. Even the principal methods that characterize archaeology itself are becomingly increasingly more scientific in nature, but, as in the natural sciences, there will always be a place in it for subjective judgment, for the hunch, the inspired guess, for sudden insight, and for speculation. Techniques of seriation are now being used by many archaeologists to help in the construction of relative chronologies, and computer-aided methods of numerical taxonomy help in the classification of ancient artifacts. Experiments are being conducted with ever greater frequency to understand how artifacts were made and used, and how earthworks and buildings were constructed and deteriorate with time.

The applications of science in archaeology may be grouped under five main headings: dating, palaeoecology, man himself, his artifacts, and prospecting for archaeological sites. Scientific methods of dating have had a major impact on archaeology, particularly on prehistory, as they provide more or less precise chronologies that previously could only be guessed at: not surprisingly, much of this guesswork proved to be wide of the mark. Moreover, scientific methods have proved invaluable in unmasking hoaxes and forgeries; the technique of measuring the amount of fluorine absorbed from ground water into bone came into prominence through its contribution to the detection of the fraudulent "Piltdown man" (*see* FRAUDS). Varve counting in Europe was the first method to give a precise yardstick of the time that has elapsed since the last glaciation (*see* VARVES). Archaeo-magnetic dating, based on measurement of changes in the direction and declination of the earth's magnetic field, is beginning to make a major impact, as it enables fired structures and silted deposits to be dated directly; measurement of energy given off and trapped within ceramics and burnt flint since firing forms the basis of thermoluminescent dating, which gives dates to man's commonest artifact, pottery (*see* THERMOLUMINESCENCE). DENDROCHRONOLOGY, the counting of annual growth rings in trees, gives very precise dates for timber: in Europe, it has confirmed and further refined the accuracy of much 1st-millennium BC chronology built up by cross-dating with the Mediterranean civilizations. It has also provided a yardstick for measuring the amount of cosmic radiation in the past, a corrective to the principal isotopic method of dating, radiocarbon, which has had the profoundest impact so far of any of the scientific methods of dating archaeological materials and deposits (*see* RADIOCARBON DATING).

Palaeoecology, the study of man's past environment (*see* ECOLOGY), has contributed much to archaeology by enabling detailed vegetational and climatic histories since the end of the Pleistocene to be built up, by enabling man's impact on the environment to be assessed, and by giving invaluable information about his diet and his exploitation and husbandry of animals and plants. The study of buried soils (pedology), pollens (palynology), insects (palaeoentomology), and snail shells (conchology) found within them has yielded detailed information on the history of the landscape and of man's use and modification of it. The study of seed impressions on ceramics, and of seeds and other plant residues gathered from archaeological deposits, is shedding important light on the domestication of plants and on man's diet, as is now the analysis of carbonized food residues. The examination and identification of animal bones has likewise added much to our knowledge of man's diet, as well as his exploitation and domestication of animals.

The anatomical and pathological examination of the remains of man himself tells us much about past patterns of mortality, diseases, diet, stature, and physical and mental evolution. Some progress has also been made in investigating the history of peoples by the study of blood groups from the traces of blood preserved in bone marrow, and by measuring very large samples of skeletons from ancient burials.

Information gleaned from artifacts by the application of scientific methods falls into three categories: manufacture, use, and trade. A large number of techniques are employed to elucidate the ways in which ancient artifacts were made. Neutron activation analysis, optical spectroscopy, heavy mineral and particle analysis, thin-sectioning, and wet chemistry are all used to determine the elements of which they were made, and the information that these methods yield often tells us much about the sources of the raw materials, and about the very places of their manufacture. Metallography indicates the methods by which metal artifacts were made, and thin-sectioning how pots were formed. Microscopic examination reveals traces of wear, and has led to the identification of the uses to which many bone and flint implements were put.

Various scientific methods are nowadays used by archaeologists to prospect for buried structures and underwater wrecks, principally those of magnetic location and resistivity surveying. Increasing use is also being made of various kinds of sonar equipment. (*See* AIR PHOTOGRAPHY; SURVEYING.)

**Scraper.** *See* STONE TECHNOLOGY.

**Sculpture, Greek and Roman.** Monumental sculpture in stone was introduced into Greece *c.* 650 BC from Egypt. Archaic sculptures are normally of standing figures—the nude male *Kouros* or the draped female *Kore*—in traditional and somewhat inflexible poses, though there were attempts at different action poses for temple pediment scenes. The development of sculpture from 650 to *c.* 480 BC was achieved by the increasingly better representation of the anatomical structure of the human body (for the male figure), and by the sophistication and intricacy of the treatment of drapery (for the female). Seated figures were also represented, and relief sculptures on metopes or on pediments of temples introduced new themes (*see* METOPE). The principal survivals today are of limestone or marble, but wood and bronze, beaten or cast, were also used.

The greatest period of Classical sculpture began *c.* 480 BC, and the best-known examples of this are the pediments and metopes of the Temple of Zeus at OLYMPIA (465–457 BC) and the sculptures of the PARTHENON at Athens (447–431 BC)—the "Elgin Marbles," now in London at the British Museum. One of the most renowned sculptors of the Classical period was Phidias, responsible for massive gold and ivory statues of Zeus (at Olympia) and Athene (at Athens). He was artistic overseer for both temples.

An Archaic Greek male *Kouros*, in traditional pose, from Anavysos, *c.* 540–515 BC.

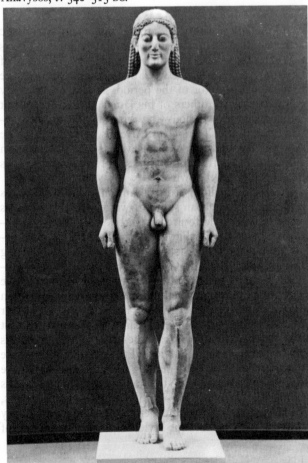

A Greek bronze figure, *c.* 470–450 BC, found in the sea off Cape Sunium.

In the 4th century BC, there was renewed artistic activity after a lull during the Peloponnesian Wars (431–404 BC). One original statue, the Hermes of Olympia, survives of the work of Praxiteles, perhaps the best-known sculptor of the period, and there are many Roman copies of others of his famed works. Important buildings of the period—the Mausoleum at HALICARNASSUS and the Temple of Artemis at EPHESUS—bore sculptures, and the names of several sculptors famed in antiquity for both temple works and individual statues have been handed down.

The main medium of Etruscan sculpture in Italy was terra-cotta rather than stone; it was closely linked in its rather stilted style to archaic Greek sculpture, and appears not to have achieved a parallel development between the 7th and the 1st centuries BC. Thus Hellenizing Rome looked towards Greece for the sculptors to decorate her city, and the earliest sculptures of Roman style date from the early 1st century BC. Portraiture, with often a most unflattering degree of realism, was a popular theme in sculpture, but the main use to which the art was put was to commemorate the historical achievements of Rome under the republic and the empire. Often these sculptures are in relief—ranging from the idealism of the Ara Pacis of Augustus, to the military realism of Trajan's campaigns as portrayed on his column. Later reliefs, under 3rd- and 4th-century emperors, show a tendency towards a more Baroque style, with more crowding of scenes and ornamentation, especially on ceremonial buildings, such as the triumphal arch. But this kind of official art was by no means the only sculpture current. Many far humbler pieces, among them reliefs on tombstones, grave monuments, and military dedications, survive and in many Roman provinces, particularly on the fringes of the empire, they show the fusion of Roman and native elements to good advantage.

**Scythians.** Nomads from Central Asia who probably first moved into South Russia as bearers of the Timber Grave culture in the 13th century BC, and were responsible for driving the CIMMERIANS into the Near East. At the beginning of the 7th century BC, they also moved into IRAN and ANATOLIA and appear in Assyrian records. They later returned to South Russia and Royal Scythian burials are found in the Kuban and on the Pontic steppes. They were in contact with the Greeks, who manufactured goods in the Scythian style for the Scythian market, particularly at Olbia. Herodotus writes about the Scythians at some length. Objects from Kul Oba and from burials in the Kuban and on the Dnieper (Seven Brothers Barrow, Kostromskaya, Kelermes, Chertomlyk) display various styles, with a predominance of nomadic animal styles. The incursion of Scythians into Eastern Europe has not been definitely proved archaeologically.

**Seals.** The use of seals and WRITING on clay tablets appeared together in Mesopotamia, towards the end of the 4th millennium BC. The seals were distinctive: they were shaped like cylinders with a vertical perforation, and were carved with a design. These seals were rolled on the damp clay of a tablet or jar stopper and left a frieze-like impression. The shape, type of stone, or design of the seals vary according to the date, but they are not as useful for dating purposes as one might imagine, since they are often found in much later contexts and were used by subsequent owners, with or without recarving.

From Early Dynastic times onwards some seals are inscribed, sometimes with the name of the owner and his patronymic, and this can give us useful information. Cylinder seals came to be used on tablets or their clay envelopes wherever cuneiform writing was used (in Iran, Anatolia, Syria, and Palestine), especially during the 2nd millennium BC, which was a period of great epistolary activity. Parallel to the use of cylinder seals we find the use of stamp seals, but this is restricted to sites in Northern Mesopotamia, Iran, and Anatolia. They appear as early as the Halaf period (5th millennium BC). In Anatolia, stamps appear at ÇATAL HÜYÜK in the middle of the 6th millennium, but it is not known how they were used. Stamp seals were used by the Hittites, and they replaced cylinder seals during the 1st millennium BC, since the increased use of parchment as a writing material, as opposed to tablets, made them more suitable than cylinder seals.

**Sea People.** The name given in Egyptian texts to peoples of many different origins who were on the move in the 13th century BC, due to economic and political pressures which are as yet unclear. As a result, Dorians, Aeolians, and Ionians moved into Greece and the Aegean islands, probably destroyed the Mycenaean kingdom, and drove the inhabitants eastwards (Trojan War, *c.* 1200 BC). The Thraco-Phrygians were also driven into Anatolia, where they brought about the fall of the Hittite Empire. Homeless peoples swept southwards along the coasts of Asia Minor and Syria, burning and looting as they went, and were only stopped by Ramesses III in 1174 BC on the borders of Egypt. It was at this time that the PHILISTINES settled in Palestine.

**Segesta.** A Sicilian town, an ally of Athens in the 5th century BC, and famous for its unfinished Greek Doric temple.

**Seibal.** An ancient Maya site located on the Rio Pasion in the Southern Maya Lowlands, situated on a high bluff about 10 mi. (16 km) upriver from the modern town of Sayaxche in the Department of Peten, Guatemala. Recent excavations by the Peabody Museum, Harvard University, under the direction of Gordon R. Willey and A. L. Smith, have shown that the site was occupied as early as 800 BC; it expanded in size and importance throughout the Preclassic Period and reached its height in Late Preclassic times. The site then went into an eclipse and was virtually abandoned from AD 300 to 600. Population influx between AD 600 and 700, probably from Northeast Peten, led to a revival in the site's fortunes.

Between AD 770 and 800, Seibal was invaded by non-Classic Maya peoples, who probably spoke Chontal Maya and have been identified as the Putun. They controlled Seibal until approximately AD 900. Although the rest of Classic Maya civilization was declining at this time, Seibal underwent a brief florescence. The Putun erected a series of famous (and beautifully preserved) carved monuments at Seibal, built several distinctive structures, including a round temple, and imported their own temperless pottery known as Fine Orange.

**Seine-Oise-Marne culture.** The last Neolithic culture in Northern France and Southern Belgium, named after three rivers. It lasted from before 2500 to about 2000 BC, and is known principally from a series of collective tombs, freestanding megalithic gallery graves, and chalk-cut tombs, and settlements have also been recorded.

**Seleucids.** These are named after Seleucus (356–280 BC), one of Alexander the Great's generals, who founded the Seleucid Empire after the death of his leader. He captured Babylon in 312 BC, and the Seleucid era is reckoned from this date. His empire stretched from Asia Minor and Mesopotamia to Afghanistan, with its capital at Seleucia on the River Tigris. Many new cities were founded, several of them called Seleucia, Antioch, or Apamaea, and settled with Greek veterans, leading to the fusion of Hellenistic and Oriental cultures. The Eastern provinces gradually broke away, and the Parthian capture of their capital in 141 BC marks the decline of the Seleucids. Under Antiochus VII, Seleucid fortunes

revived for a time but the empire finally disintegrated, leaving the Parthians in control to the east of the River Euphrates and the Romans to the west.

**Sequence dating.** A method of relative dating devised by W. M. Flinders PETRIE to establish an historical sequence for Egypt's Predynastic Period. It can only be used to determine whether one type of artifact is earlier or later than another: it cannot show the length of time between the two.

During the 1893–4 season in Egypt, while excavating at Naqada, opposite Quft (Coptos), Petrie uncovered nearly 3,000 graves belonging to a previously unknown people. They were buried unmummified, lying on their sides in the foetal position in pit graves, surrounded by grave goods of every kind: pottery, hard stone vessels, strings of beads, flint knives, ivory combs, copper implements, slate palettes, and some small human and animal figurines. At first Petrie dated this new people to the troubled First Intermediate Period which followed the fall of the Old Kingdom (*c.* 2160–2040 BC), but further excavations by others, as well as by himself, discovered identical grave goods in burials which obviously predated the Dynastic Period. Examples of the new ware were also found in 1st Dynasty burials. Clearly, then, the new people predated the 1st Dynasty but there was no break in continuity between the Predynastic and the Dynastic Periods. (*See* NAQADA CULTURE I; NAQADA CULTURE II.)

Petrie had already made detailed records of the position and type of each object in each burial; after further detailed recording of his excavations at Hu (Diospolis Parva) in 1898–9, he was able to prepare a corpus of each type of grave good found. Every grave contained one or more pottery vessels so, using the pottery corpus, which contained over 700 types, he distinguished nine main shapes, of which the Wavy-handled form seemed most obvious in its development. Gradually, all pottery vessels were placed in sequence relative to the Wavy-handled ware's development. These sequences were checked, using corpuses of the other grave goods, and the system was found to be valid.

The range was divided into 50 sections numbered 30 to 80, the earliest pottery vessels being placed at 30, the latest at 80, just prior to the beginning of the 1st Dynasty. The sequence began at 30 so as to accommodate earlier material. Each of the numbers between 30 and 80 was called a sequence date and newly excavated material was assigned a sequence date and placed within the series. Petrie further subdivided the series into two main sections, sequence dates 30–37 and 38–80, the latter number later revised to 76, which were allotted to the two Naqada cultures. Even the revised S.D. for the end of the Predynastic Period had later to be brought down to 63, when it was realized that Petrie's Semainian period was contemporary with the early 1st Dynasty.

Although Petrie originally called the two main divisions of his system Amratian (S.D. 30–37) and Gerzean (S.D. 38–63) after find-sites, most Egyptologists prefer the terms Naqada I and II, mainly because the latter terminology shows more clearly the continuity between the two civilizations, but also as a tribute to Petrie and his original discovery of the previously unknown Predynastic civilizations at Naqada.

Although sequence dates are still used and the division into two main sections is still valid, the whole system now needs revision.

**Serapeum.** A term given to the vast underground galleries at Saqqara which housed the embalmed bodies of the Apis bulls. In 1850, the French Egyptologist Auguste Mariette noticed a limestone sphinx almost hidden by sand in an area northwest of the Step Pyramid of Djoser. It seemed identical to others he had seen in Cairo in the possession of a dealer, who claimed they all came from Saqqara, where they had formed an avenue leading out into the Western Desert. Remembering the Greek historian Strabo's description of the road to the Temple of Serapis being lined by sphinxes, he began digging in the area he thought might cover the next sphinx. After he found it he searched for the next sphinx and the next, until eventually he had uncovered the whole avenue. At the end lay a small temple built by a 30th-Dynasty pharaoh, before which stood a semicircle of statues of Greek poets and philosophers.

Later, in 1851, after Mariette had excavated many important monuments and small objects unconnected with his search for the Serapeum, his workmen uncovered a large blocked doorway. Within, leading from vaulted galleries, were 24 vaulted burial chambers, each lined with fine limestone blocks and containing a huge granite sarcophagus. Some weighed more than 60 tons (60,963 kg). But the vaults had been robbed in antiquity, and virtually all that remained were votive stelae, set in the walls between the vaults, giving the dates of birth and death of each Apis. These have provided much valuable information about the length of reign of Late Period kings and confirmation of their order of succession; only now, however, are they being properly published. After his discovery of these Greater Vaults, as he called them, Mariette uncovered the Lesser Vaults, which included an intact burial of two Apis bulls dating to the reign of Ramesses II. With them he found many *shabtis* (tomb figures), various objects inscribed with the name of Prince Khaemwese, Ramesses' fourth son, and four canopic jars for the embalmed viscera. The wooden coffins did not, however, contain Apis mummies but only bones and animal fragments in a badly preserved condition.

The Apis bull cult can be traced back to the very beginning of Egypt's Dynastic history and almost certainly predates it, as bulls were buried in cemeteries of the BADARIAN CULTURE. But although the worship of the Apis, PTAH's earthly manifestation, is recorded throughout the Old and Middle Kingdoms, the earliest Serapeum burials, in the Lesser Vaults, date only to the reign of Amenophis III of the 18th Dynasty. This catacomb continued in use until the 26th Dynasty, when a new set of galleries (the only ones at present open to the public) was excavated by Psammetichus I. They continued in use until the Ptolemaic Period. It now seems likely that, during the Old and Middle Kingdoms and probably

even into the New Kingdom, the dead Apis was eaten by the king in a ritual feast to restore his strength. The Ramesside mummies, consisting of bones and fragments, probably confirm that the practice still existed. In fact it is not until the 26th Dynasty that the Apis was embalmed intact and given a state funeral. In 1941 an alabaster embalming table used to prepare Apis mummies was found at Memphis, together with some embalming equipment and ox bones. Even more interesting were some limestone reliefs of the mummified bulls being carried to their tombs in wheeled cars. The datable articles among these belong to the 26th Dynasty.

A bronze statuette of the Apis bull, dedicated to Petiese, 26th Dynasty, *c.* 600 BC.

There was only one Apis at any one time, which was selected for his special markings from bull calves throughout Egypt. Once installed in his quarters beside the Temple of Ptah at MEMPHIS, he lived out his life in luxury, surrounded by his own harem of cows. At his death the whole of Egypt went into mourning, and he was embalmed and interred in the manner of a pharaoh. Members of the royal family often participated as mourners at his funeral. The dead Apis was just as important as the living, for he then became the funerary god Osiris-Apis. It is actually the latter name which was used by the Greeks, in the form Serapis, for the new god invented by Ptolemy I to unite in religion his Macedonian fellow-countrymen and his Egyptian subjects.

Thus Strabo's Serapeum was not a temple of Serapis but Mariette's tomb of Osiris-Apis.

For many years Egyptologists had known that the cow which bore the Apis was revered as a divine mother. Sacred cows had been found buried with their divine sons in the Bucheum at Armant, but it was not until 1970 that W. B. EMERY discovered at Saqqara the burial place of the Mothers of the Apis, which he called the Iseum because the cows were associated with Isis. The gallery, robbed in antiquity, had contained burials dating back only to the reigns of Psammuthis and Hakor of the 29th Dynasty, but a papyrus found during excavations listed Mothers of the Apis back to the 26th Dynasty. Clearly, therefore, more galleries must lie nearby.

**Shaft tomb.** A type of tomb current in China up to the 1st century BC. It consisted of a vertical pit shaft in which the coffin was placed, with or without access ramps. (*See* TOMB ARCHAEOLOGY IN CHINA.

**Shamanism.** A religious ideology found among herdsmen and hunters throughout the world, though it seems to be North Asian in origin. Belief was in the sky and the underworld, in supernatural possession and transmission of the spirit to another being, often an animal: hence the importance of animal costume in Shaman ritual and of the animal style in art. Shaman concepts may well be the basis of the animal art of the SCYTHIANS and SARMATIANS.

**Shang Dynasty.** The earliest ruling house in China (*c.* 1600–1027 BC), for which the archaeological evidence confirms the later written historical records. An earlier Dynasty, the Hsia, is mentioned in these texts, but as yet they cannot be linked with any excavated remains. The Shang is the first Dynasty from which written records survive, mainly as inscriptions on ORACLE BONES and bronze RITUAL VESSELS. In the texts the Shang are described as having occupied several capitals in succession. The last of these, Yin, has been conclusively identified as the major city excavated at AN-YANG. Large deposits of inscribed oracle bones found there enabled this city to be identified, and further confirmed the list of Shang kings set out in the texts. Two other major Shang sites, both of which pre-date An-yang, have been excavated: CHENG-CHOU and Erh-li-t'ou. Neither of these can be definitely established as a capital though their chronological relationship is clear, with Erh-li-t'ou being the earlier.

The development of bronze casting in the Shang, from the initial stage of early weapon forms and primitive ritual vessels at Erh-li-t'ou to the full flowering of bronze casting in the late Shang, can be followed at these three sites. However, bronze casting was not confined to this area of North China, which was the center of Shang power. Important bronzes have been excavated further south in Hupei and Anhui provinces. These suggest that other bronze-casting centers existed, and that Shang control was by no means as absolute as later texts imply. Shang power must nonetheless have been

very great, for they controlled a labor force sufficient to build the elaborate cities and great tombs which have been excavated. Their military force depended on soldiers armed with dagger-axes and bows, the sword being unknown in China until the late CHOU DYNASTY. However, small daggers and knives were in use, implying a relationship between the Shang and the KARASUK CULTURE of South Siberia. The introduction of the CHARIOT in the late Shang period likewise suggests a connection with Southern Russia, possibly the Caucasus.

**Shih-chai-shan.** One of a group of 1st-century BC sites near Lake Tien in Yünnan province in Southwest China. In the graves at this site a large group of bronzes has been excavated which, although related to the mainstream of Chinese bronze casting, has certain very unusual features. In the prominence of drums it has important links with Southeast Asia, but the carefully modeled groups of figures, and the designs of boats and animals in combat are all peculiar to this area. In some respects, further links with the Western areas of China, such as Szechuan and Kansu, show an innate conservatism, preserving weapon types of the SHANG DYNASTY (*c.* 1600–1027 BC), for example, long after they had disappeared in the rest of China.

**Shouldered adze.** A polished stone adze of the Neolithic period, distributed along the coastal area of China from Shantung southwards and in Central Southern China. It is also a prominent form in Southeast Asia.

**Sialk.** *See* TEPE SIALK.

**Siberia.** The colonization of Siberia by man, quite late in the Palaeolithic, peopled a new continent larger than Europe, and opened the way to the Bering Strait land bridge (the sea level was then lower, since so much water was locked-up in ice) and America.

The earliest sites known at present date from a little over 20,000 years ago, and are concentrated in Southern Siberia around Lake Baikal and the upper Yenissei River. Two of the best known are Mal'ta and Buret'. Traces of huts are known from these sites, as well as small art objects, such as carved figurines of geese. The burial of a child at Mal'ta included a kind of belt buckle. The racial features of the child seem to be mongoloid, and it is reasonable to assume that the Palaeolithic peoples of Siberia, as well as of America, were of this type. Towards the end of the Palaeolithic the settlement of Siberia becomes much more widespread.

These peoples must have been able to survive extremely cold winters, and we have some clue as to how they were able to do so: the tiny female statuettes from Mal'ta and Buret' are evidently clothed in skin suits, like those worn by the Eskimo, with parka hoods and moccasins sewn on to the trousers. No doubt this important adaptation made the colonization of "Beringia" and arctic America possible for the first time.

Rock engravings have been found recently in Siberia, some of which may be Palaeolithic. (*See also* AFANASIEVO CULTURE; ANDROVONOVO CULTURE; KARASUK CULTURE; TAGAR CULTURE; PASYRYK.)

**Sicily.** There has been settlement from prehistoric times on this Mediterranean island. It was colonized by the Greeks in the 8th century BC, resulting in the establishment of cities such as SYRACUSE, Leontini, Naxos, Messana (Zanele), Megara, GELA, AGRAGAS, and Selinus. These came into conflict with the Phoenician colony of CARTHAGE early on in their history: the Phoenician settlement of Sicily was, however, confined to a small portion of the island, and, in a battle at Himera in 480 BC, the Syracusan fleet beat the Carthaginians. But this was only a prelude to further attempts at control by Carthage throughout the 4th and 3rd centuries BC, until Sicily became a Roman province—the first territory gained by Rome—in 227 BC.

The capital of the province thus created was at Syracuse, and Sicily became one of the major grain producers for Rome: large estates, worked mainly by slaves, existed in many parts of the island. The island was extremely prosperous until well into the 4th century AD, as is shown by large villas such as the Piazza Armerina and others in a similar sumptuous style.

**Sidon.** An important Phoenician harbor north of TYRE, mentioned in texts from the mid-2nd millennium BC onwards, and destroyed by the Assyrians in 677 BC. A number of coffins have been found, among them that of Ahiram, bearing a 10th-century BC Phoenician inscription, as well as several Greco-Roman coffins of the 5th and 4th centuries BC.

**Sieving.** In order to recover all the small artifacts and other pieces of evidence from the soil which he digs, the archaeologist needs to process all the earth from his site through a fine mesh. Several systems are now in operation, using either dry screening in a shaker-frame, or wet sieving with flowing water.

**Silk.** The thread that can be drawn off the cocoon spun by the grub of the moth *Bombyx mori*. Its use for weaving fine cloth originated in China in the Neolithic period. Elaborate methods of weaving this thread were developed by the HAN DYNASTY (206 BC–AD 220), and, from that period onwards, textiles were exported in large numbers along the SILK ROUTE to the Roman world and later to Byzantium.

**Silk route.** The trade route from China to Western Asia across Central Asia through the oases on either side of the Tarim Basin. Excavations along this route have brought to light scraps of SILK exported from China, together with wooden figures and furniture which show clear Chinese influence. In the other direction, horses, in particular, and other luxuries were imported into China. Buddhism was also brought this way from the Indian subcontinent. The TOMB FIGURES of the T'ANG DYNASTY (AD 618–906) include horses, camels, and foreign dancers which can all be associated with this trade route.

**Sinjerli.** The site in Southeastern ANATOLIA of the ancient city of Sam'al, center of an independent state at the beginning of the 1st millennium BC (*see* ARAMAEANS;

HITTITES). It was excavated by the Germans from 1888 to 1892. A walled citadel contained two buildings of the BÎT HILANI type. Many sculptured reliefs were found, together with a stele of the Assyrian King Esarhaddon (670 BC).

**Sippar.** An ancient Sumerian city identified with the site of Abu-Habba, and lying on a canal which linked the Rivers Tigris and Euphrates. It was an important religious and trading center of Southern MESOPOTAMIA. The city was surrounded by a rectangular enclosure with a temple and a ZIGGURAT dedicated to Shamash. A scribal school and many tens of thousands of tablets, predominantly from the Old Babylonian and Neo-Babylonian periods, have been found.

**Sirāf.** A medieval port on the Persian Gulf between Bushire and Bandar 'Abbās, the most important medieval Islamic site in Iran to have been excavated. Its geographical position made it a city of great prosperity in the early Islamic period, and its remains have been largely untouched since it was abandoned in late medieval times. Excavations in 1966–73 uncovered the Great Mosque, a palatial residence, various defensive and military edifices, a warehouse, a *hammām* (bath house), and a pottery, as well as part of the bazaar, private houses of various dates, an *imāmzādeh* (shrine of a saint), and a monumental cemetery. A Sassanian fort has also been identified beneath the Islamic buildings. The finds included much unglazed and glazed pottery, of particular importance being the abundant imported Chinese and Far Eastern wares, and the excavations provided important stratigraphical information for the dating of these various wares. Small amounts of stucco and stone, and large quantities of GLASS were also found.

**Site catchment analysis.** The decision to locate a settlement at a particular point is determined by the resources which its community will have to use in their daily activities. This is especially true where movement is difficult or where the technology of transport is still in a primitive stage; but in any case it makes sense to reduce time and effort in traveling. While this may be overridden in some circumstances by other needs, such as a defensible position on high ground, it makes a working assumption for the archaeologist in trying to reconstruct the economic basis of ancient settlements.

The supplies of food and raw materials which arrive in a village can be considered to come from a "catchment area," in the same way as the water reaching a river, and by looking at the resources within access of a prehistoric site, some estimate can be made of prehistoric land and resource use. This can be done crudely by looking at all the land within, say, a 2-mi. (3.2 km) radius of a site; or it can be made more accurately by estimating relative accessibility within an hour's walking distance, and by weighting the areas immediately adjacent in comparison with those on the fringes of the territory. It is thus possible to construct diagrams of the different types of terrain within access of a settlement, and to look for consistent patterns of preference among contemporary sites in the same area. Particularly fertile classes of soil often stand out in such analyses.

This technique does not, of course, give unambiguous answers, but complements the detailed analysis of the animal and plant remains and other evidence found in excavation. It does, however, force the excavator to look beyond his site to the land which supported it.

**Skara Brae.** A Late Neolithic (*c*. 2000 BC) nucleated village on the mainland of Orkney in Scotland. It consisted of several rectangular houses carefully built of stone, connected by narrow passages, which contained stone fittings interpreted as beds and dressers. This is a form of settlement which is hardly known elsewhere in the British Neolithic.

**Slab grave.** *See* CIST TOMB.

**Slavs.** The origins of the Slavs can be found in the Late Bronze Age in Southeast Central Europe. A series of migrations established the East Slavs on the River Dnieper, the West Slavs round the Oder and Vistula Rivers, and the Southern Slavs in the Balkans. From these groups Russians, Ukrainians, Czechs, Poles, Serbs, Croats, and Macedonians are all descended.

By the 9th century AD several Slavonic kingdoms had been established. The empire of Great Moravia was centered roughly on modern Czechoslovakia and Poland. The kingdom of the Bulgars was centered on the Balkans, and to the northeast of these lay the kingdoms of Kiev and NOVGOROD, which were composed of a mixture of Eastern Slavs and Scandinavians. In AD 881 these were amalgamated by Oleg into the state of Kievan Russia. The Slavs were converted to Christianity from the 9th century AD onwards. Bulgaria was converted in AD 865, while Russia became officially Christian under Vladimir (AD 978–1015), following Greek Orthodox religion. The Slavs were constantly under pressure from Byzantium, and only Russia and Poland managed to remain intact as states, though the other kingdoms maintained their language and traditions.

**Smelting.** *See* METAL TECHNOLOGY, PREHISTORIC EUROPE.

**Smyrna.** A city on the Aegean coast of Asia Minor, on trade routes to Persia. The earliest Greek occupation was at the beginning of the 10th century BC, and in the 7th century BC a new fortified town was laid out on the site. It was destroyed *c*. 600 BC by the Persians. Refounded in a slightly different site by the Macedonian kings, it became one of the principal cities of Asia Minor throughout the Hellenistic and Roman periods.

**Somme sequence.** In addition to being one of the first places where the great antiquity of man was recognized, the Somme valley in France includes the type-site of the ACHEULIAN (St. Acheul, a suburb of Amiens) and the ABBEVILLEAN (Abbeville). The sequence of the Palaeolithic here was studied by Commont before 1918 and by Breuil in the 1930s, and it is now being revised.

**Spain.** After the prehistoric period, Phoenicians, Greeks, and Carthaginians all founded settlements in Spain, the earliest of which were Tartessus and Cadiz (Gades), traditionally Phoenician colonies. Greek colonists also arrived in the 7th century BC, and had colonies near Malaga, on Ibiza, and at Marseilles (Massilia), which later established trading posts at AMPURIAS and elsewhere. The Carthaginians, however, controlled large parts of Mediterranean coastal Spain in the 3rd century BC, though much of the rest was still the preserve of native Celts (the so-called Iberian Celts, or Celtiberians). This coastal strip came under Roman control in 206 BC, when the Carthaginians were driven out.

The Roman Conquest of the remainder of Spain, despite successes such as that at NUMANTIA, was not finally achieved until the beginning of the reign of Augustus (27 BC), from which time Spain became a peaceful and valuable asset to the Roman world. Her cities, though little now remains of them, were among the greatest in the Roman world—Emerita Augusta (Mérida), Corduba (Cordova), Hispalis (Seville), Barcino (Barcelona), and Carmona were among the most prominent—and her Northwestern corner was exploited for gold, iron, and tin until well into the 4th century AD.

**Spiro Mound.** A temple mound of the Caddo culture in the MISSISSIPPIAN TRADITION of Oklahoma. The site is noted for the fine assemblages of Southern Cult, or Southern Death Cult, ritual objects and dates from AD 1450 to 1650. Many of the designs on the carved shell gorgets and embossed sheet copper ornaments probably came from Mesoamerica, perhaps from the Huastec culture of Veracruz. These designs include dancing eagle warriors, skulls, and weeping and open eyes.

**Split** (Salona). A Roman city on the Adriatic coast of Yugoslavia. Remains survive of part of the Roman town, with walls, gates, and baths, but the main building is the palace of Diocletian (emperor AD 285–305) which lies nearby in the heart of the modern town. This was built within strong four-square walls with heavily guarded gates and towers, not for military reasons, but because Diocletian, a soldier emperor, wished to retire in luxury within familiar surroundings.

**Squier, E. G.** (1821–88), and **Davis, E. H.** (1811–88). A journalist and a doctor, respectively, who together wrote the first descriptive study of the mounds of Eastern North America. Their book, *Ancient Monuments of the Mississippi Valley*, was published in 1848 as the first scientific publication of the Smithsonian Institution. Its particular importance is that they, like JEFFERSON before them, largely abandoned speculation about the origins of the mounds and based their work on their own archaeological findings. They used a simple functional classification for describing the mounds and formulated hypotheses about their possible uses. Large numbers of mounds in Ohio, their native state, were surveyed. However, in the end they accepted the idea that the mounds were built by a race of moundbuilders unrelated to the present inhabitants of America—who were felt to be incapable of producing such sophisticated buildings or artifacts. Squier afterwards explored the mounds of the Western part of New York State, but in this case he decided that some of the findings were similar to the products of the modern Iroquois. But this did not change his opinion that the mounds of Ohio were built by a lost race who had perhaps migrated to Mexico.

**Stadium.** A running track in antiquity, usually about 200 yd. (183 m) long, and surrounded by seats for spectators. Surviving examples include those at OLYMPIA, DELPHI, Epidauros, and ATHENS.

**Starčevo culture.** Named after the type-site near Belgrade in Yugoslavia, this group of early farmers making painted pottery in the style of contemporary groups in Bulgaria and Northern Greece is dated to the 5th millennium BC. They developed into the VINČA CULTURE, whose eponymous site lies just across the Danube.

**Steam engines.** Stationary steam engines are, for the most part, museumpieces and very few early examples remain on their original sites. The oldest steam engine in existence, the Hawkesbury engine, now at Dartmouth, England, has been moved three times since it was first installed at Griff Colliery, Warwicks. Another, but a much later Newcomen-type engine, is preserved at Elsecar, Yorks., where it was used for colliery drainage from 1787 to 1923. Many Boulton- and Watt-type steam engines survive. Two, dated 1835, are still in use at the Ram Brewery, Wandsworth, London. The reliability of the steam engine made it popular with water supply companies and for sewage pumping, and improved models for these purposes were still being built at the end of the 19th century. Two such engines (1884) are preserved at the pumping station at Papplewick, Notts., England, while Ryhope Pumping Station in Co. Durham has two 1868 engines. A number of North American waterworks have their original engines. The oldest still operating is probably at the Ottawa Waterworks in Canada, where the equipment dates from 1874. The oldest working steam engine in the world (1812) is at Crofton Pumping Station, Wilts., England, on the Kennet and Avon Canal.

Development of the steam engine continued throughout the early years of the present century, especially to meet the demand from textile manufacturers. The most advanced type is represented by the 1906 horizontal compound engine at Dee Mill, Shaw, England, which is preserved by its owners, Courtaulds Ltd. On the European mainland, as in the United States, regrettably little attention has been paid to the preservation of steam engines, but at Vijfhuizen, in the Netherlands, the British-built Cruquius engine (1849) worked continuously until 1933 and is now the centerpiece of a museum devoted to the history of polder drainage. The destruction of examples of America's greatest contribution to the development of steam engines, the Corliss engine, is deplorable: the few that have survived are now in museums.

**Stein, Sir Aurel** (1862–1943). An English orientalist, traveler, and archaeologist, who worked in Iran, Central Asia, and China.

**Stele.** The term for an upright, generally carved or inscribed, stone, especially a Greek gravestone. The fashion for elaborately decorated stones began *c.* 600 BC at Athens, and was continued into the 5th century BC.

In Mesoamerican archaeology, stelae are flat, columnar monuments often carved with calendrical and hieroglyphic inscriptions. They appear as early as the Preclassic Period and continue into the Postclassic. The OLMECS appear to have used such monuments, judging from the Stele C at TRES ZAPOTES, and the so-called "stele-cult" of the Maya, which appeared *c.* AD 300 and continued for six centuries, was an important aspect of the Lowland Maya civilization.

**Stepped adze.** A polished stone adze of the Neolithic period in China, roughly rectangular in shape, flat on one side, and with a step on the other. It is distributed along the coastal area of China from Shantung southwards, and is also an important implement in Southeast Asia.

**Steward, J. H.** (1902–72). A North American anthropologist and archaeologist who emphasized that the goals of both disciplines were the same: the understanding of cultural change and the plotting of that change on spatial and temporal planes. In his editing of the monumental *Handbook of the South American Indians*, 1946–50, he was able to develop this approach. The South American continent was marked out into broad cultural areas and into individual cultures, and these were then discussed in their development through time and space.

**Stoa.** A Greek building with a long open colonnade, used particularly in temple enclosures and in the AGORA. Several such buildings are known at ATHENS: the most famous is the Stoa Poikile (painted stoa), which bears episodes from Athenian history in pictures, and was built *c.* 460 BC.

**Stonehenge.** Perhaps the best known of British, or even of European prehistoric monuments, Stonehenge is a highly atypical construction which has few comparable parallels. The monument began in the later Neolithic period as a simple banked enclosure, of the kind now generally referred to as a HENGE (though somewhat misleadingly, as the term means "hanging" and is a description of a later feature, the three-stone trilithons). Such monuments are later than the majority of megalithic tombs (*see* MEGALITH), and the stone construction at Stonehenge is an elaboration dating to a period when stone tombs were not generally in use, in the Early Bronze Age. The stones used were of two kinds: the inner horseshoe arrangement of characteristic "bluestones," geologically attributable to a source in Wales; and the larger sarsens, a natural weathered covering of the chalk downlands, used for the trilithons. There is now some controversy as to whether the bluestones were brought by human agency, or as glacial erratics during the Ice Age; if the latter case is true, then Bronze Age man must have scoured Southern England for scattered examples. Equally remarkable are the sarsens, for the trilithon constructions, mortised on top for security, represent a great engineering achievement both in their erection and in their shaping—cleverly adjusted to take account of optical illusion.

The purpose of the site can only be a ritual one, connected with the seasonal gathering of local tribes, and it may have had an astrological significance.

**Stone technology.** The Stone Age is a division based originally on stone tools, and evidence for it, especially in its earlier stages, comes most often from such tools. Accordingly, an early objective of research into prehistory was to discover and date the earliest stone toolmaking. Because Palaeolithic tools were already rather well made, cruder and cruder pieces, sometimes called eoliths, were collected from deposits of Pliocene or Miocene date. Doubts were raised about whether these were truly "artifacts," (i.e., made by man), and, ever since, the question of criteria for recognizing human stone technology has been a key one.

Generations of prehistorians have experimented in

Flint side scrapers of Quina type, characteristic of the Charentian Mousterian, from caves in Southwest France.

making their own stone tools, and have learned to distinguish "mechanical" fractures from "thermal" fractures. While thermal fracturing, usually from frost action, is common in nature, mechanical fracturing is rare; when it has happened from several different directions, it is almost certain evidence of human activity.

A mechanical fracture detaches a flake from the original flint or other rock core. The main flake surface where it has come away from the core has certain highly characteristic features. These include first, a distinct point of percussion on the ridge between the main flake surface and the platform or butt on which the original blow was directed; second, a swelling or bulb near this point on the main flake or "bulbar" surface; and third, rings of percussion or undulations spreading concentrically from the point. There are two other features which occur only on some flakes: a scar on the bulb and radial fissures or *striae* near its edge. This type of fracture is called conchoidal. When rock is hit, the shock waves radiate out conically from the point of impact and fracture occurs along these wave lines. An actual cone sometimes survives at the point of percussion.

The flakes removed vary greatly. They may be thick and clumsy, with blunt edges and the original cortex or surface of the rock over much of the back. Alternatively they may be thin and fine, and have been removed with a hammer of soft material like antler, instead of a hard hammer stone. If the flint worker requires a flake with a sharp edge round it, or if he requires a special shape like a long narrow blade, then it is necessary first to prepare the core with preliminary flakes until it is the right shape for the removal of the desired flake. When applied to producing flakes with a sharp edge round them, this is called the Levallois technique.

Once the various flakes have been removed, Stone Age men often applied secondary flaking, called retouch. Sometimes retouch was applied systematically to a core until it was a core tool of the desired shape. Retouch falls into two main types. Abrupt or blunting retouch can be applied to the edges of flakes at a steep angle. It may be for blunting the edge to make finger pressure possible, and it sometimes helps to make a sharp strong point. The other kind of retouch, invasive retouch, travels further in from the edge at a more or less steep angle.

Prehistorians have long tried to learn what stone tools were used for by experimenting themselves and by comparing the tools with those in use today amongst stone-using people. This has helped to confirm the identification of one or two obvious types, like axes and arrowheads; but for most Palaeolithic tools, like hand-axes and chopping tools, nothing has been learned.

An alternative approach, now being widely tried but still a long way from giving reliable results, is the study of wear traces on the tools. This may be in the form of tiny chips knocked off in use, or of polish and minute scratches visible only under the microscope. The gloss on sickles, produced by cutting down crops, has thus been detected.

The best clues to usage so far come from circumstantial evidence or context. For example, handaxes are found around the carcasses of large game animals. Axes have been found in their original hafts, and arrowheads sometimes have marks or discoloration where the shaft was. On the whole it is unlikely that the tool shapes recognized by archaeologists were used for a single purpose only.

Some of the more common tool shapes known are: the rough pebble tools, lumps with a few flakes removed from one end to form a rough cutting edge; handaxes chipped over both surfaces and often pointed at one end; cleavers, made of large flakes with a wide cutting edge at one end; "scrapers" (sometimes called *racloirs* because they may well have been used for cutting or planing); burins, with a chisel-like engraving end; awls, with a sharp point and sometimes traces of rotary wear; and leaf-shaped (foliate) points, possibly spear- or arrowheads.

At the end of the Palaeolithic, a variety of tiny blades or microblades were made: these often have abrupt retouch, sometimes to make them into pointed or triangular barbs. It is known that they were often made by notching and snapping off the thicker (bulbar) end of the bladelet, which becomes a characteristic waste product called a "microburin." Such retouched microblades are called microliths.

The trend towards blade manufacture, which marks the Upper Palaeolithic, results in a much longer cutting edge from a given weight of raw material. Blades, in addition to being twice as long as they are wide, often have parallel scars running down their backs. The tiny microblades gain an even greater length of cutting edge from a block of flint by a factor of as much as 10 times. Advanced stone technology is also often characterized by pressure flaking, which produces a beautifully finished tool with straight and strong edges. In the Neolithic, stone axes were highly polished by laborious grinding on a rubbing stone. Circular knives were sometimes also ground to a sharp edge in this way.

At first in the Stone Age, there were few distinct tool types and none of the advanced techniques of core preparation and retouch. In Europe this stage goes back possibly a million years, but in Africa it existed over 2 million years ago.

**Stratigraphy.** The basic "law" of excavation is the common-sense principle that lower layers are older than overlying ones. The realization that chronological sequences could be built up by careful observation of superposition was first developed in geology in the 19th century, and it caused great improvement in excavation techniques when used by archaeologists.

**Strong, Duncan** (1899–1953). One of the founders of modern Peruvian archaeology. During the 1930s and 1940s he excavated extensively on the coast of Nazca, in Pachacamac, Paracas, and the Virú valley.

**Sue ware.** A high-fired wheel-thrown type of Japanese ceramic found in tombs of the Kofun period (4th–7th century AD). This particular ceramic derived from the pottery of the Old Silla period in Korea. (*See* GREAT TOMBS PERIOD.)

**Sui Dynasty.** The ruling house (AD 589–618) which reunified China after several centuries of division and interregnum. The capital was established at CH'ANG-AN, and thus laid the foundations for the rule of the succeeding T'ANG DYNASTY. Chinese domination extended into Central Asia, and contact with Western Asia is evident from the influence of Sussanian motifs in textiles and Buddhist paintings. A number of important chambered tombs have been excavated, which were furnished with earthenware TOMB FIGURES.

**Sultantepe.** *See* HARRAN.

**Sumer, Sumerians.** The name given to the southernmost part of Mesopotamia. The Sumerians are its earliest identifiable inhabitants, but opinions differ as to whether they were indigenous or invaders from elsewhere who brought with them the innovations characteristic of the URUK period, among them the art of WRITING. By the beginning of the 3rd millennium BC, they were organized into a series of city states, and the EARLY DYNASTIC period is one of great prosperity. They suffered a period of political eclipse under the Semitic rulers of AKKAD and the GUTI, but several city states seem to have maintained or recovered their independence. Under a series of brilliant rulers, such as Gudea at LAGASH and Ur-Nammu at UR, there was a Sumerian revival, known as the Neo-Sumerian or Ur III period, presided over by a Dynasty of kings at Ur. With the Amorite invasions at the end of the 3rd millennium BC, however, the Sumerians lost their national identity. (*See* AMORITES; SUMERIAN; the chronological table, p. 198.)

**Sumerian.** The earliest recorded language of the southernmost part of Mesopotamia, used during the 3rd millennium BC, and later preserved as the language of religion and ritual. It is an unclassified language which has not so far been convincingly related to any other, living or dead. The cuneiform script was first developed for writing Sumerian, and thus it can be read, while vocabularies containing translations into AKKADIAN have led to its decipherment (*see* SUMER, SUMERIANS; WRITING).

**Sung Dynasty.** The Sung (AD 960–1279) reunified China after the divisions of the 10th century following the collapse of the T'ANG DYNASTY. It was always threatened by nomadic tribes: first the Jürchen, who took the title of the CHIN DYNASTY, and later the Mongols, who ruled China as the YÜAN DYNASTY. When the Jürchen drove the Sung from their Northern capital of K'ai-feng in AD 1126, they moved their court to Hangchou in the South. This was a period of great literary and artistic achievement. Some buildings still stand and have been investigated. The excavations of the foundations of pagodas have proved a fruitful source of precisely dated Buddhist bronzes and ceramics, and tombs belonging to the imperial family show that the monumental style of the T'ang Dynasty continued at least into the first part of the Sung Dynasty. Excavation of lesser tombs has revealed regional differences, including, in the South, the placing of decorated urns around the coffin. In additior

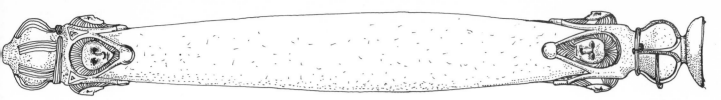

A ceremonial scepter or whetstone, which was probably surmounted by a bronze stag, from the Sutton Hoo ship burial.

investigation of a number of kiln sites has produced evidence of many types of ceramics in the Sung Dynasty.

**Sunium**. A promontory at the Southern tip of Attica with a Temple to Poseidon, built *c*. 440 BC. It was also a harbor, fortified during the Peloponnesian Wars in the late 4th century BC.

**Surveying**. The normal methods of land surveying (e.g., leveling and planetabling) have long been used by archaeologists to make maps and plans of ancient earthworks and standing structures, and of features found in excavation; however, increasing use is now being made of AIR PHOTOGRAPHY as a time-saving method. Numerous techniques have been developed in the last 30 years to search for buried and underwater features. Various sonar devices are employed to detect sunken wrecks and the internal structure of such massive monuments as the pyramids of Egypt and Mexico.

Two techniques, magnetic location and resistivity surveying, have proved especially valuable in prospecting for structures buried beneath the ground, and they are now widely used by archaeologists. Sensitive instruments are used to detect minute anomalies in the earth's magnetic field caused by iron objects, fired structures such as hearths and kilns, and the high humus content of filled-in pits and ditches. Resistivity surveying measures the resistance of the ground to electrical current passed through it: the lack of moisture in buried walls, floors, and cavities (e.g., tombs) gives higher resistance, and the greater moisture in filled-in pits and ditches lower resistance, than undisturbed ground. However, even such a traditional method of detection as water divining continues to be useful in the hands of skilled operators, although its scientific basis is still not understood. The drilling of bore holes provides valuable information on the nature, depth, and extent of archaeological deposits.

**Susa**. Biblical Shushan, in Southwestern IRAN, which controlled important East-West trade routes and was the end of the Achaemenid Royal Road from Lydian Sardis. The earliest levels excavated go back to the 4th millennium BC, and are characterized by particularly fine painted pottery. It was the capital of ELAM in Akkadian times. There are several mounds: one with the ruins of the Achaemenid palace and APADANA; one with an acropolis, on which Darius built a citadel in *c*. 500 BC, and which was probably the center of the prehistoric settlement and of the Elamite upper city; and one known as the *Citée royale*, which was the Elamite lower city, with residential and commercial quarters. (*See* the chronological table, p. 198.)

**Sutton Hoo**. The site, in Suffolk, England, of a group of burial mounds near the River Deben. In the largest, the burial of a 7th-century AD East Anglian king was excavated in 1939, and the finds have been described as the richest treasure from British soil.

The burial was laid in a ship propelled by 38 oars. The ship timbers had perished, but the iron clench nails had left an impression in the sand. A burial chamber amidships contained a rich panoply of objects. These included a solid gold buckle decorated with rich interlace ornament, a gold and garnet mounted purselid, a gold and garnet sword pommel and mounts for the sword harness, a pair of gold shoulder clasps, various small gold and garnet strap ends, buckles and fittings, a Byzantine silver dish with the stamp of the Emperor Anastasius, a set of 10 silver bowls also possibly of Byzantine origin, parts of a lyre, a decorated shield, a gilt bronze helmet, an ornamental whetstone or "scepter" surmounted by a bronze stag, hanging bowls, bronze cauldrons, drinking horn mounts, drinking vessels, a pair of silver spoons inscribed "Saul" and "Paul," and a variety of iron objects, as well as 37 Merovingian gold coins. If a body had originally been placed in the mound, no obvious trace remained. The exact date of the burial has been disputed—it lies somewhere between AD 625 and 650. The identity of the king is similarly unknown, though King Raedwald has been suggested as a possibility.

**Sybaris**. A Greek city in Southern Italy, legendary for its luxury and wealth. Its power, as the main channel for Etruscan trade with Greece, was shortlived because of her rivals' jealousy. Remains of Sybaris have recently been located near modern Sibari.

**Syracuse**. A Corinthian city, founded *c*. 733 BC on the East coast of Sicily. Its size and importance established it as leader of the Greek cities in Sicily, and it played a substantial part in struggles with ATHENS and CARTHAGE: it became the capital of Roman Sicily in the 3rd century BC. Many traces of the ancient city remain: temples (including one on the site of the present cathedral), a THEATER, and an AMPHITHEATER.

**Syria–Palestine**. The area comprises the Eastern Mediterranean seaboard with its parallel ranges of mountains and its great river valleys, part of the same geological fault as the Great Rift valley in Africa, leading from the Red Sea up through the Wadi Araba to the Dead Sea, the Jordan valley, the Sea of Galilee, and prolonged by the Bekaa, and the Orontes and Ghab depression. To the east of this Levantine area lies the Syrian plateau, and deserts border it to east and south; to the north the

Left-hand chart:

| Period | Year | MESOPOTAMIA Northern | MESOPOTAMIA Southern | ANATOLIA | PALESTINE | GREECE (Helladic) and the AEGEAN (Minoan and Cycladic) |
|---|---|---|---|---|---|---|
| BRONZE AGE | 1500 | 1st Dyn. of Babylon | | MB | MB II | Middle |
| | 2000 | Isin/Larsa | | EB III B | MB I | |
| | | Post Akkad-Ur III | | EB III A | EB-MB/EB IV | |
| | 2500 | Akkadian | | EB II | EB III | Early II |
| | | Early Dynastic I-III | | | EB II | |
| | 3000 | Gawra | Jemdet Nasr =Protolit. C and D | EB I | EB I | |
| | | | Uruk =Protolit. A and B | | Jericho LC | Early I |
| | 3500 | Northern Ubaid | Ubaid 4 | LC IV | | LN |
| CHALCOLITHIC | 4000 | Halaf | Ubaid 3 | LC III | Jericho Pottery N A and B | |
| | 4500 | | Ubaid 2 (Hajji Muhammad) | LC II | | |
| | | | | LC I | | |
| | 5000 | Hassuna-Samarra | Ubaid 1 (Eridu) | EC | | |
| | 5500 | Hassuna Umm Dabaghiyah | | LN | | EN |
| NEOLITHIC | 6000 | Jarmo | | EN | Jericho Pre-Pottery N 'A' | |
| | 6500 | | | | | |
| | 7000 | | | Aceramic | Jericho Pre-Pottery N 'B' | |

Right-hand chart:

| Year | Assur | Arpachiyah | Tepe Gawra | Uruk | Eridu | Ur/Al 'Ubaid | 'Amuq | Hama | Ugarit | Chagar Bazar | Mersin | Troy | Beycesultan | Tepe Giyan | Tepe Sialk | Susa | Tepe Hissar |
|---|---|---|---|---|---|---|---|---|---|---|---|---|---|---|---|---|---|
| 1500 | C, D | | IV | | | | K | | | | | VI | III | | | | |
| 2000 | E | | V | | | | J | | J | I | | V | V | IVC | | | III B |
| 2500 | F, G-H | | VI, VII | | | | I, H | J | III A3, III A2 | 2-3, 4-5 | I, II | III, II, I | XVI, XIX | IVB, IVA | | De, Dc-a | III A, II B, II A |
| 3000 | | | VIII | III | | | G, F | K | III A1 | | XII, XIII | | XL | V D | | Cb-c, Ca | I C, I B |
| 3500 | | | XII, XIII | XIV | V, VI | III, II | E | | III B | | XIV, XV | | | VC2 | III 6-7b | B, A | I A |
| 4000 | TT1 | | XIX | XVIII | VIII | I | | L | III C | | XVI | | | VC1, VB | III 4-5, III 1-3 | | |
| 4500 | TT5, TT6 | | XX | | XIV | | D | | IV A | 6 | XVIII | | | VA | II | | |
| 5000 | TT10 | | XXVI | | XV, XIX | | C | | IV B, IV C | 15 | XXI | | | | I | | |
| 5500 | TT15? | | | | | | B | M | V A | | XXVI | | | | | | |
| 6000 | | | | | | | A | | V B | | XXXIII | | | | | | |
| 6500 | | | | | | | | | V C | | | | | | | | |

E = Early   M = Middle   L = Late   B = Bronze   C = Chalcolithic   N = Neolithic

A chronological chart showing the correlation between some of the early cultures of the ancient Near East and the various excavated levels of the main archaeological sites.

highlands of ANATOLIA form a natural frontier, along which runs a main East-West road via ALEPPO to and from the Rivers Euphrates and Khabur and their access to MESOPOTAMIA and beyond. The rich and narrow coastal plain, with its many harbors, has always been a gateway for trade and the main mountain passes inland to the North-South route of the river valleys have always been strategically important. Of these, the Homs gap, the Nahr el Abiad, and Orontes valleys are the only routes inland from the Northern part of the coastal strip and have always been vital, as the sites of QATNA, Qadesh, Homs (the Classical and Christian Emessa), UGARIT, Latakya, Antioch/Antakya, and the 'AMUQ indicate. The principal sites are along the natural trade routes and the building of a dam on the Euphrates, east of Aleppo, has led to recent large-scale salvage excavation of many sites in that area.

Early settlement sites in Palestine, the Southern part of this area, are represented by the Epipalaeolithic Kebaran culture of the coast (before 10,000 BC). This is succeeded by the NATUFIAN (c. 10,000–8000 BC), with sites further inland and extending into Syria. Many of these, and a large number of burials, have been investigated, especially around Mount CARMEL, and the principal ones are Ain Mallaha in Galilee and Abu Hureyra and Mureybet I in the Euphrates dam area, all three characterized by a microlithic (small blade) flint industry and incipient food-producing techniques. Occupation continued in Mureybet II throughout the 8th millen-

nium BC, and excavation has shown that the settlement was larger, with circular houses and perhaps the first attested case of cereal cultivation. The first rectangular structures appear in Mureybet III alongside round ones, OBSIDIAN was imported, and wall paintings and horn cores were used for decoration. Mureybet II and III, and the site of Tell Aswad near Damascus, with its numerous figurines, are probably contemporary with Pre-Pottery Neolithic A (PPNA) JERICHO while Mureybet IV, a later occupation of Tell Abu Hureyra, and ÇAYÖNÜ near Diyarbekir are contemporary with Pre-Pottery Neolithic B (PPNB) Jericho—a culture which may have been brought from the North but which shows some continuity with the preceding culture, especially at Beidha in the South, Tell Ramad near Damascus, and Mureybet. At Beidha there is an unbroken sequence from round huts to rectangular stone-built houses with buttresses, but in Jericho the building material was mud brick. In the gypsum area of Southern Syria during the late 7th millennium BC, a composite of lime and gray ashes was shaped into vessels and fired to form what is known as "white ware." This occurs at a number of sites and was exported to ÇATAL HÜYÜK (period VIB) in Anatolia. It was replaced by pottery, which first appears at Umm Dabaghiyah (see MESOPOTAMIA), and rapidly develops into the dark, burnished wares of 'Amuq A. The flint industry changes and there are the first examples of domesticated animals.

Climatic changes c. 6000 BC were probably responsible for the abandonment of Pre-Pottery Neolithic B sites except for those along the coast. The Neolithic period is characterized by the wide spread of pottery ('Amuq A and B), increased farming, herding, and trade. Early

Neolithic architecture appears at BYBLOS. In the Middle Neolithic period, Northern Syria was influenced by the HALAF culture and there was a shift from the Anatolian sphere of influence to the Mesopotamian. Halaf imports are found as far south as Ard Tlaïti in the Bekaa, and the Wadi Rabah in Palestine. New "Canaanite" flint blades make their appearance ('Amuq C). The abrupt end of the Halaf culture *c.* 4500 BC heralds a period of decline (Ugarit IIIC, Late Neolithic Byblos), and the beginning of the UBAID. Meanwhile in Palestine, pottery had also appeared in the Yarmukian phase, which was succeeded by the Munhata (= Jericho Neolithic A) and the Wadi Rabah cultures (contemporary with 'Amuq C and D). Cist (stone slab) tombs at Kabri have produced stone vessels, a bone figure and an obsidian mirror. The Ghassulian culture, represented by Teleilat GHASSUL near the Dead Sea, was that of a settled community of farmers at the end of the 4th millennium BC. It is characterized by mud-brick houses on stone foundations, well fired pottery, elaborate stone vessels, and a rich flint industry, though two copper axes were also found. Several other sites belonging to this culture have been found in the Plain of Esdraelon, in the coastal plain near Gaza, and near Beersheba at Tell Abu Matar, where a strongly troglodyte community lived.

At the beginning of the Bronze Age a series of settlements was founded by newcomers, who probably came from the North and East, at ARAD, MEGIDDO, JERICHO, BETH SHAN, and TELL EL FAR'AH, and later at LACHISH, Tell el Hesi, and TELL BEIT MIRSIM. Some interesting burials have survived and, on the basis of pottery they contain, the new groups have been labeled Proto-Urban A, B, and C. In Syria, however, urban development took place early. A huge walled URUK site at Habuba Kabira in the Euphrates dam area has recently been excavated by a German team. We have important Early Bronze Age levels at Byblos, Ugarit, HAMA, Qatna, MARI, and, more recently, at TELL MARDIKH, where archives may throw more light on the history of the area, which is otherwise known only from references in Mesopotamian texts. During the last part of the 3rd millennium BC, the Amorite nomads were moving in from the desert and settling on its fringes. Burials found at Jericho, TELL EL AJJUL, Lachish, Megiddo, Ugarit (*porteurs de torques*), Qatna, and Tell 'As have been associated with the AMORITES, and the term E.B.–M.B. is used by some archaeologists to describe this phase in Palestine.

The urban civilization of the Middle Bronze Age was brought in by another wave of newcomers, and those who settled in Palestine are known as Canaanites. A new type of pottery and a dagger with a raised midrib are associated with them at Byblos, Ugarit, Tell Beit Mirsim, Tell el Ajjul, Ras el 'Ain, and Beth Shemesh. Contacts between Byblos and Egypt are well documented. The Hapiru tribesmen begin to appear in texts (the Mari and Amarna Letters) and have been tentatively equated with the Hebrews and also with the Hyksos tribes. Huge cities with earth ramparts, which are often plastered to form a glacis (slope), now appear throughout Syria–Palestine at CARCHEMISH, Ugarit, Tell Mardikh, Tell Turan, Tell Acharneh, Qatna, Qadesh, HAZOR, Tell

Jeriseh, Jericho, Lachish, Tell el Ajjul and even at Tell el Yahudieh in Egypt, just south of the Delta—a site where a distinctive type of pottery (Tell el Yahudieh juglets) is found. It seems likely that a new type of warfare, associated with the horse and chariot, was responsible for this development, which had appeared earlier in Anatolia. It has been suggested that these innovations were the work of the Hyksos nomads, some of whom may have been related to the HURRIANS.

Rich Middle Bronze Age tombs have been found at Jericho and the Late Bronze Age is particularly well represented at Ugarit. The political history of the area is well documented by the Amarna Letters (*see* AKKADIAN) in the 15th and 14th centuries BC, and it is clear that the little kingdoms of Syria–Palestine were being disputed by the Egyptians and Hittites. The Israelites entered Palestine during the 13th century BC; they were barely settled before the SEA PEOPLE swept through the coastal cities of Syria–Palestine in *c.* 1200 BC. The upheaval led to further changes in population and to the establishment of the Philistines in Palestine and the Phoenicians along the central part of the coast. The Syro-Hittite cities grew up in North Syria, where an influx of Semitic nomads led to the founding of a series of Aramaean kingdoms.

From the 9th century BC onwards, the rich centers of Syria and Palestine attracted Assyrian raids which are recorded in the Old Testament and in Assyrian annals, inscriptions, and reliefs. The fall of Lachish was illustrated by Sennacherib. Nebuchadnezzar carried off the population of JERUSALEM into exile in 587 BC, and Cyrus the Great allowed them to return in 538 BC (but not all did so, as proved by Jewish business archives found in NIPPUR). The Nabataeans established a kingdom on the caravan route from the Red Sea, but they were the last independent Oriental kingdom in the area, which came under Roman domination in 37 BC, though the Herodian Dynasty maintained a certain degree of autonomy. (*See* MASADA; the chronological table, p. 198.)

**Tagar culture.** A semisettled culture in South Siberia (*c.* 700–100 BC). Here, as in the surrounding steppes, the representations of animals were important and are seen on small knives, and belt and harness plaques. Broad daggers used by these people are also found much further west in the Anan 'ino culture in Russia, and to the east on the Northern borders of China.

**Tagua-Tagua.** A site in Central Chile where unifacial tools, blades, and bone tools have been found in association with mastodon bones. The site has been dated to 9400 BC, but typologically it could be older.

**Taima-Taima.** An early stratified site in Northwest Venezuela. The earliest phase has radiocarbon dates ranging from 12,000 to 14,000 years BP (before the present). Bifacial tools, scrapers, blades, and leaf-shaped points are associated with bones of several faunal species, including mastodon and horse.

**Tairona.** A lowland tribe occupying foothills of the

Andes up to 3281 ft. (1,000 m) in the Sierra Nevada of Santa Marta, Colombia, from *c.* AD 1000 to 1500. They lived in large nucleated villages in the mountain folds, cultivated maize, and irrigated their fields. Their pottery is a complex, elaborate ware, painted black and red, and with modeled zoomorphic designs and *appliqué*.

**Talud-Tablero.** An important architectural feature on Mesoamerican sites, consisting of a sloping batter or apron (talud) surmounted by a horizontal, rectangular panel with inset (tablero). It first appeared at TEOTI-HUACAN, where it is the dominant style for temple pyramids. It was then introduced at KAMINALJUYU, in the Guatemalan Highlands, and is also present on one structure at TIKAL, in the Southern Maya Lowlands.

**Tambo Colorado.** An Inca town which functioned as an administrative center, *c.* 1476–1532, in the Pisco valley, Peru. Well preserved architecture reflects the characteristics of Inca architecture combined with local coastal traits.

**T'ang Dynasty.** One of the greatest of the Chinese Dynasties, ruling from its capital, CH'ANG-AN, a large portion of Central Asia AD 618–906. In the years before the rebellion of An-lu-shan in AD 755, it ruled perhaps the most important nation in the world. At Ch'ang-an, Japanese and Sassanian coins have been excavated, and an engraved tablet granting land to a group of Nestorian Christians proves contact with distant countries. Apart from excavations of both palaces and temples at Ch'ang-an, the major excavations relating to this period have been of tombs. The imperial tombs are situated outside the present-day city of Sian on the site of Ch'ang-an and there are a few important tombs at LO-YANG. Edicts prevented the burial of precious materials on any significant scale, so the most important finds have been groups of earthenware figures and vessels decorated with "three-color" lead glaze.

**Tanis.** A site in the Eastern Delta in Egypt, now called San el-Hagar. It was excavated extensively by Auguste Mariette (*see* SERAPEUM), W. M. Flinders PETRIE and, from 1929 until his death in 1966, the French archaeologist Pierre Montet. They uncovered massive mudbrick temple enclosure walls built by Ramesside and 21st-Dynasty pharaohs, enclosing buildings, dedicated to the goddess Anta, dating from the 19th to the 30th Dynasty. Great quantities of sculpture and statuary were found, mostly belonging to Ramesses II, but including many royal 12th-Dynasty statues and some curious sphinxes. The latter, at first associated with the Hyksos invaders of Egypt, led some authorities to identify Tanis with Avaris, the Hyksos Delta capital. The mass of Ramesside statuary and building activity led them to speculate further that Tanis might also be the Ramesside capital Pi-Ramessu, traditionally built by the Hebrews, founded on the site of Avaris. However, none of the Ramesside material can be proved to have been originally at the site. In fact, the presence of reused Old Kingdom blocks suggests that they, like the Ramesside material,

were brought from elsewhere. Perhaps most important, the location of Pi-Ramessu is described in great detail in literary sources and does not conform with that of Tanis.

In 1939 Montet uncovered six brick-built chambers within the 21st-Dynasty enclosure wall containing burials of royalty and officials of the 21st and 22nd Dynasties. Most had been plundered, but the burial of Psusennes I in a stone-lined chamber, together with those of one of his generals and two later kings, Amenemope and a Sheshonq, were intact. Elaborate collars, inlaid bracelets and pectorals, amulets, earrings, and finger-rings made of gold, electrum, silver, and semiprecious stones were comparable in form with those found in TUTANKHAMUN'S TOMB but of inferior workmanship. Psusennes' golden funerary mask, however, was almost as fine as the earlier king's. Three of the coffins were of solid silver, one with a hawk's head. The grave goods included fine gold and silver cups and vessels, bronze *shabtis* (tomb figures), and canopic jars.

Much of the huge site remains unexcavated. Possibly more royal burials, certainly more evidence, lies undiscovered which may finally settle the original identity of Tanis.

**Tarascans.** The name given, erroneously, by the Spaniards to a tribe living in the state of Michoacan, in Mexico. They are famous for their skill in metallurgy and for their fighting abilities, which enabled them to resist all attempts by the Aztecs to conquer them. The shapes of their pottery, the presence of small copper "money axes," and their language suggest long-distance coastal trade with Northern Peru. Their chief ceremonial center, Tzintzuntzan, near Lake Patzcuaro, has a unique construction of five temples built on circular projections from a rectangular bank.

**Tardenoisian.** One of a group of MESOLITHIC cultures which may be regarded as transitional to farming, in the sense that in their later stages evidence of domestic animals is found. Typical tools are chisel-shaped arrowheads. The culture follows the SAUVETERRIAN in France, where it was first recognized, and it dates mainly from before 4000 BC.

**Tarquinia** (Tarquinii). An Etruscan city, famous for its tombs with a series of grave paintings from the 6th to the 1st century BC. Remains of the city walls, with a gate dating from the 4th century BC, survive.

**Tarragona** (Tarraco). A town on the Northeastern Mediterranean coast of Spain, founded as a colony by Scipio on the site of an earlier native settlement. Built up by Augustus, it retains its citadel walls, the AMPHITHEATER, and part of its AQUEDUCT.

**Tarsus.** In 1934, the Americans initiated excavations on the mound of Gözlüküle on the South coast of ANATOLIA. A sequence of levels from the beginning of the 4th millennium to the 6th century BC was recorded, and this fills many gaps in the sequence established at the other major Cilician site of MERSIN.

**Ta-wen-k'ou culture.** A Neolithic culture of the painted pottery group in China, found predominantly in Shantung province. Dating from *c.* 3500 BC, it precedes the LUNG-SHAN CULTURE.

**Taxila.** One of the two main cities of Gandhara (Northwest frontier province of ancient India, now Pakistan), Taxila at its height was a cosmopolitan center, influenced both by the indigenous cultures of contemporary India and by successive Western civilizations—Achaemenid, Greek, Parthian, and Roman. It was probably occupied from the 6th century BC, and was destroyed *c.* AD 500, probably by the White Huns (Hunas). There were three successive cities at Taxila: the Bhir mound, Sirkap, and Sirsukh. (*See also* INDIA.)

**Te-hua.** The kiln site in Fukien province in China, at which a dense creamy-white porcelain, known as *blanc de chine*, was made from the MING DYNASTY (AD 1368–1644) onwards. (*See* CERAMICS, CHINA.)

**Tell, Tepe, or Hüyük.** Names, used in the Near East, for artificial mounds formed by the accumulation of ancient ruins. This phenomenon is due to the extensive use of mud brick as a building material which, unlike wood or stone, cannot be reused, rapidly deteriorates if unprotected by plastering, bakes, and is therefore preserved when exposed to fire. Successive rebuilding will lead to the formation of a mound, so that better-built and better-maintained buildings, such as palaces or temples, will eventually be at a lower level than surrounding houses. As the mound becomes steeper, fewer houses can be built at the summit and thus are built on the slopes, which are often terraced. When a mound becomes too steep, the settlement will spread around the base of the tell. Excavation of a mound is a complicated process since buildings in use at the same date may be at different levels and the upper level of a "parent" mound may be the same date as the lowest levels of a secondary mound built up against it. Some tells have been excavated and published as a series of horizontal layers and this has resulted in considerable archaeological confusion. STRATIGRAPHY, or the careful identification of successive building levels, is vitally important.

**Tell Ahmar.** The site of Til Barsip, later called Kar-Salmanasar, capital of the Aramaean state of Bit-Adini, situated at a crossing of the River Euphrates south of Carchemish. It was excavated by the French from 1927 to 1931, where they found an Assyrian palace of the 9th century BC onwards, decorated with wall paintings of the 8th and 7th centuries BC. From this palace, the Assyrian kings could control the Syrian and Cilician states. Earlier buildings and an Early Bronze Age cemetery were also found.

**Tell al 'Ubaid.** *See* UBAID.

**Tell Arpachiyah.** A small site in Northern Mesopotamia, excavated by M. E. L. Mallowan in 1933 and inhabited from the middle of the 6th to the early part of the 4th millennium BC. Levels TT1–4 produced pottery of the Northern UBAID style, TT5 was transitional, TT6–10 contained some of the finest HALAF pottery yet found, as well as tholoi (*see* THOLOS) or beehive houses in *pisé* (mud brick) on stone foundations. There were at least five further levels, producing pottery belonging to the Early Halaf, decorated with animals. Stone amulets and figurines were also found. (*See* the chronological table, p. 198.)

**Tell Asmar.** *See* DIYALA.

**Tell Atchana.** The site of the ancient city of Alalakh where the kings of Yamhad (ALEPPO, Syria) had a palace in the 18th and 17th centuries BC. In the ruins of this palace (level VII) and the adjoining temple, were found, among other treasures, a large number of tablets and seal impressions, many of them bearing Hurrian names, and some elephant tusks. In level IV, another palace and archive were found, documenting the 15th century BC, and the relations of the Hittites and Mitannians. The statue of King Idrimi was carved with an important historical inscription of the late 16th century BC, and NUZI ware was also found. Earlier levels going back to *c.* 2000 BC (though dated earlier by the excavator), and later ones up to *c.* 1200 BC also produced interesting material and a sequence of temples and palaces.

**Tell Beit Mirsim.** A site in Palestine, excavated by the Americans under W. F. ALBRIGHT from 1926 to 1932. A clear stratigraphic sequence was obtained from the Early Bronze Age period III to the 6th century BC (*see* SYRIA–PALESTINE).

**Tell Brak.** A frontier outpost in Akkadian times and throughout history, on a tributary of the River Khabur on the Syrian-Iraqi border. It is being excavated by a British team (1977) and was excavated from 1937 to 1939 by M. E. L. Mallowan. The earliest levels of this huge mound have not been reached but HALAF, UBAID, and URUK sherds have been found. In the JEMDET NASR period (end of the 4th—beginning of the 3rd millennium BC), there was a succession of four "Eye Temples"—so-called because of votive amulets with large eyes found in them. The foundations had been strewn with FAIENCE beads and the plan was cruciform, with a decorated altar. SEALS and other types of amulet were also found. Though the EARLY DYNASTIC was represented, the next important remains belong to the Akkadian period, when Naram-Sin built a palace. Tablets were also found. Later, part of the mound was abandoned but Khabur ware characterizes the early 2nd millennium BC levels, and NUZI ware appears in the 15th century BC. The site was abandoned before the end of the 2nd millennium BC, though a Roman fort was later built there.

**Tell Chuera.** An important site in North Syria, west of the upper reaches of the River Khabur. Buildings of the EARLY DYNASTIC period and temples of a distinctive type have been found which contained vessels, statues, and seal impressions. A late 3rd-millennium BC processional way, leading to a temple, is lined with stelae.

**Tell el Ajjul.** A site near modern Gaza in Palestine. It was particularly important in the Middle Bronze Age when it was strongly fortified. A large building of that date has been found and also tombs containing gold and silver jewelry. (*See* SYRIA–PALESTINE.)

**Tell el-Amarna.** *See* AKHENATEN.

**Tell el Far'ah.** A site west of the Jordan excavated by the French from 1946 onwards. Chalcolithic remains were found, but the site was particularly important in Early Bronze Age periods I and II, when it was walled. Several burials have been found. After a gap it was re-occupied in Middle Bronze Age II, until the 9th century BC, and it may have been Tirzah, the capital of Omri, before he moved to SAMARIA. It was finally destroyed by the Assyrians in 722 BC. (*See* ASSYRIA, ASSYRIANS; ISRAEL, ISRAELITES; SYRIA–PALESTINE.) Tell el Far'ah should not be confused with FARA in Mesopotamia or TELL FARA in Palestine.

**Tell es-Sawwan.** A remarkable 6th-millennium BC site near Samarra, recently excavated by Iraqi archaeologists. The buildings are the earliest known in which moldmade bricks are used. Veined alabaster vessels and figurines are found in the earlier levels, where the pottery is plain and crude. In levels III and IV, monochrome pottery appears, but it is replaced by polychrome pottery in level V. The designs are geometric or naturalistic. In level IIIA, a buttressed wall was built along the line of an earlier ditch round the settlement. Many graves were found in levels I, II, IV, and V. (*See* MESOPOTAMIA.)

**Tell Fakheriyah.** This is perhaps the site of Washukanni, the capital of the kingdom of Mitanni (*see* HURRIANS), in Northern Mesopotamia on the River Khabur. Some tablets, statues, and ivories of the 2nd millennium BC have been found here.

**Tell Fara.** A Palestinian site excavated by the British from 1928 to 1930. The city flourished from the Middle Bronze Age period II, to the Iron Age, and many contemporary tombs were found. Neighboring Chalcolithic and Early Bronze Age sites were also excavated. (*See* SYRIA–PALESTINE.) Tell Fara should not be confused with FARA in Mesopotamia or TELL EL FAR'AH in Palestine.

**Tell Halaf.** *See* HALAF.

**Tell Hariri.** *See* MARI.

**Tell Harmal.** A site on the outskirts of Baghdad, excavated by the Iraqis in 1945. The walled city of Shaduppum belongs to the first centuries of the 2nd millennium BC, and contains a temple guarded by terra-cotta lions. A large number of cuneiform tablets were found. (*See* MESOPOTAMIA.)

**Tell Judeideh.** *See* 'AMUQ.

**Tell Mardikh.** A large fortified site in Northern Mesopotamia, 34 mi. (55 km) southwest of ALEPPO. Recent excavations have uncovered important Middle Bronze Age remains, including a city gate and some fine sculpture. An inscription on a basalt statue, found in 1968, identified the site as the ancient Ebla. The city was previously known from cuneiform texts, including inscriptions of the kings of AKKAD and of Gudea of LAGASH. Soundings revealed that a late Early Bronze Age city extended over the whole area, and was later covered by the Middle Bronze Age city.

Excavations in the southwest part of the acropolis revealed a large palace, built on terraces against the slopes of the mound; this was either destroyed by Naram-Sin of Akkad in *c.* 2250 BC, or else by Sargon some 50 years earlier. The first 42 tablets were found there in 1974 and, in 1975, the "library" of the palace was uncovered. It opened off a large courtyard, surrounded—at least on the two surviving sides—by porticos linked by a massive corner tower. The "library" contained *c.* 16,630 tablets and fragments, most of which had been arranged on wooden shelves. There are commercial, administrative, financial, economic, lexical, historical, literary, and agricultural texts written in cuneiform (*see* WRITING) in a hitherto unknown Northwest Semitic language, called Eblaite by the excavators. Bilingual Sumerian and Eblaite vocabularies are particularly important. The texts mention several rulers and a tentative order of succession has been established over five generations. The city of MARI is mentioned frequently and seems to have been a very rich and powerful rival of Ebla, with territories including ASSUR. The conquest of Mari must have made Ebla the most powerful kingdom in the area.

In addition to the tablets, a wooden chair and table were found in the palace. These were decorated with friezes of combats between heroes and animals in shell inlay. Carved steatite and lapis lazuli fragments were also found, as well as wooden doors carved with figures in relief, and cylinder seal impressions. All these are close to the Mesopotamian artistic traditions of the late Early Dynastic III and early Akkadian periods. This level, called Mardikh IIB1 (*c.* 2400–2250 BC), and the succeeding level, Mardikh IIB2 (*c.* 2250–2000 BC), contained pottery similar to that from phases I and J in the 'AMUQ sequence. From the evidence so far available, it would seem that Ebla may have adapted the Sumerian cuneiform script for writing a Semitic language before the Akkadians, and what has previously been called Akkadian art may, in fact, owe much to Syrian influence.

**Tello, Julio C.** (1892–1949). A great Peruvian archaeologist, who undertook numerous excavations and identified many cultural groups, including CHAVIN, CHIMU, HUARI, and NAZCA.

**Tell Uqair.** A site in Southern Mesopotamia, excavated by the Iraqis from 1940 to 1942. A temple on a platform belonging to the Late URUK or JEMDET NASR period (end of the 4th millennium BC) is known as the "Painted Temple," because of leopards and imitation cone mosaic painted round the cult platform. Pottery from the Late UBAID period onwards was found, and so were pictographic tablets of the Jemdet Nasr period.

**Tenayuca.** A CHICHIMEC site in the northern suburbs of Mexico City. Its large pyramid is the best surviving example of pyramids of Chichimec and Aztec type, and shows how the great pyramid of TENOCHTITLAN must have appeared. The original building was covered at 52-year intervals by no less than six successive pyramid and temple buildings. Only part of the seventh stairway remains, but the whole of the sixth pyramid has been restored.

Unlike pyramids belonging to earlier cultures, there are two parallel stairways leading to two temples on the top of the one structure. We are uncertain to what gods they were dedicated, but one was probably the rain god, Tlaloc, and the other a tribal god. Recent excavations have shown traces of TALUD-TABLERO-style architecture, indicating TEOTIHUACAN occupation in the Classic Period.

**Tenochtitlan.** The Aztec name for their capital, on a marshy island in Lake Texcoco, now drained. The downtown area of present-day Mexico city is now on the site.

**Teotihuacan.** The great city of Teotihuacan is about 30 mi. (48 km) northeast of Mexico City. It grew out of a Preclassic village and at the height of its prosperity covered an area of about 8 sq. mi. (21 km²). It was the dominating political and economic force in Mexico during the Classic Period, c. AD 200.

The center consists of a long ceremonial way oriented about 17° east of north, and known by its Aztec name of "Avenue of the Dead." Lining the avenue on both sides are substructures of small temples and residential buildings, with the enormous Pyramid of the Sun on the east side and the courtyard named the "Ciudadella," or Citadel, by the Spaniards. This encloses the Temple of QUETZALCOATL. At the north end of the Avenue is a court surrounded by temple substructures and the Pyramid of the Moon. The whole city was laid out on a rectangular plan like a modern city. Very large compounds were built to fit in with the basic plan. Most of these can only be traced by following the lines of the foundations. A dwelling compound at Teotihuacan consisted of a number of open courts surrounded by cloisters, with rooms opening off them. Usually there was a small temple for the inhabitants of the compound. It can be inferred that the compounds were the dwellings of extended families and their servants.

The orientation of the whole city was determined by that of the Pyramid of the Sun, which faces the setting sun on the horizon on the day when the sun passes right overhead, a ritual orientation found in many Mesoamerican cities. Tunnels driven into the pyramid showed that there were Preclassic figurines in the rubble fill, demonstrating clearly that it dates back to that period. This pyramid and the Temple of Quetzalcoatl, built at the beginning of the Classic Period, are the oldest visible buildings on the site.

Other buildings, of later date in the Classic Period, all have the same architectural style, the diagnostic

A view, from the Pyramid of the Moon, of the Avenue of the Dead and the Pyramid of the Sun at Teotihuacan.

feature of which is known as TALUD-TABLERO. In the Temple of Quetzalcoatl, the tableros were carved with the undulating body of a feathered serpent and marine shells, and projecting heads of the feathered serpent and of the rain god, Tlaloc, were set into the wall. There were altogether 360 heads, corresponding to the days of the year. The only other known building with these calendrical affinities is the Pyramid of the Niches at EL TAJIN, which was probably inspired by Teotihuacan.

A mapping project undertaken by the University of Rochester, in which over 5,000 buildings were examined and surface finds collected from the whole area, showed that there were over 400 workshops for the making of OBSIDIAN tools and weapons, 300 potteries, and a number of workshops for other crafts. They also found that the city was divided into a number of *barrios*, or districts, devoted to the various crafts. Of special interest was one *barrio* in which all the pottery and other artifacts were in the style of Oaxaca, with a tomb constructed in the same style, but with the buildings in the style of Teotihuacan. It is uncertain whether the *barrio* was set aside as a quarter for merchants visiting the city, or was an embassy, or was possibly for hostages forced to live in Teotihuacan as a guarantee of the good behavior of their territory, but it indicates a very close connection between the two areas.

The influence of Teotihuacan extended also to the Maya, since the city was undoubtedly a great trading community. It may also have been a great imperialist state, since Classic buildings at KAMINALJUYU, among the Highland Maya in Guatemala, were built in the talud-tablero style, and cylindrical vases with slab tripod feet and conical lids were very common. The impression given by the archaeology is that Kaminaljuyu had been colonized by Teotihuacan. Teotihuacan influences also reached the Lowland Maya. Pottery has been found at a number of sites both in Yucatan and among the Southern Maya—even as far south as COPAN in Honduras. At TIKAL, the ruling Dynasty was closely linked with Teotihuacan, as can be seen from Stele 31, which shows a ruler arrayed in typical Maya regalia but with two warriors in the style of Teotihuacan. They may have been bodyguards. We do not know the exact status of this ruler, but he may well have been a puppet appointed by Teotihuacan and provided with a kind of praetorian guard.

The early part of the 7th century AD saw the collapse of Teotihuacan, and a general upset of the settled order, but many of its traditions (the worship of Quetzalcoatl, for instance) and the technology of the city were absorbed by the more barbarous newcomers.

**Tepe.** *See* TELL, TEPE, OR HÜYÜK.

**Tepe Gawra.** A site near Mosul in Northern Mesopotamia, excavated by the Americans in 1927 and from 1931 to 1938. It was occupied from the beginning of the 5th to the middle of the 2nd millennium BC. The earlier levels were the most significant. Level XXVI, the lowest found, belonged to Neolithic settlers who used undecorated pottery, and it was succeeded by levels XXV–

XX, in which there is decorated HALAF pottery. UBAID pottery is found in levels XIX–XIII, and this latest level also contained three interesting temples. Level XII was destroyed by fire and corresponds to the Early URUK phase in the South, called Early Gawra in the North. Level XI, or Middle Gawra, has the first of an interesting sequence of temples (until level VIII), and a round building containing many rooms (other round buildings had been found in levels XX and XVII). Many rich tombs were found. The next important level is VIII, which marks the end of the Late Gawra period and is contemporary with the JEMDET NASR period in the South, and in which there is an interesting temple. The remaining levels cover the 3rd and first half of the 2nd millennia BC. Interesting pottery was recovered and there were stamp SEALS from the Halaf levels onwards. (*See* the chronological table, p. 198.)

**Tepe Giyan.** A site in Iran, excavated by the French and situated east of Kermanshah. It was occupied from the 5th to the beginning of the 1st millennium BC, and has produced a rich series of intramural graves and a large range of 3rd and 2nd millennia BC pottery. The gray and black burnished wares, generally associated with the arrival of the INDO-EUROPEANS, appear at the end of the sequence, and there is a large building of Assyrian type. (*See* the chronological table, p. 198.)

**Tepe Hissar.** A site near Damghan in Northern Iran, near the Caspian Sea, where more than 1600 prehistoric burials and a Sassanian palace have been found. The main occupation of the mound dates from *c.* 3500 to 1600 BC, and an interesting pottery sequence and metal objects have been recovered. (*See* the chronological table, p. 198.)

**Tepe Sialk.** A site in Iran, near Kashan, south of Teheran. During the second half of the 6th millennium BC, there is painted pottery, a little metalwork, stone tools, and weapons, and the dead were buried beneath their huts. Mud-brick architecture then appears in Sialk II (*c.* 5000 BC). After a move to another mound, the pottery becomes more sophisticated, the wheel and stamp SEALS appear, and copper is cast in molds. After evidence of destruction, there appear monochrome pottery, clay tablets in Proto-Elamite (*see* WRITING), and more evidence of the use of metal at the beginning of the 3rd millennium BC. At the end of the 2nd millennium BC the appearance of iron and of a new type of painted, spouted pottery, found in tombs of the 10th and 9th centuries BC outside the settlement, herald the arrival of newcomers. Around the 9th to 8th century BC the site was destroyed and abandoned. (*See* the chronological table, p. 198.)

**Tepe Yahya.** A site near Kirman in Southern Iran, where current American excavations (1977) are uncovering a city which stood on an important trade route between Mesopotamia and the Indus Valley, possibly via Shahr-i-Sokhta, and the Persian Gulf via BAMPUR. Important Neolithic levels have been found. Tablets written in Proto-Elamite script have appeared in a late 4th-millennium BC context and were written on the site. Chlorite seems to have been quarried nearby and workshops produced distinctive bowls (previously thought to have been made of steatite) which were exported throughout the Near East during the first half of the 3rd millennium BC. The site continued to be inhabited until the beginning of our era.

**Tequendama cave.** A cave outside Bogota, in the highlands of Southeast Colombia. It contained stratified preceramic remains dating from 9000 to 1000 BC. Large stemmed points occur from the earliest levels.

**Terp.** A term used to describe a type of settlement found in Frisia, which superficially resembles the tells of the Near East. Because of frequent flooding, the houses were built on artificial mounds standing some 10 or 20 ft. (3 or 6 m) above the surrounding ground. The mounds range in date from the pre-Roman Iron Age to the Carolingian period, most of them being Roman or later. Related mounds are known by the terms warf, werft, wurt, or wierde.

**Terra Sigillata.** Red-glazed, stamped pottery of Roman imperial date, made in several centers in Italy and the Roman provinces. The best known is perhaps the plain and relief decorated pottery of the 1st–3rd century AD from Southern, Central, and Eastern Gaul (called Samian ware from Pliny's description of similar wares from the island of Samos). Other centers of production were Northern Italy—a successor to ARRETINE WARE—the Eastern Mediterranean, Spain, and North Africa.

**Textiles, Industrial archaeology.** The textile industry, in all industrialized countries, presents a formidable and probably insoluble conservation problem. By the mid-19th century, cotton and woollen mills had become so large, in such areas as New England, in the United States, and South Lancashire and the West Riding of Yorkshire in England, that any modern yearnings to preserve them as monuments are certain to remain unsatisfied, unless a fruitful alternative use can be found for them after the textile manufacturers have moved on. During the past 25 years the demolition of these huge buildings, some of them architecturally splendid, has been on such a scale as to make recording both an urgent and a costly process. The New England Mill Survey, conducted from the Smithsonian Institution in Washington, shows how such a task can be planned and carried out.

In general, old textile machinery finds its way to museums, such as the Merrimack Valley Textile Museum, at North Andover, Mass. It is rare, for obvious reasons, to find it preserved on its original site. An exception is the Watkins Mill Complex (1860) at Lawson, Clay County, Miss. This plant, complete with its wood-fired steam engine and much of its old machinery, is the best-preserved example of a mid-19th-century woollen mill to be found anywhere. The mill now forms part of the Missouri State Park system. The water-

powered Crown and Eagle Mills (1825–30) at North Uxbridge, Mass., are one of the outstanding examples of early 19th-century industrial architecture. Production ceased in 1924, and, despite a recent disastrous fire, certainly deliberately started, work is now under way to convert the mills into apartments.

A very rare example of a late 19th-century mill complex which is still operating with its original machinery is the Cosmos Imperial Mills (1883) at Yarmouth, N.S., Canada. In the great majority of cases, however, the archaeology of the Victorian textile industry consists of buildings emptied of the machinery which was the reason for their existence.

**Theater.** The Greek theater consisted of two elements: the *orchēstra*, a space for acting and dancing which was usually circular; and the *auditorium*, a spectators' area, which was probably originally no more than a hillside or slope on which spectators could sit. These arrangements were formalized into the D-shaped plan, with rockcut or wooden seats around the *orchēstra*, familiar from many sites (e.g. Epidauros). The *skēnē*, at first only a temporary canvas booth, was adapted during the course of the 5th century BC to form a backdrop and accommodation for the actors. The Roman theater took over the Greek pattern, though often with a much more elaborate *skēnē* (or, in Latin, *scaenae frons*); good examples survive at POMPEII and ORANGE.

**Thebes.** The ancient Egyptian capital city and religious center on the east bank of the Nile, about 435 mi. (700 km) south of Cairo. Thebes is now delineated in the North by the Temple of Karnak, and in the South by the Temple of Luxor. Recent excavations at Karnak have uncovered the temple quay, which once stood on the ancient river bank, and a complete Aten temple, which had been dismantled and used as filling within later pylons and temple walls. At Luxor, the beginning of an avenue of sphinxes has been found, connecting with the Temple of Karnak over 1.2 mi. (2 km) away.

Although over 400 private and over 80 royal tombs are known in the Theban necropolis on the west bank, more are still being discovered. The earliest royal tombs are pyramid-capped *saff* tombs belonging to 11th-Dynasty princes (*see* PYRAMID), but the finest and best known are those of New Kingdom date in the Valley of the Kings, in the North of the necropolis, and the Valley of the Queens further South. Apart from the Tombs of the Nobles, some of the most colorfully decorated are those near the workmen's village at DEIR EL-MEDINA. Work on the line of huge mortuary temples running from Qurna in the North to Medinet Habu in the South includes restoration of the third tier of HATSHEPSUT's temple at Deir el-Bahri and a full recording of the Ramesseum's inscriptions. Further discoveries are being made at AMENOPHIS III's palace at Malkata.

**Thera** (Santorini). One of the Cycladic Islands, and the site of a Mycenaean settlement, under excavation in recent years. The island was volcanic, and the Bronze Age town was destroyed by an eruption which may also have caused the destruction of Minoan sites in CRETE, *c.* 1400 BC.

**Thermoluminescence.** An important dating technique. After firing, particles in pottery give off energy which is trapped in interstices in the matrix. Since this occurs at a constant rate, and can be measured in terms of light emissions when released by reheating the ceramic matrix, thermoluminescence provides an invaluable method of dating and checking the authenticity of the commonest archaeological artifact—pottery.

**Thessalonica.** A Macedonian and Roman city and port in the North of Greece. In Roman times it was the capital of the province of Macedonia, and it became particularly important in Byzantine times, from which period many of its surviving churches and monuments date.

**Theveste** (Tebessa). A Carthaginian, then Roman, city in Western North Africa. It has substantial remains of buildings from the Roman imperial period: an arch of Caracalla, an amphitheater, a Christian BASILICA from the late 4th century AD with an associated cloister and BAPTISTERIUM, and Byzantine fortifications.

**Tholos.** A round building, with or without a colonnade. The form was used for temples (as at Delphi), for tombs, or for official buildings (as in the PRYTANEIUM of the Athenian AGORA). The type was also used by the Romans: examples exist in the Forum at Rome (the Temple of Vesta) and at TIVOLI, among other places.

**Three Kingdoms.** The Koguryo, Old Silla, and Paekche kingdoms in Korea. The foundation of the Paekche and Old Silla kingdoms in South Korea coincided with the fall of the Chinese colony LO-LANG in the 4th century AD, while Koguryo had been in existence since the 1st century BC. Most of the excavations have been of tombs, which show considerable Chinese influence, as does some of the metalwork found in them.

**Thule culture.** The name given to an Arctic culture of Northern Canada, Northwest Alaska, and Western Greenland (*c.* AD 1000–1800). The Thule people lived in circular houses, partially dug into the ground and roofed with whalebones, turf, and stone. They lived by hunting and fishing whales, walrus, seals, and caribou. Harpoon points were made of bone or thin slate. Skin-covered boats on wooden frames were used: the open ones are known as *umiaks*, the closed ones *kayaks*. Dog sledges were used for travel across land and ice, with the dogs attached in a fan shape, rather than in tandem, as in the Northwestern Arctic. Ivory, bone, and stone were used to make ornaments, which included combs and stylized human and bird sculptures. Simple geometric designs such as V- and Y-shaped elements were used as decorative motifs. It is the final Eskimo culture of the Northern Maritime tradition. (*See also* ESKIMOS.)

**Tiahuanaco.** A site, a style, and a culture. The site, a

large complex of ceremonial and religious buildings, is situated near Lake Titicaca in Bolivia. Between AD 600 and 1000 it was the center of an important religious cult, of which the principal deity, the Staff God, is depicted on a large monolithic gateway. The religious beliefs of Tiahuanaco, expressed in an extremely distinctive art and architectural style, spread as an imperial system through Southern Peru and Bolivia. To the North, the religious style is connected with the expansion of the militaristic HUARI Empire, and formed the unifying elements of the MIDDLE HORIZON Period throughout most of Peru.

**Tikal.** A giant Classic Period Maya site, recently excavated and partly restored by the University of Pennsylvania, and one of the largest in the New World. It is a sprawling ruin located in the PETEN jungles of Guatemala, dating from the Middle Preclassic Period. The site is marked by six statuesque limestone temple pyramids, some rising 200 ft. (61 m) or more. Giant paved plazas, shrines, palatial residences, ballcourts (*see* BALLGAME, MESOAMERICA), some 3,000 buildings, hundreds of monuments, stelae, and altars dot the remote, rugged 6 sq. mi. (15 km²) of the site. Recent settlement pattern studies estimate that Tikal, at its peak, probably had a population of about 50,000. In addition to its immense size and wealth, it also has the oldest Maya monument known, Stele 29, dating from AD 292. Like most Maya sites of the Southern Lowlands, Tikal was abandoned at the end of the 10th century AD.

**Timgad** (Thamugadi). A military colony founded in AD 100 by Trajan in Africa. It is rectangular in form, with an almost complete town layout and suburbs outside the walls.

**Tin.** The addition of metals such as arsenic or tin to a pure copper has the effect of hardening it and improving its casting properties. As arsenic has obvious disadvantages of toxicity, tin became the usual additive from the late 3rd millennium BC onwards in Europe and the Near East to make the alloy bronze. Derived from the mineral cassiterite, supplies before the Roman period were obtained from panning streams rather than from mining. (*See also* BRONZE, PREHISTORIC EUROPE.)

**Ting ware.** A creamy-colored Chinese porcelain made in Hopei province in the Sung (AD 960–1279) and Yüan (AD 1280–1368) Dynasties. (*See* CERAMICS, CHINA.)

**Tiryns.** A rocky outcrop near Argos, Greece, and an important Bronze Age center. An Early Bronze Age settlement with one main round house surrounded by others was succeeded in 1600–1400 BC by a large house, which was followed in its turn by a Mycenaean palace enclosed within a massive wall. (*See also* GREECE, ARCHAEOLOGY OF; MYCENAEAN ARCHAEOLOGY.)

**Tivoli** (Tibur). A Roman city, captured by Rome in the 4th century BC, and later a fashionable resort with many fine villas. It has remains of many buildings: a Hercules temple, a Sybilline temple, and a round temple of Vesta. Near the town, Hadrian built a large villa during his reign (AD 118–138), one of the most original buildings in the ancient world. It was sumptuously decorated, and contained copies of some of the buildings and statues that the emperor had seen on his travels.

**Tlatilco.** An Early-Middle Preclassic village site in the basin of Mexico, near the former Western shore of Lake Texcoco. Today, the site is used as a brickyard, which ultimately led to the discovery of the famed Tlatilco cemetery. Hundreds of Preclassic burials, often with lavish grave offerings of figurines and beautiful formative pottery, have been unearthed, along with village refuse pits. The grave goods reveal a marked Olmec influence or presence at the site. The remarkable array of different figurines, both larger, hollow forms and smaller hand-modeled ones, reveals a striking diversity among Tlatilco society in clothing types, hairstyles, and skin decoration, as well as indicating various occupations in their society: e.g., dancers, acrobats, and ballplayers (*see* BALLGAME, MESOAMERICA).

**Toldos, Los.** A stratified cave in Patagonia, Southern Argentina, which has produced a sequence of unifacial tools, fishtail points, and preceramic material dating from 12,600 to 4000 years ago.

**Toltecs.** One of the first of the CHICHIMEC tribes to invade the valley of Mexico in the beginning of the 7th century AD. After absorbing many of the civilized peoples already settled there, they adopted many of their customs and technology, producing a culture similar to that of TEOTIHUACAN, but with a warrior-dominated society, the worship of the tribal god Tezcatlipoca, and greater emphasis on human sacrifice. Sometime in the 10th century they established their capital at Tula, some 37 mi. (59 km) north of modern Mexico City. Their great culture hero was Ce Acatl Topoltzin QUETZALCOATL. There is reason to believe that a legend describing the conflict between the Chichimec god Tezcatlipoca and Quetzalcoatl, who was god of the old religion, is actually based on true events and strife in the Toltec state, which ended in the departure of the Quetzalcoatl faction in the year AD 987. After conquering many Maya cities this faction established itself at CHICHEN ITZA, and transported its old architectural style, based on the use of columns and large arcade-like halls, but also incorporated many Maya features. This group of Toltecs was apparently ousted by further immigrants from Central Mexico about 300 years later.

**Tomb archaeology in China.** Archaeology in China has tended to concentrate on the excavation of tombs, some of the most remarkable monuments in the world. From the early Bronze Age in China, in the SHANG DYNASTY (*c.* 1600–1027 BC), the main type of tomb in use was the SHAFT TOMB. The vertical pits, at the bottom of which the coffin and grave goods were placed, were rectangular in plan and had one or more access ramps. With variations, such shaft tombs continued in use throughout the CHOU DYNASTY (1027–221 BC) and came to be covered above ground with mounds. The HAN

The Temple of Quetzalcoatl at Tula, with the huge standing figures that supported the flat roof.

DYNASTY (206 BC–AD 220) tombs excavated at MA-WANG-TUI are a late example of this type. Meanwhile on the Northern borders of China, and throughout South Siberia as far east as Korea, a different type of tomb lined with stone slabs, known as a CIST TOMB, was current. This difference in practice between China and the areas immediately adjacent emphasizes the distinctiveness and independence of the Chinese tradition.

The most important innovation in tomb design took place in the Han Dynasty with the introduction of the CHAMBERED TOMB. The earliest examples seem to have been rockcut tombs such as those of the 2nd century BC at MAN-CH'ENG, in Hopei province. There, the creation of a group of chambers linked by passages and a long access passageway was probably dictated by the terrain. This was followed in the 1st century BC by the widespread development, in Honan province in Northern Central China, of brick-lined chambered tombs. At first, the lining bricks were large hollow clay slabs; these were followed by small clay bricks from which vaults and low domes could be constructed. The several chambers of any one tomb tended to be arranged in a cluster at this date.

In the succeeding period of division, after the fall of the Han Dynasty, the plan of the tombs was simplified. In the Southeast, ruled by the WESTERN CHIN DYNASTY and the EASTERN CHIN DYNASTY, tombs usually had one dominant chamber, while in the North use of several subsidiary chambers with a longer access passage persisted. In both, the structure was of brick and was often surmounted by a dome, which usually required slightly bowed walls to support it.

Several important elements of tomb organization and furnishing became universal in the T'ANG DYNASTY (AD 618–906). They include the use of a decorated stone bed on which the coffin was placed; an incised slab on which the biography of the dead was written; and an elaborate stone coffin. All these items, when made of a black marble-like stone, were covered with figures and decorative detail in fine incised lines. This drawing in stone echoes the style of the paintings found on the walls of tombs, particularly in the T'ang period, although painting had been used to decorate tombs, in the North especially, from the Han period.

The Han also originated the custom of lining the approach road to the tomb (called a spirit road) with large stone sculptures of animals and figures of officials. The imperial tombs of the T'ang Dynasty exhibit some of the most magnificent examples of such sculptures, but the best known are those along the road to the tombs of the emperors of the MING DYNASTY near Peking.

After the T'ang Dynasty, especially in the North, chambered tombs were increasingly constructed to resemble rooms, and details of the wooden architecture of the time were faithfully reproduced. Tombs of the Liao, Northern Sung, and Chin Dynasties (10th–13th century AD) all provide interesting examples of this feature. By the Ming Dynasty, such detail had been simplified and the chambers were often square and severe, though sometimes massively constructed in stone. From such late periods not only have the spirit roads survived, but also

the buildings constructed above ground which were used for sacrifices to the ancestors.

**Tomb figures.** Figures of animals, men and spirits were placed in tombs in China from the late CHOU DYNASTY, 4th century BC. The earliest examples were made of wood, or occasionally bronze, but from the HAN DYNASTY (206 BC–AD 220) they were made of earthenware, which was often decorated with lead glaze. In the Han Dynasty, in addition to figures, many model buildings were made. Thereafter figures predominate. The most magnificent groups were made in the T'ANG DYNASTY (AD 615–906), but figures continued to be placed in some if not all tombs up to and including the CH'ING DYNASTY (AD 1644–1911).

**Totonacs.** The Totonacs occupied the central part of Veracruz, Mexico, in the Postclassic Period. It is assumed by some archaeologists that they also occupied the area in the Classic Period. Consequently, Classic Period artifacts from the area and the site of EL TAJIN are often loosely termed Totonac. Many of these artifacts are believed to have been associated with the ballgame (see BALLGAME, MESOAMERICA; PALMATE STONE); but finds also include carved backing plates for mirrors, made up of a mosaic of pieces of iron pyrites. The diagnostic feature of the art style of the period is a very tight scroll in which straight lines are combined with well rounded curves. The scrolls are short and thick with a double border. Figurines are sometimes daubed with black asphalt paint.

At the time of the Conquest, CEMPOALA was the great city of the Totonacs, and is said to have had a population of 30,000. It paid tribute to the Aztecs. Cortez visited the site on his way from Veracruz to Mexico and persuaded the Totonacs to rebel against the Aztecs.

The best-known Totonac artifacts are figurines about 15 in. (38 cm) high, with large flattened heads, suggestive of fronto-occipital deformation, and laughing faces. This latter feature is unique in Mesoamerican art.

**Transhumance.** The practice, in mountainous areas, of utilizing high pastures in the summer and taking stock to sheltered valleys in the winter. This is evidenced archaeologically by seasonally occupied sites.

**Tree-ring dating.** *See* DENDROCHRONOLOGY.

**Tres Zapotes.** An important Late Preclassic Olmec site, located near the Tuxtla Mountains, in Veracruz, Mexico. Only about 2 mi. (3.2 km) in length, and marked by numerous unevenly scattered earthen mounds, Tres Zapotes was occupied into later times than either LA VENTA or SAN LORENZO. However, its colossal stone heads and other typically Olmec cult materials suggest it was at least partly contemporaneous with the Middle Preclassic Olmec florescence. The most significant discovery at Tres Zapotes is Stele C, one of the oldest dated monuments found in the New World. The stele has an inscribed Long Count date of 31 BC on one side, with a bas-relief of a rather abstract jaguar mask on the reverse. (*See also* OLMECS.)

**Trialeti.** A site in the Caucasus where burial tumuli (mounds) have been found. These contained chariots, gold objects, jewelry, and pottery which have been variously dated but probably belong to the second quarter of the 2nd millennium BC.

**Trier** (Augusta Trevirorum). An important city, capital of the Treveri, a German tribe. Later, it was the chief city of the Roman province of Belgica, adopted by Constantius and Constantine in the 4th century AD as an imperial capital. It preserves many remains of its Roman past: the AMPHITHEATER (built *c.* AD 100), a Constantinian BASILICA (now a Protestant church), a double church (under the present-day cathedral), BATHS, and the *Porta Nigra*, part of the former wall circuit which enclosed 750 ac. (303 ha).

**Tripolye culture.** This appeared during the course of the 4th millennium BC, when the painted-pottery cultures of the Balkans (*see* GUMELNITSA CULTURE) expanded around the Western end of the Black Sea into Moldavia, following the corridor of forest-steppe to the north of the steppe area proper. Marginal groups of this culture probably first domesticated the horse.

**Triumphal arch.** A form of monument used by the Romans to commemorate victories, emperors, the making of peace, or for religious reasons. The earliest arches are found in the 2nd century BC and examples of the type, usually a single large carriageway with or without flanking side passages, are found in all the provinces.

**Troy.** An ancient city on the Northwest coast of Asia Minor, lying in the plain of the River Scamander, and celebrated as the scene of the Greek siege recounted by Homer in the *Iliad* (*see* HOMERIC ARCHAEOLOGY). The site was discovered by Heinrich SCHLIEMANN, who excavated on the Hissarlik hill between 1870 and 1890; American excavations followed in 1932–38.

Nine main periods of occupation were distinguished, beginning in the mid-3rd millennium BC, and ending with the Greco-Roman city of Ilium. The most important phases were between 2400 and 2200 BC (Troy II), when Troy was a walled city of some wealth, destroyed by fire. The celebrated gold treasure (called "Priam's" by Schliemann, but actually far too early) was found in this destruction layer. Troy VI was once again a fortified city, after a period when the settlement had been little more than a village. During this second rich phase (1900–1300 BC), Troy was once again walled, and had many trade contacts with Mycenaean centers in Greece. This city was destroyed by earthquake, and rebuilt in less magnificent style (Troy VIIa). This settlement was destroyed by fire *c.* 1200 BC, and may have been the Troy destroyed by the Greeks. In period VIIb, however, it was rebuilt, but abandoned *c.* 1100 BC. Greek settlement followed in the 8th century BC, and then it became a Hellenistic and Roman town, which incorporated the Hissarlik hill within its ambit, and crowned it with a Temple of Athena Ilias.

From Homer's description of Troy in the *Iliad*, it is impossible to distinguish which of the phases of Troy as excavated belong to the period of war with the Greeks.

**Tulum.** The Postclassic Maya site of Tulum, located on the Eastern shores of the Yucatan, in Quintana Roo, Mexico, is one of the few walled Maya cities known. The site, enclosed by a 2,625-ft. (800 m) long wall which stands over 6 ft. (2 m) tall, has on the inside a series of civic and residential squat flat-roofed buildings. Several of them are famed for wall paintings. The site represents the efforts of Maya culture primarily in the last declining Late Postclassic years, and shows some broad similarities to MAYAPAN, with which it is partly contemporaneous.

**Tumulus.** A Latin term used to describe round burial mounds in Europe (*see* BARROW), known in German as *Grabhügeln* or in French as *Tertres funeraires*. Mostly Bronze Age in date, the custom of erecting mounds over important graves survived into the Roman period and beyond, especially to mark important graves or war cemeteries.

**Tumulus period.** The middle phase of the Bronze Age in Central Europe, from 1600 to 1200 BC, named after the common round burial mounds (*see* TUMULUS), which survive in large numbers on the poorer soils of Germany. They contain burials of both men and women, often richly equipped with metal weapons and ornaments.

**Turquoise.** This was almost as highly prized as JADE in Mesoamerica. Very small fragments, *c.* 0.079 in. (2 mm) square, were worked into mosaics on wooden foundations to make ornaments, chiefly in the form of masks.

**Tutankhamun's tomb.** Tutankhamun was the Egyptian boy king who ruled for only nine years at the end of the 18th Dynasty. He was probably a half-brother of the heretic AKHENATEN but, after that king's death and that of another half-brother, Smenkhare, he was compelled to leave the new capital of Akhetaten and return to THEBES, where he allowed the worship of Amun-Re to be re-established. As a pawn of the AMUN priesthood, it is highly likely that he was granted a full pharaonic burial. Early this century, while excavating in the Valley of the Kings at Thebes, Theodore Davis and J. E. Quibell discovered the intact burial of Yuya and Thuya, the parents of Queen Tiye (mother of Tutankhamun). But of even greater interest was the small underground chamber they uncovered in 1907, which contained an alabaster figure and a broken box inscribed with the names of Tutankhamun and Ankhesenamun, his wife. Later a pit was found nearby containing about a dozen white pottery jars filled with linen, some bearing Tutankhamun's name, bags of chaff and natron, broken pots, animal and bird bones, a small cartonnage mummy mask, some floral collars, and two brooms. These were recognized by H. E. WINLOCK as being embalmers' equipment, always buried near the tomb, and the remains of the funerary banquet which was held during the burial. This indicated that Tutankhamun must be buried somewhere in the vicinity and it was in search of

The entrance to Tutankhamun's tomb (in the foreground) in the Valley of the Kings, Egypt.

his tomb that Howard Carter, a British Egyptologist, working on behalf of Lord Carnarvon, spent six seasons clearing the valley floor to bedrock.

Finally, in his 7th and last season only one small area remained on the approach to the tomb of Ramesses VI: this had been previously unexplored only because it lay under Ramesside workmen's huts. In the Fall of 1922 the huts were removed; on November 4 a step was uncovered, and on November 6 the top of a doorway was found. Work was stopped until Lord Carnarvon could be contacted, and so it was not until November 24 that the doorway at the foot of 16 steps was completely cleared so that the seals on the plaster could be read as belonging to Tutankhamun. However, it was also evident that the doorway had been opened and resealed twice and that Tutankhamun's seals were on the intact part of the plaster. Thus the tomb had been entered more than once since its original sealing, presumably by robbers, and so would not be intact. On the other hand, the necropolis officials had felt it worthwhile to reseal what was left.

On the following two days the stone and rubble blocking the descending passage behind the sealed doorway were removed until a second sealed doorway was reached. During this clearing further evidence of ancient entry was provided by a narrow tunnel cut through the passage's rubble which had been filled in with material of a different color from the original. Clear evidence of plundering lay in the pottery fragments and smashed alabaster vessels mixed with the filling. Water skins found might have been used to carry water needed for plastering the doorways or they might have belonged to the robbers and been intended to carry away precious oils and unguents. Further signs of opening and resealing were obvious on the second sealed doorway, but Carter's fears were instantly removed when he made a small

breach in it and inserted a candle through the gap. Before his astounded gaze lay the Antechamber of the tomb of Tutankhamun. The date was November 26, 1922.

The Antechamber was one of only four rooms and was only about 12 ft. × 26 ft. (3.66 × 7.92 m), but it was to take nearly four months to clear. Apart from three animal-sided gilt couches, four dismantled chariots, and the golden throne with inlaid figures of the king and his wife on the back panel, there were other chairs and folding stools, exquisite alabaster vessels, a painted wooden casket containing royal robes, a golden shrine, other boxes, some inlaid, containing staves, walking sticks, musical instruments, bows and arrows, whips, dried meats, jewelry and various articles of clothing. Among these treasures lay a handful of heavy gold rings tied up in a piece of linen where the robbers had dropped them. Other signs of their activities lay in jars and boxes with lids askew, objects bundled haphazardly into the wrong containers, and the disorderly piling of the Antechamber's contents: the necropolis officials' attempt to restore order.

On February 17 Carter was finally able to investigate the plastered doorway in the northern wall of the Antechamber, which was guarded by two life-sized sentinal statues of the king. His first impression when he cleared a small gap was of a wall of gold: what he saw in reality was the outermost of four gold-plated wooden shrines which protected the king's quartzite sarcophagus. Between the walls of the outermost shrine and those of the Burial Chamber and between the walls of the shrines themselves were alabaster vessels and lamps, staves, batons, and fans, even a silver trumpet, and many more objects of a magical or religious significance. Carter also noticed, however, parts of two necklaces dropped beside a hole which robbers had made in the partition wall between the Antechamber and the Burial Chamber. Nevertheless, the seal on the second gilded shrine was intact, so that when the lid of the sarcophagus was finally raised a nest of coffins protecting the royal mummy came into view. There were three anthropoid coffins, two gilded and inlaid, the innermost of solid gold; the famous gold mask was placed over the mummy's head and numerous amulets, jewelry, and ceremonial articles were found on the body. A third room, termed the Treasury, which led from the Burial Chamber through an unblocked doorway, had been visible throughout the operations in the adjoining room but had been deliberately left until everything of interest in the Burial Chamber had been removed. In this room were shrines containing gilded figures of the king and gods, a portable shrine surmounted by the black jackal of Anubis, the king's gold canopic canopy covering the alabaster chest, and jars, model boats, *shabti* (tomb model) figures, magnificent jewelry, and, most strangely, two mummified stillborn children in miniature coffins.

By the end of November 1927, only the Annexe leading from the west wall of the Antechamber was left to investigate. Although the necropolis officials had made some attempt to restore order in the adjoining room to the confusion caused by the robbers, this was not the case in the Annexe. Gilded beds and chairs, stools, boxes and baskets of food, alabaster vases and pottery vessels, weapons, and *shabtis* lay piled on top of one another in utter chaos. On one box the footprints and on an unguent vessel the greasy fingerprints of ancient thieves could still be seen.

In all, the clearance of the tomb took Carter and his helpers 10 years. Every single object was scientifically recorded and photographed before being moved. Many objects needed conservation treatment: wood was treated with melted paraffin wax and beadwork had to be re-threaded on the spot so that the ancient stringing order was preserved. The magnificent contents of the tomb of this insignificant king were later removed to their present resting place, the Cairo Museum.

**Tutishcainyo.** One of the oldest sites in the Upper Amazon, South America, where there is good evidence of human occupation. It is an old alluvium deposit near Pucallpa, Peru, on an oxbow lake. The lowest level of occupation, called Early Tutishcainyo, contained evidence of habitations and pottery. A few hundred people lived in dwellings of wattle-and-daub construction, whose foundations are marked only by postholes—which probably contained supports for house floors well above the ground and were made of cane or wood. Pottery was of several standardized forms, with shapes suggesting a cuisine in which vegetable foods were varied and important. The decoration techniques and designs indicate a fairly advanced pottery technology. Geometric patterns employed were mostly rectilinear or involve a curvilinear scroll. An example of an incised cat-head is one of the oldest feline representations in the New World, far predating CHAVIN, whose influence was felt here 1,000 years later. The site dates from *c.* 2500 BC.

**Tyre.** An important Phoenician city which originally stood on an island off the Lebanese coast, but which was linked to the mainland by a causeway when Alexander the Great besieged it in 332 BC. It was the site of one of the factories for the purple dye known as "Tyrian Purple," which was obtained from the murex shell and was much prized in antiquity. Hiram, King of Tyre (970–936 BC), was a contemporary of Solomon's (*see* ISRAEL, ISRAELITES).

**Tz'u-chou ware.** A large group of Chinese stonewares made in Hopei, Honan, and Shansi provinces. They were decorated in bold designs in contrasting slips in the SUNG DYNASTY (AD 960–1279) and later with enamels. (*See* CERAMICS, CHINA.)

**Uaxactun.** One of the first Classic Maya centers to receive intensive archaeological investigation. Work carried out over 12 years in the PETEN, by the Carnegie Institution of Washington, revealed a very long and complete ceramic sequence running from the Preclassic to Late Classic Periods. This ceramic analysis laid the comparative basis for all Lowland Maya chronology. The site has many of the usual Lowland Maya architectural features, but was a small center in contrast to nearby TIKAL, to which it probably owed politico-religious allegiance.

**Ubaid.** The TELL of Al 'Ubaid near UR, which was excavated by the British in 1919 and from 1922 to 1924, and which has given its name to a period in Mesopotamian chronology. Indeed, the early levels (Ubaid I, now called Ubaid 3 by some) produced evidence of 5th-millennium BC settlement with primitive reed huts, painted pottery, stone and clay tools, but no metal. A cemetery was also excavated and contained burials dating from Ubaid II (*c.* 4200 BC, now called Ubaid 4 by some) until the end of the 3rd millennium BC. Ubaid pottery, painted with geometric designs, is of a type found over a wide area, from Southern Iran and the Arabian peninsula to Syria, and shows continuous development in Southern Mesopotamia over a long period of time, with earlier stages represented at other sites (*see* the chronological table, p. 198). At the northern end of the mound, an EARLY DYNASTIC temple had been built on a platform surrounded by an oval enclosure (discovered in 1937) like that at Khafajah in the DIYALA. Copper reliefs, animals, and ornamental clay nails, which had adorned the façade, were found and are now in the British Museum in London.

**Ucayali sequence.** In the jungle of Eastern Peru, a number of sites near the town of Pucallpa have been excavated. Based upon the many pottery styles, a 4,000-year sequence has been established. (*See* TUTISHCAINYO.)

**Ugarit.** An ancient Syrian city near the coast, north of Latakya, identified with the large mound of Ras Shamra, excavated by the French since 1929. The earliest levels go back to Early Neolithic times (levels VB and VA) and there is an important sequence of early pottery through Middle Neolithic (=HALAF—levels IVC, B, and A) and Late Neolithic (=UBAID—level IIIC, and Late Ubaid—level IIIB). Little is known of the history of Ugarit during the first part of the 3rd millennium BC, but the city was destroyed during the second half and tombs, christened *Porteurs de Torques*, have been found which belonged to newcomers, perhaps the AMORITES. During the 2nd millennium BC, the city became increasingly important with a large palace, important historical and literary archives, rich objects including bronzes and ivories, and built tombs. The city was destroyed by the SEA PEOPLE in *c.* 1200 BC. Its harbor, Minet el Beida, has also been partly excavated. (*See* SYRIA–PALESTINE; the chronological table, p. 198.)

**Uhle, Max** (1856–1944). The father of Peruvian archaeology who, from his excavations in the 19th century, established the Early, Middle, and Late TIAHUANACO and INCA Ceramic sequence. Although greatly corrected and elaborated, this chronological sequence still stands today. (*See* ANDEAN CHRONOLOGY.)

**Únětice period.** The first period of the Bronze Age in

Central Europe, named after a type-site in Czechoslovakia (German *Aunjetitz*). It marks a northward shift in the centers of the metallurgical industry from their Copper Age focus in Southeast Europe. Among its innovations were the two-piece mold and the use of TIN to make bronze (*see* BRONZE, PREHISTORIC EUROPE).

**Ur.** An important Sumerian dynastic city, identified with Tell Muqqaiyyar in Southern Mesopotamia. It was investigated as early as 1625 by Pietro della Valle and by Sir William Kennet LOFTUS and others in the middle of the 19th century. The British returned to the site in 1918 and Sir Leonard WOOLLEY directed a joint expedition with the University of Pennsylvania until 1934. The city was founded in the 4th millennium BC on a promontory between a branch of the River Euphrates and a canal. UBAID and URUK levels are separated by a Flood level and burials of these, and all subsequent levels, were found.

In EARLY DYNASTIC times it was the seat of two Dynasties and one ruler, Mesanepada, deserves mention. The city was walled under Ur-Nammu, during the 3rd Dynasty of Ur, and he also built the fine ZIGGURAT, now restored, and its *temenos* or sacred enclosure.

*Kings of the 3rd Dynasty of Ur*
Ur-Nammu (2112–2095 BC)
Shulgi (2094–2047 BC)
Amar-Suen (2046–2038 BC)
Shu-Sin (2037–2029 BC)
Ibbi-Sin (2028–2004 BC)

The last king of the Dynasty was taken prisoner to ELAM. Some small town houses were excavated and belong to the first centuries of the 2nd millennium BC (Larsa period). There are also Kassite buildings, and the Chaldaean kings built or rebuilt many palaces and temples in the 1st millennium BC. Along the southeast wall of the *temenos*, a Royal cemetery was uncovered, with almost 2,000 tombs ranging from Early Dynastic to Akkadian times. Of these the richest were the Royal tombs of the middle of the 3rd millennium BC, which were distinguished from the others in that they were built tombs and that from 3 to 74 attendants were sacrificed in them. Bulls and onagers, drawing chariots and sledges, were also sacrificed. The tombs contained jewelry and ornaments, gold daggers and vessels, objects of electrum (an alloy of gold and silver) and silver, and cylindrical SEALS—often of LAPIS LAZULI and sometimes bearing the name of the owner of the tomb, e.g., A-kalam-dug or Pu-abi (previously read Shub-ad). Many objects were decorated with mosaics of shell, lapis, red stones, and paste on a bitumen base and these include gaming boards, the sound boxes of lyres and harps, and the famous "Royal Standard" with scenes of war and peace. Other burials also contained rich grave goods, and numerous tablets were recovered. Nearby stood the rifled hypogeum of the kings of the 3rd Dynasty.

**Urartu, Urartians.** A kingdom centered on the highland plains around Lake Van, where the River Euphrates takes its source, and surrounded by the mountains of Eastern Anatolia, dominated by Mount Ararat. The name first appears in the 13th century BC, but the Urartians seem to have been descendants of the HURRIANS, who were established in the area during most of the 2nd millennium BC, when it was known as the Nairi lands. The Urartian kingdom was already in existence by the end of the 10th century BC, and its increasing power threatened Assyrian access to raw materials, especially metal, so that the two powers were constantly at war. Under Menua, Argishti I, Sarduri II, and Rusa I in the 8th century BC, the Urartian kingdom expanded beyond its Vannic homeland.

Important sites have been excavated in Soviet Armenia (Arin Berd, Karmir Blur), in Iran (Bastam), round Lake Van (Patnos, Çavuş Tepe, Kayalıdere, Adılcevaz, and Van/Toprakkale), and further west at Altıntepe. Strategic sites were selected, with good natural defenses and access to water supplies. These were then well fortified and equipped with towers, elaborate storerooms, rockcut tombs, columned buildings, and square temples—the most famous of which, that of Khaldi at Muṣasir, was depicted on an Assyrian relief after it had been sacked by the Assyrians in 714 BC. Muṣasir has not been located with any certainty but lists of booty give an indication of Urartian wealth. Bronze weapons and armor, cauldrons, weights, furniture fittings, decorated metal plaques and strips all reveal an eclectic art uniting Assyrian conventions and the animal art of the steppes.

The Urartians adapted the cuneiform script to their own language, which seems to be a late dialect of Hurrian and which, because bilingual inscriptions have been found at Kelishin and Topzawa, has been deciphered (*see* WRITING). Urartian pottery was generally a fine, red burnished ware, and there are huge pithoi (storage jars) at many sites. Pressure from the CIMMERIANS, Phrygians (*see* PHRYGIA, PHRYGIANS), and SCYTHIANS led to the disappearance of the kingdom *c.* 590 BC.

**Urban archaeology, Medieval.** Extensive bomb damage in many European cities in World War II, coupled with recent redevelopment programs in town centers, has led to an accelerated amount of archaeological activity in towns during the last 20 years. Research into medieval towns has been particularly intensive in Northern and Central Europe and Britain—relatively little work has been done in the Mediterranean area.

Within the Roman Empire a network of towns served as administrative centers and focuses for trade and industry. Many of these towns survived, in spite of the barbarian incursions of the MIGRATION PERIOD. In Trier (Germany) continuity of town life is reflected in the unbroken sequence of pottery. In Tournai (Belgium), where Childeric was buried in AD 482, the medieval town grew up round the site of the Roman fort. The Anglo-Saxon incursions of Britain effectively put an end to town life (though some sites were occupied on a reduced level), and Roman sites often underlie late Saxon English towns.

In Northern Europe and Scandinavia fortified villages grew up from the 3rd century AD onwards, and, from the 7th century AD, trading posts evolved as intermediaries between town and village. Intensified trade increased the importance of these posts and places like DORESTAD in Frisia and HELGÖ in Sweden had far-flung trade links. This pattern continued until urban centers evolved in many parts of Northern and Central Europe during the 10th century. During the 11th and 12th centuries burgher towns grew up and thereafter the city state or chartered town came into existence, with a constitution based on the borough, legal supremacy, and independence. In Central Europe town growth was accelerated by the granting of market charters which defined the privileges and rights of the merchants in the named center. Town guilds played a major part in the administration of urban affairs and in the control of trade and industry.

In many European towns excavation has shed light on individual development: WINCHESTER, Southampton, and York (England); Dublin (Ireland); Trondheim and Bergen (Norway); Haithabu (Hedeby, North Germany); Ribe and Arhus (Denmark); and Antwerp (Belgium) are notable in this respect.

**Urbanization, Prehistoric Europe.** The definition of the process of urbanization in terms that satisfactorily encompass all its various global manifestations has been one of the most difficult tasks confronting archaeologists. However, it now appears from the combined efforts of anthropologists, sociologists, historians, geographers, and archaeologists that the following are the critical conditions for the birth of urbanization: the growth of settlements beyond a few hundred inhabitants; the development of long-distance trade for desired goods; the development within a society of a situation in which obligations are no longer exclusively prescribed by kinship, in which obligation by contract, whether permanent or transient, is gaining ground, and in which power is concentrated in dominant families or clans; and the existence of other communities in the same or neighboring regions at a similar stage of development, with which they are in regular contact. When these conditions interact to produce a developing, and not merely a steady, situation, urbanization gets under way. In prehistoric Europe urbanization began at different times; however, none of its societies was of dominantly urban character, for the overwhelming majority of the population continued to live an essentially rural existence. In Southeast Europe urbanization seems to have begun by 4000 BC, in Greece leading eventually to the growth of Mycenaean civilization; in Italy it began early in the 1st millennium BC and led to Etruscan civilization. In Celtic Europe, except in Northern and Western Britain and Ireland, it began late in the 1st millennium BC, with the development of *oppida* (*see* HILLFORT), but in Northern, Germanic Europe, and in Russia, it did not start for another 1,000 years.

**Urnfield period.** The name given to the later part of the Bronze Age in Central Europe, characterized by the spread of cremation burial in urns instead of inhumations under tumuli, as in the Middle Bronze Age. Other developments include the use of small hillforts and the spread of specialized bronze horse-gear and weapons.

**Uruk** (or Warka). The Biblical Erech. An important site in Southern Mesopotamia, excavated by the Germans since 1912 with breaks during both World Wars. The site has given its name to a chronological period, also known as Protoliterate A and B, which, roughly speaking, covers the centuries from *c.* 3500 to 3100 BC. During this period (levels XIV–IVa), which succeeded an earlier UBAID 4 phase (levels XVIII–XV), the distinctive pottery types are coarse bowls known as "beveled rim bowls" or *Glockentöpfe*, found all over SUMER, but also in Southwestern Iran, in the North, in Syria, and even at Abydos in Egypt. There are also vessels with long tubular spouts or strap handles in a monochrome slipped and burnished or plain ware, which is often wheelmade.

In levels VI–V, buildings on stone foundations appear suddenly, though there is no cultural break. By level IV there are magnificent and complex temples with rooms on either side, two stairways, and niched walls. Brick-built columns and half columns appear and they are decorated with mosaics of colored clay cones, arranged in geometric patterns. The main sites which have produced Uruk period material are ERIDU, NIPPUR, TEL BRAK, TELL UQAIR, and Grai Resh and Habuba Kabira in the North. At Uruk, the main groups of buildings are the successive shrines of Anu and the E-anna precinct, both of which became the core of later ziggurats. Level IV was destroyed and the buildings of level III belong to the JEMDET NASR period (Protoliterate C and D), among which is the White Temple of Anu. The E-anna precinct and ZIGGURAT remained sacred until Seleucid times. A temple built by the Kassite King Karaindash deserves special mention as it was decorated with gods and goddesses in relief brickwork. The latest Anu temple also dates to Seleucid times and was called the *bît resh*, and there is a third large Seleucid temple complex and a Parthian temple.

Uruk was an important center in EARLY DYNASTIC times at the beginning of the 3rd millennium BC, but few remains of this period have been excavated. Among the objects found during the excavations are cylinder SEALS and impressions, a group of amulets, small metal objects (*see* CIRE PERDUE), and stone vessels known as the *Sammelfund* and dating to the Jemdet Nasr period, though some may be earlier. There is also a beautiful stone head and a stone vase bearing a cult scene. (*See* the chronological table, p. 198.)

A reconstructed plan of Temple D in level IVa at Uruk, dating from the second half of the 4th millennium BC.

The Palace of the Governor at the Maya city of Uxmal, in Yucatan, Mexico.

**Uxmal.** A Late Classic Maya site, located about 50 mi. (80 km) south of Merida, in Yucatan, Mexico. It is the largest site built in the Puuc style. The most important buildings are the Pyramid of the Magician, the Palace of the Governor, and the Nunnery Quadrangle. These names were applied by Europeans and the original designations and functions of the buildings are unknown.

A small ballcourt, now in ruins, and the Nunnery, have later additions to decorative stonework, in the form of feathered serpents similar to those of CHICHEN ITZA, suggesting that, although there are no pure Toltec buildings, Uxmal may have been occupied by Toltecs for at least a time. Tradition tells us that Uxmal was the home of the Xiu family. Xiu, a Central Mexican rather than a Maya name, seems to corroborate the architectural evidence of Toltec occupation.

**Valdivia.** A stratified site on the South coast of Ecuador where a long sequence of fine pottery, dating from 2700 to 1500 BC, overlying a preceramic deposit with a radiocarbon date of 3200 BC, was uncovered in a shell midden (mound). At the time of excavation claims were made that the ceramic tradition was introduced from Japan, although further work in both regions has shown that this is chronologically unlikely.

**Valencia** (Valencoid subtraditions). With its red-colored jars, this ceramic complex is one of the best known in Venezuela and is found on a number of mound sites in the North Central part of the country. Its huge human figurines, with flat, wide heads, are very distinctive. The complex is late, AD 1000–1500, and may have been derived from the Arauquim complex further inland.

**Vallhagar.** A settlement in Sweden, on the island of Gotland, excavated in the 1950s and shown to have been occupied in the 5th and 6th centuries AD. It was an agricultural community, whose dwellings, with their associated outbuildings, were arranged within fields delimiting roughly square areas. The buildings were of tripartite form with stone walls and a central hearth. This type of aisled longhouse is a long-established tradition in Europe, spanning the period from prehistoric times to the Middle Ages.

**Varves.** Silt layers deposited annually in the lakes formed at the margins of the retreating ice which was formerly over Scandinavia. The Swedish pioneer geologist, Baron de Geer, discovered in the late 19th century that these could be counted and correlated or linked over long distances. This gave him a timescale of 12,000 years, and fixes the end of the Ice Age at about 10,000 years ago.

**Vegas.** Sites that have been found on ancient shorelines and terraces in the Santa Elena peninsula region of Southeast coastal Ecuador. Stone artifacts are mainly unifacial and include gravers, denticulates, and spokeshaves, as well as cobble choppers and pestles. They may date from *c*. 5000 BC.

**Veii.** An Etruscan city near and to the north of Rome, destroyed by the latter in 396 BC. The site was progressively abandoned in antiquity, but in Etruscan times it was surrounded by a strong wall and a rampart built in the 5th century BC.

**Vendel period.** The main phase of the MIGRATION PERIOD in Sweden. It is named after Vendel in Uppland, where a rich series of burial mounds was excavated. Other important Vendel cemeteries are known at Valsgarde and Old Uppsala. The dead in these cemeteries were often buried in boats, accompanied by rich treasures. Vendel influence is apparent in the SUTTON HOO burial in England.

**Verona.** A North Italian town, given Roman civic status in 49 BC. It has two large gates dating from the 1st century AD, a THEATER, and an AMPHITHEATER; the last two were included within the city walls, which were rebuilt in the 3rd century AD.

**Vicus.** A pottery style from graveyards in the Piura valley, on the Northern coast of Peru. Derived from the CUPISNIQUE style and dated *c.* 200 BC–AD 200, the modeled wares most resemble the GALLINAZO style.

**Vikings.** A group of peoples who first appear in history in the late 8th century AD, when they ravaged the coast of Northern Europe. The term embraces the Norse, who raided and settled in Northern Britain, Iceland, Greenland, and finally North America; the Swedes, who established a trade route from the Baltic through Russia to Byzantium and beyond; and the Danes, who were a serious threat in England and Ireland.

The Viking raiders were descended from the native peoples of MIGRATION PERIOD Scandinavia. Possible causes of the raids were internal disputes in Scandinavia, a population boom and laws of primogeniture which left many without land, and a thirst for booty and adventure. After the initial forays Vikings formed peaceful colonies. In the Northern and Western Isles of Scotland the Norse outnumbered the indigenous population, and the best-surviving example of their characteristic settlements of longhouses there is at Jarlshof in Shetland. In the Scottish isles and the Isle of Man ship burials have been found, and in Greenland Eric the Red's settlement at Brattahlid has been extensively excavated. At L'Anse aux Meadows in Newfoundland, the Norwegian author Helge Ingstad excavated a Viking settlement, dated by radiocarbon to around the 10th century AD. The extent of Viking influence in Russia has been disputed, but one influential school of thought

argues that the Vikings founded the great towns of European Russia, and as corroborative evidence Scandinavian finds from Novgorod, Staraja Ladoga, Kiev, and from a cemetery at Gnezdovo, the predecessor of Smolensk, have been cited.

Viking Scandinavia was primarily agrarian, but the raids brought new wealth, and many Vikings became traders. Towns grew up to handle the new merchandise, and of these the great trading station of Birka is known both from documentary evidence and from excavation. Even larger was Hedeby, on the neck of the Jutland peninsula, while towns like Sigtuna and Lund developed later in the Viking period.

Initially pagan, the Vikings worshiped gods such as Odin and Thor. Denmark and Norway were gradually converted to Christianity during the 10th century, and Sweden followed in the early 11th century. A late 10th-century stone from Jelling in Jutland carries a representation of the Crucifixion, the earliest in Scandinavia, set up by Harald Blue Tooth. Their paganism made the Vikings a particular threat to the clerics, whose monasteries were a rich source of plunder. The image of the Viking as a bloodthirsty adventurer owes much to the accounts of their clerical victims and to the sagas set down in Iceland later in the Middle Ages, such as *Heimskringla*, *The Saga of Burnt Njal*, and the *Vinland Saga*, the latter an account of the Viking settlements in America.

The Vikings used an alphabet known as the furthark (runes), which was probably devised in the 2nd or 3rd century AD, but which was not widely used before the Migration Period. It may have had a magical significance, but was also used for everyday purposes. Many decorated stones have been found in Scandinavia with runic inscriptions.

A few fortifications are known in Scandinavia. The Danevirke was a linear earthwork built across the neck of the Jutland peninsula, as a defense against Carolingian invasion. It was later added to at various times up to the 1160s. In Denmark are to be found four military camps, of which Trelleborg is the most notable. All are circular, with boat-shaped buildings set in a square in each sector.

The Vikings were great boat builders, as the remains of ships now preserved in Roskilde and Oslo show. The OSEBERG SHIP and the Gokstad ship are particularly notable. A reconstruction of the Gokstad ship was sailed to America in 1893, and was highly praised by her captain.

Various animal art styles evolved from those of Migration Period Scandinavia, notably style III, and the Borre, Jellinge, Mammen, Ringerike, and Urnes styles, some of which were developed in the colonies. The Urnes style (named after the decoration on the stave church at Urnes in Norway) represents the culmination of the artistic tradition, with intertwining animals from which emanate tendril-like fronds that interlace gracefully.

**Vila Nova de São Pedro.** An important CHALCOLITHIC (Copper Age) site, near Santarém in the Estremadura region of Portugal. An unenclosed settlement was

The remains of a Norse settlement at Birsay, Orkney, 10th–12th century AD.

succeeded by one surrounded by at least two bastioned stone walls (*see* LOS MILLARES), probably dating from *c.* 2500 BC. A final phase belonged to the BEAKER CULTURE.

**Villanovan culture.** An enormously wealthy culture, the first society between the Rivers Po and Tiber in Central Italy to use iron for its implements, which flourished in the earlier centuries of the 1st millennium BC. It laid the foundations of the urban centers from which Etruscan civilization blossomed in the second half of the millennium.

**Villa, Roman.** The Roman villa was primarily a farmhouse, built usually in the courtyard style, with outbuildings for storing equipment and for livestock. Residential villas, often set within an area of landscape beauty or on the seashore, developed in the late 2nd century BC. In the Roman provinces, villas are normally associated with agriculture, and often reach quite a high degree of luxury and sophistication. More information is now being gathered about their outbuildings and estates: the main house, often with mosaic floors and hypocausts, was often merely the central residential point of a large complex of buildings and fields.

**Vinča culture.** Named after the type-site near Belgrade in Yugoslavia, excavated in 1910 by M. Vassits, this Neolithic culture spans the period from the end of the STARČEVO CULTURE, *c.* 4500 BC, down to 3000 BC. It was one of the group of cultures important in the development of COPPER metallurgy.

**Viru Valley Project.** Sponsored by the United States Government in the 1960s, this project focused on a selected valley on the North Central coast of Peru. Concentrated archaeological excavations and surveying of the whole area formed the basis for newly discovered cultural sequences, developmental theories, and settlement pattern studies.

**Viscachani.** A large, open site, near La Paz in highland Bolivia, that has produced stone tools, including leaf-shaped points. Although typologically dated *c.* 9,000 years BP (before the present) the small size of the leaf points suggests that they may be more recent.

**Waira-Jirca.** The earliest ceramic phase (1800–1150 BC) on the KOTOSH site, in the Eastern Andes of Central Peru. The well made, dark brown pottery, with incised geometric designs often filled with red paint, resembles early jungle pottery from the Ucayali (*see* UCAYALI SEQUENCE; TUTISHCAINYO) and is ancestral to Kotosh-Kotosh and ultimately CHAVIN.

**Warehouses.** A major casualty of new methods of cargo handling and distribution, left behind by the introduction of containers, pallets, and bulk cargoes. Postwar demolition has continued the process begun by wartime bombing and the surroundings of ports and railway stations now look very different from 30 years ago. Fine examples have miraculously survived, however, where conversion to another use has been possible or where the

site has not been required for another purpose. In England, Albert Dock, Liverpool (1845), is providing additional premises for Liverpool Polytechnic, and parts of St. Katherine's Dock, London (1820s and 1830s) have become apartments. In Scandinavia, old warehouses at Copenhagen and Stockholm are now hotels.

**Wari.** *See* HUARI.

**Warka.** *See* URUK.

**Wāsit.** An Arab garrison town in Southern Iraq, founded in AD 703–704. Five years of intermittent excavation were undertaken at the site between 1936 and 1942. In the 1942 season the mosque of the al-Ḥajjāj was excavated, and its neighboring palace located. A small shrine (the *Manāra*) and the ruins of numerous private houses, *hammāms* (bath houses), and other buildings were also uncovered. Of particular interest among the small finds were numerous terra-cotta figurines of the Īl-Khānid period (late 13th–14th century).

**Waterpower.** Before the development of dynamos, the power generated by water could be applied only within a very restricted radius, but during the 18th and early 19th centuries engineers displayed remarkable ingenuity in designing water-driven pumping systems which operated over impressively long distances. One survivor, *c.* 49 ft. (15 m) in diameter, at Blisland, in Cornwall, England, worked flat iron rods over a total length of $1\frac{1}{2}$ mi. (2.4 km), to pump water from a china clay pit.

A number of waterpowered forges survive in Europe and an encouragingly large proportion of them have been restored. Notable examples are at Annaberg, East Germany—the Frohnauer Forge (1616); Dobřiv, Czechoslovakia; Essen-Margarethenthal, West Germany; Körsan, Sweden; and Sticklepath, Devon, England.

The use of waterpower for driving mill machinery is excellently documented by surviving mills, although the machinery itself has in nearly every case disappeared. Restored and working cornmills can still be seen at a number of places, however, examples being Børkop Mill, East Jutland, Denmark; High Mill, Skipton, Yorks., England; and Preston Mill, East Lothian, Scotland.

In Central Europe, and especially on the Danube, boat mills were once common. One boat contained the waterwheel and grinding machinery and the other was used for storage, the large undershot waterwheel being fixed between the two boats. None survives on its original site. The last example in Vienna was broken up in 1935, but a few still exist in Romania, on the Rivers Olt, Mures, and Gomes: they need frequent repair and have to be protected from damage by floating ice. A carefully renovated 19th-century boat mill is preserved in Hungary, at the open-air museum, Ráckeve. Where there is a considerable difference between high and low tides water can be impounded in an estuary at high tide and released to drive a waterwheel over the period of low tide. One of the best surviving examples of such a mill is on the River Deben at Woodbridge, Suffolk, England.

The application of waterpower to the generation of electricity is now of great importance throughout the world. Among early hydroelectric stations to survive in something close to their original form are the Ottawa Hydro Station No. 2 in Canada (building 1891, equipment 1908), one of the oldest still operating in the world; Wilson Dam and Power Station, Colbert County, Ala., United States, the first hydroelectric operation in the Tennessee Valley System; and Orlu, near Aix-les-Thermes, France (1897).

**Wessex culture.** The Early Bronze Age in Britain, covering the centuries in the middle of the 2nd millennium BC, was marked by the appearance of a number of spectacularly rich burials which stand out from the mass of those which belong to this time. Not only are weapons and objects of copper and bronze found in these graves, but also exotic materials such as gold and amber, which seem to have been particularly prized.

Because the majority of these rich graves come from the Wessex area—the counties of Wiltshire, Dorset, and Hampshire—this group has been called the Wessex culture, though burials of similar kinds are known from both East Anglia and Scotland. Nor should this group truly be called a culture, since it represents only a single stratum of society. Humbler burials of the same period have only ordinary kinds of domestic pottery as grave goods, in the tradition of BEAKER CULTURE and earlier Neolithic cooking and storage pots.

One of the outstanding examples of these Wessex rich burials is that from the TUMULUS known as the Bush Barrow, in Wiltshire. This contained a magnificent sheet gold pectoral in the shape of a lozenge, a gold belt-hook, two daggers (one with a hilt ornamented with minute gold nails), a bronze ax, and a stone mace head with a shaft ornamented with geometric bone mounting.

Such objects have often been compared with the magnificent finds from the shaft graves at MYCENAE, with which they are almost contemporary; but any direct connection is now discounted, and the growth in power and prestige of local chieftains, with their growing ability to obtain rare materials by trade, is seen as their immediate context.

**Western Chin Dynasty.** Important tombs of this period (AD 265–316) have been excavated in Kiangsu and Chekiang provinces in Southeastern China. Large groups of YÜEH WARE, with rare items of jewelry, are the most important finds.

**Wheeler, Sir Robert Eric Mortimer** (1890–1976). An English archaeologist, who revolutionized excavation standards wherever British archaeological influence was felt, inventing the grid system of investigating sites. He founded Britain's largest archaeological institute (London) and similar institutions in several other countries, reorganized Indian and Pakistani archaeology, and greatly popularized archaeology in Britain.

**Wichqana.** An archaeological complex (1200–800 BC) from the Ayacucho valley of Central highland Peru. The type-site is stratified and was a ceremonial center with Chavinoid features, but the pottery is a local product, with both PARACAS and CHAVIN affinities.

**Wilmerding.** A model industrial town, built from 1889 onwards by George Westinghouse to serve his Brakes Works in Turtle Creek valley, outside Pittsburgh, United States. The houses were, for their time, unusually well constructed. All of them had gas, running water, baths, and modern drainage, and most had gardens. During the early years of the present century, many of the houses were sold to the families who lived in them, but the company continued to own and rent out more than half the original total. In addition to the houses, Westinghouse built and maintained churches, schools, and parks.

**Winchester.** The capital of late Saxon England, founded by Alfred the Great (AD 871–899). Extensive excavations were carried out on various sites in the city between 1961 and 1970, the most important being that of the Old Minster (the late Saxon cathedral), the first phase of which was found to date from the 7th century AD. At Lower Brook Street, a succession of medieval streets with the associated buildings was examined, as was Wolvesey Palace, built by Henry de Blois c. 1130. The Winchester project was the first large-scale campaign of excavation of a medieval English city, and did much to trace the development of the town from the pre-Roman Iron Age to post-medieval times.

**Windmill.** Once a characteristic feature of most European countries, windmills have disappeared at an alarming rate during the present century. They have, however, great popular appeal, and mainly for this reason it has been relatively easy to find the money to restore and preserve them, either on their original site or transferred to open-air museums, such as those at Koog aan den Zaan and Arnhem in the Netherlands, and Skansen, in Stockholm, Sweden. Probably the most notable windmill landscape in the world is at Kinderdijk, in the Netherlands, where there are 19 mills of different types within a small area: 8 were built in 1738, 9 in 1740, and 2 are more recent. In 1850 there were 9,000 windmills in the Netherlands and nowadays more than 2,000 are still active, a figure reached nowhere else in the world.

**Windmill Hill culture.** The name given to the Early and Middle Neolithic period in Southern England (c. 3500–2500 BC), after a large enclosure in Wiltshire. It includes small settlements, large enclosures, and communal burial monuments (long barrows and chambered tombs). Pottery was both plain and decorated, and flint and other hard rocks were quarried and mined for axes, and also widely distributed.

**Winlock, Herbert Eustis** (1884–1950). An American Egyptologist who set new standards as a field archaeologist and a recorder of excavations. Early in his career at el-Lisht he participated in the discovery of the burial of Senebtisi, a wealthy lady at the court of Ammenemes I, which produced splendid Middle Kingdom jewelry. Later, at Deir el-Bahri, he continued E. Naville's work, exhaustively clearing and minutely recording the temples of Queen HATSHEPSUT and MENTUHOTEP II. As a result of his careful work the intact burials of two of Mentuhotep's harem were found in a supposedly cleared area. In connection with the Hatshepsut temple, Winlock uncovered the second tomb of Senenmut, the temple's architect, and the burial of Queen Meryet-Amun, and he laboriously reconstructed Hatshepsut's shattered statues which he found smashed and buried near the temple's causeway.

He also carried out extensive excavations in the surrounding area of the Theban necropolis, which led to the discovery of a number of important 11th-Dynasty tombs, including the intact burial of Wah, and, most spectacular of all, a hidden cache of model figures and groups in the tomb of an important official called Meketre. The tomb had been excavated twice before by less careful Egyptologists. These lively little models included boats of every kind, Meketre's country estate and his cattle count, and showed butchers, carpenters, weavers, bakers, and beermakers at work.

**Woodland tradition.** The group of cultures of Eastern North America which developed from the ARCHAIC TRADITION of hunters and gatherers (at around 1000 BC) to the Hopewellian farmers who, at their climax between AD 100 and 200, built huge earthworks sometimes enclosing hundreds of acres. This tradition is defined by three major characteristics: the beginning of substantial agriculture, the building of elaborate burial mounds, and the manufacture of Woodland pottery (marked with fabric or cord impressions). The area of the Woodland cultures includes the country south and east of a line from the Maritime Provinces of Canada to Minnesota, and from there south to the borders of Louisiana and Texas. The most distinctive difference from preceding Archaic cultures and the later MISSISSIPPIAN TRADITION is that Woodland traits only occur in Eastern North America. The pottery, with its grit temper, fabric impressions, and stamped and incised impressions occurs nowhere else in North or Mesoamerica, and is more characteristic of Neolithic cultures of Eastern Asia than of other American ones. The origin of burial mounds is equally problematical: they vary from simple tumuli to large circular mounds erected over tombs; there are also more complex earthworks in the form of animal and bird effigies. However, burial mounds are more of an Old World trait than a Mesoamerican one, and yet there are no cultures to connect the Eastern Woodlands with Asia. Maize farming was introduced into North America from Mesoamerica sometime after 1000 BC.

The Woodland tradition may be divided into four chronological periods. The first is termed Burial Mound I period which lasted from 1000 BC to 300 BC. This was a period of transition from the Archaic tradition, and is typified by the ADENA culture of the Ohio valley. In Burial Mound II period the whole of the Eastern Woodlands was dominated by the Woodland tradition (300 BC–AD 700). The HOPEWELL culture, centered in Southern

Ohio, typifies this period. Between AD 700 and 1700 the Mississippian tradition, with many Mesoamerican traits, including the erection of temples built on mounds, fused with the Woodland tradition in many areas. Even in this later period the Woodland tradition survived in many subareas, such as Ohio and the Great Lakes, while the Mississippian became most firmly established in the lower Mississippi valley and in the Southeast of the United States. The dating of these periods is, however, as elsewhere, approximate, and depends on RADIOCARBON DATING, and dating through cross-referencing of traits.

**Woolley, Sir Leonard** (1880–1960). A British archaeologist, the excavator of CARCHEMISH, UR, and TELL ATCHANA.

**Writing.**
*Near East.* In the ancient Near East, the earliest form of writing that we know is cuneiform which, as its name indicates, is made up of wedge shapes. These were produced by means of a stylus on clay tablets which were afterwards dried in the sun or baked, thus ensuring their survival. It was developed in Southern MESOPOTAMIA by the Sumerians at the end of the 4th millennium BC and originated as picture writing which, owing to the materials used, rapidly evolved into cuneiform written from left to right, while becoming increasingly ideographic and phonetic. It was adopted and adapted by the Semites for the writing of AKKADIAN, and was subsequently used for a variety of Semitic dialects throughout the ancient world and, most notably, for Assyrian and Babylonian. It was further adapted for the writing of Elamite, Hittite, Urartian, and, finally, Persian just before 500 BC. At UGARIT, simplified cuneiform signs were used for an alphabet of 32 letters which was developed around the 15th century BC. The Achaemenid Persians also reduced the number of cuneiform signs but they used these syllabically and not properly alphabetically.

G. F. Grotefend and others used copies of the inscriptions at PERSEPOLIS, made in 1765 by Karsten Niebuhr, in early attempts at decipherment, but when RAWLINSON copied a huge trilingual inscription at BEHISTUN, it led to his successful decipherment of both Persian and Babylonian cuneiform in the middle of the last century. Since then, thousands of stonecut inscriptions and clay tablets have been copied and translated and have provided us with increasing knowledge of the literature, political, commercial, and religious life, and day-to-day activities of those who wrote them. At certain periods, such as the beginning and the second half of the 2nd millennium BC, epistolary activity was particularly widespread and cuneiform was used all over the Near East. Letters and contracts were enclosed in clay envelopes which bore a summary of the contents and were often sealed by witnesses.

Other forms of writing coexisted with cuneiform. Proto-Elamite may well be as early as cuneiform and is very possibly related, as the use of the same writing materials would indicate. The Indus Valley also evolved an early script (*see* INDIA). A pseudo-hieroglyphic script was developed at BYBLOS, probably in the late 3rd millennium BC. In the middle of the 2nd millennium BC the HITTITES began using a form of writing known as Hittite hieroglyphic. This differs from the later hieroglyphic inscriptions in Luwian found in the Neo-Hittite cities of Southeastern Anatolia and North Syria, which have been to some extent deciphered owing to the discovery of a bilingual one at KARATEPE. Various scripts were used in the Aegean and Eastern Mediterranean, but there must have been many other forms of writing which have not survived because they were used on perishable materials.

It is possible that the alphabet used at Ugarit was an adaptation in cuneiform of an earlier alphabetic script. Early Canaanite inscriptions have been found on objects dated to the 18th and 17th centuries BC. They may well be alphabetic and seem to be related to the Palaeo-Sinaitic alphabet of the 16th century BC. By the end of the 2nd millennium BC a 22-letter, North Semitic alphabet had developed which was written from right to left, and from it stem the scripts used for Hebrew, Phoenician, ARAMAIC, and Greek. On Assyrian reliefs we see scribes standing side by side and writing in cuneiform on tablets, and in the alphabet on parchment. Gradually the latter replaced the former and the use of cuneiform became increasingly restricted, until it finally died out just before our era.

*Mesoamerica.* In the New World only very limited forms of writing developed. Examples of Mesoamerican writing have survived in a few pictographic manuscripts and in inscriptions carved on monuments. Broadly speaking, writing falls into two main categories: the glyphic writing of the MAYA and other Lowland peoples influenced by the OLMECS; and purely pictographic writing of the Mixtecs (*see* MIXTEC), AZTECS, and other Nahua-speaking people of the Postclassic Period.

The characters, or glyphs, of the Maya and related people were generally inscribed in cartouches: they were either in the form of heads of gods, or were highly stylized designs which bear little relation to the objects which they portray. Until recently, the only glyphs understood were those connected with the calendar (*see* CALENDAR, MESOAMERICA). However, a number of place-name glyphs have now been discovered, as well as some historical or dynastic glyphs. When more is known about these, our knowledge of Maya history is likely to increase. Most Maya glyphs are nouns, but there are hints of the beginning of syllabic writing.

The purely pictographic manuscripts of Central Mexico are less sophisticated, consisting of realistic drawings of material objects, in which color sometimes plays an important part. The beginnings of a syllabic system appear in the symbols for placenames. In these, two or more pictures of objects, which, if strung together would have a sound approximating to the name of the place indicated, are used to represent it. For example, the symbol for the town of Tecpatepec consists of a bundle of flint knives on top of a drawing of a hill. The word for flint is "tecpatl" and that for hill is "tepetl." The two words placed together, with a little

simplification, produce Tecpatepec. Abstract ideas are difficult to convey in pictographs but there are a number of examples in the codices: travel, or a journey, is conveyed by footprints; conquest, by a burning temple beside a name glyph, or an arrow inserted into the name; birth, by an umbilical cord attached to a drawing of the person concerned (*see* CODICES, MESOAMERICA).

(*For China and the Far East,* see ORACLE BONES; SHANG DYNASTY. *For Egypt, see* HIEROGLYPHS. *For Greece, see* LINEAR A; LINEAR B; EPIGRAPHY, GREEK AND ROMAN.)

**Yang-shao culture.** The most important early Neolithic culture in China (*c.* 4500 BC), found predominantly in Central and Western China. Important sites have been excavated at PAN-P'O-TS'UN and MIAO-TI-KOU. The people kept domesticated animals, and millet was their main crop. They occupied their villages semipermanently, suggesting that a slash-and-burn agriculture was practiced, although fishing and hunting played an important part in the economy. The culture is best known for the high quality of its painted pottery, which was handmade but finished on a turntable.

**Yaxchilan.** A major Maya site, situated near the Usumacinta River in Chiapas, Mexico, which shares certain architectural features with the Classic Maya site of PALENQUE, located nearby. The site is most famous for its beautifully carved hieroglyphic inscriptions on stone lintels and stelae. Unfortunately, no major archaeological research has yet been carried out there. Prominent themes on the Yaxchilan monuments, during Late Classic times, are conflict and warfare.

**Yayoi Period.** A new culture (400 BC–AD 400) which replaced the JOMON PERIOD in Japan. The people, who may have come from outside Japan, introduced rice cultivation, the use of metals (bronze and iron), and weaving. To these were added, in the middle of the period (100 BC–AD 100), large quantities of bronzes and glass imported from China. A well ordered farming life and new types of burial indicate that radical changes had taken place. The elite were buried in double urns, with grave goods which included weapons and mirrors imported from China. There was a specialized bronze industry making spearheads which had much in common with those used in Northeast Asia, and a type of bronze bell which is wholly peculiar to Japan.

**Yi Dynasty.** Korea was ruled by the Yi Dynasty from AD 1392 until 1910. In 1394 they established their capital at Seoul and rejected Buddhism in favor of Chinese neo-Confucianism. Ceramics, though still made on a large scale, were less refined than those of the KORYO DYNASTY. There were more than 186 stoneware factories and 136 porcelain factories, but of these only the sites at Keryong-san, Pusan, and Kwangju have been investigated. A special office, the sa'ong-won, was set up to administer the manufacture of ceramic wares for court and ceremonial use.

**Yi-hsing ware.** A hard, fine stoneware in red, brown, or

buff, usually unglazed, made at Yi-Hsing in Kiangsu province in China from the Ming Dynasty (AD 1368–1644) onwards. (*See* CERAMICS, CHINA.)

**Ying-ch'ing.** The name of a transparent bluish glaze used on Chinese porcelains made at Ching-te-chen in Kiangsi province from the SUNG DYNASTY (AD 960–1279). This type of porcelain formed the basis for the later largescale manufacture of PORCELAIN with underglaze blue decoration. (*See* CERAMICS, CHINA.)

**Yoke, Mesoamerica.** A large and heavy U-shaped stone, believed to be a ritual copy of a wooden protector worn resting on the hip by Totonac players of the ballgame. They are generally ornamented with carved designs, either zoomorphic or geometrical, with double-edged scrolls. They probably date from the Classic Period. (*See also* BALLGAME, MESOAMERICA.)

**Yüan Dynasty.** The Mongols established this Dynasty (AD 1280–1368) when they conquered China. They set up their capital in Peking, and recent excavations have explored the walls and buildings of this period. A few Yüan tombs have been excavated and an occasional cache of blue-and-white porcelain found.

**Yüeh ware.** Chinese stonewares with olive green glaze made in kilns in Kiangsu and Chekiang provinces (3rd–10th century AD). (*See* CERAMICS, CHINA.)

**Zaculeu.** The ruins of Zaculeu are located in the mountains of Highland Guatemala, about 3 mi. (5 km) from Huehuetenango. The site dates from the Classic Period to the Postclassic, when it was destroyed by the Spanish (AD 1525). Architecture at Zaculeu is very different from Lowland Maya styles, lacking, for example, roof combs and typical corbel vaulting. The site has been extensively excavated and restored, and these efforts point to prominent Central Mexican influences, dating from the Postclassic Period. These contacts resulted in flat-roofed structures, rather than vaulted buildings, and far cruder construction techniques than were used centuries earlier in the Lowlands.

**Zapotecs.** One of the two principal language groups of the state of Oaxaca in Mexico (MIXTEC being the other). Most of the valley of Oaxaca, a fertile, heavily populated region in Precolumbian times, is occupied today by Zapotec peoples, as it probably was in prehistoric times. The principal sites of the Zapotecs were MONTE ALBAN and MITLA.

**Ziggurat.** A massive Mesopotamian mud-brick structure, with a temple or shrine on the top and another at the bottom. Access to the top was obtained by a series of ramps or stairways rising in several stages. Opinions differ as to the purpose of the ziggurats, but it seems likely that they developed from the platforms on which the inhabitants of SUMER raised their temples above the alluvial plain (ERIDU, TELL UQAIR, UBAID, URUK). The most impressive surviving ziggurats are at BORSIPPA, CHOGA

ZAMBIL in Elam, Dur Kurigalzu (*see* KASSITES), UR (largely restored), and Uruk, but most important towns had them and the custom was adopted in Assyria (ASSUR, KHORSABAD). Nothing remains of the ziggurat at BABYLON, the origin of the Tower of Babel.

**Zimbabwe.** The labyrinthine stone walls of Zimbabwe are located in Rhodesia on the high plateau that forms the watershed between the Limpopo and Zambesi Rivers. Commencing with the 16th-century account of the Portuguese writer Joao de Barros, Zimbabwe has generated a considerable amount of literature relating to the age of the ruins and the character of the builders. Nearly all of this, with a few notable exceptions, consists of ill-informed speculation designed to establish that the builders could not have been the local population but were an intrusive group of intellectually and racially superior foreigners.

Excavations, particularly those of Gertrude Caton Thompson in 1929 and Peter Garlake between 1964 and 1970, have provided archaeological evidence that points unequivocally to the fact that the Zimbabwe complex was built and inhabited between AD 800 and 1500 by a people indigenous to South Central Africa. Their prosperous economy was based on agriculture and stock raising, and on the extensive exploitation of trade in gold, copper, and other natural resources. The pottery, ironwork, sculpture, and architecture, although showing certain idiosyncratic local features, is indistinguishable from similar material recovered from other less spectacular, and less well known, Iron Age sites of similar date in South Central Africa.

At the height of its power, during the 15th century, Zimbabwe represents a considerable development in centralization, both political and religious. It was clearly the center of a commercial enterprise with far-reaching connections, as is shown by the presence of valuable foreign imports from China (e.g., celadon ware) and India which occur in the archaeological deposits alongside luxuries of African manufacture, such as gold and copper ornaments, H-shaped copper ingots and double iron gongs.

By the time of the Portuguese domination of the Southeast African coastal ports, through which the Zimbabwe trade had to pass, political power in South Central Africa had passed to the Mwene Mutapa Empire and the extensive stone buildings of Zimbabwe were abandoned.

**Ziwiye.** A site in Iran, near the Iraqi frontier and to the south of Lake Urmia. It has given its name to a 7th-century BC treasure of gold, silver, and ivory which was found in a bronze coffin there in 1947, and is now divided up between the Museum of Tehran and several United States museums. An American survey in 1964 identified a fortress and a palace which may have been built by the MANNAEANS.

# Index

# Index

The illustrations are reproduced by courtesy of the following official bodies, museums, photographers, cartographers, and individuals, all of whom the Publishers wish to thank for supplying and permitting the reproduction of their material. (The numbers following each name refer to the pages on which the illustrations appear.)

Alinari, 16, 148; Peter Bellwood, 74; Rosemary Blott, 26, 56, 167, 203, 207, 214; Cambridge University Collection: copyright reserved, 12, 33, 39; Peter Carter, 10, 135; S. Célébonovic, 195; Mrs. P. Christie, 83; Peter Clayton, 124, 149, 150, 178, 210; Dominique Collon, 7, 14, 31, 213; Department of the Environment: Crown copyright, 48, 53, 100; Adrian Digby, 133, 146, 161; The Directorate General of Antiquities, Baghdad, 13; Crispin Fisher, 19, 57, 75, 95, 113, 137, 140, 143, 156, 198; French Government Tourist Office, 126; Hagley Museum, 2; Imitor, 105; Ann Kendall, 52, 108, 130, 172, 184; Lloyd Laing, 171, 175, 215; Charles Leva, 127; Eric de Maré, 117; National Archaeological Museum, Athens, 187, 188; Naturhistorisches Museum, Vienna, 85; Norwegian Railways, Oslo, 181; Ohio Historical Society, 9; Peabody Museum of Archaeology and Ethnology, 145; Phaidon Press, 166; J. Powell, 147; Smithsonian Institution, Photo: No. 49.808, 102; Jean Stokes, 8, 27, 63, 97, 168, 169; Stora Kopparberg, 65; The Trustees of the British Museum, 25, 50, 70, 91, 116, 121, 151, 164, 165, 174, 190; The Trustees of the British Museum (Natural History), 28; U.S. National Park Service, 17, 177; University of Alaska Museum, 79; University Museum, Philadelphia, 122; Caroline Washbourn, 42, 88, 118, 197; Dr. Philip Whitting, 43.